T0180760

Communications in Computer and Information Science 1948

Rationale
The CCIS series is devoted to the publication of proceedings of computer science conferences. Its aim is to efficiently disseminate original research results in informatics in printed and electronic form. While the focus is on publication of peer-reviewed full papers presenting mature work, inclusion of reviewed short papers reporting on work in progress is welcome, too. Besides globally relevant meetings with internationally representative program committees guaranteeing a strict peer-reviewing and paper selection process, conferences run by societies or of high regional or national relevance are also considered for publication.

Topics
The topical scope of CCIS spans the entire spectrum of informatics ranging from foundational topics in the theory of computing to information and communications science and technology and a broad variety of interdisciplinary application fields.

Information for Volume Editors and Authors
Publication in CCIS is free of charge. No royalties are paid, however, we offer registered conference participants temporary free access to the online version of the conference proceedings on SpringerLink (http://link.springer.com) by means of an http referrer from the conference website and/or a number of complimentary printed copies, as specified in the official acceptance email of the event.

CCIS proceedings can be published in time for distribution at conferences or as post-proceedings, and delivered in the form of printed books and/or electronically as USBs and/or e-content licenses for accessing proceedings at SpringerLink. Furthermore, CCIS proceedings are included in the CCIS electronic book series hosted in the SpringerLink digital library at http://link.springer.com/bookseries/7899. Conferences publishing in CCIS are allowed to use Online Conference Service (OCS) for managing the whole proceedings lifecycle (from submission and reviewing to preparing for publication) free of charge.

Publication process
The language of publication is exclusively English. Authors publishing in CCIS have to sign the Springer CCIS copyright transfer form, however, they are free to use their material published in CCIS for substantially changed, more elaborate subsequent publications elsewhere. For the preparation of the camera-ready papers/files, authors have to strictly adhere to the Springer CCIS Authors' Instructions and are strongly encouraged to use the CCIS LaTeX style files or templates.

Abstracting/Indexing
CCIS is abstracted/indexed in DBLP, Google Scholar, EI-Compendex, Mathematical Reviews, SCImago, Scopus. CCIS volumes are also submitted for the inclusion in ISI Proceedings.

How to start
To start the evaluation of your proposal for inclusion in the CCIS series, please send an e-mail to ccis@springer.com.

Sławomir Nowaczyk · Przemysław Biecek ·
Neo Christopher Chung · Mauro Vallati ·
Paweł Skruch · Joanna Jaworek-Korjakowska ·
Simon Parkinson · Alexandros Nikitas et al.
Editors

Artificial Intelligence

ECAI 2023 International Workshops

XAI^3, TACTIFUL, XI-ML, SEDAMI, RAAIT, AI4S, HYDRA, AI4AI
Kraków, Poland, September 30 – October 4, 2023
Proceedings, Part II

For the full list of editors *see next page*

ISSN 1865-0929 ISSN 1865-0937 (electronic)
Communications in Computer and Information Science
ISBN 978-3-031-50484-6 ISBN 978-3-031-50485-3 (eBook)
https://doi.org/10.1007/978-3-031-50485-3

This Springer imprint is published by the registered company Springer Nature Switzerland AG
The registered company address is: Gewerbestrasse 11, 6330 Cham, Switzerland

Paper in this product is recyclable.

Editors

Sławomir Nowaczyk
Halmstad University
Halmstad, Sweden

Przemysław Biecek
Warsaw University of Technology
Warsaw, Poland

Neo Christopher Chung
Warsaw University
Warsaw, Poland

Mauro Vallati
University of Huddersfield
Huddersfield, UK

Paweł Skruch
AGH University of Science and Technology
Kraków, Poland

Joanna Jaworek-Korjakowska
AGH University of Science and Technology
Kraków, Poland

Simon Parkinson
University of Huddersfield
Huddersfield, UK

Alexandros Nikitas
University of Huddersfield
Huddersfield, UK

Martin Atzmüller
Universität Osnabrück
Osnabrück, Germany

Tomáš Kliegr
University of Economics Prague
Prague, Czech Republic

Ute Schmid
University of Bamberg
Bamberg, Germany

Szymon Bobek
Jagiellonian University
Kraków, Poland

Nada Lavrac
Jožef Stefan Institute
Ljubljana, Slovenia

Marieke Peeters
HU University of Applied Sciences Utrecht
Utrecht, The Netherlands

Roland van Dierendonck
Rotterdam University of Applied Sciences
Rotterdam, The Netherlands

Saskia Robben
Amsterdam University of Applied Sciences
Amsterdam, The Netherlands

Eunika Mercier-Laurent
University of Reims Champagne-Ardenne
Reims, France

Gülgün Kayakutlu
Istanbul Technical University
Istanbul, Türkiye

Mieczyslaw Lech Owoc
Wroclaw University of Economics and Business
Wrocław, Poland

Karl Mason
University of Galway
Galway, Ireland

Abdul Wahid
University of Galway
Galway, Ireland

Pierangela Bruno
University of Calabria
Rende, Italy

Francesco Calimeri
University of Calabria
Rende, Italy

Francesco Cauteruccio
Marche Polytechnic University
Ancona, Italy

Giorgio Terracina
University of Calabria
Rende, Italy

Diedrich Wolter
University of Bamberg
Bamberg, Germany

Jochen L. Leidner
Coburg University of Applied Sciences
Coburg, Germany

Michael Kohlhase
FAU Erlangen-Nürnberg
Erlangen, Germany

Vania Dimitrova
University of Leeds
Leeds, UK

Preface

The European Conference on Artificial Intelligence (ECAI) is the premier European conference on Artificial Intelligence. In 2023, ECAI took place in Kraków, Poland, from the 30th of September till the 4th of October. The program included workshops on specialised topics of high relevance for the scientific community. They were held during the first two days of the conference, in parallel with tutorials and side events such as the Doctoral Consortium or STAIRS (the 10th European Starting AI Researchers' Symposium). This two-volume set includes the proceedings of the following workshops:

1. XAI^3: Joint workshops on XAI methods, challenges and applications
2. TACTFUL: Workshop on Trustworthy AI for safe & secure traffic control in connected & autonomous vehicles
3. XI-ML: International Workshop on Explainable and Interpretable Machine Learning
4. SEDAMI: The Semantic Data Mining Workshop
5. RAAIT: Workshop on Responsible Applied Artificial Intelligence
6. AI4S: Workshop on Artificial Intelligence for Sustainability
7. HYDRA: HYbrid models for coupling Deductive and inductive ReAsoning
8. AI4AI: AI for AI Education

Each section of this book contains the papers from one of the workshops, following a preface from the organisers. We would like to thank all participants and invited speakers, the Program Committees and reviewers, and the ECAI conference and workshop chairs—we appreciate your efforts in making the workshops successful events. We are also grateful to Springer for their help in publishing the proceedings.

October 2023

Sławomir Nowaczyk
on behalf of the volume editors

Organization

ECAI Workshop Chairs

Tom Lenaerts	Université Libre de Bruxelles, Belgium
Paolo Turrini	University of Warwick, UK

XAI^3 Workshop Chairs

Sławomir Nowaczyk	Halmstad University, Sweden
Biecek Przemysław	Warsaw University of Technology, Poland
Neo Christopher Chung	University of Warsaw, Poland

TACTFUL Workshop Chairs

Mauro Vallati	University of Huddersfield, UK
Paweł Skruch	AGH University of Science and Technology in Kraków, Poland
Joanna Jaworek-Korjakowska	AGH University of Science and Technology in Kraków, Poland
Simon Parkinson	University of Huddersfield, UK
Alexandros Nikitas	University of Huddersfield, UK

XI-ML Workshop Chairs

Martin Atzmueller	Osnabrück University & DFKI, Germany
Tomáš Kliegr	Prague University of Economics and Business, Czechia
Ute Schmid	University of Bamberg, Germany

SEDAMI Workshop Chairs

Szymon Bobek	Jagiellonian University, Poland
Martin Atzmueller	Osnabrück University & DFKI, Germany
Nada Lavrac	Jožef Stefan Institute, Slovenia

RAAIT Workshop Chairs

Marieke Peeters	HU University of Applied Sciences Utrecht, The Netherlands
Roland van Dierendonck	Rotterdam University of Applied Sciences, The Netherlands
Saskia Robben	Amsterdam University of Applied Sciences, The Netherlands

AI4S Workshop Chairs

Eunika Mercier-Laurent	University of Reims Champagne Ardenne, France
Gülgün Kayakutlu	Istanbul Technical University, Turkey
Mieczyslaw Lech Owoc	Wrocław University of Economics and Business, Poland
Karl Mason	University of Galway, Ireland
Abdul Wahid	University of Galway, Ireland

Hydra Workshop Chairs

Pierangela Bruno	University of Calabria, Italy
Francesco Calimeri	University of Calabria, Italy
Francesco Cauteruccio	Polytechnic University of Marche, Italy
Giorgio Terracina	University of Calabria, Italy

AI4AI Workshop Chairs

Diedrich Wolter	University of Bamberg, Germany
Jochen L. Leidner	Coburg University of Applied Sciences, Germany
Michael Kohlhase	FAU Erlangen-Nürnberg, Germany
Ute Schmid	University of Bamberg, Germany
Vania Dimitrova	University of Leeds, UK

Contents – Part II

SEDAMI

RAAIT

Hydra

AI4AI

Contents – Part I

XAI^3

Tactful

XI-ML

SEDAMI

Semantic Data Mining (SEDAMI 2023)

The general goal of data mining is to uncover novel, interesting, and ultimately understandable patterns, cf. (Fayyad 1996), i.e., relating to valuable, useful and implicit knowledge. Looking at the development of data mining in the last decades, it can be observed that not only the data mining tasks used to be more restricted, but also the applied data mining workflows were simpler. Thus, recent advances of data mining and machine learning apparently bring new challenges in its practical use in data mining, including interpretability, introduction and preservation of knowledge, as well as the provisioning of explanations.

Using semantic information such as domain/background knowledge in data mining is a promising emerging direction for addressing these problems, where the knowledge is typically represented in a knowledge repository, such as an ontology, or a knowledge base. The main aspect of semantic data mining, which we focus on in this workshop, is the explicit integration of this knowledge into the data mining and knowledge discovery modeling step, where the algorithms for data mining/modeling or post-processing make use of the formalized knowledge to improve the overall results.

The aim of this workshop, is to get an insight into the current status of research in semantic data mining, showing how to include/utilize/exploit semantic information and domain knowledge in the context of machine learning and data mining, focussing on domains and research questions that have not been deeply investigated so far and to improve solutions to classic tasks.

We encourage contributions on methods, techniques and applications that are both domain-specific but also transversal to different application domains. In particular, we solicit contributions that aim to focus on semantic data mining for providing and/or enhancing interpretability, the introduction and preservation of knowledge, as well as the provisioning of explanations - thus addressing important principles, methods, tools and future research directions in this emerging field. This will increase the visibility of the above research themes, and will also bridge research tasks from different fields of artificial intelligence connected to the machine learning and data mining community.

The workshop received six submissions, of which four papers were accepted for presentation. The papers went through a blind peer-review process in which each submission was reviewed by at least three reviewers. We would like to thank Program Committee members for their detailed and constructive reviews, the authors for their well-prepared presentations, and all workshop attendees for their engagement and participation.

September 2023

Szymon Bobek
Martin Atzmueller
Nada Lavrac

Organization

Workshop Co-chairs

Szymon Bobek	Jagiellonian University
Martin Atzmueller	Osnabrück University & German Research Center for AI (DFKI), Germany
Nada Lavrac	Jožef Stefan Institute, Slovenia

Program Committee

Johannes Fürnkranz	Johannes Kepler University Linz
Agnieszka Lawrynowicz	Poznan University of Technology
Dietmar Seipel	Wuerzburg University
Jose Palma	University of Murcia
Eric Postma	TiCC, Tilburg University
Weronika T. Adrian	AGH University of Science and Technology
Marek Sikora	Silesian University of Technology
Przemysław Biecek	Polish Academy of Science, University of Wroclaw
Marc Plantevit	LRE – EPITA
Grzegorz J. Nalepa	Jagiellonian University
Jerzy Stefanowski	Poznan University of Technology, Poland

Leveraging Graph Embedding for Opinion Leader Detection in Dynamic Social Networks

Yunming Hui(✉), Mel Chekol, and Shihan Wang(✉)

Utrecht University, Utrecht, The Netherlands
y.m.hui@outlook.com, {m.w.chekol,s.wang2}@uu.nl

Abstract. Detecting opinion leaders from dynamic social networks is an important and complex problem. The few methods in this field are poor in generalisation and cannot fully consider various dynamic features. In this paper, we propose a novel and generic method based on dynamic graph embedding and clustering. Inspired by the existing knowledge about dynamic opinion leader detection, the proposed method can exploit both the topological and temporal information of dynamic social networks comprehensively. It is also generalisable, as shown experimentally on three different dynamic social network datasets. The experimental results show that the proposed method runs faster than competitors.

Keywords: Social Network Analysis · Opinion Leader Detection · Dynamic Graph Embedding · Dynamic Networks

1 Introduction

In social networks, opinion leaders are individuals whose opinions significantly influence others [6]. They can be experts in a given subject or users who have a significant number of followers on social media. As online social platforms such as Twitter and Instagram continue to grow and the flow of information becomes more rapid, the role that opinion leaders can play also continues to grow. In recent years, there has been increasing attention on how to automatically detect opinion leaders from social networks [3,33].

In reality, social networks are dynamic. One key aspect of this dynamic is reflected in the change of *topology*. For example, individuals may join or leave the network and connections between individuals keep changing. Such topological dynamic is critical to the detection of opinion leaders, as changes in network structure may result in individuals previously identified as opinion leaders losing their influence, or the emergence of new opinion leaders. The dynamics of social networks can also be reflected in the change of *semantic properties* of individuals with respect to their influence. In social networks, an individual's influence not only depends on the strength of their social connections, but also is affected by semantic features such as expertise, reputation and expressiveness [17]. The change in individual semantic properties is also important for opinion leaders because opinion leaders inherently have requirements on identity.

S. Nowaczyk et al. (Eds.): ECAI 2023 Workshops, CCIS 1948, pp. 5–22, 2024.
https://doi.org/10.1007/978-3-031-50485-3_1

The mentioned dynamic factors are crucial for opinion leader detection in social networks [9]. However, the vast majority of existing research tends to overlook such dynamic nature. A few studies that consider them and dynamically identify opinion leaders also suffer from generalization [8,14,27,34]. They rely on certain semantic information that is only available on specific social networks. In fact, only the dynamics of topological features are present in most social networks used by state-of-the-art systems. Thus, a generic solution that can consider both the dynamics of semantic and topological features, while relying on the dynamics of topological features, is still lacking in dynamic opinion leader detection.

Recently, graph embedding has been widely used in social network research to transform nodes into low-dimensional vector representations [5]. In particular, the dynamic graph embedding technique is able to retain information about the temporal changes of a graph in the vector representations. Such representation can preserve temporal, topological and semantics information of a graph [4,5,39]. Even if the node representations are generated only based on topological information, they can still capture some aspects of semantics through the relationships and contextual information present in the graph structure [38]. Additionally, it also allows us to infer or capture implicit relationships that are available in a given graph. Inspired by this, we propose a novel method based on dynamic graph embedding to detect opinion leaders in dynamic social networks.

Specifically, we first perform graph embedding of dynamic social networks and then cluster individual nodes based on the vector representations. Opinion leaders, as a special class of individuals, share similar topological and semantic characteristics [1,3,7]. Since the node representations generated by our chosen dynamic graph embedding method (TGNs [31]) can represent these two characteristics of nodes well, the opinion leaders will be clustered into the same cluster. Then the problem is converted into selecting the cluster containing all opinion leaders which is far more easier. Based on the significant and effective metrics for detecting opinion leaders (i.e. centrality metrics), we also design a method for selecting the cluster. In order to verify the generalisability and feasibility of our method, we evaluated the detection results on three real datasets using the influence spreading mode.

Our method can be generalised to different dynamic social networks (that none of the existing methods is capable of). It can consider temporal topological information alone but also provides ways to incorporate temporal semantic information. Moreover, our method is competitive with state-of-the-art on dynamic social network datasets with dynamic topology, while achieving superior runtime performance. Furthermore, it is a model-agnostic framework that allows the comprehensive exploitation of temporal information of both topological and semantic features in social networks.

2 Problem Definition

We present three commonly used models in social networks and based on them define the problem of dynamic opinion leader detection.

2.1 Social Network Models

Social networks can be predominantly characterized by three models: the static graph model, the snapshot graph model, and the continuous graph model.

Static Graph Model. When a social network is static, it is represented by a directed static graph $G = (V, E)$, where V is the node set and E is the edge set. Each node in V represents an individual which can be attributed to represent the properties of the individual, such as age, organizational status, etc. Each edge in E represents an interaction between individuals, such as following, sending a message, etc. It can also be attributed to indicate the properties of the interaction. The direction of an edge represents the initiator of an interaction. As an example shown in Fig. 1(a), nodes 1–7 represent users 1–7, respectively. Edge $(1, 4)$ represents an interaction initiated by user 1 to user 4, and the other edges have similar meanings.

Snapshot Graph Model. In the discrete case, a dynamic social network existing between t_s and t_e is represented with a series of directed graphs, denoted by $G = \{G_1, \cdots, G_i, \cdots, G_n\}$. The time interval $[t_s, t_e]$ is divided into n sub-intervals and the length of each sub-interval is $l = (t_e - t_s)/n$. For each snapshot $G_i = (V_i, E_i)$, V_i is the node set at time $t_s + (i-1) * l$ and E_i is the edge set including all edges within time interval $[t_s + (i-1) * l, t_s + i * l]$. As the example shown in Fig. 1(b), the time interval [0, 40] is divided into 4 intervals and 4 snapshot graphs are generated correspondingly. In the first snapshot, all the nodes exist in the social network at time 10 and the timestamps of all the edges are within the time interval $[0, 10]$.

Continuous Graph Model. In the continuous case, a dynamic social network existing between time t_s and t_e is represented by a directed graph with edges and nodes annotated with timestamps, denoted by $G = (V, E, T)$. V and E are the collections of nodes and edges over time $[t_s, t_e]$. Edges and nodes have the same format as in the static graph model and therefore can also be attributed. $T : V, E \rightarrow t \in [t_s, t_e]$ is a function that maps each node and edge to timestamps between time t_s and t_e. Taking *node*3 in Fig. 1(c) as an example, $T(v_3) = [1, 31]$. It indicates that node 3 exists in the social network from timestamp 1 to timestamp 31, and $T(e(v_1, v_7)) = 32$ means the interaction between two nodes happens at timestamp 32.

In summary, the three models contain increasing amounts of evolving information of social networks. The static graph model contains no evolving information while the continuous graph model contains the full evolving details. Consequently, the complexity of these three models increases in order and the problems defined on them become more difficult to address [13].

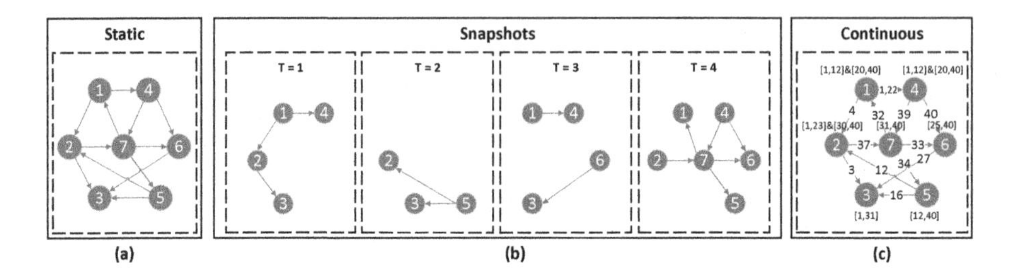

Fig. 1. An example social network represented with three different graph models. There are 7 users in this (dynamic) social network. Within a total of 40 time units, users may join/leave the network or interact with each other.

2.2 Dynamic Opinion Leader Detection

Definition 1 (Problem definition). *Given a social network represented with a continuous model* $G = (V, E, T)$. *The target of the dynamic opinion leader detection problem is to find a finite set of individuals. These individuals should have two main characteristics. One is the possession of a specific identity and authority and the reliance on them to influence other individuals. Another is that their influence, as evaluated based on the dynamic diffusion model, is also higher than that of other ordinary individuals.*

To maximise the use of temporal information of dynamic social networks, we define the dynamic opinion leader detection problem on the continuous graph model. In fact, temporal information plays an essential role in analysing and identifying opinion leaders. Take the network in Fig. 1 as an example. In-degree and out-degree of a node is the most naive way to measure whether a user is an opinion leader or not. The higher the out-degree of a user is, the more likely the user is an opinion leader. Thus, node 7 is most likely to be the opinion leader as it has both the highest in-degree and out-degree. However, considering the information diffusion procedure, it is clear that opinion leaders should accept something new before the majority of users to spread influence better. Therefore, node 7 should not be considered as an opinion leader because it participates in this dynamic social network at the last time. Instead, node 1 has more chance to be an opinion leader as node 1 may influence 4 nodes (nodes 2, 3, 4, 6) in this network, while node 7 can influence at most 2 nodes (nodes 1, 5). Therefore, it is clear that the temporal factor is not negligible and crucial to the opinion leader detection problem.

3 Related Work

In this section, we review the related work in opinion leader detection with a focus on dynamic opinion leader detection.

3.1 Opinion Leader Detection

Static Opinion Leader Detection. Opinion leaders have a high impact on the topology of social networks, which makes centrality metrics an important criterion for measuring opinion leaders in static opinion leader detection. Frequently used centrality includes degree centrality, betweenness centrality and closeness centrality [30,40]. Since these centrality metrics are often measured from a narrower aspect of centrality, they are not comprehensive. Therefore, a variety of methods have been developed, such as PageRank [28] and LeaderRank [20]. To counter the limitations of a single centrality metric, researchers also used various metrics in combination [12].

With the development of machine learning, many studies also use machine learning methods (mainly clustering or graph neural networks (GNNs) techniques) for opinion leader detection [2,15]. Opinion leaders, as a group of people with similar characteristics, can be well clustered into the same cluster by proper use of clustering techniques. Several methods followed this idea and applied the clustering algorithms to identify opinion leaders [2,11]. Later on, Yang et al. [41] used the DeepWalk graph embedding method to generate embedding vectors of users, and then combined them with network topology information to propose a local centrality index of network nodes to identify high-impact nodes. Luo et al. [21] used SNE (Social Network Embedding) model to obtain embedding vectors for each user. These embedding vectors were used to calculate the structure and text similarity between network nodes to improve efficiency.

3.2 Dynamic Opinion Leader Detection

Centrality metrics as an effective and easy-to-calculate metric have been applied to dynamic opinion leader detection as well. However, GNNs have not been used for related research yet. Song et al. [34] proposed a method for dynamic social networks consisting of users and comments. The researchers first rank the influence of comments by sentiment analysis. They also degenerate the dynamic social network into a static social network to calculate the degree of centrality and proximity prestige of each user. Then, opinion leaders are detected by considering three generated features. Only limited temporal information is considered in this study. It is reflected in the calculation of the influence of the comments: the longer the interval between sending the comments the less influence they have on each other. Huang et al. [14] followed this study and proposed a similar method. They improved the work by representing the relationship between the time factor and strength of impact between comments. A similar framework of generating snapshot networks to identify dynamic opinion leaders is also followed by Oueslati et al. [27]. The researchers first evaluated the influence of the post by semantic analysis of the post. Then, opinion leader detection is done based on the influence of the posts sent by each user. Only the impact of the post is counted in each snapshot graph and considered as a temporal feature in the detection. No temporal information has been used in the calculation of every user's influence. Chen et al. [8] proposed a distinct methodology. They do dynamic opinion leader detection on a post-and-follow dynamic social network. They first propose a method to transfer the dynamic network into a weighted static social network. The weights of edges are calculated based on the similarity of the two nodes and the time difference between the appearance of the two nodes (the only utilised temporal information). Then, they do community detection based on this weighted static social network and future detect the opinion leader with different attributes of nodes.

In summary, the limited existing methods of dynamic opinion leader detection do not make sufficient use of temporal information. Moreover, they are designed based on unique datasets containing information that is not always included in other datasets. Therefore, the generalisation of these methods is poor. Our method focuses on solving these problems.

To further clarify our focus, we also briefly mention and distinguish one related but different problem, namely dynamic information maximization. It identifies an initial set of nodes of predefined size k with the biggest influence spread in a dynamic social network. Please refer to [18] for a detailed review. This problem is different from opinion leader detection as it does not place any constraints on the identity of the node. When opinion leaders are difficult to be labelled in large-scale social networks, the influence of detected opinion leaders can be used to quantify the performance of opinion leader detection methods [3]. Aggarwal et al. [1] first proposed a method to evaluate the influence of a given set of nodes in a dynamic social network. This hill-climbing algorithm is then used to get the final seed set starting from a simple selection of individuals with the highest influence. Zhuang et al. [43] first construct a subgraph by probing a set of nodes in the underlying graph such that the influence diffusion can be best observed. Then, the seed set that can maximize the influence on the underlying graph is found on the subgraph. Unlike these two methods that select all individuals at once at the beginning stage, Michalski et al. [24] proposed a method that models dynamic social network using snapshots graph model and activates seeds based on sequential seeding in temporal networks. Notably, none of the existing dynamic information maximization methods applied dynamic graph embedding to capture various temporal features of dynamic networks.

4 Methodology

4.1 Overall Design and Framework

The overall framework of our method is presented in Fig. 2 and the specific flow of the method is shown in Appendix 7.2. Opinion leaders, as a special category of people, share the same characteristics, such as higher influence, accepting ideas and starting to spread them before most individuals do [16,37]. Based on this feature, we propose to categorise different individuals based on their (temporal) properties and then select the opinion leaders from all the categories. Such a choice is much simpler in computation compared to choosing opinion leaders from all the nodes. This is because the number of clusters (e.g. less than 10) is

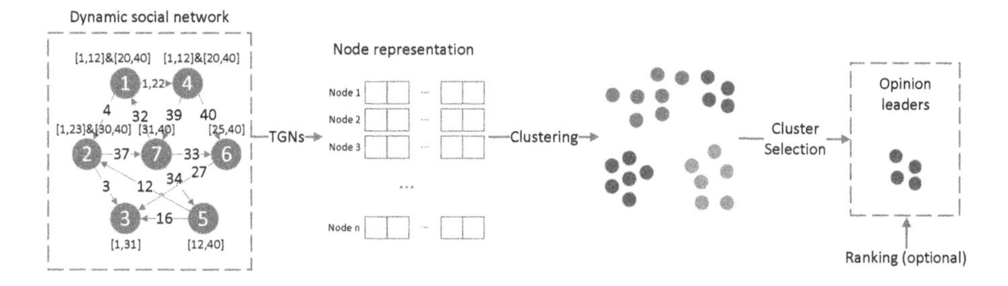

Fig. 2. Framework of the proposed method

usually smaller than that of opinion leaders (that is a small percentage of a large number of individuals and can be over a thousand).

So, we first transfer the dynamic graph into node representations (low dimensional vectors) with the dynamic graph embedding method. Then, the nodes are clustered based on node representations. This approach seeks to group nodes together based on the similarity of their embeddings, which encapsulate their structural roles within the network and how these roles evolve over time (especially influential factors). The principle here is that nodes within the same cluster should have similar features, as reflected in their embeddings. The resulting clusters can reveal patterns in the nodes' behaviors and roles that persist or evolve over time, and help us better understand the underlying structure and dynamics of the network [4,5,39]. In this manner, at a design level, our method makes better use of temporal information compared to existing methods.

Following these steps, the dynamic opinion leader detection problem is converted to select the cluster that contains all opinion leaders. Previous research has indicated that the centrality metrics can well reflect the probability of an individual being an opinion leader [3]. We therefore also design the algorithm for selecting the cluster containing all opinion leaders based on various centrality metrics. In real social scenarios, the number of nodes in this cluster may be higher than the required number of opinion leaders (e.g. we only care about the top ones). If needed, the opinion leaders in this cluster can also be ranked to select the most influential ones. In the next subsections, the method will be described in detail.

4.2 Dynamic Graph Embedding

In this framework, the node representations should be able to well represent the dynamic of topological features as well as the semantic features. Within various dynamic graph embedding methods introduced in Appendix 7.1, we employed the TGNs method which is good at retaining dynamics of both topological and semantic features and has been shown to perform significantly better than other existing dynamic graph embedding methods [31].

The TGNs method uses the encoder-decoder model. It has two core modules, a memory module and an embedding module. The memory module is used to represent the node's topological evolving history in a compressed format which allows TGNs to memorize long-term dependencies for each node in the graph. In the memory module, each node is represented with a low-dimensional vector which is updated when changes related to the node happen using Recurrent Neural Network (RNN). The main goal of the embedding module is to better aggregate the information of neighbouring nodes through Graph Neural Network (GNN) based on the information generated by the memory module. When the semantic features of nodes are available, the embedding module can incorporate the semantic information of nodes into the final node representations. Please refer to the original paper for details about the TGNs method [31]. In this way, the generated node representation shall encapsulate various features of nodes within the network both topologically and semantically, as well as how these features evolve over time.

4.3 Clustering and Cluster Selection

Next, we used the classical k-means [19] algorithm to cluster the nodes using their node representations. We followed the previous studies in social network analysis and used centrality metrics to determine the opinion leader clusters [3]. To apply three commonly used centrality metrics in our dynamic setting, we convert the dynamic social network represented with a continuous model into a snapshot model in this step. Then, we can calculate the three centrality metrics in each snapshot separately and add them proportionally. In addition, in dynamic social networks, opinion leaders should accept and disseminate ideas to others before most people do [37]. This means that the higher the centrality metric in the earlier snapshots the more likely they are to become opinion leaders. In other words, the high centrality metric in later snapshots, is not as useful as that in earlier snapshots. Node 7 in Fig. 1 is a good example. We therefore designed a decay function to reflect this pattern which will be explained in the following paragraphs.

Formally, we use the following equation to express the probability of an individual node being an opinion leader in a dynamic social network:

$$LScore(v) = \sum_{t=1}^{n} decay(\frac{t-1}{n}) \cdot (m_1 BC(v,t) + m_2 CC(v,t) + m_3 DC(v,t)), \quad (1)$$

where n is the number of snapshots and v is a node in the node set V. $BC(v,t)$, $CC(v,t)$ and $DC(v,t)$ is the betweenness centrality, closeness centrality and degree centrality of node v in t-th snapshot respectively. m_1, m_2 and m_3 are adjustable parameters to control the weighting of these three centrality metrics in the LScore. The decay function can be selected from the following five functions: $f_1(x) = 1 - x$, $f_2(x) = (x-1)^2$, $f_3(x) = 1 - x^2$, $f_4(x) = \cos(x)$, and $f_5(x) = (x+1)^2$.

Table 1. Statistics of three datasets. In the latter two datasets, the start and end times are anonymous indexes of time steps.

Dataset	Node Number	Edge Number	Start Time	End Time	Interval Length
UC-IRV	1,889	59,835	2004-04-15	2004-10-26	7 days
Bitcoinalpha	3,783	24,186	0	164246400	7,776,000 (90 days)
Bitcoinotc	5,881	35,592	0	164442412	7,776,000 (90 days)

These five decay functions represent different decay modes. The f_1 is a linear decay, which means that the contribution of centrality to importance decreases linearly. f_2 and f_3 are non-linear in decay, meaning that the effect of centrality on importance decays at different rates over time. The decaying effect of f_4 and f_5 is relatively small.

We further calculate the average probability of all nodes in a cluster and name it ALScore which is calculated as follows:

$$ALScore(c) = \frac{\sum_{i=1}^{|c|} LScore(v_i)}{|c|} \tag{2}$$

where $|c|$ is the number of nodes in cluster c and v_i is a node in cluster c. The cluster with the highest ALScore is considered as the cluster containing the opinion leaders. Sometimes the number of opinion leaders needed will be larger than the number of the top cluster containing opinion leaders. In such cases, more than one cluster can be considered, then individual nodes can be ranked to satisfy the requirement.

5 Experiments and Results

The code used for experiments can be found at here.

5.1 Experimental Setting

Dataset. Three different datasets used to carry out experiments are UC-IRV [29], Bitcoinalpha[1] and Bitcoinotc[2]. All of them can be structured as continuous graph models (defined in Sect. 2.1). The statistics of 3 datasets are shown in Table 1. The detailed information of datasets is explained in Appendix 7.3.

Parameter Setting. We used the source code[3] of the graph embedding method TGNs provided by the authors. The main parameters of TGNs used in experiments are as follows: the dimension of node embedding is 172, the learning rate

[1] http://snap.stanford.edu/data/soc-sign-bitcoin-alpha.html.
[2] https://snap.stanford.edu/data/soc-sign-bitcoin-otc.html.
[3] https://github.com/twitter-research/tgn.

is 0.001, the batch size is 200, the number of neighbours to sample is 20, the embedding model us graph attention network whose number of layer is 1 and number of heads used in attention layer is 2. The number of clusters is set to be 8 for UC-IRV and 7 for Bitcoinalpha and Bitcoinotc. The decay function we used is $decay_2$. m_1, m_2 and m_3 are all set to 1. The process of parameter optimization is shown in Appendix 7.4.

Evaluation Metric. Since it is difficult to label opinion leaders for large social networks, evaluating the influence of opinion leaders is a common method for evaluating the dynamic graph embedding method. The estimation of influence of nodes depends on the **diffusion model** which describes the rules of propagation of an individual's influence in a social network. Simulations based on the diffusion model can determine the number of individuals that an individual can influence.

The dynamic diffusion model we selected is Susceptible-Infectious (SI) model which is also used by Osawa et al. [26]. In the SI model, nodes can have two states S and I. A node in state S means it does not have information and a node in state I means it contains information. This model uses the snapshot form of a dynamic graph. If a node is in state I at time t, it tries to activate its neighbours at time $t+1$ with probability. In experiments, the affected probability of each node is set to 0.5. The ability of opinion leaders to spread influence is evaluated by the total number of nodes influenced by opinion leaders throughout the whole period. A larger number of influenced nodes means a higher impact on this network. In our experiments, due to the randomness in the diffusion process, we repeat the process 100 times and average the computation.

Baselines. We selected two kinds of baselines, static and dynamic opinion leader detection methods. The static opinion leader detection method we selected is **LeaderRank** [20]. It has a good performance among the static methods but ignores the dynamics of topological features. We therefore consider it as a representative of the static methods for comparison. Due to the unique data requirements and non-public datasets, all the existing dynamic opinion leader detection methods are difficult to be compared. Although the dynamic influence maximisation problem has some differences from the dynamic opinion leader detection problem, the requirement for the selected nodes to have high influence is the same. Therefore, two dynamic influence maximisation methods are selected to compare the influence of detected opinion leaders with ours. They are selected to represent two different mechanisms. **INDDSN** [1]: A method quickly estimates the influence of an individual in a dynamic social network and selects all individuals at once at the beginning stage. The forward version with better performance is used. **SSA** [24]: A state-of-art method selects individuals in a decentralised manner, which results in a higher spread of influence.

5.2 Clustering Result Analysis

The clustering results of three datasets are shown in Table 2. From the table, it can be seen that the size of clusters containing all opinion leaders are relatively

Table 2. Clustering results of three datasets. The numbers indicate the number of nodes in the cluster. The clusters containing opinion leaders are bolded.

Cluster	1	2	3	4	5	6	7	8
UC-IRV	292	**300**	162	288	251	214	166	226
Bitcoinalpha	671	621	**347**	333	560	728	523	–
Bitcoinotc	928	600	989	1,196	781	**243**	1,144	–

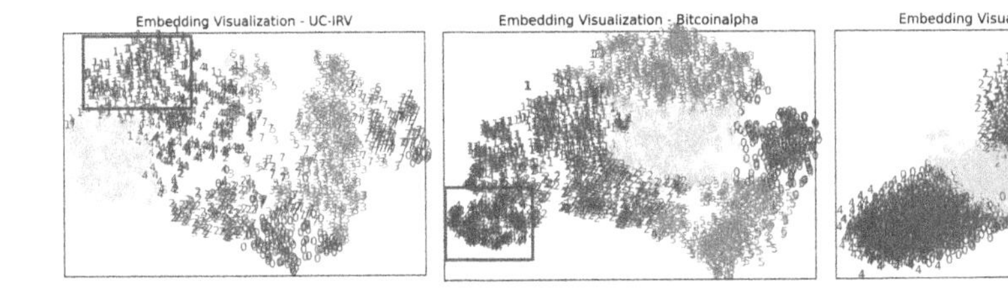

Fig. 3. Visualization of node representations of three datasets. The clusters containing opinion leaders are marked with the blue rectangular box.

small. This matches the characteristics of the opinion leader group that only a small set of individuals tend to lead the public in social networks [35].

To further validate our generated clusters, we also employed t-SNE [23] to visualise the node representation (See Fig. 3). A remarkable phenomenon from the visualization results is that all clusters containing opinion leaders are in the corners, i.e. the furthest away from all other clusters.

This phenomenon hints at the idea that opinion leaders possess distinct qualities or exert a significant level of influence that sets them apart from the general population within the dataset. Their placement in the corners of the visualization signifies that they are not only separate from other clusters, but their influence may also radiate outwards, impacting the entire network in a manner that distinguishes them from regular nodes. This phenomenon also confirms the feasibility of the method, i.e., the characteristics of the cluster containing the opinion leaders can be contained in the node embeddings (from dynamic graph embedding).

5.3 Performance Evaluation

We compared the influence of detected opinion leaders by the proposed method as well as the running time with three baselines.

Influence. As shown in Fig. 4, INDDSN has the best performance among the three baseline methods. The proposed method has similar or better performance on Bitcoinalpha and Bitcoinotc. In UC-IRV the performance of INDDSN is a little bit better than the proposed method. It is worth noting that the network of UC-IRV is dense and smaller than another two datasets which makes the

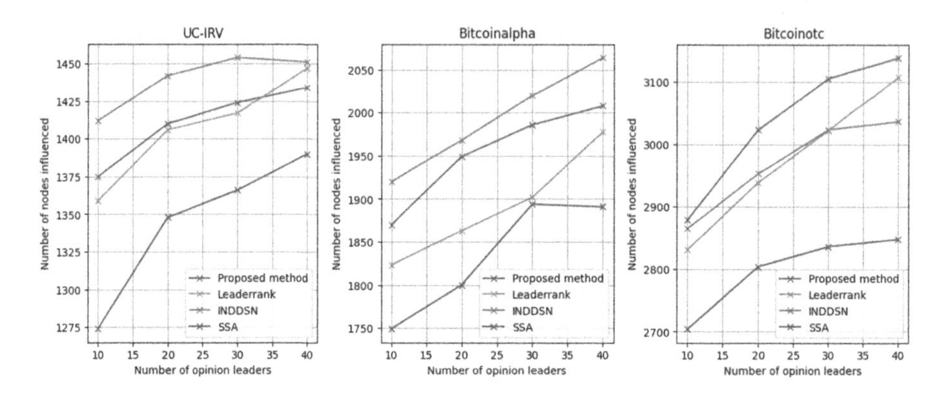

Fig. 4. Number of nodes influenced with different numbers of opinion leaders

difference less significant. Besides, as the number of opinion leaders increases, INDDSN's performance begins to deteriorate, and sometimes the number of people it can influence even decreases. This indicates that performance is difficult to guarantee when the number of opinion leaders is in high demand, and sometimes it is even lower than the static algorithm.

Running Time. The runtime performance of all methods with different numbers of opinion leaders is shown in Fig. 5. The running time of LeaderRank and the proposed method is similar for different numbers of opinion leaders as they produce the rank of each node at one time. The running time of INDDSN and SSA grows as the number of opinion leaders increases. The running time of INDDSN is the highest and is two to eight times higher than the running time of our proposed method.

Discussion. While the influential performance of the proposed method is similar to the state-of-art baseline INDDSN, our method still has superiority given the long running time of INDDSN. Even worse INDDSN uses a hill climbing algorithm. As the number of opinion leaders and the number of individuals in the social network increases, the time taken to search the neighbourhood solution space grows. When to stop searching is critical to the performance of the results, but how to set it up is tricky requiring a large number of experiments for each social network. Moreover, experimental results demonstrate that the advantages of our proposed method increase as the network size increases. This is particularly valuable because scalability is increasingly important for developing new solutions in social network analysis as there will be a high requirement for a larger size of the network in practical problems.

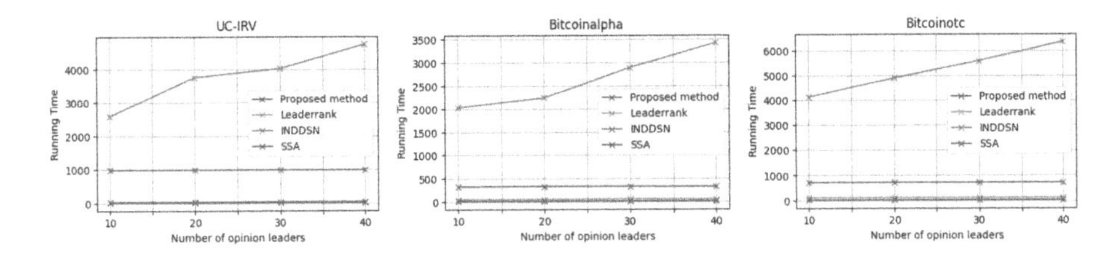

Fig. 5. Running time of different methods with different numbers of opinion leaders

6 Conclusion and Future Work

In this paper, we illustrate the importance of the dynamic nature of social networks for opinion leader detection. We proposed a novel method to detect opinion leaders from a continuously dynamic social network represented by the continuous model. We leveraged dynamic graph embedding and clustering algorithms to identify a group of opinion leaders who share similar temporal features. The results of generated clusters show that our method captures temporal and topological features of nodes. Compared to existing methods, our proposed method is less restrictive on the type of social network dataset. The method is evaluated on the influence of detected opinion leaders and running time, showing similar performance to other methods but higher operational efficiency. For future work, we want to explore new dynamic graph embedding methods by integrating influence-related knowledge into the node representations, which may bring better performance.

7 Appendix

7.1 Related Work on Dynamic Graph Embedding

Dynamic graph embedding methods can map the dynamic graph to a set of low-dimensional dense vectors. Each of these vectors represents a node. This representation improves the feasibility and efficiency of various network analysis tasks [4,39]. The purpose of dynamic graph embedding methods is that these low-dimensional vectors can not only maintain the topological information, but also the graph evolving information.

Following the static graph embedding methods [4], most early dynamic graph embedding methods update the graph representations quickly when social network changes [32,42]. The low-dimensional vector representation obtained by these methods does not represent the actual evolving information of graphs. Instead, only topological information about the graph after the change is captured. Recently, some proposed dynamic graph embedding methods can represent both topological and evolving information in the representations. Among them, several methods use random walk, which extends the random walk in static graphs by the addition of temporal constraints [10,25]. More methods use Recurrent Neural Network (RNN) to update node representations when changes on edge happened [22,31,36]. In this work, we apply this type of dynamic graph embedding method to consider the temporal evolution of social networks.

7.2 Methodology Summary

Following the above two subsections describe our design ideas and methodological principles, the pseudo-code of our method is shown in Algorithm 1.

Algorithm 1. Graph Embedding Based Dynamic Opinion Leader Detection

Require: dynamic graph: G, number of opinion leaders needed: k, number of cluster c, hyperparameter: m_1,m_2,m_3
Ensure: set of opinion leaders S
1: $node\_embeddings \leftarrow TGNs(G)$
2: $clusters \leftarrow k\text{-}means(node\_embeddings, num\_clusters)$
3: $score\_clusters \leftarrow$ calculate ALScore of each cluster in $clusters$ with Eq. 2
4: $S \leftarrow$ cluster with the highest ALScore
5: **if** size of $S > k$ **then**
6: calculate LScore of each node in S with Eq. 2
7: sort S according to LScore
8: $S \leftarrow$ top k nodes in S
9: **end if**
10: return S

The dynamic social network is first transferred to node embeddings using TGNs. Then, the nodes are clustered based the node representations. Next, the ALScore of each cluster is calculated using Eq. 2. The cluster with the highest ALScore is selected as the cluster containing all opinion leaders. If the number of nodes in cluster is higher than the number of opinion leaders needed. The LScore of these nodes is calculated with Eq 1 and these nodes are ranked according to the LScore. The top k nodes are the final opinion leaders.

7.3 Dataset Description

Here is a detailed explanation of three used datasets.

- **UC-IRV** [29] UC Irvine messages dataset includes the users that sent or received at least one message in a Facebook-like Social Network originating from an online community for students at the University of California, Irvine. The database contains a total of 59,835 online messages, each message contains the sender, receiver and time of sending. The dataset is used to form a directed dynamic social network. Each edge represents a message which is directed from the sender of the message to the receiver of the message.
- **Bitcoinalpha**[4] Bitcoinalpha is a who-trusts-whom network of people who trade using Bitcoin on a platform called Bitcoin Alpha. The dataset contains

[4] http://snap.stanford.edu/data/soc-sign-bitcoin-alpha.html.

a total of 24,186 credit rating records from one user to another. Each record contains the person who made the credit rating and the person who was rated, the rating level and the time the rating was made. The dataset is used to form a directed dynamic social network. Each edge represents a credit rating record which is directed from the rating maker to the rate.
- **Bitcoinotc**[5] Bitcoinotc is similar to Bitcoinalpha, but it is collected from another Bitcoin platform, Bitcoin OTC. The number of records in this dataset is 35,592. The format of records is the same as that of Bitcoinalpha.

7.4 Parameters Optimization

In the proposed method, there are five important parameters: number of clusters c, m_1,m_2,m_3 and type of decay function. We tested different combinations of parameters in all three datasets.

We first optimize the number of clusters c. As we discussed in the last section, ALScore can roughly reflect the average probability that all nodes in a cluster might be opinion leaders. When we choose the value of c, we want the ALScore of the cluster with the highest ALScore to be the highest. The ALScore of the cluster with the highest ALScore varying with the value of c, other conditions being equal, is shown in Table 3. It can be seen that the best results are achieved when c is set to be 7 or 8. We recommend that in subsequent experiments c will be set to 7 or 8 for best results.

Table 3. ALScore of the cluster with the highest ALScore varying with the value of c

c	5	6	7	8	9
UC-IRV	0.41	0.42	0.43	**0.45**	0.44
Bitcoinalpha	0.46	0.48	**0.49**	0.48	0.46
Bitcoinotc	0.52	0.55	**0.56**	0.55	0.54

Following, we optimize m_1,m_2,m_3 and type of decay function. The test the influence of opinion leaders detected with combinations of different type of decay function and centrality metrics in dataset UC-IRV and Bitcoinalpha. The results are shown in Table 4. For the decay function, $decay_2$ can always bring the best performance. Therefore we suggest that the preferred decay function is $decay_2$, which will also be used in the next experiments. For the centrality indicator, closeness centrality performs significantly lower than the other two centrality indicators. Considering the time-consuming calculation of closeness centrality, we suggest ignoring closeness centrality, i.e., setting m_3 to 0. Betweenness centrality and degree centrality perform similarly, so we suggest setting both m_1 and m_2 to 1 so that they contribute equally to LScore. This will also be used in the following experiments.

[5] https://snap.stanford.edu/data/soc-sign-bitcoin-otc.html.

Table 4. The influence of opinion leaders detected with combinations of different types of decay functions and centrality metrics

Dataset	UC-IRV			Bitcoinalpha		
Centrality metric	Betweenness	Degree	Closeness	Betweenness	Degree	Closeness
decay_1	1247	1245	1219	1645	1636	1631
decay_2	**1261**	**1257**	**1183**	**1679**	**1664**	**1628**
decay_3	1232	1217	1213	1636	1630	1566
decay_4	1196	1191	1180	1597	1601	1513
decay_5	1200	1203	1187	1611	1608	1521

References

1. Aggarwal, C.C., Lin, S., Yu, P.S.: On influential node discovery in dynamic social networks. In: Proceedings of the 2012 SIAM International Conference on Data Mining, pp. 636–647. SIAM (2012)
2. Arvapally, R.S., Liu, X., Jiang, W.: Identification of faction groups and leaders in web-based intelligent argumentation system for collaborative decision support. In: 2012 International Conference on Collaboration Technologies and Systems (CTS), pp. 509–516. IEEE (2012)
3. Bamakan, S.M.H., Nurgaliev, I., Qu, Q.: Opinion leader detection: a methodological review. Expert Syst. Appl. **115**, 200–222 (2019)
4. Barros, C.D., Mendonça, M.R., Vieira, A.B., Ziviani, A.: A survey on embedding dynamic graphs. ACM Comput. Surv. (CSUR) **55**(1), 1–37 (2021)
5. Cai, H., Zheng, V.W., Chang, K.C.C.: A comprehensive survey of graph embedding: problems, techniques, and applications. IEEE Trans. Knowl. Data Eng. **30**(9), 1616–1637 (2018)
6. Chan, K.K., Misra, S.: Characteristics of the opinion leader: a new dimension. J. Advert. **19**(3), 53–60 (1990)
7. Chen, Y.C., Cheng, J.Y., Hsu, H.H.: A cluster-based opinion leader discovery in social network. In: 2016 Conference on Technologies and Applications of Artificial Intelligence (TAAI), pp. 78–83. IEEE (2016)
8. Chen, Y.C., Hui, L., Wu, C.I., Liu, H.Y., Chen, S.C.: Opinion leaders discovery in dynamic social network. In: 2017 10th International Conference on Ubi-media Computing and Workshops (Ubi-Media), pp. 1–6. IEEE (2017)
9. Cordeiro, M., Sarmento, R.P., Brazdil, P., Gama, J.: Evolving networks and social network analysis methods and techniques. In: Social Media and Journalism-Trends, Connections, Implications, pp. 101–134 (2018)
10. Du, L., Wang, Y., Song, G., Lu, Z., Wang, J.: Dynamic network embedding: an extended approach for skip-gram based network embedding. In: IJCAI, vol. 2018, pp. 2086–2092 (2018)
11. Duan, J., Zeng, J., Luo, B.: Identification of opinion leaders based on user clustering and sentiment analysis. In: 2014 IEEE/WIC/ACM International Joint Conferences on Web Intelligence (WI) and Intelligent Agent Technologies (IAT), vol. 1, pp. 377–383. IEEE (2014)
12. Gao, C., Wei, D., Hu, Y., Mahadevan, S., Deng, Y.: A modified evidential methodology of identifying influential nodes in weighted networks. Phys. A **392**(21), 5490–5500 (2013)

13. Hafiene, N., Karoui, W., Romdhane, L.B.: Influential nodes detection in dynamic social networks: a survey. Expert Syst. Appl. **159**, 113642 (2020)
14. Huang, B., Yu, G., Karimi, H.R., et al.: The finding and dynamic detection of opinion leaders in social network. Math. Prob. Eng. **2014**, 7 (2014)
15. Jain, L., Katarya, R., Sachdeva, S.: Opinion leaders for information diffusion using graph neural network in online social networks. ACM Trans. Web **17**(2), 1–37 (2023)
16. Katz, E., Lazarsfeld, P.F.: Personal Influence: The Part Played by People in the Flow of Mass Communications. Routledge (2017)
17. Li, Y., Chen, W., Wang, Y., Zhang, Z.L.: Influence diffusion dynamics and influence maximization in social networks with friend and foe relationships. In: Proceedings of the Sixth ACM International Conference on Web Search and Data Mining, pp. 657–666 (2013)
18. Li, Y., Fan, J., Wang, Y., Tan, K.L.: Influence maximization on social graphs: a survey. IEEE Trans. Knowl. Data Eng. **30**(10), 1852–1872 (2018)
19. Lloyd, S.: Least squares quantization in PCM. IEEE Trans. Inf. Theory **28**(2), 129–137 (1982)
20. Lü, L., Zhang, Y.C., Yeung, C.H., Zhou, T.: Leaders in social networks, the delicious case. PLoS ONE **6**(6), e21202 (2011)
21. Luo, J., Du, Y., Li, R., Cheng, F.: Identification of opinion leaders by using social network embedding. In: 2019 IEEE 5th International Conference on Computer and Communications (ICCC), pp. 1412–1416. IEEE (2019)
22. Ma, Y., Guo, Z., Ren, Z., Tang, J., Yin, D.: Streaming graph neural networks. In: Proceedings of the 43rd International ACM SIGIR Conference on Research and Development in Information Retrieval, pp. 719–728 (2020)
23. Van der Maaten, L., Hinton, G.: Visualizing data using t-SNE. J. Mach. Learn. Res. **9**(11), 2579–2605 (2008)
24. Michalski, R., Jankowski, J., Bródka, P.: Effective influence spreading in temporal networks with sequential seeding. IEEE Access **8**, 151208–151218 (2020)
25. Nguyen, G.H., Lee, J.B., Rossi, R.A., Ahmed, N.K., Koh, E., Kim, S.: Continuous-time dynamic network embeddings. In: Companion Proceedings of the the Web Conference 2018, pp. 969–976 (2018)
26. Osawa, S., Murata, T.: Selecting seed nodes for influence maximization in dynamic networks. In: Mangioni, G., Simini, F., Uzzo, S.M., Wang, D. (eds.) Complex Networks VI. SCI, vol. 597, pp. 91–98. Springer, Cham (2015). https://doi.org/10.1007/978-3-319-16112-9_9
27. Oueslati, W., Arrami, S., Dhouioui, Z., Massaabi, M.: Opinion leaders' detection in dynamic social networks. Concurrency Comput. Pract. Exp. **33**(1), e5692 (2021)
28. Page, L., Brin, S., Motwani, R., Winograd, T.: The pagerank citation ranking: bringing order to the web. Tech. rep. Stanford InfoLab (1999)
29. Panzarasa, P., Opsahl, T., Carley, K.M.: Patterns and dynamics of users' behavior and interaction: network analysis of an online community. J. Am. Soc. Inform. Sci. Technol. **60**(5), 911–932 (2009)
30. Risselada, H., Verhoef, P.C., Bijmolt, T.H.: Indicators of opinion leadership in customer networks: self-reports and degree centrality. Mark. Lett. **27**(3), 449–460 (2016)
31. Rossi, E., Chamberlain, B., Frasca, F., Eynard, D., Monti, F., Bronstein, M.: Temporal graph networks for deep learning on dynamic graphs. arXiv preprint arXiv:2006.10637 (2020)

32. Sankar, A., Wu, Y., Gou, L., Zhang, W., Yang, H.: DySAT: deep neural representation learning on dynamic graphs via self-attention networks. In: Proceedings of the 13th International Conference on Web Search and Data Mining, pp. 519–527 (2020)
33. Sharma, K., Bajaj, M., et al.: A review on opinion leader detection and its applications. In: 2022 7th International Conference on Communication and Electronics Systems (ICCES), pp. 1645–1651. IEEE (2022)
34. Song, K., Wang, D., Feng, S., Yu, G.: Detecting opinion leader dynamically in Chinese news comments. In: Wang, L., Jiang, J., Lu, J., Hong, L., Liu, B. (eds.) WAIM 2011. LNCS, vol. 7142, pp. 197–209. Springer, Heidelberg (2012). https://doi.org/10.1007/978-3-642-28635-3_19
35. Tang, J., Lou, T., Kleinberg, J.: Inferring social ties across heterogenous networks. In: Proceedings of the fifth ACM International Conference on Web Search and Data Mining, pp. 743–752 (2012)
36. Trivedi, R., Farajtabar, M., Biswal, P., Zha, H.: DyRep: learning representations over dynamic graphs. In: International Conference on Learning Representations (2019)
37. Valente, T.W., Pumpuang, P.: Identifying opinion leaders to promote behavior change. Health Educ. Behav. **34**(6), 881–896 (2007)
38. Wu, L., Zhao, H., Li, Z., Huang, Z., Liu, Q., Chen, E.: Learning the explainable semantic relations via unified graph topic-disentangled neural networks. ACM Trans. Knowl. Discov. Data **17**(8), 1–23 (2023)
39. Xue, G., Zhong, M., Li, J., Chen, J., Zhai, C., Kong, R.: Dynamic network embedding survey. Neurocomputing **472**, 212–223 (2022)
40. Yang, L., Qiao, Y., Liu, Z., Ma, J., Li, X.: Identifying opinion leader nodes in online social networks with a new closeness evaluation algorithm. Soft. Comput. **22**(2), 453–464 (2018)
41. Yang, X.H., et al.: Identifying influential spreaders in complex networks based on network embedding and node local centrality. Phys. A **573**, 125971 (2021)
42. Yu, W., Cheng, W., Aggarwal, C.C., Zhang, K., Chen, H., Wang, W.: NetWalk: a flexible deep embedding approach for anomaly detection in dynamic networks. In: Proceedings of the 24th ACM SIGKDD International Conference on Knowledge Discovery & Data Mining, pp. 2672–2681 (2018)
43. Zhuang, H., Sun, Y., Tang, J., Zhang, J., Sun, X.: Influence maximization in dynamic social networks. In: 2013 IEEE 13th International Conference on Data Mining, pp. 1313–1318. IEEE (2013)

Post–mining on Association Rule Bases

Dietmar Seipel[1(✉)], Marcel Waleska[1], Daniel Weidner[1], Sven Rausch[1], and Martin Atzmueller[2,3]

[1] Department of Computer Science, Knowledge-Based Systems Group (KBS), University of Würzburg, Am Hubland, 97074 Würzburg, Germany
dietmar.seipel@uni-wuerzburg.de
[2] Institute of Computer Science, Semantic Information Systems Group (SIS), Osnabrück University, Wachsbleiche 27, 49090 Osnabrück, Germany
martin.atzmueller@uni-osnabrueck.de
[3] German Research Center for Artificial Intelligence (DFKI), Hamburger Street 24, 49084 Osnabrück, Germany

Abstract. Association rule mining identifies potentially unknown correlations between columns in a relational database and is therefore a central task in the data mining process. In many cases though, the resulting set of association rules is by far too big and confusing for a *domain expert* to extract useful knowledge. Moreover, the domain expert might often expect that particular association rules are generated by the data mining process and would like to be able to *search*, e. g., *for similar rules* according to their expectation.

In this paper, we propose to store association rules in a *rule base* which will offer functionality for the management of the rules. The rule base can also offer *subsumption* features for condensing huge sets of derived association rules to smaller subsets of interesting rules that can be investigated by the domain expert. The rule base can store association rules derived in different attempts of rule mining. And depending on the result of a rule mining attempt, further attempts can be initiated. The *post–processing* of the rule mining result, for example, can derive further association rules by grouping the values of attributes in their consequences; it can also initiate another round of pre-processing of the base relation to group certain values of certain attributes to sets (tiles), and thus to derive correlations between sets of attribute values in further steps of association rule mining.

Keywords: Data Mining · Association Rules · Rule Bases · Subsumption

1 Introduction

Artificial intelligence in general can be divided into two approaches, symbolic and subsymbolic [14,26,30]. Examples for *subsymbolic models* are the popular and widely used Artificial Neural Networks. They analyze statistical correlations and make predictions, based on the known history of events in a data-driven fashion, i. e., typically without considering, how this prediction could be explained logically. This approach is similar to decision making based on human experience. We can decide, based on past events, for example, without having to think about the root cause(s) of these. Also,

S. Nowaczyk et al. (Eds.): ECAI 2023 Workshops, CCIS 1948, pp. 23–35, 2024.
https://doi.org/10.1007/978-3-031-50485-3_2

we expect effects because we have seen them in the past. In contrast to that, there is the so-called *symbolic approach*. This method decides, based on logical deduction, i.e., with respect to a learned set of rules. Therefore, a domain expert has the opportunity, to adapt the set of rules and, for example, to add own coherences afterwards, to optimize the model through his own experience. The symbolic way of deciding is similar to human logical thinking, where conclusions are made by analyzing the causes and their likely effects.

The latter approach, in particular, also lends itself to facilitating *interpretability* and *explainability* in the decision making process [9,11,37], since decisions can be explicated in terms of rules, and the reasoning process can be transparently explained, e. g., via keeping track of the deductive steps, or by reconstructing the respective derivation processes. Furthermore, rules can be extracted from a database in order to support decision making, such that a user is supported by interpretable knowledge, e. g., in the form of associations or correlations from a database. Then, this also supports computational sensemaking [5] via comprehensible representations. Here, pattern mining approaches are interesting options, e. g., in the form of associative patterns or profiles, e. g., [6,7]. For this purpose, *association rules* are a prominent form of knowledge facilitating interpretability and understandability as a key feature. For supporting the process of identifying useful and actionable knowledge from a large set of association rules, however, it is necessary to provide adequate approaches for the management, analysis, and query-based access to the respective association rule bases.

In this paper, we tackle these issues by proposing such functionality for the management of association rules in the corresponding *rule bases*, such that useful knowledge can be extracted, e. g., by *subsumption of rules* or *searching for similar rules*.

Our core contributions are summarized as follows:

1. We provide operations for compressing an association rule base, i.e., using subsumption and joining association rules based on the values of associations in order to both condense as well as extend association rules in the association rule base.
2. Furthermore, we present methods for similarity search in an association rule base using simple queries.
3. Finally, we present a formal representation using the declarative logic programming toolkit Declare [34], and illustrate our methods using examples, also relating to a real-world application in the context of analyzing data of heating systems.

The rest of the paper is structured as follows: Sect. 2 discusses some related work on association rules in general and on some post-mining techniques. Section 3 provides the definitions necessary to understand the data mining workflow, which is presented in Sect. 4. In addition to the basics of association rule mining, this section also defines some post-mining steps. Then, operations on association rule bases are presented in Sect. 5, followed by small, illustrating examples in Sect. 6; we start with a toy example for demonstration, and provide a more complex realistic example from the heating domain. Finally, Sect. 7 concludes the paper with a discussion of the presented work along with some thoughts on future work.

2 Related Work

In this section, we provide an overview of the concept of association rule mining as well as approaches in the representation and post-mining methods for such rule bases.

Association Rule Mining

Searching for correlations in databases via inductive analysis [23] to create rules using association rule [1,33] mining is an established method in the field of knowledge discovery in databases [16,17] and explainable AI in general [4,25]. Over the years, different approaches have been developed to address specific areas of interest and domains. As a result, many different measures have been developed to find the most relevant rules for a given task. An overview of the most common ones is presented in [21]. However, as can be seen, for example, in [8,28,31,41], there is still current research in this area. This is necessary, e. g., because the nature and scope of the given data can change over time, or specific data characteristics need to be addressed.

The Post Mining Processes

In this evolution, not only the measures for finding rules in the data, but also the methods that work with the resulting rule base need to be adapted. While a large set of potentially relevant rules is generated, most of them are very similar in terms of what they say and are therefore redundant, e. g., considering subsumption [20]. To solve this problem, pruning of such redundant rules is presented in [12], also targeting specific approaches for efficient pruning [38,42]. Another approach is to use constraints, as shown in [10].

Post-processing [27] or post-mining [29] association rules are prominent directions for the intelligent management of association rules. This can also include rule interestingness measures for filtering association rules [18,19,32]. In [27] rule post-processing from an application-driven perspective is considered, discussing different options for selecting, summarizing and querying rules. Redundancy management of patterns given by association rules has also been investigated in the context of observational calculi, e. g., [23,33]. In [29] a knowledge-based interactive approach to prune and filter rules using an ontology is described, also integrating user expectations. The approach presented in [22] tackles a similar goal by providing interesting itemsets using domain knowledge, which is then applied for constraining the resulting set of association rules to the most interesting ones. In [39] an approach using a new definition of maximal non-redundant association rules for the domain of tennis data was developed. This provides a method for incorporating logic programming into the data mining workflow to traverse the mining process in a declarative manner. Following this approach, the data mining workflow is presented in a more general form and new features are introduced for a domain expert to manage the rule base. Furthermore, in [36] a declarative approach for knowledge discovery in databases is proposed, utilizing meta-learning on the respective dataset and rule base.

In contrast to the approaches discussed above, the approach presented in this paper provides a framework on top of an association rule base. This facilitates the management of those rules, such as pruning, filtering and searching for similar rules, but also inferring further rules in the association rule base.

3 Background Material

This section gives an insight into the theoretical background of association rule mining. For this purpose, we define the basic concepts of itemsets and transactions, which are prerequisites for most data mining algorithms such as Apriori [2] or FP-Growth [24]. In this work, we focus on the Apriori algorithm for association rule mining. In order to find the most frequent itemsets and rank the resulting association rules according to their meaningfulness, we also explain the support and confidence metrics.

Itemsets, Transactions. For a set $\mathcal{I}$ of items, the transaction base $\mathcal{T} \subseteq 2^{\mathcal{I}}$ is a finite set of subsets. The elements $t \in \mathcal{T}$ are called transactions (it holds $t \subseteq \mathcal{I}$). Let $I \subseteq \mathcal{I}$ be an itemset:

1. The transaction set of I is $\mathcal{T}_I = \{ t \in \mathcal{T} \mid I \subseteq t \}$.
2. The frequency/support of I is the number/percentage of transactions containing I: $\mathit{freq}(I) = |\mathcal{T}_I|, \;\; \mathit{support}(I) = |\mathcal{T}_I| / |\mathcal{T}|$.
3. I is called a k–itemset, if $k = |I|$. I is called min–frequent, if $\mathit{support}(I) \geq min$, i.e. $\mathit{freq}(I) \geq Min$, for $Min = min \cdot |\mathcal{T}|$.

For $|\mathcal{I}| = m$, there are 2^m Itemsets, and for large m it is computationally rather expensive test all of them for being frequent.

Association Rule, Support and Confidence. An association rule r has the form $L \Rightarrow R$, for itemsets $L, R \subseteq \mathcal{I}$.

1. The support of r is the percentage of transactions containing both L and R: $\mathit{support}(L \Rightarrow R) = \mathit{support}(L \cup R) = \frac{|\mathcal{T}_{L \cup R}|}{|\mathcal{T}|}$.
2. The confidence of r is the percentage of transactions containing $L \cup R$ related to the percentage of transactions containing L: $\mathit{confidence}(L \Rightarrow R) = \frac{\mathit{support}(L \cup R)}{\mathit{support}(L)} = \frac{|\mathcal{T}_{L \cup R}|}{|\mathcal{T}_L|}$.
   c.f. conditional probabilities: $P(R \mid L) = \frac{P(L \cup R)}{P(L)}$.
3. If $\mathit{support}(r) = s$ and $\mathit{confidence}(r) = c$, then we write $L \overset{s,c}{\Rightarrow} R$.
   Then $L \cup R$ is an s–frequent itemset.

We can find association rules with a minimum support s and confidence c using the well-known *Apriori algorithm* [2]. It first incrementally searches for frequent itemsets from which association rules are then created. For a detailed discussion, we refer to [2].

4 The Data Mining Workflow

The data mining workflow describes the entire process from the data stored in a relational database to a dense representation of the most meaningful association rules in a rule base. With this rule base, a domain expert is able to analyze and (potentially) extract knowledge from the given data in a reasonable amount of time. In order to be able to run through this process in an automated way, various tools are needed. In this work, we use and describe Weka for association rule mining from our data in a transaction base, as well as the Declare toolkit. This is used for several transformations, including the post-mining process, as well as providing additional functionality to a rule base, which can be used by the domain expert.

From Relation to Transaction Base

Usually, the data to be analyzed is stored in a relational database. Therefore, we must first convert these relations into a set of transactions:

1. The items are attribute/value pairs $A = v$.
2. Every tuple is mapped to a transaction:
   $(v_1, \ldots, v_n) \mapsto \{ A_i = v_i \mid 1 \leq i \leq n \}$ For every attribute A, the transaction contains exactly one pair $A = v$ with A in the first position.
3. Thus, all transactions have as many items as there are attributes.
4. If an itemset I contains contradicting items $A = v$ and $A = v'$ for the same attribute A, where $v \neq v'$, then $\mathit{freq}(I) = 0$ and I is not frequent (for $\mathit{Min} \geq 1$); e. g., $I = \{ \mathit{Married} = \mathit{yes},\ \mathit{Married} = \mathit{no},\ \ldots \}$.

Rule Mining using Weka

We can apply the Apriori algorithm to the data represented in a transaction base. In the context of this work, we use the well–known data mining tool Weka [40].

Post–mining on Association Rule Base

In [35], the following notions of *redundancy* and *subsumption* have been introduced on sets of association rules. They form heuristics to reduce a set of association rules to a more dense subset of potentially interesting rules for a domain expert.

Redundancy. For this, we need a new definition of redundancy: we call an association rule $r_1 = L_1 \Rightarrow R_1$ *redundant*, if there is another association rule $r_2 = L_2 \Rightarrow R_2$, such that

$$L_2 \subseteq L_1,\ R_1 \subseteq R_2 \text{ and } \mathit{conf}(r_2) = 1.$$

Note that, if a rule r_1 is redundant, then its confidence does not have to be 1 in general; e. g., for a redundant rule $r_1 = L_1 \Rightarrow R_1$ and a rule $r_2 = L_2 \Rightarrow R_2$ with $\mathit{conf}(r_2) = 1$, such that $L_2 = L_1$ and $R_1 \subsetneq R_2$, we have $\emptyset = L_2 \cap R_2 = L_1 \cap R_2$, and we get

$$1 = \mathit{conf}(r_2) = \frac{|L_2 \cup R_2|}{|L_2|} = \frac{|L_1 \cup R_2|}{|L_1|} > \frac{|L_1 \cup R_1|}{|L_1|} = \mathit{conf}(r_1)\,.$$

Subsumption. We say that an association rule $r_1 = L_1 \Rightarrow R_1$ *subsumes* another association rule $r_2 = L_2 \Rightarrow R_2$,
if

$$L_1 \subseteq L_2,\ R_2 \subseteq R_1 \text{ and } \mathit{sup}(r_1) \geq \mathit{sup}(r_2)\,,\ \mathit{conf}(r_1) \geq \mathit{conf}(r_2)\,.$$

A rule r is called *maximal*, if it is not subsumed by any other rule $r' \neq r$. Both definitions have first appeared in the lecture on Advanced Databases [35].

Note, that subsumption is different from logical implication. But, often logical implication seems to be a consequence of it. And in practice, most domain experts seem to agree, that the maximal association rules are the most *interesting* ones.

5 Operations on the Association Rule Base

The operations of this section produce association rules with a high confidence and support (frequency). In Declare, the association rule base can be reduced by *subsumption*, which returns the non–subsumed rules. In practical projects, we have also used a technique for deriving more useful association rules for the *tactical analysis* of *tennis matches* by joining rules found by Weka and a search mechanism for finding the most interesting association rules for *heating systems*.

Below, we first theoretically describe the operations on the rule base found by Weka. After that, we show some examples from a practical project in the heating domain.

5.1 Subsumption in the Rule Base

Given a transaction base (`Transactions`), the following Declare rule computes subsumptions and maximal non–subsumed association rules `Maximal`:

```
tuples_to_association_rules(
      Transations, Implications) :-
   weka_association_lists_to_rules(
      Transactions, rules:Rules),
   maplist( xml_rule_to_implication,
      Rules, Implications ),
   association_rule_subsumes_others(
      Implications, Subsumptions),
   association_rules_subsumes_maximal(
      Implications, Maximal).
```

In Sect. 6, we will investigate a small example, where `Subsumptions` shows that 1 rule subsumes 19 others, 2 subsume 14 others, 3 subsume 8 others, and 5 subsume 3 others. Also the maximal association rules will be shown.

5.2 Joining Association Rules

Frequently, association rules are derived that differ only in the prediction of the range V_i of a single attribute `A`:

$$L \stackrel{s_1,c_1}{\Longrightarrow} R \cup \{ A \in V_1 \},$$
$$L \stackrel{s_2,c_2}{\Longrightarrow} R \cup \{ A \in V_2 \}.$$

In that case, another rule joining the respective disjoint ranges V_1 and V_2 can be derived with the sum of the confidences and frequencies:

$$L \stackrel{s,c}{\Longrightarrow} R \cup \{ A \in V_1 \cup V_2 \},$$

where $s = s_1 + s_2$ and $c = c_1 + c_2$.

This rules was especially useful for deriving interesting association rules from *tennis matches*, cf. [39]. If the coordinate A where the ball hits the ground was in the tiles V_1 and V_2, respectively, under the same precondition α, then A is in the joined, bigger tile $V_1 \cup V_2$ with the sum and the supports and confidences.

5.3 Similarity Search in Sets of Association Rules

Frequently, the domain expert will try to search for certain association rules in the rule base generated by Weka. It can occur that Weka found an association rule

$$As_1 \cup \{ A \} \Rightarrow As_2,$$

but the domain expert had expected another rule

$$As_1 \cup As_2 \Rightarrow \{ A \},$$

which exchanges the atom A of the precondition by the set As_2 of atoms from the conclusion, and As_1 denotes the atoms remaining in the precondition.

In the domain of heating systems and the time series data of the sensors within the system, we found such a situation:

```
As1 = Leistung Kessel norm,
      HKRL niedrig, Leistung HK niedrig
As2 = Puffer sekRL hoch, Volumenstrom HK niedrig
A = KesselRL hoch
```

In that case, a query searching for an association rule $L_1 \Rightarrow R_1$ in our rule base will return all association rules $L_2 \Rightarrow R_2$, where L_2, R_2 contains L_1, R_1 ordered according to the following heuristic distance value (penalty):

$$\alpha \cdot |L_1 \setminus L_2| + \beta \cdot |R_1 \setminus R_2| +$$
$$\gamma \cdot |L_2 \setminus L_1| + \delta \cdot |R_2 \setminus R_1|.$$

We have used the weights $\alpha = \beta = 3$, i.e. the query atoms not contained in the rule were weighted by 3, and $\gamma = \delta = 1$, i.e. the rule atoms not contained in the query were weighted by 1. We are also using a more penalty function, which obviously generalizes the previous one; the domain expert can compare the heads and bodies with individual weights for the atoms in the difference sets: $b(L_1, L_2) + a(R_1, R_2)$

5.4 Other Methods

Obviously, there are other methods to enhance processing on association rule bases, like constraint-based [10] or interestingness-driven [19,32] methods or interactive visualization-driven techniques [13]. Specifically, this can also be tackled using approaches like using *observational calculi* in the first place, to deal with redundancy, and to find the most relevant association rules [23,33]. The data mining workflow sketched in this paper seems to be a special application of observational calculi; but the methods we are using – like Weka with the well known a–priori algorithm – seem to form a more state–of–the–art approach. Moreover, from a practical point of view, we can reuse all of the implemented interfaces and methods to focus on the specific adaptations which we derive from the background knowledge of the domain experts.

6 Examples

In the following, we use a complete toy example for illustrating the penalty functions, and another realistic example from a practical project in the heating domain, where the domain expert was trying to find useful association rules that could help improving the performance of a heating system.

6.1 A Complete Toy Example

As a small illustrating example, we consider the following set of transactions in the form of association tuples:

```
Transactions = [
    [a:1, b:1, c:3], [a:1, b:1, c:4],
    [a:2, b:1, c:3], [a:2, b:2, c:5] ].
```

From this transaction base, Weka generates 66 association rules, which we parse to XML using Declare.

The Prolog Data Format. In short form, the rules can be represented as Prolog structures `F:C:(L-->R)`. We use the arrow `-->` in Declare. `L` and `R` are lists of associations $A = V$, `F` and `C` denote the frequency and confidence.

```
2:1:([a:1]-->[b:1])                2:1:([c:3]-->[b:1])
1:1:([c:4]-->[a:1])                1:1:([b:2]-->[a:2])
1:1:([c:5]-->[a:2])                1:1:([c:4]-->[b:1])
1:1:([c:5]-->[b:2])                1:1:([b:2]-->[c:5])
1:1:([a:1,c:3]-->[b:1])            1:1:([b:1,c:4]-->[a:1])
1:1:([a:1,c:4]-->[b:1])            1:1:([c:4]-->[a:1,b:1])
1:1:([a:2,c:3]-->[b:1])            1:1:([a:2,b:1]-->[c:3])
1:1:([b:2,c:5]-->[a:2])            1:1:([a:2,c:5]-->[b:2])
1:1:([a:2,b:2]-->[c:5])            1:1:([c:5]-->[a:2,b:2])
1:1:([b:2]-->[a:2,c:5])            2:0.67:([b:1]-->[a:1])
2:0.67:([b:1]-->[c:3])             1:0.5:([c:3]-->[a:1])
1:0.5:([a:1]-->[c:3])              1:0.5:([a:1]-->[c:4])
1:0.5:([a:2]-->[b:1])              1:0.5:([a:2]-->[b:2])
1:0.5:([c:3]-->[a:2])              1:0.5:([a:2]-->[c:3])
1:0.5:([a:2]-->[c:5])              1:0.5:([b:1,c:3]-->[a:1])
1:0.5:([a:1,b:1]-->[c:3])          1:0.5:([c:3]-->[a:1,b:1])
1:0.5:([a:1]-->[b:1,c:3])          1:0.5:([a:1,b:1]-->[c:4])
1:0.5:([a:1]-->[b:1,c:4])          1:0.5:([b:1,c:3]-->[a:2])
1:0.5:([c:3]-->[a:2,b:1])          1:0.5:([a:2]-->[b:1,c:3])
1:0.5:([a:2]-->[b:2,c:5])          1:0.33:([b:1]-->[a:2])
1:0.33:([b:1]-->[c:4])             1:0.33:([b:1]-->[a:1,c:3])
1:0.33:([b:1]-->[a:1,c:4])         1:0.33:([b:1]-->[a:2,c:3])
```

Subsumption. Only 17 of these rules are maximal w.r.t. subsumption:

```
2:1:([a:1]-->[b:1])               2:1:([c:3]-->[b:1])
1:1:([c:4]-->[a:1,b:1])           1:1:([a:2,b:1]-->[c:3])
1:1:([c:5]-->[a:2,b:2])           1:1:([b:2]-->[a:2,c:5])
2:0.67:([b:1]-->[a:1])            2:0.67:([b:1]-->[c:3])
1:0.5:([c:3]-->[a:1,b:1])         1:0.5:([a:1]-->[b:1,c:3])
1:0.5:([a:1]-->[b:1,c:4])         1:0.5:([c:3]-->[a:2,b:1])
1:0.5:([a:2]-->[b:1,c:3])         1:0.5:([a:2]-->[b:2,c:5])
1:0.33:([b:1]-->[a:1,c:3])        1:0.33:([b:1]-->[a:1,c:4])
1:0.33:([b:1]-->[a:2,c:3])
```

Grouping. It can be interesting to group an association rule $F_1:C_1:(L_1 \texttt{-->} R_1)$ together with all generated related association rules $F_2:C_2:(L_2 \texttt{-->} R_2)$, where L_2 is a subset of L_1 and R_1 is a subset of R_2. In the following, we have grouped some rules (odd lines) with their related rules (following even, indented lines) using Declare:

```
1:1:([c:4]-->[a:1,b:1])
   1:1:([c:4]-->[a:1])    1:1:([c:4]-->[b:1])
1:1:([c:5]-->[a:2,b:2])
   1:1:([c:5]-->[a:2])    1:1:([c:5]-->[b:2])
1:1:([b:2]-->[a:2,c:5])
   1:1:([b:2]-->[a:2])    1:1:([b:2]-->[c:5])
1:0.5:([c:3]-->[a:1,b:1])
   2:1:([c:3]-->[b:1])    1:0.5:([c:3]-->[a:1])
...
```

Here, all bodies contain only one association. E. g., for a rule $F:C:(L\texttt{-->}[A_1,A_2])$ and $F_1:C_1:(L\texttt{-->}[A_1])$, $F_2:C_2:(L\texttt{-->}[A_2])$ it becomes visible how the confidences and frequencies are related. Obviously, it holds $C_1 \geq C$, $C_2 \geq C$ and $F_1 \geq F$, $F_2 \geq F$.

Similarity Search. Searching for the association rule `F:C:([b:'1']->[c:'4'])`, first returns a proper hit with penalty 0, whereas the last returned rule has a penalty of $3*1+3*1+1+2 = 9$. In the following, the leading parameter is the respective penalty.

```
0-(1:0.33:([b:1]-->[c:4]))
1-(1:0.33:([b:1]-->[a:1,c:4]))
1-(1:0.5:([a:1,b:1]-->[c:4]))
5-(1:0.5:([a:1]-->[b:1,c:4]))
5-(1:1:([b:1,c:4]-->[a:1]))
8-(1:1:([c:4]-->[b:1]))
9-(1:1:([a:1,c:4]-->[b:1]))
9-(1:1:([c:4]-->[a:1,b:1]))
```

6.2 A Practical Heating Example

As part of a research project, data from heating systems in buildings was examined. Sensor data was collected every minute using IoT devices and transmitted to a database via mobile networks. The sensors were attached to components in the heating room, such as the flow and return pipes of the heating circuits, the exhaust temperature, or the gas boiler. This allowed for a highly detailed observation of the central heating system's operational behavior.

The data was analyzed in collaboration with domain experts to derive meaningful insights into the operational behavior and to optimize this behavior where possible. Before these sensor data are converted into association rules, we have pre–processed them. We filtered missing and wrong values like outliers and illogical readings. Similar to [39], we converted the discrete values into intervals or labels. For example, we introduced times intervals and temperature labels such as morning, noon, afternoon, evening and night and cool, mild, moderate and warm respectively. We then created association rules using the Weka tool [40]. After that, we did post–mining as explained before.

For Weka, we chose a parameter that gave us 4000 association rules for six different buildings. With this, we then filtered maximal non–redundant rules, as shown in Table 1.

Table 1. Maximal Non–Redundant Rules in Different Immovables

Streetname	Maximal Non–Redundant Rules
Breitenfelder	1775
Johanis	559
Mariaterwielkehre	962
Oldenburger	654
Segeberg	2069
Sturmvogelweg	836

Listing 1 shows an example, where an association rule was found between the outdoor temperature or the time of day and the temperature of the boiler return:

Listing 1. Maximal Non–Redundant Heating Association Rules

```
46797:1.00:(
  ['Outdoor Temp.':'Moderate']-->['Boiler Return':'>=30'])
41714:0.99:(
  ['Outdoor Temp':'Mild']-->['Boiler Return':'>=30'])
15323:0.99:(
  ['Daytime':'Afternoon']-->['Boiler Return':'>=30'])
20435:0.99:(
  ['Daytime':'Evening']-->['Boiler Return':'>=30'])
```

The idea of the domain expert was that the outdoor temperature or the time of the day should be part of the premise `Bs2` of the found association rule. This can be modeled by the more general penalty function of Subsect. 5.3.

For this purpose, we created an association rule with preferences of the domain expert and compared it with all maximal non–redundant association rules and sorted them by penalty. For the query `['Outdoor Temp.':'Moderate']->[Boiler Return':'>=30']` the penalties and rules in Listing 2 are returned, where the penalty weights for the head atoms are 0 and the weight function for the body atoms is $b(L_1, L_2) = 3 \cdot |L_1 \setminus L_2| + 1 \cdot |L_2 \setminus L_1|$:

Listing 2. Penalties for the Maximal Non–Redundant Rules, Sorted by Penalty descending

```
4: ['Weekday':'Sunday']-->['Boiler Return':'>=30']
4: ['Weekday':'Saturday']-->['Boiler Return':'>=30']
4: ['Weekday':'Monday']-->['Boiler Return':'>=30']
4: ['Outdoor Temp.':'Warm']-->['Boiler Return':'>=30']
4: ['Boiler Forward':'>=30']-->['Boiler Return':'>=30']
4: ['Month':'July']-->['Boiler Return':'>=30','Boiler Forward':'>=30']
4: ['Boiler Spread':'Negativ']-->['Boiler Forward':'>=30']
5: ['Boiler Spread':'Negativ']-->
      ['Boiler Return':'>=30','Boiler Forward':'>=30']...
```

7 Discussion and Future Work

In this paper, we have proposed to store association rules in a *rule base*, providing the functionality for management of the rules, i.e., for *subsumption* reducing the rule base, for *searching* and *filtering* the rule base, as well as for inferring new rules by *joining* individual association rules. We demonstrated and illustrate our methods using several examples, specifically also relating to a real-world application in the context of analyzing data of heating systems.

In future work, interesting directions will include the option to compare different sets of association rules for a given set of transactions. The given metrics can be useful to optimize the process of association rule mining as well as for the analysis of the rule base by the domain expert. In addition, another interesting option is to directly work on the frequent itemset information in order to enhance the association rule generation process directly using the proposed methods, where this potentially also extends to further pattern mining approaches like subgroup discovery [3] and exceptional model mining [15]. This specifically includes exploratory and interactive settings where the domain expert is closely involved in a human-in-the-loop process. Furthermore, the analysis of further datasets and applications is another direction to consider, specifically for comparing different options and to assess their impact with respect to different characteristics of the respective representations and datasets.

References

1. Agrawal, R., Imieliński, T., Swami, A.: Mining association rules between sets of items in large databases. In: Proceedings of ACM SIGMOD, vol. 22, pp. 207–216. ACM (1993)
2. Agrawal, R., Srikant, R.: Fast algorithms for mining association rules. In: Proceedings of the 20th VLDB Conference, Santiago de Chile, pp. 487–499 (1994)
3. Atzmueller, M.: Subgroup Discovery. WIREs Data Min. Knowl. Disc. **5**(1), 35–49 (2015)
4. Atzmueller, M.: Onto explicative data mining: exploratory, interpretable and explainable analysis. Abstract. Dutch-Belgian Database Day, TU Eindhoven (2017)
5. Atzmueller, M.: Declarative aspects in explicative data mining for computational sensemaking. In: Seipel, D., Hanus, M., Abreu, S. (eds.) WFLP/WLP/INAP -2017. LNCS (LNAI), vol. 10997, pp. 97–114. Springer, Cham (2018). https://doi.org/10.1007/978-3-030-00801-7_7
6. Atzmueller, M., Hayat, N., Trojahn, M., Kroll, D.: Explicative human activity recognition using adaptive association rule-based classification. In: Proceedings of IEEE International Conference on Future IoT Technologies, IEEE, Boston, MA, USA (2018)
7. Atzmueller, M., Lemmerich, F., Krause, B., Hotho, A.: Who are the spammers? Understandable local patterns for concept description. In: Proceedings of 7th Conference on Computer Methods and Systems. Oprogramowanie Nauko-Techniczne, Krakow, Poland (2009)
8. Bao, F., Mao, L., Zhu, Y., Xiao, C., Xu, C.: An improved evaluation methodology for mining association rules. Axioms **11**(1), 17 (2021)
9. Barredo Arrieta, A., et al.: Explainable artificial intelligence (XAI): concepts, taxonomies, opportunities and challenges toward responsible AI. Inf. Fusion **58**, 82 – 115 (2020)
10. Bayardo, R.J., Agrawal, R., Gunopulos, D.: Constraint-based rule mining in large, dense databases. Data Min. Knowl. Disc. **4**(2–3), 217–240 (2000)
11. Biran, O., Cotton, C.: Explanation and justification in machine learning: a survey. In: IJCAI-17 Workshop on Explainable AI (2017)
12. Brin, S., Motwani, R., Silverstein, C.: beyond market baskets: generalizing association rules to correlations. In: Proceedings of ACM SIGMOD, pp. 265–276 (1997)
13. Bruzzese, D., Buono, P.: Combining visual techniques for association rules exploration. In: Proceedings of the Working Conference on Advanced Visual Interfaces, pp. 381–384 (2004)
14. Calegari, R., Ciatto, G., Omicini, A.: On the integration of symbolic and sub-symbolic techniques for XAI: a survey. Intelligenza Artificiale **14**(1), 7–32 (2020)
15. Duivesteijn, W., Feelders, A.J., Knobbe, A.: Exceptional model mining. Data Min. Knowl. Disc. **30**(1), 47–98 (2016)
16. Fayyad, U., Piatetsky-Shapiro, G., Smyth, P.: From data mining to knowledge discovery in databases. AI Mag. **17**(3), 37–54 (1996)
17. Frawley, W.J., Piatetsky-Shapiro, G., Matheus, C.J.: Knowledge discovery in databases: an overview. AI Mag. **13**(3), 57–57 (1992)
18. Freitas, A.A.: On rule interestingness measures. Knowl.-Based Syst. **12**(5–6), 309–325 (1999)
19. Geng, L., Hamilton, H.J.: Interestingness measures for data mining: a survey. ACM Comput. Surv. **38**(3), 9-es (2006)
20. Gottlob, G.: Subsumption and implication. Inf. Process. Lett. **24**(2), 109–111 (1987)
21. Hahsler, M.: A probabilistic comparison of commonly used interest measures for association rules (2015). https://mhahsler.github.io/arules/docs/measures
22. Hahsler, M., Buchta, C., Hornik, K.: Selective association rule generation. Comput. Stat. **23**(2), 303–315 (2008)
23. Hájek, P., Havránek, T.: Mechanizing Hypothesis Formation. Springer, Berlin (1978). https://doi.org/10.1007/978-3-642-66943-9

24. Han, J., Pei, J., Yin, Y.: Mining Frequent Patterns Without Candidate Generation. In: Proceedings of ACM SIGMOD, pp. 1–12. ACM Press (2000)
25. Hipp, J., Güntzer, U., Nakhaeizadeh, G.: Algorithms for association rule mining - a general survey and comparison. SIGKDD Explor. **2**(1), 58–64 (2000)
26. Ilkou, E., Koutraki, M.: Symbolic vs sub-symbolic AI methods: Friends or enemies? In: CIKM (Workshops), vol. 2699 (2020)
27. Imieliński, T., Virmani, A.: Association rules... and what's next? — towards second generation data mining systems. In: Litwin, W., Morzy, T., Vossen, G. (eds.) ADBIS 1998. LNCS, vol. 1475, pp. 6–25. Springer, Heidelberg (1998). https://doi.org/10.1007/BFb0057713
28. Mahdi, M.A., Hosny, K.M., Elhenawy, I.: Fr-tree: a novel rare association rule for big data problem. Expert Syst. Appl. **187**, 115898 (2022)
29. Marinica, C., Guillet, F.: Knowledge-based interactive postmining of association rules using ontologies. IEEE Trans. Knowl. Data Eng. **22**(6), 784–797 (2010)
30. McMillan, C., Mozer, M.C., Smolensky, P.: Rule induction through integrated symbolic and subsymbolic processing. In: Advances in Neural Information Processing Systems, vol. 4 (1991)
31. Olson, D.L., Araz, Ö.M.: Association rules. In: Data Mining and Analytics in Healthcare Management: Applications and Tools, pp. 35–52. Springer, Cham (2023)
32. Piatetsky-Shapiro, G., Matheus, C.J.: The Interestingness of deviations. In: Proceedings of AAAI-94 Workshop on Knowledge Discovery in Databases (KDD-94), pp. 25–36. ACM Press, New York (1994)
33. Rauch, J.: Observational Calculi and Association Rules. Springer, Berlin (2013). https://doi.org/10.1007/978-3-642-11737-4
34. Seipel, D.: Declare – a declarative toolkit for knowledge–based systems and logic programming (2005)
35. Seipel, D.: Advanced Databases, Lecture Notes of a Course at the University of Würzburg (since 2015)
36. Seipel, D., Atzmueller, M.: Declarative knowledge discovery in databases via meta–learning–towards advanced analytics. In: Proceedings of the International Workshop on Semantic Data Mining (SEDAMI 2021), co-located with the 30th International Joint Conference on Artificial Intelligence (IJCAI 2021). CEUR Workshop Proceedings, vol. 3032, pp. 1–5. CEUR-WS.org (2021)
37. Vollert, S., Atzmueller, M., Theissler, A.: Interpretable machine learning: a brief survey from the predictive maintenance perspective. In: Proceedings of IEEE International Conference on Emerging Technologies and Factory Automation (ETFA 2021), IEEE (2021)
38. Webb, G.I.: Efficient search for association rules. In: Proceedings of ACM SIGKDD International Conference on Knowledge Discovery and Data Mining, pp. 99–107 (2000)
39. Weidner, D., Atzmueller, M., Seipel, D.: Finding maximal non-redundant association rules in tennis data. In: Hofstedt, P., Abreu, S., John, U., Kuchen, H., Seipel, D. (eds.) INAP/WLP/WFLP -2019. LNCS (LNAI), vol. 12057, pp. 59–78. Springer, Cham (2020). https://doi.org/10.1007/978-3-030-46714-2_4
40. Witten, I.H., Frank, E.: Data Mining: Practical Machine Learning Tools with Java Implementations. Morgan Kaufmann, Burlington (2000)
41. Zhang, A., Shi, W., Webb, G.I.: Mining significant association rules from uncertain data. Data Min. Knowl. Disc. **30**, 928–963 (2016)
42. Zhang, S., Webb, G.I.: Further pruning for efficient association rule discovery. In: Stumptner, M., Corbett, D., Brooks, M. (eds.) AI 2001. LNCS (LNAI), vol. 2256, pp. 605–618. Springer, Heidelberg (2001). https://doi.org/10.1007/3-540-45656-2_52

Improving Understandability of Explanations with a Usage of Expert Knowledge

Maciej Szelążek[1](✉), Szymon Bobek[2], and Grzegorz J. Nalepa[2]

[1] AGH University of Science and Technology, Kraków, Poland
szelazek.m@gmail.com

[2] Jagiellonian Human-Centered Artificial Intelligence Laboratory (JAHCAI) and Institute of Applied Computer Science, Jagiellonian University, Kraków, Poland
{szymon.bobek,grzegorz.j.nalepa}@uj.edu.pl

Abstract. Data analysis is one of the most important parts of data mining and machine learning tasks. In recent years, explainable artificial intelligence methods have been used very often to support this phase. However, the explanations themselves are very often difficult to understand by domain experts, who play one of the most important roles in the phase of data analysis. In this work, we proposed a procedure to combine domain knowledge with ML and XAI methods to improve the understandability of explanations. We demonstrated the feasibility of our approach on a publicly available medical dataset. We describe a procedure for obtaining intuitively interpretable information about distinguishable groups of patients and defining differences between them with the usage of clustering, rule–based encoded domain knowledge, and SHAP values.

1 Introduction

Explainability (XAI) methods are becoming increasingly important with the spread of practical applications of Machine Learning (ML). XAI could be used to recognize internal dependencies of a model by determining the influence of features on the prediction result, and finally help get better insight into data and the model in pre–modeling phase of data mining (DM) and ML workflows. In this phase, the main focus is on domain understanding, data cleansing, feature selection, etc. The success of this stage is determined by a proper understanding of the data and the domain. Therefore, in most cases, the pre–modeling phase is a combined effort of different stakeholders including domain experts and data scientists. In recent years, XAI methods have been used to improve the communication between data scientists and nontechnical stakeholders by explaining the model decisions. However, the target users of most current XAI algorithms such as SHAP, Lime, Anchor, Lore, etc. are usually data scientists [15,19,23]. This limits their usage to model–debugging, or feature–selection tasks, while their potential of generating explanation for broader audience including domain experts is not fully utilized. In our research, we focus on augmenting existing XAI methods with an additional layer of domain knowledge that will increase their understandability. We base our procedure on the SHAP algorithms, which are among the most mature and widely used for both research and practical applications.

S. Nowaczyk et al. (Eds.): ECAI 2023 Workshops, CCIS 1948, pp. 36–47, 2024.
https://doi.org/10.1007/978-3-031-50485-3_3

SHAP importance score allows us to determine the contribution of individual input parameters to ML model decisions. Expert knowledge is usually not limited to recognizing the importance of features but also encodes complex relationships between them. Thus, the transition from a simple feature attribution scheme, which most modern XAI methods follow, to more expressive explanations is not straightforward and limits the usefulness of such explanations from the expert perspective. One of the goals of the research presented in this article was to fill this gap, developing a method that will improve the understandability of XAI explanations for non–technical users, but also provide a formalized way to encode expert knowledge into the explanation process to let data scientists get better insight into the domain [22]. To achieve this goal, we combined rule-based knowledge representation, clustering, and explainability methods according to the Semantic Data Mining paradigm [13].

The rest of the paper is organized as follows. In the 2 section, we describe our motivations. The articles related to our research are presented in Sect. 3. The methodology of is shown in 4. The results obtained and their evaluation are presented in Sect. 5.

2 Motivation

One of the goals of our research was to develop a method to integrate model explanations with additional domain knowledge to enhance the interpretability of XAI results. One way to do this is to recognize the relationship between instance values and their impact on the model's decision [11]. We applied it by designing a set of rules for the features to capture expert knowledge of certain relationships that are hidden without experience in a particular area. Such an approach has at least two advantages, the one–time implementation of additional information allows its later reuse. The second is the ability to automate the entire procedure whose results will be understandable to a non–specialist user.

In order to find patterns in the data and relate them to the explainability results, we had to consider several issues like:

1. Identify features that are not intuitive or even impossible to understand without having domain knowledge.
2. Implementation of domain knowledge in the form of rules
3. Transformation of the rules into new, binary features set
4. Defining patterns in data to recognize similarities between instances (Clustering)
5. Defining relations between the clusters using: a) ML model and SHAP results to determine distinctive patterns of features significance for each group b) Rule-based encoded domain knowledge c) Data distribution analysis

In Fig. 1 are the workflows of two approaches for explaining unsupervised learning models. In our study, we used the schema shown in 1A. Schema 1B represents the basic workflow in which the relations in the dataset are defined by the importance of SHAP features on the basis of unsupervised model decisions. Approach 1B, despite its simplicity, may be less generic. Depending on the model used for the unsupervised learning task, the appropriate method to create explanations should be selected.

In our study, we do not analyze the explainability scores of the model that creates the labels. This approach (Fig. 1A.) is universal due to the independence of the internal structure of the model, as we only use the input data and the output results for the Semantic Data Mining analysis.

3 Related Works

In our research, we want to expand the available set of information in order to create explanations that are easier to interpret, especially without detailed knowledge of the data. This approach is inspired by the concept of Semantic Data Mining [20]. It relies on the Semantic Data Mining tasks that systematically incorporate domain knowledge, especially formal semantics, into the process. As noted by the authors of [17], the main aspect of Semantic Data Mining is the explicit integration of this knowledge into algorithms for modeling or post-processing. In our study, we use domain knowledge that describes medical data for diabetes in the form of additional rules to code the original data and recognize its impact on the outcome (in our case, health status) [14]. One of the methods to look for relationships in the data is to compare the distributions between groups [4,6]. We used information obtained on the original and additional feature distributions as a basis for interpreting the XAI results. [7]

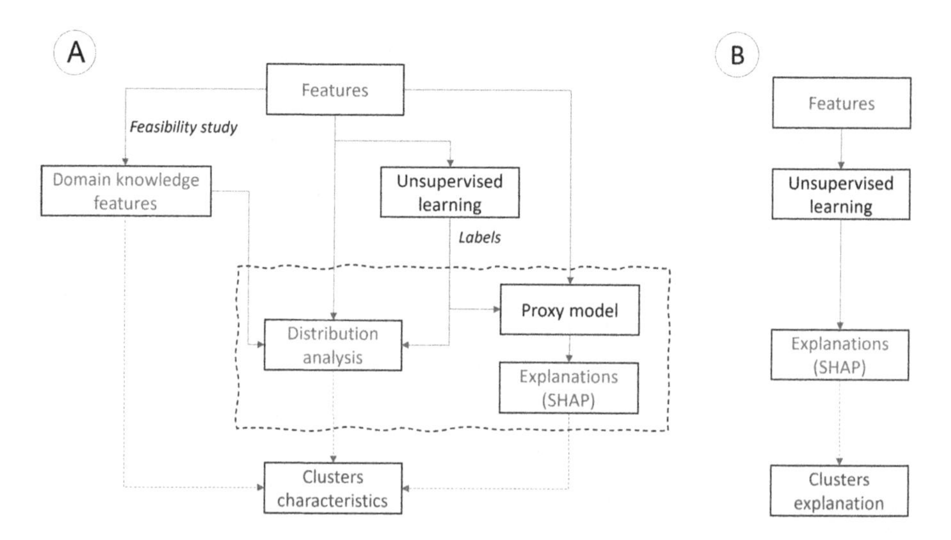

Fig. 1. Comparison of workflow used in our study (A) vs basic workflow for unsupervised learning explanations (B)

Despite many existing explainability algorithms, there is still no scientific consensus on the explicit recognition of multifaceted dependencies of model input parameters [9]. This problem was noticed by the authors of [10], especially in the case of multi–modal relationships, where different aspects of a phenomenon are represented by individual modalities/channels.

In our study, we used the proxy model to determine differences between clusters (Fig. 1A.). This term is defined by the authors of [3] under the name "surrogate model" as "usually directly interpretable model that approximates a more complex model. We evaluated the results of explainability from various perspectives in a similar way to the idea described by the authors in [5]. In our research, we explore the possibilities of recognizing relations between the instances using additional features coded from domain knowledge–based rules, original dataset distributions, and SHAP importance score.

4 Transforming Domain Knowledge into a Set of Rules

4.1 Dataset

The 'Pima Indians Diabetes' (PID) dataset [21] is a collection of data about the incidence of diabetes, originally from the National Institute of Diabetes and Digestive and Kidney Diseases. PID dataset was designed to detect relations between diabetes and parameters that describe the health status of the subjects. There are 768 cases in the database. Dataset includes information if a patient has or does not have diabetes, and 8 features:

- Pregnancies – Number of pregnancies
- Glucose – Plasma glucose concentration a 2 h in an oral glucose tolerance test
- BloodPressure – Diastolic blood pressure [mm Hg]
- SkinThickness – Triceps skin fold thickness [mm]
- Insulin – 2–Hour serum insulin [mu U/ml]
- BMI – Body mass index
- DiabetesPedigreeFunction – Indicator based on the diabetes mellitus history in relatives and the genetic relationship of those relatives to the patient.
- Age

After conducting exploratory analysis, we have noticed a significant amount of zeros values in the original dataset. The most important feature in this regard was Insulin with 374 zero values out of 768. In Fig. 2 we can see silhouette scores for all features (A), data excluding Insulin measurements (B) and after removing a small number of zeros (C) of the BMI (11 measurements), Blood Pressure (35 measurements) and Glucose (5 measurements) features. After cleaning the data and excluding Insulin, 724 cases remained as input to the unsupervised learning model. Based on the 2C plot, model was set to find similarity for 4 clusters.

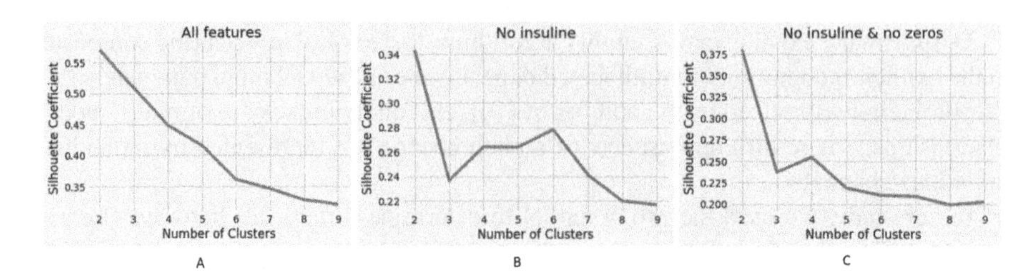

Fig. 2. Silhouette scores for different subsets of data

4.2 Feasibility Study of Rules for Features Assessment

The most time–consuming part of our approach is the preparation of rules coding the original dataset. Incorporation of domain knowledge requires a thorough exploration of the possible sources of this knowledge. In practice, decision support systems are often developed in collaboration with end users or domain experts. In such cases, users are an important source of expertise.

In our case, the two main goals of domain data mining were: 1) Determine the thresholds that would allow assessing the value of features, shown in Fig. 3, 2) Obtain information on the real impact of the feature on the outcome, in this case susceptibility to diabetes.

Let's consider influence assessment issue using the BMI feature as an example. BMI is one of the most important features related to diabetes susceptibility. It is a universal factor that is often used as a health index based on the weight–to–height ratio. The main advantage is its simplicity of calculation and interpretation. Some interpretations of the BMI factor separate the correct limits for men and women due to differences in body build [2], but this approach does not follow the guidelines of the World Health Organization (WHO), the Centers for Disease Control and Prevention (CDC) [1]. As described by the authors of [18], BMI is a useful index associated with susceptibility to various diseases such as asthma. The controversy related to BMI is oversimplification, which does not distinguish between muscle mass and fat mass. This leads to a situation where similar, high values can be obtained by a person with excessive, unhealthy weight and an athlete with a lot of muscles and a negligible share of body fat. One of the postulates of physicians analyzing this topic is the proposal to take into account the circumference of the waist as a factor that distinguishes these cases.

In a detailed analysis of this feature, we can observe that the limits determining the correct values do not depend on age, although with age there is a tendency for a statistical increase in BMI [8]. In the dataset we use in our research, all the respondents are older than 21 years, therefore the following thresholds describing obesity are universal for the entire dataset (Fig. 3), however, considerations concerning children and adolescents are not so clear. In adolescents and children, the different growth rates and generally large changes over several years mean that BMI should be assessed in relation to the BMI distribution of the local peer group and with the use of additional measurements [12]. One of the goals of our research was to assess patient health based on medical measurements and to determine the factors of influence that are the most risky in terms of health loss. The ambiguity in the interpretation of the BMI value means that as a single information is not crucial for pro–health activities recommendations. However, BMI is important information in relation to additional indicators that describe the patient's health condition.

The rules have been prepared to give semantic meaning to the values in the dataset. Without additional knowledge, in basic approach, XAI algorithms let us obtain information such as "BMI was the most influential feature considered by the model for the cluster assignment decision". The same data, after being processed by domain–based rules, allow us to designate the most influential groups of features in the context of dependencies understandable to a non–specialist user. In practice, the number of classes and the complexity of the rules depend on the individual goals of the analysis. The next section describes the results we obtained after applying our procedure.

4.3 Creating Rules

In our research, we consider the way of implementing the domain knowledge information that describes the underlying dataset to obtain meaningful results. For this purpose, we conducted a feasibility study to acquire thresholds for features real–life influence assessment. Next, we turned that information into a set of rules to classify the original data in a form of binary–coded features. Each rule r_f takes form of:

$$r_f = \prod_{j \in T_f} I(x_j \in s_{jf})$$

where T_f is a set of thresholds for feature f, I is the indicator function that is equal to '1' when threshold x_j is in a specified subset of values s for the j–th threshold and '0' otherwise. We are using numerical features, so s_{jf} is an interval in the value range of the threshold:

$$(x_{jf,lower} < x_j)\ AND\ (x_j < x_{jf,upper})$$

For example, if we need to incorporate domain–based assessment of the BMI feature that states 'BMI less than 35 and more than 30', we add a new feature – 'obesity type 1' in the instance that will be equal to '1' if it satisfies that condition and '0' otherwise. Visualization of additional features related to the level of healthy value exceedances is shown in Fig. 3.

After choosing the appropriate way to encode additional information, we proceeded to analyze the dataset. We use the clustering technique to identify patterns in the data. This is a form of unsupervised learning that allows us to group instances according to their similarity. In the next step, we create a proxy model using the original data as input. The model was aimed at predicting the clusters formed by unsupervised learning. Then we used XAI scores and distribution statistics to relate all available data in the context of the clusters. The main stages of our research include: 1) Transformation of domain knowledge into a form of rules, and then features, used for ML methods. 2) Unsupervised learning to determine patterns in the data. 3) Training ML model for identifying the relations between model input and designated clusters. 4) Explainability analysis using SHAP values. 5) Recognition of patterns and relations between clusters using explainability results, distribution statistics, and rule–based features analysis for individual clusters.

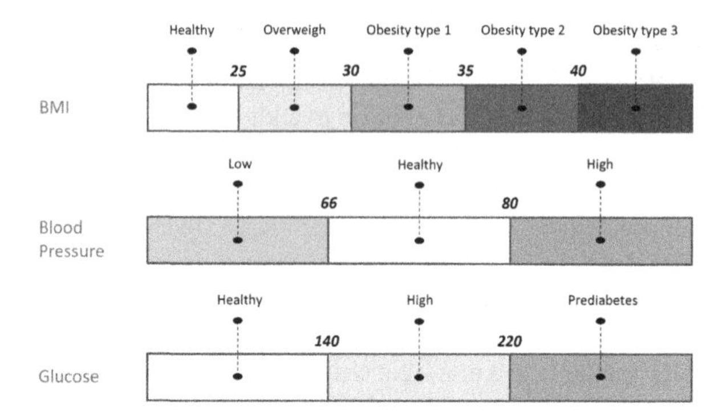

Fig. 3. Visualization of domain–based rules used to create an additional set of features

Clustering is used as a source of patterns that we want to identify and determine the internal relationships that distinguish clusters from each other. The objective of the case study presented in Sect. 5 was to divide patients into groups according to their susceptibility to diabetes and recognize the characteristics of each group.

5 Evaluation

In our procedure, we draw conclusions about relationships between patients by merging information from several sources (shown in Fig. 1): 1) Distribution characteristics of the original data 2) Distribution characteristics of the features derived from domain knowledge 3) XAI results of the proxy model

During the study, we tested 4 types of models: Logistic Regression, K–Nearest Neighbors (KNN), Random Forest Classifier, and Support Vector Machine. We chose the Random Forest Classifier for further analysis because it achieved the highest accuracy.

The Table 1 contains clustering results. Cluster 0 has the highest number of people with diagnosed diabetes (45% of all) in terms of both the number of people with diabetes and their proportion. Cluster 3 represents the most "healthy" group. Clusters 1 and 2 have similar proportions when it comes to diabetics, and to identify preliminary differences between these groups, we analyzed the distributions of feature measurements.

Table 2 shows the mean feature values according to the clusters. Bold font indicates the highest values for column, italic – the lowest. The results show that in clusters 0 and 3 people with the worst and the best scores were collected, respectively, which is consistent with the shares of diabetics in these clusters. Compared to the information in Table 1, we can observe differences between clusters 1 and 2. In cluster 2 patients have a higher average for the number of pregnancies and age, while noticeably lower values for features BMI and Diabetes Pedegree Function (represent genetic susceptibility to diabetes). The largest difference (almost 15 times) in favor of patients in cluster 2 compared to cluster 1 is noticeable for the Skin Thickness feature, which represents information about adipose tissue.

Table 1. Division of patients into clusters of the unsupervised learning model.

Cluster	Sum	Outcome	Quantity	Diabetes share
0	153	0	40	
		1	113	74%
1	194	0	127	
		1	67	35%
2	147	0	100	
		1	47	32%
3	230	0	208	
		1	22	10%

Table 2. Mean values of features for clusters.

Cluster	Pregnancies	Glucose	BloodPressure	SkinThickness	BMI	DiabetesPedigreeFunction	Age
0	**5,0**	**168,7**	**76,6**	25,1	**35,1**	**0,55**	**38,7**
1	3,5	121,7	73,7	**33,6**	34,9	0,50	31,9
2	4,6	121,9	75,9	*2,3*	30,7	*0,42*	37,7
3	*2,9*	*90,8*	*66,2*	21	*29,8*	0,44	*28,2*

Table 3 shows the summarized values of binary features according to the clusters. We can use this to provide context to the original dataset. The SHAP explainability results for the proxy model are shown in Fig. 4 The Glucose_preDiabetes feature in all clusters was 0.

The major differences considering the domain knowledge features include the following:

- Glucose – The most significant differences between the Cluster 0 and others groups are observed on the Glucose parameter due to the highest mean value. This is due to the presence of 83% of all patients with excesses in this group. Clusters 1 and 2 contain only 16 cases each (out of 185 observations), and 0 cases in cluster 3.
- BMI – people in clusters 0 and 1 have a significantly higher average BMI than clusters 2 and 3. The distinction between these groups can be made by analyzing additional data. We can see that despite the highest average for cluster 0, the largest number of people with exceeded the Obesity type 1 threshold and above are in cluster 1. The lower level of BMI is cluster numbers 2 and 3. The smallest number of overruns is in cluster 2, but it is cluster 3 that has the lowest average BMI. This is due to the fact that cluster 3 has the highest share of people without excesses of this parameter (27% compared to 22% in cluster 2).
- Blood Pressure – the most distinctive group is cluster 3 which has the highest proportion of people with problems with too low blood pressure (54% of all exceedances of this type). Cluster 0 has the largest share of people with too high blood pressure (35%). In cluster 1, the proportions of excesses related to too high and too low blood pressure are similar.

Table 3. Sum of domain–based binary features for clusters.

Cluster	BMI_obese3	BMI_obese2	BMI_obese1	BMI_overweight	Glucose_hi	BloodPressure_hi	BloodPressure_lo
0	32	33	57	20	**153**	**54**	24
1	**34**	**53**	**58**	40	16	51	46
2	12	18	42	42	16	40	25
3	12	37	55	**64**	0	18	**111**

The major interpretation differences of SHAP explainability results include:

- Glucose – SHAP results show inverse proportion to the highest measurement values. More informative is the assessment based on absolute SHAP values. For cluster 0 the results are more than 2x higher than for clusters 1 and 2, and significantly lower in cluster 3. This is consistent with the interpretation of Glucose as one of the most significant characteristics that differentiates the clusters, both in terms of mean and number of exceedances.
- BMI – For this feature, we can observe a relation between the SHAP sign and the high and low values of BMI. Clusters 0 and 1 have a similarly high BMI average, but cluster 1 has significantly higher SHAP results. This may be related to the highest overall number of cases with Obesity type 2 in cluster 1. The situation is similar for the two clusters with the lowest average BMI. In both cases, SHAP values are positive, but for cluster 3 they are significantly higher than for cluster 2. Cluster 3 also has a higher number of cases of type 2 Obesity and Overweight compared to cluster 2.
- Age – Interpretation of the results for Age is not consistent. In cluster 3 it was the most significant parameter, proportional to low age. Analysing the results for cluster 1 (low mean Age), SHAP values are negative, but for the high mean Age in cluster 2 they are also negative. This means that the significance of Age is related to other parameters that characterise the cluster.

Summarizing the results obtained, the patient groups determined by the unsupervised model are characterized by:

- Cluster 0 – Glucose problems, higher Age, genetic susceptibility to diabetes, highest average Pregnancies, high percentage of diabetics. The most significant feature, according to SHAP, defining this cluster was the high values of the Glucose parameter.
- Cluster 1 – Despite the small proportion of participants with increased Glucose, this group is distinguished by the highest proportion of patients with excess BMI and significantly higher average Skin Thickness feature than in the other groups. The most significant characteristics according to SHAP that define this cluster were low Glucose values and high BMI values.

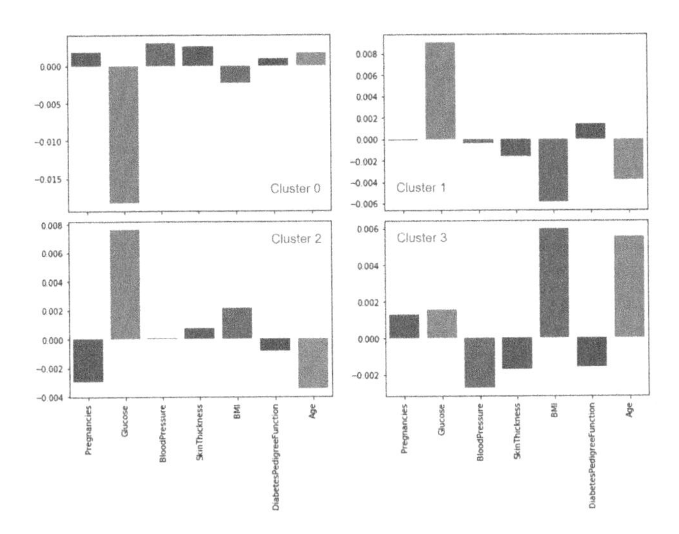

Fig. 4. SHAP explanations of proxy model

- Cluster 2 – The group with the correct glucose results, the lowest number of excess BMI, and the lowest average Skin Thickness. These features and Diabetes Pedigree Function are the most significant differentiation from cluster 0 because the mean number of pregnancies and the age are similar. The most significant features according to SHAP that defined this group were low Glucose values and high Pregnancy values.
- Cluster 3 – The most 'healthy' group, with the lowest averages for almost all parameters. Despite the relatively high number of excess BMI, there are a small number of patients with the highest obesity (type 3 Obese). A distinguishing feature of this group is also the significantly higher number of cases with too low Blood Pressure, as well as the lowest average Age and Pregnancies. The most significant characteristics, according to SHAP, defining this cluster were low BMI, Blood Pressure and Age.

In the course of the research, the method in which domain knowledge was transformed into an additional set of features proved to be an important factor in facilitating the interpretation of the original data. Parameters on a binary scale can be represented in 2 ways. Taking into account 4 levels of exceedances for the BMI feature (equivalent to creating 4 additional parameters), so that each exceeded threshold means 1 and a measurement below the threshold – 0, when describing a person with maximum exceed of BMI (Obesity type 3), all 4 parameters will have a value of 1. This approach to the creation of the dataset turned out to be better in terms of training the prediction model. The second way to represent binary characteristics is to assign 1 value only to the highest exceedance threshold for an individual. In this case, the value of the Obesity type 3 parameter will be equal to 1, while the other features describing BMI exceedances will be equal to 0. This approach is more intuitive for analyzing the distributions of exceedances within clusters and was used to create a Table 3.

6 Summary

We described a procedure for obtaining intuitively interpretable information about distinguishable groups of patients and defining differences between them with a usage of clustering, rule–based encoded domain knowledge, and SHAP values. On the basis of the data patterns found and the analysis of information with different origins, we determined the characteristic attributes of each group. This potentially allows us to automate the procedure and provide final conclusions in the form of easy–to–understand information even by non–specialist user.

This type of analysis is an important part of, for example, recommendation systems. Users of patient prediagnostic decision support are healthcare facilities that have an established set of treatment actions, the equivalent of the clusters in our study. The evaluation of the health of the clients is performed based on the knowledge of specialists and the diagnosis scripts prepared for them. By determining the associations between patient health indicators and the medical services they use, we can shorten the time between identifying the needed treatment and actually starting it. Applying our procedure in practice would require an in–depth analysis of the available domain knowledge as well as the company's experience.

One of the possibilities for further enhancement of our research is to use counterfactual explanations to estimate how much the value of a feature should change to assign a subject to a different category/cluster, other than the original. One of the implementations of that method is Diverse Counterfactual Explanations (DiCE) [16]. With a properly designed procedure, we can use the DiCE algorithm to estimate the goals of a treatment. This information could be useful in planning the intensity of therapy. Development in this direction may allow for faster and automated assessment of the patient's health. This type of information can be used to shorten the diagnostic process and limit the number of intermediate stages before the patient can reach a suitable specialist for his needs.

Acknowledgements. This paper is funded from the XPM (Explainable Predictive Maintenance) project funded by the National Science Center, Poland under CHIST-ERA programme Grant Agreement No. 857925 (NCN UMO-2020/02/Y/ST6/00070).

References

1. Body mass index : considerations for practitioners, August 2. https://stacks.cdc.gov/view/cdc/25368, pamphlet (or booklet)
2. Akindele, M., Phillips, J., Igumbor, E.: The relationship between body fat percentage and body mass index in overweight and obese individuals in an urban African setting. J. Public Health Africa **7**, 15–19 (2016)
3. Arya, V., et al.: One explanation does not fit all: a toolkit and taxonomy of AI explainability techniques. CoRR abs/1909.03012 (2019). https://arxiv.org/abs/1909.03012
4. Breiman, L.: Statistical modeling: the two cultures (with comments and a rejoinder by the author). Stat. Sci. **16**(3), 199–231 (2001)
5. Collaris, D., van Wijk, J.J.: Explainexplore: visual exploration of machine learning explanations. In: 2020 IEEE Pacific Visualization Symposium (PacificVis), pp. 26–35 (2020)

6. Ćwiek-Kupczyńska, H., et al.: Semantic concept schema of the linear mixed model of experimental observations. Sci. Data **7**(1), 70 (2020). https://doi.org/10.1038/s41597-020-0409-7
7. Hastie, T., Tibshirani, R., Friedman, J., Franklin, J.: The elements of statistical learning: data mining, inference, and prediction. Math. Intell. **27**, 83–85 (2004)
8. of Health, U.S.D., for Disease Control, H.S.C., for Health Statistics, P.N.C.: National health and nutrition examination survey (nhanes), 1999–2000 (2012). https://doi.org/10.3886/ICPSR25501.v4
9. Holzinger, A.: Explainable AI and multi-modal causability in medicine. i-com **19**(3), 171–179 (2020). https://doi.org/10.1515/icom-2020-0024
10. Jin, W., Li, X., Hamarneh, G.: Evaluating explainable AI on a multi-modal medical imaging task: Can existing algorithms fulfill clinical requirements? In: AAAI Conference on Artificial Intelligence, March 2022
11. Klein, L., El-Assady, M., Jäger, P.F.: From correlation to causation: formalizing interpretable machine learning as a statistical process (2022). https://arxiv.org/abs/2207.04969
12. Kleiser, C., Schaffrath Rosario, A., Mensink, G.B., Prinz-Langenohl, R., Kurth, B.M.: Potential determinants of obesity among children and adolescents in germany: results from the cross-sectional kiggs study. BMC Public Health **9**(1), 46 (2009). https://doi.org/10.1186/1471-2458-9-46
13. Lawrynowicz, A.: Semantic data mining: an ontology-based approach, April 2017
14. Li, Z., Zhang, C., Zhang, Y., Zhang, J.: Semanticaxis: exploring multi-attribute data by semantic construction and ranking analysis. J. Vis. **24**(5), 1065–1081 (2021). https://doi.org/10.1007/s12650-020-00733-z
15. Lundberg, S.M., et al.: Explainable AI for trees: From local explanations to global understanding. CoRR abs/1905.04610 (2019). https://arxiv.org/abs/1905.04610
16. Mothilal, R.K., Sharma, A., Tan, C.: Explaining machine learning classifiers through diverse counterfactual explanations. In: Proceedings of the 2020 Conference on Fairness, Accountability, and Transparency, ACM, January 2020. https://doi.org/10.1145/3351095.3372850
17. Nalepa, G.J., Bobek, S., Kutt, K., Atzmueller, M.: Semantic data mining in ubiquitous sensing: a survey. Sensors **21**(13) (2021). https://www.mdpi.com/1424-8220/21/13/4322
18. Novosad, S., Khan, S., Wolfe, B.N., Khan, A.: Role of obesity in asthma control, the obesity-asthma phenotype. J. Allergy **2013**, 538642 (2013)
19. Ribeiro, M.T., Singh, S., Guestrin, C.: Anchors: high-precision model-agnostic explanations. In: AAAI Conference on Artificial Intelligence (2018)
20. Sirichanya, C., Kraisak, K.: Semantic data mining in the information age: a systematic review. Int. J. Intell. Syst. **36**(8), 3880–3916 (2021). https://onlinelibrary.wiley.com/doi/abs/10.1002/int.22443
21. Smith, J.W., Everhart, J.E., Dickson, W., Knowler, W.C., Johannes, R.S.: Using the adap learning algorithm to forecast the onset of diabetes mellitus. In: Proceedings of Annual Symposium on Computer Application in Medical Care, p. 261. American Medical Informatics Ass. (1988)
22. Suchanek, F., Weikum, G.: Knowledge bases in the age of big data analytics. Proc. VLDB Endowment **7**, 1713–1714 (2014)
23. Visani, G., Bagli, E., Chesani, F.: Optilime: optimized LIME explanations for diagnostic computer algorithms. CoRR abs/2006.05714 (2020). https://arxiv.org/abs/2006.05714

Visual Patterns in an Interactive App for Analysis Based on Control Charts and SHAP Values

Iwona Grabska-Gradzińska[1(✉)], Maciej Szelążek[2], Szymon Bobek[1], and Grzegorz J. Nalepa[1]

[1] Faculty of Physics, Astronomy and Applied Computer Science, Jagiellonian University, Kraków, Poland
iwona.grabska@uj.edu.pl

[2] Faculty of Applied Computer Science, AGH University of Science and Technology, Kraków, Poland

Abstract. The aim of this paper is to describe the tool for combining the information of control charts, widely used for statistical quality control with the information obtained from the process of explanation the classification decision made using the machine learning model. Control charts are used to monitor production and show deviations from normal behavior, especially when upper and lower control limits of measured parameters are defined. Analysis of SHAP explanations allowed us to show some dependencies of classification process. Our application, which allows the user to compare the information taken from both control charts and SHAP plots, helps the user discover anomalies, especially dependencies between exceeding the limits of controlled parameters and the relevance of these values in SHAP calculations.

Keywords: Explainable machine learning · SHAP values · control charts

1 Introduction

Machine learning models are increasingly being used to replace or supplement human decision-making in tasks requiring some kind of prediction. The more complex and dynamic systems rely on artificial intelligence classification methods, the more the need for tools that explain the operation of artificial intelligence. This process can be aided by indicating the relationship between machine learning classification decisions and the parameters of other systems of evaluation processes.

One of the methods developed in recent years to explain the performance of machine learning systems is the use of algorithms to determine Shapley values for individual features used in a machine learning model. However, it is not an unambiguous method, and is treated by researchers more as a basis for interpretation rather than as a direct indication of the reasons for classifying objects in this way [13].

S. Nowaczyk et al. (Eds.): ECAI 2023 Workshops, CCIS 1948, pp. 48–59, 2024.
https://doi.org/10.1007/978-3-031-50485-3_4

Interpreting the results of algorithms based on Shapley numbers requires the cooperation of machine learning specialists and subject matter experts. The latter often use methods for maintaining systems based on the idea of control charts. Predictive methods for assessing system dynamics have been known for a long time, examples being the work of the American engineer Walter Shewhart in the first half of the 20th century. Most of specialists of industrial processes maintenance are familiar with these type of system dynamics description. Methods for statistical evaluation of variability are still being developed, often in association with ML [1,12,19]. The development of ML algorithms allows their use in applications related to predictive maintenance or forecasting of potential errors. [5]. Explainability methods are a step toward increasing users' awareness of the model's reasoning for making predictions. This makes it possible to optimize the effectiveness of the model, but also to detect undesirable model responses, thereby increasing the model's credibility [18,23].

The interpretation of artificial intelligence decision explanation algorithms in industrial processes requires the collaboration of experts in both areas: experts in the field of machine learning and experts in the field of the industrial process being analyzed or, as we will show further on, in the field of analysis of any type of issue that we have classified by artificial intelligence methods and which we wish to justify. Supporting the explanation of phenomena with visual methods makes it easier to carry out reasoning, so both in the field of machine learning and in the case of quality control processes, certain visual codes of graphs and relationships have been developed to facilitate understanding of the problem [20].

The aim of this article is to present method Shap-Enhanced Control Charts (SECC) which allows to combine information on the exceedance of system parameters limits with visualizations of the SHapley Additive exPlanations model proposed by Scott Lundberg [15]. The questions to be answered by experts using the combined data plots are:

- whether overruns of system parameter limits translate into the relevance of a parameter value in machine learning classification
- whether having no given limit we can propose one based on machine learning data
- whether there are patterns of relationships between parameter values and value relevance in machine learning.

The method is implemented in application built in Streamlit, an open-source platform dedicated to creation of the visualizations and dashboards in pure Python, available at https://iwonagg-decisionsupportstreamlit-main-59xn5u.streamlit.app/. All visualizations presented in this paper are generated based on this app. Moreover, thanks to the possibility of interacting with the data, the user is provided with tools for finding relationships and correlations between data obtained in the machine learning process and other data characterizing the product, which can be useful for further analysis.

The article is divided into several sections. Section 2 presents related works. In Sect. 3 the method is described. In Sect. 4 the usecases are presented, based on two datasets described in Sect. 4.1.

2 Related Works

The scientific literature reports several works in the field of conformance checking [7,17]. Typically, the term conformance checking refers to the comparison of observed behaviors, as an event log, with respect to a process model. At first, most of the conformance checking techniques were based on procedural models [14]. In recent years, an increasing number of researchers are focusing on the conformance checking with respect to declarative models, based on reactive business rules [4]. Conformance checking is also one of the goals of eXplainable Artificial Intelligence (XAI) methods, because their task is to link the model output with known, interpretable information. One of the motivations for our research is evaluation of the explainability results using transfer learning from expert knowledge as a base of conformance checking.

XAI is a dynamically evolving part of AI field, focusing on approaches that provide transparent and insightful explanations for decisions made by black-box models. We can distinguish between model–agnostic and model–specific methods. The first ones can be used to estimate the impact of features regardless of the type of model and its construction. These include Lime, SHAP or Anchors [16,21]. Model–specific methods are less versatile because of the affiliation to the model class e.g. saliency maps [11] for gradient–based models. In our experiments, we based on the SHAP method.

The second motivation for our study is to expand the knowledge of the dataset using XAI indicators. In particular, to identify additional value limits related to the significance of the feature's impact on the model decision. There are a number of solutions using explainable clustering as one of the tools in data mining analysis such as KnAC or CLAMP [2,3]. Rule–based explainers such as Anchors and LUX [10] can be considered as knowledge generation methods, because they extract interpretable knowledge from the black-box in the form of a set of rules.

In our work, we are enhancing the current state–of–the–art methods by combining conformance checking of the model using expert knowledge, while generating additional knowledge from data based on XAI. At the same time, we demonstrate practical applications of the developed approach. For this purpose, we use domain knowledge limits for indicators describing medical condition, as well as technological specifications as a base for assessment sensors measurements gathered during the manufacturing process. We then associated information with different origins to interpret the discovered relations and present them in the form of interactive visualizations.

3 Shap-Enhanced Control Charts (SECC)

This method is based on the two fields of data analysis: the analysis of the importance of given parameter in ML classification, using SHAP values and impact of excedance of limits defined in control charts system.

3.1 Basis of SHAP Calculation and Visualisations

For each dataset on which we perform classification, we determine the set of features that are relevant to the learning model. SHAP algorithms allow us to determine the relevance factor of a feature for positive and negative classification. Usually red and blue colors are used for visualisation.

The SHAP values can be used for many types of analysis. One of the most important possibilities is to show, for every element rejected in the process of classification, the impact of every parameter taken into consideration in the process of machine learning. In Fig. 1 the example is shown of such single explanation. The problem is, that the interpretation of the SHAP values is not obvious and sometimes need the factual background to be performed [6,9]. Without experts background it is difficult to determine whether high SHAP values are related to any part of the distribution, or perhaps are proportionally related to the values of individual parameters. This is important because if high explainability significance for a parameter means at the same time high values of this parameter, we can assess that if the model creates predictions that recognize defective products, SHAP determines the causes of this defect.

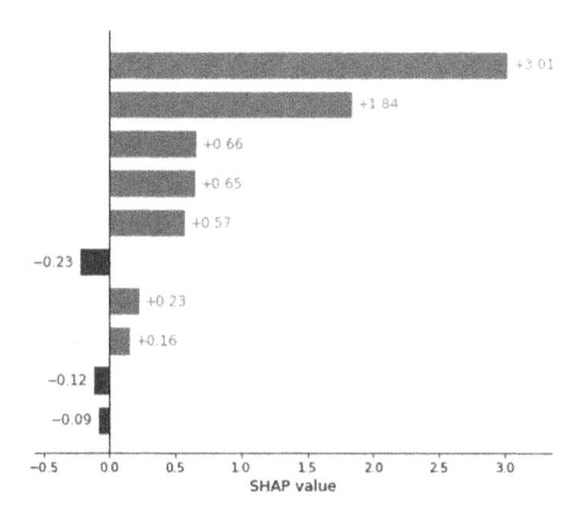

Fig. 1. SHAP bar chart example. The color is connected with negative or positive impact on classification and the width of bar is connected with the relevance of the parameter. (Color figure online)

3.2 Basis of Control Chart Usage

In the case of the quality control process, a frequently used analysis is based on a chart called the Shewhart chart, i.e. the variation of values over time including limit exceedances. The operator focuses on a single parameter and observes the variation of its value over time, and is particularly interested in the exceedances of values defined as lower and upper limits, i.e. alert values for the assessment of system performance. Figure 2 shows an example of a control chart used in a Statistical Quality Control system.

The limits – upper and lower – can be defined on the basis of external expertise or, with a normal distribution of the parameters for the data set. Factors causing nonconformities in the process under investigation on the control card are presented as:

- points not falling within the designated range (outside the control lines)
- clear sequences of consecutive points
- above or below the line of average values
- increasing or decreasing.

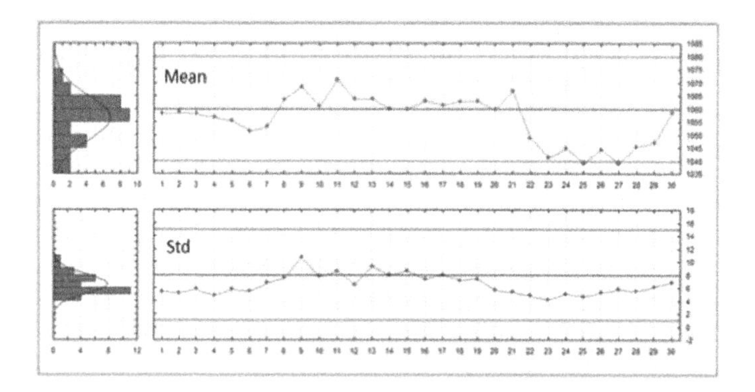

Fig. 2. Example of a control chart. The upper chart presents values of the chosen parameter, the lower chart presents the standard deviation. The blue line represents the values of the parameter, and the red ones - the upper and lower limits of this parameter. On the left corresponding histogram is given. The detailed description of the chart and its source dataset are presented in [22]. (Color figure online)

3.3 Combining the SHAP Charts and Values and Limits Plots

We assume that the parameter analysed by the operator, as relevant, has also been taken into account in the machine learning process. In order to make an analysis combining data from the two analytical processes, let us combine information from the control card for one parameter with the SHAP values for this parameter (see Fig. 3).

In the analysis based on the limits exceedance the combined information of limit value, parameter value and SHAP value is needed. In the data slice shown in Fig. 3 we can see two overruns combined with different SHAP values (zoomed in the Fig. 4), but every single overrun is hard to interpret unless we can put it in context. Visual patterns can be taken into consideration while reasoning. While analysing the data according to increasing SHAP values we can look for some dependencies between parameter values and SHAP data in the context of

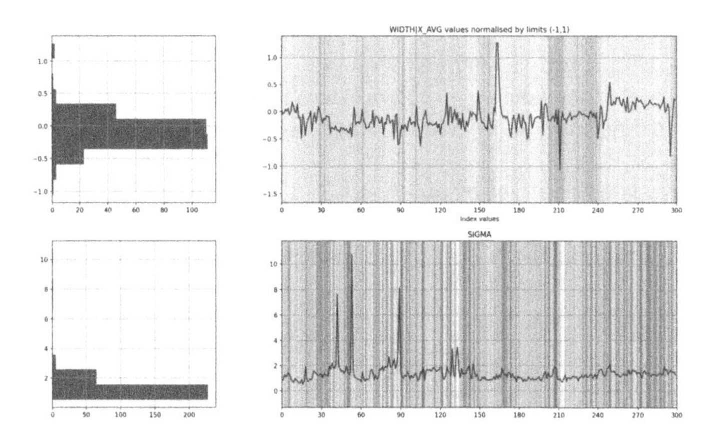

Fig. 3. Example of control chart combined with the SHAP values for the parameter shown in plot. The blue line represents values of the parameter, the yellow ones stand for limits and the background shows the SHAP values for the parameter. (Color figure online)

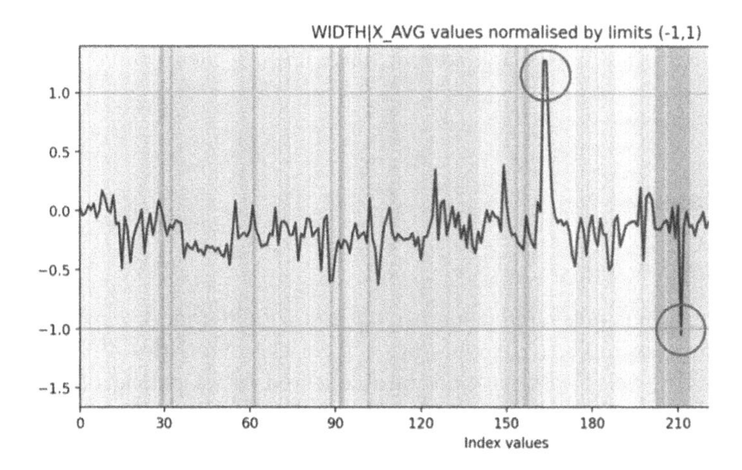

Fig. 4. Example of control chart combined with the SHAP values for the parameter shown in plot. The blue line represents values of the parameter, the yellow ones stand for limits and the background shows the SHAP values for the parameter. (Color figure online)

limits. A pattern similar to the one shown in Fig. 5A can be an argument for such connection, pattern similar to the one shown in Fig. 5B denies the relationship. Examples of real data charts meeting these patterns are shown in Sect. 4.2.

While analyzing the relationship between limits and SHAP values three cases can be taken into consideration:

- When the SHAP values importance meets the exceedance of the limit. Limits are set by experts.
- When there is no connection between SHAP parameter importance and the limits exceedance. Limits are set by experts. It is worth noticing, that it does not mean, that limit was defined wrongly. The control cart parameter limits may involve a wider range of problems than those considered for classification, and their origin may be related to other aspects of the process described by the model.
- When there is no limit set by an expert, but while analysis of the relationship between SHAP importance and parameter values, the threshold of significance can be proposed on the base of the visual pattern shown in the chart.

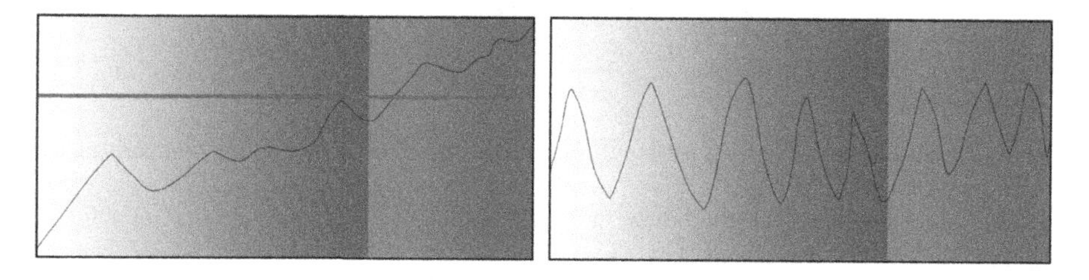

Fig. 5. Visual pattern of combined data, where there is a connection between SHAP values and limit (in the left) and pattern, where no such connection is visible (in the right).

4 Usecases

4.1 Dataset Used

The model usage is presented using two datasets of different origins and different features as an example to demonstrate typical characteristics of data collected for the quality control process and data collected for classification by machine learning methods. One of them is data on the steel rolling process in the steel mill. The data collected from the sensors are the physical parameters of the rolled object (thickness, width, cross-section, etc.) and the parameters of the production process (temperature, etc.). The objects analysed are steel coils. The problem of machine learning classification is to distinguish between good and bad coils (rejected during the complaints process). The parameters of industrial process shown in line plot can be used as well to take care of the production line to avoid the technical problems leading to the increased number of bad coils. The exceedances of limits indicate the possible need for repair process.

The first dataset (A) we used to conduct the analysis was obtained from a steel plant, specifically from the Hot Rolling Process. The data was gathered via sensors positioned along the production line. After consulting with experts from the Quality Department, we conducted a feasibility study and finalized the selection of relevant parameters. The evaluation of steel strip quality is based on the feature set employed in our research, which corresponds to the Statistical Process Control system currently implemented by the company [8].

In order to ascertain the significance of variations between distributions, we trained a Machine Learning model to categorize products as either "good" or "bad". Nonetheless, this classification is not primary objective of this study, but the visualisation of the results to enhance interpretation of the XAI. For that reason, we evaluate the importance of features on the model's decision by utilizing SHAP values.

The second dataset (B) is medical data on patients diagnosed with diabetes. The problem of machine learning classification is to predict diagnosis of diabetics. The parameters shown in line plot can be used to indicate the need of in-depth diagnostics to make sure that parameters overruns are not the sign of the disease process.

4.2 Connection Between Limits and SHAP Values

As mentioned before, while comparing the control chart with SHAP values diagrams it can be easly shown if the limits exceedance is correlated with SHAP values or not. Let's show the examples of three cases:

- overlap between the experts' limit and relevance of SHAP values.
- lack of connection between the experts' limit and relevance of SHAP values.
- the threshold of significance proposition on a base of the visual pattern shown in the chart.

The first situation can be represented by the glucose parameter from the dataset A. The expert based limit of accepted value of parameter is 140 mg/dl. As we can see in Fig. 6, there is strong correlation between upper limit and importance of SHAP value of glucose parameter.

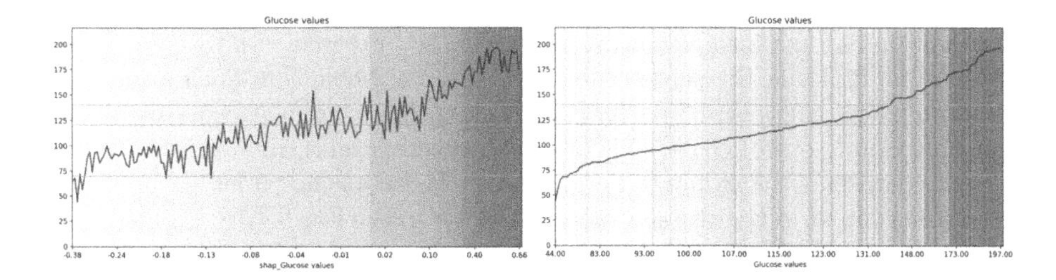

Fig. 6. Combined chart of SHAP values and limit (140 mg/dl) excedance for glucose parameters sorted by the SHAP glucose (in the left) and value of glucose (in the right).

The second situation is shown on the base of parameter of the BMI for the same dataset and the temperature of the steel coils from the other dataset. As we can see in the Fig. 7 and 8, there is no unambiguous connection between the SHAP value relevance and exceeding the limit. Especially in the second case we can see, that none of the overruns were classified negatively.

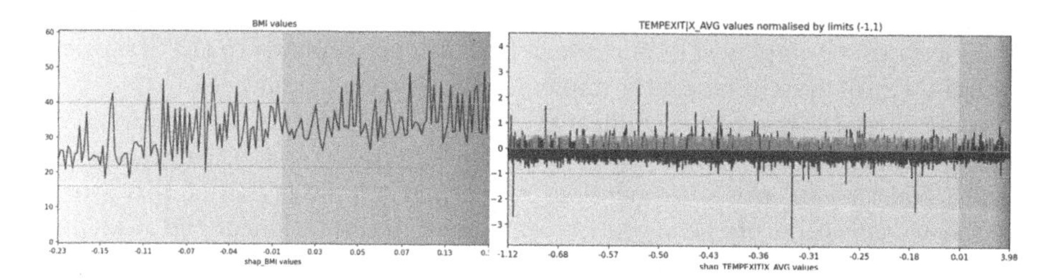

Fig. 7. Combined chart of SHAP values and limit exceedance for BMI parameter from dataset A sorted by the SHAP BMI (in the left) and temperature parameter from dataset B (in the right) sorted by SHAP temperature.

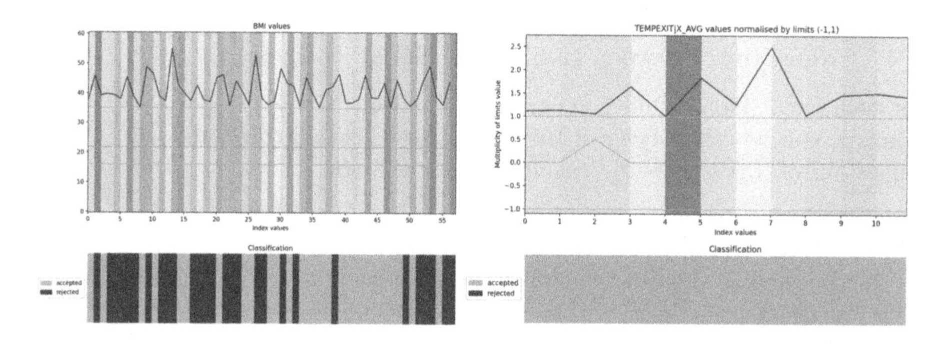

Fig. 8. Combined chart of SHAP values and limit exceedance for BMI parameter from 'dataset A (in the left) and temperature parameter from dataset B (in the right). Data filtered by the upper limit. The result of classification can be seen below: negative in navy blue and positive in gray. (Color figure online)

Finally let's take into consideration the most interesting third case, when there are no limits in the sense of experts' base threshold, but such a line can be proposed on the base of pattern analysis in the combined chart of SHAP importance and control chart. One of the parameters taken into account in the diabetics dataset is the number of pregnancies. There was no "limit" of pregnancies in the context of the risk of diabetes, but let us see Fig. 9. We can place the threshold line behind 6 pregnancies - the importance of higher values of pregnancies parameter is always high in the SHAP results schema. After establishing the 7 pregnancies as limit we can filter the cases (Fig. 9).

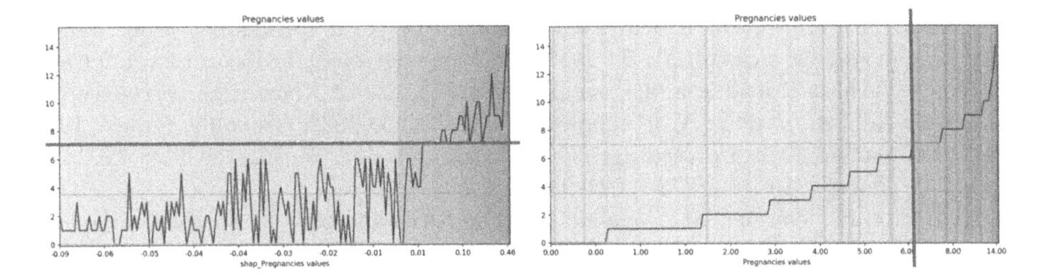

Fig. 9. Combined chart of SHAP values and limit exceedance for the number of pregnancies parameter sorted by the SHAP pregnancies (in the left) and number of pregnancies (in the right). The proposed on the base of visualisation threshold value is 7.

5 Conclusions

The combination of SHAP values and control charts parameters, especially limit exceedances are not broadly described in the literature, but separate use of both approaches is fundamental for industrial processes analysis. The combined approach, connecting the information taken from SHAP calculations and from control charts exceedance, presented in SECC method, gives us possibilities to reason beyond the scope implied by both the first and second approaches.

This approach is dedicated to practical industrial analysis, where the control charts are in everyday use. The customizable and flexible application for comparing the control charts visualizations with the combination of the SHAP values and additional information can be used as a tool for reasoning based on dependencies, which appear in the graphical visualization. Some examples of conclusions made on the base of the application were shown. In the future maybe the other types of anomalies can be extracted from the data after visual patterns recognition and described and interpreted in the context of dataset.

References

1. Boaventura, L.L., Ferreira, P.H., Fiaccone, R.L.: On flexible statistical process control with artificial intelligence: classification control charts. Expert Syst. Appl. **194**, 116492 (2022)
2. Bobek, S., Kuk, M., Brzegowski, J., Brzychczy, E., Nalepa, G.J.: KnAC: an approach for enhancing cluster analysis with background knowledge and explanations. Appl. Intell. **53**(12), 15537–15560 (2022). https://doi.org/10.1007/s10489-022-04310-9
3. Bobek, S., Kuk, M., Szelążek, M., Nalepa, G.J.: Enhancing cluster analysis with explainable AI and multidimensional cluster prototypes. IEEE Access **10**, 101556–101574 (2022). https://doi.org/10.1109/ACCESS.2022.3208957
4. Chesani, F., Mello, P., Montali, M., Riguzzi, F., Sebastianis, M., Storari, S.: Checking compliance of execution traces to business rules. In: Ardagna, D., Mecella, M., Yang, J. (eds.) BPM 2008. LNBIP, vol. 17, pp. 134–145. Springer, Heidelberg (2009). https://doi.org/10.1007/978-3-642-00328-8_13

5. Davari, N., Veloso, B., Ribeiro, R.P., Gama, J.: Fault forecasting using data-driven modeling: a case study for metro do Porto data set. In: Koprinska, I., et al. (eds.) Machine Learning and Principles and Practice of Knowledge Discovery in Databases: International Workshops of ECML PKDD 2022, Grenoble, France, 19–23 September 2022, Proceedings, Part II, pp. 400–409. Springer, Cham (2023). https://doi.org/10.1007/978-3-031-23633-4_26
6. de Bruijn, H., Warnier, M., Janssen, M.: The perils and pitfalls of explainable AI: strategies for explaining algorithmic decision-making. Gov. Inf. Q. **39**(2), 101666 (2022)
7. Dunzer, S., Stierle, M., Matzner, M., Baier, S.: Conformance checking: a state-of-the-art literature review, pp. 1–10 (2019). https://doi.org/10.1145/3329007.3329014
8. Eckes, G.: The Six Sigma Revolution: How General Electric and Others Turned Process Into Profits. Wiley (2002)
9. Gosiewska, A., Biecek, P.: Do not trust additive explanations (2020)
10. Guidotti, R., Monreale, A., Ruggieri, S., Pedreschi, D., Turini, F., Giannotti, F.: Local rule-based explanations of black box decision systems (2018)
11. Kadir, T., Brady, M.: Saliency, scale and image description. Int. J. Comput. Vis. **45**, 83–105 (2001). https://doi.org/10.1023/A:1012460413855
12. Khader, N., Yoon, S.W.: Online control of stencil printing parameters using reinforcement learning approach. Procedia Manuf. **17**, 94–101 (2018). 28th International Conference on Flexible Automation and Intelligent Manufacturing (FAIM2018), 11–14 June 2018, Columbus, OH, USAGlobal Integration of Intelligent Manufacturing and Smart Industry for Good of Humanity
13. Kumar, E., Venkatasubramanian, S., Scheidegger, C., Friedler, S.A.: Problems with Shapley-value-based explanations as feature importance measures (2020)
14. de Leoni, M., Munoz-Gama, J., Carmona, J., van der Aalst, W.M.P.: Decomposing alignment-based conformance checking of data-aware process models. In: Meersman, R., et al. (eds.) OTM 2014. LNCS, vol. 8841, pp. 3–20. Springer, Heidelberg (2014). https://doi.org/10.1007/978-3-662-45563-0_1
15. Lundberg, S.M., Lee, S.: A unified approach to interpreting model predictions. CoRR abs/1705.07874 (2017). http://arxiv.org/1705.07874
16. Lundberg, S.M., Lee, S.I.: A unified approach to interpreting model predictions. In: Guyon, I., et al. (eds.) Advances in Neural Information Processing Systems, vol. 30. Curran Associates, Inc. (2017)
17. Maeyens, J., Vorstermans, A., Verbeke, M.: Process mining on machine event logs for profiling abnormal behaviour and root cause analysis. Ann. Telecommun. **75**, 1–10 (2020). https://doi.org/10.1007/s12243-020-00809-9
18. Matzka, S.: Explainable artificial intelligence for predictive maintenance applications. In: 2020 Third International Conference on Artificial Intelligence for Industries (AI4I), pp. 69–74. IEEE (2020)
19. Pashami, S., et al.: Explainable predictive maintenance (2023)
20. Pereira, M., Bento, M.I., Ferreira, L., Sá, J., Silva, F., Baptista, A.: Using six sigma to analyse customer satisfaction at the product design and development stage. Procedia Manuf. **38**, 1608–1614 (2019). 29th International Conference on Flexible Automation and Intelligent Manufacturing (FAIM 2019)
21. Ribeiro, M., Singh, S., Guestrin, C.: Anchors: high-precision model-agnostic explanations. Proc. AAAI Conf. Artif. Intell. **32** (2018). https://doi.org/10.1609/aaai.v32i1.11491

22. Szelążek, M., Bobek, S., Nalepa, G.J.: Semantic data mining-based decision support for quality assessment in steel industry. Expert Syst., e13319 (2023). https://doi.org/10.1111/exsy.13319. https://onlinelibrary.wiley.com/doi/abs/10.1111/exsy.13319
23. Vilone, G., Longo, L.: A quantitative evaluation of global, rule-based explanations of post-hoc, model agnostic methods. Frontiers Artif. Intell. **4** (2021)

RAAIT

Preface – Responsible Applied Artificial InTelligence (RAAIT) Workshop

Huib Aldewereld[1], Roland van Dierendonck[2], Maaike Harbers[2], Sophie Horsman[3], Fabian Kok[1], Stefan Leijnen[1], Marieke Peeters[1], Saskia Robben[3], and Pascal Wiggers[3]

[1] HU University of Applied Sciences Utrecht, Heidelberglaan 15, 3584 CS Utrecht, The Netherlands
marieke.peeters@hu.nl
[2] Rotterdam University of Applied Sciences, Wijnhaven 107, 3011 WN Rotterdam, The Netherlands
[3] Amsterdam University of Applied Sciences, Wibautstraat 3b, 1091 GH Amsterdam, The Netherlands

1 About the Workshop

Artificial Intelligence (AI) increasingly affects the way people work, live, and interact. It is applied in all kinds of domains, such as healthcare, education, media, creative industry, retail, defence, transportation, law, and the financial sector. While AI has great potential to enhance well-being and help solving societal challenges, it also comes with severe risks of negative social and ethical consequences, such as discrimination, reinforcing existing biases, and causing a big carbon footprint. Over the past years, many high-level principles, and guidelines for 'responsible' or 'ethical' AI have been developed, and a lot of theoretical research on responsible AI has been done. However, this work often fails to address the challenges that arise when applying AI in practice.

This one-day workshop on Responsible Applied Artificial InTelligence (RAAIT) facilitated connecting and sharing experiences with fellow researchers and AI practitioners who bring Responsible AI to practice. In our vision, RAAIT includes the design, development, and deployment of Responsible AI applications in a practical context, while considering ethical and societal aspects.

2 Keynotes

Keynote speaker at the event was:

- Emma Beauxis-Aussalet (PhD) - The (long) path towards guaranteeing the levels of error of AI systems in practice
  If we buy a bag of screws, we would not accept that it contains an unknown amount of defective screws. Especially if we build planes with such screws. Why should we

then accept that AI systems result in unknown amounts of error in their output? Especially if we build critical algorithmic systems in healthcare or policing. We must also consider that AI systems become discriminatory if more errors systematically occur for certain populations. Measuring AI errors is critical to achieve safe, trustworthy, and fair systems. Yet this task is much more complex than it seems, and the road is still long for the AI industry to guarantee the levels of error of their systems. In this talk, we will discuss the challenges that arise in such endeavours. We will outline the theoretical and practical aspects to consider, and discuss the gaps between research and practice. We will draw inspiration from domains in which errors are more strictly measured and regulated, and point at opportunities for future work to address the case of AI errors in practice.

3 Accepted Papers

In total, we received 17 submissions, 9 of which were accepted for presentation, and 7 of which were eligible for publication in the proceedings. Contributions address technological aspects of responsible applied AI as well as social or socio-technical factors, such as the design process (e.g., through co-creation) and the organisational governance structure and processes to ensure responsible application of AI. We proudly present the papers accepted to the first edition of this annual workshop on Responsible Applied AI. The papers range from a focus on the design or the development of Responsible Applied AI systems to deployment in practice:

- Max Knobbout, *ALFR++: A novel algorithm for Learning Adversarial Fair Representations*
- Laura de Groot, *The Machine Vision Game: Making Machine Vision Development Trade-Offs Tangible*
- Senthuran Kalananthan, Alexander Kichutkin, Ziyao Shang, András Strausz, Javier Sanguino and Menna Elassady, *MindSet: A Data-Debiasing Interface using a Visual Human-in-the-Loop Workflow*
- Felix Friedrich, Manuel Brack, Patrick Schramowski and Kristian Kersting, *Mitigating Inappropriateness in Image Generation: Can there be Value in Reflecting the World's Ugliness?*
- Floor Schukking, Levi Verhoef, Tina Mioch, Coert van Gemeren and Huib Aldewereld, *Improving Adoption of AI Impact Assessment in the Media Sector*
- Danielle Sent, Tina Wünn and Linda W. P. Peute, *Trust in Artificial Intelligence: Exploring the Influence of Model Presentation and Model Interaction on Trust in a Medical Setting*
- Martin van den Berg, Julie Gerlings and Jenia Kim, *Empirical Research on Ensuring Ethical AI in Fraud Detection of Insurance Claims: A Field Study of Dutch Insurers*
- Steven Vethman, Marianne Schaaphok, Marissa Hoekstra and Cor Veenman, *Random Sample as a Pre-Pilot Evaluation of Benefits and Risks for AI in Public Sector*

- Jacintha Walters, Diptish Dey, Debarati Bhaumik, Sophie Horsman, *Complying with the EU AI Act, On which areas should organizations focus when considering compliance with the AIA?*

All of these papers are published in this volume, except for the following papers published in other venues:

- Knobbout, M. (2023). ALFR++: A novel algorithm for Learning Adversarial Fair Representations. Accepted to ECAI 2023, European Conference on AI 2023, Krakow, Poland.
- Brack, M., Friedrich, F., Schramowski, P., & Kersting, K. (2023). Mitigating Inappropriateness in Image Generation: Can there be Value in Reflecting the World's Ugliness?. arXiv preprint: 2305.18398.

4 Closing Remarks

The RAAIT workshop provided a first gathering of the community, bringing together the various aspects related to Responsible Applied Artificial Intelligence, and offering an opportunity for discussions on the future, with the objective of mapping methods and tools to the design, development, and deployment of Responsible AI. The afternoon was used to reflect on the contributions presented and to identify gaps, opportunities, and challenges for the research field. For more information about the RAAIT workshop, please visit https://raait-ecai-2023.com/.

The organizers wish to thank the keynote speakers, all authors that submitted and/or presented their work, the RAAIT Program Committee members for their help in reviewing the submissions, and the local organization and all chairs of ECAI 2023 for making the event possible.

Acknowledgements. The authors would like to acknowledge the SPRONG RAAIT project funded by SIA (for more information, please visit https://raait.nl).

Complying with the EU AI Act

Jacintha Walters(✉), Diptish Dey, Debarati Bhaumik, and Sophie Horsman

University of Applied Sciences Amsterdam, 1091 GC Amsterdam, The Netherlands
jacintha.walters@gmail.com

Abstract. The EU AI Act is the proposed EU legislation concerning AI systems. The goal of this paper is to determine on which areas organizations should focus with regards to compliance with the AIA. This paper identifies several categories of the AI Act. Based on this categorization, a questionnaire is developed that serves as a tool to offer insights by creating quantitative data. Analysis of the data shows various challenges for organizations in different compliance categories. The influence of organization characteristics, such as size and sector, is examined to determine the impact on compliance. The paper will also share qualitative data on which questions were prevalent among respondents, both on the content of the AI Act as on the application. The paper concludes by stating that there is still room for improvement in terms of compliance with the AIA and refers to a related project that examines a solution to help these organizations.

Keywords: EU AI Act · compliance preparedness · organization challenges

1 Introduction

The EU AI Act (in this paper abbreviated as AIA) is a proposed regulation (law) by the European Commission that aims to regulate the application of artificial intelligence in the European Union. The proposed regulation was published in 2021 and is currently under review by the European Parliament and the Council of the European Union. It defines which AI systems are categorized as high-risk and the rules applicable before a high-risk AI can be used [1]. At the time of writing, it is unknown when the AIA will become in effect [2].

One of the challenges in complying with the AIA is that AI systems are developed and maintained by a chain of actors, including software developers, data scientists, and engineers. The challenges for organizations are further complicated because of the interdisciplinary character of legal, technical, and domain-specific responsibilities. For an organization to comply, it must be able to interpret the contours implied by the act and translate this information into relevant requirements.

Supported by the University of Applied Sciences Amsterdam.

S. Nowaczyk et al. (Eds.): ECAI 2023 Workshops, CCIS 1948, pp. 65–75, 2024.
https://doi.org/10.1007/978-3-031-50485-3_5

This paper identifies areas where organizations face challenges when considering current and future compliance with the AIA. The following steps are undertaken to identify these areas. Initially, categories of concern within the AIA are identified. Based on this categorization, a questionnaire is constructed to gather insights into how organizations handle the requirements associated with each category. The questionnaire is further refined through expert reflection, and trial runs to ensure its effectiveness.

2 Relevant Literature

Usman *et al.* observes that organizations can be subject to multiple regulations, which may lead to several challenges. First, there can be conflicting requirements. Second, some regulations are not well-defined, leaving the development team unsure how to implement them. After implementation, it can be challenging to verify that the software system meets all the requirements [3].

Research on privacy regulations showed that many small medium enterprises (SMEs) do not possess sufficient knowledge of the regulations to achieve compliance. Besides the risk of fines, compliance is essential to sustain if organizations want to supply services to other compliant organizations [4].

There can be a significant difference in compliance for different sectors. And one study performed in Malaysia concluded that Government-owned organizations generally demonstrate a lower degree of compliance than other organizations [5].

Most existing research on the AIA has a theoretical perspective, focusing mainly on the quality of the content of the AIA rather than on the application. One study concludes that the AIA is a good attempt but has several weaknesses. For instance, many parts are ambiguous, making it hard for organizations to define rules to self-assess against [6]. Another study concludes that the AIA is generally well-constructed but advises that the proposal should not rely so heavily on internal controls. External oversight is a necessity [7].

A notable research gap exists regarding the future compliance of organizations with the AIA and their level of preparedness. The existing literature covers two parts. First, compliance with existing regulations like GDPR. Second, critical analysis of the content of the AIA. There is a lack of insight into how organizations will navigate compliance with the AIA and the extent to which they are prepared. This paper aims to address this research gap by providing insights into the level of preparedness and the challenges organizations will face in complying with the AIA.

3 Methodology

3.1 Identifying Categories in the AIA

Figure 1 shows an overview of the relevant documentation for AIA compliance. The AIA focuses on subjects such as technical documentation, user communication and risks to human rights and discrimination. However, to ensure a manageable questionnaire size, a decision was made to exclude certain subjects discussed in the AIA. The subjects of robustness, cybersecurity, logging, reporting, and audit preparedness were omitted from the questionnaire. This exclusion was primarily driven by the need to reduce the questionnaire's length, making it more feasible for potential respondents to complete. Although relevant to AI development, these subjects are broader and primarily associated with IT development.

Based on this selection, Fig. 2 shows a hierarchical breakdown of relevant key subject areas from the AIA used as a basis for the questionnaire. The breakdown in Fig. 2 is a result of highlighting key subject areas of the AIA and breaking them down into categories. This was done by focusing on the parts that are most relevant for organizations and summarizing the important information.

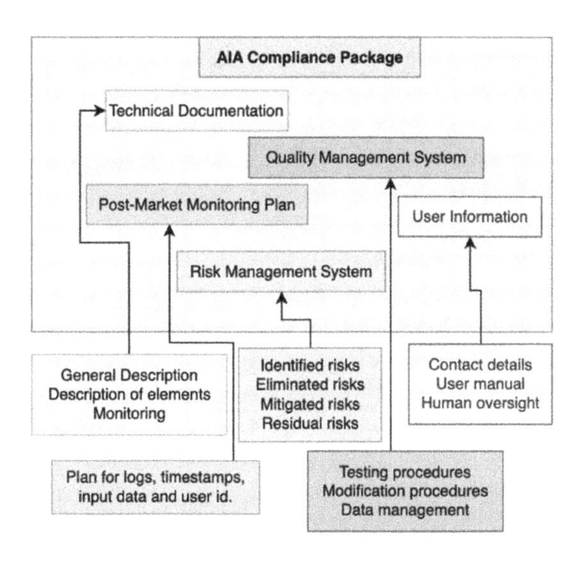

Fig. 1. Overview of the AIA compliance documentation

3.2 Creating and Refining the Questionnaire

The categories in Fig. 2 were used to create a questionnaire that assesses compliance with the AIA. The final questionnaire contains 5 parts: data & model internals, technical documentation, user communication, model monitoring (including human oversight), and risk management (including quality management and risk management).

The construction of the questionnaire involved several iterative steps to improve its validity and reliability. Existing questions were rephrased to transform open-ended questions into closed questions. Proxy questions were incorporated to ensure fair and reasonable responses. For example, the statement

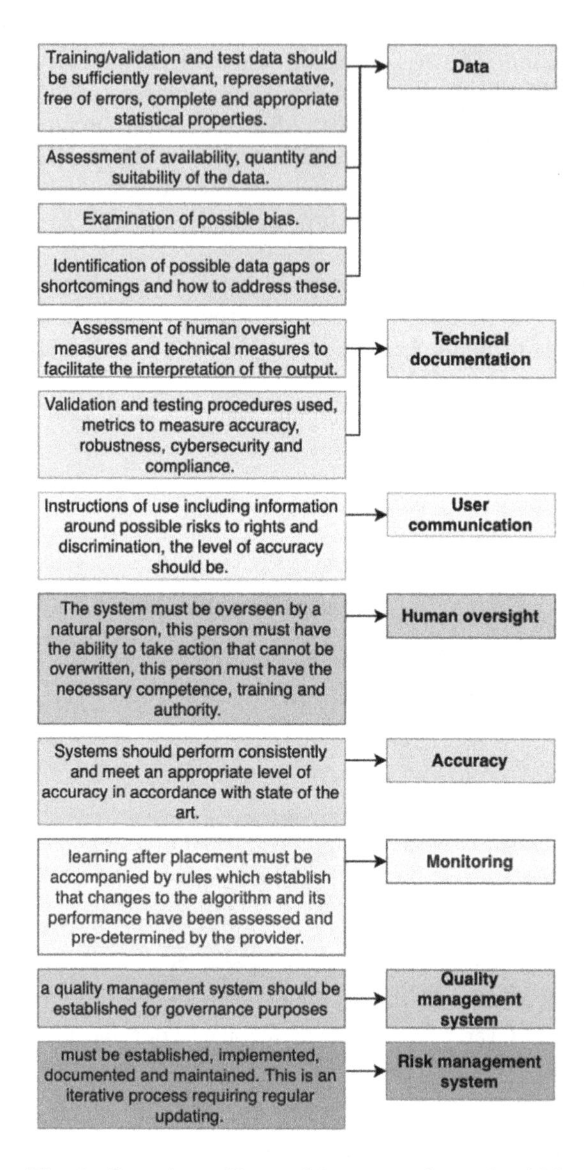

Fig. 2. Overview of key subject areas from the AIA

"My organization identifies and mitigates risks associated with a dataset" is supported by the question, "How often does your organization mitigate risks in a dataset?".

The questionnaire contains around 90 questions, which took respondents about 15 min to answer.[1] Feedback was gathered on the questionnaire from two organizations through an online interactive trial run. Most questions are 'state-

[1] Questionnaire: https://hva.eu.qualtrics.com/jfe/form/SV_9sFXWLoj5uFoaua.

ment questions', 'how often' questions and 'who' questions as can be seen in the template questions in Figs. 3, 4 and 5. "Statement questions" rely primarily on respondents' perspectives, whereas other questions are more objective. This observation is used to compute a "compliance score".

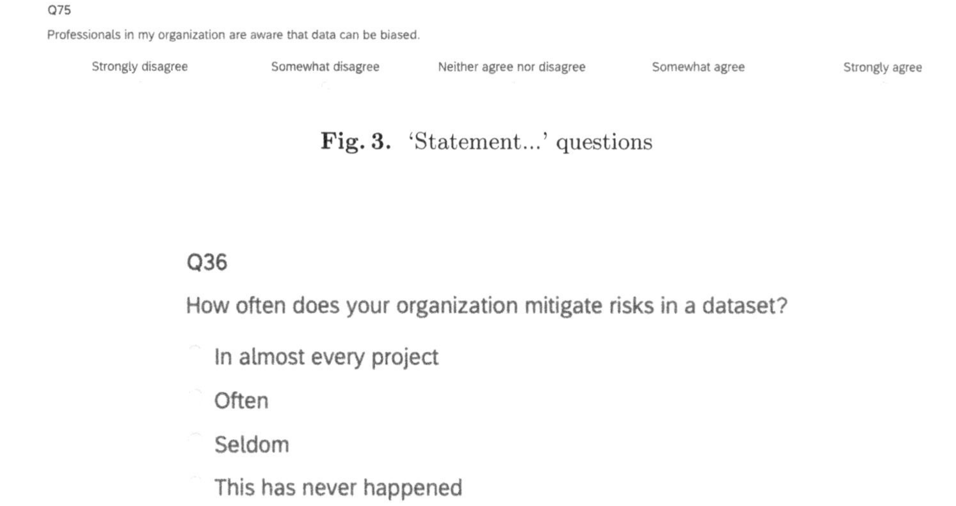

Fig. 3. 'Statement...' questions

Fig. 4. 'How often...' questions

Interactive interviews are conducted with multiple respondents based on the questionnaire. An online questionnaire is also circulated to obtain a broader range of responses. In total, seven responses were obtained through interactive interviews, supplemented by eight responses gathered online.

3.3 Response Rating

Each of the fifteen responses is rated using a three-point range. The scoring process aims to quantify the responses for each questionnaire category to enable numeric comparison. The questionnaire data is rated using a rule-based system. The rule-based system involves manually creating rules that are used to score each entry in the dataset automatically.[2]

The following categories from the questionnaire are used: data and model internals, technical documentation, user communication, model monitoring, and risk management. Generally, each question has a "perfect" answer worth 2 points, followed by "reasonable" answers worth 1 point. If a question had multiple options that should be selected, each option is worth 1/2 point. The remaining answers score 0 points. The perfect answer aligns closely with the requirements stated in the AI Act. The point distribution for each question is summarized in Fig. 6.

[2] Code: https://gitfront.io/r/user-7646844/ZTQB4rfx5SYN/CustomLLM/.

Q48

With which stakeholders are test results communicated?

- Compliance professionals
- Digital marketing professionals
- Model development professionals
- Production and maintenance professionals
- None

Fig. 5. 'Who...' questions

The overview of how the automated scoring process was implemented is shown in Fig. 7. Each respondent's score for each category is calculated along with the reflection score. The reflection score is a measure of how well an organization understands its own compliance with the AI Act. Figure 7 shows that this score is calculated by determining the ratio of "statement questions" and other questions (process). Statement questions rely primarily on respondents' perspectives, whereas other questions are more objective. The reflection score determines if an organization over- or underestimates itself.

Question	Answer	N. of questions	Scoring
Statement	1-6 scale	25	Strongly agree → 2 points Somewhat agree → 1 point Neutral → 0.5 point Disagree → 0 points
How often...	MC	24	For every model → 2 points For most models → 1 point For a few or never → 0 points
Do you...	Yes/No	14	Yes → 2 points No → 0 points
Who...	MC	9	0.5 point per stakeholder
To what extent...	0-10 scale	5	Not scored, but used to gain insight into the organization characteristics.
How many...	MC	4	If someone is responsible → 2 points If multiple people are partially responsible → 1 point If no one is responsible → 0 points
When...	MC	3	In every iteration of a project → 2 points Once at a relevant time → 1 points Sometimes or at the wrong time → 0 points
What type...	MC	2	Differs per question. Generally if a suitable method is present 2 points, if they are working on it 1 point otherwise 0 points.
Overig	MC	3	Differs per question.

Fig. 6. Points given per question type

For example, if an organization strongly agrees that they communicate accepted risks of the system with the user, but also states that they never measure a model's risk, there appears to be an overestimation by the respondent. Conversely, if an organization scores low on statement questions but high on other questions, it may be underestimating its compliance. The reflection score is added to show the validity of the responses and to help organizations better understand their own compliance.

4 Results

4.1 Identifying Focus Areas

The average percentage score for each category of the questionnaire is shown in Fig. 8. The overall average compliance score for all respondents and categories is 57%. The average reflection score is 1.0, suggesting that organizations demonstrate good self-awareness. Figure 8 reveals variations in compliance scores across different categories. The questionnaire results show that many organizations lack procedures for technical documentation and do not have someone trained to determine compliance requirements. Regarding data and model internals, organizations struggle with training employees on data and model bias. User communication presents challenges in determining metrics for measuring model risks on rights and discrimination. Risk management systems are found to be lacking in some organizations. Model monitoring shows a mixed trend, with some organizations adequately updating models when needed and having protocols in place to determine if data is outdated.

4.2 Organization Characteristics' Influence

Organizations with 1–50 employees scored lower than organizations with 51+ employees. As for the industry, the dataset is too small to draw any conclusions. There is a large variance in compliance scores for the IT sector, from 26% to 67%. One organization felt that their ISO certification helped them to comply with the AIA. Organizations with more AI experience in years did not score better compared to organizations relatively new to AI.

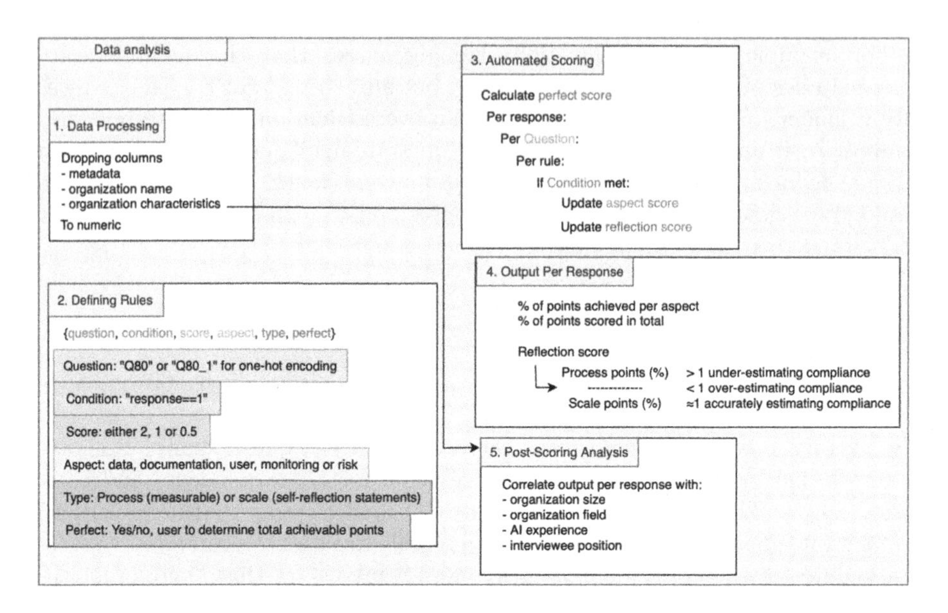

Fig. 7. Scoring system of questionnaire data

4.3 Prevalent Questions

Besides the challenges mentioned in Sect. 4.1, this paper also contributes to better understanding the challenges of organizations by identifying common questions among respondents. The interactive interviews identified several prevalent questions among respondents, both on the content of the AIA as on the application within their organization. These questions are either directly asked by the organization, or extracted from the answers on the questionnaire. For instance, when asked what data risks organizations have dealt with in the past years, almost all organizations gave an answer relating to GDPR compliance. In reality, there are many other risks besides GDPR compliance that the AIA is concerned with, so the question would be, 'What other risks besides data privacy should my organization be concerned with?'.

The identified prevalent questions among most organizations are as follows: Questions on the content of the AIA:

1. Should technical documentation also be written for non-technical people?
2. Does the AIA stipulate that we need someone to monitor the AI models full-time?
3. Does the AIA require me to work with encrypted data only?
4. How should we deal with missing data according to the AIA?
5. What other data risks besides data privacy should my organization be concerned with?
6. What does the AIA mean by high-risk AI?
7. Does the AIA require an external audit?

8. Which documents should be included in the compliance documentation?
9. Does the AIA mention metrics that should be used to determine a model's risks for rights and discrimination?
10. What does the AIA mean by 'human oversight'?

Questions on the application of the AIA within their organization:

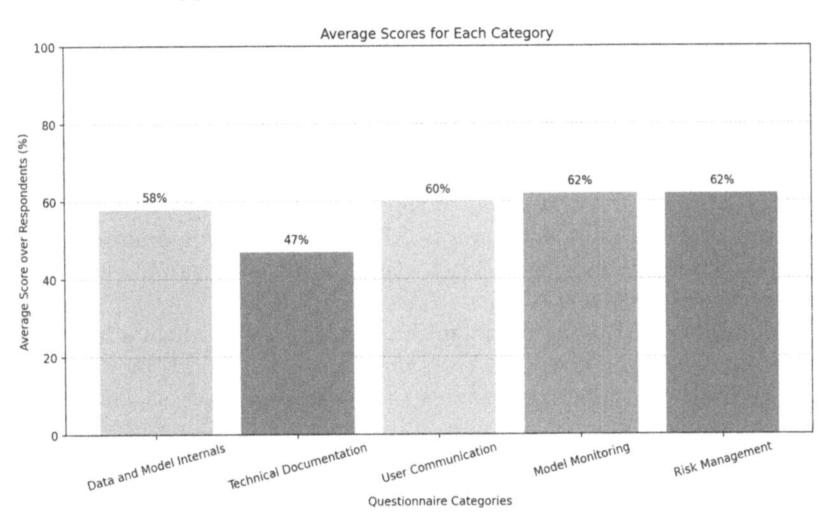

Fig. 8. Percentage of points per questionnaire category

1. To which extent does my ISO certification help towards AIA compliance?
2. Does GDPR training also include data bias and model bias training?
3. What are the biggest risks to AIA compliance when data is gathered in-house?
4. Our organization uses data from customers; what are some of the biggest risks when aiming for AIA compliance?
5. We only use ChatGPT and other out-of-the-box AI models; should we still be concerned with the AIA?
6. What can we do to improve AIA compliance concerning our technical documentation?
7. We currently don't communicate anything about our models with our users; how can we better communicate information with the users for AIA compliance?
8. Our organization is very small, and no one is specialized in compliance; where do we even begin to achieve AIA compliance?
9. We currently have no idea if we communicate with our stakeholders according to the AIA; how should we assess this to make improvements?
10. The AIA stipulates that accuracy should be according to the state of the art. This seems very vague; how should I go about achieving state-of-the-art accuracy?

These questions can be useful for future research to understand the needs of organizations.[3]

5 Conclusion

This paper examines in which areas organizations seem to be struggling with regards to current and future compliance with the AIA. A conceptual framework has been constructed based on a review of the act. A questionnaire is formulated based on the framework. Fifteen organizations answered the entire questionnaire.

A compliance score is calculated using a rule-based system that awards points for answers following the contents of the AIA. Organizations achieve an average compliance score of 57% compared to the 'perfect' score. This score indicates there is room for improvement towards AIA readiness. Organizations are best prepared on model monitoring and risk management but score the lowest, with 47%, on technical documentation.

The duration of AI usage by organizations does not result in a higher compliance score. The same goes for IT organizations compared to non-IT organizations. Overall, this paper contributes to the growing body of knowledge on the impl042weementation of the AIA. The paper is the first to identify focus areas for different categories of the AIA to help organizations better prepare. Organizations will need help dealing with the questions and challenges they are facing.

6 Future Research

Several approaches for future research are identified. First, the predictive power of the questionnaire should be tested to see if the questionnaire can predict if an organization will pass the self-assessment. More qualitative data should be gathered by observing the AIA compliance processes. This data can then be used to refine the questionnaire for different organizations' sizes and sectors.

Acknowledgement. I want to acknowledge that this research has been conducted as part of my master thesis for the Master Applied AI program at Amsterdam University of Applied Sciences (HvA). I am grateful for the guidance and support provided by Diptish Dey, Debarati Bhaumik, and Sophie Horsman, who served as my advisors throughout the research process. I would also like to thank the Centre for Market Insights (a research lab within the HvA) for their assistance and resources in facilitating this study.

[3] Future research from one of the authors of this paper has focused on examining how organizations can be supported with these questions: https://www.babelfish.nl/blog/unraveling-aia-with-llm.

References

1. The Act: The Artificial Intelligence Act. https://artificialintelligenceact.eu/the-act/. Version 21 Apr 2021
2. European Commission: Proposal for a regulation laying down harmonized rules on artificial intelligence (Artificial Intelligence Act) and amending certain EU legislative acts (2021). https://eur-lex.europa.eu/legal-content/TXT/?uri=CELEX%3A52021PC0206
3. Usman, M., Felderer, M., Unterkalmsteiner, M., Klotins, E., Mendez, D., Alégroth, E.: Compliance requirements in large-scale software development: an industrial case study. In: Morisio, M., Torchiano, M., Jedlitschka, A. (eds.) PROFES 2020. LNCS, vol. 12562, pp. 385–401. Springer, Cham (2020). https://doi.org/10.1007/978-3-030-64148-1_24
4. da Conceca Freitas, M., Mira da Silva, M.: GDPR compliance in SMEs: there is much to be done. J. Inf. Syst. Eng. Manag. (2018). https://doi.org/10.20897/jisem/3941
5. Chua, H.N., Herbland, A., Wong, S.F., Chang, Y.: Compliance to personal data protection principles: a study of how organizations frame privacy policy notices. Telematics Inf. (2017). https://doi.org/10.1016/j.tele.2017.01.008
6. Veale, Zuiderveen Borgesius, F.: Demystifying the draft EU artificial intelligence act. CRi Comput. Law Rev. Int. (2021). https://arxiv.org/pdf/2107.03721.pdf
7. Ebers, M., Hoch, V.R.S., Rosenkranz, F., Ruschemeier, H., Steinrtter, B.: The European commissions proposal for an artificial intelligence act critical assessment by members of the robotics and AI law society (RAILS). J. **4**(4), 589–603 (2021). https://doi.org/10.3390/j4040043

Trust in Artificial Intelligence: Exploring the Influence of Model Presentation and Model Interaction on Trust in a Medical Setting

Tina Wünn[1,2], Danielle Sent[1(✉)], Linda W. P. Peute[2], and Stefan Leijnen[1]

[1] Research Group Artificial Intelligence, HU University of Applied Sciences, Utrecht, The Netherlands
danielle.sent@hu.nl

[2] Department of Medical Informatics, Amsterdam UMC Location University of Amsterdam, Amsterdam, The Netherlands

Abstract. The healthcare sector has been confronted with rapidly rising healthcare costs and a shortage of medical staff. At the same time, the field of Artificial Intelligence (AI) has emerged as a promising area of research, offering potential benefits for healthcare. Despite the potential of AI to support healthcare, its widespread implementation, especially in healthcare, remains limited. One possible factor contributing to that is the lack of trust in AI algorithms among healthcare professionals. Previous studies have indicated that explainability plays a crucial role in establishing trust in AI systems. This study aims to explore trust in AI and its connection to explainability in a medical setting. A rapid review was conducted to provide an overview of the existing knowledge and research on trust and explainability. Building upon these insights, a dashboard interface was developed to present the output of an AI-based decision-support tool along with explanatory information, with the aim of enhancing explainability of the AI for healthcare professionals. To investigate the impact of the dashboard and its explanations on healthcare professionals, an exploratory case study was conducted. The study encompassed an assessment of participants' trust in the AI system, their perception of its explainability, as well as their evaluations of perceived ease of use and perceived usefulness. The initial findings from the case study indicate a positive correlation between perceived explainability and trust in the AI system. Our preliminary findings suggest that enhancing the explainability of AI systems could increase trust among healthcare professionals. This may contribute to an increased acceptance and adoption of AI in healthcare. However, a more elaborate experiment with the dashboard is essential.

Keywords: trust · explainability · artificial intelligence · healthcare · dashboard

1 Introduction

Many countries have been experiencing rapidly rising healthcare costs and a shortage of medical staff. At the same time, the growing field of Artificial intelligence (AI) in healthcare aims to extract important information from data and assist in medical decision-making, offering potential solutions for cost and staffing issues, and promising improved

S. Nowaczyk et al. (Eds.): ECAI 2023 Workshops, CCIS 1948, pp. 76–86, 2024.
https://doi.org/10.1007/978-3-031-50485-3_6

healthcare outcomes. However, despite its potential, the adoption of AI in healthcare remains limited [1, 2]. One of the key barriers in implementation is lack of transparency of AI algorithms, which is the level to which the underlying operating rules and inner logic of the technology are understandable to the users [2, 3]. Explainable AI (XAI) is an emerging field in artificial intelligence that deals with methodologies and procedures that provide explainable models of why and how an AI algorithm produces predictions [4]. It addresses the need for transparency and interpretability in AI models, which historically have resembled a 'black box', delivering outputs without a clear understanding by the user of how they were arrived at. This lack of transparency/interpretability can pose significant challenges in sectors such as healthcare, where understanding the decision-making process is necessary for ethical and safety considerations. While XAI has promising prospects for healthcare, uncertainties persist about the kind of explanations that would be most suitable for healthcare professionals and how to present this information to help end users understand the AI [5, 6]. Transparency and explainability have shown to foster trust in AI systems in various contexts [7, 8], but their specific impact in healthcare, a high-risk setting, requires further exploration.

Our objective is to explore the subjects of trust and explainable AI in greater depth. We aim to better understand trust in AI, its relation to explainability, and the resulting implications for the healthcare domain. We strive to accomplish this designing a dashboard prototype that acts as an interface between AI models and end-users to present model characteristics and outputs to the user and to enable the user to interact with the model, with which we conduct an exploratory case study, assessing it for explainability, perceived ease of use, and perceived usefulness, while also determining users' levels of trust in the AI model.

2 Preliminaries

2.1 Trust

For a definition of trust, we use the one presented by Madsen and Gregor [9] who describe trust as 'the extent to which a user is confident in, and willing to act on the basis of, the recommendations, actions, and decisions of an artificially intelligent decision aid'. Jacovi et al. [10] define trust in the context of AI as a combination of a human's perception that the AI is trustworthy and the acceptance of vulnerability to its actions. In this case, the physician is aware that he is vulnerable to the risk of relying on the AI model, understanding possible adverse consequences. It is important to stress that the AI itself does not actually have to be trustworthy, the user only has to perceive it as being such. An AI model can be completely untrustworthy (e.g., always giving incorrect diagnoses), but if the user believes that it is trustworthy, they can still trust the AI. In other words, the correlation between trustworthiness and perceived trust can be very low. Here we can differentiate between warranted and unwarranted trust; trust is warranted if it is the result of trustworthiness, and otherwise it is unwarranted. It is also noteworthy that trust is very dynamic; it changes over time and over contexts, and once it is established it does not mean that it will stay [7].

Trust between two humans and trust between a human and AI depend on different factors [3]. These factors can be grouped in four categories: user (e.g., age, gender, understanding of technology), environment (e.g., task difficulty, perceived risks/benefits, task characteristics), model performance and traits (e.g., reliability, explainability, validity), and model presentation (e.g., transparency, appearance, ease of use) as shown in Fig. 1. It is difficult to know the relative influence that each factor has on trust, however, factors concerning technology seem to be more influential than factors related to the environment or the user [11]. Explainability, and concepts related to it such as transparency and reflections of reliability of AI, plays a significant role in establishing trust [8]. It might help with aligning users' expectations with the actual performance of the system, which is important for forming warranted trust.

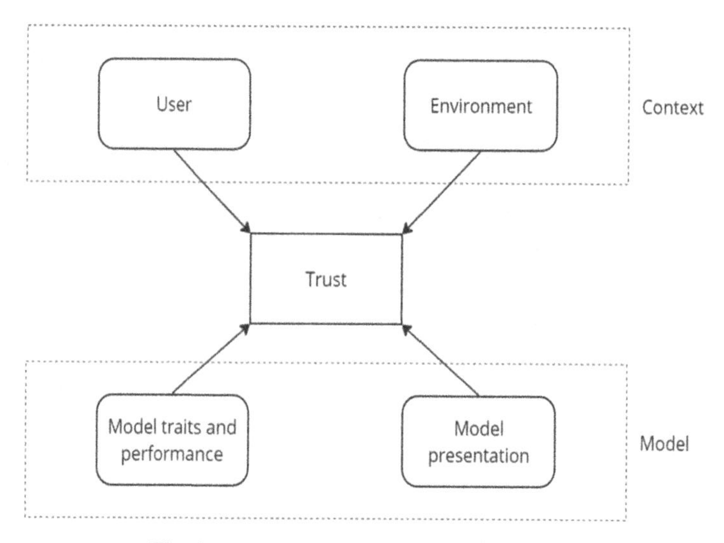

Fig. 1. Categories of factors influencing trust

Trust has been widely acknowledged to play an important role in user acceptance of technology. It has been incorporated many times into frameworks such as the Technology Acceptance Model (TAM), Unified Theory of Acceptance and Use of Technology (UTAUT) [12]. These frameworks help researchers understand and predict technology acceptance and adoption behaviours in various contexts. Abbas et al. (2018) have extended the Technology Acceptance Model (TAM) from a healthcare technology perspective [13]. They integrate trust as a factor that influences perceived ease of use, perceived usefulness, and behavioural intention. The TAM model described three categories of factors influencing trust: human-, organisational- and technology factors. We slightly adapted their model, renaming the first two categories and splitting the latter into two different categories to include the factors influencing trust in the way we have categorised them and arrive at the extended TAM in Fig. 2.

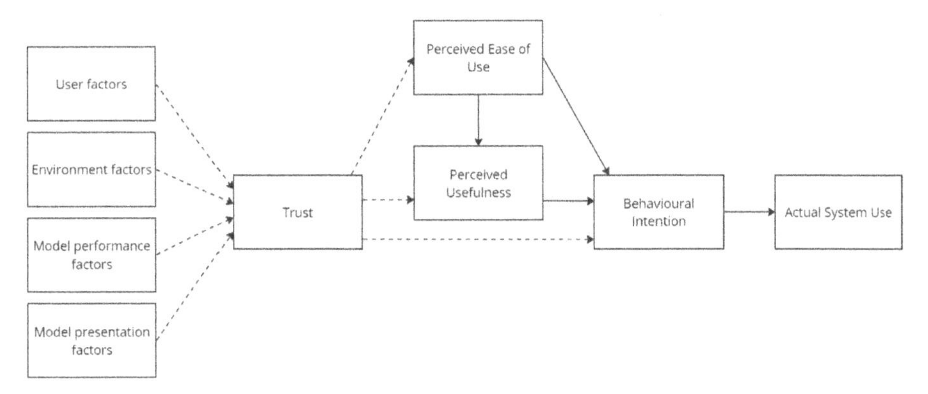

Fig. 2. Extended Technology Acceptance Model

Ideally, trust is assessed in a 'natural' situation and environment and not in a contrived experimental setup. As previously established, trust is a construct influenced by numerous factors, thereby developing differently across varied settings. This is, however, often not possible due to the high-risk context for healthcare settings, typically concerning patient safety and/or privacy. For example, measuring trust in a hospital decision-support system intended for the use in life-critical situations cannot be done in a real-life situation due to ethical concerns.

2.2 Explainable AI

Explainable Artificial Intelligence (XAI) is a field that is concerned with the development of new methods that explain and interpret AI models [14]. Local methods provide explanations that are restricted to single predictions, while global methods explain the whole model. An overview of categories of XAI is presented in Fig. 3.

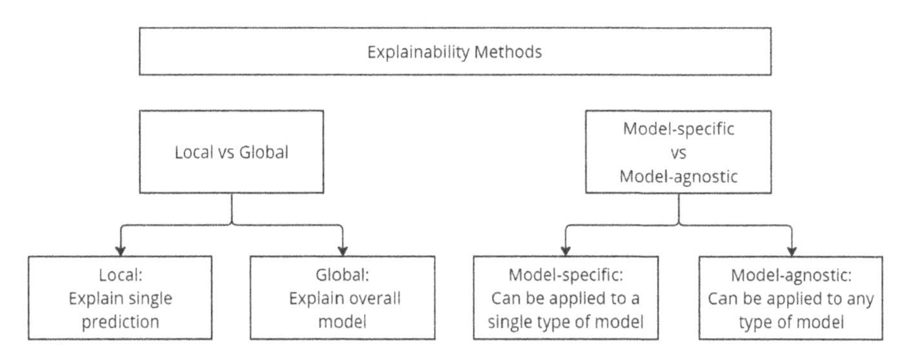

Fig. 3. Categories of XAI

The primary objective of Explainable AI (XAI) in healthcare is to assist medical professionals in understanding the underlying mechanisms that lead to specific results, thereby facilitating clear and comprehensible communication of medical decisions to patients. However, existing XAI techniques are often designed with AI developers in mind, focusing on system or model evaluation rather than providing insights that healthcare professionals would find useful. This disconnect can make it challenging for medical practitioners to interpret the data, especially considering their possible limited technical expertise.

It has been argued that people attribute human-like traits to artificially intelligent agents and expect explanations about their behaviour to mirror those of humans [15]. Therefore, people would expect explanations about the behaviour of an AI system to be similar to an explanation about the behaviour of a human. Previous research has found that humans tend to form 'contrastive explanations', meaning they tend to explain the cause of an event in comparison to a counterfactual (another event that did not happen) rather than the event itself [16] : humans do not explain the event itself, but why it happened instead of some other, hypothetical, event.

2.3 Explainability and Trust in Artificial Intelligence

Developing trust(-worthiness) is one of the key motivations for XAI. The goal of explainable AI is for the user to develop warranted trust. This can be achieved by increasing the trustworthiness of the AI system itself, increasing the trust of the user in a trustworthy AI and increasing the distrust of the user in a non-trustworthy AI. Therefore, the goal of XAI is to target three concepts in our conceptualisation of trust: trustworthiness, warranted trust and warranted distrust as can be seen in Fig. 4.

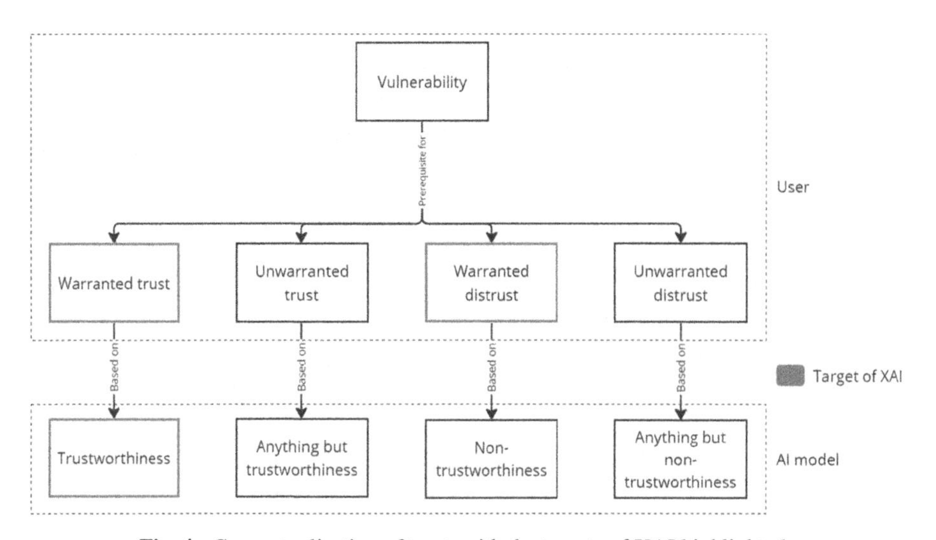

Fig. 4. Conceptualisation of trust, with the targets of XAI highlighted.

3 Method

3.1 Dashboard

If an AI-based decision-support tool would be implemented in healthcare, the interaction between the tool and the user would likely happen through a dashboard. In the following section, we present an illustrative example where we develop a dashboard prototype for the display of the output of DESIRE, an AI model that has been developed for optimising patient discharge after major surgery [17]. It predicts if a patient can be safely released from the hospital two days post-surgery. The objective of our dashboard is to present the recommendation/output by the DESIRE model along with additional information to make the AI model explainable to the user, and, consequently, increase warranted trust in the model.

The dashboard had several different options. First, basic information about the AI model was presented, such as its purpose, how it was trained, using which data, and a list of input features. This acts as global explanation. Four screens were intended for local explanations: 'Input features', 'Change values', 'Counterfactuals', and 'Similar patients'. The Input features screen displayed the input features of the model, their case-specific values, and the relative importance of the five most influential input features (Fig. 5a). This allows users to identify any abnormal values that might have arisen from faulty data entry, and that could explain potentially unexpected model predictions. By highlighting the top five influential input features, users gain a clearer understanding of the main drivers impacting the AI model's decisions. The screen Change values had the option to change input values or 'grey out' input values and recompute the advice for the given patient. The user could thus interactively explore the behaviour of the model and the impact of input feature variations on its predictions. It allows to test the robustness of the predictions under different hypothetical scenarios, which relates to the concept of contrastive explanation. The screen Counterfactuals displayed the minimal change needed in patient values that lead to a different prediction (Fig. 5b). This allowed users to compare their patient's prediction to a hypothetical contrary prediction, which also relates to contrastive explanation. For easier interpretation, the features where values have been modified in the counterfactual scenario are highlighted. This emphasises features that contribute to the shift in prediction. The last screen Similar patients showed patients who share similarities with the current patient, along with their respective predictions. The goal of this screen is to gain a broader understanding of how the model performs across a range of comparable cases. Inconsistencies in an AI model's recommendations for comparable patients, where healthcare professionals would anticipate consistent advice, can reveal discrepancies in model performance. At each of the screens a certainty score of the prediction was presented, which serves as an indicator of how certain the model is about its advice.

3.2 Participants and Setting

Participants in this study were healthcare professionals specialising in the surgical field. Participant recruitment was done through convenience sampling at the Dutch university medical centres Amsterdam UMC and Erasmus MC. Due to time constraints, only four healthcare professionals were willing to participate.

First, participants completed a questionnaire capturing characteristics such as age, gender, experience working and studying in the healthcare field, experience using AI, and their general attitude towards AI. Participants were shown static images of the five dashboard screens and after each one they were asked to fill out a questionnaire. The questionnaire was designed to measure two key aspects: the perceived explainability of the AI model and the level of trust in its predictions. The first screen that was shown to the participants was the plain screen containing basic information about the AI model. The order of presentation of the remaining screens was randomised to minimise the influence of order effects. Subsequently, participants were shown all the screens containing a local explanation again. They were asked to rank them, according to how useful they found them for their decision-making process. Perceived explainability was evaluated with the validated Explanation Satisfaction Scale [18]. Trust was measured using an adapted version of the Recommended Scale for explainable AI (XAI) [18]. Items that were not suitable in our context were dropped from the scale, either because they are only relevant after considerable use of a system, or they are not applicable for non-interactive screens. The four items taken from the Recommended Scale relate to how a user feels about an AI model and how trustworthy they perceive it to be. We added a fifth item asking the participant if they would follow the advice that the AI model gives. This incorporates the user's acceptance of vulnerability to the AI model's actions in the trust measurement. Additionally, two items from the Technology Acceptance Model (TAM) questionnaire were adapted to our context and added to assess Perceived Usefulness (PU) and Perceived Ease of Use (PEU). All items were rated on a five-point Likert scale. To analyse the results of the questionnaire, a trust and an explainability score were calculated. The scores were determined by quantifying and aggregating the answers to the respective questionnaire items.

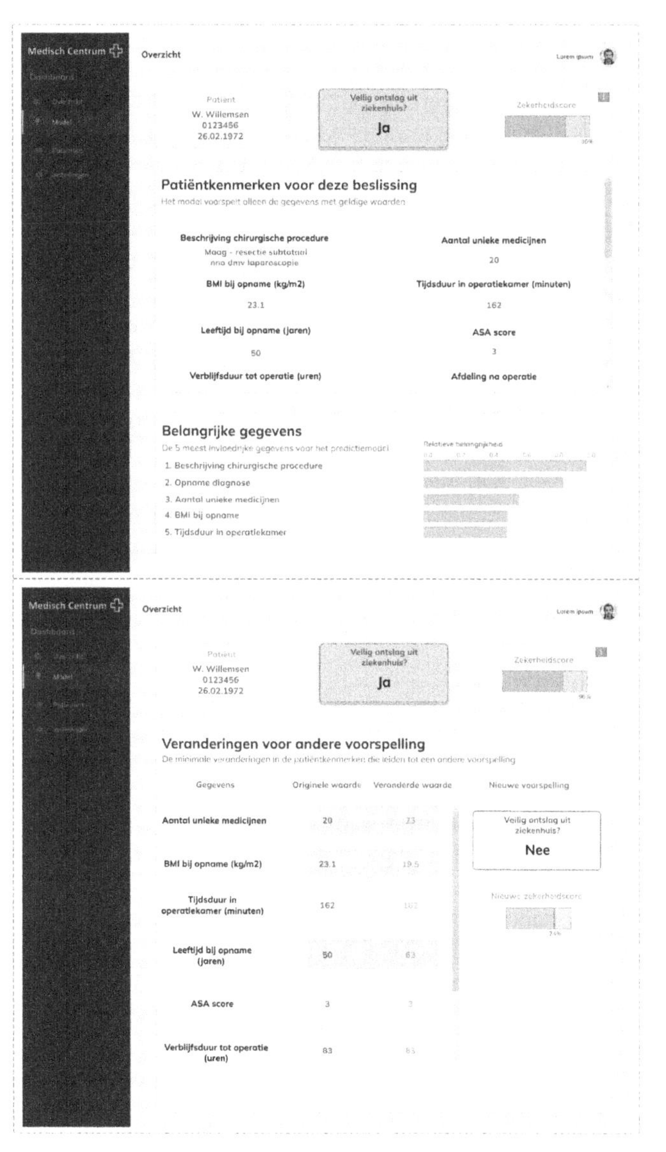

Fig. 5. Two screens of the dashboard. Figure 5a represents the input features and their relative importance. Figure 5b represents the counterfactuals and the values that will lead to a different conclusion. Translations: Veilig ontslag uit ziekenhuis = Safe discharge from hospital, Zekerheidscore = Certainty score, Patiëntkenmerken voor deze beslissing = Patient characteristics for this decision, Belangrijke gegevens = Important data, Veranderingen voor andere voorspelling = Changes for different prediction

4 Results

Based on the questionnaire concerning participant characteristics, there appears to be a predominantly positive attitude towards AI among the participants. Furthermore, the majority indicated having at least some level of experience with AI in both their daily lives and professional environments. The screen showcasing input features was found to receive the highest level of trust, while the counterfactual screen received the lowest score. No significant difference between them with regards to elicited trust was found. Similarly, for the explainability scores for the different screens, some variation can be seen, but no significant differences. The similar patients screen earned the highest score, while the change values screen received the lowest. Interestingly, the change values screen also exhibited the largest standard deviation, indicating more diverse opinions among the participants regarding its explainability compared to the other screens.

The input features screen received the highest score for PU, and both the input features and Plain screen share the highest score for PEU. Overall, participants ranked the similar patients screen as the most useful screen for decision-making. The change values and counterfactual screen share the lowest rank. Participants were most divided about the input features screen, with two assigning it the highest rank and two ranking it at the lowest.

5 Discussion

No significant difference in levels of trust and explainability was observed between the screens. This could imply that the individual participants' experiences and reactions remained comparably consistent, irrespective of the distinct components presented on each screen. Alternatively, it could suggest that individual variations existed, but these balanced out when analysed at the collective group level, resulting in no substantial differences. It is important to note that this does not prove that there is no real difference between the screens; we might not be able to detect it, either due to the small sample size or due to a small difference between screens.

Of particular interest is that the two screens based on the concept of contrastive explanation, namely Change values and Counterfactual, appeared to underperform across various metrics: they received the lowest trust levels, the lowest explainability scores, and were assigned the lowest rankings by participants. This finding suggests either that this kind of explanation is not ideal for making AI explainable in this specific context and that participants may not consider it particularly useful in their decision-making process, or it could indicate that our efforts to integrate this concept within a dashboard interface were not fully successful. In our results, we observed a strong positive correlation between explainability and trust. While we observed a strong positive correlation between explainability and trust in the AI system, it is important to remember that correlation does not imply causation. This relationship suggests that as explainability increases, so does trust. However, it does not necessarily mean that higher explainability causes an increase in trust. It is possible that other factors not accounted for in this study contribute to this relationship. Considering the small sample size, the results of this study should be interpreted with caution. Future studies with larger sample sizes would help increase the reliability of the results. It would also be beneficial to involve participants with a diverse range of experiences with AI to increase the representativeness of the findings.

For a future, and larger, experiment, we intend not to only ask for trust directly, but ask the physicians to what degree they intend to accept (or not) the advice of the AI model, to make a direct connection between the action and trust in the system. It might also be interesting to use more than one patient case (as we did in this study) but have several cases such that the decision to be made is a different one during the experiment.

To be able to capture differences in perceived trust and explainability, we are also interested whether a co-called conjoint analysis with screens of our dashboard could provide us with more valuable results. During such an experiment, users are 'forced' to choose between two screens as to which of these is perceived to increase trust most.

Additionally, our study treated trust as a static quality, assessed at one point in time, rather than a dynamic process. Trust is likely to change with increasing interaction and experience with the system. Our conclusions can therefore only be applied to the initial exposure to a system. Future research could incorporate longitudinal designs with repeated measurements to capture the evolving nature of trust.

References

1. Peterson, E.D.: Machine learning, predictive analytics, and clinical practice: can the past inform the present? JAMA **322**(23), 2283–2284 (2019)
2. He, J., Baxter, S.L., Xu, J., Xu, J., Zhou, X., Zhang, K.: The practical implementation of artificial intelligence technologies in medicine. Nat. Med. **25**(1), 30–36 (2019)
3. Hoff, K.A., Bashir, M.: Trust in automation: integrating empirical evidence on factors that influence trust. Hum. Factors **57**(3), 407–434 (2015)
4. Arrieta, A.B., et al.: Explainable artificial intelligence (XAI): concepts, taxonomies, opportunities and challenges toward responsible AI. Inform. Fusion **58**, 82–115 (2020)
5. Liao, Q.V., Pribic, M., Han, J., Miller, S., Sow, D., Question-driven design process for explainable AI user experiences. arXiv preprint arXiv:2104.03483 (2021)
6. Markus, A.F., Kors, J.A., Rijnbeek, P.R.: The role of explainability in creating trustworthy artificial intelligence for health care: a comprehensive survey of the terminology, design choices, and evaluation strategies. J. Biomed. Inform. **113**, 103655 (2021)
7. Hoffman, R., Mueller, S.T., Klein, G., Litman, J.: Measuring trust in the XAI context. Technical Report, DARPA Explainable AI Program (2018)
8. Glikson, E., Williams Woolley, A.: Human trust in artificial intelligence: review of empirical research. Acad. Manag. Ann. **14**(2), 627–660 (2020)
9. Madsen, M., Gregor, S., Measuring human-computer trust. In: 11th Australasian Conference on Information Systems. Citeseer, vol. 53, pp. 6–8 (2000)
10. Jacovi, A., Marasovic, A., Miller, T., Goldberg, Y., Formalizing trust in artificial intelligence: prerequisites, causes and goals of human trust in AI. In: Proceedings of the 2021 ACM Conference on Fairness, Accountability, and Transparency, pp. 624–635 (2021)
11. Hancok, P.A., Billings, D.R., Schaefer, K.E., Chen, J.Y.C., De Visser, E.J., Parasuraman, R.: A meta-analysis of factors affecting trust in human-robot interaction. Hum. Factors **53**(5), 517–527 (2011)
12. Ghazizadeh, M., Lee, J.D., Ng Boyle, L.: Extending the technology acceptance model to assess automation. Cogn. Technol. Work **14**, 39–49 (2012)

13. Abbas, R.M., Carroll, N., Richardson, I.: In technology we trust: extending TAM from a healthcare technology perspective. In: 2018 IEEE International Conference on Healthcare Informatics (ICHI), pp. 348–349. IEEE (2018)
14. Linardatos, P., Papastefanopoulos, V., Kotsiantis, S.: Explainable AI: a review of machine learning interpretability methods. Entropy **23**(1), 18 (2020)
15. De Graaf, M.M.A., Malle, B.F.: How people explain action (and autonomous intelligent systems should too). In: 2017 AAAI Fall Symposium Series (2017)
16. Miller, T.: Explanation in artificial intelligence: insights from the social sciences. Artif. Intell. **267**, 1–38 (2019)
17. Van de Sande, D., et al.: Predicting need for hospital-specific interventional care after surgery using electronic health record data. Surgery **170**(3), 790–796 (2021)
18. Hoffman, R.R., Mueller, S.T., Klein, G., Litman, J.: Metrics for explainable AI: challenges and prospects. arXiv preprint arXiv:1812.04608 (2018)

Improving Adoption of AI Impact Assessment in the Media Sector

Floor Schukking, Levi Verhoef, Tina Mioch, Coert van Gemeren(✉), and Huib Aldewereld

University of Applied Sciences Utrecht, Utrecht, The Netherlands
{floor.schukking,levi.verhoef,tina.mioch,coert.vangemeren, huib.aldewereld}@hu.nl

Abstract. We present an evaluation of tools for assessing the impact of AI in the Dutch media sector. Our evaluation of the ECP AIIA tool shows the need for clear guidelines in the adoption of various AI applications within Dutch media organisations. We conclude that the adoption of impact assessment tools, such as the ECP AIIA, is not held back by common media practice, but rather by commercial considerations.

1 Introduction

Artificial Intelligence (AI) can be a valuable tool for media applications, and media companies have shown a growing interest in the responsible application of it. AI is increasingly used in, for example, content personalisation, automatic subtitling, and labeling of archive content [3,10]. However, applying AI responsibly is challenging and media organisations struggle with this task.

Previous research has shown that available tools or guidelines to support the design of responsible AI are not used by the participating media organisations. Reasons for this are that tools and guidelines are perceived to be not sufficiently tailored to their needs, it is not clear which of the tools fits best, and in what phase of a project which tools should be used [8]. Many media organisations also mentioned that most considerations around ethics are done implicitly and that ethical criteria and risks concerning AI are not documented [8].

Within other domains, e.g., information privacy, the use of governance methodologies for assessing and mitigating the impact of new technologies is already more established [2,9]. Within these fields, impact assessments are used to consider complex social and technical questions combining values from the public, outside experts, and policymakers. Many different impact assessment frameworks for AI exist (see, e.g., [9] for an overview). A number of well-known assessment frameworks in the Netherlands are the Data Ethics Decision Aid (DEDA) [11], Electronic Commerce Platform Netherlands (ECP) AI impact assessment (AIIA) [5], and the AI impact assessment of the Dutch Government [6]. Other well-known international impact assessments include ALTAI [1] and IEEE 7010 [4]. Of these, the AIIA appears to be the most straightforward tool to use for Dutch media organisations due to its compact format compared

S. Nowaczyk et al. (Eds.): ECAI 2023 Workshops, CCIS 1948, pp. 87–92, 2024.
https://doi.org/10.1007/978-3-031-50485-3_7

to the DEDA. As mentioned above, media organisations currently do not use these impact assessments as they are deemed impractical. Media organisations suggest that impact assessments should be particularly tailored towards media organisations which leads to the following research question:

Which adaptations to an AI impact assessment like the ECP AI Impact Assessment are necessary to make it applicable and practical within the context of media companies?

In the remainder of this paper we first briefly describe the intent of AI Impact self-assessment tools, in general, and ECP AIIA, in particular. Next, in Sect. 3 we describe our approach to finding the answer to our research question and the results. Finally, in Sect. 4 we reflect on the results and discuss potentials for future research.

2 AI Impact Self-assessment

Within the media sector there is a growing recognition of the importance of the responsible application of Artificial Intelligence. With the ever increasing improvements in usable AI applications for media purposes (e.g., Generative AI for content creation, tools for filtering, automatic subtitling, and automatic trailer generation), the media sector realises the importance the responsible use of such tools. The declaration of intent for the responsible use of AI in the media sector [7], is a clear example that shows how serious this is for the media sector. The declaration of intent has been signed already by some of the largest media companies in the Netherlands, including NPO, RTL, and Talpa, which together cover more than 75% of the Dutch Television market.

Although the intentions are clear, the processes to achieve the responsible use of AI tools was not. As mentioned in the introduction, a previous research among media companies showed that the available tools or guidelines to support the responsible use of AI are not used.

There are several self-assessment tools available, including DEDA [11] and ECP AI Assessment Tool [5]. Ethical self-assessments are tools, usually in the form of a structured questionnaire, to be used by a company to predict the impact of their intended use of AI-systems. These questionnaires evaluate the use of AI on ethical and legal aspects in a structured manner. By performing an ethical AI assessment, it should warn companies for (negative) side-effects of the implementation of AI.

The ECP AI Assessment (AIIA) consists of three phases; **1.** necessity phase (step 1); **2.** description phase (steps 2–5); **3.** decision and reporting phase (steps 6–8) (also see Fig. 1). The first phase, the first step, consists of eight questions that are meant to ascertain whether there is a necessity for executing an AIIA assessment. If only one of these first eight questions is answered with "yes", ECP advises to perform a full assessment.

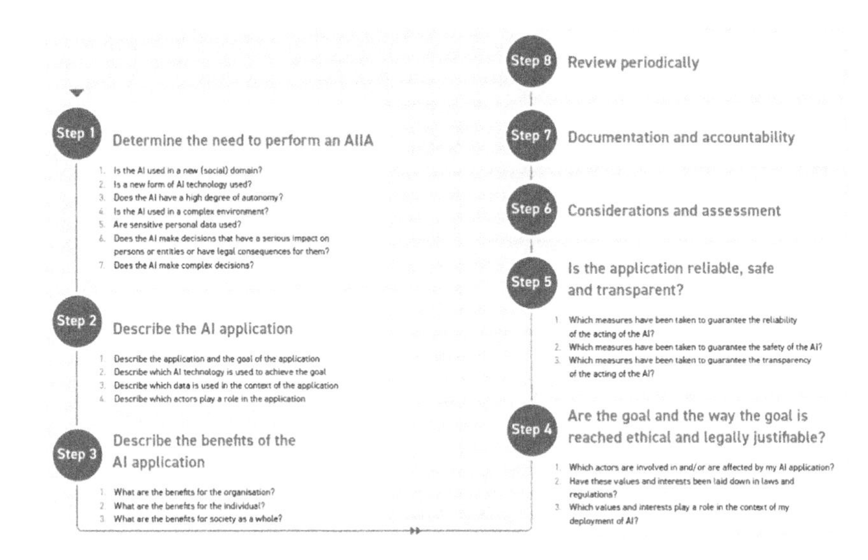

Step 1
Determine the need to perform an AIIA
1. Is the AI used in a new (social) domain?
2. Is a new form of AI technology used?
3. Does the AI have a high degree of autonomy?
4. Is the AI used in a complex environment?
5. Are sensitive personal data used?
6. Does the AI make decisions that have a serious impact on persons or entities or have legal consequences for them?
7. Does the AI make complex decisions?
Step 2
Describe the AI application
1. Describe the application and the goal of the application
2. Describe which AI technology is used to achieve the goal
3. Describe which data is used in the context of the application
4. Describe which actors play a role in the application
Step 3
Describe the benefits of the AI application
1. What are the benefits for the organisation?
2. What are the benefits for the individual?
3. What are the benefits for society as a whole?
Step 4
Are the goal and the way the goal is reached ethical and legally justifiable?
1. Which actors are involved in and/or are affected by my AI application?
2. Have these values and interests been laid down in laws and regulations?
3. Which values and interests play a role in the context of my deployment of AI?
Step 5
Is the application reliable, safe and transparent?
1. Which measures have been taken to guarantee the reliability of the acting of the AI?
2. Which measures have been taken to guarantee the safety of the AI?
3. Which measures have been taken to guarantee the transparency of the acting of the AI?
Step 6
Considerations and assessment
Step 7
Documentation and accountability
Step 8
Review periodically

Fig. 1. A schematic overview of the first steps of the ECP AI Impact Assessment tool. Details per question are provided in the documentation, see [5].

The next phase, consisting of steps two to five (see Fig. 1, consists of the description of the application, the description of the gains, the analysis of the ethical and legal responsibilities, and the analysis of the reliability, safety and transparency of the application. Each of these steps contain a number of questions, some further detailed in sub-questions.

The last phase, consisting of steps six to eight (see Fig. 1), details the questions to help make a decision, the documenting of the decision, and the periodic evaluation. In this research we have focused on the first two phases (steps 1–5), as these match closely with the need of the media companies.

3 Method and Results

To answer the research question presented above, we used a qualitative, mixed-methods methodology.

The research was performed as a case study at a large Dutch media company. First, we investigated the working processes and ethical awareness of the media company through an unstructured, participatory observation of the data science team in their day-to-day activities during an AI development project to decide on how and where the AIIA could be used in their current processes. During the evaluation period of three months the researcher did not observe planned, as in during meetings, or unplanned moments where ethical implications or considerations of the examined project or other projects of the company were discussed. Ethical consideration seem to be made based on intuition or common sense and not documented, as acknowledge by the data science manager. As AI projects become more complex and autonomous, finding aid through an assessment such as the AIIA could make such common sense intuitions more structured and explicit.

Next, an exploratory interview was held with the project managers to assess challenges with the AI impact assessment. For each step of the AIIA Table 1 shows the questions that were asked to the participants that did the AIIA. After finishing all the steps of the AIIA, we asked several more questions which can be found in Table 2.

Table 1. Questions asked after doing a step of the AIIA

1	*Do these questions make you evaluate the project in a useful way?*
2	*Were there any questions that were not relevant or useful?*
3	*If so: would any of these questions be relevant or useful for other project?*
4	*What were the important insights gained in this step?*

Table 2. Questions asked after completing the AIIA

1	*What were the substantive insights gained during this assessment?*
2	*What are the insights gained about the usage of ECP AI Assessments?*
3	*Was any step particularly useful?*
4	*Was any step not useful?*
5	*Would you consider doing ECP AI Assessments for new projects?*
6	*If not: Why not?*
7	*What is needed to make doing an assessment worthwhile?*
8	*If so: Why? What is important about doing an assessment?*

We conclude that the company mostly deemed the time investment of 2.5 hours to fill in the AIIA as too much, and that the expected value of executing an AIIA differs largely between parts of the assessment. For instance, step **4** ("Are the goal and the way the goal is reached ethically and legally justifiable?", see Fig. 1) was seen as most interesting, whereas steps **1–3** were deemed of no or little use. Based on the outcomes of the interview, the following adaptations were suggested:

- Step **1** through **3** of the AIIA contain steps to analyze if an assessment is necessary and describing the AI project and its benefits. These three steps took 1 h and 20 min to document, however the description, actors and benefits of projects at the media company were already documented internally for each project. These three steps felt as obsolete to the participants, and we therefore

propose step **1–3** to be highly shortened by time boxing or to be left out of the AIIA completely, if the project is documented well in advance.
- Step **4** felt as the most valuable part of the assessment to the participants. The participants suggested to include the company's values in this step.
- To better integrate the AIIA within company processes, participants who take part frequently are advised to read the documentation of the AIIA. Incidental participants are advised to read page 68 and 69, while recurring participants should additionally read pages 70–80, to gain more in-depth knowledge of the AIIA and ethical considerations.
- Create a company-wide template for the documentation of the AIIA, including all questions and existing documentation.
- Projects at this media company were often continuations of previous projects. If the risk profile and ethical implications overlap between projects, the same findings can be copied or it can be evaluated if a new assessments needs to be performed.

Following these adaptations we except the duration to be minimized from 2, 5 to 1 h for well-documented projects, while ethical and juridical analyses remain covered.

Finally, a structured, non-participating observation was used to assess the functioning of the adapted AIIA within the organisation. Data scientists were observed during application of the improved assessment. Attention was paid to the time required to perform the various steps of the assessment, and the results were qualitatively evaluated with the data scientists. Overall, the participants were positive about the adapted assessment, and stated that they are interested in implementing it into their work processes. The reduction in time required to perform the assessment was key in lowering the threshold to use the assessment.

4 Discussion

Adapting and applying the AIIA contributed to creating an awareness in the media organisation about the importance of reflecting on ethical aspects in the development and deployment of AI. Next to the fear of a large time investment, which could be solved with some minor adaptations, it seems that the main reason why impact assessments were not used is because of unfamiliarity and ignorance about the value and application of such assessments. We expect that impact assessments, like AIIA, are relevant for other media organisations, and will look further into this in future research.

Moreover, it appears that the media organisation's original assumption, which we shared initially, that impact assessments should be adapted towards the media practice does not hold. The main issues found in the adoption were not because of particular requirements from media practice, but from commercial considerations (i.e., time investment versus pertained value).

Acknowledgments. This research was conducted as part of DRAMA (Designing Responsible AI for Media Applications). The project is funded by SIA, RAAK Publiek DRAMA (100290-100). DRAMA is a partnership between Utrecht University of

Applied Sciences (HU), Rotterdam University of Applied Sciences (HR), Amsterdam University of Applied Sciences (HvA), and several media parties. The project focuses on supporting and guiding media organizations in embedding responsible AI within their organizations. This work was carried out at the Lectorate of AI of Utrecht University of Applied Sciences.

References

1. Ala-Pietilä, P., et al.: The assessment list for trustworthy artificial intelligence (ALTAI). Eur. Comm. (2020)
2. Ayling, J., Chapman, A.: Putting AI ethics to work: are the tools fit for purpose? AI Ethics **2**, 405–429 (2021). https://doi.org/10.1007/S43681-021-00084-X. https://link.springer.com/article/10.1007/s43681-021-00084-x
3. Chan-Olmsted, S.M.: A review of artificial intelligence adoptions in the media industry **21**, 193–215 (2019). https://doi.org/10.1080/14241277.2019.1695619. https://www.tandfonline.com/doi/abs/10.1080/14241277.2019.1695619
4. IEEE Standards Committee: IEEE Recommended Practice for Assessing the Impact of Autonomous and Intelligent Systems on Human Well-Being: IEEE Standard 7010-2020. IEEE (2020). https://doi.org/10.1109/IEEESTD.2020.9084219
5. Electronic Commerce Platform Netherlands: Artificial intelligence impact assessment (2018). https://ecp.nl/artificial-intelligence-impact-assessment/. Accessed 17 Apr 2023
6. Government of the Netherlands: AI impact assessment (2023). https://www.government.nl/documents/publications/2023/03/02/ai-impact-assessment. Accessed 17 Apr 2023
7. Media Perspectives: Intentieverklaring voor media (2021). https://mediaperspectives.nl/intentieverklaring/
8. Mioch, T., Stembert, N., Timmers, C., Hajri, O., Wiggers, P., Harbers, M.: Exploring responsible AI practices in Dutch media organizations (2023, under review)
9. Stahl, B.C., et al.: A systematic review of artificial intelligence impact assessments. Artif. Intell. Rev., 1–33 (2023)
10. Trattner, C., et al.: Responsible media technology and AI: challenges and research directions. AI Ethics **2**, 585–594 (2021). https://doi.org/10.1007/S43681-021-00126-4. https://link.springer.com/article/10.1007/s43681-021-00126-4
11. Utrecht Data School: Data ethics decision aid (DEDA) (2023). https://dataschool.nl/en/deda/. Accessed 17 Apr 2023

MindSet: A Bias-Detection Interface Using a Visual Human-in-the-Loop Workflow

Senthuran Kalananthan[1], Alexander Kichutkin[2(✉)], Ziyao Shang[1], András Strausz[1], Francisco Javier Sanguino Bautiste[3], and Mennatallah El-Assady[1,4]

[1] Department of Computer Science, ETH Zürich, Switzerland
{skalanan,zshang,strausza}@ethz.ch

[2] Department of Mathematics, ETH Zürich, Switzerland
akichutkin@ethz.ch

[3] Department of Information Technologies and Electrical Engineering, ETH Zürich, Switzerland

[4] AI Center, ETH Zürich, Switzerland

Abstract. Handling data artifacts is a critical and unsolved challenge in deep learning. Disregarding such asymmetries may lead to biased and socially unfair predictions, prohibiting applications in high-stake scenarios. In the case of visual data, its inherently unstructured nature makes automated bias detection especially difficult. Thus, a promising remedy is to rely on human feedback. Hu et al. [14] introduced a three-stage theoretical study framework to use a human-in-the-loop approach for bias detection in visual datasets and ran a small-sample study. While showing encouraging results, no implementation is available to enable researchers and practitioners to study their image datasets. In this work, we present a dataset-agnostic implementation based on a highly flexible web app interface. With this implementation, we aim to bring this theoretical framework into practice by following a user-centric approach. We also extend the framework so that the workflow can be adjusted to the researcher's needs in terms of the granularity of detected anomalies.

Keywords: User Interfaces · Dataset Bias · Bias in Machine Learning

1 Introduction

Since the appearance of the CNN [20] and subsequently the transformer [34] architectures, deep learning yielded remarkable achievements in various computer vision tasks. We have seen improvements in all the different branches of visual pattern recognition, such as image segmentation [23], classification [19], or most recently in image generation [25]. Moreover, these techniques have long left academia and have been deployed in real-life scenarios, often involving such

S. Kalananthan, A. Kichutkin, Z. Shang and A. Strausz—Equal contribution.

S. Nowaczyk et al. (Eds.): ECAI 2023 Workshops, CCIS 1948, pp. 93–105, 2024.
https://doi.org/10.1007/978-3-031-50485-3_8

where an ethical and fair decision is indispensable [22]. Unfortunately, prior research has shown that many models fall short of this criteria [5,8,18].

The primary challenge in developing fair and trustworthy models comes from the lack of a precise quantitative formulation of bias [7]. In the context of visual data, which involves datasets composed of visual components and is visually interpreted, this challenge has gained even greater prominence. As a result, either proxy measures are used aiming to grasp parts of the contained biases [35] or human judgments are included. While the prior can provide specific, typically technical, fairness guarantees, it often falls short in ensuring a universally fair model [17]. On the other hand, humans can naturally detect visual biases, and their assessments can be later included in the Machine Learning pipeline. Even when personal judgments are influenced or led astray by prejudices, this can be counteracted by collecting a large sample of opinions. According to the *wisdom of the crowd* hypotheses [28], when sufficient and diverse opinions are gathered, the common understanding of a diverse crowd would lead to more reasonable and thorough judgments of possible biases. It is worth noting that the diversity of the sample is an integral part of this concept.

Biases could occur in various stages of the ML pipeline, including data input, training, and model applications [2,22]. Deep learning techniques have been shown to rely heavily on the training data, and biases included in the training will be reflected by the models' prediction [32]. Since raw images are unintelligible for computers and learned representation may carry biases already, it is natural to involve human judgments at this stage and employ them to filter the training data. Hu et al. [14] propose a three-stage study technique to detect sample biases in visual datasets. In their evaluation, they show that the framework allows for finding both commonly known and dataset-specific yet unknown biases among images. However, the authors did not develop any implementation for their study but used static forms that were tailored for a single dataset and were not made available to the public.

In this work, we face the challenge of bringing this theoretical framework into practice by developing an interactive web interface that implements the framework of Hu et al. [14]. By making this tool accessible to various users, we allow examinations, applications, and future extensions to the framework. In particular, we:

- Create a user-friendly online survey platform for detecting biases in image datasets
- Enable the examination of any image dataset and the fine-tuning of the study with respect to the dataset
- Extend the framework by Hu et al. with an interactive dashboard for study parameter selection

2 Related Work

2.1 Bias Discovery

Fabrizzi et al. [10] gives a framework for categorizing machine-centric bias detection methods for image data. Most notably, they argue that even in carefully curated bias-aware datasets, disparities exist, making methods for bias exploration crucial. They cluster prior works as follows:

1. Reduction to tabular data: such methods convert visual data into a tabular form and use bias detection techniques designed for tabular datasets e.g. count/demographic parity [9] or causality [36]
2. Biased image representations: Bias detection methods in this category analyze distances and geometric relationships among images utilizing the lower dimensional representation to identify the presence of bias. This includes distance-based methods [15] and interventions [3]
3. Cross-dataset bias detection: Methods in this category aim to identify the distinct signature of each dataset by comparing various datasets, e.g. [32,33]
4. Other methods: They include a wide range of methods such as crowdsourcing frameworks to ad-hoc trained classification models. Examples are [24] and [31]

To the best of our knowledge, prior human-in-the-loop methods for bias identification all focused on tabular data. A line of work relied on the assumption that humans can evaluate small graphical causal models. Silva [41] offers a visual interface to detect biases based on the causal relationships between the features. D-BIAS [12] follows a similar methodology but also allows to alter the causal links and thus actively mitigate bias. Other works use individual or group-level fairness measures to detect asymmetries among features, that are then visualized in different ways. Examples are FairRankViz [40] for bias detection in graph mining or DiscriLens [37], which offers novel visualizations of group-level bias attributes. In conclusion, there does not yet exist a human-centric approach for bias detection in visual datasets.

2.2 *Wisdom of the Crowd* bias detection

We summarize the study procedure by Hu et al. [14] in more detail, as this serves as the basis of our interface. We only describe the main stages of the study here and defer any specifics or changes to Sect. 3. The study can be described by the following three stages:

1. *Question generation*: The study starts by asking the participants to enter question-answer pairs that describe a similarity among the set of images that are currently shown. Participants are encouraged to ask questions starting with *What, Where, When* or *How* and avoid questions describing common characteristics of objects. These questions are then merged to filter reformulations of the same concept.
2. *Answer collection*: The collected questions are shown to the users again but with a different sample of images. The user is then asked to enter an answer to the question if at least half of the images share the same answer; otherwise, the user should skip it. Afterward, similar answers are merged to avoid ambiguities from different spellings or synonyms.

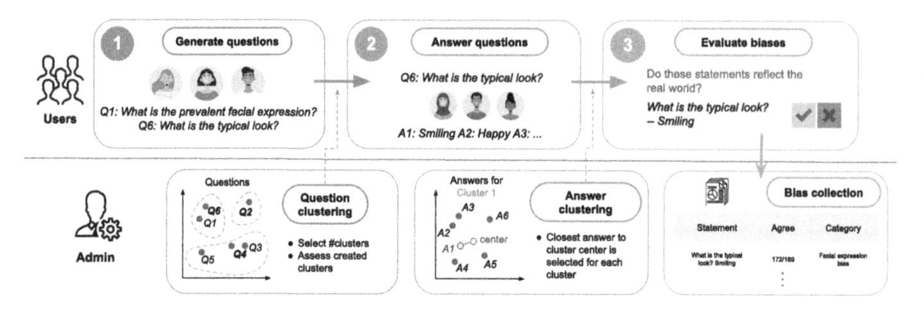

Fig. 1: Workflow illustrating the three step study framework and the corresponding admin tasks.

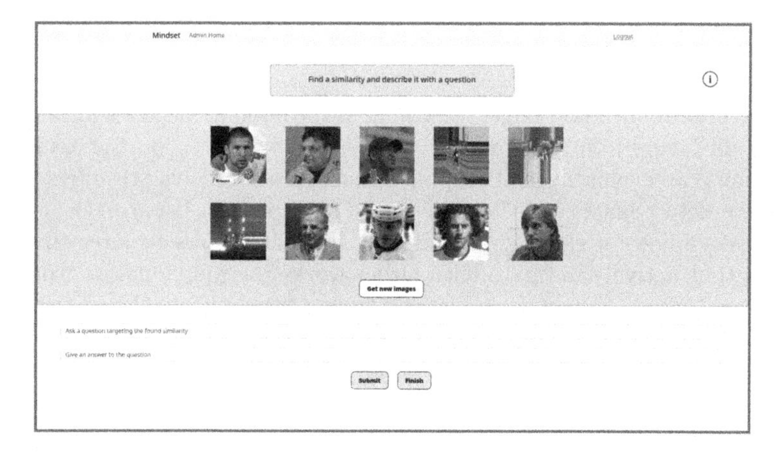

Fig. 2: Stage 1 with 10 images shown: Users enter a pair of question/answer that characterize the image set.

3. *Bias Judgement*: Lastly, questions and their corresponding answers are used to generate universal statements describing a possible bias. Users are then asked whether this statement is true in the real world or is a specific attribute of the dataset.

3 The MindSet Interface

To better support bias mitigation in visual datasets, we implement a user-friendly interface for the study framework of Hu et al. [14]. The implementation is publicly accessible[1].

3.1 Implementation Details

In the following, we describe our implementation as well as all extensions to the framework of Hu et al. [14]. Figure 1 shows an overview of the workflow.

[1] http://a10-bias-assessment-with-human-feedback.course-xai-iml23.isginf.ch/.

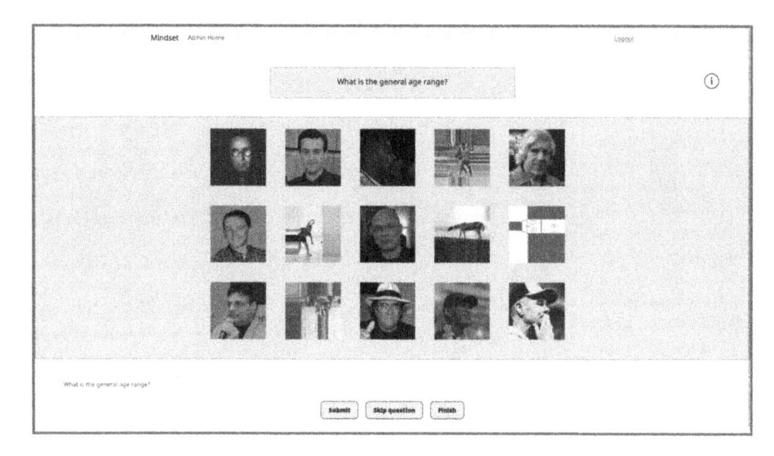

Fig. 3: Stage 2 with 15 images shown: According to the image set, users provide an answer to the given question.

User Types. We differentiate between two types of users, *participants* and *study admins*. To deal with spurious inputs, we ask users to first register with their email accounts. Registrations of participants can be verified by the participant itself through a code sent by email. Registration of study admins has to be accepted by the developers.

Participants can only access the current stage of the study and are notified when the study progresses to the next stage. Study Admins can choose to move their study from one stage to another and see overview statistics as well as detected biases. Admins are also responsible for setting the number of images (randomly sampled from the whole dataset) provided to each participant during each step and choosing parameters when proceeding with the study to the next stage.

Study Workflow. The interface for stages 1, 2, and 3 are depicted, respectively, in Fig. 2, Fig. 3, and Fig. 4, where participants are guided through the interface at the start and further aided with hints. We aim to create a neutral interface with as little text as possible to avoid influencing the participant. Participants receive a short introduction to every state and are guided through the interface before starting the study. A hint is also available in case the participant loses track. A difference from the original framework is that we do not provide any suggestions at any stage of the study in order to avoid influencing the participant.

Administrator View. We create a separate overview for study administrators where they can manage their currently ongoing study.

One of the main tasks of study administrators is to proceed with the study from one stage to the next one. To process Step 1 (question generation), the administrator needs to extract certain representative questions from

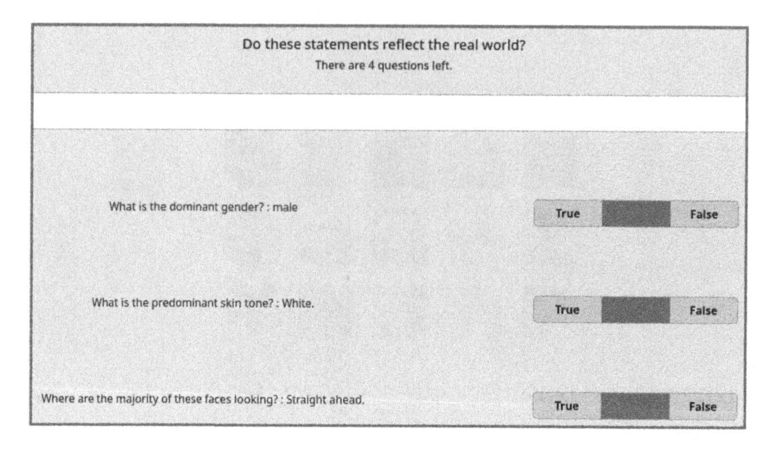

Fig. 4: Stage 3: users evaluate whether the biases are reflected in real life.

existing questions. The extraction is done via clustering. Each question is first embedded into a vector by an NLP model, for which we currently use the `all-MiniLM-L12-v2` pre-trained sentence transformer. Then, the embeddings are clustered using K-means clustering. For each resulting cluster, the question whose embedding is closest to the cluster centroid is chosen to represent that cluster. Thus, the administrator has to choose the number of questions they want to keep. This decision is aided by an interactive visualization of the elbow method [29] and the clustering for the currently chosen setting.

For the elbow method, the administrator specifies a range of centroid numbers. The visualization would be able to plot the Within Cluster Sum of Squares (WCSS) of all centroid numbers within that range. Generally, the elbow point of this graph would be a sound choice for the number of clusters. The administrator can hover over the data points on the visualization to see their actual WCSS values. Next, if the administrator clicks on one of the data points, a preview of the clustering results will be presented.

To create the preview, the embedding for each question is reduced to a 2D vector using Principal Component Analysis [11]. The cluster to which each point belongs would be encoded using the color (hue) of the points. Hovering on the points, the administrator would be able to see the actual question behind the point. The preview also contains a legend containing the questions chosen for

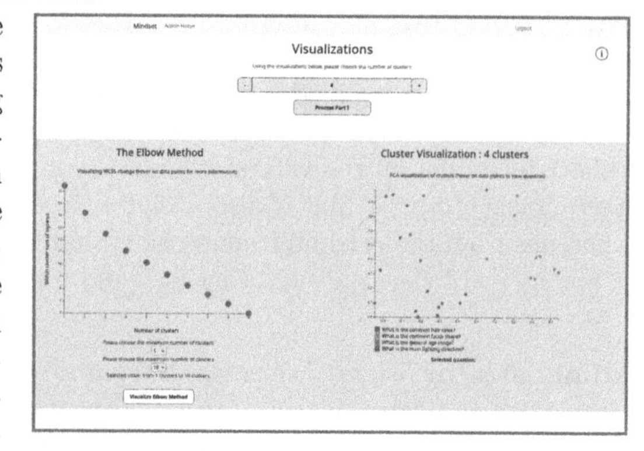

Fig. 5: Interface for processing inputs after Step 1, the admin is provided with visualizations of the WCSS distribution and the clusters.

each centroid. An example state of the dashboard for processing Step 1 is shown in Fig. 5

Once the study administrator decides to finish Stage 2, the answers are processed. For each question, all its answers are embedded. Then, the answer that is closest to the centroid is chosen. At this step, our implementation also deviates from [14], as they decide to construct statements from the question-answer pairs. Although such simple statements may be easier to understand at Stage 3, since statements must be generated with language models, they may be slightly imprecise or contain biases originating from the language model. To avoid this, we directly present the question-answer pairs to the participants.

During the final stage, the administrator can see a table overview of the biases detected in the dataset. This overview contains a list view containing the text of each bias statement, the number of users that agree with the statement, and the ratio of users agreeing, where the administrator can label biases, filter biases based on the labels, and save labels into the database. The users are also able to download the table as a .csv file.

Demo Study. To showcase the workflow, we used the CelebFaces Attributes Dataset (CelebA), a comprehensive collection comprising more than 200,000 celebrity images [1]. Additionally, we have prefilled the database with dummy text data for demonstration purposes, allowing for a comprehensive illustration of the system's functionality.

3.2 Use Cases

The following section will outline two possible use cases for the proposed workflow and showcase the flexibility of our application.

Human-Assisted Compilation of Bias-Aware Datasets. In an ideal scenario, researchers would examine their dataset for biases that might amplify societal stereotypes before training models. To that end, Wang et al. [38] proposed the measure of dataset leakage that describes how much information an image is leaking about a protected attribute when this attribute is obscured. For instance, assume that we protect for gender and consider a set of images containing adult males and females. Then, after obscuring the people in the visual data, dataset leakage will be measured on the extent to which it is still possible to infer the gender attribute from the remaining objects on the images.

Training a model on data with high dataset leakage exhibits the risk of further increasing these biases. The authors only provided a measure but not a solution for improving the dataset. To this end, we can leverage human feedback through our proposed workflow and interface. Our application allows researchers to pinpoint the objects leaking societal stereotypes to subsequent models. The first two steps localize strong signals in the data, while the third step judges whether these signals might be responsible for, in this case, gender biases. We allow the researcher to tag these findings for further processing.

An example workflow, in this case, would be that: at first, the researcher measures the data leakage of his dataset according to Wang et al. [38] revealing that it leaks societal biases about gender, which is a protected attribute here. Then, utilizing our crowdsourcing application, the researcher localizes the objects within images that leak information about the protected attribute. For instance, human feedback might suggest that an overly large portion of images containing females contain cooking utensils. The human crowd decides that this does not reflect the real world. Thus, this signals the researcher that the dataset amplifies old societal gender stereotypes. The researcher then can tag this finding on the summary page as such, that cooking utensils in his images strongly correlate with females being depicted. Assuming that he has a certain level of control over the data collection process, he can adjust the dataset to mitigate this phenomenon. Afterward, the process may be repeated over several iterations until a satisfactory upper limit on the data leakage is reached. Hence, our workflow can be leveraged together with a quantitative measure of dataset bias to build an iterative loop that results in a bias-aware dataset.

Bias Reducing Training of Generative Models. The idea of generative models is not new. They have been around as early as the 1960 s with the introduction of the ELIZA chatbot [39]. However, with recent advances, the topic has attracted a lot of new attention outside the scientific community. Frameworks such as Stable Diffusion (Rombach et al. [25]) can produce images that are difficult to be recognized as synthetically generated at first sight. However, similar to any other machine learning models, they tend to mirror biases reflected in their training data. To this end, we can utilize our workflow to examine the outputs of generative models more closely. We can consider a set of outputs of a deep generative model as a synthetically produced dataset. This dataset can then be analyzed in our study interface similarly to any other dataset. The first two steps point towards anomalies in the outputs, while the third step gives human feedback on whether these anomalies reflect the real world. As in Sect. 3.2, the researcher can use the tagging feature of the interface to categorize found anomalies. There are frameworks allowing the researcher to steer its generative model towards certain attributes. One such instance for GANs [13] are Style-Based Generators as introduced by Karras et al. [16]. They allow the researcher to steer the generative models to address these biases. To this end, our application can be incorporated into a training loop for generative models aiming to minimize exhibited biases. First, the models produce outputs. These outputs are considered the input dataset for the next step, which is crowdsourced for bias discovery using our application. The discovered biases can be directly addressed by guiding the outputs of the generative models. These steps can then be repeated until a satisfactory performance is reached.

4 Discussion

MindSet could be used in various situations, such as examining machine-generated images or detecting biases in common visual datasets, and has a large

potential for adaptations and extensions.
However, the framework is not complete yet and is subject to some constraints, which will be discussed in this section.

4.1 User Selection

The MindSet framework does not specify rules on how to choose study participants. This task is left completely to the study admin. However, participant selection is crucial. Depending on the individual participants and possible incentives or rewards, there is a risk of selection bias being introduced into the framework by the participants. This would defy its intended purpose. By design, there is a risk of self-selection and under-coverage. Failing to choose participants from a broad and diverse background can lead to the user selection mechanism failing to capture a sufficient representation of the population [4]. In that case, detected biases would only represent a one-sided perspective from a particular population group and would likely fail to capture the majority of existing biases in the specific dataset. However, it is not the emphasis of the *MindSet* framework to direct the user selection for a survey. It assumes that the study admin is familiar with guidelines on selecting participants such that the survey can be used to infer usable insights. Such guidelines can be found in plenty of literature in medical [21] or business domains [30].

Another point to consider is the effect of incentives or rewards. For instance, there could be a monetary incentive to include as many *Question-Answer pairs* as possible in Step 1. This could potentially lead to participants submitting *Question-Answer pairs* which are not suitable to the subset of images they are presented with and lead to an accumulation of redundant information. Again, *MindSet* does not aim to provide a specific study setup but rather focuses on enabling practitioners to perform bias detection in image datasets through crowd-sourcing. There exists a rich literature on how incentives and rewards can be used to optimize survey setups such as in Singer and Ye [27].

4.2 Measuring Bias

Biases in image-based machine learning workflows are usually measured in variations of the following two ways. First, given an existing and available protected attribute (e.g. race) for a set of images, we can measure the performance of subsequent machine learning applications conditioned on the protected attribute (e.g. Facial recognition accuracy for different ethnicities [6]). However, this approach is more output-focused rather than working with the dataset at hand. To that end, another popular approach is to look at label distributions within the dataset [26].
If the distribution is skewed towards specific labels, it implies a higher occurrence than for other labels. The performance of subsequent applications could then depend on label occurrences. However, this approach has its limitations. First, it assumes that the dataset is well-annotated, which, besides larger benchmark datasets, is not necessarily the case. Also, a class label does not capture

the intra-class variability within the images. For instance, a subset of 100 images labeled as containing a human does not tell us anything about the distribution of important attributes such as age, gender, and race. The dataset might suffer from label bias [32], and subsequent real-life applications might take the subset of 100 images as the ground truth for how humans are defined, posing the risk of discriminatory decisions. As mentioned in the first section, automated systems have difficulties detecting intra-class biases towards often specific attributes, while humans have an innate understanding of images and their details.

The *MindSet* framework leverages human nature to detect biases in images where algorithms would fail. However, we need to define our own measure of bias. No general all-encompassing measure is available, but we could exploit heuristics to construct a proxy variable for how biased a dataset is. The output of the interface is a table containing the number of participants agreeing with the statements aggregated in Step 3. If there is a strong agreement towards a particular statement, this implies that the dataset seems to capture a real-world property very well. A low agreement suggests that the dataset depicts properties that do not occur in reality. If there are many statements with which the participants agree, it implies that the dataset seems to capture overall real-life properties very well. However, if there are many statements with low agreement numbers (e.g. disagreeing with the statement), it suggests that the dataset fails at representing real-life properties. Overall, this provides the admin with a quantitative and qualitative assessment of possible biases in his image data. First, by observing the number of statements with high and/or low agreements, the admin gets a sense of how many and how strongly the dataset captures real-life features or fails to do so. The individual statements themselves give a qualitative pointer to the admin about which features, in particular, are well or badly captured by the dataset.
This heuristic attempts to measure bias by examining how strongly a human crowd agrees with statements describing a dataset. Nonetheless, the robustness of this measure likely correlates with the selection of survey participants. The response to statements might differ from group to group, and selection biases are possible.

4.3 Conclusion and Future Work

The *MindSet* interface is a practical implementation of the crowdsourcing framework proposed and validated by Hu et al. [14]. It makes additions to the original framework to increase usability. The demo case using the CelebA data-set [1] in Sect. 3 serves as a proof-of-concept for the interface.
However, it was not yet validated in a real-life environment. It would be interesting to see how it holds up when interacting with real human participants as part of a bias detection workflow and if it works with arbitrary image datasets as well. Overall, the validity of the interface is based on the case study done by Hu et al. [14], which tested the theoretical framework in a real-life environment. The interface enables the survey to be conducted in a scalable and user-

friendly manner. A bias measurement is provided using a heuristic, giving the admin a quantitative and qualitative response to the dataset used. The biggest uncertainty remains the selection of users. As a workflow depending largely on human feedback, the selection of participants can influence the results of the workflow drastically. However, *MindSet* is a platform for enabling surveys, while the ultimate responsibility regarding study setup lies with the practitioner. It is important that the practitioner acknowledges the possibility of selection bias and acts in a responsible way. In terms of future use cases, a possible adaptation of our interface would be converting it into a deductive interaction workflow for evaluating synthetic image generation pipelines. Our interface could be used to compare real-world and synthetic data and probe whether the data generation repeats, amplifies, or mitigates real-life biases.

Lastly, *MindSet* could be extended to enable the direct refinement of the dataset. Given the detected biases, it would be convenient if the user could fine-tune the dataset based on the study results, preferably through an interactive workflow that contains data refinement methods.

References

1. Large-scale celebfaces attributes (celeba) dataset. https://mmlab.ie.cuhk.edu.hk/projects/CelebA.html
2. Baer, T.: Understand, manage, and prevent algorithmic bias: a guide for business users and data scientists. Apress, New York, NY (2019)
3. Balakrishnan, G., Xiong, Y., Xia, W., Perona, P.: Towards causal benchmarking of bias in face analysis algorithms. In: European Conference on Computer Vision (2020)
4. Bethlehem, J.: Selection bias in web surveys. Int. Statist. Rev. **78**(2), 161–188 (2010). https://doi.org/10.1111/j.1751-5823.2010.00112.x
5. Buolamwini, J., Gebru, T.: Gender shades: intersectional accuracy disparities in commercial gender classification. In: Conference on Fairness, Accountability and Transparency. PMLR (2018)
6. Cavazos, J.G., Phillips, P.J., Castillo, C.D., O'Toole, A.J.: Accuracy comparison across face recognition algorithms: where are we on measuring race bias? IEEE Trans. Biometrics, Behav. Identity Sci. **3**(1), 101–111 (2021). https://doi.org/10.1109/TBIOM.2020.3027269
7. Corbett-Davies, S., Gaebler, J., Nilforoshan, H., Shroff, R., Goel, S.: The measure and mismeasure of fairness. J. Mach. Learn. Res (2023)
8. De-Arteaga, M., et al.: Bias in bios: a case study of semantic representation bias in a high-stakes setting. In: Proceedings of the Conference on Fairness, Accountability, and Transparency (2019)
9. Dulhanty, C., Wong, A.: Auditing ImageNet: towards a model-driven framework for annotating demographic attributes of large-scale image datasets. ArXiv (2019)
10. Fabbrizzi, S., Papadopoulos, S., Ntoutsi, E., Kompatsiaris, Y.: A survey on bias in visual datasets. Comput. Vis. Image Underst. 223 (2021)
11. F.R.S., K.P.: LIII. On lines and planes of closest fit to systems of points in space. The London, Edinburgh Dublin Philos. Mag. J. Sci. **2**(11) (1901)
12. Ghai, B., Mueller, K.: D-bias: a causality-based human-in-the-loop system for tackling algorithmic bias. IEEE Trans. Vis. Comput. Graph. (2022)

13. Goodfellow, I., et al.: Generative adversarial nets. In: Ghahramani, Z., Welling, M., Cortes, C., Lawrence, N., Weinberger, K. (eds.) Advances in Neural Information Processing Systems, vol. 27. Curran Associates, Inc. (2014)
14. Hu, X., et al.: Crowdsourcing detection of sampling biases in image datasets. In: Proceedings of The Web Conference 2020. WWW '20, Association for Computing Machinery, New York, NY, USA (2020). https://doi.org/10.1145/3366423.3380063
15. Kärkkäinen, K., Joo, J.: FairFace: face attribute dataset for balanced race, gender, and age for bias measurement and mitigation. In: 2021 IEEE Winter Conference on Applications of Computer Vision (WACV) (2019)
16. Karras, T., Laine, S., Aila, T.: A style-based generator architecture for generative adversarial networks. In: Proceedings of the IEEE/CVF Conference on Computer Vision and Pattern Recognition (CVPR) (2019)
17. Kleinberg, J., Mullainathan, S., Raghavan, M.: Inherent Trade-Offs in the fair determination of risk scores. Conf. Innov. Theoret. Comput. Sci. **67**, 23 (2017). https://doi.org/10.4230/LIPIcs.ITCS.2017.43
18. Koenecke, A., et al.: Racial disparities in automated speech recognition. Proc. Natl. Acad. Sci. **117**(14) (2020)
19. Krizhevsky, A., Sutskever, I., Hinton, G.E.: ImageNet classification with deep convolutional neural networks. Commun. ACM **60**(6) (2017)
20. Lecun, Y., Bottou, L., Bengio, Y., Haffner, P.: Gradient-based learning applied to document recognition. Proc. IEEE **86**(11), 2278–2324 (1998)
21. Martínez-Mesa, J., González-Chica, D.A., Duquia, R.P., Bonamigo, R.R., Bastos, J.L.: Sampling: how to select participants in my research study? An. Bras. Dermatol. **91**, 326–330 (2016)
22. Mehrabi, N., Morstatter, F., Saxena, N., Lerman, K., Galstyan, A.: A survey on bias and fairness in machine learning. ACM Comput. Surv. **54**(6) (2021). https://doi.org/10.1145/3457607
23. Minaee, S., Boykov, Y., Porikli, F., Plaza, A., Kehtarnavaz, N., Terzopoulos, D.: Image segmentation using deep learning: a survey. IEEE Trans. Pattern Anal. Mach. Intell. **44**(7) (2021)
24. Model, I., Shamir, L.: Comparison of data set bias in object recognition benchmarks. IEEE Access 3 (2015)
25. Rombach, R., Blattmann, A., Lorenz, D., Esser, P., Ommer, B.: High-resolution image synthesis with latent diffusion models. In: 2022 IEEE/CVF Conference on Computer Vision and Pattern Recognition (CVPR) (2022). https://doi.org/10.1109/cvpr52688.2022.01042
26. Rudd, E., Günther, M., Boult, T.: Moon: a mixed objective optimization network for the recognition of facial attributes, 9909 (2016). https://doi.org/10.1007/978-3-319-46454-1_2
27. Singer, E., Ye, C.: The use and effects of incentives in surveys. Ann. Am. Acad. Polit. Soc. Sci. **645**(1), 112–141 (2013). https://doi.org/10.1177/0002716212458082
28. Surowiecki, J.: The Wisdom of Crowds. Anchor (2005)
29. Syakur, M., Khotimah, B., Rochman, E., Satoto, B.D.: Integration k-means clustering method and elbow method for identification of the best customer profile cluster. In: IOP Conference Series: Materials Science and Engineering, vol. 336. IOP Publishing (2018)
30. Taherdoost, H.: Sampling methods in research methodology; how to choose a sampling technique for research. How to choose a sampling technique for research (2016)

31. Thomas, C., Kovashka, A.: Predicting the politics of an image using webly supervised data. In: Advances in Neural Information Processing Systems 32 (2019)
32. Tommasi, T., Patricia, N., Caputo, B., Tuytelaars, T.: A deeper look at dataset bias (2017). https://doi.org/10.1007/978-3-319-58347-1_2
33. Torralba, A., Efros, A.A.: Unbiased look at dataset bias. In: CVPR 2011 (2011)
34. Vaswani, A., et al.: Attention is all you need. In: Advances in Neural Information Processing Systems, pp. 5998–6008 (2017)
35. Verma, S., Rubin, J.: Fairness definitions explained. In: Proceedings of the International Workshop on Software Fairness (2018)
36. Wachinger, C., Rieckmann, A., Pölsterl, S.: Detect and correct bias in multi-site neuroimaging datasets. Med. Image Anal. 67 (2020)
37. Wang, Q., Xu, Z., Chen, Z., Wang, Y., Liu, S., Qu, H.: Visual analysis of discrimination in machine learning. IEEE Trans. Vis. Comput. Graph. **27**, 1470–1480 (2020)
38. Wang, T., Zhao, J., Yatskar, M., Chang, K.W., Ordonez, V.: Balanced datasets are not enough: estimating and mitigating gender bias in deep image representations. In: Proceedings of the IEEE/CVF International Conference on Computer Vision (2019)
39. Weizenbaum, J.: Eliza-a computer program for the study of natural language communication between man and machine. Commun. ACM **9**(1) (1966)
40. Xie, T., Ma, Y., Kang, J., Tong, H., Maciejewski, R.: FairRankVis: a visual analytics framework for exploring algorithmic fairness in graph mining models. IEEE Trans. Vis. Comput. Graph. (2022)
41. Yan, J.N., Gu, Z., Lin, H., Rzeszotarski, J.M.: Silva: interactively assessing machine learning fairness using causality. In: Proceedings of the 2020 CHI Conference on Human Factors in Computing Systems. CHI '20, Association for Computing Machinery, New York, NY, USA (2020)

Empirical Research on Ensuring Ethical AI in Fraud Detection of Insurance Claims: A Field Study of Dutch Insurers

Martin van den Berg[1](✉), Julie Gerlings[2], and Jenia Kim[1]

[1] HU University of Applied Sciences Utrecht, Heidelberglaan 15, 3584 CS Utrecht, The Netherlands
martin.m.vandenberg@hu.nl
[2] Copenhagen Business School, Howitzvej 60, 2000 Frederiksberg, Denmark

Abstract. The insurance industry in the Netherlands applies artificial intelligence (AI) in different processes and acknowledges that AI should be implemented in an ethical and responsible manner. Therefore, the Dutch Association of Insurers supported the industry by publishing an ethical framework. However, the framework is a set of high-level requirements, and the question is how these requirements are translated into local practices. Our research question is how ethical requirements are applied by insurance companies when using AI systems to detect fraud in insurance claims. To answer this question, we conducted interviews with representatives of four different organizations. The study demonstrates the awareness amongst interviewees that AI needs to be applied in a responsible way. The ethical framework provides a good starting point for insurers to develop their own practical ethical guidelines. Empirical evidence confirms that accountability, safety, transparency, non-discrimination, and human agency are priorities in the process of AI implementation. The research shows that translation of the ethical framework into operational and actionable instructions is done in-house by each organization and requires a multidisciplinary approach and cooperation between teams.

Keywords: Ethical AI · Responsible AI · Insurance · Fraud detection

1 Introduction

The insurance industry applies artificial intelligence (AI) in different processes and acknowledges that AI must be applied in an ethical and responsible manner [1]. Therefore, the Dutch Association of Insurers published an ethical framework which is binding for its members [2]. However, the framework is a set of high-level requirements, and the question is how these requirements are applied in practice. An IBM report indicates a "disparity between intent and implementation of AI ethics" [3]. The World Economic Forum calls this the "intention-action" gap [4]. Our research question is how ethical requirements are applied by insurance companies when using AI systems to detect fraud in insurance claims. Our research indicates that insurance firms are aware of the risks, limitations, and challenges of applying AI and have ethical frameworks in place to

S. Nowaczyk et al. (Eds.): ECAI 2023 Workshops, CCIS 1948, pp. 106–114, 2024.
https://doi.org/10.1007/978-3-031-50485-3_9

mitigate these risks. They found ways to narrow the intention-action gap. The main contribution of this research is that it provides practitioners and researchers with insights on how to implement ethical AI. This paper is organized as follows: Section 2 provides a short overview of the process of fraud detection. In Sect. 3 the research method is discussed and in Sect. 4 the results. Finally, Sect. 5 contains the discussion, conclusion, limitations, and opportunities for future research.

2 Process of Fraud Detection

Fraud detection of insurance claims is the process of determining the risk an insurance claim is fraudulent and results in lower premiums for honest consumers [1]. The process of fraud detection has the following steps:

- A private policy holder submits a claim to the insurance firm where s/he has a policy.
- The insurance firm processes the claim in its systems. Part of this processing is to check the claim for suspicious or anomalous information that may indicate fraud. This involves checking if the claim has been submitted elsewhere and checking the claimant's history of insurance fraud.
- The claim is either automatically approved, or manually checked by a claim handler. Some insurance firms have a partly automated system to evaluate whether the claim should go to a claim handler or to direct pay-out. Some systems are based on business rules, others are a combination of business rules and AI.
- If a claim handler finds the claim of a certain level of risk or something that is out of context, s/he transfers the claim to a fraud investigator who investigates the claim in more detail. Fraud investigators operate and decide independently whether the claim is fraudulent or not.
- In the end, claims that have been found fraudulent are disapproved by the insurance company and can be reported to an external warning system. The insurers can report their fraud investigations and incidents to the Dutch Association of Insurers. This association also provides guidance in the form of frameworks and best practices, as well as fraud trend-analysis and alerts on modus operandi.

3 Research Method

The research has been conducted in a qualitative and explorative manner during the first half of 2023. To gain a practical understanding of status and challenges in applying ethical AI, we conducted five interviews with experts in the field from four different organizations in the Netherlands (see Table 1). The interviews were recorded and transcribed. Interviews were conducted by two researchers and lasted about one hour each. The transcripts were coded through axial coding [5] and analyzed with NVivo.

Table 1. List of experts.

	Function	Organization	Year of experience in insurance
E1	Manager Centre Against Financial Crime	A	15
E2	Chief Analytics Officer	B	19
E3	Head of Anti-Fraud	B	14
E4	Ethicist	C	7
E5	Actuary	D	18

This study has limitations. First, the results are based on only five interviews with representatives of organizations in the Netherlands. Second, interviewees may be biased on their perception of the firm's practices. And lastly, the interviewees all belong to the managerial levels in their organizations and might not fully represent the challenges encountered by the employees who interact with the AI systems in practice (such as developers and end-users).

4 Results

An articulated and deep understanding of the ethical challenges in the process of fraud detection in general was seen across all interviewees. The leading guideline used by the companies is the ethical framework of the Dutch Association of Insurers which is binding for the association's members. This guideline is inspired by national and EU laws and regulations, with a more rigorous approach at times.

> *"In the ethical framework it says even if the National law or the European law allows something, and the ethical framework of the Insurance Association says no, we do not do that. We ask our members to follow the rules of the ethical framework, so we narrow our own boundaries, even if there's more possibilities within the (European) law." (E1)*

> *"We have a strong ethical framework, which is a nine-page legal document which explains to what type of things a model should adhere to. These consist of the seven principles of trustworthy AI from the high-level expert group of the EU that published this paper." (E2)*

Ethical guidelines have been incorporated in different ways at the firms interviewed. According to the interviewees, the incorporation of the framework is thorough and well thought about. The interviewed companies have typically started out with workshops to create awareness about the framework and guidelines in general.

> *"I've done some ethical workshops with our fraud department. And as we were implementing the ethical framework internally, we've looked at the fraud detection process within [Company] to see if there's any risks involved that touch upon points from the ethical framework." (E4)*

However, awareness is not sufficient when it comes to building responsible AI. The data scientists who work on developing and iteratively testing the model need practical instructions that translate the ethical principles into actionable tasks.

"...but if you're a data scientist, you want to have something much more practical. So, we created an AI assessment that covers all the seven principles in the ethical framework, but in a questionnaire type of way. It asks you what type of data you are going to use. Does it contain [personal identifiable information]? And if so, is your data protection officer involved? And did he or she check the baseline for data processing?" (E2)

Moreover, it is not a one-time assessment; every iteration of the model demands a review of the data used and a possible update of the checklist.

"...the assessment starts and ends basically never because once it is in production, you also need to come back to the assessment every six months or every year, depending on the type of use case that you're doing, and you need to update this document." (E2)

The ethical framework is based on the 'Ethics guidelines for trustworthy AI' [6] which contains seven principles that AI systems should meet to be deemed trustworthy. These principles were mentioned multiple times during the interviews, with special focus on accountability, safety, transparency, non-discrimination, and human agency.

4.1 Accountability and Safety

The interviewees indicated that they prefer developing their AI solutions in-house, to have full control and full accountability. They stress the importance of ensuring that the model is robust and safe and continually testing to see if it needs to be updated or retrained.

"...And the main reason for that [developing in-house] was to be in control yourself. To ensure we comply with our ethical framework, law, and legislation." (E3)

"Everything is being tested repeatedly... sometimes we retrain the model based on the outcome of tests and, we did some shadow runs. We run the model for quite some time to do it in parallel but not in production and see what the performance would be." (E2)

4.2 Transparency

Transparency towards internal stakeholders is regarded as very important by the interviewees, mainly as a means to gain employees' trust and acceptance and improve their understanding of the AI system. One such internal stakeholder is the managerial level, for whom it is important to understand how the model works, as they need to sign off on it and therefore are accountable for it. This need for transparency and explainability often drives the preference towards less complex, but more explainable, models.

"When I look at the senior managers and directors, they also want to understand. They tend very much towards the less complex models for the time being. Maybe in time it will change. Yes, but for the time being when I look at it and I see how the people at the top think, I think they are quite careful..." (E5)

Other important stakeholders are the internal end-users of the model, i.e., the claim handlers and the fraud investigators. Since they need to work with the outputs of the model, they need to understand what these outputs are. In addition, they need to be prepared to answer questions about these outputs from the customer, if such questions arise.

"Before we started this, we assessed all risks. And there's one risk we described. We must be clear about what the outcome of this model means. We must be clear that the claim handler must understand, but also the fraud investigator must understand how this model works and what they are seeing." (E3)

"...you can explain the model well, but it is sometimes too in-depth for the claim handlers. That's why I came up with competence, to be able to understand such a model properly. For the current colleagues who work in claims, they have learned things in a different way... But because they do not yet have that competence, they need to get to know those AI models well, but they also need to know how the score is arrived at... if the claim handler does not understand why he is asking for certain information and the customer asks, why are you asking this? Yes, then it will be difficult. So, you need some kind of further training... The customer wants a good explanation." (E5)

There is, however, a sensitive aspect to the transparency principle, which has to do with how much information can and should be disclosed to the customer. On the one hand, the companies have a moral (and sometimes legal) obligation to disclose the use of an algorithm in their fraud detection process and to explain what the algorithm does. On the other hand, full transparency about proprietary in-house algorithms is problematic in terms of competition between firms, and it also creates a risk of gaming the system.

"They must inform clients when they are processing their personal data. But that will not mean you have to tell them all the details of what you're doing in your process. But you must explain why something is taking up a little bit more time before they get a decision on their claim, for instance. But it's always difficult." (E1)

An additional tension is found between the pros and cons of providing detailed explanations about the outputs of the model to internal users. Some companies provide the claim handler with the risk score outputted by the model, as well as a detailed explanation in natural language about the features that contributed to this score. The advantage of this approach is that it gives the claim handler an indication on what is suspicious in the claim and where s/he should look first.

"Very important thing we built in. So, the model, of course, gives a score. But to the person who receives the claim, there's an explanation. You received this

claim to be handled manually because XYZ and then it gives the explanation in human language...For instance, a highly unusual price for a claim like this or a combination of certain factors. This same claim amount has been issued before, or an email address or this bank account was used in a similar claim before, but with another policyholder... So, there are different rules in the claim process." (E2)

However, this level of explainability also has some potential disadvantages, as it might create a bias or a tunnel vision of the handler. Therefore, some of the interviewed companies chose not to provide detailed explanations; instead, they order the cases by levels of risk, so that the most suspicious cases are handled first, but they expect the handlers and investigators to do the investigation "from scratch" to avoid potential bias by the model.

"So, it might give a score to a certain case and that case might be prioritized. And then the human comes in and starts to do their own research......we talked about in our explainable AI workgroup, how important it is for the human not to just see all the factors that the AI has determined as fraudulent because that might already bias them in a certain direction. It might already color their judgement." (E4)

The level of explainability in models such as random forest or boosting (XGBoost) may seem simple on a general level, however reasoning through the decision from a single claim evaluation can be very difficult. Therefore, firms have introduced SHAP and LIME as explainable components in their model framework. These explainable frameworks can assimilate an instance (case) and show which features are most likely to have the highest impact on the evaluation.

"We use a relatively easy simple machine learning algorithm where you can get quite good results with SHAP or LIME with it." (E2)

In combination with simpler models that do not involve deep learning, firms overcome the challenge of extracting information about the reasoning of the ML models choices. Now, the challenge is to ensure understanding from the stakeholders who need the information.

"I talked with a colleague who also worked with these models, and he said yes, you can explain the model well, but it is sometimes too in-depth for the claim handler..." (E5)

Though SHAP and LIME plots have been extensively promoted as explainable and interpretable, they still cause confusion to many stakeholders outside the data science domain since they are not contextual to the people who receive them. Moreover, claim handlers and fraud investigators tend to be analytical people who seek information until they understand in detail what is going on. Therefore, the plots can be too detailed, or may show the wrong context, to be useful for these stakeholders. One firm has generated indicators based on the plots, which are formulated in natural language to overcome this challenge.

"So, the claim handler sees on his screen the claim. Based on our model the claim gets a risk score of High, Medium, or Low. Our model will also add a simple explanation in three to five lines. So not just red, orange, green or a difficult explanation or code, but explanations like: 'watch this invoice or look at this address, it's known in another case. See claim number x.' So, the data scientists must make a translation from the code to send it to the claim handler to make it clear for them how to interpret this risk." (E3)

4.3 Non-discrimination

The interviewees indicated that they prioritize the clients and their experience rather than solely focusing on detection of more fraud. Using ML to identify suspicious claims and ending up wrongly accusing someone of fraud can have tremendous consequences for the individual. Moreover, it can tear the image of a company and the entire industry down. Therefore, firms have high standards for what data is being fed into the models to minimize the risk of discrimination or bias towards specific groups. For example:

"For the detection of fraud, area codes are a no go. You cannot create any fallout of your straight through process just on an area code. I do know that you can use it for risk management, for risk evaluations. And for instance, my car insurance premium is a bit lower than two zip codes to my left. But that's a risk assessment issue and not a fraud assessment issue." (E1)

One example of the complexity of practically implementing ethical guidelines is how to eliminate discriminatory features from the data going into the model. The basics of supervised ML start with learning from historic data and build upon that to establish a probability of a new claim falling into one of the categories. According to the interviewees, the features going into the AI-model are carefully chosen to minimize the risks of discrimination and biases. Therefore, some features, such as 'country of origin' or 'nationality' might be excluded or altered before they go into the model. However, some features are less easily identified as problematic, as they do not seem discriminatory by themselves, but they do serve as a proxy for a discriminatory feature.

"We're putting a lot of effort into bias detection. We created some tools ourselves to detect whether there is a statistical bias for the model to affect certain people who are vulnerable. So, either based on a religion, sexual orientation, a social class... there are 25 attributes that are prohibited to use because they are discriminatory. These are clear for everyone. The true harm is in the proxies of those 25 attributes. So, we are now in a late phase of deploying also this bias detector based on features that might be a proxy to discriminatory features." (E2)

In the example presented by the interviewee, it turned out that even though 'country of origin' was excluded from the data, there was a proxy feature for this information hidden in the 'marital status' feature, since one of its values was 'Married outside of the Netherlands' (a proxy for a foreign country of origin). This was discovered by a dedicated bias detection tool built by the company.

"If you are married, you both take a mortgage. It has some impact on the product. So, you are allowed to ask that: married? Yes or No. But in this case the bias detector discovered that there was a strong proxy to this marital status attribute. And it was just because we had different categories in this attribute. It could be Yes, it could be No, but it could also be Yes, married outside of the Netherlands, which was a different category, which was not being used by us deliberately in the model. But marital status was part of the model. And now, potentially this could be a proxy for ethnical background... So, we did a recode of this attribute to simple Yes or No." (E2)

4.4 Human Agency

Human oversight is another crucial aspect of implementing ML in the fraud detection process. The model is used only to assess the risk and output a score; the rest of the process, which includes the investigation, and the final decision is always performed by a human expert. This is also expressed in how the model is being named and talked about, and it is part of ensuring the intended use of the model. As the quote below shows, there is a deliberate distinction between 'fraud detection' and 'fraud risk', which emphasizes that it is the investigator, and not the model, who detects fraud.

"We call it a fraud risk model because the model itself doesn't detect fraud. It's always the human who must assess this risk and must decide if it is a possible fraud or not. An important thing in the development of our tool was a human in the loop. So first, the system presents to the claim handler, these are the fraud risks identified. Then the claim handler must look at it and must assess these risks. He might ask some questions to the client or ask for additional information ...and then he says, well, I don't trust this claim to be valid. Maybe it's fraud. Then it goes to the fraud investigator. And then he also looks at it. Are there enough indicators for fraud? If so, okay, we take over this claim and start a fraud investigation. The investigation has to point out if it is possible fraud or not. So, it's a human who always makes the decision." (E3)

5 Discussion and Conclusion

Our research provides an up-to-date overview of the practical use of AI in fraud detection of insurance claims in the Netherlands. Based on the five interviews we conducted, we conclude that:

- Interviewees acknowledge the limitations of the AI and determine its place in the whole process accordingly, so that the cooperation between the model and the human experts is optimal.
- The implementation of AI is taken seriously: it is a long process, and a lot of effort is put not only in the technical aspects but also in the human and organizational aspects.
- There is a lot of awareness among interviewees of the ethical principles that need to be met to implement AI responsibly. The Dutch Association of Insurers provides an ethical framework. Translation of the ethical framework into operational and actionable instructions is done in-house by each company.

- Compared to extant literature where the intention-action gap was described [e.g., 7, 8], this study indicates that the insurance industry in the Netherlands is actively and seriously working on ways to narrow the gap and to implement ethical AI in practice.

The main takeaway from this research is that the implementation of AI in fraud detection is a business transformation that requires many ethical and organizational considerations. Education and inclusion are crucial to ensure a successful integration of AI into the fraud detection process, and an optimal human-machine cooperation. All interviewees are aware of the risks, limitations, and challenges of applying AI and insurance firms have ethical frameworks in place to mitigate these risks. This research sheds light on the way insurance firms are implementing ethical AI and how they use ethical frameworks.

Further, and more detailed research is necessary to identify which factors, such as education, contribute most to a successful implementation of ethical AI and in what manner. Moreover, research is needed to learn how certain tools, such as bias detection tools, can help narrow the intention-action gap.

References

1. EIOPA (European Insurance and Occupational Pensions Authority). AI Governance Principles towards ethical and trustworthy AI in the European insurance sector. https://www.eiopa.europa.eu/eiopa-publishes-report-artificial-intelligence-governance-principles-2021-06-17_en. Accessed 26 Aug 2023
2. Verbond van Verzekeraars. Ethisch kader. https://www.verzekeraars.nl/branche/zelfreguleringsoverzicht-digiwijzer/ethisch-kader-datatoepassingen. Accessed 26 Aug 2023
3. Goehring, B., Rossi, F., Rudden, B.: AI ethics in action. An enterprise guide to progressing trustworthy AI. IBM Institute for Business Value (2022). https://www.ibm.com/thought-leadership/institute-business-value/en-us/report/ai-ethics-in-action. Accessed 26 Aug 2023
4. Guszcza, J., Skeet, A.: How businesses can create an ethical culture in the age of tech. World Economic Forum (2020). https://www.weforum.org/agenda/2020/01/how-businesses-can-create-an-ethical-culture-in-the-age-of-tech/. Accessed 26 Aug 2023
5. Williams, M., Moser, T.: The art of coding and thematic exploration in qualitative research. Int. Manage. Rev. **15**(1), 45–55 (2019)
6. European commission: Ethics guidelines for trustworthy AI (2016). https://digital-strategy.ec.europa.eu/en/library/ethics-guidelines-trustworthy-ai. Accessed 26 Aug 2023
7. Morley, J., Floridi, L., Kinsey, L., Elhalal, A.: From what to how: an initial review of publicly available AI ethics tools, methods and research to translate principles into practices. Sci. Eng. Ethics **26**(4), 2141–2168 (2020)
8. Georgieva, I., Lazo, C., Timan, T., Van Veenstra, A.F.: From AI ethics principles to data science practice: a reflection and a gap analysis based on recent frameworks and practical experience. AI Ethics **2**(4), 697–711 (2022)

Random Sample as a Pre-pilot Evaluation of Benefits and Risks for AI in Public Sector

Steven Vethman[1(✉)], Marianne Schaaphok[1], Marissa Hoekstra[2], and Cor Veenman[1,3]

[1] Netherlands Organisation for Applied Scientific Research (TNO) - Data Science, The Hague, The Netherlands
steven.vethman@tno.nl

[2] Netherlands Organisation for Applied Scientific Research (TNO) - Vector, The Hague, The Netherlands

[3] Leiden University - Leiden Institute of Advanced Computer Science (LIACS), Leiden, The Netherlands

Abstract. Public organisations have adopted AI into their public service aiming to tap into the promised potential for society, such as increasing efficiency and effectiveness of current processes. Recent studies from the European Commission share, however, that critical issues of AI use only tended to surface when they were already in operation and thus had already affected citizens. To prevent negative impact to citizens, we propose public organisations to use random sampling as a safe, yet valuable practical evaluation step before considering a pilot. This safe pre-pilot evaluation step enables evaluation of the AI system without applying it in any decisions or actions that already affect citizens. We pose six arguments on the added value of random sampling in the evaluation step of AI systems: 1) it provides high quality data for evaluation and validation of assumptions; 2) it supports gathering input for fairness evaluation; 3) it creates a benchmark to compare AI to alternatives; 4) it enables challenging assumptions in the organisation and the AI development; 5) it supports a discussion on the limitations of AI 6) and it provides a safe space to evaluate and reflect. In addition, we discuss limitations and challenges for random sampling in the evaluation, such as temporary loss of efficiency, class and representation imbalances, organizational hesitancy and societal experiences. We invite the participants of this workshop to reflect with us on the potential benefits and challenges, and in turn distill the practical requirements where using a random sample for evaluation is safe and useful.

1 Introduction

With the upcoming AI Act, the European Commission (EC) is providing an EU regulatory framework for the responsible development and use of AI. Groundwork for this regulation started in April 2019, when the High-Level Expert Group

S. Nowaczyk et al. (Eds.): ECAI 2023 Workshops, CCIS 1948, pp. 115–126, 2024.
https://doi.org/10.1007/978-3-031-50485-3_10

on AI presented their Ethical Guidelines for Trustworthy AI [7]. These guidelines set forward seven key principles in terms of requirements that Trustworthy Applied AI should meet. Agreeing with these principles in abstract terms is easy. However, turning them into practice has proven to be challenging, especially for public organisations using AI to aid their public services. A recent report from the Joint Research Centre (JRC) of the EC on AI use in the public sector showed that many projects reached "the adoption phase before finding some unexpected, yet critical, issues" [11]. Typical issues reported were: "legal issues, biased recommendations and staff resistance". In other words, the AI application was already adopted in the way of working of the public service, albeit in a pilot, whilst the legal embedding was still uncertain, the risks and harms related to bias were unknown or unaccounted for, and the identified benefits and possible drawbacks of the AI application did not find a sufficiently large support base.

The term *pilot* is often used to describe adoption in a small controlled setting for experimentation purposes, i.e. a pilot may be a way to find out about these critical issues. However, especially in high risk settings such as essential public services, adoption of AI in terms of a pilot, when the AI system is too premature, can already have too much direct impact on citizens. Often, public organisations start the development of an AI solution with an available data set, which has been compiled to report on the current way of working. This data set is therefore based on the experiences and policies of current operations, in which unconscious societal biases of the people involved are embedded. It occurs too often that public services are not equally accessible to all demographics. Accordingly, the collected data sets have an incomplete or skewed representation of the underlying data distribution that represents all relevant citizens. Moreover, information about these demographics, also known as sensitive attributes, such as nationality or gender are often left out of data collection for good reasons. That is, such attributes are left out from privacy and fairness considerations. It creates so-called fairness through unawareness [10], such that public servants cannot directly differentiate action or treatment based on the collected sensitive data. However, discrimination can also be indirect, e.g. through proxies of the sensitive attributes, such as geographic regions that are linked to ethnic groups. Without information about the sensitive attributes, evaluation of the AI system in terms of fairness is impeded and still leads to the risk of negative impact due to biased selections of the AI. Evaluation methodologies are needed, that are safe to citizens, such that they are not selected by an opaque and insufficiently validated AI system. Especially, when risks and harms are unknown and the added value of the AI application is still uncertain in the organizational embedding.

In this paper, we propose the use of a random sample in a safe pre-pilot phase to evaluate the effectiveness and risks of the use of AI before adoption in a pilot. That is, the risks and possibly undesired selection properties of the AI system are in this phase replaced with a random selection procedure. This enables to test the selection properties of the AI on the data set from the random sample, for which biases from policies and experiences of the current way of working have deliberately been mitigated. The random sample can provide a benchmark as well as help challenge the assumptions made in the data and during translation from organization goal to model objective. We emphasize that we focus on random sampling in the context of the evaluation of AI algorithms and not in the data collection and development phase, which would require larger sample sizes. We draw our arguments from public use cases, experiences with use cases in among others our AI Oversight Lab[1], talks with governmental bodies and peers, as well as the growing body of literature.

In the next section, we discuss the position of our methodology compared to developed impact assessments and widely-used data science methodologies. In the third section, we introduce a fictional high risk use case of AI adoption to concretely illustrate each argument in this paper. The fictional use case makes the discussion more concrete by putting focus on the lessons learned, without directly referring to wrongful practices of specific organisations. The fourth section discusses our five arguments for using a random sample for evaluation purposes before running a pilot. The fifth section presents challenges and critical remarks concerning our proposed additional pre-pilot development phase. The sixth section provides the conclusion. We hope that the insights of this paper ignite a discussion at this workshop on under which conditions random sampling can be a safe and valuable evaluation step in AI development for the public sector.

2 Background

A lot of work has been done on guidelines [7] and impact assessment frameworks [6,14] to help organizations with responsible development and use of AI. These frameworks aim to identify benefits and risks of AI systems in an early phase. However, recent work [18] and experiences by public organizations show that the practical application of these frameworks is not evident. There are challenges such as contextualization (how do these generic guidelines fit within the context of ones organization and application?), subjectivity (evaluations and impact assessments can be affected by individual beliefs and experiences of the evaluator) and knowledge deficits (does the organization have the required knowledge on technical, societal and legal issues?). [18] states that many impact assessments are based on subjective answers from people within the organization which introduces the risk of human biases. They argue that concrete, contextualized and more objective solutions or procedures should be developed and/or incorporated into the risk assessment process to improve the utility and reliability of AI risk assessments.

Furthermore, we would like to set current AI development practices in the context of a widely-used data science methodology called Cross Industry Standard Process for Data Mining (CRISP-DM) [9,13,17]. In CRISP-DM, one starts with a business or societal goal in the real world. By making a set of assumptions, said goal is translated into a modelling goal within the limits of available data. After the data are collected and prepared, the model is optimized and

[1] https://appl-ai-tno.nl/projects/ai-oversight-lab/.

tested on the available data. That is, the data that represents the historical way of working, including assumptions on missing information. After a satisfactory performance is measured in the historical data set, CRISP-DM suggests an evaluation step to gauge the effectiveness of the application in the real world. In most cases this results in doing a pilot. Referring back to the JRC report, we state that this evaluation step is often taken too early as discovering critical issues while impacting citizens is undesirable. We state that the evaluation step in CRISP-DM needs a prior effort to safely establish a realistic benchmark as well as to facilitate a critical reflection on the data and the goal translation.

Our proposed random sample adds a pre-pilot evaluation phase that makes the assessments of effectiveness and risks more concrete and objective. It allows to evaluate and compare alternatives on high quality data. Only after such diligent considerations can public organisations decide whether the potential impact of running a pilot is desirable.

3 Fictional Use Case for Illustration of Arguments

In practice we see many governmental organisations, such as inspectorates and municipalities working on risk-models to identify and prioritize cases (organisations or individuals) for inspection in order to make their inspections more effective [8]. The expected positive impact is to make more effective use of the capacity of inspectors, to reduce the impact on compliant organisations/citizens and to increase compliance in general. Such risk-models can be considered high-risk AI applications, because the outcomes may influence whether or not an individual or organisation will receive an essential public service, which has direct economic and/or social consequences.

Here we propose a hypothetical case as a running example. It considers an organisation that is piloting a risk-model to prioritize inspections to detect fraud by social welfare recipients. Inspectors of the organisation use the outcomes of the AI system to determine which recipients to inspect first. The risk-model is trained on data representing the current way of working (before adoption of AI). Here choices for whom to inspect were based on earlier insights of inspectors or warning signs of fraudulent behavior such as a suspicious neighbour. We would like to emphasize that with the choice of this example we do not argue that AI should or should not be used for the detection of this type of fraud. We choose this setting for relatability, due to the numerous examples of AI adoption for this purpose. We also choose this High Risk setting to underline that such cases in particular need safe experimentation and critical reflection before deciding whether the AI system should be adopted in operation, albeit in a pilot.

In this example, we propose the random sample evaluation in the following way. The organisation uses a random selection procedure to allocate 100 inspections of recipients for whom it is not yet known whether they are fraudulent or not. Inspectors investigate these recipients to acquire information on whether they are fraudulent. Note that only the selection process is adapted to a random sample, the inspection itself and possible follow-up actions remain the same to the current way of working. In the evaluation step one can ask post-inspection to (other) inspectors: which of these 100 would you have suggested for an inspection? And, similarly to the AI application: which of these 100 would the AI application have given a high risk score. An error-analysis could answer how many fraudulent citizens the AI or inspectors would have correctly suggested for inspection, how many compliant recipients would have been given a high risk score and how many fraudulent recipients would have been missed by either alternative. That is, you measure the effectiveness and risks of each alternative, whilst only the random sample has affected the recipients.

4 Arguments

In this section, we present five arguments for a random sample in a pre-pilot evaluation to gain practical insight in the benefits and risks of adoption of AI solutions in the public sector.

4.1 Testing Assumptions

First, random sampling is a means to gather data of higher quality for evaluation before running a pilot. In the development of AI algorithms assumptions have to be made on the data distribution. In context of our running example, an important assumption concerns the proportions of fraudulent and non-fraudulent social welfare recipients. For example, this affects discussions on the added value of an AI algorithm (were fraudulent recipients hard to find?), as well as the choice of the type of the AI algorithm (are fraudulent recipients a sizable class with different behaviour or are they uncommon outliers that need to be detected). Additionally, organizations are often limited to the available data from the current way of working. Is data on how the public service is currently performed a sufficiently reliable data set to validate these assumptions? When pursuing a developed algorithm towards operationalization, it is essential to verify the assumptions on the data and the representativeness of the data [2]; does the data set based on the current way of working represent a realistic setting in which the developed algorithm may be applied?

Collecting a random sample in the pre-pilot phase leads to high quality data where certain historical biases in the current way of working are limited. Inspectors choosing who to check for fraud are not free from subconscious human bias, which results to their choices potentially reflecting systemic discriminatory tendencies. Intended systematic preferences in organizational/political policy to give more checks to foreign-born subsidy recipients have also been reported. Moreover, inspectors might do some desk research before choosing who gets a full inspection for fraud, such that those who commit fraud in unforeseen ways are less targeted for full inspections. A data set based on random sampling where these biases are limited constitutes another, arguably cleaner, data set upon which the outcomes of the algorithm can be evaluated.

Moreover, the "cleaner" data set also allows a comparison with the distribution of the data set for development purposes which represents the current way of working. In the context of our example, this could mean that the proportions of fraudulent and non-fraudulent welfare recipients of both data sets can be compared. This comparison can provide a sanity check whether the development data set is a suitable representation of the real (or desired) world for training the AI application. This can empower the organization to decide whether alternatives or additional measurement such as extended data collection are required. For example, in our fictional use case the data set for development could contain significantly more fraudulent recipients from a specific region, because people and institutes in that region were more observant and proactive in issuing warnings. The random sample data set can show that this group is over-represented in the training set.

4.2 Fairness Calibration

Second, random sampling supports the gathering of valuable input for quantitative fairness metrics that can help signal undesirable differentiation and negative impact towards certain groups. The way in which the data collection has been performed in the current way of working can lead to the practical issue that relevant quantitative fairness metrics cannot be measured. Since data collection is often designed for administration purposes rather than the purpose of developing AI models, important labels or variables for fairness evaluations may be missing. For example for the fairness metric Equalized Odds, you need an indication per social demographic of the ratio of fraudulent and non-fraudulent recipients to see how the predictions of the algorithm deviate from these ratios [10]; acquiring this indication requires a data collection procedure that is not driven by warning signals or intuition of inspectors on who is worthy of an inspection. If reporting phone calls have mainly come from certain neighbourhoods, the data set may have misleading ratios as the calls disproportionately concern the dominant demographics from those neighbourhoods. Similarly, for the analysis of proxies for protected classes, the value of the protected class is required for the samples. We note that from a nondiscriminatory perspective, organisations have reasons to not store these sensitive attributes in their current way of working [12]. However, the ability and importance to evaluate against sensitive attributes is recognized in the current version of the AI Act as of June 14 2023 [5], which allows for the collection of sensitive attributes with the mere purpose of fairness evaluations. A random sample provides an opportunity to design and reflect on a safe data collection process, whilst not simultaneously dealing with implications of operationalizing AI.

4.3 Alternatives Comparison

Third, random sampling facilitates an evaluation of AI in terms of alternatives. Performing a random sample provides a benchmark to which not only the AI algorithm, but also the current way of working and other alternatives can be compared. This moves the perspective of the evaluation from an isolated evaluation of AI (focusing on the absolute risks and benefits of implementing it) towards a relative evaluation where the downsides and benefits of alternatives are also actively considered. In practice, we see that development and implementation of AI often rely on go/no-go moments which represent the alternatives of either implementing the AI in the public services or maintaining the public service as is. We argue that the benefits and downsides of alternatives such as maintaining the current way of working deserve as diligent of an evaluation such that the consequences of a no-go decision are also clearly understood. In the execution of public service, legal concepts such as proportionality (are the means suitable, necessary and not excessively burdening citizens to achieve the objective?) and subsidiarity (are there no alternative means which impose less burden to attain similar goals?) are key and should be considered carefully [4].

4.4 Reflection on Goal Translation

Fourth, random sampling is a means to challenge the assumptions made in the data processing as well as those made to translate the societal goal to modeling criteria. Closely related to the first and third argument, we would like to emphasize that executing a random sample, and therefore partially or temporarily changing the way of working, creates a setting of critical reflection on the current way of working. This is an opportunity to discover blind spots regarding unwanted impact with respect to any public values important to the public organization. For the development of the AI algorithm, this reflection may also help checking the explicit assumptions made in terms of data processing and those made to translate the real world goal to the model goal within the available data. For example, in our fictional example, the real world goal is to use the capacity of the inspectors more effectively to reduce fraud. The current model goal is whether a recipient is likely of committing fraud. It can be discussed whether this focus on fraudulent behavior prediction is the right translation of the real world goal to the model goal. Alternatively a model can also focus on prioritizing cases such that capacity is used most efficiently. For example a model that schedules the cases according to the ability of inspectors or the expected difficulty, duration, and impact of the inspection. Another reflection may pertain to the translation of the societal goal to reduce fraud to a single technical definition of fraud for the model. Is a measure that aggregates different types of fraud desirable? I.e. is it justifiable to consider fraud committed on purpose equivalent to unintentional misunderstanding of the exact duties for receiving welfare [15]?

4.5 Understanding Limitations of AI

Fifth, evaluating with a random sample facilitates the conversation on the limitations of an algorithm. The application of algorithms can lead to automation bias and can give people a false sense of objectivity. This can lead to insufficient validation of the algorithm outcomes and decrease the incentive for a human touch in exceptional cases. Comparing the current way of working and the algorithm on a random sample allows to challenge the false sense of objectivity in the perception of the algorithm's outcomes. AI's association of objectivity often comes from the inhuman/ emotionless characteristic of computers as well as the fact that the AI generalizes, i.e. it provides suggestions based on pattern found on a large number of examples. We argue however, that a generalized pattern based on historical practice, may be void of an individual subjectivity from a particular inspector, but is not void of a shared (undesirable) subjectivity. Think of systemic racism, or misogyny, xenophobia, which are forms of societal oppression not individual isolated phenomena. These may for example systemically alter which groups in society receive inspections. Random samples can show the differences between inspections based on a random sample, the current way of working and the algorithm. This can contribute to the conversation about the possibilities and limitations of the algorithm, such that the trust that is placed in the system is more adequate and responsible.

4.6 Safe Space

Sixth, our overarching argument for a random sample is that it provides a relatively safe environment for the evaluation of the AI algorithm and alternatives. Safe meaning here that critical issues such as the biased recommendations mentioned in the JRC report, do not yet impact the citizens during evaluation of the AI algorithm. As described in Sect. 3 only the random sample decides which recipients are inspected and the AI-based recommendations are evaluated on the results of these inspections. This ensures that citizens are not yet impacted by the recommendations of the AI system. A fundamental assumption here is that it is more safe for citizens and society when inspections are conducted at random rather than steered by human inspectors or by AI. That is, the harm experienced by a social welfare recipient to undergo a full inspection, completely by chance, is less than when the inspection is based on an inspector's intuition, warning signals, or an AI application, which are often considered opaque and inexplicable.

This additional evaluation phase also provides space in the organization to start the safe discussion on the social embedding of quantitative metrics. For example, consider the question of human accuracy versus computer accuracy; is 80% accuracy of a human valued similarly to 80% accuracy of the algorithm or do we require a higher standard for systematic evaluations? Or think of the previously mentioned discussion on whether unintentional fraud and intentional fraud should be aggregated when partially automating your public service. These discussions are essential to be able to translate evaluations to decisions on operationalization and recognize their capabilities and limitations. Conscious, transparent and documented decisions on these topics support the accountability and hence the responsible use of AI.

5 Discussion

The notion that random sampling will provide clean data is of course not new and there are multiple arguments why random sampling on a large scale for the training of AI models is often not possible. Hence we do not propose that random sampling should be the basis for AI development, but should merely be used in the pre-pilot phase to test assumptions, evaluate effectiveness and risks and compare alternatives. In this setting, we expect that the required sample size for evaluation purposes can be much smaller than for development of AI algorithms [16]. However, also for this application there are limitations and challenges that need to be considered.

5.1 Temporary Loss of Efficiency

Often the aim of using AI is to make a certain process faster and more efficient; in case of governmental institutions this results in helping more people. Especially since many organisations are looking at AI solutions to help dealing with their increasing workload. Performing a random sample will take up space and time from the current employees, which might result in less efficiency for a specific period of time. Assuming that an alternative finds more fraud, during the time of random sampling less cases of fraud are detected. From a societal perspective this means that taxpayer's money is lost. One should keep in mind here that the loss of efficiency is based on the assumption that the current way of working is more effective than the random sample, which is often unknown. In the context of fraud in social welfare in the Netherlands, most cases consist of unintentional fraud linked to the complexity of eligibility rules [3]. Because of this, inspectors may therefore have the unfounded notion that almost every visit was useful due to their skillful intuition who is committing fraud, whilst in practice almost all social welfare recipients have a difficult time to have an overview of their financial situation and the rules pertaining social welfare.

5.2 Imbalance in Class and Representation

Secondly, major class imbalances can prove a challenge for the random sample. Considering a scenario where only 10% of social welfare recipients are fraudulent. In that case, a smaller random sample is required to find the correct distribution than in cases where the classes are balanced (50% is fraudulent) [1]. To illustrate, assume that we have a population of N = 10 000 for which we assume a 10–90% distribution, where 10% is non-compliant. In this case, a random sample of approx. n = 50 is required to get estimate with a margin of 8%. If we assume a 50-50% distribution in the same population a random sample of approx. n = 150 is required to achieve an estimate within a margin of 8%. However, in many cases not only the distribution in the population but also information about the minority classes is required. In this case, the 5 samples (10% of n = 50) of non-compliant recipients are not sufficient. To achieve a suitable representation of the minority class(es) a larger random sample is required. Especially when fairness evaluation requires substantial representation of multiple demographics.

Related to the class imbalance there is also a challenge regarding small sensitive groups. In order to measure whether the AI application functions desirable for all relevant demographics, the individuals from these sensitive groups should contain samples both positive and negative. Since sensitive groups can be minorities, performing a random sample can be challenging in cases with large class imbalances and small minorities. Alternatively, stratified random sampling could prevent this problem, whilst this would also mean that the inspections are allocated based on the demographic membership of social welfare recipients.

5.3 Organizational Hesitancy

From an organizational perspective, inspectors might be reluctant to perform random samples instead of following their intuition or warning signs, as they consider it a waste of time. This drawback is even more pertinent when an inspection is very costly in terms of time spent by inspectors or time spent by welfare recipients. There is a related challenge as inspectors might execute an inspection less elaborately, if they know it is based on random selection rather than insight. This could affect the reliability and quality of the random sample.

On the higher organizational level of program manager, team lead or department head, hesitancy can occur due to the fact that the advantage and necessity of better evaluation and monitoring is not always properly understood. A meaningful size of a random sample takes often a substantial time to execute, which is in contrast to the entrepreneurship and innovation mindset of "move fast and break things". Random sampling has value in being diligent, avoiding errors and investing in sustainable innovation, whilst managers are often rewarded for short-term gains in efficiency or effectiveness. Especially with the sensitive nature of leading a team that experiments with AI for public service (due to increased scrutiny from society), the turnover in these positions is fast. Managers may therefore be disincentivized to do initiatives which are perceived to only have long-term benefits and prefer to run a pilot in operations to show the rewards from the investment in AI development. Hence from their perspective this does not directly weigh up against the short-term downside of loss of efficiency.

5.4 Experience of a Random Inspection

Lastly, as flip side of Sect. 4.6, the use of a random sample can still lead to citizens experiencing increased stress as they feel they are under suspicion and, in our example, marked as (potentially) fraudulent by the public organisation. Even though it is a random selection, who undergoes the inspection is still selected from the larger population. To experience that you are selected whilst others are not, may feel unfair. Especially those, who have seen public organisations making mistakes, are critical about the government and therefore may doubt the randomness of the selection. Based on the current way of working the assumption can live within society that if you follow the rules you will not be inspected. In this case an inspection may still feel as an invasion to the citizen. On the other hand a random sample can also be experienced by individuals or society as a just way to inspect and validate the way of working and to maintain societal support for public services.

6 Conclusion

Public organisations want to tap into the potential societal benefits of adopting AI into their public service. Unfortunately, we are all familiar with too many instances where critical issues of adoption of AI only surfaced when they were already in operation and thus had affected citizens. We propose public organisations to use random sampling as a safe, yet valuable practical evaluation step without possible negative impact on citizens. Random sampling is a means to gather higher quality data for evaluation, including input for common fairness metrics. Additionally, a random sample provides a benchmark to compare performance of alternatives to. Relating the current way of working to alternatives also sets the scene where assumptions of the model, data processing and goal translation can be challenged. This comparison also facilitates discussions that lead to understanding of the limitations of AI and a more adequate level of trust. Most importantly, it provides a safe environment to evaluate AI systems without negatively impacting citizens.

Critical reflection on random sampling indicates that class and demographic imbalances provide challenges for desired evaluation of effectiveness and risks such as fairness. Moreover, the random sampling can be met with organisational hesitancy due to expected loss of efficiency, which in turn affects the reliability of the inspections. Lastly, the aspect of safety of a random sample is only as valid as the assumption that equal unconditional chance for inspection is considered fair and experienced less burdensome than being selected for an inspection based on an inspector's intuition or an AI's suggestion. We invite the participants of this workshop to reflect with us on the potential benefit and challenges, and in turn distill the practical requirements where using a random sample for evaluation is safe and useful.

Acknowledgement. We would like to thank all our colleagues in the AI Oversight lab[2], our external partners, as well as all other public and private organisations that have facilitated transparency on this urgent yet sensitive topic such that the lessons described in this paper could be learned.[2]https://appl-ai-tno.nl/projects/ai-oversight-lab/

References

1. Bethlehem, J.: Applied Survey Methods, a statistical perspective. John Wiley and Sons Inc (2009)
2. Clemmensen, L., Kjærsgaard, R.: Data representativity for machine learning and AI systems (2022)

3. Dannenberg, E.: Factsheet overtredingen van de inlichtingenplicht - meer maatwerk en eenvoudigere regels (2021). https://www.divosa.nl/publicaties/factsheet-overtredingen-van-de-inlichtingenplicht/factsheet-overtredingen-van-de
4. EUR-Lex Access to European Union Law: glossary proportionality. https://eur-lex.europa.eu/EN/legal-content/glossary/principle-of-proportionality.html
5. European Parliament: amendments adopted by the European parliament on 14 June 2023 on the proposal for a regulation of the European parliament and of the council on laying down harmonised rules on artificial intelligence (artificial intelligence act) and amending certain union legislative acts (2023). https://www.europarl.europa.eu/doceo/document/TA-9-2023-0236_EN.html
6. Gerards, J., Schäfer, M., Muis, I., Vankan, A.: Fundamental rights and algorithms impact assessment (FRAIA). Utrecht University, Tech. rep. (2021)
7. High-Level Expert Group on Artificial Intelligence: ethics guidelines for trustworthy AI. Tech. rep, European Commission (2019)
8. Hoekstra, M., Chideock, C., Veenstra, A.: Quick scan AI in de publieke dienstverlening ii. Tech. rep. (2021)
9. Martínez-Plumed, F., et al.: CRISP-DM twenty years later: from data mining processes to data science trajectories. IEEE Trans. Knowl. Data Eng. **33**(8), 3048–3061 (2021). https://doi.org/10.1109/TKDE.2019.2962680
10. Mehrabi, N., Morstatter, F., Saxena, N., Lerman, K., Galstyan, A.: A survey on bias and fairness in machine learning. ACM Comput. Surv. (CSUR) **54**(6), 1–35 (2021)
11. Molinari, F., Van Noordt, C., Vaccari, L., Pignatelli, F., Tangi, L.: AI watch beyond pilots: sustainable implementation of AI in public services (KJ-NA-30868-EN-N (online)), 14 (2021). https://doi.org/10.2760/440212(online)
12. Reventlow, N.J.: Data collection is not the solution for Europe's racism problem (2020). https://www.aljazeera.com/opinions/2020/7/29/data-collection-is-not-the-solution-for-europes-racism-problem
13. Schröer, C., Kruse, F., Gómez, J.M.: A systematic literature review on applying CRISP-DM process model. Proc. Comput. Sci. **181**, 526–534 (2021). https://doi.org/10.1016/j.procs.2021.01.199, https://www.sciencedirect.com/science/article/pii/S1877050921002416
14. Stahl, B., et al.: A systematic review of artificial intelligence impact assessments. Artif. Intell. Rev. (2023)
15. Steen, M., Timan, T., Vethman, S.: Using an extended error matrix to promote transdisciplinary collaboration and jointly work towards social justice (2022). https://marcsteen.nl/docs/ESDiT_2022__Error_Matrix.pdf
16. Valizadegan H, Amizadeh S, H.M.: Sampling strategies to evaluate the performance of unknown predictors. In: Proceedings SIAM International Conference Data Mining (2014)
17. Wirth, R., Hipp, J.: CRISP-DM: towards a standard process model for data mining (2000)
18. Xia, B., Lu, Q., Perera, H., Zhu, L., Xing, Z., Liu, Y., Whittle, J.: Towards concrete and connected AI risk assessment (C2AIRA): a systematic mapping study. In: 2023 IEEE/ACM 2nd International Conference on AI Engineering - Software Engineering for AI (CAIN), pp. 104–116. IEEE Computer Society, Los Alamitos, CA, USA (2023). https://doi.org/10.1109/CAIN58948.2023.00027

AI4S

Preface to the Workshop on Artificial Intelligence for Sustainability (AI4S)–ECAI 2023

Eunika Mercier-Laurent[1], Gülgün Kayakutlu[2], Mieczyslaw Lech Owoc[3], Karl Mason[4], and Abdul Wahid[4]

[1] University of Reims Champagne Ardenne, Reims, France
eunika.mercier-laurent@univ-reims.fr
[2] Istanbul Technical University, Istanbul, Turkey
kayakutlu@itu.edu.tr
[3] Wroclaw University of Economics and Business, Wroclaw, Poland
mieczyslaw.owoc@ue.wroc.pl
[4] School of Computer Science, University of Galway, University Road, Galway, Ireland
{karl.mason, abdul.wahid}@universityofgalway.ie

Artificial Intelligence generates twofold effects: produces various kinds of waste and has a potential to help addressing the sustainability goals, produce smarter and greener hardware, software and applications. Sustainability requires solving complex problems, often with hybrid AI approaches.

In parallel, knowledge is vital for successful innovation, facing environmental challenges, in smart cities, education and resource management, among others. Knowledge Management principles are also applied to energy life cycle, optimization, and combination of renewable energies for sustainable power and heating. Raising prices of natural gas drives growth in renewable energies. Industries like steel, glass, chemical manufacturing sites are looking for AI based control systems for the Grid connected micro-grids. Circular energy explores heat generated by data centers and the waste steam for a sustainable environment as like creating fish farms or agricultural sites, or recreating cooling water which are additional processes that demand AI-based scheduling using meteorological data. Clean energy solutions require evolution of manufacturing processes and holistic approach supported by rigorous analytics, high quality data and the recognition of infrastructure dependencies. This workshop focuses on the innovation for sustainable energy and overall sustainability expressed by 17 UN goals. To increase sustainability in agriculture, it is vital to incorporate green technologies into farming, e.g., renewable generation. However, there are significant challenges associated with enhancing the sustainability of agriculture. This workshop focuses on utilizing Artificial Intelligence (AI) to improve farming practices.

The objective of this multidisciplinary session was to gather both researchers and practitioners to discuss methodological, technical, organizational and environmental aspects of AI used for various facets of sustainability.

We received 39 paper submissions covering various fields concerned with sustainability such as energy, agriculture, water and coral protection. Of these submissions, 27 papers were accepted for presentation. These papers went through a rigorous review process in which each paper was reviewed by at least two members of the Program Committee in a single blind review process.

The Workshop on Artificial Intelligence for Sustainability (AI4S 2023) was held in Krakow in conjunction with the European Conference on Artificial Intelligence (ECAI 2023) on September 30 and October 1, 2023. During these very interesting two days, we had three invited talks on very timely topics:

- In Search for Model-Driven eXplainable Artificial Intelligence by Prof. Antoni Ligeza, AGH – University of Science and Technology, Krakow, Poland
- AI for fakes detection by Prof Mieczyslaw L. Owoc, University of Economics, Wroclaw, Poland, and
- Multi-Agent Systems and Sustainability by Prof. Anne Nowé, Vrije Universiteit Brussel, Belgium.

The original call for papers, workshop program, and other additional details can be found on the "AI4S 2023" website (https://sites.google.com/view/ai4s/home).

This workshop was organized by members of the IFIP Technical Committee 12 – AI. Members of the organizing committee, Karl Mason and Abdul Wahid were supported by Science Foundation Ireland under Grant number [21/FFPA/9040].

Thanks to all authors, the workshop chairs, local organizers, ECAI, funding agencies and workshop attendees for making this workshop a success.

Organization

Workshop Chairs and Organizing Committee

Eunika Mercier-Laurent	University of Reims Champagne Ardenne, France
Gülgün Kayakutlu	Istanbul Technical University, Turkey
Mieczyslaw Lech Owoc	Wroclaw University of Economics and Business, Poland
Karl Mason	University of Galway, Ireland
Abdul Wahid	University of Galway, Ireland

Local Representatives

Weronika T. Adrian	AGH University of Science and Technology, Poland
Krzysztof Kluza	AGH University of Science and Technology, Poland

Program Committee

Imene Brigui	Ecole de Management, Lyon, France
Noël Conruyt	University La Reunion, France
Anne Dourgnon	EDF, France
Konstantin M. Golubev	General Knowledge Machine Research Group, Ukraine
Knut Hinkelmann	University of Applied Sciences, Switzerland
Mario Lazoche	University Nancy I, France
Antoni Ligeza	AGH University of Science and Technology, Poland
Nada Matta	Universite de Technologie de Troyes, France
Cristina Monsone	University of Gyor, Hungary
Maciej Pondel	Wroclaw University of Economics and Business, Poland
Otthein Herzog	Universitaet Bremen, Germany
Vincent Ribiere	Bangkok University, Thailand
Michael Stankosky	George Washington University, USA
Frederique Second	Inria, France
Guillermo R. Simari	Universidad Nacional del Sur, Argentina

Adesina Simon Sodiya	Federal University of Agriculture, Abeokuta, Nigeria
Junlin Lu	University of Galway, Ireland
Eric Thivant	University of Lyon 3, France
Hiroshi Takeda	Osaka University, Japan
Mario Tokoro	Keio University, Tokyo, Japan
Caroline Wintergerst	University of Lyon 3, France
Krystian Wojtkiewicz	Wroclaw University of Science and Technology, Poland
Janusz Wojtusiak	George Mason University, Fairfax, USA
Rachael Shaw	Atlantic Technological University, Ireland
Daniel Kelly	University of Galway, Ireland

Go-Explore for Residential Energy Management

Junlin Lu(✉), Patrick Mannion, and Karl Mason

University of Galway, Galway, Ireland
J.Lu5@nuigalway.ie, {patrick.mannion,karl.mason}@universityofgalway.ie

Abstract. Reinforcement learning is commonly applied in residential energy management, particularly for optimizing energy costs. However, RL agents often face challenges when dealing with deceptive and sparse rewards in the energy control domain, especially with stochastic rewards. In such situations, thorough exploration becomes crucial for learning an optimal policy. Unfortunately, the exploration mechanism can be misled by deceptive reward signals, making thorough exploration difficult. Go-Explore is a family of algorithms which combines planning methods and reinforcement learning methods to achieve efficient exploration. We use the Go-Explore algorithm to solve the cost-saving task in residential energy management problems and achieve an improvement of up to 19.84% compared to the well-known reinforcement learning algorithms.

Keywords: Residential Energy Management · Reinforcement Learning

1 Introduction

Reinforcement learning (RL) has been widely used in autonomous energy control problems [4,6,7,12,14]. It is a paradigm where the agent learns from the interaction with the environment and solves the optimal decision-making problem. It only needs a reward function to give feedback from the environment as the evaluation of its behavior, therefore it is crucial that reward functions are well designed.

In most RL applications in residential energy management, saving energy cost is always one of the most important tasks [5,8,16,17]. The reward function can be therefore constructed as feedback on the cost or the energy consumption. However, a raw cost reward function, e.g., directly using the cost as a reward, can lead the agent to local optima especially when intermittent renewable energy generation is incorporated. This is because such reward is highly stochastic and deceptive and the limit of the exploration mechanism cannot guarantee thorough exploration. The agent may occasionally find a relatively low price time interval and stay there forever even if there is a better price interval in the future as it may think this area in state space is the global optimum.

Supported by Irish Research Council & University of Galway.

S. Nowaczyk et al. (Eds.): ECAI 2023 Workshops, CCIS 1948, pp. 133–139, 2024.
https://doi.org/10.1007/978-3-031-50485-3_11

We use the cutting-edge algorithm Go-Explore [2,3], which combines planning and RL to achieve efficient exploration for the agent to find and robustify the policy in an environment with stochastic raw reward signals. To the best of our knowledge, this is the first application of the Go-Explore algorithm in energy management problems. Our experimental results show that the Go-Explore agent surpasses the performance of the baseline RL algorithms.

2 Background Knowledge

2.1 Markov Decision Process and Reinforcement Learning

A sequential control task is always modeled as a Markov decision process (MDP). MDPs are defined with a tuple $(\mathcal{S}, \mathcal{A}, \mathcal{T}, \mathcal{R}, \gamma)$ [15]. $\mathcal{S}$ and $\mathcal{A}$ are the state space and action space. They are the set of all possible situations the RL can see in the environment and all actions it can take. $\mathcal{T}$ is the transition dynamics of the environment. $\mathcal{R}$ is the reward function that defines the task and the feedback to the RL agent. γ is the discount factor for the agent to determine the importance of the long-term return.

RL is a method capable of solving the MDP when the transition $\mathcal{T}$ is unknown or partially known. In this work, we focus on model-free RL, where the agent learns through trial and error. This can be done either directly in a policy-based paradigm, indirectly in a value-based paradigm, or through a combination of both in an actor-critic paradigm. While different paradigms have been proposed, the ultimate goal remains the same: to maximize the cumulative reward. RL aims to learn the optimal policy that leads to the highest achievable cumulative reward by iteratively improving its behavior through interactions with the environment.

2.2 Go-Explore

While RL is supposed to be able to solve sequential control problems. It often struggles to learn an optimal policy when the environment is too complex to explore and the reward signal is sparse and deceptive. Ecoffet et al. mentioned that a thorough exploration can be the solution [3]. They pointed out that two main challenges in achieving efficient exploration are the phenomenon referred to as "detachment" and "derailment." These are the agent's tendency to forget how to return to previously discovered promising states, i.e. detachment, and failing to first return to the promising state and then start exploration from it, i.e. derailment. To handle those two challenges, they proposed a family of algorithms "Go-Explore" to simply memorize the promising cell (a cohesion of similar states) and firstly return to the state before exploration [2,3]. This means that the agent can always remember "good" cells. To be able to return to those cells, the Go-Explore algorithm requires a simulator that is capable of being reset to a specific cell. This feature allows the agent to revisit and explore promising cells more efficiently. There are two phases of the Go-Explore algorithm.

Phase 1: Explore Until Solve. The phase starts by sampling the initial cell from the archive and starts exploration. The Go-Explore agent explores the environment as a usual episode iteration and stores promising cells in the archive along the trajectory it goes through. When an episode ends, a new cell is sampled from the archive and the simulator is reset to one state in the cell and the agent starts exploring from it. During the new round of exploration, if it finds any new promising cell, it will store it in the archive. If the agent finds any better trajectory to an existing cell, it will update the archive. This process is repeated until the problem is solved. Note that the solution is not guaranteed to be optimal and still needs further robustification to improve it.

Phase 2: Robustification. After successfully finishing phase 1, there should be some high-standard trajectories. However, these trajectories are not optimal due to the stochasticity of the environment and the related general policy is yet learned. Phase 2 is to learn a policy that is able to imitate the same routine of the trajectory of the agent in Phase 1 and improve upon it.

3 Model

3.1 Residential Energy Consumption Model

To effectively manage residential energy loads, it is advantageous to categorize household appliances into different types. Residential loads can be classified into three categories mentioned in literature [8,9].

1. Shiftable loads.
   These are loads that can be rescheduled to take advantage of cheaper energy costs. Their operation time can be adjusted to align with periods of lower electricity prices.
2. Non-shiftable loads.
   Non-shiftable loads encompass essential appliances that cannot be rescheduled or turned off, such as refrigerators and alarm systems. They operate continuously and require a consistent power supply.
3. Controllable loads.
   Controllable loads refer to appliances where the power consumption can be flexibly adjusted by the user. This category includes appliances like air conditioners and lighting systems.

In the scheduling process, a reinforcement learning (RL) agent is employed to manage the shiftable loads, while the non-shiftable and controllable loads are referred to as "background loads". It is assumed that shiftable appliances operate at their rated power when switched on.

Household energy demand draws power from both the grid and renewable generation. To minimize costs, the agent prioritizes the utilization of energy sourced from renewable sources when it is available. The grid adopts a dynamic price scheme, see price detail in Sect. 4.1.

In this study, the selected shiftable appliance is the "Bosch WAJ28008GB Washing Machine," rated at 1 kW. We assume that the washing machine needs to operate for 2 h per day. If the agent fails to run the washing machine throughout the day, it will be compelled to operate during the final 2 h of the day.

3.2 Markov Decision Process Setup

In this section, we will present the construction of the MDP of this work.

State Space. The state space comprises several variables, including:

1. Price: Represents the last hour's dynamic average price of electricity from the grid.
2. Renewable generation: The amount of the average renewable generation in the last hour.
3. Background loads: Refers to the average background loads of the last hour.
4. Remaining task: The number of hours left for the shiftable load to operate.
5. Time by hour: Represents the current hour of the day.

Action Space. The action is a binary choice, where 0 is for not running and 1 is for running. If action 1 is picked, the appliance will start working based on the price, background loads, and renewable generation of this hour.

Reward Function. This is a single-objective RL problem, therefore the only reward function we used is the hourly cost.

$$r_t = -price_t \cdot max[p_t^s + p_t^b - p_t^r, 0] \tag{1}$$

where $price_t$ is the electricity price at time t, p_t^s is the power of shiftable loads, p_t^b and p_t^r is the power of background loads and renewable generation separately. The reward is calculated by multiplying the price of electricity at time t by the maximum value between $(p_t^s + p_t^b - p_t^r)$ and 0. This formulation encourages minimizing the total power consumption and maximizing the utilization of renewable generation, as a higher cost for the maximum term will result in a higher penalty.

3.3 Go-Explore Model

The details of the Go-Explore model are presented in this section. The Go-Explore archive stores three types of entries, e.g. the cell, the trajectory leads to the cell, and cell-related information, i.e. a tuple $(number\ of\ visits, cost)$. $number\ of\ visits$ is the number of how many times this cell is visited, and $cost$ is the energy cost of the trajectory. Each cell representation is the tuple $(remaining\ task, time\ by\ hour)$.

Phase 1: Explore Until Solve

1. **Sample a cell from the archive:** There is only one initial cell stored in the archive. As the episode proceeds, there are more cells added to the archive. Then the cell will be sampled with the probability calculated from the scores. In this work, we use a plain score that is the reciprocal of the number of visits. All cells' score is normalized to fit in the [0, 1] interval as a probability distribution.

2. **Explore from the sampled cell:** The simulator is reset to the sampled cell, and randomly samples actions as exploration from that cell.
3. **Update the archive:** The archive is updated if a better trajectory is found or a new cell is found. In this work, a better trajectory is the trajectory that resulted in less cost to reach the cell than the original trajectory.
4. **Repeat** the aforementioned three steps until the problem is solved.

We separate the robustification phase into two parts: policy cloning and robustification. This is to provide a training process on a higher granularity.
Phase 2.1: Policy Cloning. A PPO agent is trained by simply imitating the demonstration from Phase 1. It does not know anything about the true reward signal but will receive a reward of 1 if the next state is aligned with the demonstration, otherwise, the reward is 0. The agent trained in this phase is noted as "Go-Explore (no robustification)".
Phase 2.2: Robustification. With the policy cloning agent, we further train it with a true reward signal. The agent trained in this phase is noted as "Go-Explore (robustification)".

4 Experiment

4.1 Datasets

We use two datasets used in the work of Lu et al. [8].

- **Electricity Price:** The dataset for electricity prices is sourced from the PJM dataset [11]. The training data covers the period from 01/05/2021 00:00 to 02/05/2021 00:00. The evaluation data spans one month, starting from 01/05/2021 00:00 to 31/05/2021 00:00.
- **Background Load and Renewable Generation:** The renewable generation and background load is sourced from the Smart* dataset for Sustainability within the "Home C" of UMass dataset [1]. The training data covers the period from 01/05/2014 00:00 to 02/05/2014 00:00. The evaluation data spans one month, starting from 01/05/2014 00:00 to 31/05/2014 00:00.

4.2 Baseline Algorithm

We two renowned RL algorithms as the baseline, i.e. proximal policy optimization (PPO) [13] and deep Q-network (DQN) [10]. Both algorithms have been instrumental in solving challenging decision-making problems in diverse domains. We also use the PPO algorithm for the policy cloning and robustification phase in our Go-Explore implementation that shares the same hyperparameters as the pure PPO agent. The learning rates for PPO and DQN are all 0.001, while the discount factor is 1 and the batch size is 64. The other hyperparameters are detailed in Table 1.

Table 1. Hyperparameters

Alg.	Number of Episodes	Hidden Layer	KL-target	Entropy Weight
PPO	60	[32, 32, 32]	0.01	0.001
DQN	5000	[32, 32, 16]	-	-

5 Result and Discussion

Table 2 presents the results of the Go-Explore algorithm and the baselines. The monthly cost values are denoted in Euro (€). The cost-saving column specifically compares the results of the "Go-Explore (robustification)" simulation with the other three simulations. It showcases the absolute value of cost saving and the relative improvement of cost saving compared to the DQN-agent cost. The Go-Explore (robustification) agent saves €18.98 which reduced 19.84% cost than the DQN agent, achieving the highest saving in simulations. It is noted that the improvement between the versions with/without robustification is very close. This is because the environment is relatively deterministic as the action can only influence a limited number of states so the agent cannot exploit many benefits in the robustification phase. However, if the stochasticity of the transition increase, e.g. in a multi-agent setting, a robustification version can be better.

Table 2. Experiment Result

Algorithm	Cost Saving vs. DQN-agent (€95.65)
PPO	€16.49 (17.23%)
Go-Explore (no robustification)	€18.97 (19.83%)
Go-Explore (robustification)	€18.98 (19.84%)

6 Conclusion

We use the Go-Explore algorithm to solve the cost-saving task in residential energy management and have achieved a cost-saving of up to 19.84%. The combination of planning and RL is promising in hard-exploration real-life problems. Future extensions of this work can be:

- Apply the "policy-based Go-Explore" [3] to improve the training efficiency.
- Extension of the environment to a multi-agent environment.

References

1. Barker, S., et al.: Smart*: an open data set and tools for enabling research in sustainable homes. SustKDD **111**(112), 108 (2012)
2. Ecoffet, A., Huizinga, J., Lehman, J., Stanley, K.O., Clune, J.: Go-explore: a new approach for hard-exploration problems. arXiv preprint arXiv:1901.10995 (2019)
3. Ecoffet, A., Huizinga, J., Lehman, J., Stanley, K.O., Clune, J.: First return, then explore. Nature **590**(7847), 580–586 (2021)
4. Glavic, M., Fonteneau, R., Ernst, D.: Reinforcement learning for electric power system decision and control: past considerations and perspectives. IFAC-PapersOnLine **50**(1), 6918–6927 (2017)
5. Haq, E.U., Lyu, C., Xie, P., Yan, S., Ahmad, F., Jia, Y.: Implementation of home energy management system based on reinforcement learning. Energy Rep. **8**, 560–566 (2022)
6. Huang, C., Zhang, H., Wang, L., Luo, X., Song, Y.: Mixed deep reinforcement learning considering discrete-continuous hybrid action space for smart home energy management. J. Mod. Power Syst. Clean Energy **10**(3), 743–754 (2022)
7. Ilager, S., Ramamohanarao, K., Buyya, R.: Thermal prediction for efficient energy management of clouds using machine learning. IEEE Trans. Parallel Distrib. Syst. **32**(5), 1044–1056 (2020)
8. Lu, J., Mannion, P., Mason, K.: A multi-objective multi-agent deep reinforcement learning approach to residential appliance scheduling. IET Smart Grid **5**(4), 260–280 (2022)
9. Lu, R., Hong, S.H., Yu, M.: Demand response for home energy management using reinforcement learning and artificial neural network. IEEE Trans. Smart Grid **10**(6), 6629–6639 (2019)
10. Mnih, V., et al.: Human-level control through deep reinforcement learning. Nature **518**(7540), 529–533 (2015)
11. PJM: 2021 PJM dataset (2021). https://dataminer2.pjm.com/feed/rt_fivemin_mnt_lmps. https://www.pjm.com/markets-and-operations
12. Ren, M., Liu, X., Yang, Z., Zhang, J., Guo, Y., Jia, Y.: A novel forecasting based scheduling method for household energy management system based on deep reinforcement learning. Sustain. Urban Areas **76**, 103207 (2022)
13. Schulman, J., Wolski, F., Dhariwal, P., Radford, A., Klimov, O.: Proximal policy optimization algorithms. arXiv preprint arXiv:1707.06347 (2017)
14. Shuvo, S.S., Yilmaz, Y.: Home energy recommendation system (HERS): a deep reinforcement learning method based on residents' feedback and activity. IEEE Trans. Smart Grid **13**(4), 2812–2821 (2022)
15. Sutton, R.S., Barto, A.G.: Reinforcement Learning: An Introduction. MIT Press (2018)
16. Xu, X., Jia, Y., Xu, Y., Xu, Z., Chai, S., Lai, C.S.: A multi-agent reinforcement learning-based data-driven method for home energy management. IEEE Trans. Smart Grid **11**(4), 3201–3211 (2020)
17. Yu, L., et al.: Deep reinforcement learning for smart home energy management. IEEE Internet Things J. **7**(4), 2751–2762 (2019)

Remote Learning Technologies in Achieving the Fourth Sustainable Development Goal

Iwona Chomiak-Orsa[1(✉)] and Klaudia Smolag[2]

[1] Wroclaw University of Economics, 118/120 Wroclaw, Komandorska, Poland
iwona.chomiak@ue.wroc.pl

[2] Czestochowa University of Technology, 69 Czestochowa, Dabrowskiego, Poland

Abstract. The Sustainable Development Goals (SDGs) defined in the UN resolution guide the development and socio-economic transformation that should be achieved by 2030. One of the defined goals is to ensure access to quality education and promote lifelong learning. The problem of universal access to education in developed countries may seem to be of little concern because, systemically, every child is subject to compulsory schooling. However, if one looks at the problem of the quality of educational processes and the creation of educational solutions to support development at every stage of life, the picture changes greatly. The increasing use of AI in educational processes using simulation and gamification is also an important factor influencing the development of educational tools and processes.

As a contribution to the discussion in this area, the authors of this article wished to present the results of a study which presents the impact of the development of distance learning technologies on the accessibility of teaching and the educational offerings of universities in the 2020–2022 pandemic period.

The research conducted as well as the conclusions of this research provided the impetus to broaden the research perspective to include new problems. This contributed to the formulation of further research questions, enabling a more holistic view of the problem of achieving the fourth sustainable development goal of providing quality education and promoting lifelong learning. In this article, the authors present a synthesis of the results of the conducted research on the scope of educational needs of young adults, professionally active and studying part-time. The research conducted for this article used research tools such as a literature analysis and a survey conducted in two sections.

Keywords: distance learning · sustainability · education processes · machine learning

1 Introduction

The development of information and communication technologies has not only changed the accessibility of information. The creation of tools that make it possible to communicate in any situation, at any time of the day and from anywhere has introduced a new

S. Nowaczyk et al. (Eds.): ECAI 2023 Workshops, CCIS 1948, pp. 140–147, 2024.
https://doi.org/10.1007/978-3-031-50485-3_12

quality in the implementation of business, educational, administrative or private processes. The spread of technology has met the needs arising from the 2015 UN resolution setting the directions for socio-economic change in the 2030 perspective. The development and increased availability of information and communication technologies has created unique opportunities for improving the quality and accessibility of educational services. We could observe this process during the outbreak of the pandemic, which forced a kind of revolution in the ways in which educational processes are conducted. Education, which made only marginal use of ICT to develop its offer towards e-learning and distance learning, evolved 100% into remote processes in the face of the pandemic and the compulsion of social isolation - from traditionally delivered processes - in an extremely short time.

The evolution in the area of educational processes has not only altered the quality of these processes but, above all, has contributed to an increase in the range of educational services and the creation and dissemination of new forms of education. This trend meets and fits in with the UN agenda in the context of the fourth goal indicating the need to provide quality education for all and to promote and enable lifelong learning. The evolution of educational services determined by the development of information and communication technologies has changed the perspective on the perception of learning processes and the educational needs of society. There is an increasing emphasis on creating lifelong learning attitudes. In addition, the development of technology necessitates continuous learning and upgrading of one's competences, especially digital competences. Digitalization, automation and the use of artificial intelligence exclude direct human involvement in production processes - this contributes to the disappearance of professions on the one hand and the creation of new, previously unknown ones on the other. It is safe to say that the development of communication technologies used in educational processes influences the implementation of the fourth goal of the UN resolution. The above determinants contributed to the authors' formulation of the research questions:

Q1.: how do ICTs influence changes in educational provision, especially in educational provision for adults?

Q2.: how have the educational needs of young adults changed over the last two years?

To answer the above research questions, the authors conducted a research procedure. The first stage of the research process was to analyse the literature available in scopus and google scholar databases. In order to verify the theoretical considerations, the authors planned a two-stage research on a group of 230 part-time IwB students, EU in Wroclaw. In the first stage, first-year students of the faculty were surveyed in 2020. The second stage of research was planned and conducted two years later, i.e. in 2022, among the same group of students who were currently in their third year of studies at the Faculty of Business Informatics, EU in Wroclaw. Synthetic research results and conclusions will be presented in the following sections of the article. However, a detailed analysis of the results of the conducted research will be the subject of further publications by the authors.

Due to the guidelines of the article, the authors only marginally touch upon the problem of applying AI in educational processes. Instead, they consider the application of

AI in educational processes to be an extremely important problem and plan to undertake further research dedicated to this very topic.

2 Theoretical Background

2.1 Sustainable Development

Because of rapid economic change, technological progress, urbanisation and industrialisation, the environment has been devastated and ecosystems disturbed. This has determined the need to search for concepts, strategies that enable economic development while caring for the environment and natural conditions. The concept of sustainable development, which was first formulated in a UN report (WCED) in 1987, emerged from these values (Katila et al., 2019; Allen et al., 2018) This report started a trend in both scientific research and business strategies, which assumed that development activities should be undertaken with particular consideration for the environment and equality issues. A follow-up to the 1987 report is the 2030 Agenda for Sustainable Development, adopted in 2015 by 193 UN countries, which, by defining 17 Sustainable Development Goals (SDGs) and associated 169 targets, points to actions that should take place in three dimensions: economic, social and environmental (Pizzi et al., 2020; Pedersen, 2018; Mukarram, 2020). Balancing the activities that condition economic growth with attention to environmental aspects is the most commonly discussed issue in the literature. However, issues related to the implementation of social measures such as equalisation of opportunities, reduction of social exclusion or the problem of developing, improving the quality and increasing the accessibility of educational processes for all social groups regardless of age are addressed much less frequently. This problem is defined in the fourth goal of Agenda 2030. Much attention is paid to improving the quality and development of educational processes for children and young people. Less attention, h**owever, is focused on building '**lifelong learning' attitudes and implementing solutions to support such attitudes (Chankseliani, McCowan, 2021). The trend of virtualisation of educational processes and implementation of e-learning meets the expectations resulting from the above guidelines. The creation of an increasingly broader educational offer for adults, which is available via platforms and does not require direct participation in workshops, significantly increases the accessibility of educational processes for a wider audience (Nowacka & Rzemieniak 2022). The promotion of self-development courses, educationally proactive social attitudes, in the long term will not only enable the realisation of the objectives arising from goal 4, but will also contribute to the creation of a more informed society in the other areas defined in the 2030 Agenda.

2.2 Education in Business Strategies

One of the attributes of a developed economy is a well-structured education system, both at the level of compulsory and supplementary education. Moreover, highly developed societies are characterised by an attention to the continuous improvement of qualifications and social competences. Technological progress, which can be observed in every area of life, forces people to continuously improve their skills and competences. On the other hand, technological progress is becoming a determinant for the creation of new professions while others are disappearing. This becomes a determinant for adults in the search for knowledge and competences in new professional spaces. The problem of employee improvement and professional development is not only part of sustainable development strategies, but is also becoming a requirement for the development and improvement of organizations. Creating employee development plans, creating promotion paths or motivating employees by creating training offerings that enable employee self-development is becoming one of the most important elements of an organisation's development strategy (Jelonek, Chomiak-Orsa 2018;). Simulation tools for learning and development processes are increasingly being used in the modelling of employee development paths (Chomiak-Orsa 2020). Artificial intelligence tools using predictive algorithms are used to support the selection of competences that are most expected by the employee, but can also determine a better place for the employee in the labour market.

On the other hand, AI can be used to model educational processes according to reported changes in the preferences and expectations of educational process stakeholders. The increasing use of deep learning tools makes it possible to develop educational offerings without much teacher intervention. These trends in the use of advanced IT solutions may become the future in the development of educational offerings, especially for adult audiences.

As a result, employees have the opportunity to improve their skills either through training provided by their workplace or by choosing training in the market and applying for a subsidy from their employer. Such facilities change the employee's perspective on their contribution to the organisation in which they work. Yet another group are adults who participate in educational processes because they adopt a 'lifelong learning' philosophy in life (Kopnina, 2020). For these people, the most important thing is to raise their awareness and knowledge, which is not necessarily related to their working life and the improvement of their professional competences.

The above self-development processes and strategies for improvement through employee education are supported by a growing number of offers and an increasing range of educational services. Particularly large changes in this market were caused by the pandemic period, which contributed to the acceleration of educational services delivered in virtual processes (Rashid, 2019; Ashari et al., 2021; Averar et al. 2019). The pandemic period forced the transition to virtualisation of educational processes 100%, this changed the shape of the market for educational services but also the attitudes of the recipients of this group of products. The increase in the availability of educational services through the virtualisation of access was part of the trend to disseminate and improve the quality of educational services and promote lifelong learning attitudes stemming from the fourth goal of the 2015 UN Agenda.

2.3 Distance Learning Technologies

As a result of the development of information and communication technologies, the implementation of the fourth goal of sustainable development has gained a different perspective of implementation and much broader possibilities. The aim of modern educational processes is to teach students both the substantive content of a given theoretical area but also to improve competence in the use of developing technologies (Semenets-Orlova et al., 2019; Zhang et al. Al., 2020; Hajduova et al. 2020). The remote form of teaching makes it possible to deprecate geographical access barriers, expand the educational offer and make it more accessible at a time convenient for the student. All the above-mentioned advantages of remote educational processes increase the accessibility of educational processes for all groups of potential recipients. Remote learning has become one of the widely available forms of education that allows the learning process to be implemented regardless of the time and space constraints of the audience, which is particularly important for adults. The most intensive development of remote learning took place during the COVID-19 pandemic (Chomiak-Orsa & Smolag 2022). The basis of remote learning is now Internet access, applications that enable teaching and learning and computer equipment (laptop, computer, microphone, camera), which is defined as e-learning. During the pandemic, there was a significant development of ICT solutions that supported remote education, both at the stage of creation of learning materials and delivery and communication between teachers and learners. As proposed by D. H. Taylor, ICT technologies that can support learning opportunities in five different types of e-learning can be divided into:

- self-study lessons,
- virtual classrooms,
- simulations and virtual worlds,
- online collaboration,
- online resources.

Increasingly, the above technological solutions use artificial intelligence algorithms to personalize content for learners which makes e-learning processes even more attractive.

3 Research Methodology

3.1 Research Tools

To write the first part of the article, literature research was carried out in the form of snowballing and in-depth analysis of abstracts. The second part of the article contains a synthetic description of the results of the survey research. The research tool used was anonymous questionnaires, sent to a targeted group of respondents. The respondents were part-time students of the Wroclaw University of Economics.

3.2 Research Procedure

1. selection of the group of respondents,
2. preparation of survey form.
3. implementation of the survey - October 2020,
4. validation of the collected results, rejection of wrongly filled in questionnaires.
5. analysis of results, conclusions from the first survey.
6. survey of the same group of respondents - October 2022.
7. validation of the collected results, rejection of wrongly filled in questionnaires.
8. analysis of results.
9. development of research conclusions.

4 Empirical Results and Discussion

4.1 Results

The aim of the first stage of the survey was to identify the demand for supplementary educational processes among students of part-time studies at UEW. The questionnaire was divided into factual blocks, which respectively collected information on: the metrics of respondents, the characteristics of the employer, the range of training offered by the employer, the educational needs of respondents, the characteristics of time spent on supplementary education. The first stage of the research was intended by the authors to provide information about the educational needs, types of training available in remote, hybrid or traditional form for respondents and to identify potential attitudes of respondents towards lifelong learning processes. The second stage of the research was carried out using the same survey form. The aim of the survey was to analyse changes both in the educational offer available on the market and in the attitudes of respondents. Only selected results of the survey will be presented below, primarily indicating the range of remote training offerings available to respondents in the surveyed periods, as well as respondents' potential needs and their willingness to devote their free time to selected educational processes.

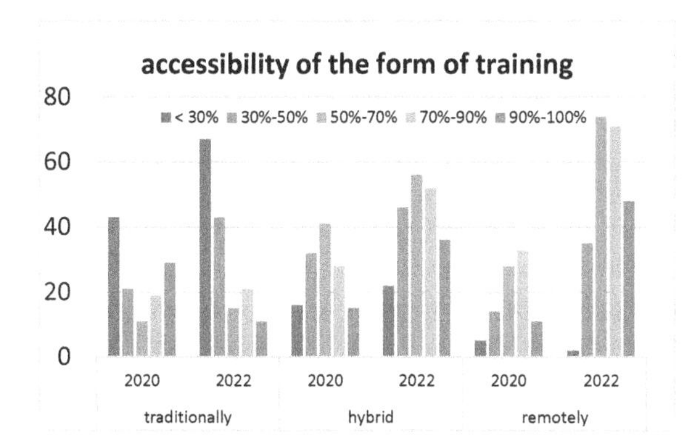

Fig. 1. .

As Fig. 1 indicates, the offer of remotely delivered education has definitely increased between 2020 and 2022. As late as 2020, respondents could still choose between the form of training delivery, while in 2022 the offer of training delivered in the traditional way has definitely decreased.

Figure 2 shows the potential interest and involvement of respondents in allocating their free time to training. As can be seen, the majority of respondents indicated that they would definitely choose training carried out remotely, devoting on average around 8 h per quarter to it - which can be taken as one longer training course of several days per year.

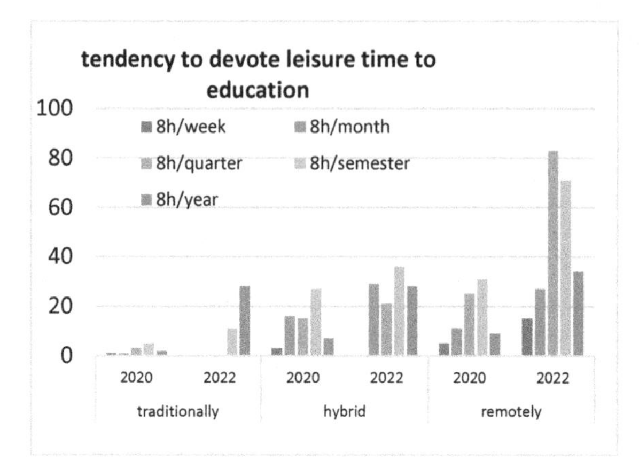

Fig. 2. .

4.2 Discussion

In the previous section of the article, the results of the answers obtained from only two blocks were presented. The authors decided to choose just these two in order to illustrate the prevailing trends in the attitudes of young adults concerning the forms of decision-making and the amount of time they are willing to devote to raising their competences. It is important to add that the above questions related to the educational processes of the training courses the respondents would opt for outside of the training offered at their workplace. The trend shows an increased interest in educational processes, especially those offered remotely.

It is significant that this trend reflects an evolution in the attitudes of young adults, which is correlated with the sustainable development guidelines defined by the fourth objective of the Agenda. Adopting a philosophy of lifelong learning is becoming a natural lifestyle. This is becoming a determinant of the increase in respondents' expectations in terms of educational provision.

5 Conclusion

The Sustainable Development Goals (SDGs) defined by the UN in 2015 indicate the expected directions of socio-economic change. The holistic approach to development that resonates from these directives is very important for the future fate of not only the societies of individual countries, but for our entire planet as a single ecosystem. Many scientific publications as well as business studies point to the importance of sustainability in terms of natural resource management, poverty alleviation, social or livelihood disparities. However, little attention is paid to the change in awareness, which takes place in very slow processes. Therefore, the authors of this article believe that problems related to changing attitudes primarily in the educational field may be crucial for the implementation of the remaining guidelines of the UN agenda.

The results presented in the article represent only a small part of the research conducted. Individual sections of the study will be presented more extensively in subsequent articles.

References

Allen, C., Metternicht, G., Wiedmann, T.: Initial progress in implementing the sustainable development goals (SDGs): a review of evidence from countries. Sustain. Sci. **13**, 1453–1467 (2018)

Ashari, H., Abbas, I., Abdul-Talib, A.N., Mohd Zamani, S.N.: Entrepreneurship and sustainable development goals: a multigroup analysis of the moderating effects of entrepreneurship education on entrepreneurial intention. Sustainability **14**(1), 431 (2021)

Avelar, A.B.A., da Silva-Oliveira, K.D., da Silva Pereira, R.: Education for advancing the implementation of the sustainable development goals: a systematic approach. Int. J. Manag. Educ. **17**(3), 100322 (2019)

Chankseliani, M., McCowan, T.: Higher education and the sustainable development goals. High. Educ. **81**(1), 1–8 (2021)

Chomiak-Orsa, I.: Intelligent personalization – the result of the evolution of web solutions. In: Soliman, K.S. (eds.) Education Excellence and Innovation Management: A 2025 Vision to Sustain Economic Development During Global Challenges, pp. 18038–18048 (2020)

Chomiak-Orsa, I., Smoląg, K.: E-learning w czasie pandemii Covid-19: pozytywne aspekty i bariery zdalnej nauki z perspektywy studentów. Organ. Manag. **191**(2), 231–241 (2022)

Hajduová, Z., Smoląg, K., Szajt, M., Bednárová, L.: Digital competences of polish and Slovak students—comparative analysis in the light of empirical research. Sustainability **12**(18), 7739 (2020)

Jelonek, D., Chomiak-Orsa, I.: The application of modern teaching methods as the development determinant of personal and interpersonal competences of students – Future Employees; Edulearn Proceedings, pp. 5259–5266 (2018)

Jelonek, D., Wioletta, S.: Effect of Personalization of E-learning on Learning Effectiveness in University Students. Edulearn Proceedings, pp. 961–969 (2018)

Katila, P., Colfer, C.J.P., De Jong, W., Galloway, G., Pacheco, P., Winkel, G.: (Eds.) Sustainable development goals. Cambridge University Press (2019)

Kopnina, H.: Education for the future? Critical evaluation of education for sustainable development goals. J. Environ. Educ. **51**(4), 280–291 (2020)

Mukarram, M.: Impact of COVID-19 on the UN sustainable development goals (SDGs). Strateg. Anal. **44**(3), 253–258 (2020)

Pedersen, C.S.: The UN sustainable development goals (SDGs) are a great gift to business! Procedia Cirp **69**, 21–24 (2018)

Nowacka, A., Rzemieniak, M.: The Impact of the VUCA environment on the digital competences of managers in the power industry. Energies **15**(1), 1–17 (2022)

Pizzi, S., Caputo, A., Corvino, A., Venturelli, A.: Management research and the UN sustainable development goals (SDGs): a bibliometric investigation and systematic review. J. Clean. Prod. **276**, 124033 (2020)

Rashid, L.: Entrepreneurship education and sustainable development goals: a literature review and a closer look at fragile states and technology-enabled approaches. Sustainability **11**(19), 5343 (2019)

Semenets-Orlova, I., Teslenko, V., Dakal, A., Zadorozhnyi, V., Marusina, O., Klochko, A.: Distance learning technologies and innovations in education for sustainable development. Stud. Appl. Econ. **39**(5) (2021)

Zhang, T., Shaikh, Z.A., Yumashev, A.V., Chłąd, M.: Applied model of E-learning in the framework of education for sustainable development. Sustainability **12**(16), 6420 (2020)

Fairlearn Parity Constraints for Mitigating Gender Bias in Binary Classification Models – Comparative Analysis

Andrzej Małowiecki[(✉)] and Iwona Chomiak-Orsa

Wrocław University of Economics and Business, Wrocław, Poland
andrzej.malowiecki@ue.wroc.pl

Abstract. Inequality is one of the problems of the modern world. Discrimination of various kinds can affect many areas of life. The growing importance of data in the modern world makes it all the more important to ensure that the methods used to analyze it do not return results in which unfairness is present. Unfortunately, there may be situations where there is unfairness in the predictions of machine learning models. In recent years, several IT solutions have been developed to mitigate this phenomenon. One of them is Fairlearn, a Python library dedicated to this type of task. This article presents a comparative analysis of parity constraints used in Fairlearn algorithms. The purpose of this article is to identify which of the constraints is best suited for mitigating gender bias in binary classification models. The following research methods were used: literature review, experiment and comparative analysis. The evaluation of constraints will be based on the value of measures: disparity in recall and disparity in selection rate for the column containing information about the person's gender. The values of these measures, achieved by binary classification models in which the Threshold Optimizer algorithm with selected parity constraints was implemented, will be compared in order to identify which of the Fairlearn parity constraints is best suited for mitigating gender bias in binary classification models.

Keywords: Fairlearn · parity constraints · gender bias

1 Introduction

In today's world, decisions made by machine learning models have a significant impact on human life. Therefore, it is crucial that the predictions of the created models are reliable and devoid of various types of social biases. Situations in which the negative decision of the model was mainly influenced by characteristics such as age, gender, race or origin are unfair and against the established sustainability goals.

Among many solutions created in order to mitigate this problem there is Fairlearn, an open-source, community-driven project with an associated Python library. Originally, it was created with the purpose of helping to mitigate unfairness in machine learning models (Dudik et al., 2020). This library provides access to various types of algorithms and parity constraints that can be used on different types of machine learning models.

S. Nowaczyk et al. (Eds.): ECAI 2023 Workshops, CCIS 1948, pp. 148–154, 2024.
https://doi.org/10.1007/978-3-031-50485-3_13

The purpose of this article is to identify which of the constraints is best suited for mitigating gender bias in binary classification models. The following research methods were used: literature review, experiment and comparative analysis. The evaluation of constraints will be based on the value of measures: disparity in recall and disparity in selection rate for the column containing information about the person's gender. The values of these measures will be compared in order to identify which of the Fairlearn parity constraints is best suited for mitigating gender bias in binary classification models.

2 Gender Bias in Machine Learning Models

Nowadays, the need for sustainable development is being increasingly promoted, especially by the youngest generations (Rzemieniak, Wawer, 2021). In this regard the problem of reducing inequalities becomes one of the biggest challenges of today's world. Among 17 sustainable development goals, 2 of them were established with the purpose of overcoming this problem:

- goal 5 – gender equality,
- goal 10 – reduced inequalities (SDG FUND, 2015).

Nowadays the use of machine learning in decision-making processes is becoming more widespread, covering a variety of fields (Butryn et al., 2021). With the growing role of this technology in everyday life, it is important to ensure that the model adheres to these sustainable development goals. This means that no sensitive characteristics should affect predictions made by them. Unfortunately, there are examples where models tend to make unfair or biased predictions (Barocas, Hardt, Narayanan, 2017, Mittelstadt, Wachter, Russell, 2023, Yang, Wang, Ton, 2023). There are many factors that can affect a model's fairness, including ethnicity, gender, age or race (Mehrabi et al., 2021).

This article focuses on gender bias in machine learning models. This type of unfairness was identified in numerous algorithms. One of the examples is an algorithm that was used in order to deliver ads, designed with the purpose of promoting job opportunities in the Science, Technology, Engineering and Math fields. Even though the ads were supposed to be gender-neutral, the majority of viewers were men. The simple explanation of this behaviour would be that the algorithm just imitated supposed user behaviour, which means that, due to the fact that women were supposedly less likely to click on an ad, it was displayed to fewer of them. This assumption turned out to be incorrect because women were more likely to click on an ad after it was displayed to them (Lambrecht, Tucker, 2019). This means that there were other reasons which can be summarized as a difference in "price" between both demographics. For a given example, women were considered a "prized demographic" due to the fact that they are more likely to engage with advertising than men, even though the stereotypical assumption can be made that these types of ads would not interest them (Lambrecht, Tucker, 2019).

There are two factors that allow users to check whether models learning model are making unfair predictions:

- disparity in predictions – predictions comparison for each group within a selected sensitive feature, measured using selection rate,

- disparity in prediction performance – predictive performance metrics comparison for each group within a selected sensitive feature (Microsoft, 2023).

When any of the disparity values is significant, then the assumption can be made that the given model is lacking fairness. The reason for this may be, e.g., data imbalance, indirect correlation between features or other societal biases. Correct identification of the reason is very important when implementing mitigation methods.

3 Fairlearn Overview

Fairlearn was originally started in 2018 as a Python package created for the purpose of a connected research paper by Miro Dudik with the aim of providing data scientists with a toolkit to mitigate unfairness in their machine learning models (Dudik et al., 2020).

The basis of fairness consists of two types of algorithms that allow unfairness mitigation in machine learning models:

- postprocessing algorithms – algorithms that transform predictions created by a trained model, e.g., Threshold Optimizer, which establishes different decision thresholds for each group within a selected sensitive feature so that the model complies with the selected constraint,
- reduction algorithms – algorithms that iteratively re-weight data points and retrain the model in order for the final version of it to have the best performance and at the same time comply with the selected constraint, e.g., Exponentiated Gradient or Grid Search (Dudik et al., 2020).

Both types have advantages and disadvantages that make their use vary depending on the given use case. In general, reduction algorithms are more flexible and compliant due to the fact that they allow the use of a wider range of metrics and do not require access to sensitive features during deployment (which often can be forbidden by the law) (Dudik et al., 2020). On the other hand, postprocessing algorithms are easier and faster to use due to the fact that there is no need to make any changes to the model, just to its predictions.

Besides algorithms, Fairlearn consists of other features that are designed with the purpose of helping people detect and mitigate unfairness in machine learning models, e.g., special metrics like selection rate, which is used to measure the proportion of positive predictions for each group within a selected sensitive feature (Microsoft, 2023, Pandey, 2022).

4 Fairlearn Parity Constraints

In Fairlearn, parity constraints are constraints that a model has to satisfy in order for it to be considered fair. There are different types of constraints that are designed in a way so that the user is able to choose whichever is best suitable for the given machine learning task and specific fairness criteria[1].

[1] Available parity constraints are mostly algorithm-agnostic, which means that they should be able to work with both types of Fairlearn algorithms. One of the exceptions is error rate parity, which is a constraint example that works only with reduction algorithms.

Among many available Fairlearn parity constraints, ones that will be used for the purpose of this article are:

- Demographic parity – constraint designed to assure that an equal number of positive predictions is being made for each group within a selected sensitive feature,
- True positive rate parity – constraint designed to assure that a comparable proportion of true positive predictions is being made for each group within a selected sensitive feature,
- False positive rate parity – constraint designed to assure that a comparable proportion of false positive predictions is being made for each group within a selected sensitive feature,
- Equalized odds – constraint designed to assure that a comparable proportion of true positive and false positive predictions is being made for each group within a selected sensitive feature (Dudik et al., 2020).

Some of the selected constraints are designed for the purpose of reducing specific unfairness factors, e.g., the use of demographic parity should reduce mainly the disparity in the model's predictions, while equalized odds should concentrate on reducing the disparity in its prediction performance. A conducted experiment should give an answer if that will be the case in this instance.

5 Comparative Analysis of Fairlearn Parity Constraints for Mitigating Gender Bias in Binary Classification Models

Machine learning models are used for the purpose of supporting the decision-making process in many areas, such as financial services, marketing or health care. Companies in every industry have the opportunity to benefit from the use of this technology in decision-making by using its models in the hiring process. As machine learning algorithms are increasingly being used at every stage of this process, it is all the more important to ensure that the decisions they make are not unfair (Schumann et al., 2020).

5.1 Experiment Overview

For the following experiment, "Utrecht Fairness Recruitment dataset" dataset was selected. This dataset was created by Sieuwert van Otterloo, AI researcher at Vrije Universiteit and Utrecht University of Applied Sciences. The owner of it is Utrecht ICT Institute, which has made it available on Kaggle with a license: CC BY-SA 4.0 (Kaggle, 2023).

Selected dataset contains data on recruitment decisions of 4 companies. It consists of over 500 candidates who are described using attributes such as gender, age, nationality, sports background, university grade and previous working experience. A number of sensitive features (such as gender, age or nationality) makes this dataset an appropriate choice for the experiment.

The experiment will be conducted according to the following procedure:

1. Creation of a baseline binary classification model, using the decision tree algorithm.
2. Calculation of evaluation metrics for the baseline model.
3. Calculation of the disparity in evaluation metrics for gender groups in the baseline model.
4. Addition of a balancing index to the training dataset.
5. Creation of ThresholdOptimizer instances for selected parity constraints.
6. Calculation of evaluation metrics for ThresholdOptimizer instances.
7. Calculation of the disparity in evaluation metrics for gender groups in the ThresholdOptimizer instances.

5.2 Baseline Model

The first stage of the experiment was to create a binary classification model, using the decision tree algorithm. Before that, selected dataset was prepared for the given task, which means that all non-numerical attributes were converted using LabelEncoder and all rows with gender values different than "male" or "female" were removed[2]. It is important to mention that the selected dataset is imbalanced.

After preparation, the dataset was split into training and test sets at a ratio of 2:1. The training set was used during the process of learning the decision tree model. The test set was used to evaluate models using selected evaluation metrics: selection rate, accuracy, recall and precision. After evaluation, disparities in evaluation metrics for gender groups in the baseline model were calculated. Table 1 presents results of the baseline model evaluation.

Table 1. Baseline model evaluation results.

	selection rate	accuracy	recall	precision
female	0.252632	0.826316	0.655172	0.659722
male	0.330567	0.825726	0.710037	0.799163
disparity	0.077935	−0.000590	0.054865	0.139441

According to obtained evaluation results, there is a disparity between the values of selection rate and recall, which means that the model is slightly biased.

5.3 Comparative Analysis

After successful evaluation of the baseline model, the next step was to implement a balancing index into the dataset. This index is used to ensure that in the input there is an equal number of samples that produce the result of 0 and 1. The new, balanced dataset was split again into train and test sets at the same ratio as before.

[2] There was only one different value for gender – "other". It was removed due to the fact that there were fewer observations of it: 83 to 2127 for "male" and 1790 for "female".

The newly created train set was used to train ThresholdOptimizer instances, which were also using the originally trained model. Each of the 4 instances had different parity constraints implemented: demographic parity, true positive rate, false positive rate and equalized odds.

Created models were evaluated using selected evaluation metrics. After evaluation, disparities in evaluation metrics for gender groups were calculated for each of the models. Table 2 presents a comparison of disparities in selection rate and recall between all the models, including the baseline.

Table 2. Comparison of disparities in selection rate and recall between all the models.

	disparity in selection rate	disparity in recall
Baseline model	0.077935	0.054865
Demographic parity	0.006064	0.050224
True positive rate	0.0924	0.081528
False positive rate	0.088149	0.070914
Equalized odds	0.083999	0.049147

5.4 Summary

Among the selected constraints, demographic parity achieved the lowest value of disparity in selection rate and the second lowest value of disparity in recall. The lowest value of disparity in recall was achieved by equalized odds constraint. Besides demographic parity, none of the other constraints achieved a lower value of disparity in selection rate than the baseline model. Additionally, the true positive rate and false positive rate constraints achieved higher value of disparity in recall than in baseline models.

Selected evaluation criteria indicated demographic parity as the most suitable parity constraint for a given use case. The true positive rate and false positive rate parities were indicated as unsuitable due to the fact that they achieved higher values of both metrics than in the baseline model.

6 Conclusions

In this article the results of comparative analysis of Fairlearn parity constraints in binary classification models were presented. Created decision tree models were compared using disparity in selection rate and disparity in recall measures.

The comparative analysis indicated demographic parity constraint as most suitable for the given use case. The use of equalized odds can also be advised as the disparity in recall achieved by this constraint was better than in the baseline model. The true positive rate and false positive rate constraints achieved worse results than the baseline model, so the application of them for a given use case is not advised.

In future publications the scope of compared Fairlearn features could be expanded to include comparison of different algorithms for different machine learning models (not only binary classification but also regression). Additionally, it could be worth trying to detect and mitigate model unfairness in different areas, such as corporate credit risk analysis or markets selection.

References

Barocas, S., Hardt, M., Narayanan, A.: Fairness in machine learning. Nips tutorial **1**, 2017 (2017)

Bird, S., et al.: Fairlearn: A toolkit for assessing and improving fairness in AI. Microsoft, Tech. Rep. MSR-TR2020–32 (2020)

Butryn, B., Chomiak-Orsa, I., Hauke, K., Pondel, M., Siennicka, A.: Application of Machine Learning in medical data analysis illustrated with an example of association rules. Procedia Comput. Sci. **192**, 3134–3143 (2021)

Kaggle (2023). https://www.kaggle.com/datasets/ictinstitute/utrecht-fairness-recruitmentdataset. Accessed 15 Jul 2023

Lambrecht, A., Tucker, C.: Algorithmic bias? An empirical study of apparent gender-based discrimination in the display of STEM career ads. Manage. Sci. **65**(7), 2966–2981 (2019)

Mehrabi, N., Morstatter, F., Saxena, N., Lerman, K., Galstyan, A.: A survey on bias and fairness in machine learning. ACM Comput. Surv. (CSUR) **54**(6), 1–35 (2021)

Microsoft (2023). https://learn.microsoft.com/en-us/training/modules/detect-mitigate-unfairness-models-with-azure-machine-learning/2-consider-model-fairness. Accessed 15 Jul 2023

Mittelstadt, B., Wachter, S., Russell, C.: The Unfairness of Fair Machine Learning: Levelling down and strict egalitarianism by default (2023). arXiv preprint arXiv:2302.02404

Pandey, H.: Comparison of the usage of Fairness Toolkits amongst practitioners: AIF360 and Fairlearn (2022)

Rzemieniak, M., Wawer, M.: Employer branding in the context of the company's sustainable development strategy from the perspective of gender diversity of generation Z. Sustainability **13**(2), 828 (2021)

Schumann, C., Foster, J., Mattei, N., Dickerson, J.: We need fairness and explainability in algorithmic hiring. In: International Conference on Autonomous Agents and Multi-Agent Systems (AAMAS) (2020)

SDG FUND. Sustainable development goals (2015). https://www.un.org/sustainabledevelopment/inequality

Yang, M., Wang, J., Ton, J.F.: Rectifying unfairness in recommendation feedback loop. In: Proceedings of the 46th International ACM SIGIR Conference on Research and Development in Information Retrieval, pp. 28–37 (2023)

AI in Accelerating the Creation of Renewable Energy Sources. Bibliometric Analysis

Iwona Chomiak-Orsa, Andrzej Greńczuk(✉), Kamila Łuczak, and Estera Piwoni-Krzeszowska

Wroclaw University of Economics and Business, 53-345 Wroclaw, Poland
{iwona.chomiak-orsa,andrzej.grenczuk,kamila.luczak, estera.piwoni-krzeszowska}@ue.wroc.pl

Abstract. In recent years, one of the most pressing issues facing society is the protection and conservation of our planet's resources. The United Nations 2030 Agenda for Sustainable Development, adopted by 193 countries in 2015, defines a global model for sustainable development. According to the agendas guidelines, the modernisation efforts of highly developed countries should be focused on the eradication of poverty in all its forms, while pursuing a set of economic, social and environmental goals. Energy management, the acquisition and use of renewable energy sources, innovation and attention to environmental sustainability are some of the agenda's goals. This trend includes innovations to create renewable energy sources, which are managed and monitored using artificial intelligence (AI) solutions. Therefore, the aim of this article is to highlight the importance of AI in accelerating renewable energy creation. As a research method, we used bibliometric analysis based on a set of publications from the Scopus database to achieve the stated objective. The VOSviewer programme was also used to analyse the collected bibliographic data on publications. The research shows that authors are increasingly interested in AI and renewable energy topics in recent years, as evidenced by the growing number of publications in this area.

Keywords: Artificial Intelligence · sustainability · renewable energy sources

1 Introduction

Caring for natural resources is one of the key premises of the UN resolution. Thus, of the 17 goals defined in the document, almost half directly or indirectly refer to the need to create solutions to increase the protection of natural resources and care for the sustainable use of ecosystems and environmental protection. Economic development based only on economic calculation and the criterion of profitability has led to the devastation of natural resources and an imbalance in the biological balance of the entire planet. Awareness of this threat has led to

S. Nowaczyk et al. (Eds.): ECAI 2023 Workshops, CCIS 1948, pp. 155–162, 2024.
https://doi.org/10.1007/978-3-031-50485-3_14

the adoption of the UN Sustainable Development Agenda, developed in 2015, by 193 countries.

Consequently, it is becoming increasingly important to extract natural resources without devastating the environment. One of the most important problems of the modern world is to ensure adequate energy resources and energy security. Therefore, in line with sustainable development trends, a very important direction of economic dynamisation is the effort to create and manage both industrial and individual installations of renewable energy sources [2,3,6,10,16].

This process is not possible without the use of modern ICT solutions. Moreover, AI solutions are increasingly being applied to large industrial installations such as photovoltaic or windmill farms that provide energy for businesses or conurbations. The use of this class of IT solutions is justified by the need to anticipate energy demand in the short and long term and to manage the volume of energy generation and storage [1,7,13,17]. This problem is all the more important given that current technological solutions do not allow energy to be stored in a way that will be cost-effective, which means that the ability to monitor demand in terms of acquisition, consumption and potential storage is a significant financial issue [4,20].

Expectations of optimising energy production in correlation with energy demand are driving numerous investments in the implementation of advanced information technology into the processes of energy production and consumption management. The creation of smart grids, the Internet of Things or the use of AI solutions and machine learning algorithms are currently standard [5,9,12,15,19,21]. Strong links are also being made between urban energy sources [11] or the concept of zero waste [14] and the popular approach of the smart city [18].

Therefore, we believe that a bibliometric analysis in the above-mentioned subject area is an extremely important research issue. The bibliometric analysis will be the first stage of the research work planned by us on the use of AI solutions in the management of generation and monitoring of renewable energy resources. We have observed a growing interest in the above-mentioned topics, both in the context of published scientific papers as well as reports and industry and popular science studies.

Therefore, the aim is to present the general results of a bibliometric analysis of the scientific literature on the use of AI tools in the management of renewable energy sources. The research method used was bibliometric analysis conducted on the resources of the Scopus database. The VOSviewer programme was used to visualise the results of the analysis. The article presents only a small part of the analysis, which shows quantitative trends in the publications as well as the identification of countries where the authors most frequently address this topic in their articles.

2 Research Questions

(RQ1) What is the publication trend in the area of application of AI to accelerate renewable energy sources?

(RQ2) What is the publication trend in the area of application of AI to accelerate renewable energy sources in Business, Management and Accounting sciences?
(RQ3) From which countries do papers related to AI and renewable energy originate?

3 Methodology

We decided to use bibliometric analysis as a research method. The present research was carried out according to the procedure presented below in the form of a numbered list:

1. Defining the research questions (RQ1-RQ3) → They have been developed based on the literature review and own knowledge of publication trends. The questions relate to the area of applying artificial intelligence to accelerate the development of renewable energy sources.
2. Defining the keywords - "artificial intelligence" OR "AI", "renewable energ*" → Three keywords have been defined, one of which is an abbreviation. The "*" in the third keyword will replace a number of characters at any point in a word.
3. Selection of the scientific publication database for bibliometric analysis in Scopus → We decided to choose the Scopus database because it is the most recognisable database containing up-to-date and trusted research and data that can be useful for academic work.
4. Development of the first version of the query - TITLE-ABS-KEY (("artificial intelligence" OR "AI") AND "renewable energ*") → The first search we constructed is generic and was entered into the database to achieve an overall picture of the study area.
5. Development of the second version of the query with restriction to the Business, Management & Accounting area - TITLE-ABS-KEY (("artificial intelligence" OR "AI") AND "renewable energ*") AND (LIMIT-TO (SUBJAREA , "BUSI")) → In the second search, one area-related narrowing was introduced in order to relate the study area to the field of management.
6. Entry of both queries into the Scopus database → Both queries were entered into the database and the analysis began.
7. Analysis of the number of publications in all and individual years for both searches → The results of this stage have been presented in the charts.
8. Part of bibliographic coupling for both searches - analysis of the countries from which the publications originated → The countries were analysed in terms of the number of documents, and this was presented in the visualisations developed in VOSviewer.
9. Development of conclusions based on the collected results → The summary, conclusions, as well as the concept for further research are described at this stage.

The results of the research carried out will be presented later in the article.

4 Results

Research using bibliometric analysis was carried out from 10-14.07.2023 using data from the Scopus database. Among the techniques used in the bibliometric analysis was the use of science mapping [8], and within the science mapping we focused on the bibliographic coupling part, which in this case includes the analysis of countries. Furthermore, in order to present the overall status of the number of papers in the field of AI and renewable energy sources, we analysed the total number of publications, the number of papers published in each year.

Following the research methodology presented, we entered two defined queries into the Scopus database and obtained a certain number of documents. In the case of the first query, this number was 2288 documents. Due to the relevance of the field of management of all environmental changes, as well as the need to manage projects related to the application of AI in accelerating the creation of renewable energy sources, an inclusion criterion in the Scopus database was selected - subject area as Business, Management & Accounting. The second search yielded 105 papers. The results show a significant difference in the number of documents after selecting a subject area.

The number of publications per year was then analysed for both searches. Looking at the first search (Fig. 1), between 1994 and 2005 only a few authors addressed the topic described. Since about 2007, however, the number of publications has increased. The highest number of publications combining the field of AI and renewable energy sources was recorded in 2022, with 505 papers in the Scopus database. It is reasonable to assume that the number of papers published in 2023 would also increase if the analysis were carried out in December of that year.

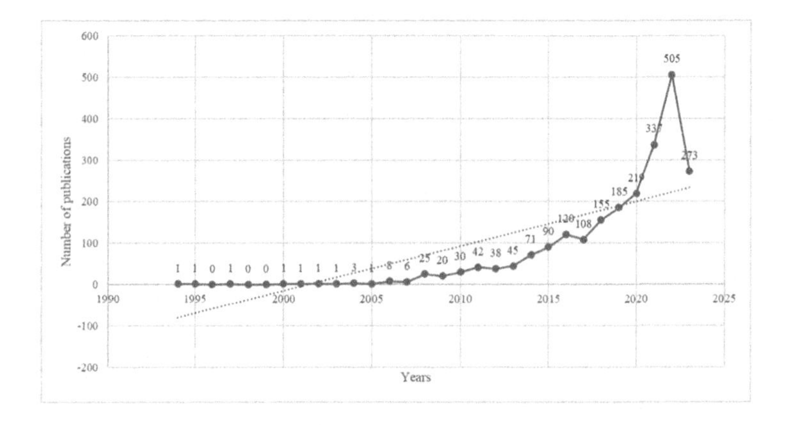

Fig. 1. Number of publications per year for the first search (1994–2023).

In the second graph, which is based on publications from the second search, considering only the subject area - Business, Management & Accounting (Fig. 2), an increasing trend is also noticeable. Between 2019 and 2022, at least 11 papers per year were produced on AI and renewable energy sources in the selected subject area. In 2023, 12 papers on the subject area have already been produced; given that this bibliometric analysis is carried out in July, it is likely that there will be more publications at the end of this year than in 2022.

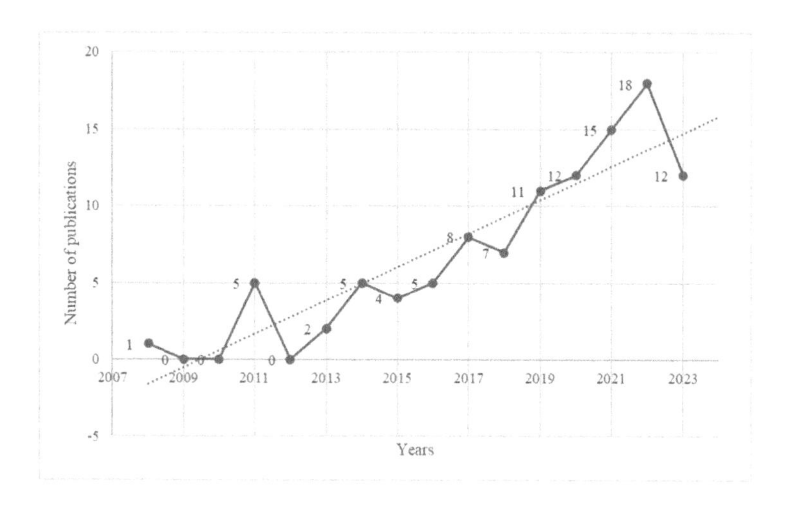

Fig. 2. Number of publications per year for the second search (1994–2023).

First part of the bibliographic coupling carried out is the analysis of the countries from which the collected documents originate. For the first search, publications came from 140 countries. We defined the following restrictions for the countries to be displayed: minimum number of documents of a country - 5, minimum number of citations of a country - 0. As a result of the conditions applied, 68 countries were displayed (Fig. 3).

The largest number of publications collected in the first search came from India (441 documents). This is followed by countries such as China (329 documents), United States (222 documents), United Kingdom (144 documents) and Germany (102 documents). The rest of the countries produced less than 100 documents in the selected area. Considering citations, China (7651 citations), United States (5334 citations) and India (4438 citations) accumulated the most.

The countries from which the documents for the second search originated were then analysed. We also defined some conditions for the analysis: minimum number of documents of a country - 5, minimum number of citations of a country - 0. Of the 46 countries, 9 met the indicated criteria (Fig. 4).

As with the first search, the largest number of publications comes from India (20 documents). The United States came second (11 documents), followed by China (9 documents), Netherlands and Germany (8 documents each). Publications from the United States (345 citations), China (223 citations), United

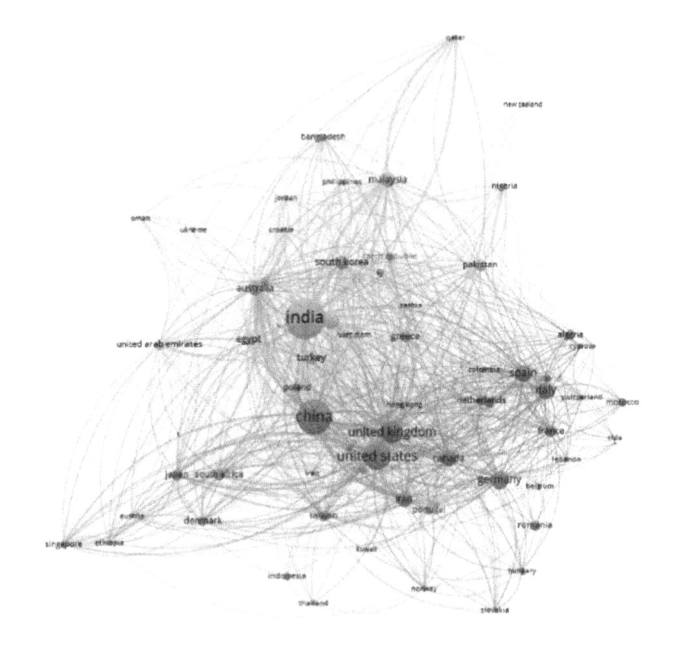

Fig. 3. Countries of documents for the first search.

Fig. 4. Countries of documents for the second search.

Kingdom (220 citations) and Netherlands (211 citations) accumulated the most citations.

Due to limitations in the number of pages of this article, we plan to conduct further parts of the bibliographic coupling, which will deal with the analysis of documentary sources, authors of documents and organizations.

5 Conclusions

By carrying out a bibliometric analysis, the following objective - to present the general results of a bibliometric analysis of the scientific literature on the use of AI tools in the management of renewable energy sources - was achieved.

It is apparent that the topic is important and research centres in many countries are addressing it. Among the countries at the forefront of research into the use of AI and the creation of renewable energy sources, the triad of 3 countries - India, China, USA - is clearly visible. In addition, among the publications cited, it is worth pointing out that the countries indicated are at the forefront. In addition, citations were supplemented by the Netherlands, Germany.

Therefore, we will undertake further research to determine which centres are leading in their research, as well as to determine whether leading representatives of the analysed topic can be identified. Further research aims to identify which research centres can be collaborated with. Furthermore, we aim to conduct further research, including determining whether there are any research gaps in the current state of knowledge.

References

1. Adami, L., Castagna, G., Magaril, E., et al.: Criticalities and Potentialities of Local Renewable Sources of Energy, pp. 103–115. The New Forest, UK (2018)
2. Colombo, E., Bologna, S., Masera, D. (eds.): Renewable Energy for Unleashing Sustainable Development. Springer, Cham (2013). https://doi.org/10.1007/978-3-319-00284-2
3. Chel, A., Kaushik, G.: Renewable energy for sustainable agriculture. Agron. Sust. Dev. **31**, 91–118 (2011). https://doi.org/10.1051/agro/2010029
4. Chen, C., Hu, Y., Karuppiah, M., Kumar, P.M.: Artificial intelligence on economic evaluation of energy efficiency and renewable energy technologies. Sustain. Energy Technol. Assess. **47**, 101358 (2021). https://doi.org/10.1016/j.seta.2021.101358
5. D'Amore, G., Di Vaio, A., Balsalobre-Lorente, D., Boccia, F.: Artificial intelligence in the water-energy-food model: a holistic approach towards sustainable development goals. Sustainability **14**, 867 (2022). https://doi.org/10.3390/su14020867
6. Dawoud, S.M.: Developing different hybrid renewable sources of residential loads as a reliable method to realize energy sustainability. Alex. Eng. J. **60**, 2435–2445 (2021). https://doi.org/10.1016/j.aej.2020.12.024
7. Dincer, I.: Renewable energy and sustainable development: a crucial review. Renew. Sustain. Energy Rev. **4**, 157–175 (2000). https://doi.org/10.1016/S1364-0321(99)00011-8
8. Donthu, N., Kumar, S., Mukherjee, D., et al.: How to conduct a bibliometric analysis: an overview and guidelines. J. Bus. Res. **133**, 285–296 (2021). https://doi.org/10.1016/j.jbusres.2021.04.070
9. Goralski, M.A., Tan, T.K.: Artificial intelligence and sustainable development. Int. J. Manage. Educ. **18**, 100330 (2020). https://doi.org/10.1016/j.ijme.2019.100330
10. Güney, T.: Renewable energy, non-renewable energy and sustainable development. Int. J. Sustain. Dev. World Ecol. **26**, 389–397 (2019). https://doi.org/10.1080/13504509.2019.1595214
11. Hajduk, S., Jelonek, D.: A decision-making approach based on Topsis method for ranking smart cities in the context of urban energy. Energies **2021**(14), 2691 (2021)
12. Hoang, A.T., Pham, V.V., Nguyen, X.P.: Integrating renewable sources into energy system for smart city as a sagacious strategy towards clean and sustainable process. J. Clean. Prod. **305**, 127161 (2021). https://doi.org/10.1016/j.jclepro.2021.127161
13. Ibrahim, R.L., Al-mulali, U., Ozturk, I., et al.: On the criticality of renewable energy to sustainable development: do green financial development, technological innovation, and economic complexity matter for China? Renew. Energy **199**, 262–277 (2022). https://doi.org/10.1016/j.renene.2022.08.101
14. Jelonek, D., Walentek, D.: Exemplifying the Zero Waste Concept in smart cities. Ekonomia i Środowisko (2022)
15. Leal Filho, W., Yang, P., Eustachio, J.H.P.P., et al.: Deploying digitalisation and artificial intelligence in sustainable development research. Environ. Dev. Sustain. **25**, 4957–4988 (2023). https://doi.org/10.1007/s10668-022-02252-3

16. Lund, H.: Renewable energy strategies for sustainable development. Energy **32**, 912–919 (2007). https://doi.org/10.1016/j.energy.2006.10.017
17. Østergaard, P.A., Duic, N., Noorollahi, Y., et al.: Sustainable development using renewable energy technology. Renew. Energy **146**, 2430–2437 (2020). https://doi.org/10.1016/j.renene.2019.08.094
18. Stepniak, C., Jelonek, D., Wyrwicka, M., Chomiak-Orsa, I.: Integration of the infrastructure of systems used in smart cities for the planning of transport and communication systems in cities. Energies **14**(11), 3069 (2021)
19. Vinuesa, R., Azizpour, H., Leite, I., et al.: The role of artificial intelligence in achieving the sustainable development goals. Nat. Commun. **11**, 233 (2020). https://doi.org/10.1038/s41467-019-14108-y16
20. Vivek, C.M., Ramkumar, P., Srividhya, P.K., Sivasubramanian, M.: Recent strategies and trends in implanting of renewable energy sources for sustainability - a review. Mater. Today Proc. **46**, 8204–8208 (2021). https://doi.org/10.1016/j.matpr.2021.03.208
21. Wach, M., Chomiak-Orsa, I.: The application of predictive analysis in decision-making processes on the example of mining company's investment projects. Procedia Comput. Sci. **192**, 5058–5066 (2021)

The Use of Semantic Networks for the Categorization of Prosumers

Iwona Chomiak-Orsa[1], Andrzej Greńczuk[1](✉), Kamila Łuczak[1], and Dorota Jelonek[2]

[1] Wroclaw University of Economics and Business, Wroclaw 53-345, Poland
{iwona.chomiak-orsa,andrzej.grenczuk,kamila.luczak}@ue.wroc.pl
[2] Czestochowa University of Technology, Czestochowa 42-201, Poland
dorota.jelonek@pcz.pl

Abstract. Business continuity is possible through maintaining market position, while growth requires gaining competitive advantage. This can only be achieved through systematic attention to the consumer and the development of the product offering. These factors primarily determine the success of an organization. Against this backdrop, the trend towards personalization of goods delivered to consumers is becoming increasingly evident. The answer to these business problems is the creation of buyer-seller relationships in which the consumer becomes a prosumer: a consumer who provides opinions, suggests solutions, tests and evaluates the advantages and disadvantages of the product. Therefore, the search for methods and tools that allow for the identification of groups of consumers susceptible to cooperation with the organization - to varying degrees - becomes a very important scientific and business problem. This is why the authors of this article defined the aim of the article as the analysis of the possibility of using semantic networks for the categorization of consumers and defining the category of prosumers. The results presented in the article were obtained through the application of triangulation of research methods, such as analytical literature review, computer simulation conducted using Protégé software, and research experiment consisting of simulation of selected problem situations.

Keywords: prosumers · semantic networks · competitiveness

1 Introduction

The concept of sustainability is not only about the environment, but also about people and all the social aspects involved. Prosumers, representing consumers, can contribute to so-called "eco-prosumption". Eco-prosumption refers to ways of producing and acquiring value in a socially and environmentally responsible form [6].

The evolution of market conditions in which modern enterprises operate has determined changes in the concepts of creating relationships and directions of cooperation with customers, who are the final consumers of manufactured goods

S. Nowaczyk et al. (Eds.): ECAI 2023 Workshops, CCIS 1948, pp. 163–169, 2024.
https://doi.org/10.1007/978-3-031-50485-3_15

[1,14]. Purchasing relationships are evolving into relationships based on customer experience [8,18]. When creating marketing strategies, companies move away from actions aimed at seeking and acquiring passive customers, whose relationship with the organization is limited only to the purchase transaction [13,15].

The information obtained in this way is a key stimulus for the organization to enrich and develop the product offer, often contributing to innovative actions [10, 11,20] carried out mainly within the framework of open innovation models [10,12, 21]. The search for mechanisms "stimulating" customers to actively participate in trade relations becomes one of the concepts of organization development, which is increasingly important and attention is paid to it in scientific studies [2,3,7].

The above determinants contribute to the fact that identifying groups of customers who may become potential prosumers becomes a very important problem for organizations. In order to correctly identify potential prosumers, it is necessary to develop tools supporting the processes of classifying and clustering customers. Such tools can be semantic networks [4,5,9,17,19], which allow the classification and clustering of groups of customers by searching for phraseological relationships and relations resulting from possessing specific similarities and equations. Semantic networks show strong versatility in application. It can be pointed out, moreover, that semantic networks can be a source for Artificial Intelligence algorithms that will treat it as input. In addition, these algorithms can update its content [16].

The above scientific observations as well as the authors' business experiences have contributed to considering the possibility of developing patterns for selected consumer groups and the relationships they can create in their interactions with an organization through the use of semantic networks. As a result, the authors of this article have defined the following research problem: Can semantic networks be used to categorize consumers in order to identify their potential to transform into prosumers? Therefore, the aim of this article is to analyze the potential use of a semantic network for the categorization of consumers and the definition of prosumer categories. To achieve the designated goal of the article, the following specific research questions have been defined:

1. How can semantic networks be used to represent prosumer categories?
2. Can the designed network be mapped using concept maps (topics)?
3. What IT tools can be used to design the target semantic network?

The research presented in the article was conducted using the following research methods:

1. Computer simulation in the form of building a semantic network in the Protégé program.
2. An experiment conducted in the form of scenario analysis to preliminarily verify the proposed solution.

As a result of the above triangulation of research methods, the authors verified the research problem and achieved the designated goal of the article.

2 Identification of the Scope of Publications

This section presents a quantitative identification of the range of publications in the area of the application of artificial intelligence tools such as semantic networks to categorise prosumer attitudes. The content analysis of the databases was based on establishing the leading keyword as "prosumer*". The use of the symbol "*" allows for the matching of the suffix of the term "prosumer". The query was then defined in the databases by specifying that the leading keyword should appear in the title, abstract, and/or keywords. In Scopus, 4,628 records were obtained, while in WoS, 3,277 results were obtained. The set of results was then narrowed down by applying limitations to the query:

- Language = "English",
- Document type = "Article" and "Conference paper",
- Years = 2010–2022.

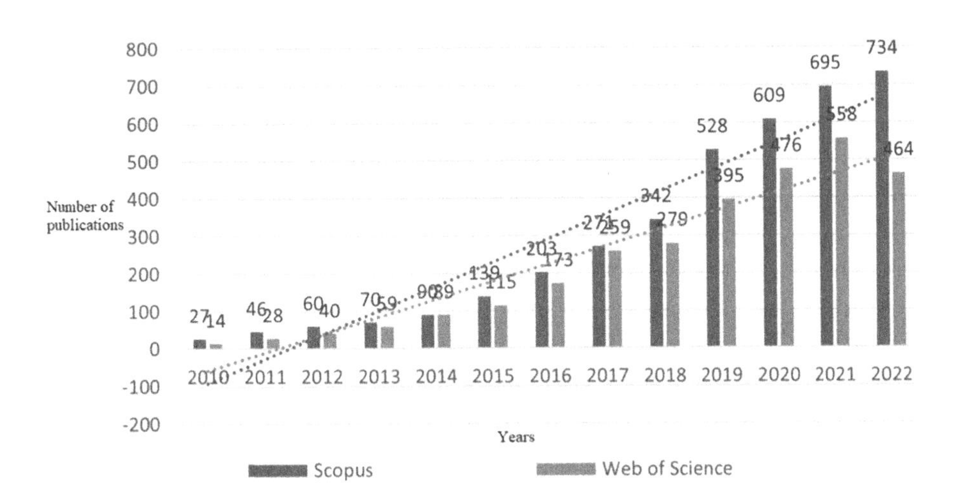

Fig. 1. Number of publications from 2010 to 2022.

On Fig. 1, it can be observed that the number of publications increases from year to year. It is worth noting that this increase is significantly greater in the Scopus database compared to the WoS database.

3 Method and Reserach Procedure

The research method used was a research experiment, consisting of developing the assumptions of a semantic network and basic concepts with their relationships. The construction of the semantic network was based on the analysis of scientific papers (documentary method). Then, a computer simulation was used to create an ontology as a method of knowledge representation. The simulation was conducted using the Protégé ontology editor.

To develop the semantic network, the following steps were taken:

1. Analysis of scientific publications on prosumers,
2. Extraction and analysis of the scope of concepts,
3. Development of:
   (a) Taxonomic relations,
   (b) Semantic relation words,
   (c) Semantic relations of concepts,
4. Introduction of concepts into the Protégé program,
5. Testing and verification of the semantic network by performing defined scenarios.

4 Research Results

As a result of the previously presented research procedure, an ontology was created with the purpose of categorizing prosumers. The categorization of prosumers depends on different criteria, which can be divided into characteristics related to the product and personal characteristics of the prosumers. Figure 2 presents the developed semantic network, which was shown using a concept map stored in the ontology.

The relation that connects the presented concepts is a taxonomic relation. After developing the semantic network in the form of a concept map, it is necessary to present the meaning of all concepts.

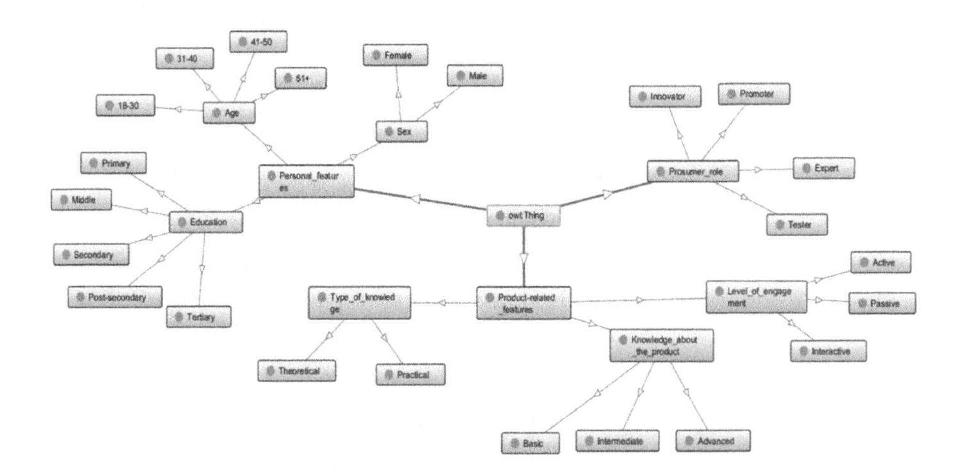

Fig. 2. Presentation of semantic network mapping using concept map.

Table 1 presents the taxonomic relations identified within the developed semantic network. After defining the taxonomic relations, it is necessary to define the semantic relations. In the case of the considered problem, one semantic relation was defined: "is called as".

Table 1. Taxonomic relations

Taxonomy	Component concepts
Prosumer role	Innovator, Expert, Tester, Promoter
Personal feature	Age, Education, Sex
Product-related features	Knowledge about the product, level of engagement, Type of knowledge
Age	18–30, 31–40, 41–50, 51+
Education	Primary, Middle, Secondary, Post-secondary, Tertiary

In the next step, selected concepts were connected by the developed semantic relation. To achieve the aim of this article, three scenarios were developed and implemented. However, presented is only one scenario, which reflects the idea.

The developed scenarios aim to verify whether it is possible to obtain answers to the given questions in the selected area. The Protégé editor and OntoGraf plugin were used to implement the scenarios. The developed scenarios will be presented in the further part of the article.

Scenario No. 1. An organization wants to identify prosumers among its clients. It has collected some personal characteristics of prosumers and those related to the product (Fig. 3).

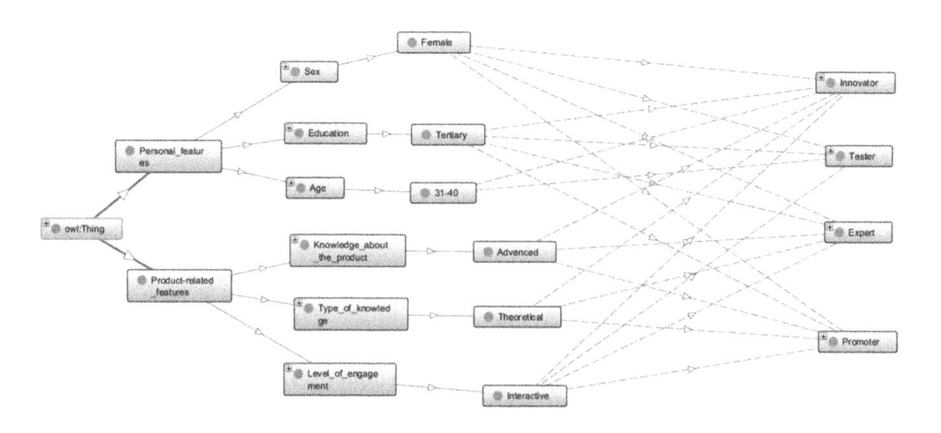

Fig. 3. Results obtained from scenario 1.

PROCEDURE: From the semantic network, "owl: Thing" should be selected, followed by: "Personal_features" -> "Sex" -> "Female", "Personal_features" -> "Education" -> "Tertiary," "Personal_features" -> "Age" ->

"31–40," "Product-related_features" -> "Knowledge_about_the_product" -> "Advanced," "Product-related_features" -> "Type_of_knowledge" -> "Theoretical," and "Product-related_features" -> "Level_of_engagement" -> "Interactive."
RESULT: As a result of scenario 1 implementation, the organization can determine that based on the indicated characteristics, the prosumers are likely to be innovators.

5 Conclusions

The goal defined in this article by the authors was to analyze the possibilities of using a semantic network for categorizing consumers and defining prosumer categories. Furthermore, the authors defined detailed research questions to support the goal. As a result of the conducted and presented research, the authors obtained the following answers:

1. Semantic networks can be a very useful tool for categorization and visualization of customer categorization into appropriate prosumer segments.
2. The designed networks can be mapped using a concept map, which is a very useful complementary tool for visualizing researched problems.
3. One of the very useful tools for designing target semantic networks is the Protégé program, which was used by the authors of this article during the research and preparation of research results.

Obtaining answers to all research questions posed by the authors is equivalent to achieving the goal, which was to analyze the possibilities of using semantic networks in the categorization of prosumers.

References

1. Anshari, M., Almunawar, M.N., Lim, S.A., Al-Mudimigh, A.: Customer relationship management and big data enabled: personalization & customization of services. Appl. Comput. Inf. **15**(2), 94–101 (2019). https://doi.org/10.1016/j.aci.2018.05.004
2. Chandler, J., Chen, S.: Prosumer motivations in service experiences. J. Serv. Theory Pract. **25**(2), 220–239 (2015). https://doi.org/10.1108/JSTP-09-2013-0195
3. Cova, B., Cova, V.: On the road to prosumption: marketing discourse and the development of consumer competencies. Consumption Markets Cult. **15**(2), 149–168 (2012). https://doi.org/10.1080/10253866.2012.654956
4. Drieger, P.: Semantic network analysis as a method for visual text analytics. Procedia. Soc. Behav. Sci. **79**, 4–17 (2013). https://doi.org/10.1016/j.sbspro.2013.05.053
5. Dudycz, H.: Mapa pojęć jako wizualna reprezentacja wiedzy ekonomicznej: Topic map as a visual representation of economic knowledge. No. nr 229 in Monografie i Opracowania - Uniwersytet Ekonomiczny we Wrocławiu, Wydawnictwo Uniwersytetu Ekonomicznego, Wrocław (2013)

6. Eizenberg, E., Jabareen, Y.: Social sustainability: a new conceptual framework. Sustainability **9**(1), 68. MDPI AG. (2017). https://doi.org/10.3390/su9010068
7. Fernandes, T., Remelhe, P.: How to engage customers in co-creation: customers' motivations for collaborative innovation. J. Strateg. Mark. **24**(3–4), 311–326 (2016). https://doi.org/10.1080/0965254X.2015.1095220
8. Gentile, C., Spiller, N., Noci, G.: How to sustain the customer experience. Eur. Manag. J. **25**(5), 395–410 (2007). https://doi.org/10.1016/j.emj.2007.08.005
9. Hills, T.T., Kenett, Y.N.: Is the mind a network? Maps, Vehicles, and Skyhooks in cognitive network science. Top. Cogn. Sci. **14**(1), 189–208 (2022). https://doi.org/10.1111/tops.12570
10. Jelonek, D.: The innovative potential of prosumption and the results of enterprises. In: Proceedings of the 7th Conference on Performance Measurement and Management Control (2013)
11. Jelonek, D., Chomiak-Orsa, I.: The application of ICT in the area of value co-creation mechanisms support as a determinant of innovation activities. Int. J. Ambient Comput. Intell. (IJACI) **9**(2), 32–42 (2018)
12. Jelonek, D., Moczała, A. (eds.): Metody i techniki projektowania innowacji. NPI Nauka i Praktyka Innowacji, Państwowe Wydawnictwo Ekonomiczne, Warszawa (2020)
13. Kingsnorth, S.: Digital marketing strategy: an integrated approach to online marketing. NY, 3rd edn, Kogan Page Inc, New York (2022)
14. Kumar, V., Reinartz, W.: Customer Relationship Management. STBE, Springer, Heidelberg (2018). https://doi.org/10.1007/978-3-662-55381-7
15. Mothersbaugh, D.L., Hawkins, D.I., Kleiser, S.B., Mothersbaugh, L.L., Watson, C.F.: Consumer behavior: building marketing strategy. NY, fourteenth edition, international student edition edn, McGraw-Hill Education, New York (2020)
16. Navigli, R., Ponzetto, S.P.: BabelNet: the automatic construction, evaluation and application of a wide-coverage multilingual semantic network. Artif. Intell. **193**, 217–250 (2012)
17. Odlanicka-Poczobutt, M.: Significance of semantic web - pitfalls and benefits of use in the common judiciary. Comp. Legilinguistics **40**(1), 21–41 (2019). https://doi.org/10.14746/cl.2019.40.2
18. Palmer, A.: Customer experience management: a critical review of an emerging idea. J. Serv. Mark. **24**(3), 196–208 (2010). https://doi.org/10.1108/08876041011040604
19. Scott, P.B.: Knowledge workers: social, task and semantic network analysis. Corp. Commun. Int. J. **10**(3), 257–277 (2005). https://doi.org/10.1108/13563280510614519
20. Seran (Potra), S., Izvercian, M.: Prosumer engagement in innovation strategies: the prosumer creativity and focus model. Manage. Decis. **52**(10), 1968–1980 (2014). https://doi.org/10.1108/MD-06-2013-0347
21. West, J., Bogers, M.: Leveraging external sources of innovation: a review of research on open innovation: leveraging external sources of innovation. J. Prod. Innov. Manag. **31**(4), 814–831 (2014). https://doi.org/10.1111/jpim.12125

Automatic Coral Detection with YOLO: A Deep Learning Approach for Efficient and Accurate Coral Reef Monitoring

Ouassine Younes[1(✉)], Zahir Jihad[1], Conruyt Noël[2], Kayal Mohsen[3], A. Martin Philippe[2], Chenin Eric[4], Bigot Lionel[2], and Vignes Lebbe Regine[5]

[1] Computer Science Department, LISI, Cadi Ayyad University, Marrakesh, Morocco
younes.ouaasine99@gmail.com, j.zahir@uca.ac.ma

[2] EA2525 LIM, I.T. Department, University of La Réunion, 97400 Saint-Denis, France
{noel.conruyt,philippe.martin,Lionel.Bigot}@univ-reunion.fr

[3] ENTROPIE, IRD, IFREMER, CNRS, University of La Reunion, University of New Caledonia, Noumea, New Caledonia, USA
mohsen.kayal@ird.fr

[4] Institut de Recherche Pour le Développement (IRD), Paris, France
eric.chenin@ird.fr

[5] Institut de Systématique, Evolution, Biodiversité (ISYEB), SU, MNHN, CNRS, EPHE, UA - CP 48, 57 rue Cuvier, 75005 Paris, France
regine.vignes_lebbe@sorbonne-universite.fr

Abstract. Coral reefs are vital ecosystems that are under increasing threat due to local human impacts and climate change. Efficient and accurate monitoring of coral reefs is crucial for their conservation and management. In this paper, we present an automatic coral detection system utilizing the You Only Look Once (YOLO) deep learning model, which is specifically tailored for underwater imagery analysis. To train and evaluate our system, we employ a dataset consisting of 400 original underwater images. We increased the number of annotated images to 580 through image manipulation using data augmentation techniques, which can improve the model's performance by providing more diverse examples for training. The dataset is carefully collected from underwater videos that capture various coral reef environments, species, and lighting conditions. Our system leverages the YOLOv5 algorithm's real-time object detection capabilities, enabling efficient and accurate coral detection. We used YOLOv5 to extract discriminating features from the annotated dataset, enabling the system to generalize, including previously unseen underwater images. The successful implementation of the automatic coral detection system with YOLOv5 on our original image dataset highlights the potential of advanced computer vision techniques for coral reef research and conservation. Further research will focus on refining the algorithm to handle challenging underwater image conditions, and expanding the dataset to incorporate a wider range of coral species and spatio-temporal variations.

Keywords: Machine Learning · Deep Learning · Underwater ecosystems · Corals · Object Detection · YOLO

S. Nowaczyk et al. (Eds.): ECAI 2023 Workshops, CCIS 1948, pp. 170–177, 2024.
https://doi.org/10.1007/978-3-031-50485-3_16

1 Introduction

Coral reefs are among the most biodiverse and productive ecosystems on Earth, supporting an extraordinary array of marine life and providing critical resources to millions of people worldwide [1]. These magnificent underwater structures play a vital role in maintaining the balance of marine biodiversity and serve as natural barriers against coastal erosion and storm surge [2, 3]. However, coral reefs face unprecedented threats, primarily due to local anthropogenic impacts and climate change, and are declining, with consequences for biodiversity and coastal societies [4, 5, 12, 13].

The degradation and loss of coral reefs not only endanger marine species but also jeopardize the livelihoods of coastal communities dependent on these vulnerable ecosystems. Effective conservation and management of coral reefs require comprehensive monitoring efforts to assess ecosystem health, identify major drivers of species dynamics, and respond swiftly to changes or disturbances [14–16]. Traditional manual survey methods, though essential, are time-consuming, labor-intensive, and often limited in scale, making them insufficient to address the challenges faced by coral reef ecosystems in the present era of accelerating environmental change [6]. Recent advancements in computer vision and deep learning have paved the way for novel approaches to automate coral reef monitoring [7]. The integration of these technologies allows for the development of robust and efficient systems capable of automatic coral detection in large-scale underwater image and video datasets. In this paper, we propose a state-of-the-art solution for automatic coral detection, employing the popular You Only Look Once (YOLO) object detection algorithm [11].

The main aim of this research is to show how YOLOv5, known for its real-time object detection capabilities, can be used to effectively and accurately detect coral colonies in underwater imagery. By using YOLOv5 instead of other deep learning techniques, our approach aims to surpass traditional methods and enhance the efficiency, scalability, and accuracy of coral reef monitoring. In the Results and Analysis section, we present a complete analysis of our automatic coral detection system, detailing the key components, architecture, and data preparation. We also discuss the challenges associated with coral detection in underwater environments, such as lighting variations and complex background structures. To address these challenges, we describe the pre-processing techniques applied to the input imagery to improve the overall performance of the YOLOv5 model. Overall, this paper aims to contribute to the growing body of research in the field of imagery tools and artificial intelligence algorithms applied to coral reef monitoring and conservation [6, 7].

2 Related Works

The authors of [8] Focuses on the classification of bleached and unbleached corals using visual vocabulary, which combines spatial, texture, and color features. The proposed methodology includes feature extraction techniques and classifiers, with a bag of features (BoF) and a linear kernel of Support Vector Machine (SVM) achieving the highest accuracy of 99.08% for binary classification and 98.11% for multi-class classification.

The authors in [9] Compares two supervised machine learning methods for detecting and recognizing coral reef fish in underwater videos. The authors present the Deep Learning method and the HOG + SVM method and evaluate their performance. The paper discusses the use of histograms of oriented gradients (HOG) for feature extraction and support vector machines (SVM) for classification in the HOG + SVM method. The Deep Learning method utilizes a deep neural network for both feature extraction and classification. The authors compare the F-measure of both methods on a dataset of underwater videos, for the HOG + SVM approach, the F-measure ranges from 0.28 to 0.49, while for the Deep Learning method, it ranges from 0.62 to 0.65.

The authors of [10] Introduces a new method for detecting and assessing the health of coral reefs using underwater images and videos. The researchers found that previous studies focused mainly on coral image classification and lacked coral health detection. To address this gap, they developed a hardware-based autonomous monitoring system for coral-reef health detection. The proposed method, called MAFFN-YOLOv5, consists of a backbone, neck, and head network architecture. The authors obtained 0.83 in the precision measure for a dataset of 3049 high-quality images.

3 Datasets

We used a dataset of 580 underwater images specifically collected for coral detection. The dataset includes 400 original images, which were augmented through image treatment to increase training data diversity. The images were captured using underwater cameras during research expeditions to various coral reef locations in the Reunion and Scattered Islands. These expeditions aimed to cover a wide range of coral reef health and habitats, depths, and lighting conditions, ensuring a comprehensive representation of underwater environments. The dataset includes different coral species, colony sizes, and orientations, providing a realistic depiction of the coral reef ecosystem (Fig. 1).

Public link to the dataset: https://drive.google.com/file/d/1YsqGLyAZ4QRZkUJHs8VsRrfj6bK7CG1C/view.

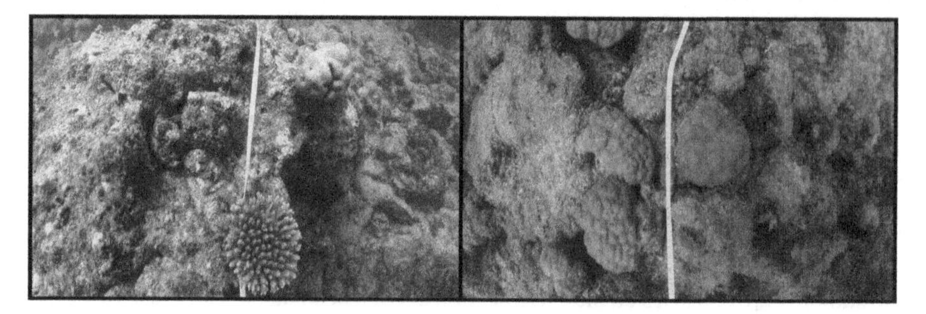

Fig. 1. Sample images from the dataset

For training and evaluating our automatic coral detection system, we manually annotated the images using the Label Studio tool. The annotation process involved drawing bounding boxes around individual coral colonies and assigning them the label "coral". This annotation scheme simplifies the task by focusing on identifying coral colonies specifically (Fig. 2).

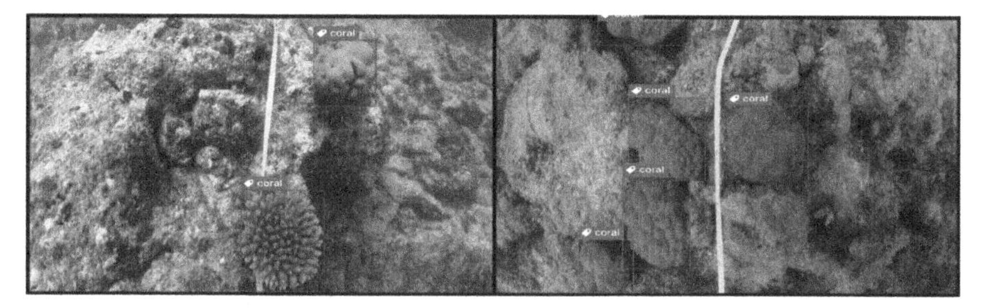

Fig. 2. Sample annotated images from the dataset

4 YOLOv5

YOLOv5, like other neural networks designed for image processing, is built upon convolutional layers. The architecture of YOLOv5 can be divided into three distinct parts, as illustrated in Fig. 3. These parts can be considered as sets of layers that form functional units. Each part serves a specific role and is composed of modified versions of existing network components found in the literature. These modified layers were carefully selected and tailored to suit the requirements of YOLOv5's architecture.

- Backbone: The initial component of the network is referred to as the backbone. Its primary function is to optimize the network by enhancing the gradient descent process. This crucial segment enables the network to achieve fast inference times, facilitating real-time applications.
- Neck: The neck component in the model generates feature pyramids, which aid in generalizing objects across various scales. These feature pyramids enhance the model's ability to identify objects of different sizes and scales, improving its robustness. YOLOv5 incorporates PANet, a feature pyramid approach, which contributes to superior predictions, increased accuracy, and improved performance.
- Head: The head model plays a crucial role in the final stage of detection. It is responsible for generating the output vectors that contain class probabilities, objectivity scores, and bounding boxes by utilizing anchor boxes. These anchor boxes serve as reference templates that aid in accurately localizing and classifying objects within the input data.

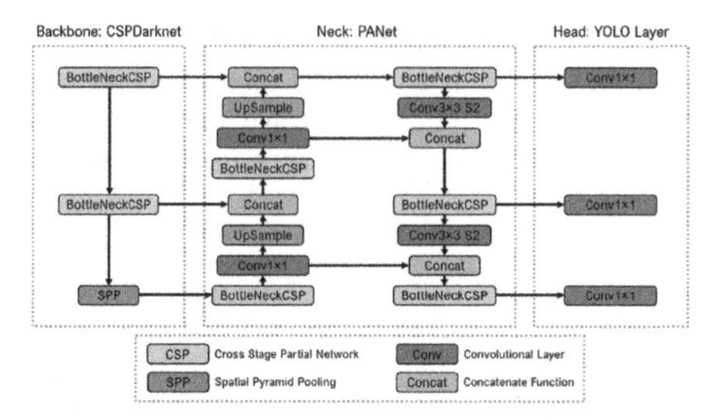

Fig. 3. YOLOv5 architecture

5 Results and Analysis

YOLOv5 is available in different variants, designated by the letters N, S, M, and L, representing NANO, Small, Medium, and Large, respectively. These variants differ in the size of the model architecture, which impacts performance and detection speed. In general, the larger variants (M and L) tend to offer higher accuracy but slower inference times, while the smaller variants (N and S) sacrifice some accuracy for faster performance. The table presents a comparison of various models in the YOLOv5 family specifically designed for coral detection tasks. Each model is evaluated based on its size, precision, recall, mean average precision, and inference time. Here is a description of each column (Table 1, Figs. 4 and 5):

Table 1. Comparison of YOLOv5 models for coral detection.

Model	Size	Precision	Recall	m Average Precision	Inference time
Yolov5n	3.9MB	0.534	0.46	0.461	50.2ms
Yolov5s	14.4MB	0.558	0.445	0.452	83.7ms
Yolov5m	42.2MB	0.598	0.481	0.47	178.5ms
Yolov5l	92.8MB	0.599	0.486	0.474	319.5ms

- Model: This column displays the different YOLOv5 models specifically tailored for coral detection that are being compared.
- Size: This column indicates the file size of each YOLOv5 model, which represents the amount of storage required for the model.
- Precision: Precision measures the accuracy of the model's predictions for coral detection. It calculates the ratio of true positive predictions to all positive predictions made by the model.
- Recall: Recall quantifies the ability of the model to correctly identify coral instances in the dataset. It represents the ratio of true positive predictions to all actual positive instances present.

- mean Average Precision: mean Average Precision is a widely used metric in object detection tasks, including coral detection. It calculates the average precision across different levels of detection confidence thresholds. Higher values indicate better overall performance in terms of precision and recall.
- Inference Time: This column represents the time taken by each YOLOv5 model to process an input image and generate the corresponding coral detection results. It is measured in milliseconds (ms).

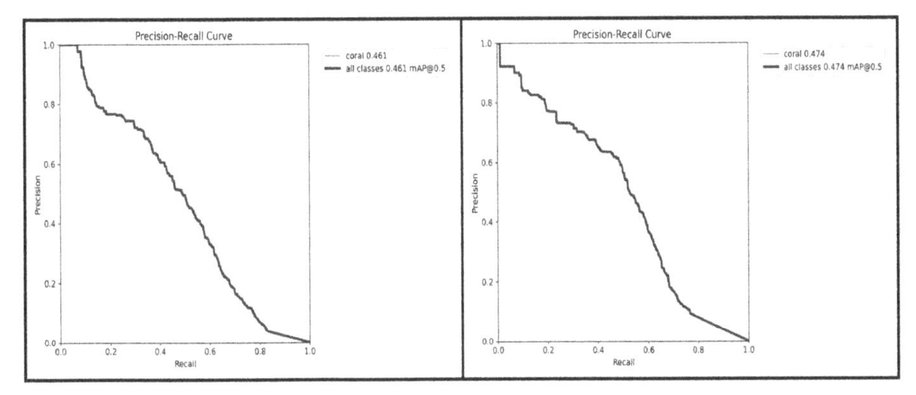

Fig. 4. Precision and recall curves for yolov5n and yolov5l models respectively from left to right.

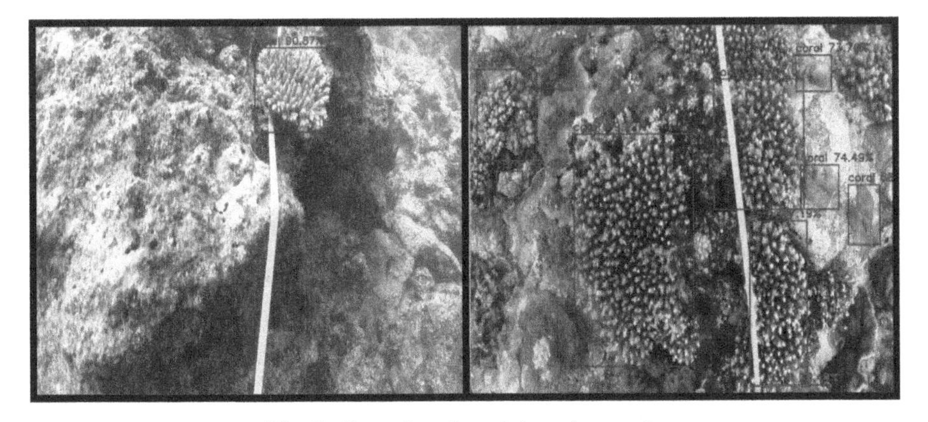

Fig. 5. Examples of coral detection results

6 Conclusion

In this paper, we have presented an automatic coral detection system using the You Only Look Once (YOLO) algorithm, a state-of-the-art deep learning approach for efficient and accurate object detection. Our proposed system addresses the need for scalable and accurate coral reef monitoring, a critical task for understanding and conserving these vulnerable ecosystems. Our approach is specifically tailored to handling difficult image data, which often contains corals with various shapes and sizes, as well as images featuring an uneven distribution of corals.

While the utilization of our dataset comprising 580 manually annotated underwater images with precise bounding boxes has been beneficial for training and evaluating the automatic coral detection system, it is important to acknowledge some limitations. Currently, our approach primarily focuses on images with a low concentration of corals. To improve the system's effectiveness in detecting corals in images with a high concentration of corals, future work involves annotating more images and data specifically targeting such scenarios. This expansion of annotated data will enhance the model's ability to accurately detect and analyze densely populated coral areas. By automating coral detection with YOLOv5, we provide a means to gather timely and accurate data, enabling a deeper understanding of coral reef dynamics and facilitating prompt actions in response to threats. This enhanced understanding allows us to develop targeted conservation strategies, allocate resources efficiently, and implement adaptive management practices. Our research contributes to the broader field of computer vision and deep learning in marine biology and environmental sciences, fostering innovation and collaboration to tackle pressing sustainability challenges. By successfully applying YOLOv5 to coral detection, we pave the way for scalable and cost-effective monitoring solutions, thereby supporting long-term coral reef resilience and biodiversity preservation.

References

1. Woodhead, A.J., Hicks, C.C., Norström, A.V., Williams, G.J., Graham, N.A.J.: Coral reef ecosystem services in the Anthropocene. Funct. Ecol. **33**(6), 1023–1034 (2019). https://doi.org/10.1111/1365-2435.13331
2. Ferrario, F., Beck, M.W., Storlazzi, C.D., Micheli, F., Shepard, C.C., Airoldi, L.: The effectiveness of coral reefs for coastal hazard risk reduction and adaptation. Nature Commun. **5**(1),(2014). https://doi.org/10.1038/ncomms4794
3. Beck, H.E., Zimmermann, N.E., McVicar, T.R., Vergopolan, N., Berg, A., Wood, E.F.: Present and future Köppen-Geiger climate classification maps at 1-km resolution. Sci. Data **5**(1),(2018). https://doi.org/10.1038/sdata.2018.214
4. Eddy, T.D., et al.: Global decline in capacity of coral reefs to provide ecosystem services. One Earth **4**(9), 1278–1285 (2021). https://doi.org/10.1016/j.oneear.2021.08.016
5. Carlot, J., et al.: Coral reef structural complexity loss exposes coastlines to waves. Sci. Rep. **13**(1),(2023). https://doi.org/10.1038/s41598-023-28945-x
6. Kayal, Mohsen, Eva Mevrel, and Jane Ballard. "Coral demographic performances in New Caledonia, a video transect approach to operationalize imagery-based investigation of population and community dynamics." bioRxiv (2023): 2023–05
7. Gonzalez-Rivero, M., et al.: "Monitoring of coral reefs using artificial intelligence: a feasible and cost-effective approach. Remote Sens. **12**(3), 489 (2020)
8. Jamil, S., Rahman, M., Haider, A.: Bag of features (BoF) based deep learning framework for bleached corals detection. Big Data and Cogn. Comput. **5**(4), 53 (2021)
9. Villon, S., Chaumont, M., Subsol, G., Villéger, S., Claverie, T., Mouillot, D.: Coral reef fish detection and recognition in underwater videos by supervised machine learning: comparison between deep learning and HOG+SVM methods. In: Blanc-Talon, J., Distante, C., Philips, W.,

Popescu, D., Scheunders, P. (eds.) ACIVS 2016. LNCS, vol. 10016, pp. 160–171. Springer, Cham (2016). https://doi.org/10.1007/978-3-319-48680-2_15

10. Rajan, S.K.S., Damodaran, N.: MAFFN_YOLOv5: multi-scale attention feature fusion network on the YOLOv5 Model for the health detection of coral-reefs using a built-in benchmark dataset. Analytics **2**(1), 77–104 (2023)
11. Redmon, J., et al.: "You only look once: Unified, real-time object detection. In: Proceedings of the IEEE Conference on Computer Vision and Pattern Recognition (2016)
12. Hughes, T.P., et al.: Coral reefs in the Anthropocene. Nature **546**(7656), 82–90 (2017). https://doi.org/10.1038/nature22901
13. Darling, E.S., et al.: Social–environmental drivers inform strategic management of coral reefs in the Anthropocene. Nat. Ecol. Evol. **3**(9), 1341–1350 (2019)
14. Kayal, M., et al.: Predicting coral community recovery using multi-species population dynamics models. Ecol. Lett. **21**(12), 1790–1799 (2018). https://doi.org/10.1111/ele.13153
15. Riegl, B., et al.: Population collapse dynamics in Acropora downingi, an Arabian/Persian Gulf ecosystem-engineering coral, linked to rising temperature. Global Change Biol. **24**(6), 2447–2462 (2018). https://doi.org/10.1111/gcb.14114
16. Condie, S.A., et al.: Large-scale interventions may delay decline of the Great Barrier Reef. Royal Soc. Open Sci. **8**(4),(2021). https://doi.org/10.1098/rsos.201296

An Overview of Artificial Intelligence for Electric Vehicle Energy Systems Integration

Weiqi Hua[1], Daniel Mullen[2], Abdul Wahid[3(✉)], Khadija Sitabkhan[3], and Karl Mason[3]

[1] Department of Electronic, Electrical and Systems Engineering, University of Birmingham, Birmingham B15 2TT, UK
w.hua@bham.ac.uk

[2] School of Engineering, University of Edinburgh, Edinburgh EH9 3DW, UK
d.t.mullen@sms.ed.ac.uk

[3] School of Computer Science, University of Galway, Galway H91 FYH2, Ireland
{abdul.wahid,k.sitabkhan1,karl.mason}@universityofgalway.ie

Abstract. Electric vehicles are growing in market penetration annually. They are expected to play a significant role in decarbonising road transport point source emissions and supporting the global transition to Net Zero. Integrating these electric vehicles into the existing electricity networks, supply chain and refueling infrastructure presents difficulties. However, appropriately deployed artificial intelligence solutions can address many of these challenges. This paper investigates the issues facing the integration of electric vehicles into society as well as providing an introduction into artificial intelligence. This paper then provides a comprehensive overview of the applications of artificial intelligence to electric vehicle integration. Limitations of the current research in this area are outlined, and promising future research directions are discussed.

Keywords: Artificial Intelligence · Electric Vehicles · Smart Grid · Sustainability · Renewable Energy Integration

1 Introduction

Electric vehicles (EVs) are widely accepted as the most promising solution to the problems faced by fossil fuel powered vehicles. They are quieter, easier to maintain and do not directly emit carbon dioxide as well as having reduced particulate matter emissions [19]. However, production, adoption and integration into current energy systems face many difficulties. For instance, the batteries required by EVs use rare earth minerals, such as lithium [26], which are expensive to mine and production often has poor humanitarian records. EVs require the roll-out of a new, integrated and extensive charging network which is financially challenging for governments while also placing a significant additional demand on the electricity grid [7]. As many countries still rely heavily on fossil fuels to power the grid the degree of decarbonisation achieved by rolling out EVs is

S. Nowaczyk et al. (Eds.): ECAI 2023 Workshops, CCIS 1948, pp. 178–186, 2024.
https://doi.org/10.1007/978-3-031-50485-3_17

limited by the carbon intensity of power production. Integrating centralised and distributed renewable generation, carbon capture and storage and battery, and thermal storage systems into the electricity grid can provide a solution.

Artificial Intelligence (AI) is expected to play a major part in integrating EVs into energy systems infrastructure as it transitions to a decarbonised and digitised future. AI algorithms are algorithms that exhibit behaviours that are deemed to be intelligent [16]. Effectively integrating EVs into the grid requires optimisation, planning, forecasting, modelling, etc. These are tasks that many AI algorithms are designed to solve. A significant amount of research exists in the literature applying a variety of AI algorithms to different aspects of energy-transportation system integration. This paper will provide a review of these studies.

Many researchers have conducted literature reviews on the intersection of AI and EVs. Rigas et al. provided a comprehensive review of EV integration using AI in 2014, but it lacks coverage of recent advancements [14]. Zadeh et al. conducted a recent and detailed survey of deep learning for microgrid EVs, focusing on only one aspect of AI [25]. Song et al. conducted a comprehensive review of EV adoption, excluding AI aspects [18]. Abdullah et al. reviewed studies on reinforcement learning (RL) for EV charging management, but they only covered RL techniques and many other techniques in AI not discussed in their study [1]. This paper aims to address the limitations of these reviews by considering a broader range of AI algorithms and recent applications in EV integration. The contributions of this paper are as follows:

1. To provide a comprehensive overview of the applications of AI for the energy-transportation integration.
2. To discuss the limitations of the current literature and areas for future research.
3. To outline key areas in which AI methods can have the greatest impact with regards to EV energy system integration.

The paper is structured as follows. Section 2 presents an overview of EVs and their relationship to the energy sector. Section 3 discusses AI broadly. Section 4 provides a comprehensive review of AI applications for EVs. Section 5 discusses the limitations and future works. Finally, Sect. 6 concludes the paper.

2 Electric Vehicles

The market share of EVs is rapidly increasing in many countries. EVs are composed of a battery that stores power and an electric motor for propulsion. The main technical challenges in EVs are related to battery technology, including capacity, range, charging efficiency, lifespan, and cost. Other challenges include developing charging infrastructure and decarbonizing the battery supply chain, while public opinion and high costs affect EV adoption. Various EV configurations are available in the market today, such as Hybrid electric vehicles, Battery electric vehicles, and Fuel cell electric vehicles.

2.1 Transport and Climate Change

The recent Intergovernmental Panel on Climate Change (IPCC) [11] report confirms human-induced warming, projecting global warming to exceed the Paris Agreement's 1.5°C limit [8]. Surface transport contributes significantly to greenhouse gas emissions, making achieving net-zero goals challenging. The high carbon intensity of hydrocarbon fuels used in internal combustion engines hinders decarbonization efforts. Options like hydrogen and electricity are considered, with electrification being the most viable for passenger vehicles. Battery electric vehicles (BEVs) are adopted to combat climate change and improve air quality, emitting zero carbon emissions at the point of use. However, accurate environmental impact evaluation requires considering factors like power carbon intensity and production emissions through lifecycle assessments.

2.2 Batteries

Advanced battery technology is crucial for meeting the high energy demands of domestic vehicle transport. Lithium-ion (Li-ion) batteries, with their lightweight construction, high energy density, and favourable cycle life, are the most popular choice. They typically consist of a lithium metal oxide cathode, a graphite anode, and a lithium salt electrolyte in an organic solvent. Li-ion batteries offer a wide range of specific energy densities (90 to 250 Wh/kg [27]). Current state-of-the-art Li-ion technology provides an average range of 314 km, with rapid charging-enabled BEVs achieving a charging time of under an hour. [17].

2.3 Grid

The electricity for EVs comes from distributed renewable sources like solar PV or the electricity grid. Traditional grids had centralized generation and transmission, with base load and load-following plants. The carbon intensity of grid electricity depends on the mix of generators. Decentralized production and micro-grids have seen growth in European markets [2]. Smart grids offer solutions for integrating distributed energy generation and enabling real-time interaction between producers, operators, and consumers. Smart meters provide real-time data, allowing consumers to monitor energy usage and operators to manage demand. Two-way electricity flow enables consumers to export surplus power and use domestic battery capacity as operational reserves. Vehicle-to-Grid (V2G) allows EV owners to sell electricity back to the grid, reducing peak demands and generating additional income [20].

2.4 Challenges

The challenges of global BEV adoption can be categorized into consumer adoption and infrastructure development. Concerns about cost and range anxiety are preventing consumer adoption, but technological advancements are resolving these problems. Infrastructure development faces challenges in scaling up battery manufacturing and establishing sufficient charging points. Government support and public backing are crucial to overcoming these challenges and integrating BEVs into the power grid.

3 Artificial Intelligence

AI encompasses various algorithms enabling machines to exhibit intelligent behaviour, such as imitating human actions. ML, a prominent sub-field of AI, includes techniques like computer vision, NLP, neural networks, and RL. This section provides a high-level overview of AI techniques and focuses on integrating EVs into energy systems. For a comprehensive understanding, refer to Russell & Norvig's work [16].

3.1 Machine Learning

Machine Learning (ML) is a sub-field of AI that involves algorithms learning automatically from experience. Traditional AI approaches rely on hand-crafted rules, while ML algorithms learn by interacting with data or environments. ML algorithms can be categorized into supervised learning (with labelled data), unsupervised learning (without labels), semi-supervised learning (a mixture of labelled and unlabeled data), and reinforcement learning (learning optimal policies for actions in an environment).

3.2 Reinforcement Learning

Reinforcement Learning (RL) involves an agent learning to interact with an environment to maximize its rewards, such as navigating a maze. In RL, the agent observes the environment state s_t, takes an action a_t based on its policy π, and receives a reward R. RL problems are often modelled as Markov decision processes. Figure 1 illustrates how an RL agent interacts with its environment.

One notable RL algorithm is Q-Learning, which uses a Q-table to determine actions for each state. Deep Q-Network (DQN) extends Q-Learning to continuous state spaces using a neural network. The Deep Deterministic Policy Gradient (DDPG) algorithm operates in environments with continuous actions.

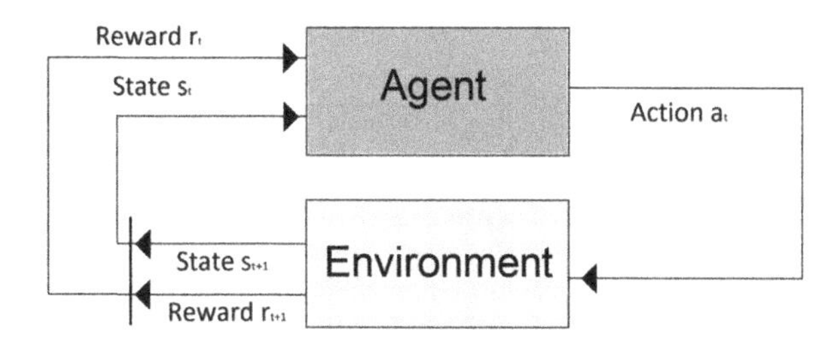

Fig. 1. Reinforcement Learning Agent Environment Interaction.

3.3 Neural Networks and Deep Learning

Neural Networks (NNs) are ML models inspired by the brain. They consist of interconnected layers of processing units, or neurons, that receive and process input signals. The weights of the connections determine the importance of each input. NNs can have multiple hidden layers, known as deep NNs. Common activation functions in NNs include the Sigmoid and ReLU functions, outlined in Eqs. (1) and (2), respectively.

$$f(x) = \frac{1}{1+e^{-x}} \tag{1}$$

$$f(x) = max(0, x) \tag{2}$$

NNs are trained using backpropagation, where the error between observed and expected outputs is calculated and used to update the weights. Variants of NNs include Convolutional NNs (CNNs) for processing high-dimensional input signals like images and Recurrent NNs (RNNs) with memory through recurrent connections. Long Short-Term Memory (LSTM) networks are a type of RNN suited for data with a temporal element.

4 Applications of AI to Electric Vehicles

AI is increasingly applied in the field of electric vehicles (EVs), benefiting various stakeholders. Table 1 summarises stakeholders, functions, and relevant studies. Further details can be found in the following subsections.

4.1 Electric Vehicle Producers

AI supports EV producers in various ways, including range prediction, range efficiency improvement, battery usage optimization, charging efficiency enhancement, cost reduction, performance enhancement, and manufacturing process adjustment. Previous studies have used AI for range prediction and improving range efficiency. Yavasoglu et al. developed an AI-based range estimation approach using a decision tree and jerk trace analysis [24]. Sun et al. employed a gradient-boosting decision tree algorithm for more accurate driving range prediction [22]. Meng et al. implemented online sequential extreme learning machines for efficiency optimization control of extended-range EVs [12].

Table 1. Stakeholders, functions, and studies for applying the AI into the field of EVs.

Stakeholders	Functions	Studies
EV producers	Range efficiency	[24]
	Battery efficiency	[5]
End users	Adoption	[4]
	Behaviours	[6]
	Scheduling	[10]
Power system operators	Intrusive load monitoring	[3]
	Non-intrusive load monitoring	[13]
	Management	[9]
Infrastructure owners	Planning	[21]
	Scheduling	[23]

4.2 End Users

AI analyzes EV adoption and charging behaviours for users and helps schedule their charging activities. De Rubens used the k-means method to investigate EV buyer motivations and potential adoption waves, highlighting price and vehicle-to-grid (V2G) capabilities as key factors for adoption [15]. Bas et al. identified influential factors and classified potential EV purchasers using machine learning techniques like support vector machines, deep neural networks, and gradient boosting models [4].

4.3 Power System Operators

Power system operators benefit from AI in load monitoring for supply-demand balance, energy conservation, and grid resilience. AI techniques, such as deep learning, decision trees, and ML-based clustering algorithms, have been applied to detect EV charging profiles and separate EV loads from non-EV loads in intrusive and non-intrusive load monitoring (ILM and NILM). NILM algorithms driven by random forests, support vector machines, bounding-box fitting, and deep generative models have been proposed. AI also aids in managing grid operations, including microgrid energy management, locational marginal pricing, optimal EV charging strategies, and vehicle-to-grid control.

4.4 Owners of EV Charging Infrastructure

AI is crucial in planning and scheduling EV charging infrastructure, aiming to reduce costs, enhance utilization efficiency, and improve coordination. AI techniques have been applied to predict infrastructure popularity, optimize charging station locations, and determine the number and placement of charging points. Scheduling of public EV charging infrastructure has been explored using methods such as Markov decision processes, internet of Vehicles frameworks, and machine learning algorithms. Additionally, autonomous AI robots have been investigated for EV integration, including mobile charging robots, Turtlebot robots for V2G simulation, and robot-based EV test beds.

5 Discussion

5.1 Limitations

The current literature on applying AI to EV integration has several limitations:

- Practicality: Most studies only apply AI in simulation, lacking real-world validation of their effectiveness in tasks like battery charging management or EV charge point scheduling.
- Vehicle-to-Grid: While V2G pilot programs exist, widespread adoption of this technology is still lacking, limiting its application in EV integration.

- Willingness of control: Consumer acceptance of AI-managed EV charging may be hindered by concerns and hesitation related to understanding and trust in AI technologies.
- Explainability: The lack of transparency and comprehensibility in AI decision-making processes raises concerns, especially in safety-critical systems or situations requiring explanations.
- Trustworthiness: Developing reliable and robust AI systems is crucial for managing EV charging/discharging and gaining consumer trust, but this topic is not extensively explored in the literature.

5.2 Future Directions

There are a number of trends that future research in the AI for the EV integration will follow:

- Advancements in AI algorithms: Improved AI algorithms will be developed and applied to address various aspects of EV integration.
- Focus on explainable and trustworthy AI: Research will address the need for explainable and trustworthy AI in EV integration.
- Peer-to-Peer (P2P) energy trading: The growing interest in P2P energy trading, facilitated by technologies like blockchain, will drive research on AI-based EV battery management within P2P networks.

6 Conclusion

This paper has provided an overview into both, the issues surrounding EV grid integration, and the field of AI. A comprehensive review of applications of AI to EV grid integration was provided. The limitations of the current research on this topic have been discussed, and future research directions have been outlined.

Key conclusions of this review are summarised as follows:

1. AI can provide significant benefits to many aspects of EV integration, e.g., battery management.
2. The deployment of many of the proposed AI solutions in real world settings would further validate the techniques by demonstrating their effectiveness outside of simulation.
3. Advanced technologies, e.g., P2P energy trading, blockchain, and V2G, are prime areas for the benefits of AI techniques to be realised for the EV integration.

Acknowledgement. This work was partially supported by Enterprise Ireland grant number: CS20212029.

References

1. Abdullah, H.M., Gastli, A., Ben-Brahim, L.: Reinforcement learning based EV charging management systems-a review. IEEE Access **9**, 41506–41531 (2021)
2. Ahlqvist, V., Holmberg, P., Tangerås, T.: A survey comparing centralized and decentralized electricity markets. Energ. Strat. Rev. **40**, 100812 (2022)
3. Ahmed, S., Khan, Z.A., Gul, N., Kim, J., Kim, S.M.: Machine learning-based clustering of load profiling to study the impact of electric vehicles on smart meter applications. In: 2021 Twelfth International Conference on Ubiquitous and Future Networks (ICUFN), pp. 444–447. IEEE (2021)
4. Bas, J., Cirillo, C., Cherchi, E.: Classification of potential electric vehicle purchasers: a machine learning approach. Technol. Forecast Soc. Change **168**, 120759 (2021)
5. Bhatt, A., Ongsakul, W., Madhu, N.: Machine learning approach to predict the second-life capacity of discarded EV batteries for microgrid applications. In: Vasant, P., Zelinka, I., Weber, G.-W. (eds.) ICO 2020. AISC, vol. 1324, pp. 633–646. Springer, Cham (2021). https://doi.org/10.1007/978-3-030-68154-8_55
6. Chung, Y.W., Khaki, B., Li, T., Chu, C., Gadh, R.: Ensemble machine learning-based algorithm for electric vehicle user behavior prediction. Appl. Energy **254**, 113732 (2019)
7. Coignard, J., MacDougall, P., Stadtmueller, F., Vrettos, E.: Will electric vehicles drive distribution grid upgrades?: the case of california. IEEE Electrification Magazine **7**(2), 46–56 (2019)
8. Horowitz, C.A.: Paris agreement. International Legal Materials 55 (2021)
9. Lei, M., Mohammadi, M.: Hybrid machine learning based energy policy and management in the renewable-based microgrids considering hybrid electric vehicle charging demand. Int. J. Elec. Power **128**, 106702 (2021)
10. Li, S., et al.: Electric vehicle charging management based on deep reinforcement learning. J. Mod. Power Syst. Cle., 1–12 (2021)
11. Masson-Delmotte, V., et al.: Contribution of working group i to the sixth assessment report of the intergovernmental panel on climate change (2021)
12. Meng, B., Wang, Y., Yang, Y.: Efficiency-optimization control of extended range electric vehicle using online sequential extreme learning machine. In: 2013 IEEE Vehicle Power and Propulsion Conference (VPPC), pp. 1–6 (2013)
13. Rehman, A.U., Lie, T.T., Vallès, B., Tito, S.R.: Non-invasive load-shed authentication model for demand response applications assisted by event-based non-intrusive load monitoring. Energy AI **3**, 100055 (2021)
14. Rigas, E.S., Ramchurn, S.D., Bassiliades, N.: Managing electric vehicles in the smart grid using artificial intelligence: a survey. IEEE Trans. Intell. Transp. Syst. **16**(4), 1619–1635 (2014)
15. de Rubens, G.Z.: Who will buy electric vehicles after early adopters? using machine learning to identify the electric vehicle mainstream market. Energy **172**, 243–254 (2019)
16. Russell, S., Norvig, P.: Artificial intelligence: a modern approach (2002)
17. Sanguesa, J.A., Torres-Sanz, V., Garrido, P.J., Martinez, F.M., Marquez-Barja, J.: A review on electric vehicles: technologies and challenges. Smart Cities 4 (2021)
18. Song, R., Potoglou, D.: Are existing battery electric vehicles adoption studies able to inform policy? a review for policymakers. Sustainability **12**(16), 6494 (2020)
19. Sovacool, B.K.: A transition to plug-in hybrid electric vehicles (PHEVs): why public health professionals must care (2010)

20. Sovacool, B.K., Kester, J., Noel, L., de Rubens, G.Z.: Actors, business models, and innovation activity systems for vehicle-to-grid (v2g) technology: a comprehensive review. Renew. Sustain. Energy Rev. **131**, 109963 (2020)
21. Straka, M., et al.: Predicting popularity of electric vehicle charging infrastructure in urban context. IEEE Access **8**, 11315–11327 (2020)
22. Sun, S., Zhang, J., Bi, J., Wang, Y.: A machine learning method for predicting driving range of battery electric vehicles. J. Adv. Transp. (2019)
23. Vanitha, V., Resmi, R., Reddy, K.N.S.V.: Machine learning-based charge scheduling of electric vehicles with minimum waiting time. Comput. Intell. **37**(3), 1047–1055 (2021)
24. Yavasoglu, H., Tetik, Y., Gokce, K.: Implementation of machine learning based real time range estimation method without destination knowledge for BEVs. Energy **172**, 1179–1186 (2019)
25. Zadeh, P.T., Joudaki, M., Ansari, A.: A survey on deep learning applications for electric vehicles in micro grids. In: 2021 5th International Conference on Internet of Things and Applications (IoT), pp. 1–6. IEEE (2021)
26. Zeng, X., et al.: Commercialization of lithium battery technologies for electric vehicles. Adv. Energy Mater. **9**(27), 1900161 (2019)
27. Zubi, G., Dufo-López, R., Carvalho, M., Pasaoglu, G.: The lithium-ion battery: state of the art and future perspectives. Renew. Sustain. Energy Rev. 89 (2018)

Merging Grid Technology with Oil Fields Power Distribution: A Smart Grid Approach

Omar Khaled Fadhl Ali Al-Eryani[1], Gülgün Kayakutlu[2](✉), Zeynep Bektas[3], and M.Özgür Kayalica[2]

[1] Bahcesehir University, Istanbul, Turkey
[2] Istanbul Technical University, Istanbul, Turkey
gkayakutlu@gmail.com
[3] Kadir Has University, Istanbul, Turkey

Abstract. This study explores how grid technology can help improve oil fields' power distribution using a fuzzy multi-criteria decision-making approach. The study compares different grid technologies based on multiple criteria, such as technical feasibility, economic viability, environmental impact, social acceptance, and regulatory compliance. The fuzzy TOPSIS method is used because it can effectively handle both crisp and fuzzy data, as well as linguistic and numerical values. After obtaining a ranking of alternatives, the study also conducts a sensitivity analysis and a robustness check to validate the results. The results show that the hybrid grid is the most preferred option for oil fields' power distribution, followed by the smart grid, the microgrid, the nano grid, and the conventional grid. This implies that integrating different grid technologies can provide more benefits and advantages than using a single grid technology. The study provides some implications and recommendations for oil fields to adopt or integrate different grid technologies to enhance their power systems and operations.

Keywords: Oil Fields · Power Grid · Power Distribution · Fuzzy TOPSIS · Fuzzy Decision-Making

1 Introduction

Oil fields are among the most energy-intensive industries in the world. They require a reliable and efficient power supply to operate various equipment and processes, such as drilling, pumping, refining, and transportation [1]. However, power distribution in oil fields is often faced with many challenges, such as high demand fluctuations, remote locations, harsh environments, aging infrastructure, and carbon emissions. These challenges can affect the performance, safety, and profitability of oil fields [2].

One possible solution to overcome these challenges is to adopt smart grid technology. A smart grid is an intelligent network that integrates advanced communication, control, automation, and monitoring systems to optimize the generation, transmission, distribution, and consumption of electricity. A smart grid can provide benefits such as improved reliability, efficiency, flexibility, security, sustainability, and customer satisfaction [3].

S. Nowaczyk et al. (Eds.): ECAI 2023 Workshops, CCIS 1948, pp. 187–193, 2024.
https://doi.org/10.1007/978-3-031-50485-3_18

The main objective of this study is to explore how grid technology can help improve oil fields' power distribution using a fuzzy multi-criteria decision-making approach. The study will compare different grid technologies based on multiple criteria, such as technical feasibility, economic viability, environmental impact, social acceptance, and regulatory compliance. The study will also conduct a sensitivity analysis and a robustness check to validate the results.

The rest of the article is organized as follows: Sect. 2 reviews the previous literature on smart grid applications in oil fields and fuzzy multi-criteria decision-making approach. Section 3 describes the methodology used in this study. Section 4 presents the results and discussion. Section 5 concludes the article and provides some recommendations.

2 Literature Review

Smart grid technology has been applied in various sectors and industries to enhance their power systems. Some examples include renewable energy integration, electric vehicle charging, demand response, microgrids, and distributed generation [3]. However, there are few studies that specifically focus on smart grid applications or other novel grid ideas in oil fields.

Ghanam et al. considered the rapidly increasing power demand and aimed to explore different grid alternatives to improve energy efficiency and reliability for generation and consumption. They focused on oil fields especially because of the common fossil fuel options of their case study area Saudi Arabia. They tried to implement of new automation system in the power grids and to search for options for the integration of renewable energy sources into the current system [4]. Hao et al. conducted a case study on the implementation of a smart grid system for an oil field using radio technology. They considered the options of high-speed load shedding, online monitoring, event reporting, oscillography, and engineering access. The results showed that the proposed radio links are adequate for the application [5]. As the last one, Nesterenko et al. conducted a study on off-grid oil fields. They represented the results of field measurements in the off-grid power system of an oil field. They found that gas piston generators instead of diesel generators are possible only with the same increase in the number of generating units for off-grid oil fields [6].

Fuzzy multi-criteria decision-making (FMCDM) is a popular technique for solving complex problems that involve multiple criteria and uncertainty. FMCDM can handle both quantitative and qualitative data, as well as linguistic and numerical values. FMCDM can also capture the vagueness and ambiguity of human judgments and preferences using fuzzy sets and logic. FMCDM has been widely used in various fields and applications, such as engineering, management, environment, health, and education [7]. However, there is no study that applies FMCDM to compare different grid technologies for oil fields' power distribution, up to our information.

3 Methodology

3.1 Data Collection and Analysis

The data for this study were collected from various sources, such as academic journals, conference papers, technical reports, industry publications, and online databases. The data included information on different grid technologies for oil fields' power distribution, such as their characteristics, advantages, disadvantages, costs, benefits, risks, and impacts [4]. The data also included information on the fuzzy multi-criteria decision-making approach, such as its steps, methods, tools, and applications. To fill in Table 1, the ratings of each grid alternative for each criterion were collected. Then, they were integrated as triangular fuzzy numbers to express the variable uncertainty and imprecision of human judgments and preferences. The data were analyzed using descriptive statistics and content analysis to summarize their main features and findings. The data was also used to construct the fuzzy multi-criteria decision-making model for this study.

3.2 Fuzzy Multi-criteria Decision-Making Approach

The fuzzy multi-criteria decision-making approach used in this study consists of four main steps: criteria selection and weighting; alternatives evaluation and ranking; sensitivity analysis; and robustness check.

Criteria Selection and Weighting

The first step is to select the criteria that are relevant and important for comparing different grid technologies for oil fields' power distribution. Based on the literature review and expert opinions, the following five criteria were selected:

- Technical feasibility: The degree to which a grid technology can be implemented in oil fields without major technical difficulties or constraints.
- Economic viability: The degree to which a grid technology can provide economic benefits or savings to oil fields in terms of capital costs, operational costs, and revenue generation.
- Environmental impact: The degree to which a grid technology can reduce or mitigate the negative environmental effects of oil fields' power distribution, such as carbon emissions, air pollution, water pollution, and land degradation.
- Social acceptance: The degree to which a grid technology can gain or maintain the support or approval of various stakeholders involved or affected by oil fields' power distribution, such as employees, customers, communities, and regulators.
- Regulatory compliance: The degree to which a grid technology can comply or conform with the existing or emerging laws or regulations related to oil fields' power distribution, such as safety standards, quality standards, and emission limits.

The next step is to assign weights to each criterion according to its relative importance or priority. This can be done using various methods, such as pairwise comparison, rating scale, or entropy method. In this study, the entropy method was used because it can objectively determine the weights based on the information content or diversity of each criterion.

The entropy method involves the following steps [8]:

- Normalize the data matrix of each criterion using a linear scaling technique.
- Calculate the entropy value of each criterion using Eq. 1.

$$E_j = \frac{1}{lnn} \sum_{i=1}^{n} p_{ij}.lnp_{ij} \tag{1}$$

where E_j is the entropy value of the jth criterion, n is the number of alternatives and p_{ij} is the normalized value of the ith alternative for the jth criterion.

- Calculate the degree of diversification of each criterion using Eq. 2.

$$D_j = 1 - E_j \tag{2}$$

where D_j is the degree of diversification of the jth criterion.

- Calculate the weight of each criterion using Eq. 3.

$$W_j = \frac{D_j}{\sum_{j=1}^{m} D_j} \tag{3}$$

where W_j is the weight of the jth criterion and m is the number of criteria.

The weights obtained by applying the entropy method are 0.21, 0.19, 0.20, 0.18, and 0.22, respectively.

Evaluation and Ranking of Alternatives

The second step is to evaluate and rank alternatives based on the criteria and weights. This can be done using various methods, such as fuzzy TOPSIS, fuzzy VIKOR, or fuzzy ELECTRE [7]. In this study, the fuzzy TOPSIS method was used because it can effectively handle both crisp and fuzzy data, as well as linguistic and numerical values. Briefly, the fuzzy TOPSIS method involves the following steps [9]:

- Construct the fuzzy decision matrix using triangular fuzzy numbers (TFNs) to represent the ratings or scores of each alternative for each criterion. TFNs are defined by three parameters: lower bound (l), middle value (m), and upper bound (u). TFNs can capture the uncertainty and imprecision of human judgments and preferences. The fuzzy decision matrix for this study is shown in Table 1.
- Then, using all necessary formulas the fuzzy decision matrix is normalized, the weighted normalized fuzzy decision matrix is calculated, the positive and negative ideal solutions are determined, the distance of each alternative from the positive and the negative ideal solutions are calculated, and the relative closeness of each alternative to the positive ideal solution is calculated.

Table 1. Fuzzy decision matrix.

Criteria → Alternatives ↓	Technical feasibility	Economic viability	Environmental impact	Social acceptance	Regulatory compliance
Conventional grid	(3,4,5)	(2,3,4)	(1,2,3)	(2,3,4)	(3,4,5)
Smart grid	(6,7,8)	(5,6,7)	(6,7,8)	(5,6,7)	(6,7,8)
Microgrid	(4,5,6)	(4,5,6)	(5,6,7)	(4,5,6)	(4,5,6)
Hybrid grid	(7,8,9)	(6,7,8)	(7,8,9)	(6,7,8)	(7,8,9)
Nano grid	(5,6,7)	(3,4,5)	(4,5,6)	(3,4,5)	(5,6,7)

- Finally, the alternatives are ranked according to their relative closeness values in descending order. The alternative with the highest value is the most preferred option, while the alternative with the lowest value is the least preferred option. The results obtained by applying the fuzzy TOPSIS method are shown in Table 2.

Table 2. Results of fuzzy TOPSIS method.

Alternative	Relative closeness	Rank
Hybrid grid	0.79	1
Smart grid	0.71	2
Microgrid	0.49	3
Nano grid	0.32	4
Conventional grid	0.13	5

Sensitivity Analysis and Robustness Check

The third step is to conduct a sensitivity analysis and a robustness check to validate the results of the fuzzy TOPSIS method. A sensitivity analysis is a technique that examines how the results change when some parameters or assumptions are varied [6]. A robustness check is a technique that tests whether the results are consistent or stable when different methods or models are used. In this study, a sensitivity analysis was performed by changing the weights of the criteria using different methods, such as pairwise comparison, rating scale, and entropy method. A robustness check was performed by using different methods for evaluating and ranking the alternatives, such as fuzzy VIKOR, fuzzy ELECTRE, and fuzzy PROMETHEE.

As the first application, by using a pairwise comparison approach criteria weights are calculated as 0.21, 0.18, 0.21, 0.16, and 0.24, respectively. The results of this fuzzy TOPSIS application with different weights are ranked as hybrid grid as the first one, then smart grid, nano grid, microgrid, and conventional grid, respectively, according to relative closeness. The second application uses the former criteria weights with the fuzzy VIKOR method. The result rank is as follows according to advantage value: smart grid, hybrid grid, microgrid, nano grid, and conventional grid, respectively.

4 Results and Discussion

Based on the results of the fuzzy TOPSIS method given in Table 2, it can be seen that the hybrid grid is the most preferred option for oil fields' power distribution, followed by the smart grid, the microgrid, the nano grid, and the conventional grid. This implies that integrating different grid technologies can provide more benefits and advantages than using a single grid technology.

The sensitivity analysis and the robustness check showed that the results of the fuzzy TOPSIS method are valid and reliable and that they reflect the preferences and judgments of the decision-makers. The hybrid grid was always ranked as the first- or second-best option, while the conventional grid was always ranked as the last or second-last option. The smart grid, the microgrid, and the nano grid had varying ranks depending on the weights and methods used, but they were generally ranked in between the hybrid grid and the conventional grid. This implies that the criteria and weights used in this study are reasonable and representative of the decision problem. It also implies that the fuzzy TOPSIS method is a robust and effective technique for comparing different grid technologies for oil field power distribution, therefore, it reflects the preferences and judgments of the decision-makers.

5 Conclusion

This study explored how grid technology can help improve oil fields' power distribution using a fuzzy multi-criteria decision-making approach. The study compared different grid technologies based on multiple criteria, such as technical feasibility, economic viability, environmental impact, social acceptance, and regulatory compliance. The study also conducted a sensitivity analysis and a robustness check to validate the results.

The main findings of this study are:

- The hybrid grid is the most preferred option for oil fields' power distribution, followed by the smart grid, the microgrid, the nano grid, and the conventional grid. It can provide more benefits and advantages than using a single grid technology, as it can combine the strengths and overcome the weaknesses of different grid technologies.
- The smart grid is also a good option for oil fields' power distribution, as it can provide many benefits such as improved reliability, efficiency, flexibility, security, sustainability, and customer satisfaction.
- The microgrid is a moderate option for oil fields' power distribution, as it can provide some benefits such as increased reliability, efficiency, and flexibility, especially in remote or isolated areas.

- The nano grid is a low option for oil fields' power distribution, as it can only provide limited benefits such as reduced power losses and improved power quality for small loads or devices.
- The conventional grid is the least preferred option for oil fields' power distribution, as it can only provide basic benefits such as power supply and transmission.

As the main implications of our study, it can be inferred that for oil fields, the authorities should consider adopting or integrating different grid technologies to enhance their power systems and operations and evaluate different grid technologies based on multiple criteria and weights that reflect their objectives and preferences by using fuzzy multi-criteria decision-making techniques to handle uncertainty and imprecision in their decision problems.

References

1. Verma, V., Singh, B., Chandra, A., Al-Haddad, K.: Power conditioner for variable-frequency drives in offshore oil fields. IEEE Trans. Ind. Appl.ns. Ind. Appl. **46**(2), 731–739 (2010)
2. Rodkin, M.V., Gvishiani, A.D., Labuntsova, L.M.: Models of generation of power laws of distribution in the processes of seismicity and in formation of oil fields and ore deposits. Russian J. Earth Sci. **10**, ES5004 (2008)
3. Escobar, J.J.M., Matamoros, O.M., Padilla, R.T., Reyes, I.L., Espinosa, H.Q.: A comprehensive review on smart grids: challenges and opportunities. Sensors **21**, 6978 (2021)
4. Ghanam, S.H., Shahrani, B.S., Essa, A.S., Hamrani, M.M., Dubaikel, F.A.: Saudi ARAMCO's efforts in smart grid. IEEE PES Conference on Innovative Smart Grid Technologies - Middle East, Jeddah, Saudi Arabia, pp. 1–9 (2011)
5. Hao, K., Shah, N., Herbert, N.: Case Study: radio application in a smart grid system for a brownfield onshore dispersed oil field. In: IEEE Petroleum and Chemical Industry Technical Conference (PCIC), Cincinnati, OH, USA, pp. 351–360 (2018)
6. Nesterenko, G., Vakulenko, V., Zyryanov, V., Potapenko, A., Prankevich, G., Aleksandrov, M.: Analysis of the frequency deviation in off-grid power system of oil field. Energy Rep. **8**, 831–838 (2022)
7. Beeram, S., M, S., Raj, S.P., K.S, R. Selection of sustainable juice extraction techniques for non-centrifugal sugar industry using multi-criteria decision-making methods. J. Food Process. Eng. **43**, e13415 (2020)
8. Shen, X., Du, H., Yuan, Y., Dong, Z. Evaluation and optimization of transfer service quality of urban rail transit based on entropy-TOPSIS method. In: 20th COTA International Conference of Transportation Professionals, Xi'an, China, pp. 4524–4536 (2020)
9. Junior, F.R.L., Osiro, L., Carpinetti, L.C.R.: A comparison between Fuzzy AHP and Fuzzy TOPSIS methods to supplier selection. Appl. Soft Comput. **21**, 194–209 (2014)

Green Hardware Infrastructure for Algorithmic Trading

Kamil Hudaszek[1(✉)], Iwona Chomiak-Orsa[1], and Saeed Abdullah M. AL-Dobai[2]

[1] Wroclaw University of Economics, Komandorska 118/120, Wroclaw, Poland
kamil.hudaszek95@gmail.com, iwona.chomiak@ue.wroc.pl
[2] Sana'a University, Sana'a, Yemen

Abstract. Every software needs hardware to be run on. Nowadays we encounter urgent need to mitigate the adverse effects of climate change. It prompted a paradigm shift towards the development of low carbon dioxide (CO2) emission hardware infrastructure. This scientific paper presents a thorough analysis of the current state of low CO2 emission hardware infrastructure, highlighting its significance in achieving sustainable and environmentally friendly technological advancements. The paper begins by highlighting the global greenhouse gas emissions and their significance in changing the climate. It emphasizes the crucial role of hardware infrastructure in this context, as the energy consumption and carbon footprint of data centers, communication networks, and other hardware-intensive systems continue to rise. Next, in the paper have been analyzed various strategies and technologies that have been developed to reduce CO2 emissions during computations. These include energy efficient designs, advanced cooling techniques, renewable energy integration, audits and controls, and optimization algorithms such modern AI tools. The advantages and limitations of each approach are discussed, with a focus on their potential for widespread adoption and scalability.

The paper concludes by outlining the future prospects and challenges associated with low CO2 emission hardware infrastructure. It emphasizes the need for continued research and innovation to overcome existing barriers and accelerate the adoption of environmentally friendly hardware systems on a global scale.

Keywords: green computing · sustainability · climate change · AI

1 Introduction

The escalating issue of climate change and its profound consequences have propelled the need for sustainable practices across various industries. One sector that has garnered significant attention in recent years is the technology industry, particularly in terms of energy consumption and carbon emissions. This article focuses on the environmental impact and greenhouse gas emissions associated with different types of hardware architecture, specifically the comparison between in-house data centers and cloud computing infrastructure.

S. Nowaczyk et al. (Eds.): ECAI 2023 Workshops, CCIS 1948, pp. 194–200, 2024.
https://doi.org/10.1007/978-3-031-50485-3_19

The continuous release of greenhouse gases into the atmosphere has resulted in a troubling rise in global temperatures, causing numerous adverse effects on our planet.

Amidst these risks, it becomes crucial to prioritize sustainability and energy efficiency across all sectors, including the technology industry. This article delves into the analysis of minimizing carbon emissions resulting from running algorithmic trading software, with a particular focus on the hardware aspect. IT systems consist of both software and hardware components, and optimizing both is essential for achieving energy efficiency.

The choice of hardware plays a vital role in carbon dioxide emissions. Innovative hardware solutions, such as energy-efficient processors, memory systems, and cooling mechanisms, contribute to a significant reduction in the carbon footprint of algorithmic trading software.

The analysis presented in this article aims to provide insights into how the selection and optimization of hardware components can contribute to minimizing carbon emissions in algorithmic trading software. By adopting energy-efficient hardware and incorporating sustainable practices throughout the software development lifecycle, the financial industry can play its part in mitigating climate change while meeting the demands of a rapidly evolving market [1].

Furthermore, this article highlights the efforts made by cloud service providers in their pursuit of sustainable practices. Cloud computing providers actively tailor hardware to specific requirements, focusing on providing leaner and more sustainable solutions. They optimize data center cooling systems to maintain temperatures at safe levels while ensuring energy efficiency. Regular energy audits and comprehensive control measures help monitor and optimize energy consumption.

2 Theoretical Background

2.1 Sustainable Development

Global energy-related CO2 emissions grew by 0.9%, or 321 Mt, in 2022, reaching a new high of over 36.8 Gt. These emissions have significant consequences that could be irreversible for over 1000 years [2]. The continuous release of greenhouse gases into the atmosphere has led to an alarming rise in global temperatures. According to the Intergovernmental Panel on Climate Change (IPCC), human activities have already caused approximately 1.0 °C of global warming, contributing to the increasing frequency and intensity of extreme weather events worldwide [3, 4].

If the current rate of emissions continues unchecked, the projected rise in global temperatures could reach 1.5 °C between 2030 and 2052 [5]. This temperature increase would have profound impacts on our planet. Rising mean temperatures would not only affect land and ocean regions but also disrupt delicate ecosystems and ecological balance. The consequences would extend beyond temperature changes, leading to more frequent heatwaves and scorching temperatures in inhabited areas. Additionally, the altered climate patterns would result in increased heavy precipitation in some regions, leading to a higher risk of floods and water-related disasters. Conversely, other areas may experience prolonged periods of drought, further exacerbating water scarcity issues.

Moreover, the impacts of global warming go beyond immediate weather events. Rising sea levels, triggered by the melting of polar ice caps and thermal expansion of water, pose significant threats to coastal communities and low-lying regions. The resulting inundation can lead to the displacement of populations, loss of valuable habitats, and increased vulnerability to storm surges and coastal erosion. Furthermore, as the oceans absorb a significant portion of the excess CO2, they become more acidic, leading to adverse effects on marine ecosystems and marine life, including coral reefs, shellfish, and other sensitive organisms [6, 7].

Given these risks and the urgent need to address climate change, every decision and action taken now becomes critical. It is essential to prioritize sustainability and energy efficiency in all sectors, including the technology industry. In 2013 data centers were accountable for 1–2% of global electricity use [8–11]. In this paper, the author delves into the analysis of minimizing carbon emissions resulting from running algorithmic trading software. While software development plays a crucial role in energy efficiency, the focus of this study lies in the hardware aspect.

IT systems encompass both software and hardware components, and optimizing both is crucial for energy efficiency. One fundamental consideration is the choice of programming language for software development. Different programming languages have varying performance characteristics and task execution times, which directly impact energy consumption. For example, a web application that calculates Fibonacci's sequence written in Node.js demonstrates superior performance compared to one developed in Python. On average, generating 30 elements in the sequence took only 16.993 ms in Node.js, while the same task took 354.307 ms in Python, nearly 21 times longer [12]. The choice of programming language can significantly influence energy consumption and carbon emissions [13, 14].

While the choice of functions within a selected programming language also plays a role in energy efficiency, this paper primarily focuses on analyzing the choice of hardware and its implications on carbon dioxide emissions. As technology advances, hardware optimization becomes increasingly vital. This includes the design of energy-efficient processors, memory systems, and cooling mechanisms. By employing innovative hardware solutions, such as low-power processors, intelligent power management systems, and efficient cooling techniques, the carbon footprint of algorithmic trading software can be significantly reduced.

The analysis presented in this paper aims to provide insights into how the selection and optimization of hardware components can contribute to minimizing carbon emissions in algorithmic trading software. By adopting energy-efficient hardware, incorporating sustainable practices throughout the software development lifecycle and modern AI tools utilization, the financial industry can play its part in mitigating climate change while still meeting the demands of a rapidly evolving market. Where AI might be used not only for energy consumption management itself, but also by different tools and processes optimization.

3 Research Methodology

3.1 Research Tools the Considerations Presented in the Article Were Developed as a Result of the Use of Such Research Tools as a Review of Scientific Literature, Analysis of Industry Reports, and Analysis of Reports on the Sustainable Development of Major Solution Providers. The Scope of Application of the Mentioned Research Tools Was as Follows:

- A classic literature review using the snowball method. Selected publications from google Scholar were analyzed. The authors used the following search criteria:

  o query:

  - "Data center energy consumption",
  - "Green data center",
  - "Data center cooling methods",
  - "Energy consumption, software optimization".

  o period: 2015–2023, o publications with highest number of citations.

- secondary research analysis of industry reports – was to understand the potential solutions to use. Reports on ICT impact on the environment in English have been analyzed for period 2016–2023,
- secondary research analysis of reports on sustainable development – was to understand the reasons for the differences in the effects of applying individual solutions.

3.2 Research Procedure

The research procedure consists in comparing the available solutions and indicating their impact on the environment.

4 Empirical Results and Discussion

4.1 Results

In this article, the author delves into a comprehensive comparison between two distinct types of hardware architecture: in-house data centers and cloud computing infrastructure. The primary focus of this analysis lies in assessing the environmental impact and greenhouse gas emissions associated with these two approaches.

To shed light on the environmental implications, a study conducted by 451 Research, an esteemed information technology research and advisory company, in 2019, scrutinized the reduction in greenhouse gas emissions achieved by transitioning from premises data centers to Amazon Web Services (AWS). The study encompassed 302 companies across 13 diverse industries, featuring annual revenues ranging from $10 million to $1 billion. Employing a carbon efficiency model, which integrated survey data, information from Amazon Web Services, and third-party industry data, the research yielded noteworthy results, showcasing a remarkable 87.93% decrease in carbon emissions. These emissions reductions were attributed to several factors: around 61% points resulted from the implementation of more efficient servers and enhanced server utilization, approximately 11% points were linked to the employment of advanced and greener data center facilities, while an additional 17% points stemmed from the reduced electricity consumption and the adoption of renewable energy sources. Consequently, the findings emphasized that Amazon Web Services demonstrated 2.5 times greater energy efficiency compared to the median performance of the analyzed American companies [15]. The remarkable efficiency can be primarily attributed to the optimal utilization of available resources and the adoption of cutting-edge server technologies. Furthermore, the research highlighted that the efficiency of data center facilities associated with cloud computing was 3.6 times higher due to the implementation of free cooling methods and the establishment of a leaner electrical infrastructure, which resulted in reduced power distribution losses. Notably, the research firm concluded that even if the analysis was confined to the top 10% most efficient companies, a significant reduction of 72% in carbon emissions would still be observed.

In addition to the aforementioned study, an insightful paper titled 'Cloud Libraries: A Novel Application of Cloud Computing' authored by Faiz Abidi and Hasan Jamal Abidi published a compelling comparison of carbon emissions derived from utilizing three Microsoft applications: Microsoft Exchange, Microsoft SharePoint, and Microsoft Dynamics CRM. The investigation revealed that the migration from on-premises solutions to Microsoft Cloud yielded an astounding reduction of up to 90% in carbon emissions [16]. To further solidify these findings, Microsoft published the 'Microsoft Cloud Carbon Studies,' which showcased energy efficiency improvements ranging from 22% to 93% upon migrating to their cloud platform. These energy savings extend beyond the ecological benefits, as they also translate into substantial financial advantages. According to the Carbon Disclosure Project, prominent US companies that embrace cloud computing have the potential to save an impressive $12.3 billion in energy costs and concurrently curtail CO_2 emissions by a staggering 85.7 million tons on an annual basis [17].

Supporting the case for cloud-based solutions, a research publication by the Lawrence Berkeley National Laboratory in 2014 unveiled a remarkable finding. The research suggested that the migration of every office worker in the United States to cloudbased solutions could potentially reduce hardware energy consumption by a remarkable 87%. This equates to an astounding 326 petajoules, which, at that time, would have been sufficient to power the bustling metropolis of Los Angeles.

Undoubtedly, the most notable disparity between on-premises solutions and cloud architecture lies in the primary operational focus of cloud service providers—their data centers. These data centers are meticulously designed and optimized to deliver unparalleled operational efficiency, maximize resource utilization, and minimize environmental impact. By prioritizing energy efficiency, employing advanced monitoring systems, and adhering to stringent modeling methods, cloud service providers constantly strive to develop and maintain sustainable solutions.

IT Equipment Efficiency

Cloud computing providers spend a significant amount of money on electricity. This is why they feel strong financial motivation to optimize such expenses. For instance, AWS designs chips by itself, they claim that their Elastic Compute Cloud (EC2) service that runs on AWS-designed Graviton 3 general-purpose processor uses up to 60% less energy than non-Graviton EC2 instances. Every provider actively tailors hardware to the specific requirements to provide leaner and more sustainable solutions.

Data Center Infrastructure Efficiency
Cloud computing providers optimize the cooling systems of their data centers to maintain the temperature at the highest safe level while ensuring energy efficiency. To achieve this goal, they employ advanced monitoring systems and modeling methods to design data centers appropriately. Additionally, they conduct regular energy audits and implement comprehensive control measures to monitor and optimize energy consumption [18].

Renewable Energy
Efforts by major cloud service providers allow purchases of green power. Google Cloud Platform is already carbon neutral and plans to be carbon-free by 2030. AWS and Microsoft Azure aim to fully operate on renewable energy sources by 2025 [19, 20].

5 Conclusion

IT systems design matters from the perspective of emitting greenhouse gases. Every architect should keep in mind the environmental cost of creating the system from the very beginning of the creation process to reduce emissions from computing and storage by optimizing both software and hardware.

The biggest cloud computing providers are in the corporate efficiency race which entails innovation and technology development. With surgical precision, they cut the energy consumption of data centers to lower their costs by creating their computer equipment tailored for specific needs and cooling techniques optimization modern AI tools utilization. Due to the effect of scale, they perform large green energy purchases. This is why using cloud computing services is a great way to develop algorithmic trading systems sustainably concerning the environment, especially for relatively small projects.

References

1. Goede, R.: Sustainable business intelligence systems: modelling for the future. Syst. Res. Behav. Sci. 38(5), 685–695 (2021)
2. Susan S., Plattnerb, G.-K., Knuttic, R., Friedlingstein, P.: Irreversible climate change due to carbon dioxide emissions. The National Academy of Sciences of the USA (2009)
3. Peters, R.L.: Effects of global warming on forests. Forest Ecol. Manag. **35**(1–2), pp. 13–33 (1990). ISSN 0378-1127
4. Rosenthal, D.H., Gruenspecht, H.K., Moran, E.A.: Journal of the IAEE's Energy Economics Education Foundation, vol. 16, no. 2, pp. 77–96 (1995)
5. Taalas, P., Msuya, J.: Global Warming of 1.5 °C. Intergovernmental panel on climate change (2019)
6. Adla, K., Dejan, K., Neira, D., Dragana, Š.: One Health, Integrated Approach to 21st Century Challenges to Health, pp. 281–327 (2022)
7. Feagin, R.A., Sherman, D.J., Grant, W.E.: Coastal erosion, global sea-level rise, and the loss of sand dune plant habitats. Frontiers Ecol. Environ. **3**(7), 359–364 (2005)

8. Masanet, E., et al.: The energy efficiency potential of cloud-based software: A U.S. Case Study, p. 1 (2013)
9. Shehabi, A.: United States Data Center Energy Usage Report, Ernest Orlando Lawrence Berkley National Laboratory (2016)
10. Elliot, S.: Environmentally Sustainable ICT: A Critical Topic for IS Research?" In: PACIS 2007 Proceedings, p. 114 (2007)
11. Elliot, S., Binney, D.: Environmentally sustainable ICT: developing corporate capabilities and an industry-relevant is research agenda. In: PACIS 2008 Proceedings, p. 209 (2008)
12. Lei, K., Ma, Y., Tan, Z.: Performance comparison and evaluation of web development technologies in PHP, Python and Node.js. In: IEEE 17th International Conference on Computational Science and Engineering (2014)
13. Pereira, R., et al.: Ranking programming languages by energy efficiency. Sci. Comput. Programm. **205** (2021)
14. Ahmad, T., Chen, H., Shah, W.A.: Effective bulk energy consumption control and management for power utilities using artificial intelligence techniques under conventional and renewable energy resources. Int. J. Electr. Power Energy Syst. **109**, 242–258 (2019). https://doi.org/10.1016/j.ijepes.2019.02.023
15. Bizo, D.: The Carbon Reduction Opportunity of Moving to Amazon Web Services, 451 Research (2019)
16. Abidi, F., Abidi, H.J.: Cloud libraries: a novel application of cloud computing. Int. J. Cloud Comput. Serv. Sci. **1**, 79–83 (2012).
17. CO2 Emissions in 2022: International Energy Agency (2022)
18. Farooqi, A.M.: Comparative analysis of green cloud computing. Int. J. Adv. Res. Comput. Sci. **8** (2017)

Investigating Air Pollution Dynamics in Ho Chi Minh City: A Spatiotemporal Study Leveraging XAI-SHAP Clustering Methodology

Polat Goktas[1,2](✉), Rajnish Rakholia[1,2], and Ricardo S. Carbajo[1,2]

[1] UCD School of Computer Science, University College Dublin, Belfield, Dublin, Ireland
{polat.goktas,rajnish.rakholia,ricardo.simoncarbajo}@ucd.ie
[2] CeADAR: Ireland's Centre for Applied Artificial Intelligence, Clonskeagh, Dublin, Ireland

Abstract. Air pollution poses an urgent challenge to public health and ecosystems, particularly in rapidly urbanizing regions. Despite the severity of this issue, there is a lack of robust analytical frameworks capable of identifying key variables and their spatial effects across landscapes. Our study directly addresses this void by applying an innovative supervised clustering approach to air quality data in Ho Chi Minh City (HCMC), Vietnam—a rapidly growing urban area grappling with escalating pollution levels. The analytical model employs Shapley Additive exPlanations (SHAP) to interpret feature importance within tree-based machine learning models, supplemented by the Unified Manifold Approximation and Projection (UMAP) technique to explore intersections between affected areas. We utilize a feature set from Rakholia et al. (2023) as input variables for each target time series, with a focus on answering key questions: What pollutants exert the most influence at different times of day? Which areas of the city are most affected? And can this method effectively pinpoint intersections of pollutant effects? Our results reveal morning traffic congestion predominantly elevates levels of Nitrogen Dioxide (NO_2), Humidity, and Carbon Monoxide (CO), while afternoon emissions are significantly impacted by Sulfur Dioxide (SO_2), CO, and Ozone (O_3) due to solar radiation and industrial activities. Through this research, we expect to contribute to the ongoing discourse on urban air pollution management, highlighting the potential of artificial intelligence-driven tools in environmental research and policy-making.

Keywords: Shapley Additive exPlanations (SHAP) · XAI · Air quality

1 Introduction

Air quality is critical for human health and the preservation of the environment's ecology. However, air pollution has become a major concern in many nations, bringing serious health hazards such as a rise in the incidence of heart disease, asthma, and lung cancer [1]. Air pollution also contributes to environmental issues such as global warming, acid rain, and depletion of the ozone layer. Rapid urbanization, uncontrolled transportation, and poorly regulated industrial environments all contribute to the issue. According to

S. Nowaczyk et al. (Eds.): ECAI 2023 Workshops, CCIS 1948, pp. 201–207, 2024.
https://doi.org/10.1007/978-3-031-50485-3_20

the World Health Organization (WHO), 9 out of 10 individuals live in areas where air pollution exceeds WHO limits [2]. According to studies, outdoor air pollution, mostly caused by Particulate Matter ($PM_{2.5}$), causes millions of premature deaths per year globally [3].

With approximately 60,000 fatalities per year attributable to air pollution-related disorders, Ho Chi Minh City (HCMC) in Vietnam has a significant air pollution crisis. As the city's economy and people have grown, so too has the harm to their health posed by the growing $PM_{2.5}$ levels in the metropolis. By 2030, it is expected that $PM_{2.5}$ levels in HCMC and other Vietnamese cities would have increased by 30% [4].

The levels of air pollutants, such as Nitrogen Dioxide (NO_2), Ozone (O_3), Sulfur Dioxide (SO_2), and Carbon Monoxide (CO), in the city exceed the WHO threshold limits, posing serious risks to human health and the environment [5]. The non-linearity and time-varying nature of the data, as well as the complex interplay between air contaminants and meteorological conditions, provide the greatest challenge to accurate air pollution forecasting [6]. Artificial intelligence (AI)-based $PM_{2.5}$ models have demonstrated better performance in dealing with non-linearity and time-varying data [7, 8].

This paper presents a supervised clustering approach based on Shapley Additive exPlanations (SHAP) values to investigate the impact of different air pollution factors, using a publicly accessible outdoor air quality dataset in HCMC. To better understand the causes of air pollution in specific areas, we employ this methodology to go deeper than simple statistical analyses of air contaminants. The main objectives of this study are to (1) identify air pollutant factors and their combinations that are likely to increase at specific time points, (2) identify affected stations or regions of the city, (3) determine the impact of increased pollutant levels on the other areas, and (4) determine the feasibility of using supervised clustering based on SHAP values to identify intersections between affected stations in the city.

2 Related Work

2.1 Application of AI in Forecasting Air Pollutants

There has been a growing trend in employing AI-based models for predicting air quality. Their ability to model non-linear associations and handle large-scale datasets makes them superior for air pollution prediction. Several AI-based models that have been used in this context include Random Forest [9], XGBoost [10], Neural networks [11], and Hybrid and Multi-output models [7, 8].

2.2 Interpreting Models with XAI – SHAP Approach in Environmental Research

The concept of eXplainable AI (XAI) has gained significant traction in recent AI research. The primary objective of XAI is to enhance the transparency and interpretability of complex AI models. One such method is the SHAP approach, which provides a cooperative game theory framework to explain the output of any machine learning model [12]. SHAP values has been effectively applied to diverse environmental research for its capacity to understand complex variable interactions, enhancing model interpretability [13–15]. Specific studies include its integration with machine learning for seasonal

$PM_{2.5}$ projections in Beijing [13], air pollution predictions [14], and highlighting critical factors in estimating NO_2 concentrations [15]. Across these applications, the inclusion of SHAP has consistently improved the transparency, interpretability, and predictive power of the respective environmental models.

3 Investigating Air Pollution Dynamics Using XAI-SHAP Clustering

3.1 Dataset and Experimental Settings

For this study, we adopt the HealthyAir dataset [16], a database of environmental air quality measurements that is freely available to the public, for our evaluation. This public database comprises 52,549 records of air quality measurements compiled by the Air Quality Monitoring Network in HCMC. These records, which span February 2021 to June 2022, were collected from six air monitoring stations distributed across diverse urban locales including residential neighborhoods, commercial zones, and densely populated areas.

The dataset captures two weather conditions—Temperature (°C) and Humidity (%)—and hourly pollutant concentrations—$PM_{2.5}$, Total Suspended Particles (TSP), SO_2, O_3, NO_2, and CO—measured in $\mu g/m^3$. Our research considers data from the following monitoring stations in HCMC:

- *Urban background*: Vietnam National University, HCMC (10.86994333, 106.7960143).
- *Residential*: 49 Thanh Da Street, Binh Thanh District, HCMC (10.81584553, 106.7174282).
- *Traffic*: 268 Nguyen Dinh Chieu Street, District 3, HCMC (10.77636612, 106.6878094).
- *Traffic + Residential*: MM18 Truong Son Street, District 10, HCMC (10.78047163, 106.6594579).

These records underwent various preprocessing stages, including unit conversions, data transformations, and missing value treatments as per established literature [7, 8]. Input variables for each potential air pollutant combination as per Rakholia et al. [8] were sorted for selected time points based on typical patterns of human activity and traffic congestion in HCMC.

3.2 Constructing and Assessing ML Classification Models

We employed a range of cutting-edge tree-based ML methods, such as decision tree, random forest, gradient-boosting decision tree (GBDT), histogram-based gradient-boosting classification tree (HistGBDT), and light gradient-boosting machine (LightGBM, version 3.3.3). The dataset was divided into training and testing sets, and classifiers were trained and tested under different configurations. The performance of ML classifiers was evaluated using metrics like accuracy, precision, recall, and *F1*-score. All experiments were run on a GPU server with specific specifications.

3.3 SHAP-Based Dimensionality Reduction

In order to highlight the value of dimensionality reduction using SHAP values, we performed supervised clustering using average SHAP values as per the feature set proposed by Rakholia et al. [8] for each target time series in the dataset. Tree-based ML models were used to categorize target areas, excluding $PM_{2.5}$ and TSP from the analysis. Additionally, the UMAP (Uniform Manifold Approximation and Projection) technique was employed to depict intersections between affected regions, providing a two-dimensional visual of high-dimensional data.

4 Study Findings and Insights

4.1 Hourly Variations in Air Pollutant Concentrations Across Monitoring Stations

We leveraged a suite of tree-based machine learning models to classify monitoring stations in HCMC into *Urban background*, *Residential*, *Traffic*, and *Traffic plus Residential*, based on NO_2 air pollution level at various time intervals (Table 1). We observe that certain models routinely achieve higher performance across different time intervals. LightGBM, HistGBDT and Random Forest classifiers, for example, perform well across all metrics, especially recall, which is essential for reducing false negatives, while the Decision Tree model results in relatively lower scores. We can see how well all tree-based ML models perform at 9 AM and 5 PM. The Random Forest model performs the best at both 9 AM and 5 PM time points, with the highest accuracy, precision, recall, and *F1*-scores. Overall, the performance of all models is higher at 5 PM than at 9 AM, except for the HistGBDT model. Notably, the models' performances underscored the influence of time and pollutant type on air pollutant concentration classification (Table 1).

Table 1. Performance comparison of tree-based machine learning models in classifying *Urban background*, *Residential*, *Traffic*, and *Traffic plus Residential* monitoring stations for NO_2 air pollution with CO, O_3, SO_2, Humidity, and Temperature at specific time points (7 AM, 9 AM, 1 PM, and 5 PM).

		Percentage Split			
Time	*Model*	*Accuracy*	*Precision*	*Recall*	*F1-score*
07:00	GBDT	89.787	89.896	89.787	88.830
	LightGBM	94.042	94.609	94.043	93.827
	HistGBDT	93.191	93.809	93.191	92.886
	Decision Tree	86.808	86.747	86.809	86.564
	Random Forest	90.639	91.032	90.638	90.024
09:00	GBDT	83.552	85.261	83.553	83.444
	LightGBM	86.184	86.578	86.184	85.946
	HistGBDT	85.526	86.502	85.526	85.293
	Decision Tree	80.263	80.812	80.263	79.915
	Random Forest	87.500	88.477	87.500	87.379
13:00	GBDT	81.364	80.970	81.366	81.109
	LightGBM	88.819	88.656	88.820	88.644
	HistGBDT	88.198	88.257	88.199	87.865
	Decision Tree	80.124	79.960	80.124	79.730
	Random Forest	86.956	87.221	86.957	86.687
17:00	GBDT	85.906	85.826	85.906	85.658
	LightGBM	86.577	86.594	86.577	86.590
	HistGBDT	77.181	77.095	77.181	75.756
	Decision Tree	85.906	85.753	85.906	85.724
	Random Forest	90.604	90.862	90.604	90.421
19:00	GBDT	92.796	92.696	92.797	92.540
	LightGBM	93.220	93.266	93.220	92.905
	HistGBDT	93.644	93.699	93.644	93.368
	Decision Tree	87.288	86.709	87.288	86.655
	Random Forest	91.525	91.454	91.525	91.015

4.2 Feasibility of Supervised Clustering Using SHAP Values

In our experiments, we were unable to distinguish stations from the air quality dataset at specific targeted time points when projected in two-dimensional space using UMAP (Fig. 1A; top left panel). To enhance station characterization from a range of air contaminants, we used a supervised clustering approach, converting raw data into SHAP values from an optimal tree-based trained ML model. We utilized the XAI- SHAP approach to offer insights into the processes behind the contribution of these factors to certain area assignments and examined the intersections between affected areas using the UMAP technique (Fig. 1B; right panel). Based on our analysis of the spatial and temporal dynamics of air pollution variables in HCMC, we have discovered that using SHAP embedding plots for interference mapping between monitoring stations can significantly improve the precision in categorizing the city's neighborhoods. This also enables us to examine the impact of increased pollution levels in different regions on the primary categorization area.

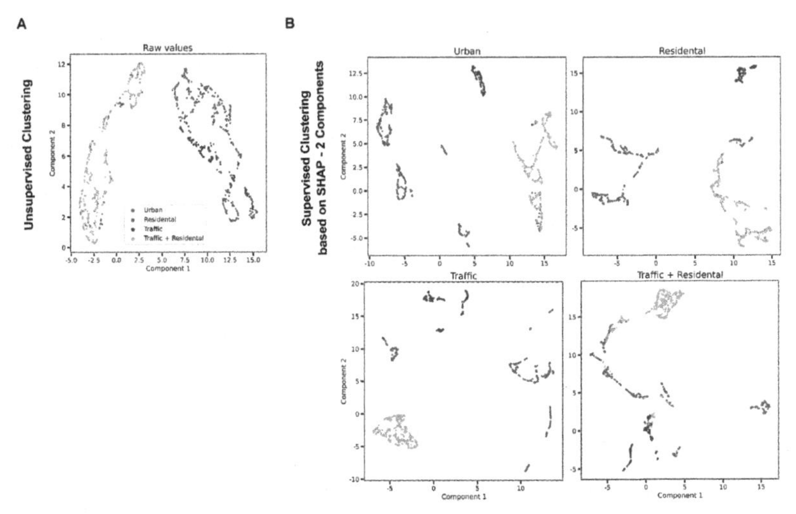

Fig. 1. UMAP visualization and SHAP-based supervised clustering for air quality monitoring stations for O_3 air pollution levels at the 7 AM targeted time point. (A) The unsupervised UMAP projection of stations from the air quality dataset, highlighting the difficulty in distinguishing stations based on raw data alone. (B) Supervised clustering approach using SHAP values derived from tree-based trained ML models, demonstrating improved station characterization based on air pollutant sets. This visualization provides insights into the processes under-lying the contributions of specific variables to station assignments and reveals the intersections between affected areas.

5 Conclusion

In this work, we present a supervised clustering approach based on average Shapley Additive exPlanations (SHAP) values to investigate the impact of various air pollutant factors in Ho Chi Minh City (HCMC), Vietnam. By employing a feature set from Rakholia et al. (2023) in tree-based machine learning models and using the eXplainable artificial intelligence (XAI)-SHAP approach along with the Uniform Manifold Approximation and Projection (UMAP) technique, we can gain a deeper understanding of the influence of various factors and the interplay between impacted regions. The benefits of our proposed methodology are as follows:

- *Enhanced classification performance*: Improved accuracy and precision in categorizing air pollution levels.
- *Interpretability*: The use of SHAP values allows for better understanding and explanation of model predictions.
- *Visualization*: The combination of SHAP and UMAP techniques provides an effective visualization of the relationships between variables and their impacts on air quality.
- *Adaptability*: The methodology can be easily adapted to other datasets, locations, and environmental challenges.

Acknowledgements. This work is part of the MSCA Career-FIT PLUS fellowship, funded by the Enterprise Ireland and the European Commission (Fellowship Ref. Number: MF20200157).

References

1. Mills, N.L., Donaldson, K., Hadoke, P.W., Boon, N.A., MacNee, W., Cassee, F.R., et al.: Adverse cardiovascular effects of air pollution. Nat. Clin. Pract. Cardiovasc. Med. **6**(1), 36–44 (2009)
2. Perez Velasco, R., Jarosinska, D.: Update of the WHO global air quality guidelines: systematic reviews - An introduction. Environ. Int. **170**, 107556 (2022)
3. Lelieveld, J., Evans, J.S., Fnais, M., Giannadaki, D., Pozzer, A.: The contribution of outdoor air pollution sources to premature mortality on a global scale. Nature **525**(7569), 367–371 (2015)
4. Amann, M., Klimont, Z., An Ha, T., Rafaj, P., Kiesewetter, G., Gomez Sanabria, A., et al.: Future air quality in Ha Noi and Northern Vietnam. IIASA Research Report. Laxenburg, Austria (2019)
5. Fan, P., Ouyang, Z., Nguyen, D.D., Nguyen, T.T.H., Park, H., Chen, J.: Urbanization, economic development, environmental and social changes in transitional economies: Vietnam after Doimoi. Landsc. Urban Plan. **187**, 145–155 (2019)
6. Xu, Z., Dun, M., Wu, L.: Prediction of air quality based on hybrid grey double exponential smoothing model. Complexity **2020**, 1–13 (2020)
7. Rakholia, R., Le, Q., Vu, K., Ho, B.Q., Carbajo, R.S.: AI-based air quality $PM_{2.5}$ forecasting models for developing countries: a case study of Ho Chi Minh City, Vietnam. Urban Climate **46**, 101315 (2022)
8. Rakholia, R., Le, Q., Ho, B.Q., Vu, K., Carbajo, R.S.: Multi-output machine learning model for regional air pollution forecasting in Ho Chi Minh City, Vietnam. Environ. Int. **173**, 107848 (2023)
9. Joharestani, M.Z., Cao, C., Ni, X., Bashir, B., Talebiesfandarani, S.: $PM_{2.5}$ prediction based on random forest, XGBoost, and deep learning using multisource remote sensing data. Atmosphere **10**(7), 373 (2019)
10. Zhong, J., Zhang, X., Gui, K., Wang, Y., Che, H., Shen, X., et al.: Robust prediction of hourly $PM_{2.5}$ from meteorological data using LightGBM. Nation. Sci. Rev. **8**(10), nwaa307 (2021)
11. Li, T., Hua, M., Wu, X.: A hybrid CNN-LSTM model for forecasting particulate matter ($PM_{2.5}$). IEEE Access **8**, 26933–26940 (2020)
12. Lundberg, S.M., Lee, S.I.: A unified approach to interpreting model predictions. In: Advances in Neural Information Processing Systems 30 (2017)
13. Wu, Y., Lin, S., Shi, K., Ye, Z., Fang, Y.: Seasonal prediction of daily $PM_{2.5}$ concentrations with interpretable machine learning: a case study of Beijing, China. Environ. Sci. Pollut. Res. **29**(30), 45821–45836 (2022)
14. Gu, Y., Li, B., Meng, Q.: Hybrid interpretable predictive machine learning model for air pollution prediction. Neurocomputing **468**, 123–136 (2022)
15. García, M.V., Aznarte, J.L.: Shapley additive explanations for NO_2 forecasting. Eco. Inform. **56**, 101039 (2020)
16. Rakholia, R., Le, Q., Vu, K.H.N., Ho, B.Q., Carbajo, R.S.: Outdoor air quality data for spatiotemporal analysis and air quality modelling in Ho Chi Minh City, Vietnam: a part of HealthyAir Project. Data Brief **46**, 108774 (2023)

An Experienced Chatbot – The Case of Technical Knowledge at Electricity of France (EDF)

Anne Dourgnon[1](✉), Alain Antoine[2], Pascal Albaladejo[3], and Fabrice Vinet[1]

[1] EDF R&D, Chatou, France
anne.dourgnon@edf.fr
[2] University of Lorraine, Nancy, France
[3] EDF DIPDE, Marseille, France

Abstract. From a practical point of view, *Knowledge Management* is both a mix of well-established corporate procedures and an emerging field of academic research. The opposition might be strong between these different points of view. To go a step forward, we had a pragmatic approach, including theory and practice, engineers, and academics. We will see how an innovation can germinate, with a classical KM problem: experts are retiring soon, how could we "transfer" their experience?

Therefore, we followed a *Data Sliming* methodology, combining Technical Expertise and Contextual Data. In this paper, we focus on an air conditioner: how and where to install it? The discussions in the team set up an innovation: a "conversationalist", i.e., a chatbot whose dialog is that of an expert.

Keywords: Knowledge Management · Chatbot · Abductive Reasoning · Deductive Reasoning · Data Sliming

1 Introduction

Knowledge Management (KM) is both a practice with a set of processes implemented in organizations (companies, institutions, etc.) and an emerging academic field. The oppositions between different conceptions of KM might be strong [Hislop, Bosua & Helms 2018; Holford 2020; Amidon, D. 2009]. Anyway, KM is a reference discipline used in other fields (Organisational theory, information systems and ICT [Antoine & Blum 2013; Serenko & Bontis 2013; Syed, Murray, Hislop & Mouzugui 2018].

To go a step forward in KM, we are adopting a pragmatic approach, including theory theory and practice, engineers, and academics, in a single development process [Lorino 2016; Thievenaz 2019]. We will pay particular attention to the notion of Open Innovation [Chesbrough 2006; Rampa & Agogué 2020].

Our aim in this paper is to show that in a large company (EDF), an innovation can germinate little by little. The starting point is very traditional in KM field: how to preserve and disseminate practical knowledge from the field in specific contexts such as the leaving in retirement of an expert? His or her experiential knowledge is even more important given the long lifespan of a power plant - several decades. What's more, during

S. Nowaczyk et al. (Eds.): ECAI 2023 Workshops, CCIS 1948, pp. 208–215, 2024.
https://doi.org/10.1007/978-3-031-50485-3_21

that period, design semantics lose their strength in favour of operational semantics. This semantic shift poses a problem in terms of capitalising knowledge and transferring it to newcomers.

This innovation was hailed as such by the EDF company (compete for R&D 2020 Trophy). It is part of the evolution of engineering professions. It is based on the *Data Sliming* concept [Kayakutlu & Mercier-Laurent 2016]: how to obtain good results based on a combination of targeted data and business knowledge. The reduction in the volume of data is made possible by expertise, capable of interpreting the context and inferring the applicable resolutions.

We will examine the process by which the problem was posed and, ultimately, in our case study, to incriminate the air conditioner. There were several possible solutions but the team (made up of engineers, technicians and schematists, then computer scientists and, to a lesser extent, academics) gradually decided to make a chatbot.

As the name suggests, a chatbot involves dialogue and conversation. We consider them in their performative dimensions. They generate new knowledge for the company and enable achievements that were not initially anticipated. Building a demonstrator in a context that encourages innovation was an important step.

In the first part, we present the "air conditioner case" in its context. It is presented here for its essentially didactic aspect, as shown in the film "The Click & Connect of the EO". The second, a very concrete point, will show the background to the "Application Sheets", in relation to the "design prescriptions". The following point is an abductive one [Lorino 2018] and of type of *Problem setting*: "how do you decide on an air conditioner?". Points 4 and 5 show how the discussions led to the production of new data that make the chatbot a living being. This innovation has been quietly working to meet its main objective: transforms the traditional uses of chatbots.

2 An Air Conditioner in the Electrical Room?

How to install an air conditioner in a power unit electrical room? This question was put very specifically to the Engineering Office (EO). The EO is studying modifications to first-generation power plants (about 30 in France) following the National Heatwave Plan and its regular updates since the 2003 alert.

The electrical room is a vast room with rows of electrical cabinets, monitored by sensors. It is essential that the air conditioner does not interfere with these sensors, which were installed when the power station was commissioned.

Half a dozen of Schematists is working in this EO. These experts translate the plant's design into diagrams on long, wide sheets called "bed sheets" in business language. The diagrams show the physical nature of the installations, for example a particular electromagnetic relay at a particular location.

This schema language is particularly rigorous. Schematists have a very specific professional skill that can be found in other industries, such as metallurgy. This skill is acquired through in-house training and, above all, through intergenerational experience. This enables the EO to play a major role in preserving and updating knowledge. Operating a power plant is a long-term process: the expert knowledge of Schematists is essential.

The leaving in retirement of the head of the EO and his replacement by Mr P gave rise to a new dynamic: how to capitalize on this knowledge?

To answer this question, one engineer (Mrs A) has capitalized on the knowledge of the EO for the EO. Documenting this knowledge requires writing skills and, above all, skills inspired by ethnomethodology. To be successful, this dual skill requires a propitious context: capitalizing knowledge requires teamwork within a professional community led by a coordinating manager (Mr P).

In this paper, we will show how the initial objective of capitalizing the EO's knowledge has evolved to become a conversational assistant or chatbot. In French, we use the term "Dialogueur" ("conversationalist"): it underlines the value of dialogue as an input. It's not only a discussion between a human and a machine or robot. Basically, the question is that the dialogue generator has been, and is, and will be fed with data. These data were produced by conversations that have taken place within the EO.

The example of the air conditioning unit to be installed in a power unit's electrical room is our guideline for explaining the importance of discursive processes. Mrs A discreet sense of observation in situ revealed a self-evident and unquestioned practice.

First, we'll show how this engineer, her colleague (Mr F) and the head of the EO (Mr P) were able to develop the Knowledge Base.

3 Produce New Documentation to Capitalize on Knowledge

Design instructions - or more precisely, prescriptions - are set out in a succession of documents, ranging from general instructions to practical, case-by-case instructions. For easy consultation, these are set out in sheets called "Principle Sheets" or "Application Sheets" (instructions are applied without discussion).

As instructions are nearly fixed from the design stage, they are rarely updated. They reflect decades of experience that must now be shared with new hands. But these newcomers don't have the same written culture as their elders. In addition, they sometimes have difficulty in understanding the sheets because of a lack of knowledge, that is the famous tacit knowledge, so obvious to the older generation that they often fail to mention it. Experts rarely talk about it, and younger people are sometimes reluctant to ask.... Yet questioning them is where the implicit is expressed.

Our approach was based on observation, questioning and dialogue. It's a long-term project; a "sprint" operation is not possible.

4 How Did the Air Conditioner Come About?

A design engineer comes to the EO with a problem concerning a fire alarm that triggers unexpectedly on a power plant. The discussion then begins in the EO.

The EO first translates this question into its own technical language. The EO is investigating these unexpected triggers and has put forward several hypotheses:

- Hypothesis #1: The EO suspects a change in the electronic circuits. First, the EO checks whether any modifications have been made to these detectors that could have altered their behaviour. The electronic cards have recently been replaced, they're from a new manufacturer. Taking a closer look (that's the role of the EO, not the Design Office), the EO concludes that there has been no change of functionality on these cards.

- Hypothesis #2: a change to the power supplies? The EO checks the power supplies for the fire detection system. Here again, no changes have been made.
- Hypothesis #3: changes around the fire detector? The EO asks his colleagues in the Installations Office (IO) for a list of everything that has recently been installed there. An air conditioner has been installed in the electrical rooms. After discussions, the EO quickly concluded that it was this new air conditioner that was interfering with the detector.

How are the areas of expertise divided between the EO and the IO? The photo below gives a good idea: the circuits installed in electrical cabinets of the electrical rooms are designed by the control engineers, translated into diagrams by the EO and installed by… The fitters. The installers are responsible for the entire installation, including what is needed for it to work properly: the air conditioner.

Fig. 1. A bay in the electrical room of a 900MW PWR power plant

Air conditioners are not strictly speaking part of circuit design skills. But in this "job for insiders", as Mr P puts it, it is invaluable to be able to spot the presence of the air conditioner on the plan. And, indeed, reading a plan is not self-evident: only insiders "see" an air conditioner on the plan below.

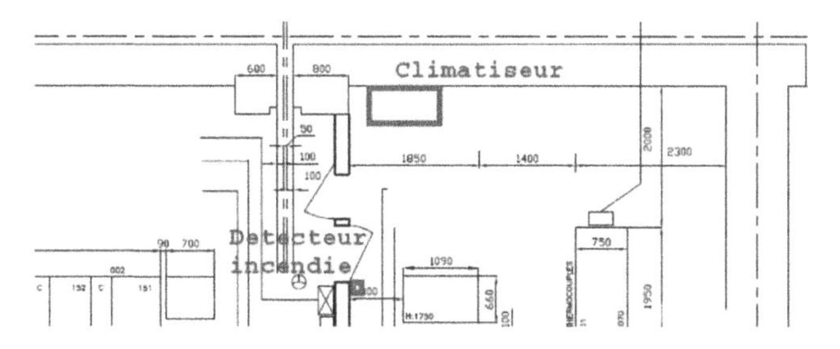

Fig. 2. Plan of the electrical room with the air conditioner and fire detector

Once this third hypothesis had been chosen, the EO discussed to find a robust and rapid solution. The whole EO took part in the discussion, and the debates were lively, with some solutions being considered and then abandoned.

- Can the air conditioner be installed in the lower section?
- Is there another place in the room to move the air conditioner?
- Are the cables long enough?
- What equipment could be affected in the new location? Etc.

A great deal of knowledge and know-how is required: about the equipment and installations (the location and nature of the sensors, the types of signals, changes, and behavior over time) but also about life in the room (the comings and goings of the operators and maintenance staff).

Following this questioning, solutions emerge, ultimately leading to a permanent solution. The plans are updated. As the discussion progressed, Mrs A drew up a note summarizing the list of questions asked and the solution chosen, with its justifications and explanations. At the end of the discussion, Mr P and Mrs A reread the note together and amend it if necessary. Every request leads to questioning and dialogue to clarify and complete it.

5 How Do Discussions Feed the Conversationalist?

A new sheet was initiated with this note. A traditional sheet is "passive": it is not possible to interact with it. To make it "active", we must give it a part of the life that took place at the EO. The initial question is noted, followed by the progression of the questions and the answers given according to the cases encountered. The lexicon and the different wording of the questions are included:

- I need to install an air conditioner, what should I do?
- How do I install an air conditioner?
- Where should I position an air conditioner?

The problem is then capitalised on to make it available to as many people as possible:

- *How are the instructions justified?* Air conditioner must be installed in an area protected from the risk of disturbance.
- *What principles should underlie this installation?* The air conditioner must be installed on the floor, in a defined area, according to the plans given.
- *What explanations are given for this principle?* The air conditioner must be kept away from certain overly sensitive sensors that it could interfere with.

The conclusion is a warning about this phenomenon of disturbance, as well as a suggestion to get in touch with the IO before each installation of an air conditioner to check the surrounding equipment. It is important to explain the disadvantages of air conditioner too close to the sensors, with a clear explanation of the consequences of any erroneous action: *we say and write what not to do.*

6 The Conversationalist and AI

6.1 AI Enables Dialogue

An instruction does not follow a straight line, and there are many design variants. The expert knows them well, but this is not the case for novices. To help them, Mr P draws and diagrams the different possibilities as he sees them (the different cases are rarely verbalized, they are drawn). Each case is associated with a design principle:

IF (Case #i) THEN (Principle #j)

These rules are used by an AI system. In forward chaining, we start from the data, for example we recognise Case #i and deduce the application of Principle #j (deductive reasoning, based on the data). In backward chaining, when we want to know if Principle #j is applicable, we look to see if Case #i arises (hypothetical reasoning, based on the goals). The expert's knowledge, his or her ability to recognise situations to which a novice would not necessarily pay attention, is apparent at every step:

- The user: "How do I install an air conditioner?".
- The conversationalist: "What room are you in?".
- The user: "In the Control Room".
- The conversationalist: "You need to install the air conditioner in an area that is sheltered from the risk of disturbance" (*justification*).
- The user: "How?".
- The conversationalist: "In which case are you?".
- The user: "Case #1".
- The conversationalist: "The air conditioner must be installed on the floor, in a defined area, according to the plans given" (*principle*).
- The user: "Why?".
- The conversationalist: "The air conditioner must be located away from certain sensors that are too sensitive and could interfere with them" (*explanation*).

6.2 The Life of the Conversationalist

The Open Innovation Team supports this innovation and gives it a breath of fresh air with *Lean Startup*. Iterative experimentation is authorised and even encouraged!

The team had the idea of using these sheets in a chatbot, a tool traditionally designed for simple, recurring questions rather than complex technical ones. The advantage of a chatbot is that it is easy to use: a question leads to an answer, or even a more detailed explanation, illustrated by diagrams. The user can give feedback on the answer, which helps to improve the tool and keep it alive.

Knowledge is not structured in the same way as it is in Expert Systems. There is no modelling of the knowledge domain: there is no way of describing the variety of knowledge involved, in the form of a semantic network, an ontology or even a hierarchy of concepts. It is the dialogue, with its succession of questions and answers, that organises the knowledge, taking account of "semantic shifts". In other words, the Data Model - or rather, the Knowledge Model - is dictated by the dialogue modes. This optimisation requires a great deal of rigour, from design to implementation. It is the price to pay to operate in a contextualised and relevant way. Especially as the application is rich in documents, diagrams, plans and links with other applications, references that need to be carefully managed.

The AI Team at EDF Solution Lab produced a very convincing prototype. The prototype is systematically tested to ensure that it complies with the dialogue set out in the sheets. Tests are exhaustive and recorded in a thick test book.

The conversationalist is directly accessible to engineers and technicians. It reaches its target audience straight away! Its commissioning is satisfactory: thanks to the completeness of its Knowledge Base, 94% of the themes are recognized. Unrecognized themes and user comments are reviewed weekly by the expert, who improves the tool and brings it to life. In fact, the life of the conversationalist can only be sustained by the questioning of users (assisted, in the future, by chatbot suggestions?).

7 Conclusions

The installation of the air conditioner has shown us that the design and production of a conversationalist leads to an innovative practice. This new practice makes it possible to capitalise on experiential knowledge following, for example, a leaving in retirement. It adapts to very specific and localised cases.

This innovation is the result of the performance of inter-professional discussions within an informal group driven largely by a team spirit and a community of "common concern" views. It saves on data and knowledge. In this sense, it contributes to the sustainable development of the company's digital economy.

The chatbot has acquired a certain notoriety: it knows how to provide relevant information in response to a clearly formulated question. The conversationalist uses the chatbot's technology but incorporates the questions as formulated by the agents involved in the EO. Cognitive AI enables them to be translated into an application [Dourgnon, Antoine & Samba 2020]. Our Chatbot-Conversationalist can answer questions formulated in natural language and avoids the time wasted searching through the mass of documents.

The codification of explicit and implicit knowledge cannot be reduced to a process of Knowledge Extraction; it is a socialised process, in which discursive exchanges within different communities play a central role. Wenger's work [Thievenaz 2019] has stimulated a great deal of academic research on Communities of Practice (CoP).

Today, many CoP have developed in companies and organisations [Mabey & Zhao 2017; Lorino 2016; APQC 2021]. A new open question arises: how can these communities be managed for the company? A new challenge for managerial practices?

Acknowledgments. We would like to thank our EDF colleagues: Marie-Astrid De Muynck, Idriss El Asry, Anne-Cécile Ladrange, Aleksandra Lewicka and Alain Ourghanlian.

References

Amidon, D.: Innovation strategy for the knowledge economy, Ed. Routledge (2009)

Antoine, A., Blum, G.: La gestion des connaissances ou le Knowledge Management (KM). Revue Internationale De Psychosociologie Et De Gestion Des Comportements Organisationnels **19**, 23–31 (2013)

APQC American Productivity & Quality Center: Atteindre l'excellence avec les Communau-tés de pratique (2021)

Chesbrough, H.W.: Open Innovation: the new imperative for creating and profiting from technology. First trade paper edition. ed. Harvard Business Review Press, Boston, Mass (2006)

Dourgnon, A., Antoine, A., Samba, M.: Ontologies combining design semantics and seman-tics used in operation and maintenance: Feedback from EDF power plants case studies. I-ESA, Tarbes, France (2020)

Hislop, D., Bosua, R., Helms, R.: Knowledge Management in Organizations: a critical in-troduction. 4th ed. OUP Oxford, Oxford, G.B (2018)

Holford, W.D.: Managing knowledge in organizations: a critical pragmatic perspective. Palgrave Macmillan (2020)

Kayakutlu, G., Mercier-Laurent, E.: Intelligence in Energy, ISTE Editions, Londres (2016)

Lorino, P.: Pragmatisme et Etude des Organisations. Economica (2018)

Lorino, P.: De Skerlock Holmes au lean management: théorie et pratique, deux dimensions insé-parables de l'enquête. Dans : A La Pointe Du Management. Ce Que La Recherche Ap-porte Au Manager. Dunod (2016)

Mercier-Laurent, E., Kayalica, O., Owoc, M.L.: Artificial intelligence for knowledge manage-ment. In: 8th IFIP WG 12.6 International Workshop, AI4KM 2021, Held at IJCAI 2020, Yokohama, Japan, 7–8 January, Technology Book 614 (2020)

Mabey, C., Zhao, S.: Managing five paradoxes of knowledge exchange in networked organ-izations: new priorities for HRM? Hum. Resour. Manag. J. **27**, 39–57 (2017). https://doi.org/10.1111/1748-8583.12106

Rampa, R., Agogué, M.: Lorsque les démarches d'exploration nécessitent de l'innovation collective. Rev. Francaise Gest. **291**, 53–71 (2020)

Serenko, A., Bontis, N.: The intellectual core and impact of the knowledge management aca-demic discipline. J. Knowl. Manag. 17, 13673271311300840 (2013). https://doi.org/10.1108/13673271311300840

Syed, J., Murray, P.A., Hislop, D., Mouzugui, Y.: The Palgrave Handbook of Knowledge Management (2018)

Thievenaz, J.: Enquêter et apprendre au travail : Approcher l'expérience avec John Dewey. Editions Raison et Passions (2019)

Wenger, E.: Communities of Practice: Learning, Meaning, and Identity. Cambridge University Press, Cambridge, UK.; New York, NY (1998)

Towards a Sustainable Future: The Use of Electrical Energy in Smart Cities

Michał Petri and Iwona Chomiak(✉)

Wroclaw University of Economics and Business, 53-345 Wrocław, Poland
iwano.chomak-orsa@ue.wroc.pl

Abstract. An intelligent city is a center that effectively manages its resources to ensure a high standard of living for its residents while maintaining ecological awareness. The effective management of energy poses a significant problem in major urban areas, mostly attributable to the intricate nature and criticality of energy networks. Intelligent energy management in residential structures is crucial to smart city efficiency. Energy management involves demand management, peak load reduction, and carbon dioxide emission reduction. Risk management, efficiency, and sustainable development are integral elements of every energy management strategy in smart cities. Risk elimination, effectiveness, and environmentally friendly growth are fundamental components that form an essential part of energy management strategies in smart cities. They are an indispensable condition for the transformation from the traditional model based on conventional sources to a more sustainable system using renewable energy. The article is a literature review presenting the role of smart grids in creating smart cities.

Keywords: Smart cities · Smart grids · Energy management · Internet of Things · Innovations · Information and communication technologies · Electricity

1 Introduction

Creating environmentally friendly and sustainable cities according to the vision for 2030, Goal 11: Sustainable Cities and Communities, cannot be achieved without continuous changes in the electricity sector. The increase in energy demand and use is inextricably linked to the depletion of non-renewable resources, climate change and global warming. As a result of the climate and energy package, there is increasing pressure to reduce the negative environmental impact of electricity production, distribution and use [1]. At the level of the European Union, all Member States have committed to increasing by 2030 share of renewable energy in EU energy consumption to at least 27%. [2]. Transitioning from traditional energy sources, such as fossil fuels, to clean and renewable electricity sources is crucial for reducing greenhouse gas emissions. In cities, where a large number of people concentrate, and many economic sectors operate, transforming the energy system to become more electric contributes to achieving climate goals and improving air quality. The development of artificial intelligence and machine learning should contribute to improving the quality of life in a sustainable way, one that respects the rights of

S. Nowaczyk et al. (Eds.): ECAI 2023 Workshops, CCIS 1948, pp. 216–222, 2024.
https://doi.org/10.1007/978-3-031-50485-3_22

beneficiaries. The article addresses the key aspects illustrating the significance of the electricity sector in achieving this goal. Access to electrical energy can be considered a social good, and therefore, state supervision in this sector is necessary [3].

The energy sector is a vital part of the economy, often operating as natural monopolies (network companies) and not subject to market regulation. State intervention is driven by the special social role of electricity supply, treated as a sphere of public utility. While electricity is a commodity, its strategic importance and impact on the functioning of the economy and society's livelihoods have led to national legislation, following EU guidelines, to create rules that substitute competition in this sector. The main aim of the publication is to identify and analyze the benefits associated with the use of electrical energy in smart energy grids, smart buildings, and demand management to minimize energy losses and increase energy efficiency. The article examines the possibilities of utilizing smart grids technologies and data analysis to monitor energy consumption and optimize its distribution in cities.

The choice of this topic was determined by the relevance of the discussed issue. Adopting such a goal is connected with the author's understanding of the idea of using electric energy in a smart city. Information and Communication Technology (ICT) systems in public administration offices, various sorts of agencies, municipal enterprises, and entities providing services to cities acquire a variety of data types that can be utilized for a variety of purposes. Typically, the amount of data collected and then processed is determined by the party in charge of the system. It should be noted, however, that part of the recorded data is not input as forms for describing major events, but can be recorded as electronic tags using Internet of Things (IoT) tools [4]. ICT solutions enable organizations to support all of its business processes [5]. At the same time, the author assumes that the technological advancement of intelligent energy grids is not at a sufficient level. According to the author, municipal authorities use ICT for individual ad hoc actions. However, they often express an opinion about the lack of utilization of intelligent grid technologies in many areas of urban activities, which would further improve the lives of smart city residents. The issue of intelligent electric energy grids is widely discussed in contemporary literature, including the field of Power Engineering or Automation and Process Control. [6]. Creating "smart buildings" and a more efficient transportation system is crucial for addressing climate change and other environmental issues. Teleinformatics technologies and the concept of a smart city create immense possibilities for taking actions. New technologies allow real-time data sharing (e.g., about the location of public transportation vehicles) and enable understanding specific behavior patterns to create tailored solutions, optimize city operations, and generate savings. Suburban expansion and urban development pose significant challenges to planners in many countries [7]. Unsustainable urbanization has social consequences such as congestion and difficulties for suburban residents to adapt, as well as environmental impacts such as the loss of natural habitats. Negative effects of this process also include communication problems and loss of agricultural land.

In India, an example of this is the pressure caused by population growth and urban saturation, resulting in the density of urban centers such as Dhanbad and Jamshedpur. In addition, as in the case of Ranchi Urban, the conversion of agricultural land into built-up land has been document [8]. In Smart City, data from Internet of Things (IoT) sensors, such as motion sensors, presence sensors, smart energy meters, etc., can be used to monitor real-time energy consumption. This data can be used to create predictions and optimize energy consumption. The function of smart grids in supplying renewable energy.

Smart Grid makes it possible for users to use electricity more effectively while simultaneously providing more efficient ways to create and deliver it Smart grids facilitate the integration of renewable energy sources and offer several environmental advantages to nations in terms of electricity generation [9]. These include environmentally acceptable alternatives to fossil fuels like wind, solar, and biomass, which are used in numerous large power plants [10]. As a result, greenhouse gas emissions that contribute to global warming can be decreased control the network's technical foundation This makes it possible for proactive maintenance to be done and allows for a quicker response time to a failure. Taking into account both technological and political considerations, a smart grid ensures security of supply with minimal risk of interruptions. The implementation of this strategy ensures energy independence through the mitigation of external vulnerabilities to energy supply, including political and economic uncertainties. When planning smart cities, regional planners need to be aware of the challenges of powering energy-dependent infrastructure. If the smart grid is to prosper and provide efficient service to its settlers. Planners must be prepared to deal with the many threats that threaten the smart grid. Utilizing advanced technologies and data analysis enables better management of the power grid in Smart Cities. Data related to energy consumption, system performance, weather conditions, and other factors are analyzed to optimize energy distribution and minimize losses. The integration of renewable energy sources is a key focus in the development of Smart Cities, which aim to promote sustainable and environmentally friendly solutions. This involves placing a growing emphasis on incorporating technologies such as solar panels and wind turbines to harness renewable energy. The management of the power grid involves the effective integration of various energy sources with the aim of enhancing the proportion of renewable energy and mitigating the release of greenhouse gas emissions.

2 Research Background

Smart City technologies play an essential part in supporting sustainability and cost reduction in urban areas, particularly in the domains of energy, water, and gas. The implementation of automated data gathering systems allows for the efficient monitoring of energy usage, additionally facilitating intelligent control systems that can enhance overall energy efficiency. Optimized lighting, heating, or cooling significantly reduces energy costs. For instance, the system can "learn" and only heat a room during the hours it is typically used, contributing to reduced energy consumption (Trindade et al. 2017). Intelligent technology can also be used to automatically optimize electricity consumption in buildings through efficient control of lighting and elevators. A smart grid is defined as a collection of energy production sources, storage and consumption points combined into a uniform structure that can be used in isolated mode (island mode) or integrated with the electricity grid (connected mode). The management of electricity flow within a smart grid is subject to economic and technical requirements. The installed capacity of smart grids can range from a few kW to several MW. Properly constructed smart grids play a key role in improving the reliability and resilience of power grids by creating a backup emergency system in crisis situations. The components of smart grids include: ordinary rotating machines, renewable energy sources (solar, wind, fuel cells and combined heat and power plants), isolation and protection devices (at the point of coupling) and intelligent network controllers at the local or distributed level that are responsible for local and distributed control operations. Creating a smart city requires implementing multidimensional strategies that encompass all the mentioned aspects. It is a process that involves using solutions from the Internet of Things (IoT), Big Data, and artificial intelligence tools to make more accurate decisions, resulting in reduced crime rates, shorter commute times, lower CO2 emissions, water and electricity savings, etc. Smart Grids are divided into five categories that meet specific requirements: commercial or industrial, community, campus, military and remote. Smart City derives its intelligence from the combination of ideology and technology, as well as collaboration among people, institutions, and businesses. Working together allows us to strive for sustainable development and achieve a better quality of life in the city. The following research hypotheses are associated with the realization of this goal: The introduction of smart technologies in energy networks brings significant economic benefits, regardless of the regulatory structure. Evidence shows that these benefits outweigh the investment costs. The European Union strives to create an internal electricity market across its entire territory, allowing for the free flow of goods (electricity) and services (transmission and distribution). The liberalization and demonopolization processes were only possible with legal reforms that effectively regulate the electricity sector. In Europe, the main driving force behind changes in the functioning of national electricity markets has been the EU institutions, legislative acts, and the case law of EU courts. Ensuring the functioning and development of competition in the energy market is one of the three fundamental assumptions for this sector in both national and European energy policies[1].

The European energy market has certain characteristics that distinguish it from other product markets. The specific nature of the electricity market results from the physical characteristics of the power system. Differences between commodity markets and the electricity market include the need to ensure a continuous balance between electricity demand and production, low price elasticity of demand in the short term, the impossibility of short-term product storage, the strategic importance of uninterrupted power system operation, and the tendency towards market monopolization due to the specific physical characteristics of the power system. The proper functioning of the electricity market is supposed to ensure rational prices, reliable energy supply with high-quality parameters, and guarantee the market profitability of entities operating in the power sector. Separating electricity as a product from its supply as network services (transmission, distribution, quality assurance, coordination of supply and demand balancing) is the most important assumption of market implementation. This allows for separate price setting for the

[1] Por. Commission of the European Communities, Green Paper European Strategy for Sustainable, Competitive and Secure Energy, Brussels, on 8 march 2006, KOM (2006), 105 final version {SEK (2006)317 and the Ministry of Economy, Energy Policy of Poland do 2025 r., Chapter I point 1, Objectives of the priority principle, Announcement of the Minister of Economy and Labor of 1 July 2005 on the state energy policy until 2025 (Official Gazette No. 42, item 562).

product and services and introduces competitive principles in electricity trading [11]. Additionally, the market must ensure equal treatment of all participants, free access to the market limited only by technical or financial barriers, freely shaping the price of electricity, and regulated pricing for network operations (tariffing) due to the existence of network monopolies. There is a lack of a binding EU legal definition of the relevant market and guidelines for its determination. The Commission's announcement on the definition of the relevant market could be useful in this regard (Commission Notice on the definition of the relevant market for the purposes of Community competition law) [12].

3 Prediction Models of Electrical Consumption in Smart Cities

With increasing costs of energy, the necessity of renewable energy sources, and climate change, the existing power infrastructure is becoming outmoded and facing many constraints such as cybersecurity, privacy, and power loss due to one-way communication [13]. A smart grid is the answer to this challenge. The smart grid system is the digital power system of the future, allowing for two-way communication between the center and the device to the center. Instead of adjusting the controlled production of electricity to "constant" demand, the aim is to flexibly match supply and demand in real time throughout the system, including the distribution network. In this approach, consumers play a key role by responding to more environmentally friendly, if less predictable, production, as well as potentially exploiting the storage of energy sources. The first part of this report focused on identifying the challenges to which such a transformation is to be an answer. Below, we will present the planned changes in the structure of the network, with particular reference to international examples.

The three most commonly used methods for predicting electrical energy are classical prediction, traditional prediction models, and intelligent prediction models [14]. Classical prediction methods include trend extrapolation, load forecasting, and load density methods. These prediction methods are widely used, but most of them analyze the relationship between some simple variables, lacking in-depth data analysis, which often results in low prediction accuracy. Traditional prediction methods include regression analysis, which establishes the relationship between dependent variables and known energy consumption data, predicting the electricity load through mathematical analysis. Time series methods include exponential smoothing and Census decomposition methods. Random time series methods include state-space methods, Box-Jenkins methods, and Markov methods [15]. The smart grid's stability prediction becomes important to make it more reliable and to increase the efficiency and consistency of the electrical supply.

4 Conclusions and Considerations

All these elements work together to ensure a more sustainable, efficient, and flexible management of the power grid in Smart Cities. Europe's electricity grid has historically been designed to route centralized and "controlled" production from large power stations to consumption points. This paper presents the challenge of leaving this centralized approach in order to adapt to technological, historical and social progress. In order to carry out this transformation in the best conditions, the author suggests four key directions of action.

Proposal 1: Launch initiatives to finance and accelerate the transformation of electricity networks. Inclusion in the pan-European discussion on methods of financing investments in power infrastructure. These investments should involve local authorities, network managers, energy distributors, consumer representatives, investor groups (banks, investment funds) and regulatory authorities (both national and European).

Proposal 2: Review of administrative procedures governing the installation of network infrastructure in order to make them fit for the intended purposes. A simplified and adequate administrative and regulatory procedure for projects enjoying greater social support, e.g. in the case of underground power lines. Opening a public discussion on regulated tariffs in order to adapt them to changes in the power system. The priority is to encourage consumers to better control their energy consumption by introducing smart meters and other technical tools enabling more effective management of energy consumption.

Proposal 3: Support self-consumption and develop the storage sector. The development of wind energy and photovoltaics should be in parallel with the development of the industrial storage sector and incentives for self-consumption. In the case of small RES installations (up to 250 kW), it is proposed to adjust the electricity purchase tariff for new contracts to favor self-use. Photovoltaic energy production can be combined with improving the energy performance of buildings by promoting production and demand management and smart meter functions. For existing larger industrial RES installations (over 250 kW), it was proposed to introduce a mechanism facilitating the management of instabilities and strengthening the position of producers.

Proposal 4: Promote the growth of the stationary storage sector in the European Union by allowing renewable energy to be stored and energy recovered from stock at the same level as initial energy. Implementation of storage at each stage of the electrical network is also being considered. Low-cost stationary storage technologies have potential for further development.

The goal of a Smart City should be a system of distributed response to the needs of its residents Due to the limited nature of the text in the publication, the discussed topics have been analyzed only to a restricted extent. Further analyses may focus on the impact of energy saving through smart solutions. They should also encompass the extensive use of Smart City concepts in human functioning, undoubtedly involving raising awareness of the importance of such an approach. Another proposed research area is the possibility and potential limitation of the number of energy-consuming devices managed by public authorities.

References

1. Kłosowski G.; Hoła A.; Rymarczyk T.; Mazurek M.; Niderla K.; Rzemieniak M., Using Machine Learning in Electrical Tomography for Building Energy Efficiency through Moisture Detection. Energies 2023, 16, 1818. https://doi.org/10.3390/en16041818

2. Phan, C., Plouhinec, C.: Key figures for renewable energies, Ministry of Transition Ecological - SDES, The statistical data and studies service Edition (2021)
3. Jasiński, P., Skoczny, T., George, Y.: Konkurencja a regulacja w energetyce, Warsaw, p. 19 (1995)
4. Stepniak, C., Jelonek, D., Wyrwicka, M., Chomiak-Orsa, I.: Integration of the Infrastructure of Systems Used in Smart Cities for the Planning of Transport and Communication Systems in Cities, Energies, pp. 2 (2021)
5. Jelonek, D., Chomiak, I.: The application of ICT in the area of value co-creation mechanisms support as determinant of innovation activities. Int. J. Ambient Comput. Intell. **9**(2), 37 (2018)
6. Trindade, E.P., Hinnig, M.P.F., Moreira, E., da Costa, J., Marques, S., Bastos, R.C., Yigitcanlar, T.: Sustainable development of smart cities: a systematic review of the literature. J. Open Innov. Technol. Market Complex. **3**(3), 1–14 (2017). https://doi.org/10.1186/s40852-017-0063-2
7. Sahana, M., Hong, H., Sajjad, H.: Analyzing urban spatial patterns and trend of urban growth using urban sprawl matrix: a study on Kolkata urban agglomeration India. Sci. Total. Environ. **628**, 1557–1566 (2018)
8. Ibid., p. 216
9. Shaukat, N., Ali, S.M., Mehmood, C.A., Khan, B., Jawad, M., Farid, U., et al.: A sustainable regional planning 16 survey on consumers empowerment, communication technologies, and renewable generation penetration within smart grid. Renew. Sustain. Energy Rev. **81**, 1453–1475 (2018)
10. Bari, A., Jiang, J., Saad, W., Jaekel, A.: Challenges in the smart grid applications: an overview. Int. J. Distrib. Sens. Netw. **10**, 974682 (2014)
11. Szczygieł L., Model rynku energii elektrycznej, [w:] Jaki model rynku energii?, red. M. Okólski, Biblioteka Regulatora, Warszawa, p. 1 (2001)
12. Commission Notice on the definition of the relevant market for the purposes of Community competition law 97/C 372/03 (Dz. U. C 372 z 9.12.1997 r)
13. Gharavi, H.; Ghafurian, R. Smart Grid: The Electric Energy System of the Future, vol. 99. IEEE, Piscataway (2011)
14. Marjani, M. Acces IEEE **5**, 5247–5261. al.et [4] L. Anthopoulos, "Smart Utopia vs. Smart Reality: Experiential Learning from 10 Smart Cities Cases" (2017)
15. Ghalehkhondabi, I., et al.: An overview of energy demand forecasting methods published in 2005–2015. Energy Syst. **8**(2), 411–447 (2017)
16. Kumar, A., Pandey, A.C., Hoda, N., Jeyaseelan, A.: Evaluation of urban sprawl pattern in the tribal-dominated cities of Jharkhand state, India. Int. J. Remote Sens. **32**, 7651–7675 (2011)
17. Standard ISO 37122:2019 Sustainable cities and communities—Indicators for smart cities; Internationa Organization for Standardization: Geneva, Switzerland (2019)

The Importance of Eco-Commerce in the Context of Sustainable Development: A Case Study Analysis

Konrad Liszczyk(✉) and Iwona Chomiak-Orsa

Wroclaw University of Economics and Business, Wrocław, Poland
konrad.liszczyk@ue.wroc.pl

Abstract. Sustainability has become a priority for many sectors of the economy, including the e-commerce sector, and the concept of eco-commerce is emerging as a key concept to support this goal. This article highlights the importance of eco-commerce as a strategic factor for companies pursuing sustainability in the SME sector, harmonizing business goals with environmental concerns. The case study considers the implementation of specific solutions in four key areas of the sector studied: business model, operational materials, order management and image communication. In addition, the empirical section also includes constraints related to the implementation of eco-commerce elements in the organization's structures, such as the cost of internal eco-innovations, changes in operational processes and the need to change organizational culture. The increasing role of process automation, especially the aforementioned operational processes related to sales and after-sales activities, is due to growing economic challenges, such as rising purchasing volumes, declining margins, rising transaction costs and intensifying competition. In order to meet these challenges, organizations must demonstrate a high degree of adaptability and self-organizational intelligence, which in the case under review takes sustainability as a leading aspect. The research process also included a review of academic and industry literature to systematize concepts related to the use of eco-commerce strategies in the context of sustainability. Findings from the analysis can inform the development of key operational practices and sustainable strategies for companies operating in the e-commerce sector.

Keywords: eco-commerce · e-commerce · sustainability · case study

1 Introduction

Today's challenges of climate change, natural resource depletion and environmental degradation require new approaches to economic development. The concept of sustainable development, based on simultaneous consideration of economic, social and environmental aspects, has become a key goal for many countries and organizations around the world. In this context, there is a growing interest in green e-commerce (eco-commerce) as a way to promote sustainable economic development. Eco-commerce refers to online

S. Nowaczyk et al. (Eds.): ECAI 2023 Workshops, CCIS 1948, pp. 223–229, 2024.
https://doi.org/10.1007/978-3-031-50485-3_23

sales activities that take into account the environmental aspects of the production, distribution and consumption of goods and services and services, guided by the doctrine of sustainable development. The aforementioned form of digital commerce is primarily aimed at minimizing the negative impact of economic activity on the environment, while maintaining the competitiveness and profitability of enterprises, which in the long run is also expected to lead to minimizing costs (Detlor, 2001). Eco-commerce, understood broadly as a philosophy of operating in the market, is an area that includes practices such as:

1) *Green procurement* - practices related to the holistic preparation and execution of orders, including pre- and post-sales service to consumers
2) *Eco-design* - designing both products, services and processes based on the principles of sustainable development

2 Eco-Commerce as a Tool for Sustainable Development

E-commerce sustainability aims to minimize the negative environmental impacts of online retail activities. Traditional retail models are often associated with increased greenhouse gas emissions, excessive energy consumption, excessive waste production and other negative impacts on the environment. E-commerce sustainability sets itself the task of addressing these issues and striving for a balance between economic growth and environmental protection. From an ecological point of view, operating in the e-commerce sector is much more focused on sustainability than traditional sales - stationary (Mohamad, Hassan, Elrahman, 2001). When shopping online, we reduce traffic on the streets and use less packaging. Research also confirms this - stationary retail generates 1.5 to 2.9 times more carbon dioxide than its digital counterpart. According to a report by Kantar, 42% of online shoppers in Poland are able to pay more for a unit product if it is communicated as - eco-friendly, biodegradable, or environmentally neutral (Table 1).

One of the concepts that operates in organizations applying the doctrine of sustainable development is the implementation of green procurement. This opens up new market opportunities for companies based on the aforementioned eco-commerce philosophy. In the context of sustainability, it is also important to consider not only the economic aspect, but also the social aspect. From an entrepreneurial perspective, which comes from being involved in ensuring the financial flow of an organization, profitability and sustainability do not always correlate positively. Nowadays, greater concern for the environment including following sustainability-driven aspects is combined with greater expenses - changing suppliers, manufacturers, or packaging to biodegradable ones can be much more costly than traditional counterparts (Engelhardt 2023). According to the *E-commerce Delivery Compass* report, more than 50% of consumers expect e-commerce stores to provide environmentally friendly delivery options, and 60% believe that online stores use excessive packaging and fillers. Users' satisfaction with met demands is primarily higher loyalty and higher retention rates. (Zhu and Thatcher 2010) From an economic point of view, the key to realizing eco-commerce are:

1. Organic products
2. Minimize packaging
3. Energy efficiency

Table 1. Eco commerce assumptions in the business model - "*Re*".

Assumptions	Area of influence	Purpose of establishment	Implementation in practice
Reduce	Green delivery	Courier companies' actions for sustainable development	Creating pick-up points - according to Gemius, this method of delivering parcels reduces CO2 emissions by nearly 75%
Reverse commerce	Selling used products	Strategy changes brand perception and reduces costs	H&M, allows clothes to be donated to the store, they go on the market as second-hand clothing
Reuse,	Warehouse processes, operating materials	Use of reusable packaging and storage operating supplies	InPost with Modivo brand - reusable packaging tests
Repurpose	Education	Related to creativity and economy of resources, looking at objects-new ways to use them	AllegroOne - exchange of electrical equipment at collection points

Source:Own elaboration

4. Transportation and logistics
5. Education and awareness

Companies for which the doctrine of sustainable development is of paramount importance in creating an e-commerce environment, point to the benefits of high market competitiveness based on increasing environmental awareness among consumers as a value (Gregor and Kaczorowska-Spychalska 2020).

3 Define the Research Methods

In the research process, a case study method was used. Due to the detailed analysis of the research problem, this method will work well in describing a complex and multifaceted case, leading to a comprehensive understanding of cause-and-effect relationships. One of the methods used was also *action research* due to, active participation inside the studied organization. (Glinka and Czakon 2021). In order to present the importance of eco-commerce in the e-commerce sector, a review of academic and industry literature on sustainability and eco-commerce application strategies was also conducted.

4 A Case Study of a Polish Fashion and Accessories e-store (SMEs)

In the face of growing environmental challenges, the eco-commerce concept has been applied by a Polish fashion e-store and accessories. The company, which has been operating continuously since 1957, decided in 2013 in the era of digital transformation to establish an internal e-commerce department. The conversion of sales of fashion and accessories items was applied on a B2C level, using such sales channels as the company's own e-shop and key regional marketplaces. The entire effort understood to be embarking on a path of sustainable development was subjected to a strategic pre-inspection. Management introduced assumptions, which have been implemented since 2021 by virtue of structured operational processes that take place periodically as part of sales tasks on the network. Based on the doctrine of sustainability, fueled by the concept of eco-commerce, points of contact between the e-commerce brand and common ecological concepts were established, including, in turn, frameworks:

1) **Warehouse area:** Reduce plastic, film or foam in the order packaging proces → Use of eco-friendly and biodegradable parcel fillers and cardboard shipping boxes, including paper tape.
2) **Goods delivery area:** orders with contractors are based on prior predictive analysis and seasonal variation, so that the quantities of goods ordered directly to the company are correspondingly higher/lower → Reducing carbon emissions, but also the economics of warehouse operation in the reception process.
3) **Courier delivery area:** Selective approach to working with courier companies that are guided by sustainability values → Selection of companies that also have an eco-commerce philosophy in their mission and vision (electric cars, pick-up point offerings)
4) **Productization area:** A key movement from the perspective of business operations, laying the groundwork for the application of the eco-commerce philosophy, i.e. starting to work with contractors who have an area of environmentally friendly, environmentally neutral or biodegradable goods in their product ranges, with elements that were created from recycled materials → In the fashion and accessories industry, the leading *fast fashion* trend had to be curtailed, in the case of accessories such as umbrellas, all technological solutions were replaced with biodegradable or recycled materials.
5) **Product presentation area:** Provide as accurate product descriptions as possible, enriched with quality photos and videos → Minimize the risk of purchase dissatisfaction and unnecessary returns.
6) **User education:** Creation of special areas inside the site dedicated to education about sustainability and applied eco-commerce practices → Through customer education, broad CSR and eco-commerce campaigns (planting trees for each purchase and percentage discounts for returning used goods) are applied. Providing this information contributes to building customer trust, enhancing loyalty and building a positive image as a socially responsible company.

One of the main areas where AI is supporting e-commerce sustainability is in logistics optimization. Machine learning algorithms analyze delivery, warehousing and transportation data, identifying optimal routes, minimizing greenhouse gas emissions and reducing losses in the supply chain. Another area where AI plays an important role is in predicting trends and demand, which is directly related to warehouse-related software. With advanced data analysis algorithms, changes in customer preferences and seasonal increases or decreases in sales can be predicted. This enables effective production planning and inventory management, which minimizes wasted resources and contributes to the efficient use of raw materials. Sustainability for the case studied includes both the use of eco-commerce elements and process optimization, which are also indirectly the result of the initial assumptions based on the application of eco-solutions in the organization's structures (Motowidlak and Tokarski 2022). Key from the entity's point of view was the optimization of warehouse processes and document processing support processes. As a first step, a warehouse management system (WMS) was introduced. The main objectives to be covered by the organization under study were to improve the efficiency of deliveries, minimize the distance traveled by people in the warehouse through efficient positioning of goods (improving labor economics), and manage goods through an intelligent system for detecting shortages and predictive behavior toward rotating goods. The table below illustrates a summary of two key ICT solutions from an implementation perspective that are driving the change toward eco-commerce solutions in the surveyed organization (Table 2).

Table 2. Process automation areas - improving labor economics

	Automation of workflow	Automation of warehouse processes
System	ERP System, Cloud solutions	ERP System, WMS System
Process description	Once the documents are scanned or received electronically, they must be indicated for the system to begin processing them. Once processed, the invoices are automatically entered into the indicated system	ABC/XYZ classification is based on analysis of historical data. The AI algorithm predicts future demand for a given product and then assigns it the appropriate category and status
The purpose of automation	The goal is to recognize data from invoices and enter it into the system, which replaces manual transcription of data. In addition, the goal is to reduce the circulation of paper document in the organization - achieving the goals of sustainability	Through classification, the system can optimize the arrangement of goods so that those that rotate more often are closer to the packing area. The algorithm will predict turnaround times and allocate dispositions to workers - labor economy
Result	The document processing time is a few seconds, which compared to manual transcription of data, which can take several, or tens of minutes-providing real time and cost savings	The system can automatically assign appropriate categories to products and goods according to ABC/XYZ classification, enabling better allocation of goods and optimization of inventory levels

*Source:Own elaboration based on (*Wrycza and Maślankowski 2019*)*

5 Discussion

The case study showed that eco-commerce is a strategic factor in supporting sustainability in the small and medium-sized e-commerce sector. Implementing eco-commerce strategies in areas such as the business model, operational processes, order management and image communication can help reduce the negative environmental impact of e-commerce, which will be fundamental in the long run, especially in an era of increasing digital transformation and the intensification of online shopping trends in the post-pandemic era. However, the implementation of eco-commerce elements requires consideration of various constraints and challenges. Companies must be ready for the costs of eco-innovation, changes in operational processes and the need to change organizational culture. (Alyahya et al. 2023). The increasing role of automation of operational processes, especially sales and post-sales, is crucial for the effective and sustainable operation of e-commerce companies in a dynamic market environment. The implementation of sustainable practices in e-commerce primarily carries three key benefits (Fig. 1):

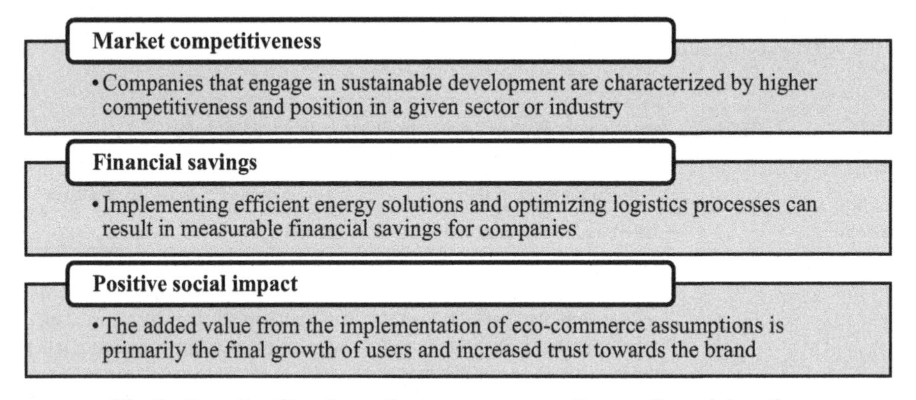

Market competitiveness
• Companies that engage in sustainable development are characterized by higher competitiveness and position in a given sector or industry
Financial savings
• Implementing efficient energy solutions and optimizing logistics processes can result in measurable financial savings for companies
Positive social impact
• The added value from the implementation of eco-commerce assumptions is primarily the final growth of users and increased trust towards the brand

Fig. 1. Benefits of implementing eco-commerce, Source: Own elaboration

The application of sustainability policies to online stores need not at all involve a strategic revolution within the organization, and the eco-commerce philosophy itself can contribute to job creation in non-environmental sectors through a structured evolution of processes.

References

Alyahya, M., Agag, G., Aliedan, M., Abdelmoety, Z.H.: A cross-cultural investigation of the relationship between eco-innovation and customers boycott behaviour. J. Retail. Consum. Serv. **72**, 1–3 (2023)

Chomiak-Orsa I. Intelligent Personalization - The Result of The Evolution of Web Solutions, Education excellence and innovation management: a 2025 vision to sustain economic development during global challenges, 18038–18048 (2020)

Detlor, B.: The influence of information ecology on e-commerce initiatives Internet research: electronic networking. Appl. Pol. **11**(4), 286–288 (2001)

Engelhardt M. Who is willing-to-pay for sustainable last mile innovations? Transportation Research Procedia, 911–913 (2023)

Gemius: https://www.gemius.pl/wszystkie-artykuly-aktualnosci/raport-e-commerce-w-polsce-2021.html. Accessed 07 Aug 2023

Glinka B., Czakon W.: Podstawy badań jakościowych, PWE, 53–72 (2021)

Gregor B., Kaczorowska-Spychalska D.: Technologie cyfrowe w biznesie Wydawnictwo PWN, 52–58 (2020)

Jelonek, D., Chomiak-Orsa, I.: The Application of ICT in the Area of value co-creation mechanisms support as a determinant of innovation activities. Int. J. Ambient Comput. Intell. **9**(2), 32–42 (2018)

Kantar: https://www.kantar.com/campaigns/sustainability-the-european-story. Accessed 07 Aug 2023

Kłosowski, G., Hoła, A., Rymarczyk, T., Mazurek, M., Niderla, K., Rzemieniak, M.: Use of the double-stage LSTM network in electrical tomography for 3D wall moisture imaging. Measurement **213**, 1–13 (2023)

Mohamad, A.H., Hassan, G.F., Elrahman, A.S.A.: Impacts of e-commerce on planning and designing commercial activities centers: a developed approach. Ain Shams Eng. J. **13**(4), 4–6 (2022)

Motowidlak, U., Tokarski, D.: Critical processes and risk factorsof disturbances in the implementation of ecological reusable packaging intocontext of e-commerce sustainable, development. Ekonomia i Środowisko **81**(3), 98–100 (2022)

Wach, M., Chomiak-Orsa, I.: The application of predictive analysis in decision-making processes on the example of mining company's investment projects Knowledge-based and intelligent information & engineering systems, **192**, 5058–5066 (2021)

Wrycza S., Maślankowski J. Informatyka ekonomiczna – teoria i zastosowania, Wydawnictwo PWN, 293–314 (2019)

Zhu, L., Thatcher, S.M.B.: National information ecology: a new institutional economics perspective on global e-commerce adoption. J. Electron. Commer. Res. **11**, 60–64 (2010)

Modelling Electricity Consumption in Irish Dairy Farms Using Agent-Based Modelling

Hossein Khaleghy[1(✉)], Abdul Wahid[1], Eoghan Clifford[2], and Karl Mason[1]

[1] School of Computer Science, University of Galway, Galway H91 FYH2, Ireland
{h.khaleghy1,abdul.wahid,karl.mason}@universityofgalway.ie
[2] School of Engineering, University of Galway, Galway H91 HX31, Ireland
eoghan.clifford@universityofgalway.ie

Abstract. Dairy farming can be an energy intensive form of farming. Understanding the factors affecting electricity consumption on dairy farms is crucial for farm owners and energy providers. In order to accurately estimate electricity demands in dairy farms, it is necessary to develop a model. In this research paper, an agent-based model is proposed to model the electricity consumption of Irish dairy farms. The model takes into account various factors that affect the energy consumption of dairy farms, including herd size, number of milking machines, and time of year. The outputs are validated using existing state-of-the-art dairy farm modelling frameworks. The proposed agent-based model is fully explainable, which is an advantage over other Artificial Intelligence techniques, e.g. deep learning.

1 Introduction

Dairy farming is vital to the Republic of Ireland's economy, with a significant volume of milk production. In January 2023, the country produced 40.4 million litres of milk for human consumption, emphasizing its economic importance [1]. The energy consumption in dairy farms is substantial, as it takes about 41.1 watt-hours of electricity to produce one litre of milk [6]. Understanding the factors affecting electricity consumption is crucial for farm owners and energy providers.

This study proposes an agent-based modelling (ABM) approach to estimate dairy farm electricity consumption on an hourly, monthly, and yearly basis. The ABM consists of nine agents representing common dairy farm equipment. By simulating each agent's behavior, the model estimates equipment-specific electricity consumption, providing an overall farm consumption estimate. ABM offers advantages over traditional and modern approaches, as it allows for targeted interventions to reduce energy use and provides transparent and interpretable results for decision-making.

Proc. of the Articial Intelligence for Sustainability, ECAI 2023, Eunika et al. (eds.), Sep 30-Oct 1, 2023, https://sites.google.com/view/ai4s. 2023.

S. Nowaczyk et al. (Eds.): ECAI 2023 Workshops, CCIS 1948, pp. 230–237, 2024.
https://doi.org/10.1007/978-3-031-50485-3_24

This paper contributes in the following ways:

1. Development of ABM approach for dairy farm electricity consumption modeling.
2. Analysis of the impact of dairy farm herd size on electricity consumption.
3. Evaluation and validation of the proposed ABM approach using the Republic of Ireland as a case study.

2 Background

Several studies have explored electricity consumption prediction for dairy farms. Sefeedpari et al. [8] used an adaptive-fuzzy inference system based on data from 50 Iranian farms. They also employed an Artificial Neural Network (ANN) in another study [7]. Shine et al. [9] developed a support vector machine model for annual electricity consumption prediction at farm and catchment levels. In their other study [10], Shine et al. employed various machine learning algorithms to predict on-farm water and electricity consumption using data from 58 pasture-based dairy farms.

While numerous studies have focused on applying machine learning algorithms to predict energy consumption on dairy farms, these approaches come with certain limitations. One significant drawback is their lack of interpretability and explainability, which can impede farm owners' and managers' understanding of energy consumption patterns. Additionally, machine learning algorithms often require large amounts of data for accurate predictions, leading to time-consuming and expensive data collection and preparation processes. Consequently, the practicality and cost-effectiveness of machine learning for predicting energy consumption on dairy farms may be compromised.

Agent-based modelling (ABM) has been widely used in various domains, including construction research [5] and climate energy policies [3]. While ABM has been utilized to predict electricity consumption in different contexts, such as office buildings [11] and electricity markets [12], no prior studies have applied ABM for predicting electricity consumption on dairy farms. This paper aims to address this gap by proposing a novel ABM approach to estimate electricity usage in Irish dairy farms, providing full explainability and valuable insights into the driving factors behind electricity consumption in this sector.

3 Agent-Based Model of Dairy Farm

3.1 Agent-Based Model

Agents are parts of a multi-agent system (MAS); These agents have some characteristics which can be helpful in solving modern issues. Learning from the environment and interacting with other agents, make the agents flexible, and help them to make autonomous decisions. Using the gained knowledge from the environment and other agents, each agent tries to decide and perform an action to solve a task [4] (Fig. 1).

The advantage of using agent-based modelling is that every aspect of the agent can be modelled and programmed [11].

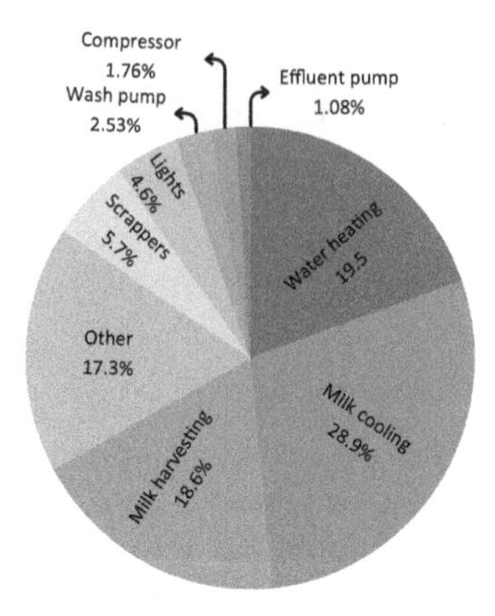

Fig. 1. Electricity consumption of each equipment on a dairy farm [6].

3.2 Model Overview

Electricity consumption on a farm is primarily driven by various equipment usages, with milk cooling being the largest contributor, followed by water heating, milk harvesting, and unmonitored consumptions like winter housing (17.3%). The agent-based model (ABM) in this study uses inputs such as herd size, milking machines, month, day, milking machine system, and water heating system to estimate electricity consumption for the specified farm and date. The ABM's architecture facilitates agent interactions and collaborative communication, enabling accurate predictions and improved forecasting outcomes for electricity consumption (Fig. 2).

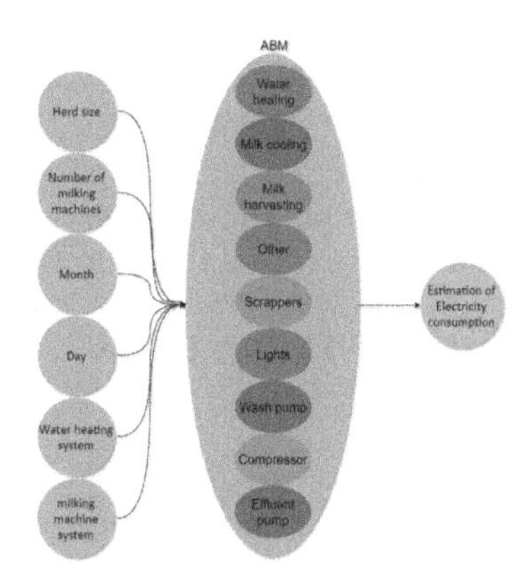

Fig. 2. Architecture of proposed ABM.

As mentioned, The proposed model consists of nine agents: Water heating agent: This agent has two modes: "enabled" implies that the ABM model considers that electrical energy is used for water heating. However, "disabled" implies using other sources of energy for water heating like using oil.

Depending on the herd size and the number of milking machines, the activation duration of the water heating system can be varied.
The total consumption of the water heating agent can be calculated as:

$$WHC = df \times (1.84 + n_{mu} \times 0.01345) + (n_c \times 0.075392) \tag{1}$$

Here, WHC is the water heating consumption (kWh), n_c is the number of cows, n_{mu} is the number of milking units, and df is the factor of date which is calculated as the chosen day divided by the total number of days on that month which will be a number between 0 and 1. The constant numbers in the equation are selected to modify the electricity consumption of the water heating agent and the constants are hand-tuned.

Milk harvesting agent: It is considered that milk harvesting happens twice a day at 7 am and 5 pm [2]. The duration of milk harvesting is dependent on herd size and the number of milking machines. The total consumption of the milk harvesting agent is calculated as:

$$MHC = df \times n_c \times mpd \times Cpl_{MHC} \tag{2}$$

Here, MHC is the milk harvesting consumption, mpd is the average of produced milk per cow per day, and Cpl_{MHC} is the consumption per liter.

Milk cooling agent: It has two modes: "DX" which represents the Direct Expansion method and "IB" which stands for the Ice Bulk method. It is assumed that the milk cooling and milk harvesting process start at the same time. The total consumption will be:

$$MCC = df \times n_c \times mpd \times Cpl_{MCC} \tag{3}$$

Here, MCC is the milk cooling consumption, and cpl_{MCC} is the consumption of the milk cooling system per liter of milk.

Lights agent, Wash pump, Compressor agent, scrapper agent, effluent pump the other agent: As it is obvious in the name lights agent is responsible for lighting the area of the dairy farm and it is assumed that it is working 24 h a day. The other agent is responsible for the unmonitored electricity consumption. The total consumption of these agents is calculated as:

$$EC = df \times n_c \times mpd \times Cpl_{EC} \tag{4}$$

Here, EC is the equipment consumption, and cpl_{EC} is the consumption of the equipment per liter of milk.

3.3 Agent-Based Model Inputs

Electricity consumption on a dairy farm depends on factors like herd size, milk cooling, and milk harvesting processes. Larger herds lead to increased milk production, raising electricity usage for cooling and harvesting equipment. Effective milk cooling is crucial for maintaining milk quality and safety, while electric milking machines also contribute to overall energy consumption. Seasonal variations, temperature fluctuations, and water heating impact energy requirements, with electric water heaters commonly used for on-demand hot water but higher operating costs if electricity rates are expensive. Optimizing electricity consumption in dairy farming involves considering these factors and adopting efficient practices for sustainable and cost-effective operations.

4 Experimental Results

The proposed ABM can generate electricity consumption data at various levels of time, from hourly to yearly, and for different time periods such as days, weeks, and months. This data can be used to analyze and optimize electricity usage across the farm, and to identify opportunities for energy savings and cost reduction.

4.1 Hourly Electricity Consumption

Table 1. Characteristics of the farm used for the case study

Inputs	Values
Herd size	75
Number of milking machines	8
Day	15
Month	June
Water heating system	Electric
Milk cooling system	DX

Making assumptions is a common simplification used in ABMs to make the simulation more manageable and representative of real-world scenarios. However, it is important to note that the actual timing of milk harvesting and water heating may vary depending on factors such as herd size, milking equipment capacity, and milk production patterns (Table 1).

It is imperative to note that alterations in milk harvesting or water heating practices would not exert any discernible influence on the overall electricity consumption. Nonetheless, such modifications could significantly impact the electricity price. In order to ensure a degree of comparability, the selected time intervals have been derived from reputable sources.

4.2 Agent-Based Model Validation

Acquiring electricity data for individual farms is time-consuming and expensive, especially when dealing with hundreds of farms. To validate the proposed agent-based model (ABM), it is compared to the Decision Support System for Energy Use in Dairy Production (DSSED) [6], which generates realistic farm energy consumption and carbon emission data (Fig. 3).

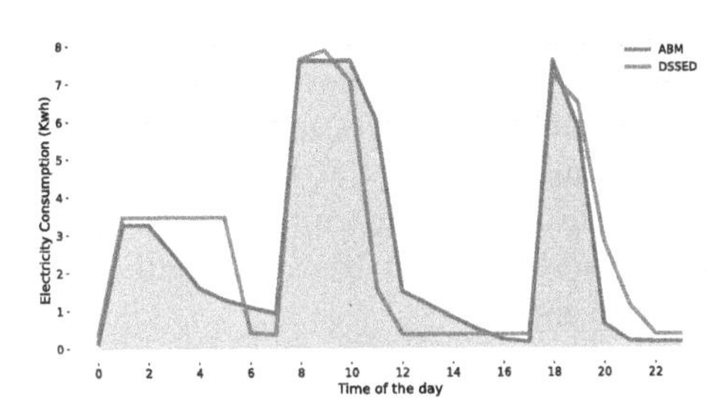

Fig. 3. Comparison between the output of the DSSED and proposed ABM.

However, DSSED has limitations, such as imposing restrictions on input values from predefined intervals, which may not fully reflect unique farm circumstances. Additionally, its hourly consumption is based on an average day, limiting flexibility and accuracy.

To investigate the effect of herd size on electricity consumption, the average overall electricity consumption on an average day of the year is calculated using both the ABM and the DSSED models for a range of milking machine numbers from 3 to 40. In addition, the percentage error is also calculated. As can be seen in Table 2, for different herd sizes the proposed ABM is capable of predicting the electricity consumption with a maximum error of 5.5%.

Table 2. Comparison of the proposed ABM output and the DSSED.

Herd size	DSSED (Kwh)	ABM (Kwh)	Error
35	47.644	45.783	3.9%
45	55.613	52.548	5.5%
55	60.624	59.307	2.1%
65	67.853	66.029	2.6%
75	73.038	72.745	0.4%
85	77.962	79.454	1.9%
95	85.294	86.114	0.9%

5 Conclusion

The proposed agent-based model for estimating the electricity consumption of dairy farms is a contribution to the field of agricultural energy management. The model's ability to estimate consumption on an hourly, daily, and annual basis provides a valuable tool for farm owners to make informed decisions regarding energy usage.

Explainability is the advantage of the model, which allows farm owners to understand the factors that contribute to their energy consumption. This can help them identify areas where energy efficiency improvements can be made and make informed decisions about future investments in energy-saving technologies.

The use of agent-based modelling is particularly useful in cases where data availability is limited. Unlike machine learning approaches that require a large amount of data to train models, agent-based modelling can provide accurate estimates with limited data inputs.

The results of the proposed model are validated using the Decision Support System for Energy Use in Dairy Production (DSSED). The comparison showed that the max percentage error for the different herd sizes is 5.2%.

For future work, calculating greenhouse gas (GHG) emissions using the proposed agent-based modelling could be a valuable extension of this study. This would enable a more comprehensive understanding of the environmental impact of dairy farming, which is a critical consideration in sustainability assessments.

Acknowledgements. This publication has emanated from research conducted with the financial support of Science Foundation Ireland under Grant number [21/FFP-A/9040].

References

1. CSO, milk sales (dairy) for human consumption. Year and statistic cent stat off (2023). https://data.cso.ie/table/AKM02. Accessed 04 May 2023
2. Milking interval relationship with pm finish time. https://www.teagasc.ie/news-events/daily/dairy/milking-interval-relationship-with-pm-finish-time.php. Accessed 08 May 2023
3. Castro, J., et al.: A review of agent-based modeling of climate-energy policy. Wiley Interdisc. Rev. Clim. Change **11**(4), e647 (2020)
4. Dorri, A., Kanhere, S.S., Jurdak, R.: Multi-agent systems: a survey. IEEE Access **6**, 28573–28593 (2018)
5. Khodabandelu, A., Park, J.: Agent-based modeling and simulation in construction. Autom. Constr. **131**, 103882 (2021)
6. Murphy, M.D., Shine, P., Breen, M., Upton, J.: DSSED: decision support system for energy use in dairy production. https://messo.shinyapps.io/AEOP/
7. Sefeedpari, P., Rafiee, S., Akram, A.: Application of artificial neural network to model the energy output of dairy farms in Iran. Int. J. Energy Technol. Policy **9**(1), 82–91 (2013)

8. Sefeedpari, P., Rafiee, S., Akram, A., Komleh, S.H.P.: Modeling output energy based on fossil fuels and electricity energy consumption on dairy farms of Iran: application of adaptive neural-fuzzy inference system technique. Comput. Electron. Agric. **109**, 80–85 (2014)
9. Shine, P., Scully, T., Upton, J., Murphy, M.: Annual electricity consumption prediction and future expansion analysis on dairy farms using a support vector machine. Appl. Energy **250**, 1110–1119 (2019)
10. Shine, P., Murphy, M.D., Upton, J., Scully, T.: Machine-learning algorithms for predicting on-farm direct water and electricity consumption on pasture based dairy farms. Comput. Electron. Agric. **150**, 74–87 (2018)
11. Zhang, T., Siebers, P.O., Aickelin, U.: Modelling electricity consumption in office buildings: an agent based approach. Energy Build. **43**(10), 2882–2892 (2011)
12. Zhou, Z., Zhao, F., Wang, J.: Agent-based electricity market simulation with demand response from commercial buildings. IEEE Trans. Smart Grid **2**(4), 580–588 (2011). https://doi.org/10.1109/TSG.2011.2168244

Personalised Electric Vehicle Routing Using Online Estimators

Elnaz Shafipour(✉), Sebastian Stein, and Selin Ahipasaoglu

School of Electronics and Computer Science, University of Southampton, Southampton, UK
{e.shafipour,s.stein,s.d.ahipasaoglu}@soton.ac.uk

Abstract. In this paper, we develop a novel approach to help drivers of electric vehicles (EVs) plan charging stops on long journeys. A key challenge here is eliciting the highly heterogeneous preferences of drivers. Here we develop an intelligent personal agent that learns preferences through multiple interactions. To minimise the cognitive burden on the driver, we propose a novel technique which applies a small-scale discrete choice experiment to interact with the driver. Specifically, the agent provides drivers with several routes with possible combinations of charging stops based on their latest beliefs about the driver's preferences. Then, through subsequent iterations, the personal agent learns and refines its beliefs about the driver's preferences. It suggests better routes closer to the driver's preferences. We evaluated our novel algorithm with real preference data from EV drivers, showing that our approach converges quickly to the optimal routes after only a small number of queries.

Keywords: Preference Elicitation · Electric Vehicles · Online Planning

1 Introduction

Electric vehicles (EVs) play a critical role in tackling climate change and achieving net-zero emissions, and many governments are supporting their widespread introduction. As EVs become more popular, better-charging infrastructure will be required. The development of this infrastructure will take time, and drivers currently have limited charging options. The situation is particularly challenging when a driver has to refuel several times on a long journey. Thus, in April 2022, we surveyed 1,278 electric vehicle drivers to better understand their problems and their choice of charging stops. According to the results, more than a third were unhappy with their charging experience. Drivers were also highly heterogeneous in their preferences for charging stations, with some prioritising time while others focusing on cost or even availability. Based on our findings from the survey, we explore in this paper how a personal intelligent agent can help EV drivers manage the currently limited charging infrastructure on long journeys. Since the drivers' preferences for charging stops are highly diverse, we are interested in using artificial intelligence (AI) tools to plan their stops on long journeys, while learning their preferences (such as the trade-off between cost, travel time, charging time, and station facilities). Although existing work [8, 10, 12] has looked at personalised routing, it does not consider dynamic preference elicitation. In more detail, we propose a novel

S. Nowaczyk et al. (Eds.): ECAI 2023 Workshops, CCIS 1948, pp. 238–245, 2024.
https://doi.org/10.1007/978-3-031-50485-3_25

method: *Online Estimators for Preference Elicitation (OEPE)*. Using this method, we find a route that uses charging stops that align with a driver's preferences (i.e., maximizes utility). Our contributions to the state of the art are as follows: (1) A new application domain we used was personalised routing in electric vehicles to find convenient charging stations. (2) The main contribution of our work is the introduction of the novel method OEPE that can learn drivers' preferences without any prior knowledge. (3) We introduced Discrete Route Choice (DRC). Through this solution, drivers can choose from multiple routes from origin to destination based on their preferences. This allows us to collect more information from drivers with fewer interactions.

2 Related Work

User-centric route planning and eliciting human preferences are very active research topics [3,7,8,10,12]. In particular, in recent works on dynamic user-centric route planning [8,10,12] authors propose personalised route planning algorithms. These algorithms can provide users with routes that meet their needs, assuming these are known a priori. Unlike their work, our method acquires a user's preferences without assuming prior information about that user. There is other recent research [13] in which the authors select an appropriate query at each stage of an interactive preference elicitation process for the user. Their method is to choose a query that minimises max setwise regret. In light of the fact that we currently do not generate questions and that we already have a few possible stations, their solution does not fit our current work. Furthermore, recent work [3] looked at obtaining user preferences through interaction. Based on feedback from human preferences, the authors propose an interactive platform for grammar-guided symbolic regression. There are other works [1,2,4,7] where the authors suggest pairs to users and ask them to choose one to elicit feedback. In contrast, we use an approach called Discrete Route Choice (DRC). We provide the driver with more than two routes with charging stops. Each choice has summarised information about the route and charging stops and allows drivers to choose their preferred one. With this method, we are able to elicit the preferences of the drivers with fewer interactions.

3 Methodology

In our model, we assume that $\mathbf{R}_{ab}$ is a set of all possible routes considering charging stops between the given origin a and destination b of the driver. Each $r \in \mathbf{R}_{ab}$ is defined with its feature $\mathbf{X}_r = \{x_1, x_2, ..., x_n\}$ where x_i is the ith feature of the route r (related to EV charging stops and the route itself). These features can include charging costs, charging speed, waiting times, and availability of restaurants, restrooms or childcare facilities during the entire journey. Additionally, the marginal contribution of each feature to the driver's utility is denoted by weight $\mathbf{W} = \{w_1, w_2, ..., w_n\}$. Each element w_i is a real number between -1 and 1. Here, we assume that each driver's preferences can be described by a utility function $u : u(\mathbf{W}, \mathbf{X}_r) = w_1x_1 + w_2x_2 + ... + w_nx_n$. In this paper, we present our novel method, OEPE, which identifies the best route based on the driver's preferences regarding the charging stops on the route between the origin and destination. This driver-in-the-loop method learns the driver's preferences interactively in order to determine the optimal route. Over time, our algorithm refines a set of *estimators*, which are plausible hypotheses. There are potential weights $\mathbf{W}$ for each estimator. A driver's route choice is predicted based on these weights. Those estimators that cannot make accurate predictions are removed, and replaced with ones that use successful ones as a basis, or which are chosen randomly.

3.1 OEPE Fundamentals

Set of Estimators: In OEPE, the personal agent keeps a set, $\mathbf{E}$, of N estimators. An estimator e is a tuple: $\{\mathbf{W}_e, \zeta_e, f_e\}$, where: $\mathbf{W}_e$ is a vector of estimated weights of the driver's utility function u; ζ_e holds the number of times that e was successful in predicting the chosen route by the driver; f_e keeps the count of failures in identifying the chosen route. The estimators are initialised at the beginning of the process and evaluated whenever a route is chosen by a driver. The estimators that are not able to make accurate predictions after several trials are removed and replaced by estimators that are created using successful ones as a basis, or purely randomly, in a fashion inspired by genetic algorithms [6].
List of Route Choices: As we mentioned before, based on the specified origin a and destination b, we have $\mathbf{R}_{ab}$ as possible routes from a to b. At each interaction with the driver, the personal agent recommends a set of route choices $\mathbf{R}^*_{ab} = \{r_1, r_2, ..., r_\theta\}$ selected from $\mathbf{R}_{ab}$ to the driver. According to the driver's preference, he/she chooses a route r^* that maximises the utility function. In order to be able to check the history of suggested routes and select one by the driver, we define a set of all suggested route choices and selected ones in $\mathbf{C}$: $\mathbf{C} = \{(\mathbf{R}^*_{ab_1}, r^*_1), (\mathbf{R}^*_{ab_2}, r^*_2), ..., (\mathbf{R}^*_{ab_k}, r^*_k)\}$where each element c of this set is $\mathbf{R}^*_{ab}$ and r^* of all interactions with the driver.
Bags of Successful Weights: To predict $\mathbf{w}_e$ precisely and with less interaction, we define the bags of successful weights. Each bag $\mathbf{B}_i$ is a set for each parameter w_i in vector $\mathbf{w}_e$. Whenever $\mathbf{w}_e$ successfully estimates the correct route selected by the driver, we keep w_i in the corresponding bag. Bags are used when generating new estimators. If one w_i is successful many times, it will be kept in the corresponding bag repeatedly. Therefore, the chance of selecting it for generating a new estimator will increase.

3.2 Process of Eliciting Preferences

Algorithm 1 illustrates the process of interacting with the driver and eliciting his/her preferences. First using the $Initialisation$ function (Line 3), all weights w_i of $\mathbf{W}_e$ are initialised with a random value drawn uniformly at random from $[-1, 1]$. Both ζ_e and f_e are set to zero. Then. We start the interaction with the driver for σ times and assume that in each interaction, the driver travels from a different origin a to a different destination b (Line 5). Later, the *GenarateRoutes* function generates Λ random routes $\mathbf{R}_{ab}$ from a to b considering the stations on the route to charge (Algorithm 2). At Line 6, we first find the shortest path r_s between the moving point of the car α to the destination b. Initially, α is set to the origin a of the driver and updated later with the location of the station s where the car is supposed to be charged and move to the next destination. To find the shortest path, we used the A^* algorithm [5]. After getting the shortest path

Algorithm 1. Eliciting Preferences

1: **procedure** ELICITPREFERENCES($\theta, \sigma, N, m, \nabla$)
2: $\mathbf{E} \leftarrow$ Initialisation(N);
3: $\mathbf{C} \leftarrow \emptyset$; $\mathbf{B} \leftarrow \emptyset$;
4: **repeat**
5: $a, b \leftarrow$ GetOriginAndDestination();
6: $\mathbf{R}_{ab} \leftarrow$ GenarateRoutes (a, b, Λ, ∇);
7: $\mathbf{W}_p \leftarrow$ PredictWeights($\mathbf{E}$);
8: $\mathbf{R}^*_{ab} \leftarrow$ GenerateChoices $(\mathbf{R}_{ab}, \mathbf{W}_p, \theta)$;
9: $r^* \leftarrow$ GetSelectedRoute $(\mathbf{R}^*_{ab})$;
10: $c \leftarrow (r^*, \mathbf{R}^*_{ab})$;
11: $\mathbf{C} \leftarrow \mathbf{C} \cup \{c\}$;
12: $\mathbf{E}_t, \mathbf{B} \leftarrow$ Evaluation $(\mathbf{E}, \mathbf{C})$;
13: $\mathbf{E} \leftarrow$ Generation $(\mathbf{E}_t, \mathbf{B}, \mathbf{C}, m)$;
14: **until** σ *iterations*

Algorithm 2. Generate random routes

1: **procedure** GENARATEROUTES(a, b, Λ, ∇)
2: $\mathbf{R}_{ab} \leftarrow \emptyset$;
3: **while** $|\mathbf{R}_{ab}| = \Lambda$ **do**
4: $\alpha \leftarrow a$; $r \leftarrow \emptyset$;
5: **repeat**
6: $r_s \leftarrow$ FindShortestRoute(α, b);
7: $\mathbf{S} \leftarrow$ GetReachableStations(r_s, ∇);
8: $s \leftarrow$ FindStation($\mathbf{S}$);
9: $\alpha \leftarrow$ GetLocation (s);
10: $r \leftarrow r \cup \{s\}$;
11: **until** reach destination
12: $\mathbf{R}_{ab} \leftarrow \mathbf{R}_{ab} \cup \{r\}$;
13: **return** $\mathbf{R}_{ab}$;

r_s between α and b, we will seek some stations around it and find all stations $\mathbf{S}$ that are within ∇ distance of r_s. Based on the car's current state of charge, we calculate (Line 8) all stations that can be accessed from α among $\mathbf{S}$. We assume that there is at least one station the car can reach. We randomly select one station s from all reachable stations. After getting to that point, we will presume that the car is recharged to a certain value and consider that station s as the next moving point. This process will be repeated until reaching the destination. All stations selected will be considered as one route. We repeat this process Λ times. Later, using the *PredictWeights* function we get the predicted weights $\mathbf{W}_p$ based on the current set of estimators $\mathbf{E}$. As we proceed to Line 8, the function *GenerateChoices* is used to find θ ($\theta < |\mathbf{R}_{ab}|$) possible routes among all possible routes by evaluating them based on the latest elicited preferences of the driver. Therefore, the function gets randomly generated routes $\mathbf{R}_{ab}$ between a and b as well as $\mathbf{W}_p$. This function calculates the utility u of each $r \in \mathbf{R}_{ab}$ as follows: $u = \sum_{i=1}^{n} w_{pi} x_{ri}$ and then the route with maximum u will be considered as the estimated route r_e. After selecting the route with maximum utility, we will select another $\theta - 1$ routes from $\mathbf{R}_{ab} \setminus \{r_e\}$ randomly. Afterwards, the agent will interact with the driver and run DRC with *GetSelectedRoute*. For this DRC, there are θ routes as choices with information about the routes' attributes and their related values, from which the driver selects his/her preferred route r^*. Accordingly, we update the list of route choices $\mathbf{C}$ with the offered routes to the driver $\mathbf{R}^*_{ab}$ and the selected one r^* by the driver. After getting the selected route by the driver, we will evaluate the estimators. Algorithm 3

Algorithm 3. Evaluating Estimator

```
1: procedure EVALUATION(E, C)
2:     F ← ∅;        ▷ F is a set that contains failed estimators
3:     for each e ∈ E do
4:         ζ_e ← CalculateSuccess(C, W_e);
5:         if ζ_e > 0 then
6:             for each w_i ∈ W_e do
7:                 B_i ← B_i ∪ {w_i};
8:         else
9:             f_e ← f_e + 1;
10:        if f_e > ξ then
11:            F = F ∪ {e};
12:    E_t = E − F; B ← {B_1, B_2, ..., B_n};
13:    return E_t, B;
```

presents the process for evaluating estimators. The key objective of this step is to find the estimators that are able to estimate the chosen route correctly.

Hence, in Algorithm 3, we want to update the ζ_e and f_e for each estimator of the estimators' list ($\mathbf{E}$). *CalculateSuccess* is used to calculate ζ_e which checks each choice c in $\mathbf{C}$ and identifies what is the optimal route r_e^* among $\mathbf{R}_c$ by assuming $\mathbf{W}_e$ as the driver's true weight. If the preferred route by driver r_c^* is equal to the estimated route using $\mathbf{W}_e$ (r_e^*) then the ζ will be increased. This process will be repeated for all choices in $\mathbf{C}$ to get the total ζ. The value returned from the function will be stored in ζ_e. Whenever there is at least one successful estimation for e, w_i in the $\mathbf{W}_e$ vector will be stored in a bag with the name $\mathbf{B}_i$. If the estimator e could not predict the correct route among previous choices, f_e is increased. Since the estimator e may still hold the correct weight after a failure, it will not be removed after its first failure. There is a *threshold* ξ for removal. After the *Evaluation* we will have $\mathbf{E}_t$ as the surviving set estimators so we will generate new $N - |\mathbf{E}_t|$ estimators to have N estimators. In this step, new estimators are partially created with random values and partially generated using previous successful weights from the *bags* $\mathbf{B}$. Accordingly, a new combination of weights that had at least one success in the previous steps can be utilised in generating new estimators.

More detail of the process of generating new estimators is indicated in Algorithm 4. The main part of producing new estimators is creating a new weight vector $\mathbf{W}'$. Weights for a proportion $(N - |\mathbf{E}_t|) \times m$ (where $m \in [0, 1]$) of the new estimators will be randomly sampled from a uniform distribution $\mathcal{U}(-1, 1)$. The other proportion $(N -$

Algorithm 4. Generating New Estimators

```
1: procedure GENERATION(E_t, B, C, m)
2:     n ← 0; η ← (N − |E_t|) × m;
3:     while |E_t| < N do
4:         for all w'_i ∈ W' do
5:             if n < η OR |B_i| = 0 then
6:                 w'_i ← random value U(−1, 1);
7:             else
8:                 w'_i ← random value B_i;
9:         hist_success ← CalculateSuccess (C, W');
10:        if hist_success > 0 then
11:            W_e ← W';
12:            ζ_e ← hist_success; f_e ← 0; E_t ← E_t ∪ {e}; n ← n + 1;
13:    E ← E_t;
14:    return E;
```

$|\mathbf{E}_t|) \times (1 - m)$ will be created as a new mixture from the respective bags, which are containing previously winning weights. If all bags are empty, then all parameters will be random. Before creating a new estimator e', in Line 9 and 10 of the Algorithm 4, the *CalculateSuccess* function (Line 9) is employed here to check if the recently generated weights $\mathbf{W}'$ would have at least one success across the choices list so far. Checking the previous successes improves the algorithm since it decreases the likelihood of wasting an estimator with weights $\mathbf{W}'$ that would not be able to make any correct prediction in the previous steps. As a result, if the output of the function is zero, $\mathbf{W}'$ will be discarded. Otherwise, it will be considered as the weight $\mathbf{W}_{e'}$ of the new estimator e'. Consequently, $\zeta_{e'}$ will be assigned with the output of the *CalculateSuccess* function and $f_{e'}$ will be assigned to zero. In the end, the created e' will be added to $\mathbf{E}_t$, and the process repeats until $|\mathbf{E}_t| = N$. Additionally, we need to have the estimated weights for u at each iteration to be able to guess the route that the driver would prefer. In this case, we would be able to recommend routes that are close to the driver's preferred route. To enable the personal agent to make better recommendations, it is necessary to estimate the weights of the driver's utility function u. For estimating the weights, we apply the $PredictWeights$ function (Line 7). In this function, we get the weighted average of the predicted w_e in which weights are ζ_e of each estimator e. $W_p = \frac{\sum_{e \in \mathbf{E}} \zeta_e w_e}{\sum_{e \in \mathbf{E}} \zeta_e}$. The number of iterations will continue for σ times.

4 Evaluation

To evaluate the performance of our novel method (OEPE), we compare it with one of the standard classification methods Decision Trees (DT) [9] and Discrete Choice Model (DCM) [11]. For this, we used data from the survey described in Sect. 1. In this survey, we asked participants what their priorities are when it comes to choosing a charging station. We gave them multiple options like *High speed of charging, Overall low charging cost, Close to food/refreshment facilities, Location with baby change facilities* and others. We then asked them to rank their preferred features. For each driver, we converted their ranked preferences to weights using the following equation: $w_i = \frac{1}{p_i}$ where p_i is the rank order of feature i for a given participant. For our analysis, we generated 200 random scenarios. For each scenario, we assumed fixed-size grids 10×10 and set the driver's origin and destination to randomly located nodes at the grid border. In addition, the car's battery level when starting the trip is randomly chosen between 50 and 90 percent. The maximum range is set to a random value between 30 and 300 miles. We create 20 stations in positions not assigned as drivers' origins or destinations. Cost, waiting time, restrooms, and food facilities are assumed to be routes' features. A random number between 1 and 100 is assigned to cost, driving time, and waiting time. For each route, the value of the facilities is determined by its proportion among all stations. For OEPE configuration, $N = 100$, $\theta = 3$, $\sigma = 20$, $\Lambda = 10$, $\xi = 2$ and $m = 0.2$. All these 200 scenarios were run 20 times for 500 survey participants considering their preferences. For each run, we tracked the estimated weights of the drivers, the chosen route and the number of interactions with the driver. We aggregated the results and plotted the average and the confidence interval ($\rho = 0.05$). Figure 1(a) shows the number of interactions each method needs for its preference error to converge to 0.01. To plot the error of preferences, we show the average error across all weights by evaluating the mean absolute error of the weights. Moreover, since we aggregate multiple results, we calculate and plot the average error. The average error across all weights for all drivers and all scenarios is shown in Fig. 1(b). As we see, OEPE the error of preferences gets closer to the driver's true preferences after a couple of iterations. It shows that our weight estimation error is consistently lower than the other algorithms starting with the second iteration, and it (almost) monotonically decreases with more iterations. On the other hand, DCM and DT do not show any signs of convergence as the number of iterations increases. Hence, using the driver's utility, we can find out which route would be the right choice r_t for the driver among all possible routes $\mathbf{R}_{ab}$ for a given origin and destination: $r_t \leftarrow \arg\max_{r \in \mathbf{R}_{ab}} (\sum_{i=1}^{n} w_{ti} x_{ri})$ Thus, at each iteration, we compared the utility of the chosen route r^* and r_t: $d = |u(\mathbf{W}_t, \mathbf{X}_{r_t}) - u(\mathbf{W}_p, \mathbf{X}_{r^*})|$. Figure 1(c) shows the percentage of the distance of the selected route r^* at each interaction compared to the best route r_t at each interaction. After more interactions with the driver, our distance quickly surpasses the other algorithms in the mean, becoming significantly better after a few iterations.

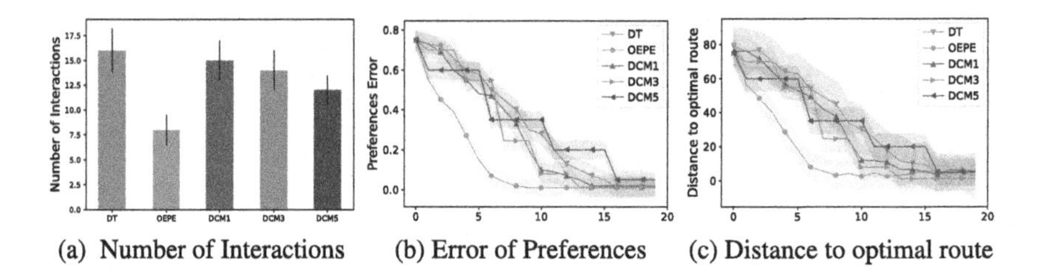

(a) Number of Interactions (b) Error of Preferences (c) Distance to optimal route

Fig. 1. Evaluation results

5 Conclusions

In this work, we aimed to facilitate the uptake of electric vehicles by providing drivers with routes and charging stops that align with their preferences. To elicit drivers' preferences without prior knowledge, we introduced Online Estimators for Preference Elicitation (OEPE). To reduce the interaction with the driver and get more information at the same time, we also used DRC to interact with the driver. Based on our results, we can suggest the optimal route to the driver in only a few iterations.

Acknowledgement. The authors acknowledge the financial support received from the Engineering and Physical Sciences Research Council (EPSRC) through a Turing AI Acceleration Fellowship on Citizen-Centric AI Systems (EP/V022067/1) and the Future Electric Vehicle Energy Networks supporting Renewables (FEVER) grant (EP/W005883/1).

References

1. Bourdache, N., Perny, P., Spanjaard, O.: Incremental elicitation of rank-dependent aggregation functions based on Bayesian linear regression. In: Twenty-Eighth International Joint Conference on Artificial Intelligence, IJCAI 2019, pp. 2023–2029. International Joint Conferences on Artificial Intelligence Organization (2019)
2. Brandt, F., Lederer, P., Suksompong, W.: Incentives in social decision schemes with pairwise comparison preferences. arXiv preprint arXiv:2204.12436 (2022)
3. Crochepierre, L., Boudjeloud-Assala, L., Barbesant, V.: Interactive reinforcement learning for symbolic regression from multi-format human-preference feedbacks. In: 31st International Joint Conference on Artificial Intelligence, IJCAI 2022 (2022)
4. Filipczuk, D., Baarslag, T., Gerding, E.H., Schraefel, M.: Automated privacy negotiations with preference uncertainty. Auton. Agent. Multi-Agent Syst. **36**(2), 49 (2022)
5. Hart, P.E., Nilsson, N.J., Raphael, B.: A formal basis for the heuristic determination of minimum cost paths. IEEE Trans. Syst. Sci. Cybern. **4**(2), 100–107 (1968)
6. Holland, J.H.: Adaptation in Natural and Artificial Systems: An Introductory Analysis with Applications to Biology, Control and Artificial Intelligence. MIT Press, Cambridge (1992)
7. Kuhlman, C., et al.: Preference-driven interactive ranking system for personalized decision support. In: Proceedings of the 27th ACM International Conference on Information and Knowledge Management, pp. 1931–1934 (2018)
8. Li, P., Wang, X., Gao, H., Xu, X., Iqbal, M., Dahal, K.: A dynamic and scalable user-centric route planning algorithm based on polychromatic sets theory. IEEE Trans. Intell. Transp. Syst. **23**(3), 2762–2772 (2021)
9. Myles, A.J., Feudale, R.N., Liu, Y., Woody, N.A., Brown, S.D.: An introduction to decision tree modeling. J. Chemom. Soc. **18**(6), 275–285 (2004)
10. Pradhan, R., Agarwal, A., De, T.: A multi-criteria route selection method for vehicles using genetic algorithms based on driver's preference. Wirel. Pers. Commun. **10**(2), 1–20 (2022)
11. Small, K.A.: A discrete choice model for ordered alternatives. Econometrica J. Econometric Soc. **55**, 409–424 (1987)
12. Tiausas, F., et al.: User-centric distributed route planning in smart cities based on multi-objective optimization. In: 2021 IEEE International Conference on Smart Computing (SMARTCOMP), pp. 77–82. IEEE (2021)
13. Toffano, F., Viappiani, P., Wilson, N.: Efficient exact computation of setwise minimax regret for interactive preference elicitation (2021)

Reinforcement Learning for Battery Management in Dairy Farming

Nawazish Ali[1](✉), Abdul Wahid[1], Rachael Shaw[2], and Karl Mason[1]

[1] School of Computer Science, University of Galway, Galway H91 FYH2, Ireland
{N.Ali3,abdul.wahid,karl.mason}@universityofgalway.ie
[2] Atlantic Technological University, Galway H91 T8NW, Ireland
rachael.shaw@atu.ie

Abstract. Dairy farming is a particularly energy-intensive part of the agriculture sector. Effective battery management is essential for renewable integration within the agriculture sector. However, controlling battery charging/discharging is a difficult task due to electricity demand variability, stochasticity of renewable generation, and energy price fluctuations. Despite the potential benefits of applying Artificial Intelligence (AI) to renewable energy in the context of dairy farming, there has been limited research in this area. This research is a priority for Ireland as it strives to meet its governmental goals in energy and sustainability. This research paper utilizes Q-learning to learn an effective policy for charging and discharging a battery within a dairy farm setting. The results demonstrate that the developed policy significantly reduces electricity costs compared to the established baseline algorithm. These findings highlight the effectiveness of reinforcement learning for battery management within the dairy farming sector.

Keywords: Reinforcement Learning · Dairy Farming · Battery management · Q-learning · Maximizing self Consumption · Time of Use

1 Introduction

The global population rise has increased food demand, including milk. Milk production rose from 735 to 855 million metric tons between 2000 and 2019. Growing demand for dairy products requires more electricity for farm activities. To reduce costs and reliance on external grids, adopting renewable energy like solar and wind is crucial [1,2].

Renewable energy generation has variability, so batteries are essential for storing electricity for future use. They play a crucial role in reducing dairy farming's electricity costs. To optimize battery performance, different techniques are used, including Maximizing Self-Consumption (MSC) and Time of Use (TOU) [3]. These methods involve regulating battery charge to reduce reliance on the power grid. With the advent of AI, many tasks have become more manageable.

Previous studies have shown RL's effectiveness for residential battery management. Ebell et al. achieved a 7.8% reduction in grid energy consumption using

S. Nowaczyk et al. (Eds.): ECAI 2023 Workshops, CCIS 1948, pp. 246–253, 2024.
https://doi.org/10.1007/978-3-031-50485-3_26

RL techniques with PV panels [4]. However, Minnaert et al. assessed energy storage options in dairy farming without utilizing RL algorithms [5]. RL's application to agriculture, especially in dairy farming, is limited in the existing literature. This study introduces RL for optimizing PV battery management in dairy farming and makes the following contributions:

1. Development dairy farm energy simulator as a baseline.
2. The implementation of Q-learning to control a battery store in a dairy farm.
3. Compare the performance of Q-learning with existing baseline battery control algorithms.

2 Background

Battery management is a significant area of research across various domains, aiming to decrease reliance on power grid imports and cut costs. While many battery load regulation methods have been studied in scientific research, dairy farm battery management has not yet explored the use of RL. This study aims to implement battery management techniques in dairy farming to reduce power grid load. The main battery scheduling methods used in scientific studies include dynamic programming, rule-based scheduling, and Reinforcement Learning.

2.1 Conventional Battery Control Methods

Numerous investigations have explored operational strategies for PV Battery systems, focusing on objectives such as efficient utilization [6]. The MSC strategy, widely used for PV battery systems, particularly in distributed PV systems, efficiently consumes PV generation [7]. This approach aims to consume PV generation at the highest permissible rate, enhancing self-consumption [6]. Braun et al. found that proper battery utilization significantly increases local consumption of PV generation [8]. Researchers have optimized PV size [9] and storage capacity [10] to maximize self-consumption and minimize grid energy supply. Luthander et al.'s study indicates that appropriately sizing batteries can enhance relative self-consumption by 13–24

Sharma et al. optimized battery size for zero-net energy homes with PV panels using the MSC strategy, potentially boosting self-consumption by 20–50% [11,12]. FiT and TOU tariffs promote PVB systems and demand-side engagement [13]. Christoph M Flath and Li et al. explored TOU tariff optimization methodologies [14,15]. Prosumers seek economic benefits through FiTs and TOU strategies [16]. Gitizadeh et al. and Hassan et al. optimized battery capacity with tariff incentives [17,18]. Ratnam et al. noted significant cost savings for PVB system users through FiTs [19].

2.2 Reinforcement Learning for Battery Control

Various applications utilize reinforcement learning algorithms to enhance energy management and efficiency. Wei et al. employed dual iterative Q-learning for smart residential battery management, optimizing charging and discharging for improved energy usage [20]. Kim et al. developed a reinforcement learning-based algorithm for smart energy-building management, dynamically determining optimal energy strategies [21]. Ruelens et al. applied reinforcement learning to enhance electric water heater efficiency by adapting to real-time demand and grid conditions [22]. Li et al. used multi-grid reinforcement learning to optimize HVAC systems for energy efficiency and comfort [23].

Foruzan et al. proposed reinforcement learning for microgrid energy management, adapting to changing requirements and renewable generation [24]. Guan et al. suggested a reinforcement learning-based solution for domestic energy storage control, reducing costs through optimized charging and discharging [25]. Liu et al. employed deep reinforcement learning for household energy management, continuously learning optimal techniques for efficiency [26]. These applications demonstrate how reinforcement learning can enhance energy consumption and management efficiency across various contexts.

3 Methodology

3.1 System Design

The grid-connected photovoltaic (PVB) system includes solar PV, battery (Tesla Powerwall 2.0 with 13.5 KWh capacity and 3.3 kW to 5 kW charging/discharging), power grid, and Dairy Farm load. PV power can go to the load, battery, or grid. The charge/discharge controller controls battery processes. The power grid powers the load, battery, PV, and battery storage as needed.

3.2 Data and Price Profile

The investigation used Load data from Finland [27] and PV data from the System Advisor Model (SAM) [28]. Hourly electricity usage was tracked for one year for a dairy farm with 180 cows, consuming 261 MWh annually. Similar-scale farms provided data, and a daily consumption profile was created from a large dairy farm's winter consumption. Sliding data series were made using monthly consumption data to estimate annual variations. Pricing data from the same area had hourly divisions into reduced, standard, and peak-hour rates: 11 pm to 7 am (reduced), 8 am to 4 pm and 7 pm to 10 pm (standard), and 5 pm to 7 pm (peak-hour) (Fig. 1).

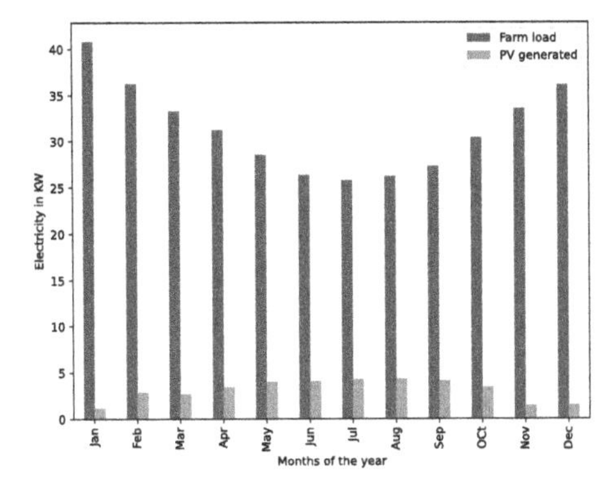

Fig. 1. Farm load and PV generation for one year.

3.3 Baseline Implementation

Two baseline algorithms are implemented which are MSC and TOU:

MSC optimizes PV power for load demand and battery charging in PV-integrated systems. The grid receives excess energy from the battery. When PV generation is low, the battery discharges to meet demand. Grid electricity is bought if demand exceeds PV and battery capacity. Weather drives MSC strategy.

TOU seeks economic gains from peak and off-peak electricity rates. Low-cost utility electricity charges the battery and discharges during high prices. Off-peak hours (23:00–8:00) charge the battery at the highest grid rate. Peak demand (5:00–7:00 PM) depletes the battery.

3.4 Application of Q-Learning to Battery Management

The proposed methodology involves the utilization of the Q-learning Reinforcement Learning algorithm for efficient battery management. The optimal policy can be derived from the greatest Q values through Q-learning. The Q-Learning algorithm operates by choosing the action that corresponds to the maximum Q-value in every state. Equation 1 illustrates the maximum Q value selection.

$$Q^*(s_t, a_t) = argmax_{a \in A} Q^{\pi}(s_t, a_t) \tag{1}$$

The state space (**S**) influences an agent's perception and behavior. State space knowledge helps the RL agent optimize reward. State space complexity affects RL algorithm performance. Time and battery charge are considered in this study.

Action Space (A) (A = {0, 1, 2}). The study considers charging (0), discharging (1), and remaining idle (2). The battery is charged by photovoltaic and utility grid electricity. To meet energy needs, action $a = 1$ discharges the battery. Purchase grid power if the PV system and battery cannot provide enough energy. The dairy farm is idle and powered by solar PV and the grid (a = 2).

Reward (R_p). To reduce grid electricity export and import, this study optimizes PV system-generated electricity. The reward function, P_r, is the grid electricity price minus 1.

4 Results and Discussion

Q-learning optimizes PV battery scheduling for solar power utilization and grid import reduction using reinforcement learning. Based on battery charge level, time of day, and energy prices, the Q-learning algorithm optimizes charging, discharging, and idle times over the year.

The Q-learning algorithm reduced the grid electricity importation from 9.45% to 10.42% as compared to the Rule base algorithm over the period of one year. As depicted in the Fig. 2a Q-learning reduced a significant amount of energy importation from the external grid. Furthermore, the proposed algorithm reduces the cost of electricity imported from the grid by 11.93% to 12.39% compared to the rule base as illustrated in the Fig. 2b.

Figure 2 compares electricity consumption and importation over one year using various methods. Grid electricity purchased is on the vertical axis and hour on the horizontal. The graph shows three bars: grid-imported electricity without proposed algorithms, TOU-procured electricity, and Q-learning-consumed electricity. Electricity management affects grid importation and consumption.

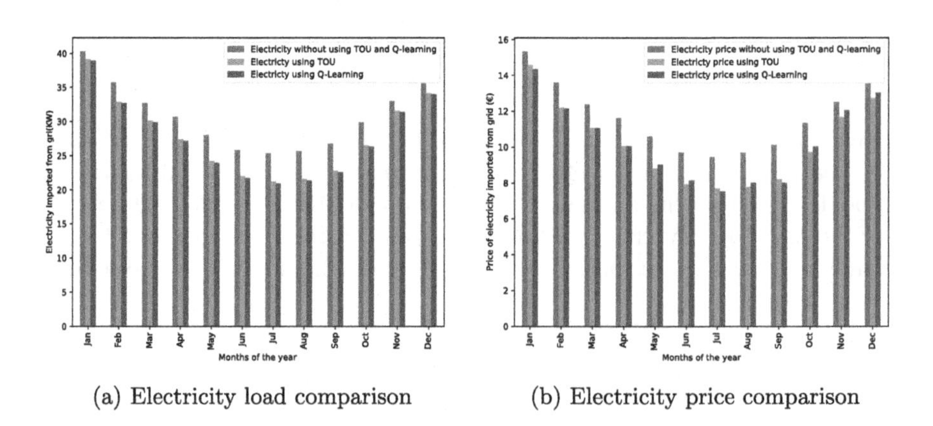

(a) Electricity load comparison (b) Electricity price comparison

Fig. 2. Comparison of the electricity load and price imported from the power grid by using Rule base and Q-learning.

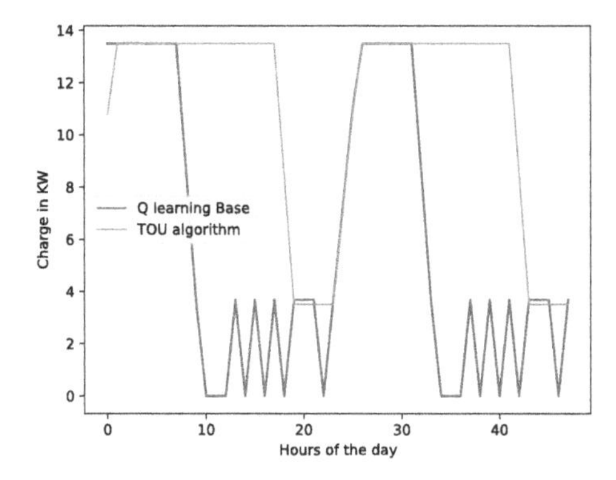

Fig. 3. Comparison of the battery charging and discharging by using TOU and Q-learning.

Figure 3 shows charging behavior over two days using various algorithms. The vertical axis shows battery charge in kilowatts, while the horizontal shows hours. Q-learning and rule-based battery charge lines. Battery charging affects system performance. Q-learning reduced electricity prices and load. The Q-learning agent charges the battery at night. The agent discharges the battery during peak prices or farm load demand to reduce grid electricity import.

Q-learning maximizes dairy farm energy use. AI algorithms optimize PV battery scheduling to reduce electricity consumption without control. Dairy farms save energy with this.

5 Conclusion

1. This paper discussed dairy farming battery load management. Two rule base algorithms in a dairy farm energy simulator reduced grid-imported electricity significantly. The rule base algorithm cuts imported electricity prices by 11.93%.
2. This study shows that RL algorithms improve solar photovoltaic battery performance. RL can make real-time decisions in a continuous action space. RL beats TOU. Q-learning cuts electricity prices by 11.93–12.39
3. RL algorithms for dairy farm battery management may lower electricity prices because they outperform TOU algorithms. RL can be improved to handle complex and large systems.
4. The Q-learning algorithm's battery management scalability for larger dairy farms could be studied. The Q-learning algorithm may be affected by weather and battery life. The study could compare Q-learning to other reinforcement learning algorithms, including deep reinforcement learning, to find the best dairy farm battery management method. Multiple batteries and better management could also be studied.

Acknowledgements. This publication has emanated from research conducted with the financial support of Science Foundation Ireland under Grant number [21/FFP-A/9040].

References

1. Upton, J., Michael, M., French, P., Dillon, P., et al.: Dairy farm energy consumption (2010). Online. Accessed 20 Apr 2023
2. Renewable energy opportunities for dairy farmers (2021). Online. Accessed 20 Apr 2023
3. Zou, B., Peng, J., Li, S., Li, Y., Yan, J., Yang, H.: Comparative study of the dynamic programming-based and rule-based operation strategies for grid-connected PV-battery systems of office buildings. Appl. Energy **305**, 117875 (2022)
4. Ebell, N., Heinrich, F., Schlund, J., Pruckner, M.: Reinforcement learning control algorithm for a PV-battery-system providing frequency containment reserve power. In: 2018 IEEE International Conference on Communications, Control, and Computing Technologies for Smart Grids (SmartGridComm), pp. 1–6. IEEE (2018)
5. Minnaert, B., Thoen, B., Plets, D., Joseph, W., Stevens, N.: Optimal energy storage solution for an inductively powered system for dairy cows. In: 2017 IEEE Wireless Power Transfer Conference (WPTC), pp. 1–4. IEEE (2017)
6. Azuatalam, D., Paridari, K., Ma, Y., Förstl, M., Chapman, A.C., Verbič., G.: Energy management of small-scale PV-battery systems: a systematic review considering practical implementation, computational requirements, quality of input data and battery degradation. Renew. Sustain. Energy Rev. **112**, 555–570 (2019)
7. Zhang, Y., Ma, T., Campana, P.E., Yamaguchi, Y., Dai, Y.: A techno-economic sizing method for grid-connected household photovoltaic battery systems. Appl. Energy **269**, 115106 (2020)
8. Braun, M., Büdenbender, K., Magnor, D., Jossen, A.: Photovoltaic self-consumption in Germany: using lithium-ion storage to increase self-consumed photovoltaic energy. In: 24th European Photovoltaic Solar Energy Conference (PVSEC), Hamburg, Germany (2009)
9. Talavera, D.L., Muñoz-Rodriguez, F.J., Jimenez-Castillo, G., Rus-Casas, C.: A new approach to sizing the photovoltaic generator in self-consumption systems based on cost-competitiveness, maximizing direct self-consumption. Renew. Energy **130**, 1021–1035 (2019)
10. Vickers, N.J.: Animal communication: when i'm calling you, will you answer too? Curr. Biol. **27**(14), R713–R715 (2017)
11. Sharma, V., Haque, M.H., Aziz, S.M.: Energy cost minimization for net zero energy homes through optimal sizing of battery storage system. Renew. Energy **141**, 278–286 (2019)
12. Nyholm, E., Goop, J., Odenberger, M., Johnsson, F.: Solar photovoltaic-battery systems in Swedish households-self-consumption and self-sufficiency. Appl. Energy **183**, 148–159 (2016)
13. Dusonchet, L., Telaretti, E.: Comparative economic analysis of support policies for solar PV in the most representative EU countries. Renew. Sustain. Energy Rev. **42**, 986–998 (2015)
14. Flath, C.M.: An optimization approach for the design of time-of-use rates. In: 39th Annual Conference of the IEEE Industrial Electronics Society, IECON 2013, pp. 4727–4732. IEEE (2013)

15. Li, R., Wang, Z., Chenghong, G., Li, F., Hao, W.: A novel time-of-use tariff design based on gaussian mixture model. Appl. Energy **162**, 1530–1536 (2016)
16. Darghouth, N.R., Wiser, R.H., Barbose, G.: Customer economics of residential photovoltaic systems: sensitivities to changes in wholesale market design and rate structures. Renew. Sustain. Energy Rev. **54**, 1459–1469 (2016)
17. Gitizadeh, M., Fakharzadegan, H.: Battery capacity determination with respect to optimized energy dispatch schedule in grid-connected photovoltaic (PV) systems. Energy **65**, 665–674 (2014)
18. Hassan, A.S., Cipcigan, L., Jenkins, N.: Optimal battery storage operation for PV systems with tariff incentives. Appl. Energy **203**, 422–441 (2017)
19. Ratnam, E.L., Weller, S.R., Kellett, C.M.: An optimization-based approach to scheduling residential battery storage with solar PV: assessing customer benefit. Renew. Energy **75**, 123–134 (2015)
20. Wei, Q., Liu, D., Shi, G.: A novel dual iterative Q-learning method for optimal battery management in smart residential environments. IEEE Trans. Industr. Electron. **62**(4), 2509–2518 (2014)
21. Kim, S., Lim, H.: Reinforcement learning based energy management algorithm for smart energy buildings. Energies **11**(8), 2010 (2018)
22. Ruelens, F., Claessens, B.J., Quaiyum, S., De Schutter, B., Babuška, R., Belmans, R.: Reinforcement learning applied to an electric water heater: from theory to practice. IEEE Trans. Smart Grid **9**(4), 3792–3800 (2016)
23. Li, B., Xia, L.: A multi-grid reinforcement learning method for energy conservation and comfort of HVAC in buildings. In: 2015 IEEE International Conference on Automation Science and Engineering (CASE), pp. 444–449. IEEE (2015)
24. Foruzan, E., Soh, L.-K., Asgarpoor, S.: Reinforcement learning approach for optimal distributed energy management in a microgrid. IEEE Trans. Power Syst. **33**(5), 5749–5758 (2018)
25. Guan, C., Wang, Y., Lin, X., Nazarian, S., Pedram, M.: Reinforcement learning-based control of residential energy storage systems for electric bill minimization. In: 2015 12th Annual IEEE Consumer Communications and Networking Conference (CCNC), pp. 637–642. IEEE (2015)
26. Liu, Y., Zhang, D., Gooi, H.B.: Optimization strategy based on deep reinforcement learning for home energy management. CSEE J. Power Energy Syst. **6**(3), 572–582 (2020)
27. Uski, S., Rinne, E.: Data for a dairy farm microgrid solution, June 2018
28. National Renewable Energy Lab (NREL): System advisor model (SAM) (2017). Online. https://sam.nrel.gov. Accessed 1 Nov 2022

A Multi-agent Systems Approach for Peer-to-Peer Energy Trading in Dairy Farming

Mian Ibad Ali Shah(✉), Abdul Wahid, Enda Barrett, and Karl Mason

School of Computer Science, University of Galway, Galway H91 FYH2, Ireland
{m.shah7,abdul.wahid,enda.barrett,karl.mason}@universityofgalway.ie

Abstract. To achieve desired carbon emission reductions, integrating renewable generation and accelerating the adoption of peer-to-peer energy trading is crucial. This is especially important for energy-intensive farming, like dairy farming. However, integrating renewables and peer-to-peer trading presents challenges. To address this, we propose the Multi-Agent Peer-to-Peer Dairy Farm Energy Simulator (MAPDES), enabling dairy farms to participate in peer-to-peer markets. Our strategy reduces electricity costs and peak demand by approximately 30% and 24% respectively, while increasing energy sales by 37% compared to the baseline scenario without P2P trading. This demonstrates the effectiveness of our approach.

Keywords: Renewable Energy · Peer-to-Peer Energy Trading · Multi-Agent Systems

1 Introduction

According to Shine et al. [1], global dairy consumption per capita is projected to increase by 19% by 2050. However, milk production requires significant energy, raising concerns about carbon emissions. To ensure the future sustainability of the dairy industry, energy resources must be used sustainably [2]. An AI system can help reduce emissions and peak demand for electricity in dairy farms.

Multi-agent systems (MAS) have shown promising results in addressing microgrid challenges [3]. Performance evaluation models have optimized profit in energy-sharing regions (ESR) [4]. Peer-to-peer (P2P) energy trading involves sharing energy within a microgrid before trading with the retailer [5].

Three types of P2P energy trading exist: centralized, decentralized, and distributed [6]. Distributed markets combine aspects of centralized and decentralized markets, employing auction-based mechanisms such as the Double Auction (DA) [5]. This research utilizes MAS, P2P energy trading, pricing and auction to contribute:

Proc. of the Artificial Intelligence for Sustainability, ECAI 2023, Eunika et al. (eds.), Sep 30- Oct 1, 2023, https://sites.google.com/view/ai4s. *2023.*

S. Nowaczyk et al. (Eds.): ECAI 2023 Workshops, CCIS 1948, pp. 254–261, 2024.
https://doi.org/10.1007/978-3-031-50485-3_27

1. Development of a P2P energy trading model using MAS to optimize the utilization of renewable energy (RE) sources and minimize reliance of dairy farms on the utility grid to achieve energy sustainability and reduce carbon emissions
2. Integrating an internal pricing advisor with the auctioneer which makes the decision-making processes more transparent

2 Related Work

MAS has been widely studied for P2P energy trading due to its potential for financial benefits, scalability, reliability, data security, user satisfaction, peak demand management, and load management [7]. Researchers have explored different approaches to achieve these objectives. Various techniques have been proposed, such as non-cooperative games for dynamic pricing [8], reinforcement learning (RL) models [9], and deep RL [10] have also been employed.

In our research, we primarily focus on the distributed approach, which offers scalability and autonomy to customers [11]. Various techniques, including DA-MADDPG [12], aggregated control models [13], and MARL models [14], have been proposed for privacy, profit maximization, and market participation. Our research consolidates these findings and integrates critical factors such as financial benefits, data security, scalability, user satisfaction, load management, peak demand management, and transparent auction mechanisms into a comprehensive simulation.

3 Methodology

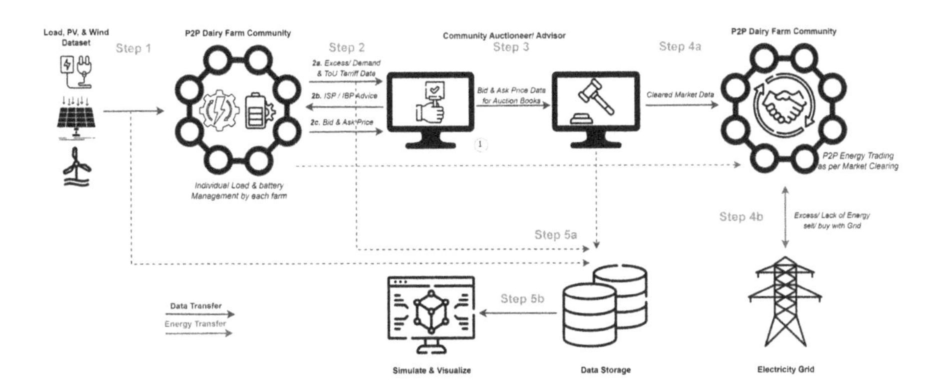

Fig. 1. Steps to Develop Distributed P2P Energy Trading Simulation with MAS

This study aims to introduce a MAS-based algorithm that facilitates distributed P2P energy trading among dairy farms. The proposed approach leverages MAS to enable dairy farms to sell excess energy produced from renewable sources to other farms in the vicinity. This approach aims to decrease their reliance on the utility grid and promote energy self-reliance. Figure 1 illustrates the process flow of the simulation model, which is explained in detail in the subsequent sections covering each step.

3.1 Datasets and Infrastructure

This study combines three datasets: Farm load data from Uski et al. [15], PV and wind energy generation data from the System Advisor Model (SAM). The infrastructure supports a scalable number of farms, with diverse sizes and PV/ wind systems. Participants are prosumers connected to the utility grid, facilitated by a central auctioneer providing Internal Selling Price (ISP) and Internal Buying Price (IBP) using the Supply Demand Ratio. The infrastructure operates on a distributed peer-to-peer model, with farms sharing generation and load data for centralized market clearance. Various agents, including farms, batteries, and traders, coordinate to meet energy demands effectively.

3.2 Model Design

The simulator consists of three steps: individual load and battery management, calculation of community's ISP and IBP, and market clearing through auction and energy trading. It can be tailored to simulate any duration, enabling a comprehensive analysis of grid load and potential profit/ loss.

The study proposes a Python-based simulation model for energy generation, consumption, and storage in a farm using renewable sources. It includes tailored load and battery management rules for dairy farming. The model enables energy trading through a P2P network or the grid. Input parameters and variables are used to calculate energy generation, consumption, and storage, considering different scenarios.

$$\lambda_{buy} = \$, \$\$, \$\$\$ = \text{night, day, peak} \tag{1}$$

$$B_{uc} = \begin{cases} B_{cc}, & \text{if } B_{cc} < \max(B_{dp}) \\ \max(B_{dp}), & \text{if } B_{cc} \geq \max(B_{dp}) \end{cases} \tag{2}$$

$$E_{tot} = \begin{cases} E_{pv} + E_w + B_{uc}, & \text{PV} = 1 \text{ or wind} = 1 \text{ bat} = 1 \\ 0, & \text{otherwise} \end{cases} \tag{3}$$

$$\begin{aligned} &\text{if } E_{\text{tot}} > E_l \& \text{SoC} < 90: \\ &\begin{cases} E_{tot} - E_l < B_{cp}, charge = 1 \\ E_{tot} - E_l > B_{cp}, charge = 1 \& sell = 1 \end{cases} \end{aligned} \tag{4}$$

$$\begin{aligned} &\text{if } E_{tot} < E_l: \\ &\begin{cases} SoC > 20 \& \lambda_{buy} = \$, Buy = 1 \& charge = 0 \\ (SoC < 50 \& \lambda_{buy} = \$) \text{ or} \\ (SoC < 20 \& \lambda_{buy} < \$\$\$), Buy = 1 \& charge = 1 \end{cases} \end{aligned} \tag{5}$$

$$\text{if } RE = 1\&bat = 0: \quad \begin{cases} \text{if } E_{tot} > E_l, \text{ sell} = 1 \\ \text{if } E_{tot} < E_l, \text{ buy} = 1 \end{cases} \tag{6}$$

$$\text{if } RE = 0 \ \& \ \text{bat} = 1: \\ \begin{cases} \text{if } SoC > 20\&\lambda_{\text{buy}} = \$, & Buy = 1\&charge = 0 \\ \text{if}(SoC < 20\&\lambda_{\text{buy}} < \$\$\$), & Buy = 1\&charge = 1 \end{cases} \tag{7}$$

$$SoC = \begin{cases} SoC + \frac{B_{ccap}}{B_c} \times 100, & charge = 1 \\ SoC - B_{dp}, & discharge = 1 \end{cases} \tag{8}$$

$$B_{ccap} = \\ \begin{cases} \max(B_{ccap}), & (RE = 1\&E_{tot} - E_l > \max(B_{ccap})) \text{ or } RE = 0 \\ E_{tot} - E_l, & RE = 1\&E_{tot} - E_l < \max(B_{ccap}) \end{cases} \tag{9}$$

$$B_{dp} = \frac{B_{uc}}{B_c} \times 100 \tag{10}$$

$$E_s = \\ \begin{cases} E_{tot} - E_l, & SoC \geq 90 \\ (E_{tot} - E_l) - B_{ccap}, & (E_{tot} - E_l) > B_{ccap}\&SoC < 90 \end{cases} \tag{11}$$

$$E_b = \\ \begin{cases} E_l, & RE = 0\&bat = 0 \\ E_l - (E_{tot} + B_{uc}), & E_{tot} < E_l\&\lambda_{buy} > \$\&SoC > 20 \\ (E_l - E_{tot}) + B_{ccap}, & \lambda_{buy} < \$\$\&SoC \leq 50 \\ E_l - E_{tot}, & RE = 1\&bat = 0 \\ E_l - B_{uc}, & RE = 0\&bat = 1\&SoC > 20\&\lambda_{buy} > \$ \\ E_l + B_{ccap}, & RE = 0\&bat = 1\&SoC \leq 20\&\lambda_{buy} < \$\$\$ \end{cases} \tag{12}$$

Equation 1 defines the energy tariff purchased from the grid, denoted as λ_{buy}, with three levels: \$, \$\$, and \$\$\$, representing night, day, and peak hours, respectively. Equation 2 calculates the present usable battery capacity (B_{uc}) based on the current battery capacity (B_{cc}) and the maximum battery discharge capacity ($\max(B_{dp})$). If B_{cc} is less than $\max(B_{dp})$, B_{uc} is equal to B_{cc}; otherwise, it is set to $\max(B_{dp})$. Equation 3 evaluates the total energy generation of the farm (E_{tot}) by summing up the energy generated by the PV system (E_{pv}), wind turbine (E_w), and B_{uc}. If any of these sources do not generate energy, E_{tot} is zero.

Equation 4 determines the optimal battery operation when renewable energy resources and batteries are available on the farm. If E_{tot} is greater than E_l (farm load) and the current battery percentage (SoC) is less than 90%, the battery is charged or discharged based on the difference between E_{tot} and E_l, and the charging capacity (B_{ccap}). If the excess energy is insufficient to charge the battery, only the battery is charged; otherwise, the remaining energy is sold in the market.

Equation 5 determines whether to charge or discharge the battery and whether to purchase energy from the grid based on E_{tot}, SoC, and the energy tariff (λ_{buy}). The conditions in this equation guide the decision-making process. Equation 6 decides whether to buy or sell energy based on E_{tot} and E_l, considering the presence or absence of a battery. Equation 7 determines whether energy should be purchased externally and whether the battery should be charged, based on SoC and λ_{buy}.

Equation 8 updates the battery percentage (SoC) based on its charging or discharging status. Equations 9 and 10 calculate the battery charging capacity (B_{ccap}) and discharge percentage (B_{dp}) using the given conditions. Equations 11 and 12 determine the excess energy available (E_s) and the amount of energy bought (E_b), respectively, based on various scenarios involving renewable energy generation, battery capacity and percentage, energy tariffs, and load demand.

After implementing individual load and battery management at farms, the subsequent action is to engage in transactions involving the sale or purchase of surplus or deficient energy to or from the community or grid, respectively.

$$SDR = \frac{TSP}{TBP} \tag{13}$$

$$\text{ISP} = \begin{cases} \frac{\lambda_{sell} \times \lambda_{buy}}{(\lambda_{buy} - \lambda_{sell}) \times \text{SDR} + \lambda_{sell}}, & 0 \leq \text{SDR} \leq 1 \\ \lambda_{sell}, & \text{SDR} > 1 \end{cases} \tag{14}$$

$$\text{IBP} = \begin{cases} \text{ISP} \times \text{SDR} + \lambda_{buy} \times \text{(1-SDR)}, & 0 \leq \text{SDR} \leq 1 \\ \lambda_{buy}, & \text{SDR} > 1 \end{cases} \tag{15}$$

IBP and ISP are computed using the SDR technique [16] for energy trading. Internal prices consider the feed-in tariff, utility grid electricity prices, and economic balance. As seen in Eqs. 14 and 15, ISP and IBP are determined through a piecewise function based on the SDR. The pricing strategy depends on the SDR, guiding the selling price between λ_{sell} and λ_{buy} (feed-in tariff and time of use) for a balanced supply-demand ratio. Prosumers aim to increase the SDR by reducing consumption when it is small, while sellers and buyers adjust consumption accordingly when the SDR is large.

In the final phase of the simulation, market clearance is conducted to facilitate energy trading among community participants and the grid based on cleared market conditions. The simulation incorporates a DA auction inspired by Qiu et al.'s work [12,17]. The auctioneer only requires load, generation, and pricing data, ensuring data security for market participants.

4 Experimental Results

We evaluated our simulation approach by conducting a one-year simulation with a one-hour time step involving 10 prosumer farms. We assessed the results using five key metrics: (i) energy purchased by farms with and without RE sources and P2P trading, (ii) energy purchased by farms with P2P trading compared to no P2P trading, all with RE sources, (iii) energy sold by farms with RE sources (P2P vs. non-P2P), (iv) peak hour energy demand from the grid by farms with RE sources (P2P vs. non-P2P), and (v) effective ISP and IBP advice based on time-of-use (ToU) tariffs.

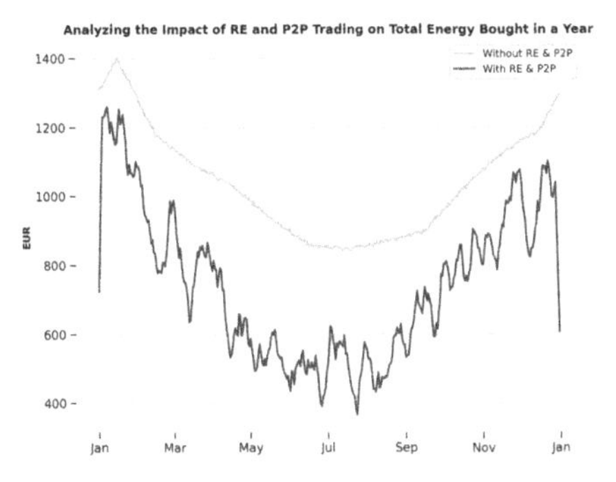

(a) Comparison of Energy Purchased by Farm Community: P2P and RE vs Non-P2P and Non-RE Sources

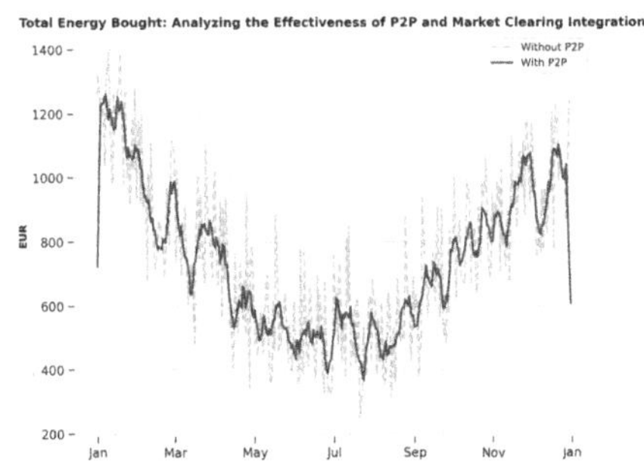

(b) Comparison of Energy Purchased by Farms: P2P vs Non-P2P, all having Renewable Energy Sources

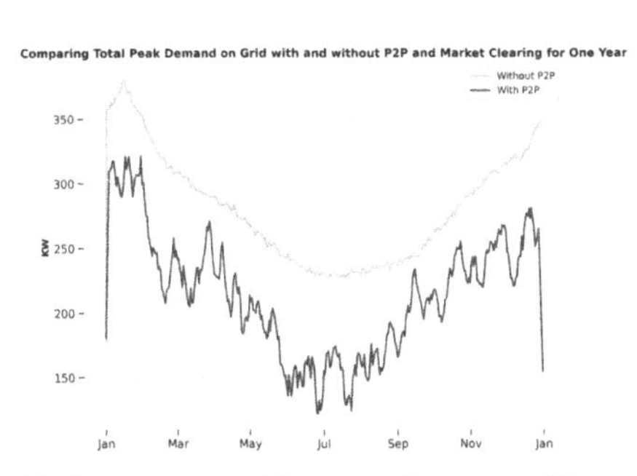

(c) Comparison of Electricity Demand of Farms from Grid: P2P vs Non-P2P in Peak Hours

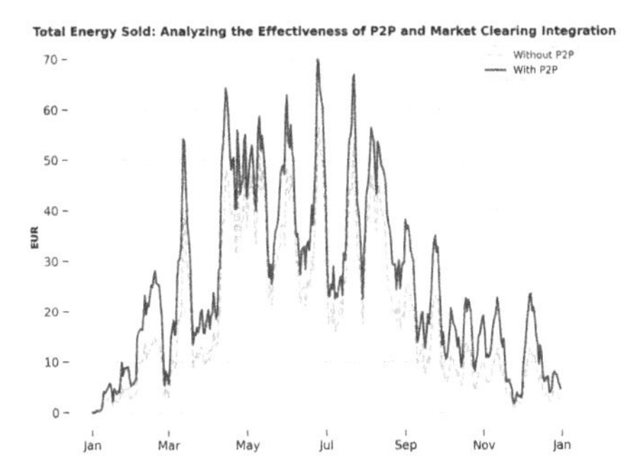

(d) Comparison of Energy Sold by Farms: P2P vs Non-P2P

Fig. 2. Simulation Results

Figure 2a compares the cost trend per day between farms without RE generation sources and P2P energy trading, and farms with RE generation sources and P2P energy trading. The results show that the community using RE sources and P2P energy trading paid approximately 30% less compared to the farms without these features. Figure 2b demonstrates the cost difference between farms with RE generation sources but no P2P trading, and farms with both RE sources and P2P trading. The results show a reduction of approximately 1% in energy purchasing costs for the community. Figure 2c illustrates the reduction in peak hour demand from the grid, with a 24% decrease observed over the course of the year. Figure 2d shows the potential earnings from selling excess energy, indicating that farms with P2P trading can earn approximately 37% more compared to selling energy solely to the grid. These results highlight the cost savings and reduced reliance on the grid achieved through P2P energy trading, RE generation sources, and market clearing strategies.

5 Conclusion and Future Work

This research demonstrates the efficacy of integrating distributed P2P energy trading, RE resources, and auction-based market clearing mechanisms within a dairy farming community. The one-year simulation with 10 farms shows that P2P trading significantly reduces energy costs and reliance on the grid. The research contributions resulted in:

1) Farm community reduced energy purchases from the grid by 30% with the use of RE sources and P2P trading compared to no RE sources and P2P trading.
2) With RE sources, the farm community increased profit from selling excess energy to peers and the grid by 37% with P2P energy trading compared to no P2P trading.
3) With RE sources, farms' electricity demand from the grid, especially during peak hours, decreased by 24% with P2P energy trading compared to no P2P trading.
4) Regular updates on market conditions were provided to participants, ensuring transparency and informed decision-making during auctions.

To improve the model, further research should investigate the influence of bidding prices on load and battery management and line losses. One potential approach is to employ multi-agent reinforcement learning (MARL) techniques to enhance market estimation and decision-making. These advancements can lead to more accurate models of market behavior and enable informed energy trading in dairy farms.

Acknowledgements. This publication has emanated from research conducted with the financial support of Science Foundation Ireland under Grant number [21/FFP-A/9040].

References

1. Shine, P., Upton, J., Sefeedpari, P., Murphy, M.D.: Energy consumption on dairy farms: a review of monitoring, prediction modelling, and analyses. Energies **13**(5), 1288 (2020)
2. Mehdi Ben Jebli and Slim Ben Youssef: Renewable energy consumption and agriculture: evidence for cointegration and granger causality for Tunisian economy. Int. J. Sustain. Dev. World Ecology **24**(2), 149–158 (2017)

3. Elena, D.O., Florin, D., Valentin, G., Marius, P., Octavian, D., Catalin, D.: Multi-agent system for smart grids with produced energy from PV energy sources. In: 2022 14th International Conference on Electronics, Computers and AI (ECAI), pp. 1–6. IEEE (2022)
4. Zhou, Y., Jianzhong, W., Long, C., Cheng, M., Zhang, C.: Performance evaluation of peer-to-peer energy sharing models. Energy procedia **143**, 817–822 (2017)
5. Zhou, Y., Jianzhong, W., Long, C.: Evaluation of peer-to-peer energy sharing mechanisms based on a multiagent simulation framework. Appl. Energy **222**, 993–1022 (2018)
6. Zhou, Y., Jianzhong, W., Long, C., Ming, W.: State-of-the-art analysis and perspectives for peer-to-peer energy trading. Engineering **6**(7), 739–753 (2020)
7. Ye, Y., Tang, Y., Wang, H., Zhang, X.-P., Strbac, G.: A scalable privacy-preserving multi-agent deep reinforcement learning approach for large-scale peer-to-peer transactive energy trading. IEEE Trans. Smart Grid **12**(6), 5185–5200 (2021)
8. Zhang, M., Eliassen, F., Taherkordi, A., Jacobsen, H.A., Chung, H.M., Zhang, Y.: Energy trading with demand response in a community-based p2p energy market. In: 2019 IEEE International Conference on Communications, Control, and Computing Technologies for Smart Grids (SmartGridComm), pp. 1–6 (2019)
9. Ali, F.S., Bouachir, O., Özkasap, Ö., Aloqaily, M.: Synergychain: blockchain-assisted adaptive cyber-physical p2p energy trading. IEEE Trans. Ind. Inf. **17**(8), 5769–5778 (2020)
10. Chen, T., Bu, S.: Realistic peer-to-peer energy trading model for microgrids using deep reinforcement learning. In: 2019 IEEE PES Innovative Smart Grid Technologies Europe (ISGT-Europe), pp. 1–5. IEEE (2019)
11. Khorasany, M., Mishra, Y., Ledwich, G.: Market framework for local energy trading: a review of potential designs and market clearing approaches. IET Gener. Transm. Distrib. **12**(22), 5899–5908 (2018)
12. Qiu, D., Wang, J., Wang, J., Strbac, G.: Multi-agent reinforcement learning for automated peer-to-peer energy trading in double-side auction market. In: IJCAI, pp. 2913–2920 (2021)
13. Long, C., Jianzhong, W., Zhou, Y., Jenkins, N.: P2p energy sharing through a two-stage aggregated battery control in a community microgrid. Appl. Energy **226**, 261–276 (2018)
14. Liangyi, P., Wang, S., Huang, X., Liu, X., Shi, Y., Wang, H.: Peer-to-peer trading for energy-saving based on reinforcement learning. Energies **15**(24), 9633 (2022)
15. Uski, S., Rinne, E., Sarsama, J.: Microgrid as a cost-effective alternative to rural network underground cabling for adequate reliability. Energies **11**(8), 1978 (2018)
16. Liu, N., Xinghuo, Yu., Wang, C., Li, C., Ma, L., Lei, J.: Energy-sharing model with price-based demand response for microgrids of peer-to-peer prosumers. IEEE Trans. Power Syst. **32**(5), 3569–3583 (2017)
17. Qiu, D., Wang, J., Dong, Z., Wang, Y., Strbac, G.: Mean-field multi-agent reinforcement learning for peer-to-peer multi-energy trading. IEEE Trans. Power Syst. **38**, 4853–4866 (2022)

Food Ontologies and Ontological Reasoning in Food Domain for Sustainability

Weronika T. Adrian[1(✉)], Katarzyna Pyrczak[2], Krzysztof Kluza[1], and Antoni Ligęza[1]

[1] AGH University of Krakow, al. A. Mickiewicza 30, 30-059 Krakow, Poland
{wta,kluza,ligeza}@agh.edu.pl
[2] Jagiellonian University Medical College, Montelupich 4, 30-155 Kraków, Poland
katarzyna.pyrczak@student.uj.edu.pl

Abstract. This paper investigates the potential of combining food ontologies and AI in the food sector for enhanced sustainability. We argue that ontology-driven AI can foster sustainable food systems, underscoring how semantic structures and AI can facilitate precision agriculture, sustainable food choices, personalized diets, and climate change mitigation. Our goal is to discuss how these innovative technologies can be harnessed to better understand, manage, and ultimately transform the food domain for a sustainable future. As a first step towards achieving this goal, we provide an overview of prominent food ontologies and knowledge graphs such as FoodOn, Food KG, SPO, Ingredients Ontology, and ONS, highlighting their structures and focal points, as well as illustrate the value of ontological reasoning through practical food domain examples, using SPARQL queries and ontological reasoning for insightful knowledge derivation.

Keywords: Food Ontologies · Ontological Reasoning in Food Systems · Sustainability in Food Systems

1 Introduction

In today's digital and interconnected society, managing complex data is crucial, especially in the multifaceted food industry. Ontologies, a key component of semantic web technologies, can effectively model connections between ingredients, recipes, dietary choices, and environmental impacts, facilitating the extraction of valuable insights. Artificial Intelligence (AI) enhancements have shown transformative capabilities across various fields. AI methods based on ontologies can lead to better understanding and managing of food-related data.

In this paper, we discuss how AI and food ontologies can enhance sustainability. We elaborate on such issues as biodiversity protection, precision agriculture, food waste reduction, sustainable supply chains, individualized diets, and climate change abatement, emphasizing the transformative potential of converging ontologies and AI in the food industry.

S. Nowaczyk et al. (Eds.): ECAI 2023 Workshops, CCIS 1948, pp. 262–268, 2024.
https://doi.org/10.1007/978-3-031-50485-3_28

The paper is structured as follows. Section 2 elaborates on how the combination of AI and food ontologies can be harnessed to promote sustainability. Section 3 provides an overview of ontologies and their application in the food domain. In Sect. 4, we delve into the concept of ontological reasoning and illustrate how reasoning can be used to extract implicit knowledge from food ontologies. We conclude our paper with a summary in Sect. 5.

2 Combining AI with Food Ontologies for Sustainability

There are many areas in which food ontologies and AI methods can significantly contribute to improving sustainability, such as biodiversity, precision agriculture, reducing food waste, sustainable supply chains, sustainable food choices, personalized diets, or even climate change mitigation [7].

Monitoring and maintaining biodiversity in agriculture can be done by predicting the impacts of different agricultural practices on local ecosystems and suggesting ways to minimize negative impacts. Food ontologies can provide a structured knowledge framework about the dependencies in food production. Employing machine learning algorithms, AI can analyze data from soil sensors, weather reports, and other variables, guiding farmers towards timely planting, irrigation, etc., and therefore minimizing waste. Ontologies offer a framework for structuring and correctly interpreting this data. Through their combined use, precision agriculture can be enacted, reducing water and fertilizer use, promoting sustainability, and diminishing agriculture's environmental footprint [11].

Another sustainability challenge is food waste [13]. Leveraging food ontologies and AI can enhance demand prediction, and mitigate overproduction. Technology can not only forecast future trends by analyzing historical sales but also minimize food waste in homes by identifying available food items and suggesting recipes to use up ingredients before they spoil.

AI can also help in creating more sustainable food supply chains. By using machine learning algorithms to analyze supply chain data, companies can identify inefficiencies and make their operations more sustainable. Food ontologies can help ensure that the data being analyzed is relevant and accurately represents the various elements of the supply chain [8].

Food ontologies can also enlighten consumers about the environmental implications of food choices, enabling more sustainable eating decisions [10]. AI can facilitate personalized diets tailored to individual health needs and preferences, reducing waste and improving health outcomes. Ontologies structure food-related data, while AI guides consumer behavior towards sustainable choices, encompassing recommendations aligning with sustainable, healthy preferences.

Another issue where food ontologies combined with AI can help in sustainable decisions is predicting climate change's impact on food production, aiding in sustainable farming strategies, and implementing adaptive agricultural practices for food security and sustainability. Food ontologies can offer a structural understanding of the correlations between various farming practices and their environmental consequences [2].

3 Ontologies in Food Domain

There are many ontologies and knowledge graphs in the field of food. Since this area of interest is very broad, each of them focuses on different aspects. Depending on the purpose of a given ontology, they also differ in size and whether they already have instances or are simply universal tools. In this paper, we focus on ontologies in the field of nutrition, their characteristics, and their structure.

3.1 FoodOn

The largest source of structured information on food is the FoodOn ontology [5]. FoodOn contains 9600 categories of products that function as food and descriptions of their processing. Food products include animal, plant, mushrooms, and processed food. However, the ecosystem of FoodOn is more than just food products and encompasses ontologies related to food harvesting, features, and production (see https://foodon.org/). FoodOn is provided open-sourced by OBO Foundry, a consortium of interoperable life science-oriented ontologies.

3.2 Food KG

Food KG [6] was created by collecting information on recipes, nutrients, and preparation times for given meals in order to be able to recommend recipes to users that fit their preferences. Thus, the ontology is geared toward customers and practical applications. The data has been combined into a single knowledge graph. The sources that FoodKG uses can be divided into 3 types, namely:

- data from recipes – recipes can come from books, blogs, or structured datasets, currently they come from a dataset prepared by the authors of the Im2Recipe project.
- nutrient data – the data comes from the USDA (United States Department of Agriculture).
- food knowledge – FoodOn was used to structure the data in terms of origin, as well as its preparation and processing.

Food KG has 3 components: Food – containing new classes, FoodOn – containing imported classes from FoodOn, and Ingredient – containing instances of recipes and ingredients.

3.3 The SmartProducts Network of Ontologies (SPO)

Another ontology that focuses on structuring food products is the SPO ontology [3]. The ontology contains three modules - external, generic, and application-specific. Each of these is also divided into separate modules.

It is interesting to note that there are two connections between the generic module and the application-specific module. The 'food' module has relationships with both the 'process' and 'product' modules.

3.4 Ingredients Ontology

The purpose of Ingredients Ontology [1] is to link ingredients with their corresponding category and the products that can be obtained from them. The notation convention used here is "language:ingredient name". This ontology is being developed all the time. Ingredient names are in the 'Named_ingredient' class, and products derived from other ingredients are in the 'OFF_ingredient' class. Also present is the 'FoodSource' class, which "assembles all possible food sources that are used for ingredients. A food source is the starting point of food, i.e. something found in nature, an animal, a plant, a mineral, or a fluid".

3.5 Ontology for Nutritional Studies (ONS)

Ontology for Nutritional Studies is the first ontology that seeks to formally systematize knowledge about food studies. The ONS has 6056 classes of [14]. ONS was created as an amalgamation of information about food and its processing, which was taken from other ontologies and a new classification of food terminology. As many as 2,809 classes were imported from FoodOn, nearly half of the current classes in ONS. Other sources included Ontology for Biomedical Investigations, Semanticscience Integrated Ontology, and The Information Artifact Ontology.

3.6 Comparison of ONS, FoodKG, SPO and FoodOn Ontologies

In Table 1, we present a comparative analysis of the ONS, FoodKG, SPO, and FoodOn ontologies in terms of selected aspects.

Table 1. Comparison of the ONS, FoodKG, SPO, and FoodOn ontologies

Selected aspect	ONS	FoodKG	SPO	FoodOn
Class defining a recipe	✓	✓	✓	✓
Class defining a meal	✓	✓	✗	✓
Class defining a component	✓	✓	✗	✗
Class defining a product substitute	✗	✗	✗	✓
Class defining food	✓	✓	✓	✓
Classes regarding drinking	✓	✗	✓	✓
Classes regarding processed food	✓	✓	✗	✓
Classes describing process of making food	✓	✗	✓	✓
Classes regarding diet	✓	✗	✓	✓
Classes regarding user preferences	✓	✗	✓	✓
Classes regarding product quality	✓	✓	✓	✓
Classes regarding taste	✓	✓	✗	✓

4 Ontological Reasoning in Food Domain

An important element of ontologies is that they have practical applications. By querying ontologies, one can get information from them that they need at a given time and that is already in the ontology. On the other hand, thanks to ontology inference, it is possible to obtain data that is not explicitly provided in the ontology. Let us analyze the problem of looking for substitution in a food recipe. An example query, based on the Food Recipe Ingredient Substitution ontology design pattern [9] for the question "What vegan product can be substituted for beef in a roast romaine recipe?" in SPARQL looks like this:

```
SELECT  DISTINCT ?recipe ?food_item
    WHERE{ ?recipe_ingr_sub rdf:type food:food_recipe_ingr_subst_spec.
        ?recipe rdf:type food:food_recipe.
        ?set rdf:type food:ingredient_set_specification.
        ?spec rdf:type food:ingredient_specification.
        ?spec2 rdf:type food:ingredient_specification.
        ?food_item rdf:type food:food_item.
        ?set_trans rdf:type food:ingredient_set_trans_spec.

        ?recipe_ingr_sub food:has_part ?recipe.
        ?recipe_ingr_sub food:has_part food:pieczen_rzymska.
        food:pieczen_rzymska food:has_component ?set.
        ?set food:has_member ?spec.
        ?spec food:is_about food:wolowina.
        ?recipe_ingr_sub food:has_part ?set_trans.
        ?set_trans food:has_member ?spec2.
        ?spec2 food:is_about ?food_item.
        ?food_item food:has_quality food:weganski.
    }
```

After running the HermiT reasoner, which supports SPARQL queries [4], the result is a vegan product that can be substituted for beef: chickpeas. These queries can be even more specific and not only look at the characteristics of the product itself but also take into account the user's preferences.

Inference in ontologies involves the derivation of data that are not expressed directly. For this reason, it is very important that the structure of the ontology is formal, which allows its automatic processing. The following shows what sample information can be obtained, thanks to ontology inference. Inference was also carried out in the Protégé application. This time the reasoner Pellet was used, which is the first reasoner to support the OWL-DL language and inference in ontologies with instances of [12].

The first inference example is presented on the Food Recipe Ingredient Substitution ontology pattern [9]. The class 'food_item' is linked to quality through the relationship 'has_quality' and 'has_no_quality'. Both the ObjectProperties 'has_quality' and 'has_no_quality' in their description have the 'food_item' class in the domain and the 'quality' class in the value range.

A new instance of 'wieprzowina' ('pork') was introduced into the ontology, without assigning it to any class, but linking it to instances of the 'quality' class using the 'has_quality' and 'has_no_quality' relationships. Before running the reasoner, the pork did not belong to any class. After running it, the pork was assigned as an instance of the 'food_item' class.

Let us consider another example of ontological inference (see Fig. 1).

Fig. 1. Sample ontology in Protégé software.

The ontology contains only three classes and one ObjectProperty, which is the relationship between the pie class and the ingredient. Two instances have been introduced - 'szarlotka' and 'jabłko' ('apple pie' and 'apple'), without assigning them to either class. In the properties of the 'apple pie' instance, the ObjectProperty 'has_ingredient' was added, linking it to 'apple'. Again, the reasoner Pellet was used. The result of the inference is presented in Fig. 2.

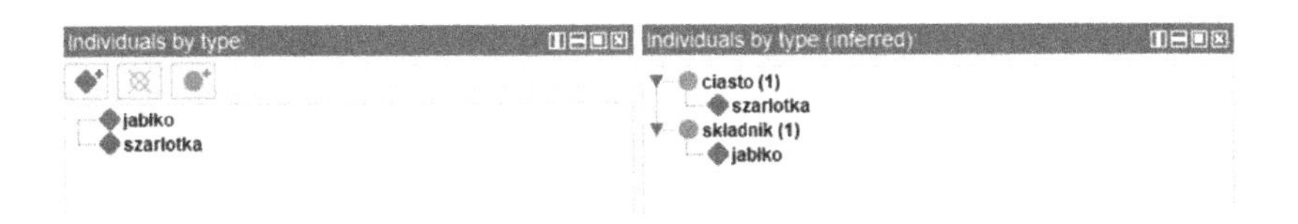

Fig. 2. The result of inference in the ontology.

After running the reasoner, one can see that the instances have been correctly assigned to classes which means new objects can be automatically classified and used in further queries and reasoning tasks.

5 Conclusions

In this paper, we argued that AI can contribute to achieving sustainability in the food sector, and food ontologies can provide the necessary data structure to facilitate these AI applications. This paper underlines the versatility of ontologies in the food domain and showcases ontological reasoning's potential in extracting implicit knowledge in complex scenarios. The integration of AI methods and food ontologies has been identified as a potential contributor to sustainability, impacting areas such as biodiversity, precision farming, waste reduction, and supply chain efficiency. We have implemented a proof-of-concept ontology based on the ontology design pattern for ingredient substitution. In the future, we plan to extend this ontology with more instances representing recipes and their ingredients, maintaining links to existing food ontologies, so that ontology-based intelligent recommendations for personalized diets can be developed.

References

1. Ingredients ontology. https://wiki.openfoodfacts.org/Project:Ingredients_ontology (2018)
2. Babaie, H., Davarpanah, A., Dhakal, N.: Projecting pathways to food-energy-water systems sustainability through ontology. Environ. Eng. Sci. **36**(7), 808–819 (2019)
3. d'Aquin, M., Motta, E., Nikolov, A., Thomas, K.: Realizing networks of proactive smart products. In: ten Teije, A., et al. (eds.) EKAW 2012. LNCS (LNAI), vol. 7603, pp. 337–352. Springer, Heidelberg (2012). https://doi.org/10.1007/978-3-642-33876-2_30
4. Glimm, B., Horrocks, I., Motik, B., Stoilos, G., Wang, Z.: Hermit: an owl 2 reasoner. J. Autom. Reason. **53**(3), 245–269 (2014)
5. Griffiths, E.J., Dooley, D.M., Buttigieg, P.L., Hoehndorf, R., Brinkman, F.S., Hsiao, W.W.: Foodon: a global farm-to-fork food ontology. In: ICBO/BioCreative, pp. 1–2 (2016)
6. Haussmann, S., et al.: FoodKG: a semantics-driven knowledge graph for food recommendation. In: Ghidini, C., et al. (eds.) ISWC 2019. LNCS, vol. 11779, pp. 146–162. Springer, Cham (2019). https://doi.org/10.1007/978-3-030-30796-7_10
7. Holden, N.M., White, E.P., Lange, M.C., Oldfield, T.L.: Review of the sustainability of food systems and transition using the internet of food. NPJ Sci. Food **2**(1), 18 (2018)
8. Jachimczyk, B., Tkaczyk, R., Piotrowski, T., Johansson, S., Kulesza, W.: IoT-based dairy supply chain-an ontological approach. Elektronika ir Elektrotechnika **27**(1), 71–83 (2021)
9. Ławrynowicz, A., Wróblewska, A., Adrian, W.T., Kulczyński, B., Gramza-Michałowska, A.: Food recipe ingredient substitution ontology design pattern. Sensors **22**(3), 1095 (2022)
10. Mazac, R., Tuomisto, H.L.: The post-anthropocene diet: navigating future diets for sustainable food systems. Sustainability **12**(6), 2355 (2020)
11. Ngo, Q.H., Le-Khac, N.-A., Kechadi, T.: Ontology based approach for precision agriculture. In: Kaenampornpan, M., Malaka, R., Nguyen, D.D., Schwind, N. (eds.) MIWAI 2018. LNCS (LNAI), vol. 11248, pp. 175–186. Springer, Cham (2018). https://doi.org/10.1007/978-3-030-03014-8_15
12. Sirin, E., Parsia, B., Grau, B.C., Kalyanpur, A., Katz, Y.: Pellet: a practical owl-dl reasoner. J. Web Semant. **5**(2), 51–53 (2007)
13. Stojanov, R., et al.: Food waste ontology: a formal description of knowledge from the domain of food waste. In: 2019 IEEE International Conference on Big Data (Big Data), pp. 5190–5194. IEEE (2019)
14. Vitali, F., et al.: ONS: an ontology for a standardized description of interventions and observational studies in nutrition. Genes Nutr. **13**(1), 1–9 (2018). https://doi.org/10.1186/s12263-018-0601-y

AI System for Short Term Prediction of Hourly Electricity Demand

Małgorzata Markowska[1], Andrzej Sokołowski[2(✉)], Grzegorz Migut[3], and Danuta Strahl[4]

[1] Wroclaw University of Economics and Business, Wroclaw, Poland
malgorzata.markowska@ue.wroc.pl
[2] Collegium Humanum - Warsaw Management University, Warsaw, Poland
sokolows@uek.krakow.pl
[3] StatSoft Poland, Kraków, Poland
g.migut@statsoft.pl
[4] WSB University, Dąbrowa Górnicza, Poland
danuta.strahl@ue.wroc.pl

Abstract. Companies supplying electrical energy rely mainly on long term agreements with electricity produsers, but on the other hand the actual demand should be precisely predicted for 48 h ahead, to take into account the actual weather conditions. Some time series models can be used for this purpose, and the best results can be achieved by combining forecasts from regression models, exponential smoothing, ARIMA models and neural networks. In practice – more popular are average demand profiles showing the average demand distribution over 24 h. We propose to build an AI system to choose the future profile. First – from the historical data – daily profiles are obtained, by cutting the time series into 24-h periods. Then, these empirical profiles are clustered with hierarchic and non-hierarchic clustering procedures to form homogeneous groups (types of profiles). Finally the classification methods are applied using weather data and observed demand from previous days (up to one week backwards). The measure for the forecasting evaluation has been proposed. Out of the tested classification methods, neural networks performed the best, followed by some voting procedures.

Keywords: Electricity Demand · Forecasting Models · Neural Networks

1 Introduction

During United Nations summit in 2015, with 160 heads of state, the document „Transforming Our World: The 2030 Agenda for Sustainable Development" [15] has been approved. Sustainable Development Goals assumes actions to change the world in which the needs of current generation will be fulfilled in a balanced way. According to Goal 7 we should ensure access to affordable, reliable, sustainable and modern energy for all, and Goal 12 tells us to ensure sustainable consumption and production patterns. With 10% of world population without access to modern electric energy we have to work

S. Nowaczyk et al. (Eds.): ECAI 2023 Workshops, CCIS 1948, pp. 269–276, 2024.
https://doi.org/10.1007/978-3-031-50485-3_29

on effective energy production and consumption in every country, and on every level. One possible way is to forecast the demand for electricity within existing system of production and distribution. Artificial Intelligence systems can help to forecast demand and optimize production.

2 Literature Remarks

Historical data is typically used in building forecasting systems. In electric energy industry prices are forecasted on hourly basis [3] and in long-term horizon [4, 10, 19] show that in last 10 years more than 170 papers were published on that subject. Probabilistic energy forecasting [6] and short-term load forecasts are important for production system and energy markets [1]. Among methods used for forecasting we can name some examples: data-driven modeling [4, 19], artificial neural networks: ANN [7, 9, 11], Deep Feed-Forward [17], deep neural networks [3], hybrid models with SSN and wavelet transform [1, 2, 12], seasonal and non-seasonal autoregressive moving average models (SARIMA/ARIMA) [8, 14], quantile regression [5], Ordinary Least Squares Regression [16], machine learning Random Forests [13], models merging Singular Spectral Analysis, Cuckoo Searchand Support Vector Machine [18].

3 Method

The aim of the paper is to propose the methodological structure of AI system for forecasting hourly demand for electrical energy. The research is based on an empirical time series. The most popular approach in short term hourly forecasting is based on time series analysis. We propose to forecast not the individual hours but daily profiles of electricity demand. Different daily profiles are used in forecasting practice. Analysis presented here is based on concrete real data, but the shape of profiles are more or less similar in a given country. It is interesting that electricity profiles are similar to water usage profiles or number of mobile phone calls. From this point of view the proposed methodology seems to be more general.

Our empirical time series covers the period from October, until May two years later (15312 h) for small region in Poland. It is presented on Fig. 1. This time series has been transformed into multivariable data set (each variable representing one hour). Each object (table row) represents one day. 21 days have been randomly selected as a test data – not the consecutive days but spread all over time series. So the learning set consists of 617 days.

Daily profiles have been clustered by Ward agglomerative method with squared Euclidean distance used to measure distances between groups on the consecutive stages of agglomerative process.

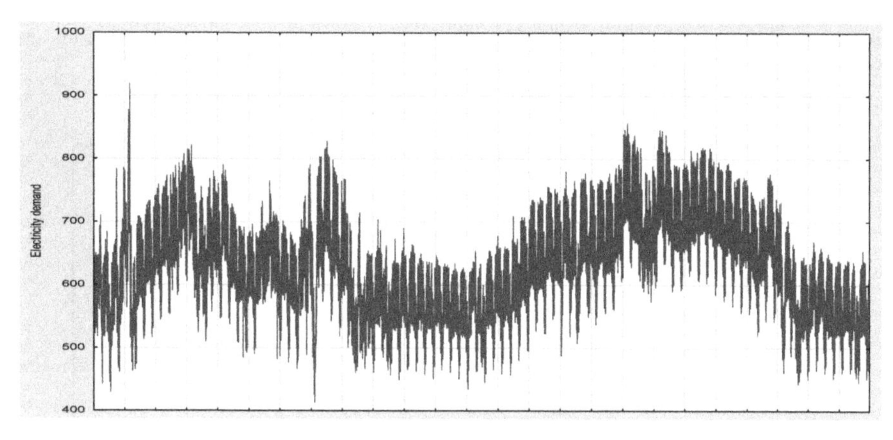

Fig. 1. Hourly electricity demand time series

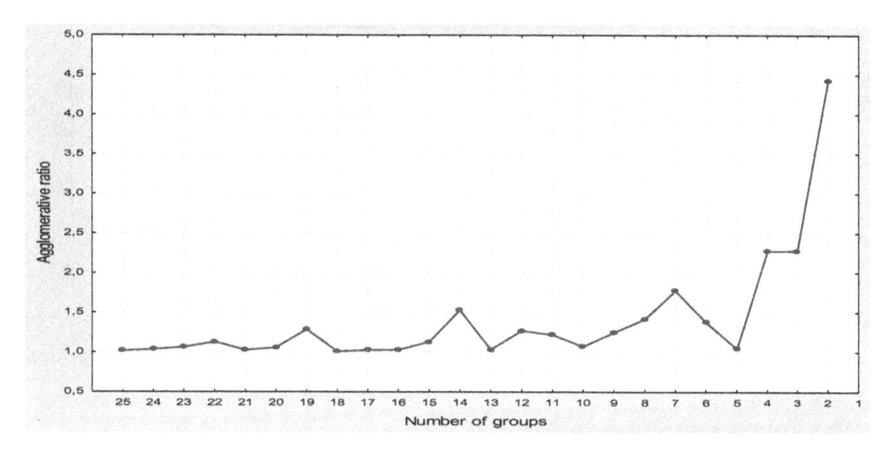

Fig. 2. Agglomerative ratios at the hierarchic joining steps

Different methods have been proposed in the literature to stop the agglomeration process and obtain the final partition. We decided to use the procedure based on the relative increase of the agglomerative distance, i.e. the distance which is used to identify which groups should be merged on the given step. The increase of this distance is somehow smooth until objects or small groups belonging to the same large group are merged. The distance visibly increased when we join together groups lying far from each other in the multidimentional space. It means that it would be fair to stop the agglomeration process before distant groups are put together. There is an additional criterion for the number of groups. If there are too many groups than the practical simplicity of forecasting profiles, not the time series, is lost. Analysing Fig. 2 we decided to identify 14 groups of profiles. The final partition has been obtained by k-means method. In cluster analysis the final groups can differ by the level or by the structure. Figure 3 presents the average profiles of 14 clusters. We numbered them from the smallest to the greatest value of the daily average. The same order has been archived by the first dimension from the Multidimensional Scaling of the whole profiles. The profiles are given on Fig. 3.

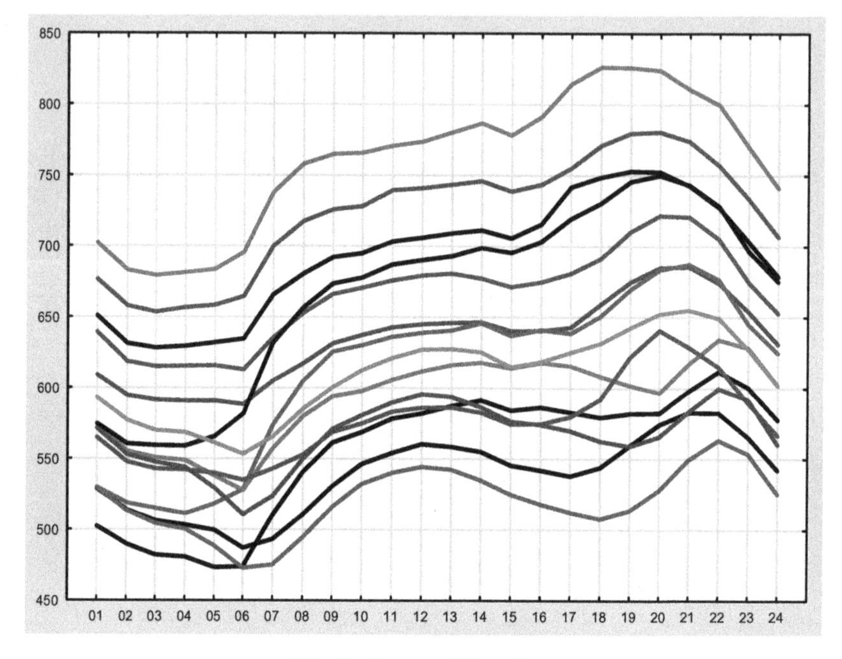

Fig. 3. Average 14 profiles

For the forecasting – identifying future profiles, the following explaining variables have been used:

- qualitative variables: week day
- dummy variables: day before holiday different from Sunday, day of the holiday, day after the holiday
- quantitative variables: average day temperature, average night temperature, seven lagged demand veriables from the days of previous seven days

In order to measure the quality of prediction we propose measure M defined by (1).

$$M = 1 - \frac{\sum_{i=1}^{k} \sum_{j=1}^{k} n_{ij} d_{ij}}{\sum_{j=1}^{k} n_{.j} \sum_{i=1}^{k} p_j d_{ij}} \tag{1}$$

The above measure is based on two matrices: **N** – classification matrix obtained by a given classification method, **D** – matrix of weights (distances between day means (per hour) of the profiles or dositances between profiles). The idea of M is to compare the results of a given method with random assignment defined by the observed probability distribution for profiles. This distribution has been obtained on the basis of learning set and is given in Table 1. The distribution in Table 1 is somehow “biased” by the summer/winter structure of the learning set, so the other possiblity is to use equal probabilities for profiles.

Table 1. Probability distribution of profiles

Profile number	1	2	3	4	5	6	7
Probability	0.063	0.036	0.054	0.042	0.044	0.143	0.075
Profile number	8	9	10	11	12	13	14
Probability	0.031	0.112	0.123	0.036	0.107	0.093	0.041

Source: own calculations

4 Results

To predict profiles both in learning and test set we used the following methods: CART, CHAID, Boosted Tree, Random Forests, SVM, K-nearest Neighbors and Neural Networks. Having results from 6 methods we also applied voting prediction by calculating mean, median and trunctated mean (rejecting lowest and highest predicted profile numbers).

Table 2. Accuracy of prediction – M measure (probability of profiles)

Method	Learning set		Test set		
	Weighted by distance between means	Weighted by distance between profiles	Weighted by distance between means	Weighted by distance between profiles	Average
CART	0.718	0.835	0.670	0.831	0.751
CHAID	0.587	0.730	0.638	0.827	0.733
Boosted Tree	0.623	0.773	0.736	0.847	0.792
Random Forest	0.733	0.833	0.789	0.902	0.846
SVM	0.800	0.872	0.751	0.837	0.794
KNN	**0.883**	**0.926**	0.535	0.775	0.655
Neural Networks	0.858	0.915	**0.843**	0.899	**0.871**
Mean votes	0.800	0.840	0.742	0.855	0.799
Median of votes	0.843	0.896	0.813	**0.919**	0.866
Trunc. Mean votes	0.791	0.851	0.817	0.889	0.853

Source: own calculations

The results evaluated by M measure are presented in Table 2 for random assignment with probabilities given by Table 1, and for equal probabilities of profiles in Table 3. The average in the last column has been calculated only for test data. Best method results are given in bold.

Table 3. Accuracy of prediction – M measure (equal probabilities)

Method	Learning set		Test set		
	Weighted by distance between means	Weighted by distance between profiles	Weighted by distance between means	Weighted by distance between profiles	Average
CART	0.715	0.991	0.711	0.819	0.765
CHAID	0.545	0.993	0.678	0.889	0.784
Boosted Tree	0.664	**0.994**	0.775	0.801	0.788
Random Forest	0.743	**0.994**	0.818	0.860	0.839
SVM	0.800	0.991	0.778	0.738	0.758
KNN	**0.882**	0.990	0.603	**0.891**	0.747
Neural Networks	0.857	0.990	**0.863**	0.834	0.849
Mean votes	0.795	0.988	0.772	0.827	0.800
Median of votes	0.844	0.991	0.838	0.864	**0.851**
Trunc. Mean votes	0.794	0.989	0.843	0.835	0.839

Source: own calculations

Neural Networks performed generally the best among individual methods. Our network consists of 22 input neurons, one hidden layer with 7 neurons, and 14 output neurons. The activation functions in hidden layer were logistic and in output layer – exponential.

All calculations have been performed on STATISTICA software.

5 Conclusions

The staff responsible for ordering the hourly amount of electricity usually for two days in advance may not be expert in statistical forecasting, having just weather forecast for the next two days and past demand from last seven days. So AI system would be very helpful for them, suggesting which profile they can use for ordering demand. Such a profile defines the size and hourly distribution of demand. In the paper we proposed the procedure which can be applied as a core for AI forecasting system. The first part of it is the analysis of historical data of a given region to identify the typical profiles. This can be done by applying cluster analysis method. Then the forecasting is performed by some classification method or voting by many methods. In our research, the Neural Network gave the best results among individuals method and median of votes combining six methods. Demand and electricity prices are usually difficult to forecast. To achieve goals of sustainable development named in Agenda 2030 we need the support of research based AI systems in the decision process. The analysis presented here can be used in the construction of AI system forecasting electric energy demand.

References

1. Amjady, N., Keynia, F.: Short-term load forecasting of power systems by combination of wavelet transform and neuro-evolutionary algorithm. Energy **34**(1), 46–57 (2009)
2. Chang, Z., Zhang, Y., Chen, W.: Electricity price prediction based on hybrid model of adam optimized LSTM neural network and wavelet transform. Energy **187**, 115804 (2019)
3. Dombi G., Dulai, T.: Hourly electricity price forecast for short-and long-term, using deep neural networks. Acta Universita Sapientiae Informatica **14**(2), 208–222 (2022). https://doi.org/10.2478/ausi-2022-0013
4. Gabrielli, P., Wüthrich, M., Blume, S., Giovanni, S.: Data-driven modeling for long-term electricity price forecasting. Energy **244** (2022). https://doi.org/10.1016/j.energy.2022.123107
5. Hagfors, L.I., Bunn, D., Kristoffersen, E., Staver, T.T., Westgaard, S.: Modeling the UK electricity price distributions using quantile regression. Energy **102**, 231–243 (2016)
6. Hong, T., Pinson, P., Fan, S., Zareipour, H., Troccoli, A., Hyndman R.: Probabilistic energy forecasting: global energy forecasting competition 2014 and beyond. Int. J. Forecast. **32** (2016). https://doi.org/10.1016/j.ijforecast.2016.02.001
7. Jasiński, T.: Use of new variables based on air temperature for forecasting day-ahead spot electricity prices using deep neural networks: a new approach. Energy **213**, 118784 (2020)
8. Kristiansen, T.: Forecasting Nord Pool day-ahead prices with an autoregressive model. Energy Policy **49**, 328–332 (2012)
9. Lago, J., De Ridder, F., Vrancx, P., Bart De Schutter, B.: Forecasting day-ahead electricity prices in Europe: the importance of considering market integration. Appl. Energy, **211**, 890–903 (2018)
10. Lu, H., Ma, X., Ma, M., Zhu, S.: Energy price prediction using data-driven models: a decade review. Comput. Sci. Rev. **39**, 100356 (2021)
11. Nitin, S., Soumya, R.M., Rishabh, D.S.: Short term electricity price forecast based on environmentally adapted generalized neuron. Energy **125**, 127–139 (2017)
12. Qiao, W., Yang, Z.: Forecast the electricity price of U.S. using a wavelet transform-based hybrid model. Energy **193**, 116704 (2020)
13. Romero, A., Dorronsoro, J.R., Diaz, J.: Day-ahead price forecasting for the Spanish electricity market. Int. J. Interact. Multimedia Artif. Intell. **5**(4), 42–50 (2019)
14. Shafie-khah, M., Parsa, M.M., Sheikh-El-Eslami, M.K.: Price forecasting of day-ahead electricity markets using a hybrid forecast method. Energy Convers. Manage. **52**(5), 2165–2169 (2011)
15. Transforming our world: the 2030 Agenda for Sustainable Development, United Nations (2015). https://sdgs.un.org/2030agenda
16. Uniejewski, B., Weron, R., Ziel, F.: Variance stabilizing transformations for electricity spot price forecasting. IEEE Trans. Power Syst. **33**(2), 2219–2229 (2017)

17. Windler, T., Busse, J., Rieck, J.: One month-ahead electricity price forecasting in the context of production planning. J. Clean. Prod. **238**, 117910 (2019)
18. Zhang, X., Wang, J., Gao, Y.: A hybrid short-term electricity price forecasting framework: cuckoo search-based feature selection with singular spectrum analysis and SVM. Energy Econ. **81**, 899–913 (2019)
19. Ziel, F., Steinert, R.: Probabilistic mid-and long-term electricity price forecasting. Renew. Sustain. Energy Rev. **94**, 251–266 (2019)

The Use of Artificial Intelligence in Activities Aimed at Sustainable Development - Good Practices

Dorota Jelonek[1(✉)] and Magdalena Rzemieniak[2]

[1] Czestochowa University of Technology, Al. Armii Krajowej 19 B, 42-200 Czestochowa, Poland
dorota.jelonek@pcz.pl
[2] Lublin University of Technology, Nadbystrzycka 38D, 20-618 Lublin, Poland
m.rzemieniak@pollub.pl

Abstract. The challenges faced by modern organizations are very diverse. Dynamic changes in market, technological, economic, demographic and, above all, climate and eco-logical processes generate a number of solutions using artificial intelligence (AI), which helps in achieving sustainable development goals. The application of the principles of sustainable development should be an element of the strategy of every organization. The aim of the article is to identify activities aimed at sustainable development in which artificial intelligence solutions were used. The article presents the results of research conducted using the desk research method on secondary sources. The researched secondary sources were scientific publications from the Scopus and Elsevier databases, source documents, research reports and publications of official statistics from 2020–2023. The Science Direct database was also used, in which topics and related entries were reviewed. The analysis of available data sources, including in particular their compilation, mutual verification and processing, allowed for the formulation of research conclusions. The achievement is the collection of a set of good practices in which artificial intelligence was used and which support the achievement of sustainable development goals in various industries. In addition, using the results of the analysis of secondary sources, key macrotrends that affect 17 sustainable development goals were identified. The article presents examples of good practices using artificial intelligence supporting the implementation of sustainable development goals.

Keywords: Artificial intelligence · AI · sustainable development · good practices

1 Introduction

To accelerate the world's efforts to achieve the Sustainable Development Goals, the years 2020–2030 have been named the Decade of Action. Currently, many reports and initiatives are being prepared that present recommendations on how to achieve the goals by 2030. However, most scientific articles and research reports undertake analyzes in a specific area of research. The application of the principles of sustainable development

S. Nowaczyk et al. (Eds.): ECAI 2023 Workshops, CCIS 1948, pp. 277–284, 2024.
https://doi.org/10.1007/978-3-031-50485-3_30

should be an element of the strategy of every organization. In this regard, the issues of sustainable development considered in the context of activities supporting the implementation of the Agenda's goals should become an area of particular interest. Activities implementing the use of artificial intelligence (AI) provide opportunities to accelerate activities in the field of achieving goals. The aim of the article is to identify activities aimed at sustainable development in which artificial intelligence solutions were used. Although analyzing the relationship be-tween these areas seems quite logical and obvious, there is not much research in this area in the scientific literature. Therefore, this subject has become the subject of theoretical considerations and empirical research undertaken in the article. Then, the description of the research subject and research period. Based on the conducted research, it can be concluded that activities in the field of implementing the Sustainable Development Goals with the use of artificial intelligence give the opportunity to accelerate the achievement of goals.

Finally, the implications and limitations of this study are provided.

1.1 The Concept of Sustainable Development in the Context of the 2030 Agenda

The concept of sustainable development is multi-contextual and multi-faceted and has a huge scientific and research potential, especially from the point of view of interdisciplinary research. This concept allows you to link management, ecology, ethics, research on development, computer science and many other disciplines and areas.

The term sustainable development has the ability to assume many meanings [1, 2]. The concept of sustainable development was established in the 1980s and is one of the most important concepts of economic development today. D. Pearce, E. Barbier, A. Markandya and R. Tumer are considered to be the creators of the concept of sustainable development [3]. Autors P.F. Barlett and G.W. Chase [3] say that "sustainable growth is about meeting the current needs of society in such a way that future generations will also be able to meet their own needs". According to H. Komiyama and K. Takeuchi [4] in the concept of development, strong emphasis was placed not only on the elimination of barriers to growth and poverty, the implementation of innovative solutions, the increase in intangible assets, but also on environmental protection and the possibility of renewing resources.

For many years, the concept of sustainable development has been an important term in the literature on the subject (Dixon and Fallon 1989 [5, 6], Lele 1991 [7], Sneddon 2000 [8], Robinson 2004 [9], Kates et al. 2005 [10–12], Daly 2007 [13]). The term "sustainable development" is very widespread today both in science [14] and business practice [15]. It is not only the best-known and most often quoted concept combining the natural environment and development, but also the best documented in publications, e.g. Agenda for Sustainable Development [16] adopted at the UN summit in New York on 25/09/2020 with 17 goals to be achieved by 2030. The agenda is a document addressed not only to governments and parliaments, international institutions, local authorities, residents, but also to business and the private sector [17].

1.2 Artificial Intelligence and the Sustainable Development Goals

The term artificial intelligence was first proposed by J. McCarthy in 1955 [18]. Artificial intelligence is a science that includes the engineering of creating intelligent machines, especially intelligent computer programs [19]. This definition has a wide range of both supporters and opponents. Opponents - mainly scientists, claim that such highly sophisticated behaviors and states as love, creativity, moral choices will always be beyond the scope of any machine or computer program. The same people often claim that artificial intelligence is nothing more than "the standard way machines work". Other objections that arise are the definition of artificial intelligence as an abstract concept, supported by technical formulations, aimed at attracting people's attention. It is also a response to many complex scientific and business problems related to the latest information technologies. Referring to J. Carthy's definition, it should be supplemented with the term - artificial intelligence is the ability of a digital computer or computer-controlled robot to perform tasks usually associated with intelligent beings [20]. It should be emphasized that this term is very often assigned to IT systems development projects. As a result, these systems are endowed with processes that are characteristic of humans, such as the ability to reason, discover meaning, generalize, or learn from experience. To enable their functioning, the architects of these systems need an extensive database of information on the designed phenomena [21, 22].

As discussions about climate change and global warming become more urgent, there is also a growing awareness of the importance of sustainable action. The prudent and thoughtful treatment of the environment is not only a moral issue: environmental degradation is also a serious threat to the global economy. Artificial intelligence can be an important tool for adopting responsible business practices. Appropriate use of artificial intelligence may allow for a revolution in the implementation of sustainable development goals. Some even claim that AI will be the driving force behind the fourth industrial revolution [23, 24]. The possibilities offered by new technical developments present great potential for achieving the objectives of the Agenda.

2 Methods

The aim of the article is to identify activities aimed at sustainable development in which artificial intelligence solutions were used. The article presents the results of research conducted using the desk research method on secondary sources. The researched secondary sources were scientific publications from the Scopus and Elsevier databases, source documents, research reports and publications of official statistics from 2020–2023. The Science Direct database was also used, in which topics and thematically related entries were reviewed. Literature review and bibliometric analyzes were conducted in WoS and Scopus databases. The exploration consisted of searching for scientific publications by titles, summaries and keywords of the phrases "artificial intelligence" and "sustainable development". As a result of searching the Scopus database, 146,341 publications were obtained, including 93,998 scientific articles, and WoS 157,543 publications, including 99,887 scientific articles. In order to determine the dominant categories, the criterion was the number of publications. The research categories of the articles were the basis for the selection of examples of good practices in the use of artificial intelligence. The analysis of available data sources, including in particular their compilation, mutual verification and processing, allowed for the formulation of conclusions from the research.

3 Results – Good Practices – Selected Examples

Based on the conducted research, the basic problem areas of environmental degradation in the world were identified (see Fig. 1). In these areas, great opportunities for sustainable practices with the help of artificial intelligence have been identified. In the field of climate protection, there is potential in the areas of autonomous electromobility, smart energy grids or weather modeling. Green energy, sustainable land use, "smart cities" or "smart homes" are other sectors of the economy where meaningful data can be intelligently analyzed and used to better effect in the future [25]. Species conservation is another pressing concern. Here, good results can be achieved through AI-based pollution control, invasive species control, disease control and prevention, and the "green economy". The same applies to the areas of water protection and air pollution control. Opportunities here include smart air filtration systems, improved water use efficiency, sustainable strategies to prevent droughts and water scarcity, clean fuels or real-time integrated, adaptive urban management [26].

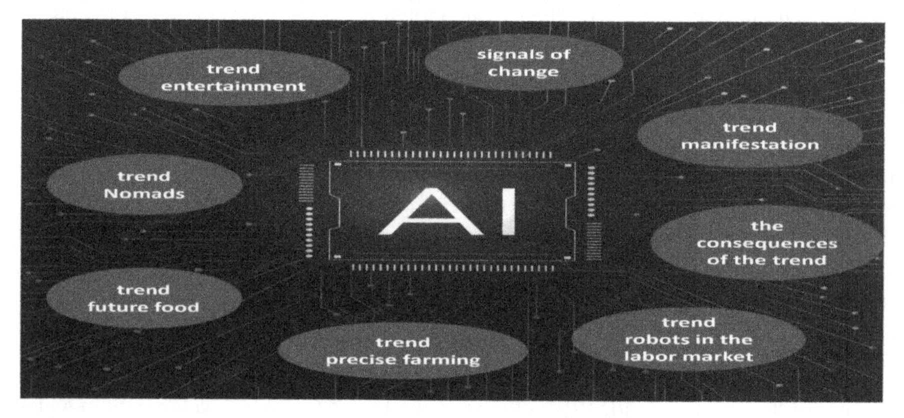

Fig. 1. Implementation scheme of AI applications in the areas written in the article.

3.1 Robots in the Labor Market

With the development of automation and artificial intelligence, almost all tasks and jobs will be performed by robots. The definition of work has been redefined after the entry into force of the basic income concept. Work is time to do what you like, what gives you pleasure, what you are good at. People still have the need to gather, educate or professionalize. The lack of compulsion to work generates various creative initiatives, new inventions aimed not only at developing interests, but also, for example, at improving the condition of the planets. Specialists from the STEM category (science, technology, engineering, maths) with high competence in the field of solutions based on AI are still developing the market. In this scenario, on the one hand, we meet conscious, creative people who want to act for the benefit of their communities or the environment, but on the other hand, there is a group of people who, after being excluded from the labor market, cannot find themselves in the new reality. This generates the development of areas related to social and psychological assistance [27].

3.2 Future Food and Precise Farming

Precise Farming assumes that the increase in demand for food products will be associated with more and more precise and effective use of current crops. The use of artificial intelligence in agriculture serves to increase yields thanks to the rational use of space, e.g. based on the collected data and the use of technologies that facilitate informed decisions regarding breeding. It also ensures lower production costs while limiting environmental contamination. It assumes the use of GPS systems, drones, devices for the rapid detection of organisms causing diseases of crop plants, B-droids (artificial bees), numerous services and applications supporting and consulting for farmers.

AI also gives you the opportunity to use scenarios related to the food of the future. The plant-based food scenario assumes that due to the possible collapse of the meat market and the fact that a balanced plant-based diet has a beneficial effect on health, our diet will be 100% plant-based in the future. The superfoods scenario assumes that the diet of the future will be based on products with an extremely rich amount of minerals, vitamins and other nutrients that are valuable for the body. The edible bugs scenario assumes that insects will be one of the main sources of protein in the future. Currently, it is the cheapest and most widely available alternative source of protein on Earth [28].

The Singaporean start-up Hoow Foods has presented its new product, which is intended to replace the hen's egg. The replacement created under the HEGG brand is in the form of a powder, and its composition is the result of artificial intelligence calculations. This is another of the growing number of food alternatives from East Asia. Many of them are already in the first stores and restaurants, and over time they may also gain popularity in Europe [29].

3.3 Nomads, Inclusiveness and Diversity

The vast majority of professions depend not on a permanent place of work, but on access to the Internet. Digital nomads come from many professions: writers, bloggers, journalists, photographers, programmers, graphic designers, teachers or psychologists conducting therapy via videoconference, as well as lawyers, doctors and marketing specialists. As a result, a huge market of mobile work style is developing and the business potential to provide working conditions for a billion digital nomads in 2035 is growing. The NomadOffice space was designed entirely using a parametric algorithm. It is enough to provide input data, and thanks to the algorithmic interpretation, the geometry of the building and the location of equipment are automatically generated. This allows optimal design in almost any location. Data such as the number of workplaces, ceiling height or building outline are flexibly modifiable as needed. NomadOffice is a global network of personalized offices for the digital nomad style of working. Each registered NomadOffice user has a digital profile in which he presents comfortable working conditions, including office equipment and necessary tools. Its entire digital environment is stored on the company's servers and is loaded onto the equipment in the location used. The client reserves an office in one of the locations of the global network for a given time and works in an identical environment regardless of where it is located. The company model is designed for traveling or stationary employees who do not have their own place of work. A mobile office is key to efficiency and reduces the time needed to prepare the environment for work [30]. Psychologically, this allows employees to feel safe and stable in the company due to the unchanging office space [31].

3.4 Entertainment with AI

With the development of artificial intelligence, the phenomena of tv screens (multi-screens), immersive viewing, second screen (using an additional device connected to the Internet), over the top (subscription-based business model), gaming world (participants of modern games may already have the impression that they become part of the virtual world), connected culture (AI changes the way we participate in culture, we are no longer just passive recipients, but we become part of the experience involving our senses), human inter(net)action (development of new technologies has impact on interpersonal relationships through time spent in the digital world), digital journey (development of AI means that physical limitations are no longer an obstacle to exploring the world) and digital well-being (development of AI is conducive to the creation of solutions to improve mental and physical condition. Future and linking entertainment with the area of health are developing in several areas - building positive habits, fighting fears, improving the mood - the idea of wellbeing). The use of artificial intelligence in entertainment gives the possibility of immersive experiences, i.e. solutions that engage the user [30].

4 Discussion - Summary

The opportunities offered by new technical developments are already being implemented. For example, in business it is now common to use systems that analyze and intelligently interpret relevant data, one of the applications being the optimization of work and production processes [28, 32]. The information that emerges during the manufacturing process can be used to improve energy consumption and machine efficiency. The positive impact on the environment results from the reduction of greenhouse gas emissions. A similar idea applies to sustainability risk assessments at company locations [33]. AI can also be used for materiality optimization and stakeholder analysis or overall emissions calculations. Such systems are already used in many areas where work related to environmental protection is carried out. Whether global climate models to predict problematic weather scenarios, smart farming for sustainable farming or smart grids to regulate energy consumption, innovative smart technologies have already been adopted in all these fields.

References

1. Dosi, G., Stiglitz, J.E.: ICC announcement: annual special issue on macro economics and development. Ind. Corp. Chang. **29**, 577–580 (2020). https://doi.org/10.1093/icc/dtaa009

2. Stiglitz, J.E.: Addressing climate change through price and non-price interventions. Eur. Econ. Rev. **119**, 594–612 (2019). https://doi.org/10.1016/j.euroecorev.2019.05.007
3. Beckerma, W, Markandy, A.: Pollution control and optimal taxation - static analysis. J. Environ. Econ. Manage. 1, 43–52 (1974), https://doi.org/10.1016/0095-0696(74)90016-3
4. Barrett, J., et al.: Microplastic pollution in deep-sea sediments from the great Australian bight. Front. Marine Sci. **7** (2020). https://doi.org/10.3389/fmars.2020.576170
5. Dixon, R.: Growth, accumulation, and unproductive activity - an analysis of the Postwar united-states-economy - Wolff. EN. Econ. Record **65**, 409 (1989)
6. Lele, S.M.: Sustainable development - a critical-review. World Dev. **19**, 607–621 (1991). https://doi.org/10.1016/0305-750x(91)90197-p
7. Sneddon, C.S.: Sustainability' in ecological economics, ecology and livelihoods: a review. Prog. Hum. Geogr. **24**, 521–549 (2000). https://doi.org/10.1191/030913200100189076
8. Manning, A., Robinson, H.: Something in the way she moves: a fresh look at an old gap. Oxford Econ. Papers-New Ser. **56**, 169–188 (2004). https://doi.org/10.1093/oep/gpf039
9. Komiyama, H., Takeuchi, K.: Sustainability science: building a new discipline. Sustain. Sci. **1**, 1–6 (2006). https://doi.org/10.1007/s11625-006-0007-4
10. Kates, R.W., Leiserowitz, A.A., Parris, T.M.: Accelerating sustainable development. Environment, 47, COVER2-COVER2 (2005)
11. Leiserowitz, A.A., Kates, R.W., Parris, T.M.: Do global attitudes and behaviors support sustainable development? Environment **47**, 22–38 (2005). https://doi.org/10.3200/envt.47.9.22-38
12. Kates, R.W., Parris, T.M., Leiserowitz, A.A.: What is sustainable development? Goals, indicators, values, and practice. Environment **47**, 8–21 (2005)
13. Daly, H.E.: Population, migration, and globalization (vol 59, pg 187, 2006). Ecol. Econ. **62**, 762 (2007). https://doi.org/10.1016/j.ecolecon.2007.03.005
14. Lin, B.C.A.: Sustainable growth: a circular economy perspective. J. Econ. Issues **54**, 465–471 (2020). https://doi.org/10.1080/00213624.2020.1752542
15. Kroll, C., Zipperer, V.: Sustainable development and populism. Ecol. Econ. **176** (2020). https://doi.org/10.1016/j.ecolecon.2020.106723
16. Weber, H., Weber, M.: When means of implementation meet Ecological Modernization Theory: a critical frame for thinking about the Sustainable Development Goals initiative. World Development **136** (2020). https://doi.org/10.1016/j.worlddev.2020.105129
17. Stiglitz, J.E.: An agenda for reforming economic theory. Front. Econ. China **14**, 149–167 (2019). https://doi.org/10.3868/s060-008-019-0009-3
18. Chen, Y.: Comparing content marketing strategies of digital brands using machine learning, Human. Soc. Sci. Commun. **10**(1) (2023). https://doi.org/10.1057/s41599-023-01544-x
19. Brasse, J., Broder, H.R., Förster, M., Klier, M., Sigler, I.: Explainable artificial intelligence in information systems: a review of the status quo and future research directions. Electron. Mark. **33**(1) (2023)
20. Kinkel, S., Capestro, M., Di Maria, E., Bettiol, M.: Artificial intelligence and relocation of production activities: an empirical cross-national study. Int. J. Prod. Econ. **261** (2023). https://doi.org/10.1016/j.ijpe.2023.108890
21. Walk, J., Kühl, N., Saidani, M., Schatte, J.: Artificial intelligence for sustainability: facilitating sustainable smart product-service systems with computer vision. J. Clean. Prod. **402** (2023). https://doi.org/10.1016/j.jclepro.2023.136748
22. Jelonek, D., Mesjasz-Lech, A., Stę, C., Turek, T., Ziora, L.: The artificial intelligence application in the management of contemporary organization: theoretical assumptions, current practices and research review. In: Arai, K., Bhatia, R. (eds.) FICC 2019. LNNS, vol. 69, pp. 319–327. Springer, Cham (2020). https://doi.org/10.1007/978-3-030-12388-8_23

23. Al Mubarak, M.: Sustainably Developing in a Digital World: harnessing artificial intelligence to meet the imperatives of work-based learning in Industry 5.0. Dev. Learn. Organ. **37**(3), 18–20 (2023). https://doi.org/10.1108/DLO-04-2022-006
24. Lei, Z., Cai, S., Cui, L., Wu, L., Liu, Y.: How do different Industry 4.0 technologies support certain Circular Economy practices? Ind. Manage. Data Syst. **123**(4), 1220–1251 (2023). https://doi.org/10.1108/IMDS-05-2022-0270
25. Ferreira, J.J., Lopes, J.M., Gomes, S., Rammal, H.G.: Industry 4.0 implementation: environmental and social sustainability in manufacturing multinational enterprises. J. Clean. Product. **404** (2023). https://doi.org/10.1016/j.jclepro.2023.136841
26. Yin, Z.H., Zeng, W.P.: The effects of industrial intelligence on China's energy intensity: The role of technology absorptive capacity. Technol. Forecast. Soc. Change **191** (2023). https://doi.org/10.1016/j.techfore.2023.122506
27. Dwivedi, Y.K., et al.: Evolution of artificial intelligence research in Technological Forecasting and Social Change: research topics, trends, and future directions. Technol. Forecast. Soc. Change **192** (2023). https://doi.org/10.1016/j.techfore.2023.122579
28. Zhao, J., Gómez Fariñas, B.: Artificial intelligence and sustainable decisions. Eur. Bus. Organ. Law Rev. **24**(1), 1–39 (2023). https://doi.org/10.1007/s40804-022-00262-2
29. https://www.wnp.pl/tech/sztuczna-inteligencja-daje-przepis-na-eksperymentalne-produkty-spozywcze,488580.html. Accessed 07 Jun 2023
30. https://infuture.institute/raporty/wplyw-trendow-na-cele-zrownowazonego-rozwoju/. Accessed 01 Jun 2023
31. Rzemieniak, M., Wawer, M.: Employer branding in the context of the company's sustainable development strategy from the perspective of gender diversity of generation Z. Sustainability **13**(2), 1–25 (2021)
32. Chomiak-Orsa, I., Rot, A., Blaicke, B.: Artificial intelligence in cybersecurity: the use of AI along the cyber kill chain. In: International Conference on Computational Collective Intelligence, pp. 406–416. Springer, Cham (2019)
33. Bildirici, M., Ersin, Ö.Ö.: Nexus between Industry 4.0 and environmental sustainability: a Fourier panel bootstrap cointegration and causality analysis. J. Clean. Prod. **386** (2023). https://doi.org/10.1016/j.jclepro.2022.135786

Hydra

HYDRA 2023: The 2nd International Workshop on HYbrid Models for Coupling Deductive and Inductive ReAsoning

Pierangela Bruno[1], Francesco Calimeri[1], Francesco Cauteruccio[2], and Giorgio Terracina[1]

[1] University of Calabria, Rende, Italy
{pierangela.bruno,francesco.calimeri,giorgio.terracina}@unical.it
[2] Polytechnic University of Marche, Ancona, Italy
f.cauteruccio@univpm.it

Preface

The second edition of the International Workshop on Hybrid Models for Coupling Deductive and Inductive Reasoning (HYDRA) marks a significant step in the ongoing effort to bridge the gap between two fundamental pillars of AI research: deductive and inductive reasoning. With these proceedings, we are excited to present a diverse collection of research contributions, ideas, and insights from the scientific community in this field.

In the ever-evolving landscape of artificial intelligence (AI), the coexistence of deductive and inductive reasoning methods offers an intriguing avenue for exploration. Deductive reasoning, with its reliance on explicit premises and logical inference rules, stands in contrast to inductive reasoning, which draws generalizations from observations, often leveraging machine learning and deep learning techniques. The convergence of these approaches promises to unlock new horizons for AI systems, endowing them with enhanced robustness and flexibility to tackle a myriad of complex challenges.

Our intent with the HYDRA workshop is to provide a platform for researchers to delve into the intriguing possibilities at the intersection of deductive and inductive reasoning. Our workshop welcomed original research contributions that span theoretical frameworks, practical applications, and experimental results. Our call aimed at grouping particularly interesting approaches that address key challenges, such as devising methods to seamlessly integrate logical and statistical models, crafting algorithms capable of reasoning with incomplete or uncertain knowledge, and creating tools for elucidating and interpreting hybrid models. Furthermore, we invited researchers to explore the ethical and societal implications of these innovative technologies, including issues related to fairness, accountability, and transparency. In its call, HYDRA included different topics:

- Hybrid inductive-deductive approaches to AI,
- Interaction of inductive and deductive techniques for AI solutions,
- Integration of Answer Set Programming (ASP) in inductive scenarios,
- Integration of Constraint Programming (CSP) in inductive scenarios,

- Integration of other logic programming paradigms in inductive scenarios,
- Integration of declarative solutions in inductive scenarios,
- Logic programming language extensions for supporting inductive processes,
- New methods for coupling peculiarities of deductive and inductive systems,
- Inductive reasoning to enhance and improve deductive systems,
- Deductive processes for intensive data flow management,
- Deductive processes in strong inductive-tailored scenarios,
- Knowledge representation and reasoning for improving and enhancing inductive processing,
- Discussions and positions on novel hybrid methods of deductive and inductive reasoning,
- Evaluation and comparison of existing deductive and inductive methods,
- Hybridizing logic programming paradigms with procedural approaches,
- Novel contexts of application for hybrid deductive and inductive systems,
- Neuro-symbolic approach to reasoning and learning.

The workshop papers underwent a single-blind peer-review process, with each submission assigned to three members of the Program Committee. Ultimately, six papers were chosen for oral presentation.

We extend our heartfelt appreciation to the numerous individuals who played pivotal roles in ensuring the success of this workshop. Our sincere thanks go to the Program Committee members for their invaluable and insightful reviews, the dedicated authors who actively participated in the workshop, and the enthusiastic attendees who engaged with our event. Your collective contributions have greatly enriched the workshop experience.

Organization

General Chairs

Francesco Calimeri	University of Calabria, Italy
Giorgio Terracina	University of Calabria, Italy

Program Chairs

Pierangela Bruno	University of Calabria, Italy
Francesco Cauteruccio	Polytechnic University of Marche, Italy

Organization Chairs

Weronika T. Adrian	AGH University of Science and Technology, Poland
Krzysztof Kluza	AGH University of Science and Technology, Poland

Publicity Chair

Weronika T. Adrian	AGH University of Science and Technology, Poland

Program Committee

Mario Alviano	University of Calabria, Italy
Alessia Amelio	University G. D'Annunzio Chieti-Pescara, Italy
Esra Erdem	Sabanci University, Turkey
Antonio Ielo	University of Calabria, Italy
Brais Muñiz Castro	Universidade da Coruña, Spain
Ester Zumpano	University of Calabria, Italy
Marco Maratea	University of Calabria, Italy
Stefano Cirillo	University of Salerno, Italy
Claudia Diamantini	Polytechnic University of Marche, Italy
Luciano Caroprese	University G. D'Annunzio Chieti-Pescara, Italy
Gianluigi Greco	University of Calabria, Italy
Lucia Migliorelli	Polytechnic University of Marche, Italy
Simona Perri	University of Calabria, Italy

Carmine Dodaro	University of Calabria, Italy
Elena De Momi	Polytechnic of Milan
Thomas Lukasiewicz	University of Oxford
Cinzia Marte	University of Calabria, Italy
Rafael Peñaloza	University of Milano-Bicocca, Italy

Do Datapoints Argue?: Argumentation for Hierarchical Agreement in Datasets

Ayush Bahuguna(✉), Sajjad Haydar, Andreas Brännström, and Juan Carlos Nieves

Umeå University, Department of Computing Science, 90187 Umeå, Sweden
{mai22aba,ens22shr,andreasb,jcnieves}@cs.umu.se

Abstract. This work aims to utilize quantitative bipolar argumentation to detect deception in machine learning models. We explore the concept of deception in the context of interactions of a party developing a machine learning model with potentially malformed data sources. The objective is to identify deceptive or adversarial data and assess the effectiveness of comparative analysis during different stages of model training. By modeling disagreement and agreement between data points as arguments and utilizing quantitative measures, this work proposes techniques for detecting outliers in data. We discuss further applications in clustering and uncertainty modelling.

Keywords: Formal argumentation · Machine learning · Adversarial learning · Deception detection

1 Introduction

The field of machine learning is concerned with algorithms that can generate data structures that can be "trained" to perform tasks using data – models are trained using datasets of *input-target* pairs to learn representations of mappings between the input and output spaces [17]. The quality of training data is often critical to the performance of ML models; while some models are optimised for being robust to outliers in data [5,15], in general ML models cannot be expected to reliably extract meaningful patterns in data if those patterns are influenced by external forces [26,32,35]. The primary goal for this study is to conceptualize "opinion" of labelled datapoints with respect to parameters of a machine learning model; how do different input-target pairs influence a model during training, and can these influences be used to distinguish clusters of agreement and disagreement in data?

A major motivation is the development of techniques for identifying perceivable differences between the influences of legitimate and malicious data. The concept of *deception* in formal dialogue is often defined as an agent attempting to persuade others towards a belief that the agent does not assume to be true [24,25,29]. There is an obvious parallel between this concept and our aim if

S. Nowaczyk et al. (Eds.): ECAI 2023 Workshops, CCIS 1948, pp. 291–303, 2024.
https://doi.org/10.1007/978-3-031-50485-3_31

we apply the lens of formal dialogue to the interactions between a party developing an ML model and other potentially malicious parties acting as data sources. Deception in such cases is referred to as a poisoning attack. We wish to identify whether a learning model is able to acquire resistance to such deception over the span of its training. With such aims for our study, an incentive for the use of argumentation frameworks emerges: as every data sample used to train or validate a model can be interpreted as an opinionated argument regarding incremental changes for model parameters, there should emerge varying degrees of consensus and opposition between the datapoints.

While academic and corporate efforts have been quick to apply ML methods for AI applications, the use of symbolic AI methods also has scope for application within several fields of uncertainty modeling [23,33], interpretable learning [19, 28] and outlier detection [1]. In this paper, we focus our efforts towards the use of formal argumentation reasoning which is utilised to develop concomitant reasoning methodology over domain- and case-specific knowledge [30]. With this in mind we can formulate the focus of our research:

- Given a preliminary ML model, how can we utilise quantitative argumentation to cluster labelled data by agreement on model parameters?

Our aims are similar to that of formal outlier and anomaly detection [14,21]. We are concerned with estimating relative risk in data [20], however we instead focus on measuring the distribution of their influences on model parameters rather than on their distribution in input and output spaces. This document is structured as follows: Sect. 2 explores inspiring work in the literature that aligns the design philosophy of this study and Sect. 3 elaborates the background for developing our proposed framework. Section 4 summarises methods for formulation of arguments and relations in the framework, and Sect. 5 details results based on experimentation with the proposed methods. We conclude in Sect. 6.2 by discussing potential applications, ethical considerations and other future work.

2 Related Work

Formal argumentation is a powerful tool for utilising relationships in information and carrying out reasoning on knowledge. Argumentation frameworks (AFs) have proven to be effective at comprehending relations, isolating contradictions and resolving disparities in ontological knowledge in non-monotonic and default reasoning [30]. Arvapally *et al.* [1] provide a framework for detecting outliers in opinions generated from online argumentation between multiple parties, by deriving mappings of agreement on topics in dialogue as opinion vectors. This opinion vector space is used to derive metrics for distance and clustering arguments, which is relevant to our requirement for detecting disagreement in parametric influence.

Bhuyan & Nieves [3] define an AF that is used to model agreement between datapoints, and use this framework to generate adversarial data for training regression models robust to anomalous or compromised training. Arguments are instantiated for datapoints sampled from datasets, and are characterised by tuples $\langle x_i, \phi, p_i \rangle$ of inputs x_i and their corresponding model predictions p_i supported by different learning functions (identified by their learning parameters ϕ), and symmetric attacks are devised between two such arguments when $x_i \approx x_j$ and $p_i \neq p_j$, or $x_i \neq x_j$ and $p_i \approx p_j$. This approach for generating arguments aligns with our goal of argumentation over datapoints and relationships inferred from their influences during training.

Potyka [22] explores the parallels between AFs and MLPs and in studying the possibility of interpreting acyclic quantitative AFs as artificial neural networks and vice versa, describing a framework for an argumentation graph with which prior knowledge can be used to derive quantitative relationships and trust measures for arguments *a posteriori* using formulations inspired from MLPs. Representations for arguments are modeled as logical units in MLPs and the strength of arguments is derived in a manner inspired by neural activation of those units.

Riveret *et al.* [23] use probabilistic argumentation to augment Markov decision processes [9,18] as decision-making models for reinforcement learning agents in order to create a rational decision-making framework that can withstand uncertainty due to the model being over- or under-constrained by information in knowledge base, such as uncertainty about the environment, agents, their interactions and systematic stochasticity. They also use this framework to characterise agent attitudes and behaviours logically and probabilistically, and describe support for normative compliance. This can be used to model behaviour of adversarial agents as stochastic processes in a deceptive learning scenario to make them robust to poisoning.

3 Theoretical Background

3.1 Use Scenario

We envision our methodology being used by software developers applying machine learning methods, using it as a quality measure for data used to validate or update a preliminary model. We imagine incremental development in which developers iteratively expand their data portfolio to continuously evaluate and improve performance. Our framework is pertinent for the landscape of online machine learning, where learning algorithms sequentially produce updated predictors based on newly available data. One common scenario for online learning is crowdsourcing of data [11], which is a common method for acquiring training data in problems where data labelling and curation is labour-intensive yet there is demand for robust solutions. Machine vision tasks like image segmentation and generative modeling, or language modeling tasks like speech-to-text and machine translation are prime examples where generation of labelled data is time-taking and requires expert knowledge without straightforward approaches to mine labels effectively. [7,10]. In such scenarios, quality control of data is necessary to ensure crowdsourced data is void of neglectful or malicious labelling [4,34].

3.2 AI Methodology

A classical argumentation framework (AF) is defined with a finite set of arguments $AR = \{\alpha_1 \dots \alpha_n\}$ and a binary relation $att \subseteq AR \times AR$ that represents attacks or conflicts within the arguments in AR, where the existence of $att(a, b)$ implies an attack between arguments a and b. We can thus devise a skeletal framework that can be refined using acquired domain knowledge.

One approach to performing reasoning on an AF is qualitative argumentation, where the primary goal is to identify subsets of AR with well-behaved properties, like being void of mutual attack (*conflict-free subsets*), capability to defend from attack (*admissible subsets*), maximising or minimising utilisation of knowledge and others. Another approach is quantitative argumentation where a prevalent approach for reasoning is the use of gradual semantics [6], which pertains to assigning measures of acceptability to arguments of argumentation frameworks. The argumentation graph is equipped with a total function defined as the *base score* which represents prior confidence for arguments. Reasoning entails evaluating a *strength* function calculated using the base score and relations for attack and support. This strength represents posterior confidence that is used to rank order arguments. A quantitative bipolar argumentation framework (QBAF) [2] extends the concept of attack with that of *support*, where both attack and support relations are defined between arguments and the strength function independently utilises these relations to evaluate arguments.

Multilayer perceptrons (MLPs) are a generalized terminology representing feed forward neural networks applicable to most machine learning problems i.e., classification, regression and reinforcement learning tasks [12]. The generic layout of MLPs have been elaborated and improved vastly in machine learning and specialised variants of these methods have found great success in AI applications. This structure has been adapted by Potyka [22] for the design of a MLP-based QBAF.

The definition of attack between arguments in the framework of Bhuyan & Nieves [3] limits the utility of argumentation to the domain of regression, as in classification problems there may not be an obvious similarity measure for inputs that would allow generating attacks of the first kind ($x_i \approx x_j$, $p_i \neq p_j$), while the valid possibility of requiring classification of vastly different inputs to the same class renders attacks of the second kind ($x_i \neq x_j$, $p_i \approx p_j$) undesirable. Expanding the scope to include classification algorithms will also allow relaxing the structure of arguments by eliminating parametric support in argument definitions. With this in mind, we can justify utilising a quantitative approach to argumentation for modeling uncertainty.

4 Methodology

When training a model $\hat{f}_\Theta$ using gradient descent, we optimise its set of defining parameters $\Theta = \{\theta_1, \theta_2 \dots \theta_n\}$ by minimising a cost function $C(\hat{f}_\Theta(x), y)$ between mappings of inputs x and expected values y. We want to model individual datapoints as representing quantitative opinion on the state of model parameters. We formulate a method that generates a hierarchical ranking of agreement among the datapoints by iteratively applying gradual semantics on partitions of the dataset.

4.1 Argumentation Framework

For a model with p parameters, we create a quantitative argumentation framework $AF = \langle AR, \mathcal{R}, \tau, \zeta \rangle$ with a set of n arguments AR corresponding to n datapoints in a batch of analysed datapoints, a binary support function $\mathcal{R} : \mathbf{R}^p \times \mathbf{R}^p \rightarrow [0, 1]$, a base score function $\tau : \mathbf{R}^n \rightarrow [0, 1]$ and a strength function $\zeta : \mathbf{R}^n \times \mathcal{R} \rightarrow [0, 1]$. We make a complete graph between all arguments in a batch of data so these functions are all total. We have an argument $\alpha \in AR$ for every tuple $\langle x, y \rangle$ for a sample input x and target y in the validation batch, and we characterise α using the definition of $\nabla_{\Theta} C(\alpha) = \langle \delta_1, \delta_2 \ldots \delta_n \rangle$ as the *cost gradient vector*, where

$$\delta_i = \frac{dC(\hat{f}_{\Theta}(x), y)}{d\theta_i}, \theta_i \in \Theta. \tag{1}$$

In gradient descent, the simplest iterative optimisation rule (omitting augmentations for model regularisation and learning momentum) can be expressed as

$$\theta_i := \theta_i - \lambda \delta_i \tag{2}$$

for a defined *learning rate* λ. In practice, averaging $\nabla_{\Theta} C$ over batches of training data instead of performing parameter updates over single datapoints individually is computationally cheaper in models having large $|\Theta|$ and leads to more stable optimisation [13,27]. It should thus be clear that $\nabla_{\Theta} C$ is representative of an opinion on learning representation, and that opposing values of δ between different datapoints characterise opposing opinions regarding evolution of model parameters. We can expect our framework to be capable of identifying arguments representing datapoints that disagree disproportionately with their respective batch of training/validation data.

We shall use $\nabla_{\Theta} C$ to compare arguments with each other and with the mean of all gradient vectors in the batch of data which we represent with $\hat{\nabla}$. The motivation for interpreting argument opinions from gradients is to overcome the limitations of using x and y to model disagreement. Therefore, the input to such a framework is a preliminary trained model, a (potentially unverified) update or validation batch and a chosen loss function, and the framework assigns a base score τ to each argument and support $\mathcal{R}$ between all arguments. These are then utilised in a strength function ζ in conjunction with the graph weights to score arguments. For numerical stability we shall scale the values of the gradient vectors by the largest magnitude among all vectors (Fig. 1).

Base Score and Support. A straightforward approach for modeling attack is the absolute difference between gradient vectors; equivalently, we can interpret

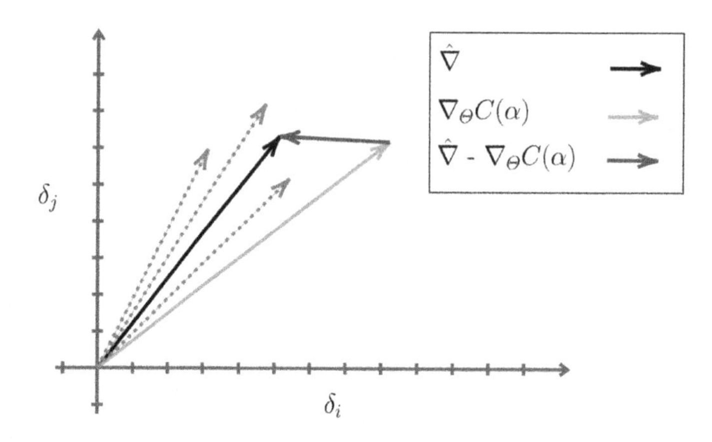

Fig. 1. Calculation of τ_{raw} from gradient vectors for an argument α in Eq. 3. The magnitude of difference of mean gradient vector from $\nabla_{\Theta}C(\alpha)$ in gradient vector space gives a measure for disagreement of α from the opinions of other datapoints in the dataset.

the reciprocal as weightage for support. Opposing values for gradients in different iterations should negate the learning performed by gradient descent in those iterations. We hence formulate the base score τ for our arguments by measuring the agreement of each argument with the mean gradient vector of the validation batch $\hat{\nabla}$. We then define the *raw score* τ_{raw} of an argument as

$$\tau_{raw}(\alpha) = \frac{|\hat{\nabla}|}{|\hat{\nabla} - \nabla_{\Theta}C(\alpha)|_{\epsilon}} \tag{3}$$

where $|\mathbf{v}|$ represents the magnitude of the vector v and $|\mathbf{v}|_{\epsilon}$ represents the magnitude with a lower bound of ϵ used in the denominator for numerical stability. We now get τ from τ_{raw} using the *softmax* function $\mathcal{S}$ which normalises a vector $\mathbf{z} = \langle z_1 \dots z_k \rangle$ of k values into a probability distribution of k outcomes as

$$\tau = \mathcal{S}(\tau_{raw}), \quad s_i = \frac{e^{z_i}}{\Sigma_{j=1}^{k} e^{z_j}}, \quad \mathcal{S} = \langle s_1 \dots s_k \rangle \tag{4}$$

We also similarly define support between two gradient vectors as being the reciprocal of the magnitude of their difference scaled by their average magnitude.

$$\mathcal{R}(\alpha_i, \alpha_j) = \frac{|\nabla_{\Theta}C(\alpha_i) + \nabla_{\Theta}C(\alpha_j)|}{2|\nabla_{\Theta}C(\alpha_i) - \nabla_{\Theta}C(\alpha_j)|_{\epsilon}}. \tag{5}$$

As mentioned before, all gradient vectors have been assumed to be scaled by the magnitude of the largest gradient vector for well-behaved scoring and weighting of the nodes and edges. We set $\epsilon = 0.01$ as a lower bound for the denominators in both τ_{raw} and $\mathcal{R}$.

Strength Function. We calculate argument strength ζ similar to Potyka's MLP-based QBAF approach in a gradual iterative manner, where we define a *raw strength* ζ_{raw} with the formulation

$$\zeta_{raw}^{i+1}(\alpha_i) = log(\frac{\zeta_i^0}{1-\zeta_i^0}) + \Sigma_{j\neq i}\mathcal{R}(\alpha_i,\alpha_j)\zeta^i(\alpha_j) \quad (6)$$

which is used to get the strength by applying softmax over the raw strength

$$\zeta^0 = \tau, \quad \zeta^i = \mathcal{S}(\zeta_{raw}^i). \quad (7)$$

This provides us with gradual semantics over the AF, allowing us to compare arguments by relative acceptability.

4.2 Recursive Partitioning

Logical units in multilayer perceptrons present an "all-or-none" behaviour to mimic action of biological neurons and this behaviour is not particularly suited for providing a total order to the logical units. Sigmoidal activations are sensitive to input in very small regions of their domain, and even in nonlinearities like ReLU which are linearly sensitive, interpreting the magnitude of activation proportionally as a probabilistic measure anywhere in a neural network is only useful at the output layer. The gradual semantics of the MLP-based QBAF lack the self-correction of the weights like traditional neural network training achieves using methods like backpropagation, yet in a QBAF the acceptability is evaluated at convergence or at an arbitrary iteration limit for the gradual semantics. Hence the methodology needs to be improved for precise analysis of argument relationships. We arrive at a preliminary ranking using the MLP gradual semantics and then partition the ranked arguments into a top and bottom half. This can be performed either by threshold or by count. We then repeat the gradual semantics on the partitioned subsets until we have ranked every argument as elements of a binary tree, thus imparting a total order on all arguments.

In our case of detecting data poison, only the lower partitions are reevaluated since we are interested in the most disagreeable arguments. We rank samples logarithmically where the top half of the dataset gets the highest rank, the next quarter gets ranked second, the next eighth gets ranked third and so on. We also preserve the value of the mean gradient vector $\hat{\nabla}$ used in Eq. 3, always using the mean over the whole dataset for base scores and strengths in all smaller partitions. In logarithmic ranking half of all weights are not needed after every partition, but the magnitudes for the rest of the weights need to be recalculated.

5 Results

We designed a testbed for a simple slope-and-intercept regression model with synthetic data to test our framework, utilising the PyTorch framework. It ingests an instance of the `torch.nn.Module` class as a learning model that exposes its gradients during training. To calculate these gradients, the framework accepts a compatible loss function, for which the `torch.nn` module provides a repository of loss functions. We have used the `torch.nn.MSELoss` mean squared error loss for our experiments. The `torch.utils.data` module also provides a `Dataset` class compatible with all training and testing operations in PyTorch. The framework expects the data input as an instance of `Dataset` to make it easy to both implement our methodology and extend its use to prior work using PyTorch. The implementation is available at https://github.com/Kocytean/GradArg.

5.1 Detecting Poisoned Data

We experiment with training regression models with synthetic data from derived linear trends, varying values for slope and intercept. We add noise with standard deviation $\sigma = 1$ to the targets. This data is considered ground truth, and for erroneous samples we simply sample from the data and add a deviation equal to a chosen multiple of σ to the target, referred to here as kσ poisoned data for $k = 1, 2, 3 \ldots$. With this synthetic ground truth and poisoned data, we perform two kinds of experiments: detection of poisoned data using a regression model trained on clean data, and filtration of poisoned data during further training of a preliminarily trained regression model.

For both kinds of experiments, we use 3σ and 4σ poisoned data batches of 8 samples with one poisoned sample in each batch, and average results over 16 experiments. Figure 2 shows results on detection experiments, depicting that 3σ errors are often difficult to completely partition and get misclassified while 4σ errors easily get detected and isolated from the validation batch. Ranks are logarithmic, where the best rank in a batch of 8 is 0 and the worst is rank 3, so misclassification of a poisoned sample by one order of risk contributes an error of 0.5. Hence we can see that with even a few epochs of training, the framework seems to begin classifying erroneous samples with quantifiable reliability.

5.2 Filtering Training Data

We also experiment on how effective our framework is in filtering data in an online learning scenario. We use a training test-bed with two identical models being trained with identical data, initially clean but eventually mixed with poisonous samples, where one of the models is equipped with the capability to filter out datapoints labelled as risky. We filter out the lowest two ranks of data in the experiment with 3σ poisoned data, and the lowest rank of samples in the 4σ experiment. With the batch size being 8, this means the model is expected to perfectly label 4σ errors as being the most risky and mistake 3σ error as being less risky than at maximum one other datapoint in the batch. Figure 3 shows that although the system does not manage to do this perfectly, it manages to reduce its cost more than the baseline and approaches the local minima of cost better than the baseline model which jumps out of the convex well quickly once it starts receiving poisoned data. This shows that for a preliminary trained model, if data is suspected to be of poor quality it is better to not train rather than to

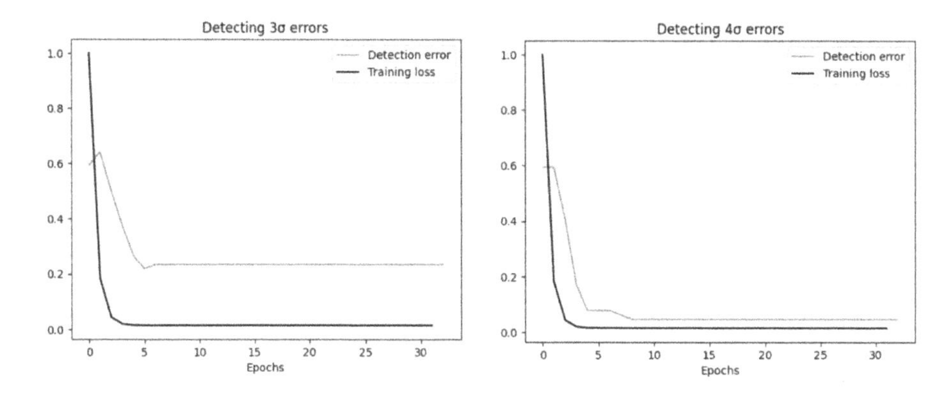

Fig. 2. Risk detection error for samples having an induced error equal to a multiple of the standard deviation of the noise function used in generation of training data, compared with the training loss. Results are an average of 16 experiments with 10 epochs of 64 training iterations and losses are scaled by the training cost of the first epoch.

hope that the changes to parameters "average out" across batches of data. But using our framework the model is able to not only resist deterioration, it is able to still achieve and maintain marginal gains.

Deviations of 2σ or lower are significantly harder to pinpoint simply by modeling agreement simply based on the datapoint alone, as we failed to train on 2σ poisoned data even when filtering out 50% of the datapoints in batches. In such cases, since deviation from the correct trend is small, the difference between the optimal loss and converged loss after introducing poisoned data is smaller but the performance of the filtered model worsens to being similar to baseline much quicker.

6 Discussion

In the experiments performed in this study, sizes of validation/update datasets were kept small in order to simulate the framework being applied on a batch level; one can envision the system being similarly applied to a larger validation/update dataset. Hence the model could take advantage of optimisations such as pruning of the support relation in order to minimise the computational cost. One straightforward approach to pruning is to eliminate weights to and from arguments with zero strength. As gradual semantics can cause strengths to oscillate, it might seem premature to prune out arguments but it should be mentioned that with recursive partitioning a zero strength argument and its weights can be revived in lower partitions and hence doesn't imply the argument immediately being labelled with the lowest rank. It can be expected that further pruning will require empirically devised thresholds for relation weights.

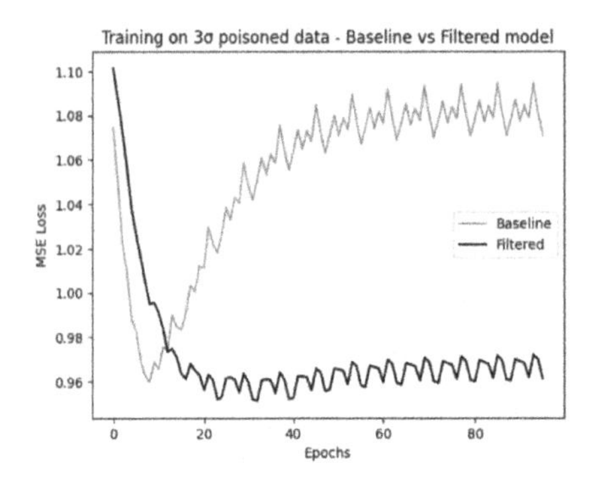

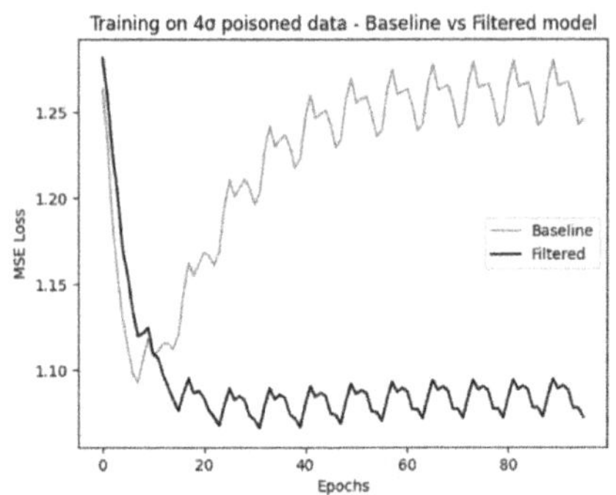

Fig. 3. Comparison of a baseline model trained on poisoned data with an identical model which filters data using the proposed quantitative AF. Showing 96 out of 128 epochs; the first 32 were performed with clean data. 25% and 12.5% of the data is filtered out in the 3σ and 4σ experiments respectively. Results are an average of 16 experiments.

6.1 Ethical Considerations

We can identify four prominent classes of stakeholders with varied interests vested in the performance of a framework that delivers on the promise of detection of adversarial data and outliers: software developers, software owners, data sources and software customers. It is necessary to consider whether the formulation of our proposed system unfairly endangers their rights or nefariously exploits their incentives. Non-discrimination is an immediate concern, as usage of the system in a practical scenario necessitates investigating whether it is biased against demographic features in data.

Explainability is also a challenge since the proposed methodology interprets agreement through algorithmic parameters in learning models and hence hinges on the explainability of the model being used [16] and the interpretability of the parameters [19]. Expecting the framework to be model-agnostic makes this more difficult. Software owners and developers might not be comfortable with permitting complete or even partial awareness of the functionality of the model as it might facilitate circumventing the detection of poisoned data. Privacy, access and modification control in an online learning context are also fields of research relevant to our study. [8,31].

6.2 Conclusions and Future Work

The base score in QBAFs provides an immediate approximation for relative strength, while the strength function takes repeated iterations to become precise. The use of recursive partitioning with Potyka's MLP-based QBAF is an attempt to enforce this capability of structured non-linear decision-making by adding a layer of structured analysis over ranking by acceptability in gradual semantics. Our current approach is model-, application- and domain-agnostic to maximise generalisability, but it is also worth researching whether better reasoning could be performed if we utilised knowledge of the domain, application or model either for more accurate immediate approximation or more complex context-aware reasoning.

Studying the robustness of quantitative argumentation methods in anomaly detection to majority attacks is necessary; how many manipulated samples can be tolerated before the framework fails? Since a loss function is also necessary as input to the framework, we can also research similar argumentation schemes to evaluate reliability of different loss functions over the same data in areas of machine learning where formulation of cost is not intuitive where different approaches may favor different formulations, such as spiking neural networks, image segmentation and generative modeling of images and audio. Another potential avenue for research is minimisation of *catastrophic interference*, a phenomenon in which sequentially trained machine learning models lose the ability to generate accurate predictions over inputs that they were trained on earlier in the learning process, for which a system similar to ours can be used to measure how opinions in datasets evolve as training proceeds.

References

1. Arvapally, R.S., Liu, X.F., Nah, F.F.H., Jiang, W.: Identifying outlier opinions in an online intelligent argumentation system. Concurrency and Comput. Pract. Exp. **33**(8), e4107 (2021). https://doi.org/10.1002/cpe.4107, https://onlinelibrary.wiley.com/doi/abs/10.1002/cpe.4107, e4107 CPE-16-0123.R3
2. Baroni, P., Rago, A., Toni, F.: From fine-grained properties to broad principles for gradual argumentation: A principled spectrum. Int. J. Approximate Reasoning **105**, 252–286 (2019). https://doi.org/10.1016/j.ijar.2018.11.019, https://www.sciencedirect.com/science/article/pii/S0888613X18304651
3. Bhuyan, M., Nieves, J.: Argumentation-based adversarial regression with multiple learners. In: 2022 IEEE 34th International Conference on Tools with Artificial Intelligence (ICTAI), pp. 96–104 (10 2022). https://doi.org/10.1109/ICTAI56018.2022.00023
4. Chen, P., Sun, H., Chen, Z.: Data poisoning attacks on crowdsourcing learning. In: U, L.H., Spaniol, M., Sakurai, Y., Chen, J. (eds.) APWeb-WAIM 2021. LNCS, vol. 12858, pp. 164–179. Springer, Cham (2021). https://doi.org/10.1007/978-3-030-85896-4_14
5. Chen, R., Paschalidis, I.C.: A robust learning approach for regression models based on distributionally robust optimization. J. Mach. Learn. Res. **19**(13), 1–48 (2018)
6. Delobelle, J., Villata, S.: Interpretability of gradual semantics in abstract argumentation. In: Kern-Isberner, G., Ognjanović, Z. (eds.) ECSQARU 2019. LNCS (LNAI), vol. 11726, pp. 27–38. Springer, Cham (2019). https://doi.org/10.1007/978-3-030-29765-7_3
7. Desmond, M., et al.: Increasing the speed and accuracy of data labeling through an ai assisted interface. In: 26th International Conference on Intelligent User Interfaces, pp. 392–401 (2021)
8. Dong, Y., Chen, X., Shen, L., Wang, D.: Privacy-preserving distributed machine learning based on secret sharing. In: Zhou, J., Luo, X., Shen, Q., Xu, Z. (eds.)

ICICS 2019. LNCS, vol. 11999, pp. 684–702. Springer, Cham (2020). https://doi.org/10.1007/978-3-030-41579-2_40
9. Doshi, P., Qu, X., Goodie, A.: Chapter 8 - decision-theoretic planning in multiagent settings with application to behavioral modeling. In: Sukthankar, G., Geib, C., Bui, H.H., Pynadath, D.V., Goldman, R.P. (eds.) Plan, Activity, and Intent Recognition, pp. 205–224. Morgan Kaufmann, Boston (2014). https://doi.org/10.1016/B978-0-12-398532-3.00008-7, https://www.sciencedirect.com/science/article/pii/B9780123985323000087
10. Fredriksson, T., Mattos, D.I., Bosch, J., Olsson, H.H.: Data labeling: an empirical investigation into industrial challenges and mitigation strategies. In: Morisio, M., Torchiano, M., Jedlitschka, A. (eds.) PROFES 2020. LNCS, vol. 12562, pp. 202–216. Springer, Cham (2020). https://doi.org/10.1007/978-3-030-64148-1_13
11. Gilyazev, R.A., Turdakov, D.Y.: Active learning and crowdsourcing: a survey of optimization methods for data labeling. Program. Comput. Softw. **44**, 476–491 (2018)
12. Goodfellow, I., Bengio, Y., Courville, A.: Deep learning: The MIT Press, 2016, 800 pp, ISBN: 0262035618. Genetic Programming and Evolvable Machines 19 (10 2017). https://doi.org/10.1007/s10710-017-9314-z
13. Hoffer, E., Hubara, I., Soudry, D.: Train longer, generalize better: closing the generalization gap in large batch training of neural networks (2018)
14. Hossain, A., Naik, D.N.: A comparative study on detection of influential observations in linear regression. Stat. Papers **32**(1), 55–69 (1991). https://doi.org/10.1007/BF02925479
15. Jagielski, M., Oprea, A., Biggio, B., Liu, C., Nita-Rotaru, C., Li, B.: Manipulating machine learning: poisoning attacks and countermeasures for regression learning. In: 2018 IEEE Symposium on Security and Privacy (SP), pp. 19–35. IEEE (2018)
16. Jeyakumar, J.V., Noor, J., Cheng, Y.H., Garcia, L., Srivastava, M.: How can i explain this to you? an empirical study of deep neural network explanation methods. Adv. Neural. Inf. Process. Syst. **33**, 4211–4222 (2020)
17. Lison, P.: An introduction to machine learning. Lang. Technol. Group (LTG) **1**(35), 1–35 (2015)
18. Littman, M.: Markov decision processes. In: Smelser, N.J., Baltes, P.B. (eds.) International Encyclopedia of the Social & Behavioral Sciences, pp. 9240–9242. Pergamon, Oxford (2001). https://doi.org/10.1016/B0-08-043076-7/00614-8, https://www.sciencedirect.com/science/article/pii/B0080430767006148
19. Molnar, C.: Interpretable machine learning - a guide for making black box models explainable. https://christophm.github.io/interpretable-ml-book/, Accessed 01 Jun 2023
20. Ning, J., Chen, L., Chen, J.: Relative density-based outlier detection algorithm. In: Proceedings of the 2018 2nd International Conference on Computer Science and Artificial Intelligence, CSAI 2018, pp. 227–231. Association for Computing Machinery, New York, NY, USA (2018). https://doi.org/10.1145/3297156.3297236
21. Peña, D.: Detecting Outliers and Influential and Sensitive Observations in Linear Regression, pp. 605–619. Springer, London (2023). https://doi.org/10.1007/978-1-4471-7503-2_31
22. Potyka, N.: Interpreting neural networks as gradual argumentation frameworks (including proof appendix). CoRR **abs/2012.05738** (2020), https://arxiv.org/abs/2012.05738
23. Riveret, R., Gao, Y., Governatori, G., Rotolo, A., Pitt, J., Sartor, G.: A probabilistic argumentation framework for reinforcement learning agents. Auton. Agents

Multi-Agent Syst. **33**(1), 216–274 (2019). https://doi.org/10.1007/s10458-019-09404-2
24. Sakama, C.: A formal account of deception. In: 2015 AAAI Fall Symposium Series (2015)
25. Sarkadi, S., McBurney, P.J., Parsons, S.D.: Deceptive storytelling in artificial dialogue games. In: Proceedings of the AAAI 2019 Spring Symposium: Story-Enabled Intelligence (2019)
26. Sayed-Mouchaweh, M., Lughofer, E.: Learning in Non-Stationary Environments: Methods and Applications. Springer, New York (2012). https://doi.org/10.1007/978-1-4419-8020-5
27. Smith, S.L., Kindermans, P., Le, Q.V.: Don't decay the learning rate, increase the batch size. CoRR **abs/1711.00489** (2017). http://arxiv.org/abs/1711.00489
28. Spieler, J., Potyka, N., Staab, S.: Learning gradual argumentation frameworks using genetic algorithms. CoRR **abs/2106.13585** (2021). https://arxiv.org/abs/2106.13585
29. Takahashi, K., Yokohama, S.: On a formal treatment of deception in argumentative dialogues. In: Criado Pacheco, N., Carrascosa, C., Osman, N., Julián Inglada, V. (eds.) EUMAS/AT -2016. LNCS (LNAI), vol. 10207, pp. 390–404. Springer, Cham (2017). https://doi.org/10.1007/978-3-319-59294-7_33
30. Toni, F.: A tutorial on assumption-based argumentation. Argument Comput. **5**(1), 89–117 (2014). https://doi.org/10.1080/19462166.2013.869878
31. Vaidya, N.H.: Security and privacy for distributed optimization & distributed machine learning. In: Proceedings of the 2021 ACM Symposium on Principles of Distributed Computing, PODC 2021, p. 573. Association for Computing Machinery, New York, NY, USA (2021). https://doi.org/10.1145/3465084.3467485
32. Westworth, S.O., Chalmers, C., Fergus, P., Longmore, S.N., Piel, A.K., Wich, S.A.: Understanding external influences on target detection and classification using camera trap images and machine learning. Sensors **22**(14), 5386 (2022)
33. Xu, J., Yao, L., Li, L., Ji, M., Tang, G.: Argumentation based reinforcement learning for meta-knowledge extraction. Inf. Sci. **506**, 258–272 (2020). https://doi.org/10.1016/j.ins.2019.07.094, https://www.sciencedirect.com/science/article/pii/S0020025519307170
34. Yu, G., Zhou, X., Hou, D., Wei, D.: Abnormal crowdsourced data detection using remote sensing image features. Int. Arch. Photogramm. Remote. Sens. Spat. Inf. Sci. **43**, 215–221 (2021)
35. Zhang, J., Li, C., Ye, J., Qu, G.: Privacy threats and protection in machine learning. In: Proceedings of the 2020 on Great Lakes Symposium on VLSI, pp. 531–536 (2020)

From Probabilistic Programming to Complexity-Based Programming

Giovanni Sileno[1](✉) and Jean-Louis Dessalles[2]

[1] University of Amsterdam, Amsterdam, The Netherlands
g.sileno@uva.nl
[2] Télécom Paris, Institut Polytechnique de Paris, Paris, France
dessalles@telecom-paris.fr

Abstract. The paper presents the main characteristics and a preliminary implementation of a novel computational framework named CompLog. Inspired by probabilistic programming systems like ProbLog, CompLog builds upon the inferential mechanisms proposed by Simplicity Theory, relying on the computation of two Kolmogorov complexities (here implemented as min-path searches via ASP programs) rather than probabilistic inference. The proposed system enables users to compute *ex-post* and *ex-ante* measures of unexpectedness of a certain situation, mapping respectively to posterior and prior subjective probabilities. The computation is based on the specification of world and mental models by means of causal and descriptive relations between predicates weighted by complexity. The paper illustrates a few examples of application: generating relevant descriptions, and providing alternative approaches to disjunction and to negation.

Keywords: Complexity-based programming · Simplicity Theory · Causal models · Descriptive models · Probability · Relevant descriptions · Negation · Kolmogorov complexity · Answer Set Programming

1 Introduction

Probabilistic forms of programming are increasingly attracting attention [1,7,14,18], and part of this success is likely because they provide an intuitive common ground between numeric and symbolic approaches. Yet, the axiomatization of probability theory relies on assuming the presence of a measurable space of events, which can in principle be contested. Given any description of the world, we can always add new elements, eg. entities previously not in focus, arrangements at other moments in time, properties not considered before. On the other hand, scalability concerns generally hinder considering an ever-growing number of variables.

In previous work [16], we have argued that the notion of "unexpectedness" introduced by Simplicity Theory (ST) [3], based on the computation of two bounded Kolmogorov complexities, provides a framework more general than Bayes' rule to compute the posterior of a certain situation. On the basis of this

S. Nowaczyk et al. (Eds.): ECAI 2023 Workshops, CCIS 1948, pp. 304–317, 2024.
https://doi.org/10.1007/978-3-031-50485-3_32

conjecture, we propose here a novel computational framework named CompLog, able to compute *ex-post* and *ex-ante* measures of unexpectedness of a certain situation, mapping respectively to posterior and prior subjective probabilities. The computation relies on the representation of causal and descriptive relationships, specified as relationships between predicates, weighted by complexity.

At syntactic level, the system we propose is inspired by ProbLog [1], yet it has its own unique characteristics. (1) CompLog enables by design the distinction between descriptive and causal dimensions, and thus in principle supports the integration of distinct dedicated tools for the two dimensions (ontologies, and causal models, for instance). (2) With adequate operators, CompLog can mimic cognitive mechanisms observable in humans. This is because the Simplicity Theory of cognition on which it builds upon has a better alignment with evaluations of relevance expressed by humans compared to Shannon's Information theory. (3) From a technical point of view, because the minimization of complexity is based upon a non-extensional search (the framework does not keep and propagate random distributions), we hypothesize that CompLog may be faster than a probabilistic equivalent system, and thus in principle it may be used efficiently both for abduction and prediction (causal, non-primarily statistical).

The present paper does not aim to demonstrate all these goals, but will present and discuss the first design choices we are taking in this line of work. Section 2 provides a brief overview to Simplicity Theory, the cognitive model underlying the inferential mechanisms we implement; on ProbLog; and on some of the problems lying at the boundary between logical and probabilistic approaches. Section 3 presents the main CompLog's components: a (simplistic) programming language, inferential mechanisms, and a preliminary implementation in ASP. Section 4 provides a few examples of application, meant to show CompLog's distinctive characteristics in comparison with functionally comparable systems.

2 Theoretical Background

2.1 Simplicity Theory

Shannon's theory of information entails that samples extracted from a uniform distribution are maximally informative. Yet, very few humans would agree with such a conclusion. Motivated by addressing this shortcoming, Simplicity Theory (ST) [3] was presented as an alternative computational model of cognition. Technically, ST introduces a measure of *unexpectedness* [5] building upon results from *algorithmic information theory*, which is defined as:

$$U(s) = C_W(s) - C_D(s)$$

where s is a situation in focus, and C_W and C_D are two Kolmogorov complexities computed via distinct bounded Turing machines.[1] The *causal complexity* C_W (also called *world complexity* or *generation complexity*) relies on a "world model" maintained by a world machine W, whose operators are expected to be about occurrences, causal dependencies, and possibly forms of causal compositionality. The *description complexity* C_D builds upon a "mind model" maintained by a description machine D, whose operators are expected to be about concept retrieval, association, and possibly various forms of descriptive compositionality. Informally, ST entails that situations are unexpected if they are (algorithmically) simpler to describe (i.e. visualize mentally) than to generate in the world (i.e. to simulate their generation according to the agent's world model). Because complexities are expressed on a logarithmic scale, one may introduce an additional constraint:

$$U(s) \geq 0$$

to capture a principle of *cognitive economy*: situations are described up to the extent they are unexpected to occur.

Previous works [2–5] have shown that this definition predicts various human phenomena observed in experimental settings, amongst which judgments on remarkable lottery draws (e.g. 11111 is more unexpected than 64178, even if the lottery is fair), coincidence effects (e.g. meeting by chance a friend in a foreign city is more unexpected than meeting any unknown person equally improbable), deterministic yet unexpected events (e.g. lunar eclipses), and many others.

Unexpectedness and Bayes' Rule. Interestingly, we have recently acknowledged [16] that Bayes' rule can be seen as a specific instantiation of ST's Unexpectedness that: (a) makes a candidate "cause" explicit and does not select automatically the best candidate; (b) takes a frequentist-like approach for encoding observables. We traced therefore the following correspondence:

$$U(s) = \min_c \overbrace{[C_W(c * s) - C_D(s)]}^{\text{posterior}} = \min_c [\overbrace{C_W(s||c)}^{\text{likelihood}} + \overbrace{C_W(c)}^{\text{prior}} - \overbrace{C_D(s)}^{\text{evidence}}]$$

where "$*$" is a (temporal) sequential compositional operator, c is a situation (candidate cause of s), and "$||$" map to the "$|$" notation in conditional probability, with an additional explicit temporal constraint (in this case c has to occur before than s). Taking unexpectedness as an alternative measure of subjective posterior probability, it could in principle replace Bayesian inference in a probabilistic deduction system.

2.2 ProbLog

ProbLog [1] is plausibly the best known amongst the available solutions for probabilistic programming. It provides a suite of efficient algorithms for various

[1] The *Kolmogorov complexity* of a string x is defined as the minimal length of a program that, given a certain optional input parameter y, produces x as an output: $K_\phi(x|y) = \min_p \{|p| : p(y) = x\}$. Note that the length of the minimal program depends on the operators and symbols available to the machine ϕ.

inference tasks, relying on a conversion of a program, queries, and evidence to a weighted Boolean formula, and thus transforming the inferential task into weighted model counting, which can be solved using state-of-the-art methods. The knowledge bases of ProbLog programs can be represented in various ways, amongst which Prolog/Datalog facts. Here is an example of code:

```
0.5 :: friendof(john, mary).
0.5 :: friendof(mary, pedro).
0.5 :: friendof(mary, tom).
0.5 :: friendof(pedro, tom).

1.0 :: likes(X, Y) :- friendof(X, Y).
0.8 :: likes(X, Y) :- friendof(X, Z), likes(Z, Y).

evidence(likes(mary, tom)).
query(likes(mary, pedro)).
```

A ProbLog program consists of facts (eg. `friendof(john, mary)`), rules (eg. `likes(X, Y) :- friendof(X, Y)`), possibly annotated with a certain probability (eg. `0.5`). Special predicates are used to specify goals (`query/1`) and observations (`evidence/1`). ProbLog also introduces the possibility to specify disjoint facts in the head of rules to capture the existence of mutually exclusive outcomes. Solving the previous program[2] returns as outcome `probability: 0.58333333`.

2.3 From ProbLog to CompLog

The outcome of the ProbLog program above can be read both as saying that Mary likes Pedro a bit, or that Mary likes Pedro in more than half of the possible world configurations specified by the program. Indeed, applications of probability theory oftentimes are used to deal with two dimensions of uncertainty: descriptive uncertainty (also *indetermination*) and causal uncertainty. This is based on the assumption that the *degree* or the extent to which it is true that, for instance, the email just received is spam may also be captured as the probability that this email is spam. Whether and when the passage between the two types of uncertainties is legitimate is still an open question, which goes beyond probability theory and involves research fields such as fuzzy logic and other quantitative approaches to logic. Here we will consider however an alternative line of arguments with respect to this issue.

Epistemic vs Ontological. On a more fundamental level, the descriptive dimension can be associated to *epistemic uncertainty*, ascribed to things that have not been unveiled yet (or proven, in a logical framing), including things that may not be proven; it is therefore primarily a matter of *conditions holding* in the world. In contrast, the causal dimension can be associated to *ontological*

[2] See eg. https://dtai.cs.kuleuven.be/problog/editor.html for an online running version of ProbLog.

uncertainty, ascribed to things that have not been created yet (or extracted, in a sampling framing); it is a matter of *events occurring* in the world. Interestingly, seen in terms of conditions/events, passing from one dimension to the other can be related to various, and very distinct, challenges studied in AI and related fields. We will cover two prototypical cases here: symbolic automated reasoning about events, and causality in Bayesian networks.

Reasoning about Events with Logic Programs. In symbolic AI, particularly in the 80 s/90 s, reasoning about the effects of events (including actions) has been a mainstream topic, eventually related to the infamous *frame problem*. It became soon manifest that it was rather difficult to perform automated reasoning about events by means of simple deduction. In order to deal with phenomena as inertia and locality of effects, several axiomatizations were proposed, the most known being *situation calculus* [10,13], *event calculus* [8,15], *fluent calculus* [17]. Looking at the event calculus, for instance, meta-level predicates are introduced to deal with two different types of entities: *fluents* (i.e. conditions that vary in time) and *events* (i.e. transitions/changes of fluents that occur at a certain point in time). Facts about the world are then reified either via `holds(C, T)` for fluents, or as `occurs(E, T)` for events, where `T` is a temporal coordinate. Other solutions share similar meta-level constructs.

Interventions with Bayesian Networks. In probabilistic inference, from a formal point of view, Bayesian Networks are known to capture only associationistic relationships. Any causal reading exists only in the mind of the modeler. To take into account interventions, like those present in causal scenarios (and relevant eg. to scientific experimentation), we need to consider an additional `do` operator [11, 12]. The `do` operator provides *local counterfactuality* by performing an operation on the Bayesian network: its presence entails that the edges from the intervened node towards its parent nodes have to be cut. Because this operation is performed at the level of the Bayesian network, and not at the level of the variables, the construct can be seen also in this case as operating at a meta-level.

Simplicity Theory as an Integrative Framework. The examples above illustrate that: (1) both logical and probabilistic inferences work primarily at the level of conditions; and (2) additional machinery is required to properly take into consideration the side effects of events. ST, in contrast, explicitly relies on two different machines to compute unexpectedness: one for the world (making events occurring), and one for the mind (determining conditions). Intuitively, this cognitive model offers a more principled solution to separate ontological and epistemic uncertainty concerns, and indeed CompLog (in contrast eg. to PropLog or other probabilistic inference systems) stems from the idea of keeping them distinct.

3 CompLog

This section presents our current design choices on CompLog going over three dimensions: the programming language, the inferential mechanisms, and their implementation.

3.1 Language

We introduce here a simplistic propositional language meant to specify both causal and associative (descriptive) relationships. We do not require it to be comprehensive, but rather to be functional for early experimentations.

Conditions and Events. The language is based upon a primary distinction between conditions and events. Events are predicates whose duration of applicability, in the descriptive frame considered, is irrelevant, whereas conditions are predicates that can be applied for some relevant amount of time. We will then use simple literals to specify conditions: `s`, `x`, `y`, `z`. We will distinguish events from conditions by means of prefixed literals: `#x`, `#y`, etc. Two special type of events will be introduced, specified by their effects: `+x` for the initiation (or creation, production, addition, etc.) of condition `x`, `-x` for the termination (or destruction, consumption, removal, etc.) of a certain condition `x`.

Declarative and Active Rules. A *declarative rule* (to be read as *if condition then conclusion*) is specified as a relation between two conditions, eg. `x -> y`. In the prolog/ASP syntax this construct would correspond to `y :- x`. An *active rule* (to be read as *if antecedent then consequent*) is specified as a relation between two events, eg. `#push => +light` (if you push the button, the light goes on). Note that the syntax is sufficiently rich to describe causal dependencies with consumption (eg. `+x => +y, -x`) and without (eg. `+x => +y`). Active rules can be also extended to fit the ECA template (*when event in condition then action*): `#push : electricity => +light`.

Race Conditions. The term "race condition" is used in concurrent systems to indicate a critical point in which only a limited amount of threads or processes have access to a resource, therefore execution may bring non-deterministic results, unless priority of access is defined up-front. Active rules in principle are susceptible to race conditions. For instance, given the following program:

```
+x => +y.
+x => +z.
```

it is not clear whether only one amongst of `+y` or `+z` should be triggered after `+x`, or both of them. To make the syntax non-ambiguous, we assume that the state of the world changes always at the activation of any causal rule[3], therefore the previous rules are interpreted as in a race condition, and only one of the

[3] There will be certainly a change of temporal coordinate, even if implicit.

two will be executed. To specify the absence of race conditions we can use the ECA template, allowing active rules with no triggering event, and introducing a *catalyst* entity which is not consumed:

```
=> +x.
: x => +y.
: x => +z.
```

Active formulas with no triggering event can be seen as related to ergodic properties of the world, underlying asymptotic growth phenomena. In a propositional setting, growth is however constrained to be non-linear and capped.

Program. A CompLog program consists of a *world model*, specified as a set of causal relationships (in the proposed language, active rules) and centered on events; and a *mental model*, specified as a set of associationistic relationships (eg. logical, in the proposed language via declarative rules), centered on conditions. If a program consists only of facts about events and active rules, it is called *active program.* If a program consists only of facts about conditions and declarative rules it is called *declarative program.* Any program can be divided into active and declarative programs, mapping isomorphically to world and to mental models.

Program Augmentation. Given a declarative program, we can read it as an active program by capturing explicitly initiation and termination mechanisms. Here we will focus only on initiation, as it has a more prominent role when thinking of the plausibility of a target situation. The transformation can be applied in two ways, with race conditions, or with no race conditions:

```
x.   x -> y.      % declarative
+x.  +x => +y.    % active with race conditions
+x.  : x => +y.   % active without race conditions
```

Complexities. Whereas in ProbLog facts and rules can be given a probability (a value between 0 and 1), in CompLog facts and rules can be given a value of complexity (a positive value). When complexity is specified within a world model, associated to an element of an active program, it has to be interpreted as a causal complexity C_W, when it is specified within a mental model, associated to an element of a declarative program, it has to be interpreted as a descriptive complexity C_D. Consider the following example:

```
4 :: eagle.
12 :: #eagle.
```

This program expresses that conceptually evoking an eagle is much easier than actually encountering it.[4]

[4] The easiness of retrieval may be due to a much more frequent appearance of the concept of eagle in discourses around the observer.

3.2 Inference

A second intuition motivating the introduction of CompLog is that the world and mental models connect to two different characterizations of computation, which can be treated separately.

Productive vs Epistemic Characterization. Causal events generally consume resources (except for catalysts); we will therefore consider a *productive* characterization of computation to simulate the world generation processes, which can be put in correspondence with graphical notations as, eg., Petri Nets. We will instead consider an *epistemic* characterization for the computation of mental objects: once a fact has been unveiled (eg. it has been proven true or retrieved from memory), it becomes part of the current resources and cannot be removed, unless non-monotonic effects apply. This view can be applied to systems based on logic, and can also be given a graphical representation, as for instance through dependency graphs.

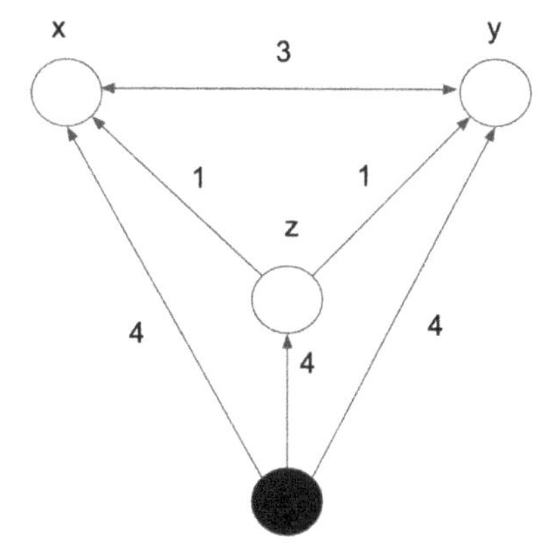

Fig. 1. Graph constructed from of a descriptive model. Coloured nodes (in black) are available resources. Numbers on edges specify the complexity of colouring the target node if the source node is coloured.

Computation as a "Colouring" Task. From the above, we hypothesize that the world and mental models can be represented as two distinct directed graphs. The nodes coloured at a certain moment in time count as resources which are available at that moment. The edges reify the complexity, i.e. the cost of colouring the target node, when the source node is coloured already. Queries specify goal nodes. With this mapping, the minimization of complexity required by the computation of Kolmogorov complexity maps to the application of min-path search algorithms. We require two distinct search algorithms, because transitions on the two graphs behave differently (respectively, with or without consumption). Consider for instance the following declarative program (mental model):

```
4 :: x. 4 :: y. 4 :: z.
1 :: z -> x. 1 :: z -> y.
3 :: x -> y. 3 :: y -> x.
```

Adding an initial state, the various relations can be represented on a graph like the one in Fig. 1. We can then augment the declarative program to generate a corresponding active program, obtaining:

```
4 :: +x. 4 :: +y. 4 :: +z.
1 :: +z => +x. 1 :: +z => +y.
3 :: +x => +y. 3 :: +y => +x.
```

Note how we have illustratively kept the same primitive values of complexity in the two models, and yet the computed derived complexities vary. For instance, $C_D(\mathrm{x}) = 4$ is equal to $C_W(\texttt{+x}) = 4$, whereas $C_D(\langle \mathrm{x}, \mathrm{y} \rangle) = 6$ is inferior to $C_W(\langle \texttt{+x}, \texttt{+y} \rangle) = 7$.[5] This divergence appears because on the descriptive program we apply an epistemic computation, which does not consume any resources; we can then generate `z` as a more efficient basis to construct both `x` and `y`. In contrast, on the active program we apply a productive computation, which (generally) consumes resources; the given program has a race condition over `+z`, and therefore it cannot be used both to trigger `+x` and `+y`. Note however how the designer can modify this behaviour in case `z` acts rather as a catalyst.

Output. In CompLog, given a query, we will compute its unexpectedness (mapping to a posterior, *ex-post* probability) as the difference between the complexities computed on the world and on the description machine, i.e. $U = C_W - C_D$. In the example illustrated in Fig. 1, we can infer for instance that $U(\langle \mathrm{x}, \mathrm{y} \rangle) = 1$, and therefore, this input would be (slightly) unexpected *if it had to occur.*

In order to generate an *ex-ante* value, relevant for predicting what will occur in the future, the determination cost needs to be added back to unexpectedness, i.e. $C_W^U = U + C_D$ [16]. On simple cases, this seems rather inefficient, as we could simply compute C_W. However, in general cases, there may be elements in the query (which describes a situation) which may turn out to be irrelevant. The optimization on C_D to compute U is functional to finding the correct framing by which to interpret the input situation. In probabilistic approaches, this is left implicit in the choice of random variables; for instance, we approach a lottery without considering the context that brought the lottery to be, nor other events that may disrupt its functioning: the framing is given by design. For further information, see the *informational principle of framing* elaborated in [16].

3.3 Implementation

Because it relies on the computation of (bounded) Kolmogorov complexities, the core inferential mechanism of CompLog are min-path search algorithms to be applied on the graphs resulting from the world and mental models. For our

[5] $\langle \ldots, \ldots \rangle$ is an operation used to specify multiple goals, all of which need to achieved, regardless of the order.

preliminary experiments, we have manually implemented the search algorithms in *answer set programming* (ASP) [9], using the ASP solver `clingo` [6].[6] This choice was motivated by the intention of keeping control on the various steps. Yet, other solutions may be more efficient.[7]

The ASP program we use to encode the inferential mechanisms of CompLog consists of model and control parts, related respectively to the given problem (specific) and to the control mechanisms (generic) required to run the inference.

The model part consists of statements reifying the edges of the graph with their cost (complexity), including the initial state (the coloured nodes) and the query (the goal nodes). The graph in Fig. 1 is for instance reified as:

```
cost(s, x, 4). cost(s, y, 4). cost(s, z, 4).
cost(z, x, 1). cost(z, y, 1).
cost(x, y, 3). cost(y, x, 3).
start(s). goal(x). goal(y).
```

The control part of the program is an axiomatization consisting of three components: a common *exploration* core, specific *constraints* depending on whether we are in the context of productive or epistemic computation (i.e. consumption or no-consumption, race conditions), and axioms for defining optimization. For the exploration axioms, we consider:

```
path(X, Y) :- reached(X, N), edge(X, Y).
reached(X, 0) :- start(X).
:- goal(Y), not reached(Y, _).
```

The first line states that every outgoing edge from a reached node may be traveled. The second specifies that the initial state consists of nodes reached at time 0. The third states that all goals should be reached eventually. The search mechanism is then extended with specific constraints. In an epistemic computation setting, time is deemed irrelevant:

```
{ reached(Y, N) } :- path(X, Y), reached(X, N).
```

which states that if the node `X` was reached at time `N`, and there is a path between `X` and `Y`, then `Y` may be reached in the same moment. In a productive computation setting, time is instead relevant:

```
{ reached(Y, N + 1) } :- path(X, Y), reached(X, N), N < 10.
```

This expression introduces a temporal aspect in going through the graph. (The boundary to `N` acts as a maximal depth of search, at the moment set as a hard-coded parameter.) We may want also to add race conditions: only one event can be caused at once (what in concurrent systems is called an *interleaved semantics*). This constraint can be encoded in the following ASP rule:

```
:- reached(X, N), reached(Y, N), X != Y.
```

[6] https://potassco.org/clingo/.

[7] Interestingly, a new probabilistic programming framework (including ProbLog inferential mechanisms) based on ASP/clingo has been recently presented: `plingo` [7].

Finally, the optimization criteria can be expressed as simply as:

```
totalcost(T) :- T = #sum{C,X,Y : path(X, Y), cost(X, Y, C)}.
#minimize {T: totalcost(T)}.
```

By solving this program, we obtain the minimal path achieving all goals (colouring all target nodes) from the start conditions, together with its cost.

4 Examples of Application

This section provides three examples of application, aiming to highlight the potential of a system like CompLog.

4.1 Most Relevant Description

Suppose we are given a certain ontology (including taxonomical and terminological aspects), here expressed in the form of declarative rules:

```
eagle -> bird. pigeon -> bird. canary -> bird.
tiger -> mammal. dog -> mammal. cat -> mammal.
dog -> pet. cat -> pet. canary -> pet.
```

Suppose we have some descriptive complexity associated to those terms (eg. related to their appearance in discourses):

```
3 :: dog. 3 :: cat. 3 :: bird.
4 :: eagle. 4 :: tiger. 4 :: pigeon.
6 :: canary.
```

as well as some measures on world complexity (eg. related to actual frequencies of encounter):

```
3 :: #pigeon. 3 :: #dog. 3 :: #cat. 3 :: #bird.
7 :: #canary.
12 :: #eagle. 12 :: #tiger.
```

By computing the various measures of unexpectedness we can settle on what is the best descriptor of the current situation (minimizing U). For instance, given `#pigeon`, we may prefer to say `bird` (as C_W(`#pigeon`) $-$ C_D(`pigeon`) < 0), whereas we would keep saying `eagle` for `#eagle`.[8]

[8] Here we are assuming that there the rules provided with the ontology are applied with no cost. Yet, for the mental mode, they should rather be thought as reifying associationistic relations, related to how often the two concepts are activated together. If the target concept is abstract/rarely used (eg. `mammal`), additional cost may be associated to declarative rules involving it.

4.2 Disjunction

Suppose we have a die with 4 faces. In ProbLog, an extraction would be specified by means of an exclusive disjunction:

```
0.25 :: die1; 0.25 :: die2; 0.25 :: die3; 0.25 :: die4.
```

The equivalent representation in CompLog would distinguish the declarative from the active part (obtained eg. by program augmentation) as:

```
2 :: die1. 2 :: die2. 2 :: die3. 2 :: die4.
2 :: => +die1. 2 :: => +die2. 2 :: => +die3. 2 :: => +die4.
```

Note that disjunction is a by-design consequence of the race conditions. Stated otherwise, exclusive disjunction in probabilistic specifications can be seen as conveying implicitly the presence of race conditions.

4.3 Negation

Probability theory allows us to compute the probability of a *negated event* (eg. $\neg$ `die1`) as the probability of the union set of events dual to the event which is negated, or, algebraically, as $1 - P(\texttt{die1})$. This possibility is enabled by the closure of the horizon of events by means of an extensional semantics, i.e. defining random events as sets, and then using set operations.

In contrast, Simplicity Theory (and thus CompLog) does not assume such a closure, as it deems cognitively unsound to infer the unexpectedness of encountering eg. a not-dog. Yet, it hints to a way to approach negation which is procedural and incremental, at a meta-level with respect to the core inference. Suppose that someone says, "I just met an animal, which was not a dog". Plausibly, the person wants to convey that she was in a context in which she would have expected a dog, but then that expectation wasn't met. Therefore, in our mind we need first to reconstruct a context in which dog is expected, then we remove the appearance of a dog, and the first animal that would appear in its stead (eg. a cat) would give us a proxy measure for the complexity looked for.

As a more concrete example, let us apply the same intuition to the case of the die, which is more extreme, being a fair lottery. We first compute the complexity of `die1`, which is 2. We then remove `die1` from the graph. We compute the node with the best complexity, eg. `die2`, which is still 2. We could take this as a proxy of the negation of the target, however, this computation also shows that the best alternative has the same level of unexpectedness of the target, which can be taken as a hint to proceed further. We can then apply another iteration: negating `die2`, finding `die3` with again complexity 2, and then we may aggregate the complexities of the two alternatives. This procedure can be formulated as a general heuristic: the search/aggregation can be stopped (i) when the best alternative has a sufficiently high complexity, or (ii) when the aggregated value has a sufficiently low complexity, with respect to the complexity of the target.

5 Conclusion and Future Works

The paper presented the general motivation, the underlying theory, the main components, and elements of an initial implementation of CompLog, a novel complexity-based programming framework. CompLog is meant to explore a space of research in the domain of computational inferential systems (not extensional, not primarily statistical, but algorithmic, and cognitively sound inference) which has not yet attracted much attention. In future works, besides further clarifying the various components, and consolidating the various definitions, we will explore additional applications, including learning mechanisms, and attempt to integrate CompLog with existing computational frameworks, symbolic and sub-symbolic. We also aim to perform experiments to benchmark performances of CompLog on tasks where probabilistic-oriented frameworks are currently used, both in terms of computability, and of empirical alignment with human behaviour.

References

1. De Raedt, L., Kimmig, A., Toivonen, H.: ProbLog: a probabilistic prolog and its application in link discovery. In: Proceedings of the 20th International Joint Conference on Artificial Intelligence, IJCAI 2007, pp. 2462–2467 (2007)
2. Dessalles, J.L.: Coincidences and the encounter problem: a formal account. In: Proceedings of the 30th Annual Conference of the Cognitive Science Society (CogSci 2008), pp. 2134–2139 (2008)
3. Dessalles, J.L.: La pertinence et ses origines cognitives. Hermes-Science (2008)
4. Dessalles, J.L.: Simplicity effects in the experience of near-miss. In: Proceedings of thee 33th Annual Meeting of the Cognitive Science Society (CogSci 2011), pp. 408–413 (2011)
5. Dessalles, J.-L.: Algorithmic simplicity and relevance. In: Dowe, D.L. (ed.) Algorithmic Probability and Friends. Bayesian Prediction and Artificial Intelligence. LNCS, vol. 7070, pp. 119–130. Springer, Heidelberg (2013). https://doi.org/10.1007/978-3-642-44958-1_9
6. Gebser, M., Kaminski, R., Kaufmann, B., Schaub, T.: Multi-shot ASP solving with clingo. TPLP **19**, 27–82 (2019)
7. Hahn, S., Janhunen, T., Kaminski, R., Romero, J., Rühling, N., Schaub, T.: Plingo: a system for probabilistic reasoning in clingo based on LP^{MLN}. In: Governatori, G., Turhan, A.Y. (eds.) Rules and Reasoning. RuleML+RR 2022. LNCS, vol. 13752, pp. 54–62. Springer, Cham (2022). https://doi.org/10.1007/978-3-031-21541-4_4
8. Kowalski, R., Sergot, M.: A logic based calculus of events. New Gener. Comput. **4**(1975), 67–95 (1986)
9. Lifschitz, V.: What is answer set programming? In: Proceedings of the AAAI Conference on Artificial Intelligence (2008)
10. McCarthy, J., Hayes, P.J.: Some philosophical problems from the standpoint of artificial intelligence. In: Machine Intelligence, pp. 1–51. Edimburgh University Press (1969)
11. Pearl, J.: Causality. Cambridge University Press, Cambridge (2009)
12. Pearl, J., Glymour, M., Jewell, N.P.: Causal Inference in Statistics: A Primer. Wiley, Hoboken (2016)

13. Reiter, R.: Knowledge in Action: Logical Foundations for Specifying and Implementing Dynamical Systems. MIT Press, Cambridge (2001)
14. Saad, F.A., Cusumano-Towner, M.F., Schaechtle, U., Rinard, M.C., Mansinghka, V.K.: Bayesian synthesis of probabilistic programs for automatic data modeling. In: Proceedings of the ACM on Programming Languages 3(POPL), pp. 1–32 (2019)
15. Shanahan, M.: The event calculus explained. In: Wooldridge, M.J., Veloso, M. (eds.) Artificial Intelligence Today. LNCS (LNAI), vol. 1600, pp. 409–430. Springer, Heidelberg (1999). https://doi.org/10.1007/3-540-48317-9_17
16. Sileno, G., Dessalles, JL.: Unexpectedness and bayes' rule. In: Cerone, A., et al. Software Engineering and Formal Methods. SEFM 2021 Collocated Workshops. SEFM 2021. LNCS, vol. 13230, pp 107–116. Springer, Cham (2022). https://doi.org/10.1007/978-3-031-12429-7_8
17. Thielscher, M.: From situation calculus to fluent calculus: state update axioms as a solution to the inferential frame problem. Artif. Intell. **111**(1–2), 277–299 (1999)
18. Winters, T., Marra, G., Manhaeve, R., De Raedt, L.: Deepstochlog: neural stochastic logic programming. In: Proceedings of the AAAI Conference on Artificial Intelligence, vol. 36, pp. 10090–10100 (2022)

Integrating Machine Learning into an SMT-Based Planning Approach for Production Planning in Cyber-Physical Production Systems

René Heesch(✉), Jonas Ehrhardt, and Oliver Niggemann

Helmut Schmidt University, Hamburg, Germany
{rene.heesch,jonas.ehrhardt,oliver.niggemann}@hsu-hh.de

Abstract. Cyber-Physical Production Systems (CPPS) are highly complex systems, making the application of AI planning approaches for production planning challenging. Most AI planning approaches require comprehensive domain descriptions, which model the functional dependencies within the CPPS. Though, due to their high complexity, creating such domain descriptions manually is considered difficult, tedious, and error-prone. Therefore, we propose a novel generic planning approach, which can integrate mathematical formulas or Machine Learning models into a symbolic SMT-based planning algorithm, thus shedding the need for complex manually created models. Our approach uses a feature-vector-based state-space representation as an interface of symbolic and sub-symbolic AI, and can identify a solution to CPPS planning problems by determining the required production steps, their sequence, and their parametrization. We evaluate our approach on twelve planning problems from a real CPPS, demonstrating its ability to express complex dependencies within production steps as mathematical formulas or integrating ML models.

Keywords: AI Planning · Cyber-Physical Production System · Machine Learning · SMT

1 Introduction

Modern production systems are faced with rapidly decreasing batch sizes, increasing product variants, and volatile resource availability [13,14]. These strains make it inevitable for manufacturing companies to rapidly adjust or reconfigure their production systems [14,20]. One approach to address these challenges is the usage of Cyber-Physical Production Systems (CPPS). CPPS are production systems of computational and physical entities that are strongly connected to the physical world. They are characterized by the complex interplay of mechanical, electrical, and informational components, making their handling complex and costly [1]. Research towards automating CPPS often remains on an operational level, including anomaly detection or diagnosis [3,8,19]. However, in order to exploit the full potential of CPPS, production planning must be automated, as well [16].

S. Nowaczyk et al. (Eds.): ECAI 2023 Workshops, CCIS 1948, pp. 318–331, 2024.
https://doi.org/10.1007/978-3-031-50485-3_33

Production planning denotes the problem of finding the correct sequence of production steps – as well as their corresponding parametrization – that are necessary to transform a given initial product state – i.e., raw materials – into a final product state – i.e., a goal product – [16]. Production planning in CPPS grows more complex, as CPPS include higher numbers of subsystems and allow for a more detailed monitoring of system components and the production process as a whole [16]. Symbolic planning approaches, such as Satisfiability Modulo Theory (SMT) techniques [5,6,16], operate on detailed descriptions of the planning problem domains, i.e., defined with the Planning Domain Definition Language (PDDL) [9]. Those descriptions allow for spanning a detailed state-space of the planning problem. However, creating and maintaining them is considered as tedious, difficult, and error-prone [10]. Sub-symbolic approaches, instead, leverage on the large amounts of hybrid system data that is generated in CPPS [24], though struggle in terms of their reasoning capabilities.

We therefore propose a novel approach benefiting from both, symbolic reasoning capabilities and sub-symbolic system modelling capabilities. Our approach allows the integration of trained Machine Learning (ML) models into SMT formulas and their subsequent solving (cf. Figure 1). This allows us to reduce the modelling effort, by substituting the manually created models with ML models, that were trained on the system data derived from the CPPS.

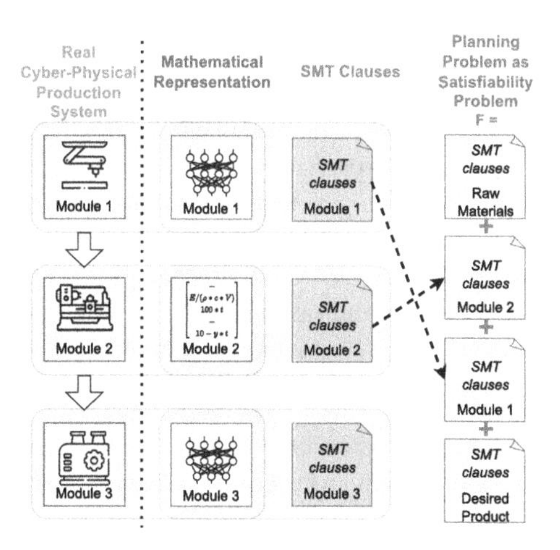

Fig. 1. Our novel planning approach combines representations of CPPS as mathematical formulations or Machine Learning models in an SMT-based planning algorithm, bypassing the need for tedious and error-prone manual domain modeling.

A crucial step of including sub-symbolic AI approaches into symbolic AI approaches lies in finding a joint representation of the state space that allows the two approaches to communicate. To derive our approach, we formulated the following research questions (RQs):

RQ1: Is there a state-space representation that can be used to (i) solve CPPS planning problems with SMT and (ii) train ML models to approximate complex dependencies within CPPS?

Multiple AI applications [2,18] in the context of CPPS proved that a factored representation in the form of a feature vector can easily be derived from CPPS time-series data. We hence create a feature-vector-based state-space representation that allows for solving of CPPS planning problems with SMT and training of ML models.

RQ2: Can production steps be described as mathematical functions, including dependencies of production step parameters, based on a feature-vector-based state-space representation of a CPPS planning problem?

To answer the RQ, we introduce an algorithm to translate the feature-vector-based state-space representation into a satisfiability problem and solve it with a state-of-the-art SMT-solver. Our algorithm can deal with dependencies that are formulated as mathematical functions and can integrate these functions in the solution space of the SMT-solver.

RQ3: Can trained ML models be translated into SMT-solvable formulas that allow their integration into an SMT-based planning approach?

We extend our planning algorithm to enable it to translate trained ML models, as representation of production steps, into SMT-solvable formulas. We demonstrate our algorithm's ability by translating trained Neural Networks (NN) into SMT formulas and integrate them into our planning approach to solve CPPS planning problems.

As a result, we present the Gene**R**ic **A**rtificial **I**ntelligence Pla**N**ning for Cyb**E**r-Physical P**R**oduction Systems[1] algorithm (RAINER). RAINER works on a feature-vector-based state-space representation and can integrate mathematical formulations of system dependencies, as well as ML models in its solving space (cf. Figure 1). Although RAINER demonstrates promising results in integrating sub-symbolic models into a symbolic planning algorithm, it lacks computational performance for complex models, leaving the gap for novel SMT solving strategies.

The contributions of this paper are:

- A novel and generic feature-vector-based representation for planning problems that allows to express effects as mathematical formulas or to learn the effects from system observations.
- RAINER, a novel planning algorithm that converts the feature-vector-based state-space representation of a CPPS planning problem, including the trained ML models, into a satisfiability problem in SMT, and subsequently solves it.
- A comprehensive evaluation of our approaches based on twelve scenarios in a real CPPS planning domain.

[1] https://github.com/RHeesch/rainer.

2 Related Work

Expressing a planning problem as a satisfiability problem in SMT has been recognized as a suitable approach for production planning in CPPS [16]. SMT defines the satisfiability of a formula in first-order logic with respect to a background theory T [4]. These background theories in SMT are semantic restrictions that limit the interpretations of various symbols, such as models of the theory of integer numbers [7]. To check the satisfiability of a formula, an SMT-solver typically first creates a Boolean abstraction, replacing each background theory constraint by a new proposition. This abstraction is then passed to a SAT solver, which searches for a satisfying assignment. Finally, a theory solver examines the consistency of the assignment in the underlying theory [4].

In 1992, Kautz et al. [15] introduced an approach to solve planning problems as satisfiability problems by encoding a fixed-length plan as the satisfiability of a propositional logic formula. Hoffmann et al. [12] extended this approach in 2007 by translating a numerical planning problem into a satisfiability problem in SMT. More recent approaches, such as Springroll [26], SMTPlan [6], and RANTANPLAN [5], aim to exploit the expressiveness of SMT for solving planning problems. These approaches require formalizations of planning problems in one of the extensions of the Planning Domain Definition Language (PDDL) [9].

PDDL was initiated in 1998 by Ghallab et al. [9] to support classical planning. Since then, different extensions and versions of PDDL have been developed, increasing the expressiveness of the language and enabling its application to more realistic problems. However, writing and maintaining formal descriptions of planning problems, e.g., in PDDL, is a notoriously hard task [21], often considered as time-consuming and error-prone [27].

Various approaches have emerged to learn PPDL descriptions from lists of state transitions or action sequences for other planning problems in the regarded domain [11,21]. Nonetheless, these approaches require lists of state transitions or action sequences created by a human operator, random exploration, or other domain-specific process [21] and are not explicitly available for CPPS. Other AI approaches, like [2,18] use factored representation in the form of a vector of attributes that can easily be derived from CPPS time-series data. Each state of the system is partitioned into a fixed set of variables or attributes; each having a value of tpye Boolean, real number, or selected from a fixed set of symbols [25]. The resulting feature vector is often a fixed-dimensional vector of numbers or symbols [23].

We therefore propose a planning approach, which translates a feature-vector-based state-space representation of a CPPS planning problem into a satisfiability problem that can be solved with the state-of-the-art Z3 solver [22]. This allows for both, *(i)* solving CPPS planning problems with SMT, and *(ii)* training ML models to approximate complex dependencies within CPPS.

3 Background

A CPPS planning problem describes the task of finding the correct sequence of available production steps within a CPPS to transform given raw materials into a goal product. To allow the integration of ML models within an SMT-based planning approach, we propose a new generic formalization of CPPS planning problems based on a feature-vector-based state space representation. Compared to, for example, ontologies, feature vectors are very generic, require less modeling effort, and are well suited for use in ML models. Subsequently, all products and possible intermediate products within the CPPS are described as vectors.

Definition 1. *A product π_i is an n-dimensional feature-vector, where n is the amount of features, necessary to uniquely describe all products within the regarded CPPS.*

$$\pi_i = \mathbb{R}^n, n \in \mathbb{N} \tag{1}$$

The input of the production process, i.e., raw materials, is denoted as I. The output of the production process, i.e., the goal product is denoted as G. All products π_i within the regarded CPPS are collected in the set Π, where $I \subseteq \Pi$ and $G \in \Pi$.

$$\Pi = \{\pi_0, \pi_1, \pi_2, ..., \pi_l\} \tag{2}$$

Definition 2. *S is the state space, spanned by the all feature-vectors in Π and denotes the space of all possible products, and thereby also defines the limits of a CPPS.*

$$S = \pi_0 \times \pi_1 \times ... \times \pi_l \tag{3}$$

Definition 3. *A production step $a_j \in A$ transforms input products from $Pre^{(j)} \subseteq S$ into output products $Pout^{(j)} \subseteq S$. $Pout^{(j)}$ denotes the vector space that can be reached by applying a_j to products from the input space $Pre^{(j)}$.*

$$a_j : Pre^{(j)} \times \Phi \times \Theta^{(j)} \rightarrow Pout^{(j)} \tag{4}$$

A is the set of production steps which are available in the regarded CPPS. Each production step a_j owns an individual set of parameters Θ^j that influences the transformation of $Pre^{(j)}$ to $Pout^{(j)}$. Parameters that are influencing all production steps but are not bound to one production step, such as environmental factors, are collected in the set of environmental parameters Φ. a_j can be approximated by the corresponding ML model m_j. All ML models are collected in the set M.

Definition 4. *A CPPS planning problem is a tuple P, defining the problem's domain as well as the raw materials I and goal product G.*

$$P = \langle S, A, \Phi, I, G, \Psi \rangle \tag{5}$$

Additional, general constraints concerning the CPPS are collected in the set Ψ.

Definition 5. *A solution to a given CPPS planning problem P is a plan* Γ. *The plan* Γ *is a sequence of production steps* a_j, *of the length k, that transform the given raw materials into the goal product.*

$$\begin{aligned} &\Gamma = (a_{j_1}, a_{j_2}, ..., a_{j_k}), with \\ &I \subseteq Pre^{(j_1)}, G \subseteq Pout^{(j_k)}, \\ &\forall i \in \mathbb{N}, i < k : a_{j_x} \in A, Pout^{(j_i)} \subseteq Pre^{(j_{i+1})} \end{aligned} \tag{6}$$

4 Solution

We propose a novel twofold approach for solving CPPS planning problems. Our approach includes *(i)* a generic modelling approach that allows for expressing complex dependencies and interdependencies in a CPPS (RQ1), and *(ii)* a novel planning algorithm, which is capable of translating CPPS planning problems into satisfiability problems in SMT, and subsequently solve them. Our novel planning algorithm can translate mathematical models and ML models into SMT, and is therefore especially suitable for CPPS planning problem domains that include complex dependencies and interdependencies that otherwise would entail elaborate manual modeling (RQ2, RQ3).

4.1 Generic Modelling Approach for CPPS Planning Problems

In Sect. 3, we introduced a formalization of a CPPS planning problem based on a feature vector representation of CPPS and their components.

For modelling the products $\pi_i \in \Pi$, we collect their features in a feature vector. The feature-vector-based representation is generic and allows for an easy integration of ML methods, as it can serve both as input and output to an ML model. Each product π_i has $n \in \mathbb{N}$ features. The features can be numeric or nominal and may vary across different products. The structure of all feature vectors in Π is identical. If a product does not own a specific feature, its value is set to NULL. If an intermediate product is the result of an assembly process of two or more components, we concatenate the input vectors and add additional features to describe the connection between the components.

Each production step a_j transforms a product from an input space $Pre^{(j)}$ into a product from an output space $Pout^{(j)}$. Where $Pre^{(j)}$ is the vector space containing all vectors or products to which the production step a_j is applicable. By adding the effect of a production step, depending on the environmental parameters Ψ and production step specific parameters Θ^j, a new vector in $Pout^{(j)}$ is calculated. pre_{a_j} reduces the vector space of all possible products S to $Pre^{(j)}$. eff_{a_j} describes the production step's effect on every single feature, including the dependencies from Φ and $\Theta^{(j)}$. The notation of eff_{a_j} in vector form allows for simple addition to calculate the effect of an action a_j to a product π_i, resulting in an output product π_{i+1}:

$$\pi_{i+1} = \pi_i + eff_{a_j} \tag{7}$$

We expand the notation of eff_{a_j} by including mathematical formulas in the individual elements of the vector. This allows us to depict functional and learnable dependencies in eff_{a_j}, leaving the possibility for a manual mathematical modelling or the use of ML models $m_j \in M$ that approximate the transformation function from the input feature vector π_i to the output feature vector π_{i+1}.

4.2 Novel Planning Algorithm for CPPS Planning Problems

As existing SMT-based planning approaches do not allow for the direct integration of ML models and require detailed PDDL descriptions of CPPS planning problems, we introduce our novel planning algorithm RAINER. RAINER translates a feature-vector-based state-space representation of a planning problem, including integrated ML models, into a satisfiability problem in SMT and subsequently solves it. Besides determining the plan Γ, RAINER additionally determines the corresponding parameter set Θ for each production step $a_j \in \Gamma$.

Algorithm 1 describes the procedure *translateSMT*, which translates a trained ML model into a set of SMT clauses that can be integrated into a satisfiability problem. We formulate *translateSMT* to fit Multilayer Perceptron Networks,

---

Algorithm 1. The procedure *tranlateSMT* translates a trained NN m_j into a set of SMT clauses $SMTclauses_j$.

Input: m_j // NN
Output: $SMTclauses_j$ // NN as a set of SMT clauses
1: **procedure** translateSMT:
2: $layer_j, neurons_j, act_j \leftarrow m_j$ // loading architecture of the NN
3: $weights_j, biases_j \leftarrow m_j$ // loading the weights of the NN
4: **for all** neuron in outputlayer **do**
5: // generate SMT clauses for the mathematical dependencies between // output layer and input layer
$Dependencies_{neuron} \leftarrow genFormula(layer_j, neurons_j, act_j, weights_j, biases_j)$
6: // append to set of SMT clauses representing the NN
$SMTclauses_j = SMTclauses_j + Dependencies_{neuron}$
7: **end for**
8: **return** $SMTclauses_j$

---

further called NN. Other operations and ML models will be integrated in further implementations of the approach. In the first step of *translateSMT*, the architecture and weights of the NN, including its activation functions, are loaded. Next, the mathematical dependencies from all features of the NN's input layer to each neuron of its output layer are translated as mathematical functions into SMT clauses. Finally, all clauses are added into a set of clauses $SMTclauses_j$, representing the trained NN in SMT.

Algorithm 2 introduces our planning algorithm RAINER, which translates a CPPS planning problem into a satisfiability problem in SMT and subsequently solves it. The algorithm creates a constant for each feature from the state space S and adds them to the set *Vars* (cf. Algorithm 2, line 1). The initial product I and goal product G are encoded as a set of SMT clauses, using the constants from *Vars*. Parameters Φ and general constraints Ψ are translated into constants *Fix* and SMT clauses *GC*. All available production steps in A are translated with the *translateSMT* function into a set of SMT clauses, serving as templates for the solver, and added to the set T (cf. Algorithm 2, line 6). Similar to the translation of the vectors I and G, the vectors pre_{a_j} and eff_{a_j} are translated

Algorithm 2. Our Planning Algorithm RAINER transforms a CPPS planning problem P into a satisfiability problem in SMT and solves it iteratively.

Input: CPPS planning problem $P = \langle S, A, \Phi, I, G, \Psi \rangle$ including ML models M
Output: Γ

```
1: // generate the constants Vars representing the features of the state space S
   Vars ← genSMTconst(S)
2: Init ← genSMTclauses(Vars, I) // generate a set of clauses denoting I
3: Goal ← genSMTclauses(Vars, G) // generate a set of clauses denoting G
4: Fix ← genSMTconst(Φ) // generate the constants Fix representing Φ
5: GC ← genSMTclauses(Ψ) // generate a set of clauses representing Ψ
6: // generate a set of clauses serving as templates of the available production steps
   T ← genSMTclauses(A, translateSMT)
7: // adding the sets of clauses GC + Init + Goal to satisfiability formula F
   F = GC + Init + Goal
8: procedure Solve:
9: for i = 0, i <= maxlength do
10:    check sat // the SMT-solver checks the satisfiability of F
11:    if F == sat then
12:       break
13:    end if
14:    i++
15:    Act_i ← genSMTconst(T) // generate the constant Act_i of the type T
16:    // generate a set of clauses Actions_i representing the available production steps
       Actions_i ← genSMTclauses(Act_i, T)
17:    F = F + Actions_i // add the set of clauses Actions_i to satisfiability formula F
18: end for
19: return model(F)
20: Γ ← model(F) // extract the plan Γ from the satisfiability model model(F)
```

into logical clauses. Furthermore, for each $a_j \in A$, for every $\theta \in \Theta^{(j)}$, a constant-template of the type real is generated and added to the set $Parameter_{a_j}$. Thus, each action template t_{a_j} is a tuple, with the two sets of logical clauses describing the vectors pre_{a_j} and eff_{a_j} as logical constraints over the constants within the set *Vars*, and the set $Parameter_{a_j}$. If an ML model is used to approximate the effect of a production step, the set of clauses $SMTclauses_j$ is generated by the procedure *translateSMT* (cf. Algorithm 1) and added to the set eff_{a_j}. Finally, the general constraints GC, initial product I, and goal product G are summed in the satisfiability formula F.

The solving process of the CPPS planning problem is iterative, as it is only possible to encode the existence of a fixed-length plan as the satisfiability of a logical formula [15]. We limit the length of a possible plan with the counter variable *maxlength*. At the beginning of each iteration, the algorithm checks the satisfiability of the F.

If the raw materials are equal to the goal product and no production step is necessary, the formula $F_{i=0}$ is satisfiable. In that case, the procedure *Solve* is exited (cf. Algorithm 2, line 12) and the satisfiable model is returned (cf. Algorithm 2, line 19). Else, an additional set of SMT clauses $Actions_i$ is added to the satisfiability formula F, marking an additionally considered production step a_j for the plan Γ. For this purpose, a new constant Act_i of type T is generated and subsequently a new set of SMT clauses $Actions_i$ is generated. This allows for the repeated execution of identical production steps with different parameter sets $\Theta^{(j)}$. Consequently, the formula F for a planning problem with k steps consists of the clauses GC, *Initial*, *Goal* and k sets of clauses describing the available production steps.

$$F_k = GC + Initial + \sum_{i=1}^{k} Actions_i + Goal \tag{8}$$

Finally, the plan Γ is extracted from the satisfiability model $model(F)$ (cf. Algorithm 2, line 20).

5 Evaluation

We tested our planning approach empirically by applying it to twelve different CPPS planning problems from a single domain. Therefore, we used the Flexible Production Simulation (FliPSi) [17], which offers four modules of a metal processing CPPS: *Mill*, *Drill*, *CNC* and *Paint* (cf. Figure 2). Each module represents a production step that transforms properties of a metal block into a new state. To include physical dependencies, we extended FliPSi with an additional production step *Heat*. The *Heat* production step heats a product with thermal energy that is absorbed by the product without losses. The sets of the production step specific parameters Θ is empty for the first four production steps. Only Θ_{Heat} includes the parameter energy input (E), denoting the energy, the module has to transfer to the product. The set Φ includes parameters denoting the density of the product (ρ), its volume (V) and its specific heat capacity (c). Within this example, there are no general constraints. Hence, the set Ψ is empty.

Based on the CPPS domain, we created 12 different CPPS planning problems. The CPPS planning problems span from four scenarios $\{s_1, ..., s_4\}$, that describe different initial products $\{I_1, ..., I_4\}$ and goal products $\{G_1, ..., G_4\}$ (cf. Figure 2). For each scenario, we varied the product material type thrice, by changing its material-specific constants ρ, c, V. We created two scenarios s_3 and s_4 as unsolvable to evaluate our algorithm's behavior for unsolvable CPPS planning problems.

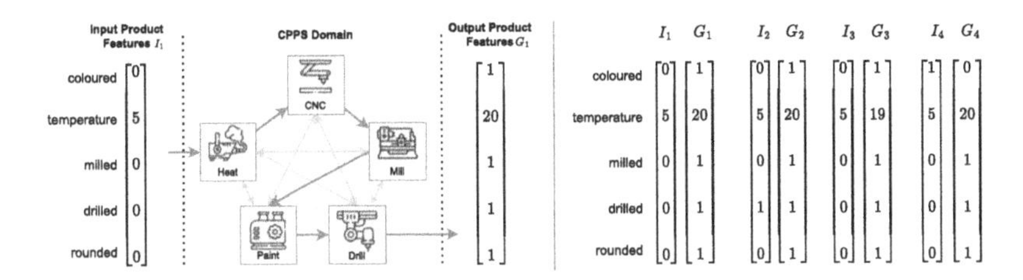

Fig. 2. *Left:* The figure shows the FliPSi domain, on which we validated our algorithm. The domain consists of five interchangeable process steps that sequentially transform an initial product I_1 into a goal product G_1. *Right:* The feature vectors for initial product I_n and goal product G_n of our four planning problems $\{s_1, ..., s_4\}$

We described the physical dependencies in the *Heat* module of our CPPS domain as mathematical formula (RQ2) and trained a Neural Network on artificially generated training data from the CPPS (RQ3). Therefore, we generated a dataset of observation of the behavior of the module *Heat.* As network architecture, we chose a fully connected Multilayer Perceptron with ReLU activations.

We applied our new planning algorithm RAINER with the state-of-the-art SMT-solver Z3 [22] to our twelve CPPS planning problems. For each problem, we evaluated RAINER on a domain describing the physical dependencies as mathematical formulas $RAINER_{math}$, and as NN $RAINER_{NN}$.

$RAINER_{math}$ and $RAINER_{NN}$ were able to find plans for all planning problems in the scenarios s_1 and s_2. Additionally, to the correct sequence of production steps, the algorithms were able to determine the correct parameter settings for all CPPS planning problems. The determined sequence and parameters are valid in the sense that the plan can be executed in the simulation and the goal product is produced from the raw materials. Furthermore, the plans are optimal in terms of the required production steps; there is no solution that leads from the raw materials to the goal product with fewer production steps. For all planning problems in the scenarios s_3 and s_4 $RAINER_{math}$ and $RAINER_{NN}$ did not find any valid plan. The results of our evaluation are summarized in Tab. 1.

Table 1. The table summarizes the results of the algorithm, using mathematical formulas ($RAINER_{math}$) and a NN ($RAINER_{NN}$) describing the physical dependencies for the twelve planning problems. *mat* denotes the material type of scenario. (✓) denotes that the algorithm found a valid or optimal plan, (x) denotes that the algorithm could not find a valid or optimal plan, (-) denotes that the algorithm could not find a plan.

planning	$RAINER_{math}$		$RAINER_{NN}$	
problem	valid plan	optimal plan	valid plan	optimal plan
s_1 mat 1	✓	✓	✓	✓
s_1 mat 2	✓	✓	✓	✓
s_1 mat 3	✓	✓	✓	✓
s_2 mat 1	✓	✓	✓	✓
s_2 mat 2	✓	✓	✓	✓
s_2 mat 3	✓	✓	✓	✓
s_3, s_4	-	-	-	-

6 Discussion

We tested our novel proposed planning approach in various CPPS planning problems from the manufacturing domain. The empirical evaluation of our novel proposed planning approach shows that our planning algorithm can find a plan as long as the CPPS can produce the goal product. Furthermore, the algorithm can determine production parameters in accordance with the description of the underlying dependencies or the integrated ML model. However, due to the iterative structure of our algorithm and its stopping criteria for finding *one* satisfiable model for the formula F, our presented algorithm does only guarantee for finding the solution with the fewest production steps.

Further, more strenuous evaluation of our algorithm needs to be performed, by employing it on more complex CPPS and product setups, and analyzing its theoretical boundaries. Additional evaluations on real world CPPS planning problems should demonstrate our algorithms capabilities for application in industry.

So far, we demonstrated our algorithm's capability to translate a simple NN into SMT clauses, enabling their integration into a satisfiability problem in SMT. To integrate other, more complex operations within ML models, such as convolutions, gates, or sampling operations, the procedure *translateSMT* has to be extended. Based on the presented approach, it is possible to integrate any ML model into the satisfiability problem, as long as the underlying dependencies between the model's input and output can be described using mathematical expressions that are solvable by the employed SMT-solver. The capabilities of the employed SMT-solver also limit the description of the physical dependencies within the CPPS as mathematical formulas.

The integration of ML models significantly increases the solving time of our novel planning algorithm. Following [6], a solving strategy that creates a set of individual satisfiability problems could boost our algorithm's performance. However, solving a satisfiability problem including the mathematical dependencies of an ML model remains a challenging task for an SMT-solver and the evaluation of our approach underlines the lack of an efficient solving strategy for integrated ML models.

7 Conclusion

In this paper, we present a novel generic AI planning approach for CPPS planning problems that allows for the integration of ML models into a symbolic SMT-based planning approach. Our proposed approach builds on a feature-vector-based state-space representation of a CPPS planning problem, allowing for both expressing a planning problem and training an ML model (RQ1). The new planning algorithm RAINER translates this representation, including ML models, into a satisfiability problem in SMT which is then solved by a state-of-the-art SMT-Solver (RQ2, RQ3).

We evaluated our novel approach on twelve CPPS planning problems from the manufacturing domain. RAINER offers various advantages compared to other, existing planning approaches:

- Its generality and ability to integrate ML models reduce the modelling effort of typical symbolic planning approaches.
- It does not rely on such comprehensive datasets as pure sub-symbolic approaches for CPPS planning problems.
- It can handle complex dependencies within CPPS' and additionally determine the correct parametrization of all process steps of the plan.

Future work will evaluate the presented approach on other, more complex real-world CPPS planning problems to demonstrate its ability to handle complexity in CPPS. However, the evaluation with FliPSi already shows that the integration of ML models significantly increases the solution time of our novel planning algorithm. Therefore, future research will also focus on improving the ability of the SMT solver to effectively solve ML models embedded in the satisfiability problem.

Acknowledgements. This research as part of the projects EKI and LaiLa is funded by dtec.bw - Digitalization and Technology Research Center of the Bundeswehr which we gratefully acknowledge. dtec.bw is funded by the European Union - NextGenerationEU.

References

1. Baheti, R., Gill, H.: Cyber-physical systems. Impact control technol **12**(1), 161–166 (2011)
2. Balzereit, K., Niggemann, O.: Gradient-based reconfiguration of cyber-physical production systems. In: 2021 4th IEEE International Conference on Industrial Cyber-Physical Systems (ICPS), pp. 125–131 (2021)

3. Bampoula, X., Siaterlis, G., Nikolakis, N., Alexopoulos, K.: A deep learning model for predictive maintenance in cyber-physical production systems using LSTM autoencoders. Sensors **21**(3), 972 (2021)
4. Bit-Monnot, Arthur, Leofante, Francesco, Pulina, Luca, Tacchella, Armando: SMT-based Planning for Robots in Smart Factories. In: Wotawa, Franz, Friedrich, Gerhard, Pill, Ingo, Koitz-Hristov, Roxane, Ali, Moonis (eds.) IEA/AIE 2019. LNCS (LNAI), vol. 11606, pp. 674–686. Springer, Cham (2019). https://doi.org/10.1007/978-3-030-22999-3_58
5. Bofill, M., Espasa, J., Villaret, M.: The rantanplan planner: system description. Knowl. Eng. Rev. **31**(5), 452–464 (2016)
6. Cashmore, M., Fox, M., Long, D., Magazzeni, D.: A compilation of the full PDDL+ language into SMT. In: Workshops at the Thirtieth AAAI Conference on Artificial Intelligence (2016)
7. Clarke, E.M., Henzinger, T.A., Veith, H., Bloem, R., et al.: Handbook of model checking, vol. 10. Springer (2018)
8. Diedrich, A., Maier, A., Niggemann, O.: Model-based diagnosis of hybrid systems using satisfiability modulo theory. In: Proceedings of the AAAI Conference on Artificial Intelligence. vol. 33, pp. 1452–1459 (2019)
9. Ghallab, M., et al.: PDDL-the planning domain definition language (1998)
10. Grand, M., Pellier, D., Fiorino, H.: TempAMLSI: temporal action model learning based on STRIPS translation. Proc. Int. Conf. Autom Planning Sched. **32**, 597–605 (2022)
11. Grand, M., Pellier, D., Fiorino, H.: Tempamlsi: Temporal action model learning based on strips translation. In: Proceedings of the International Conference on Automated Planning and Scheduling. vol. 32, pp. 597–605 (2022)
12. Hoffmann, J., Gomes, C.P., Selman, B., Kautz, H.A.: Sat encodings of state-space reachability problems in numeric domains. In: IJCAI, pp. 1918–1923 (2007)
13. Jarvenpaa, E., Siltala, N., Lanz, M.: Formal resource and capability descriptions supporting rapid reconfiguration of assembly systems. In: 2016 IEEE Int. Symp. Assembly Manuf. (ISAM). IEEE (Aug 2016)
14. Kagermann, H., Helbig, J., Hellinger, A., Wahlster, W.: Recommendations for implementing the strategic initiative INDUSTRIE 4.0: Securing the future of German manufacturing industry; final report of the Industrie 4.0 Working Group. Forschungsunion (2013)
15. Kautz, H., Selman, B.: Planning as Satisfiability. In: Proceedings of the 10th European Conference on Artificial Intelligence (ECAI 92) (1992)
16. Köcher, A., et al.: A research agenda for ai planning in the field of flexible production systems. In: 2022 IEEE 5th International Conference on Industrial Cyber-Physical Systems (ICPS), pp. 1–8 (2022)
17. Krantz, M., et al.: FliPSi: Generating data for the training of machine learning algorithms for CPPS. In: Annual Conference of the PHM Society. vol. 14 (2022)
18. Lee, J., Noh, S.D., Kim, H.J., Kang, Y.S.: Implementation of cyber-physical production systems for quality prediction and operation control in metal casting. Sensors **18**(5), 1428 (2018)
19. Li, P., Niggemann, O.: Non-convex hull based anomaly detection in CPPS. Eng. Appl. Artif. Intell. **87**, 103301 (2020)
20. Monostori, L.: Cyber-physical Production Systems: Roots. Expect. R&D Challenges. Procedia CIRP **17**, 9–13 (2014)
21. Mordoch, A., Juba, B., Stern, R.: Learning safe numeric action models. In: Proceedings of the AAAI Conference on Artificial Intelligence. vol. 37, pp. 12079–12086 (2023)

22. de Moura, Leonardo, Bjørner, Nikolaj: Z3: An Efficient SMT Solver. In: Ramakrishnan, C.. R.., Rehof, Jakob (eds.) TACAS 2008. LNCS, vol. 4963, pp. 337–340. Springer, Heidelberg (2008). https://doi.org/10.1007/978-3-540-78800-3_24
23. Murphy, K.P.: Probabilistic machine learning: an introduction. MIT press (2022)
24. Niggemann, O., Frey, C.: Data-driven anomaly detection in cyber-physical production systems. at - Automatisierungstechnik 63(10), 821–832 (2015)
25. Russell, S.J., Norvig, P.: Artificial intelligence: A modern approach. Pearson Series in Artificial Intelligence, Pearson, Hoboken, fourth edition EDN. (2021)
26. Scala, E., Ramirez, M., Haslum, P., Thiébaux, S.: Numeric planning with disjunctive global constraints via SMT. In: Twenty-Sixth International Conference on Automated Planning and Scheduling (2016)
27. Strobel, Volker, Kirsch, Alexandra: MyPDDL: Tools for Efficiently Creating PDDL Domains and Problems. In: Vallati, Mauro, Kitchin, Diane (eds.) Knowledge Engineering Tools and Techniques for AI Planning, pp. 67–90. Springer, Cham (2020). https://doi.org/10.1007/978-3-030-38561-3_4

Learning Process Steps as Dynamical Systems for a Sub-Symbolic Approach of Process Planning in Cyber-Physical Production Systems

Jonas Ehrhardt(✉), René Heesch, and Oliver Niggemann

Helmut-Schmidt-University, Hamburg, Germany
{jonas.ehrhardt,rene.heesch,oliver.niggemann}@hsu-hh.de

Abstract. Approaches in AI planning for Cyber-Physical Production Systems (CPPS) are mainly symbolic and depend on comprehensive formalizations of system domains and planning problems. Handcrafting such formalizations requires detailed knowledge of the formalization language, of the CPPS, and is overall considered difficult, tedious, and error-prone. Within this paper, we suggest a sub-symbolic approach for solving planning problems in CPPS. Our approach relies on neural networks that learn the dynamical behavior of individual process steps from global time-series observations of the CPPS and are embedded in a superordinate network architecture. In this context, we present the **p**rocess st**ep** **repr**esentation network architecture (*peppr*), a novel neural network architecture, which can learn the behavior of individual or multiple dynamical systems from global time-series observations. We evaluate *peppr* on real datasets from physical and biochemical CPPS, as well as artificial datasets from electrical and mathematical domains. Our model outperforms baseline models like multilayer perceptrons and variational autoencoders and can be considered as a first step towards a sub-symbolic approach for planning in CPPS.

Keywords: Planning · Machine Learning · Cyber-Physical Production Systems

1 Introduction

Modern production systems face the challenges of dealing with a growing variability of product variants, smaller batch sizes, and volatile resource availability [9,16]. Consequently, manufacturing companies must be able to rapidly adjust their production systems, in order to stay competitive [16]. One way to achieve this, is by employing Cyber-Physical Production Systems (CPPS) [21]. CPPS are systems of computational entities, which are strongly interconnected to the physical world [20]. By employing sensors, actuators, and data processing services, they allow for a rapid adjustment and reconfiguration of production processes [17,20]. Though, due to their high complexity, methods from Artificial Intelligence (AI) are necessary for their monitoring and control [20].

S. Nowaczyk et al. (Eds.): ECAI 2023 Workshops, CCIS 1948, pp. 332–345, 2024.
https://doi.org/10.1007/978-3-031-50485-3_34

Research in Machine Learning (ML) in the field of CPPS is vibrant, but mainly focussing on the operational level of CPPS, comprising topics like anomaly detection, diagnosis, and reconfiguration [4,6,14]. However, only by including production planning in ML research, the full potential of CPPS can be leveraged [17].

So far, most AI planning approaches for CPPS are symbolic; solvers solve planning problems that are formulated in comprehensive domain descriptions [11] with search algorithms, heuristics, or translating them into satisfiability problems [17]. Creating those domain descriptions requires manually modeling all potential product states, process steps, and their relationships, which potentiates in large CPPS. Additionally, substantial knowledge of the used formal language, as well as the CPPS is necessary, making the compilation of domain and problem descriptions difficult, tedious, and error-prone [13]. Sub-symbolic approaches instead allow for avoiding manual modeling of domains and problems. By utilizing the data that is already available and continuously recorded in CPPS, more accurate and complex models of the real world can be learned, creating projections of real-world product or machine states only from time-series data. Therefore, we propose a novel, sub-symbolic approach for planning in CPPS, which is based on time-series observations (cf. Fig. 1).

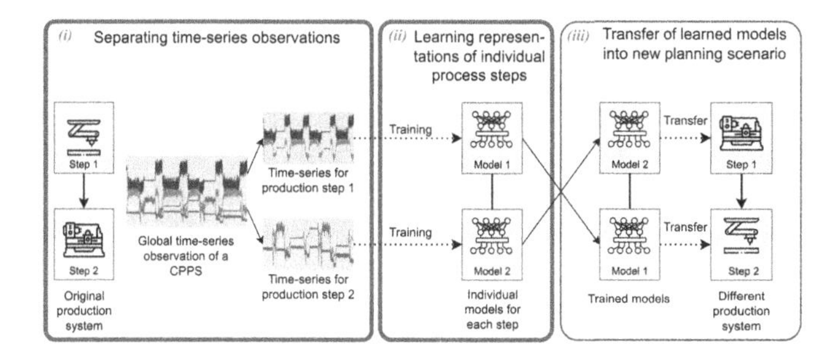

Fig. 1. Our novel sub-symbolic approach for production planning in CPPS is based on three steps: *(i)* separating global time-series observations from the CPPS into individual process steps, *(ii)* learning representations of the individual process steps in neural networks, *(iii)* using the learned representations to create plans of new production processes. Within this paper, we focus on the first two steps (highlighted in orange). (Color figure online)

The approach comprises three steps: In the first step *(i)*, global time-series observations from a production process within a CPPS are separated into individual process steps: Datasets from CPPS usually consist of high numbers of continuous and discrete sensor time-series [24]. Separating and assigning this data to individual process steps allows for an examination of the in-process step dependencies. In the next step *(ii)*, neural networks (NN) learn representations of the individual process steps from the separated time-series observations: Process steps can be modeled as dynamical systems that transform input products to output products, under consideration of parameters, environmental factors, and faults [8]. Representations of these dynamical systems can be approximated by NNs and reused for planning. In the last step *(iii)*, the trained NNs are used in a new configuration to model a new production process: As the trained NNs are generalizable representations of process steps, they can be re-applied in new contexts. By operating the NNs normally – in forward direction – the output of the process steps can be inferred. In this case, the NNs can be used for determining the necessary process steps and their parametrization to reach a given goal state from a given initial state. By operating the NNs inversely, either process step parametrizations or input states can be inferred. In this case, the NNs can be used for determining the necessary process steps and their parametrizations to reach a given initial state from a given goal state or to calculate the optimal parametrization of the process steps to reach the goal state.

Within this paper, we focus on the first two steps of our proposed approach: *(i)* separating and assigning the time-series observation to individual process steps, and *(ii)* learning the dynamical systems that represent the individual process steps. These steps require a sub-symbolic architecture to be able to learn representations of dynamical systems from time-series observations and solve them inversely, as well as learn multiple dynamical systems from one global time-series observation. We formulate the following research questions (RQ):

RQ1: Can neural networks learn the behavior of a dynamical system, based on time-series observations?

RQ2: Is there a neural network architecture that supports learning the behavior of dynamical systems from time-series observations and allows for forward and inverse operation?

RQ3: Is there a neural network architecture that can be trained on a global time-series observation, and separate it in order to learn the behavior of its individual subsystems?

As a result, we introduce the **p**roc**e**ss ste**p** re**pr**esentation network architecture (*peppr*). *Peppr* can learn the behavior of multiple dynamical systems from global time-series observations. It can be operated and trained forward and inverse, making it applicable to our approach to CPPS planning problems. We evaluate *peppr* on CPPS datasets from physical [8], biochemical [12] domains, as well as artificial datasets from electrical and mathematical domains.

2 Related Work

There are three directions in AI planning: *(i)* symbolic planning approaches *(ii)* neurosymbolic planning approaches, and *(iii)* sub-symbolic planning approaches.

Symbolic Planning Approaches use formal logic and heuristics to find a plan. They rely on detailed formal domain and problem descriptions, e.g., in Planning Domain Definition Language (PDDL) [11,13]. Hoffmann et al. [15] introduced the FF planning system, a heuristic-search planning approach. In the FF planning system, the search in the state-space is guided by a heuristic, which is derived from the PDDL problem description. Other symbolic planning approaches encode planning problems as satisfiability problems [17]. While the encoding into propositional logic is straight forward for classical planning problems, real-world planning problems like CPPS planning problems require additional extensions, such as integer or real number theories [5]. Using Satisfiability Modulo Theory for this task, like in [7], is hence considered a well-suited approach [17]. However, creating and maintaining the formal domain and problem descriptions remains tedious, difficult, and error-prone [13].

Neurosymbolic Planning Approaches leverage on ML to substitute intricately parts of the symbolic modeling and solving process. Asai and Muise [3] introduce a neurosymbolic architecture that is trained end-to-end to learn symbolic domains from image data. They propose an Autoencoder architecture which jointly learns state space representations and action models that are shaped in formalized semantics, thereby bypassing laborious manual modelling [3]. The learned models can be solved by standard heuristic search solvers [3]. Amado et al. [1] similarly combine a statistical predictive model to infer next states with symbolic heuristics in a neurosymbolic approach for planning. Their approach allows to counter the most common problems in planning: missing or noisy observations.

Sub-symbolic Planning Approaches rely on system observations, to learn underlying dynamics and reasoning. Research on sub-symbolic planning focuses on learning individual action models, planning heuristics, or creating solutions for planning problems in complete domains. Milani et al. [19] propose to learn action transitions with simple NNs. Their approach shows good results for simple state transitions and sparse feature vectors. However, they only evaluate their approach on simple symbolic domains. Ferber et al. [10] propose to learn planning heuristics with NNs. They show that NNs can approximate planning heuristics and can compete with existing solvers. Though, their learned heuristics remain problem specific and cannot be generalized over the complete domain. Toyer et al. [26] introduce Action Schema Networks, a NN architecture that is able to learn a planning domain and solve different planning problems within it. Their approach shows good results on simple PDDL planning domains, though is limited by the network architecture for a maximum number of actions.

Though there are approaches in symbolic, neurosymbolic and sub-symbolic planning, they remain restricted to artificial domains, excluding the complexity of real world domains, like CPPS.

3 Problem Formalization

A CPPS planning problem describes the task of finding a sequence of process steps and their parametrization within a CPPS to transform given input materials into a defined output product. In other words, it is a stepwise transformation of an initial product state, until it reaches a goal state within the capabilities of a CPPS. Sub-symbolic planning approaches do not consider real physical products or their semantic descriptions. Instead, they use time-series observations to construct a representation of the products and the CPPS and use them for solving the planning problem.

Definition 1. *Time-series observations χ are continuously recorded in CPPS. They consist of pointwise observations of all individual sensors $\boldsymbol{x}_i$ that form a chronologically ordered sequence of length n. Together they form a set of sufficiently observable CPPS observations S.*

$$\chi = (\mathbf{x}_0, ..., \mathbf{x}_{n-1}), \chi \in S \tag{1}$$

Definition 2. *π_l is defined as the state of the real product within the CPPS. All states of π form the set $\Pi \in \mathbb{R}^r$. A production process transforms a product state $\pi_l \in \mathcal{P}(\Pi)$ into a subsequent product state $\pi_{l+1} \in \mathcal{P}(\Pi)$, where $l \in \mathbb{N}$ is the state of the product after its last transformation.*

As a sub-symbolic approach cannot directly work on the real product states π_l, it has to derive the product states from the time-series observations $\mathbf{x}_l$, bridging the gap from the real world to its representation in the time-series.

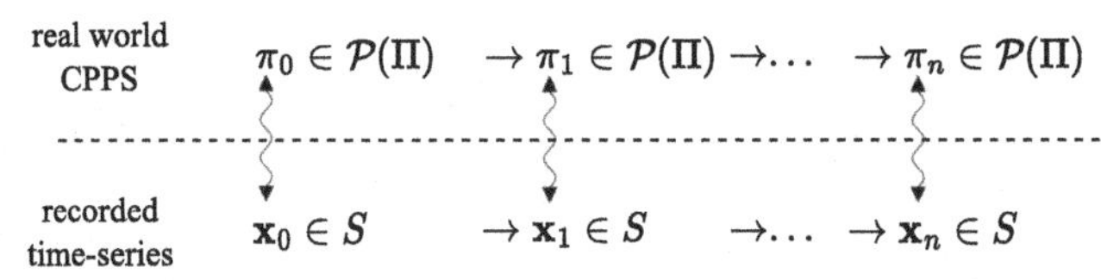

Definition 3. *m_l is defined as a process step that achieves all transformations of π within the CPPS. The set of all process steps is defined as M. m_l is defined as a dynamical system that transforms a given input product $\pi_{in,l} \in \Pi$ and a process step parameter set $\varphi_l \in \Phi$, where $\Phi \in \mathbb{R}^s$ is the space of all process parameters, into an output product $\pi_{out,l} \in \Pi$:*

$$m_l : \pi_{in,l} \times \varphi_l \rightarrow \pi_{out,l}, m_l \in M \tag{2}$$

NNs $\nu_{\theta,l}$ can approximate the underlying dynamical systems of the transformation processes. We define $\nu_{\theta,l}$ as a function that transform $s_{in,l}$, φ_l into $s_{out,l}$, where $s_{in,l}$, φ_l and $s_{out,l}$ are part of $\mathbf{x}_l$, and θ are learnable weights of the NN:

$$\nu_{\theta,l} : s_{in,l} \times \varphi_l \rightarrow s_{out,l} \tag{3}$$

Definition 4. *By training a NN ν_l with the corresponding time-series χ_l, we can approximate m_l:*

$$\nu_l \otimes m_l \tag{4}$$

Where $\otimes$ denotes a sufficient approximation of the real world process step with a trained NN.

Definition 5. *A real-world CPPS planning problem can be formulated as* P_m *and a sub-symbolic planning problem as* P_ν*, respectively:*

$$P_m = \langle \pi_0, \pi_G, M, \Phi \rangle \approxeq P_\nu = \langle I, G, N, \Phi \rangle \tag{5}$$

Where I *denotes the initial product state,* G *denotes the goal product state,* N *the set of all* $\nu \approxeq m$ *and* Φ *the parameter space.*

Definition 6. *A plan* Γ *is the solution to a planning problem, and is defined as a sequence of process steps and their parametrizations.* Γ_m *denotes a plan with real process steps,* Γ_ν *denotes a plan with NNs as substitutes:*

$$\Gamma_m = (m_0, ..., m_k) \approxeq \Gamma_\nu = (\nu_0, ..., \nu_k), k \in \mathbb{N} \tag{6}$$

Reaching G with Γ can be achieved by nesting all process steps ν. Φ and I can be calculated by computing the inverse G^{-1}

$$G = \nu_k(...(\nu_0(I, \varphi_0), ...)\varphi_k) \tag{7}$$

4 Solution

To approach CPPS planning problems, we introduce a novel sub-symbolic approach consisting of three steps (cf. Fig. 1). We subsequently present and evaluate *peppr*, a NN architecture for solving the first two steps.

4.1 A Sub-Symbolic Planning Approach for Planning in CPPS

In the first step of our novel sub-symbolic planning approach *(i)*, the global time-series observation of the CPPS χ is separated into subsets $\chi_{m,l} \subseteq \chi$ (cf. Fig. 1). $\chi_{m,l}$ contain all $s_{in,l}, s_{out,l}$, and φ_l and hence the underlying dynamical system, of the process step m_l within the CPPS. In step *(ii)*, we use $\chi_{m,l}$ to learn a representation of the underlying dynamical system of m_l with a NN ν_l (cf. Fig. 2). When trained, ν_l can infer $s_{out,l}$ based on $s_{in,l}$ and φ_l, which can be used to solve a planning problem from I to G. By inversely operating ν_l as ν_l^{-1}, $s_{in,l}$ and φ_l can be inferred with $s_{out,l}$. This mode can be used for inverse planning from G to I, and optimizing φ_l (cf. Fig. 2). In step *(iii)*, the trained NNs from N are re-applied in a superordinate network architecture Ξ. A plan Γ for a given planning problem P_ν can be calculated as an energy optimal function of Ξ (cf. Fig. 2). The optimal plan Γ_ν can be derived from the weights of Ξ.

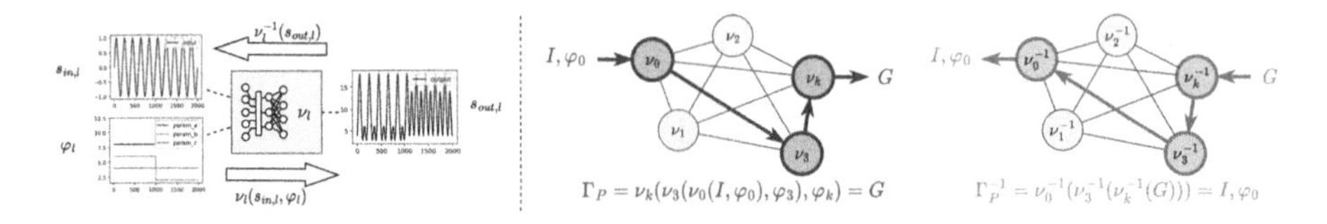

Fig. 2. *Left:* In step *(ii)* of our sub-symbolic planning approach, individual NNs ν_l are trained on $\chi_{m,l}$ to learn representations of the individual process steps m_l. *Right:* In step *(iii)* of our sub-symbolic planning approach, the trained individual NNs ν_l are applied in a superordinate network structure Ξ.

4.2 Learning Process Steps as Dynamical Systems

To solve steps *(i)* and *(ii)* of our novel sub-symbolic planning approach, we introduce *peppr*[1]. *Peppr* is a novel NN architecture, which can split global time-series observations into individual process steps and subsequently learn their representations.

We derived the *peppr* architecture based on the problem formalization in Sect. 3 and our research questions, which all correspond to the three steps of our novel sub-symbolic planning approach. We hence focused on its ability to learn dynamical systems *RQ1* and step *(ii)*, being inversely operable *RQ2* and step *(iii)*, and its ability to learn multiple individual process steps from one global observation *RQ3* and step *(i)*.

Learning Dynamical Systems from Time-Series Observations: As stated in the problem formalization (cf. Sect. 3), we define process steps m_l in CPPS planning problems as dynamical systems that transform a process input $s_{in,l}$ and process parameters φ_l into a process output $s_{out,l}$. We define our NN architecture to approximate m_l as the function $\nu_{\theta,l}(s_{in,l}, \varphi_l) = s_{out,l}$ with $s_{in,l}, \varphi_l, s_{out,l} \in \chi_{m,l}$. To enable ν_l to represent even complex dynamical systems, we define it as deep architecture with nine layers. We counter the problem of vanishing or exploding gradients in deep architectures, by employing self-normalizing network properties, such as normally distributed weight initialization and SELU activations [18].

We reduce the number of parameters in our network architecture, by applying causal convolutions [25] before and after the self-normalizing core. The encoder $\nu_{\varepsilon,l}$ transforms the high-dimensional time-series $s_{in,l}, \varphi_l$ into the lower dimensional representations $\bar{s}_{in,l}, \bar{\varphi}_l$, with the learnable encoder-network-parameters ε, so that $\nu_{\varepsilon,l}(s_{in,l}, \varphi_l) = \langle \bar{s}_{in,l}, \bar{\varphi}_l \rangle$. We decode the representations with a causal convolutional decoder $\nu_{\delta,l}$, respectively.

For learning the process step as a dynamical system, we embed $\nu_{\theta,l}$ between $\nu_{\varepsilon,l}$ and $\nu_{\delta,l}$:

$$\nu_l(s_{in,l}, \varphi_l) = \nu_{\delta,l}(\nu_{\theta,l}(\nu_{\varepsilon,l}(s_{in,l}, \varphi_l))) = s_{out,l} \tag{8}$$

[1] https://github.com/j-ehrhardt/peppr.

Inverse Operation: To enable the inverse operation of our network, we adapt the network architecture from Eq. (8). To inversely operate the causal convolutional blocks, we save intermediate representations after each convolutional layer during forward operation. Those representations are added to the feature maps during the inverse operation, adapting [27]. We adapt the core network ν_θ as an invertible NN, following the approach of [2], by splitting the output of the core network's forward mapping into y and z, where $y = s_{out,l}$ and z is a normally distributed latent vector $z \sim \mathcal{N}(0, \sigma)$. z contains all necessary information, to solve the otherwise ill-posed problem [2] of inferring $\langle \bar{s}_{in,l}, \bar{\varphi}_l \rangle$ through an inverse operation of ν_l'. The forward pass through $\nu_{\theta,l}'$ can hence be formulated as:

$$\nu_{theta,l}'(s_{in,l}, \varphi_l) = \langle \nu_{\theta,l,y}(s_{in}, \varphi_l), \nu_{\theta,l,z}(s_{in}, \varphi_l) \rangle = \langle y_l, z_l \rangle \tag{9}$$

The inverse pass through ν_l' can hence be formulated as the inverse ν_{l-1}':

$$\nu_{l-1}'(s_{out,l}) = \nu_{\varepsilon,l}^{-1}(\nu_{\theta,l,y}^{-1}(\nu_{\delta,l}^{-1}(s_{out,l})), \nu_{\theta,l,z}^{-1}) = \langle s_{in,l}, \varphi_l \rangle \tag{10}$$

For training our network architecture, we extended the forward pass by an additional inverse forward pass and weight adaption through all components of the network. We counter the levelling of weight adaptions through contrary optimization objectives, by introducing two skip layers at the beginning and end of the core network ν_θ. The skip layers are not included in the gradient tree during the backpropagation in forward, respectively inverse forward pass operation.

We penalize deviations of $\nu_l(s_{in,l}, \varphi_l)$, with a forward loss, by calculating the L2 norm $\mathcal{L}_y(\bar{s}_{out,l}, \nu_l(\bar{s}_{in,l}, \bar{\varphi}_l))$. Deviations of $\nu_l^{-1}(s_{out})$ are penalized with the inverse loss $\mathcal{L}_x(\langle \bar{s}_{in,l}, \bar{\varphi}_l \rangle, \nu_l^{-1}(\bar{s}_{out,l}))$, also by calculating the L2-norm. Additionally, we penalize the deviations of z from a normal distribution with $\mathcal{L}_z(z, \mathcal{N})$, by using Kullback-Leibler divergence. We introduce the weights $\lambda_x, \lambda_y, \lambda_z \in \mathbb{R}$ for regulating the loss functions' impact on the gradient, leading to the overall loss function:

$$\mathcal{L} = \lambda_x \mathcal{L}_x + \lambda_y \mathcal{L}_y + \lambda_z \mathcal{L}_z \tag{11}$$

Learning Multiple Dynamical Systems from a Single Global Observation: Following the approaches of [22,23], we encode the input sequences through a joint convolutional encoder and map the representation to multiple initializations of ν_θ (cf. Fig. 3). The number of initializations is defined by the number of process steps in the dataset. On the inverse pass, we average the network outputs to pass them back into the convolutional encoder ν_ε.

$$\nu(s_{in}, \varphi) = \langle \nu_{\delta,1}(\nu_{\theta,1}(\nu_\varepsilon(s_{in}, \varphi, \varepsilon), \theta_1), \delta_1), ..., \nu_{\delta,k}(\nu_{\theta,k}(\nu_\varepsilon(s_{in}, \varphi, \varepsilon), \theta_k), \delta_k) \rangle \tag{12}$$

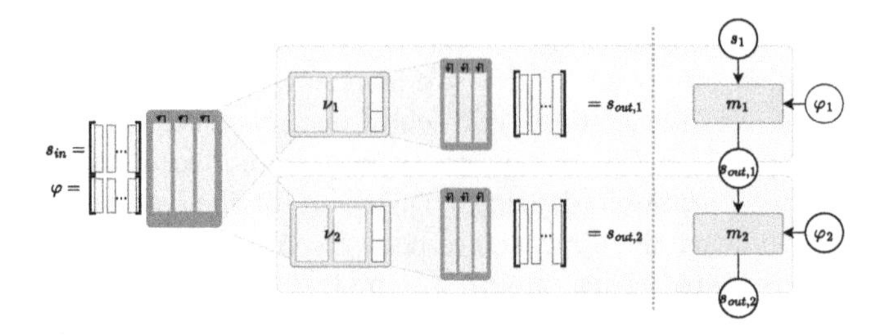

Fig. 3. Our approach toward learning multiple process steps from a global time-series observation of a CPPS. s_{in} and φ_j are encoded by a single encoder (blue). The encoded representation of the time-series observations is passed into separate instances of the self-normalized invertible cores ν_l (green) and decoded in separate causal convolutional decoders (blue). They hence form a representation of the corresponding process steps m_l in the CPPS. (Color figure online)

5 Results

We tested our proposed NN architecture empirically and theoretically. As an empirical evaluation, we applied our network architecture on datasets from a Cyber-Physical Process Plant, and a Cyber-Physical Bioreactor. As a theoretical evaluation, we tested the inference performance of our network architecture for decreasing information density within the time-series. Therefore, we employed it on two artificially generated datasets from an electronic, and a mathematical domain. All datasets were split into training (0.5), validation (0.25), and test (0.25) datasets. We benchmarked our approach against a multilayer perceptron (mlp) and a variational autoencoder (vae) using LeakyReLU activations, as baselines. All models have the same receptive field and number of hidden layers.

5.1 Empirical Results

Our empirical evaluation shows that our proposed network architecture can learn a process step as dynamical system from CPPS data (*RQ1*). The network architecture further allows for inverse operation (*RQ2*), and can learn multiple subsystems from one global observation (*RQ3*). While surprisingly the mlp performs best for learning single process steps, for learning multiple process steps, *peppr* outruns both baselines by far.

We tested our network architecture on datasets from two CPPS. Our first evaluation dataset – *physical* – comprises time-series observations from an experimental modular Cyber-Physical Process Plant [8]. Our second evaluation dataset – *biochemical* – comprises time-series observations from the batch-wise fermentation of penicillin in a Cyber-Physical Bioreactor [12].

We tested our network architecture on two criteria: *(i)* Learning individual dynamical systems from time-series observations of individual process steps (cf. *RQ 1* and *RQ 2*), and *(ii)* learning individual dynamical sub-systems from one global time-series observation of a CPPS (cf. *RQ 3*). For evaluating the model performance, we used the root mean squared error (RMSE) metric, as it is a suitable indicator for a model's ability to infer the correct behavior of a dynamical system. We ran all experiments on five different seeds and calculated the mean of their results.

Table 1 shows the results for inferring $\langle s_{in}, \varphi \rangle$, and s_{out}. For learning single process steps, the mlp and vae baseline throughout outperform our network architecture. However, the distance of *peppr* to the baseline is often only differentiable by the second or third decimal. Though, for learning multiple process steps from one observation, *peppr* outperforms the baselines by far. For inverse inference, *peppr* shows especially superior results. Good performance in learning multiple process steps is important, as CPPS usually consist of a variety of different process steps, showing dependencies and interdependencies.

5.2 Theoretical Results

As a theoretical evaluation, we tested the inference performance of our network architecture for increasing time-series complexity in two dimensions: increasing complexity of the observed dynamical systems and decreasing information density. We employed our model on two different datasets[2] from an electronic *ode*, and a mathematical *polynom* domain, containing three sub-datasets with increasingly complex observed systems, each. The *ode* dataset comprises the response behavior of a PT1 (*ds1*), a PT2 (*ds2*), and a serial coupling of a PT1 and PT2 element (*ds3*) (cf. Fig. 4 (left)), each excited by a rectangular function. The *polynom* dataset comprises three sub-datasets that describe a linear (*ds1*),

Table 1. This table summarizes the performance of our model in learning a single or multiple process steps from one global observation of a CPPS. As a performance measure, we calculated the RMSE for separate predictions of $\langle s_{in}, \varphi \rangle$, as well as s_{out}. We benchmarked our model (*peppr*) against a deep multilayer perceptron (mlp) and a variational autoencoder (vae), with causal convolutional encoders and decoders. Best results are highlighted in bold format.

scenario	dataset	mlp		vae		*peppr*	
		$\langle s_{in}, \varphi \rangle$	s_{out}	$\langle s_{in}, \varphi \rangle$	s_{out}	$\langle s_{in}, \varphi \rangle$	s_{out}
learning single steps	physical ds1	**0.51516**	**0.10064**	0.52282	0.11085	0.51652	0.11752
	physical ds2	**0.67417**	0.30789	0.67519	**0.29122**	0.67894	0.50019
	physical ds3	**1.33604**	0.49106	1.37410	**0.46205**	1.37386	0.83144
	physical ds4	0.33652	**0.12630**	**0.33624**	0.13252	0.33841	0.15207
	biochem ds1	**0.11486**	**0.14212**	0.52527	0.62893	0.13231	0.18737
	biochem ds2	**0.21476**	**0.20786**	0.52919	0.24166	0.25054	0.29749
learning multiple steps	physical ds5	0.45199	0.66620	0.45471	0.46301	**0.33264**	**0.27877**
	physical ds6	0.38904	0.32882	0.40758	0.21610	**0.38512**	**0.15509**
	physical ds7	**0.29343**	0.53858	0.29413	0.42781	0.29884	**0.24115**

[2] https://github.com/j-ehrhardt/ode-ml-datasets.

quadratic (*ds2*), and cubic (*ds3*) polynomial function, each excited by a sine function.

To test our architecture's performance in learning dynamical systems on datasets with decreasing information density, we downsampled the datasets in eight steps. For every n^{th} downsampling step, we included only every n^{th} value. This allowed us to evaluate the architecture with constant model parameters on decreasing information density.

Figure 4 (right) shows the cumulated inference error of our models when learning individual and multiple models for decreasing information density of the dataset. For learning individual process steps, the models show similarly worse performance, when the information density decreases. For learning multiple process steps, *peppr* shows superior results, even with low information density, except for the lowest information density sampling.

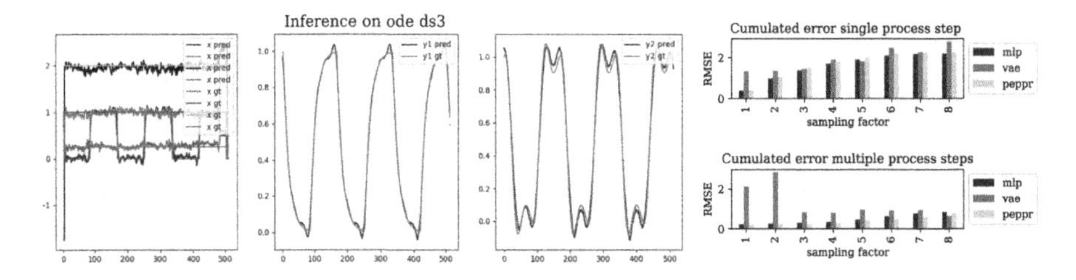

Fig. 4. *Left:* An inference step of *peppr* on the ode ds3 dataset, showing the results of two parallelly trained networks that approximate the behavior of a PT1 and PT2 element. *Right:* The cumulated inference errors of our models for decreasing information density by downsampling of the original datasets.

6 Discussion

In the following, we discuss our novel sub-symbolic approach for planning and our proposed *peppr* architecture for learning process steps from global observations of CPPS.

A Novel Sub-Symbolic Approach for Planning Problems in CPPS: In Sect. 3, we introduced a novel sub-symbolic approach for planning problems in CPPS. Our approach is based on individual NNs ν_l that learn individual process steps of a CPPS, and which are embedded in a superordinate network structure Ξ for inferring plans.

The main disadvantage of our approach lies in error propagation. If a model does not properly represent the real process step behavior, its error can be propagated through the complete superordinate network structure, and hence skew the results of its outcome, or its parametrization. Incomplete representations can occur due to monotone datasets that show little variance in the behavior of process steps, making it difficult to generalize the process steps' behavior. This pitfall can be overcome by expanding the available datasets with sufficient simulated data or modeling the process steps as Bayesian Neural Networks.

Another disadvantage of a sub-symbolic approach concerns learning preconditions of process steps. In planning problems, preconditions describe the facility of combining products and process steps, i.e., specific tools with specific materials. If represented in the sub-symbolic dataset, those preconditions can be learned and represented by Ξ. Though, this also restricts our approach to the domain it was trained on.

Learning Individual Process Steps from Global CPPS Observations: Within this paper, we evaluated an approach to learn representations of multiple process steps from a global time-series observation of a CPPS and solve them forward and inversely. This entails separating time-series and assigning them to individual process steps of the observed CPPS.

Like any Machine Learning based approach, *peppr* is highly dependent on its training dataset. If there is no representation of the dynamical systems' behavior within the training dataset, the model cannot approximate it and hence cannot contribute to solving the planning problem. This restricts our approach to CPPS that own sufficient recordings to allow for learning their representation.

Our proposed architecture performed best on learning multiple process steps from a global observation, excelling both of our baselines. Though we implemented the architecture as a deterministic model, we achieve different results in the forward and backward inference of our network. The differences in forward and backward inference can be explained by our testing setup, in which we separately evaluated the forward and the inverse pass through the network.

The low performance of our model for learning single process steps, in comparison to learning multiple process steps, can be explained by the additional information that is stored within the latent vector z within each sub-network ν_l. As the additional information allows the architecture to better solve the inverse problem than in a regular mlp or a vae. We additionally suspect the self-normalizing properties to enhance our architecture's performance.

While our approach shows good performance, it lacks explainability due to the use of deep architectures. We employed a deep model architecture for approximating even complex process steps. Future research will include an evaluation of recurrent architectures on the investigated task.

7 Conclusion

Within this paper, we introduced a novel sub-symbolic approach toward solving planning problems in CPPS, consisting of three steps, and *peppr*, a novel NN architecture that can solve its first two steps. We demonstrate that the *peppr* architecture is capable of learning individual process steps as dynamical systems (*RQ1*) and solving them forward and inversely (*RQ2*). Our architecture can separate a global time-series observation into individual sub-systems and learn their representations (*RQ3*). We evaluated the *peppr* architecture on datasets from two CPPS and tested its performance for different data complexities on theoretical datasets from an electrical and a mathematical domain. Our proposed architecture outperformed both baselines in CPPS observations containing multiple steps.

We see the *peppr* architecture as a first step towards a novel sub-symbolic planning approach for planning problems in CPPS. Future research will benchmark the *peppr* architecture with recurrent and Bayesian architectures, and introduce a learning algorithm for the superordinate network structure.

Acknowledgements. This research as part of the projects LaiLa and EKI is funded by dtec.bw - Digitalization and Technology Research Center of the Bundeswehr which we gratefully acknowledge. dtec.bw is funded by the European Union - NextGenerationEU.

References

1. Amado, L., Pereira, R.F., Meneguzzi, F.: Robust neuro-symbolic goal and plan recognition. Proc. AAAI Conf. Artif. Intell. **37**(10), 11937–11944 (2023)
2. Ardizzone, L., Kruse, J., Rother, C., Köthe, U.: Analyzing inverse problems with invertible neural networks. In: International Conference on Learning Representations (2019)
3. Asai, M., Muise, C.: Learning neural-symbolic descriptive planning models via cube-space priors: the voyage home (to strips) (2020)
4. Balzereit, K., Niggemann, O.: Autoconf a new algorithm for reconfiguration of cyber-physical production systems. IEEE Trans. Industr. Inf. **19**(1), 739–749 (2023)
5. Bit-Monnot, A., Leofante, F., Pulina, L., Tacchella, A.: SMT-based planning for robots in smart factories. In: Wotawa, F., Friedrich, G., Pill, I., Koitz-Hristov, R., Ali, M. (eds.) IEA/AIE 2019. LNCS (LNAI), vol. 11606, pp. 674–686. Springer, Cham (2019). https://doi.org/10.1007/978-3-030-22999-3_58
6. Bunte, A., Stein, B., Niggemann, O.: Model-based diagnosis for cyber-physical production systems based on machine learning and residual-based diagnosis models. Proc. AAAI Conf. Artif. Intell. **33**(01), 2727–2735 (2019)
7. Cashmore, M., Fox, M., Long, D., Magazzeni, D.: A compilation of the full PDDL+ language into SMT. In: Workshops at the Thirtieth AAAI Conference on Artificial Intelligence (2016)
8. Ehrhardt, J., Ramonat, M., Heesch, R., Balzereit, K., Diedrich, A., Niggemann, O.: An AI benchmark for diagnosis, reconfiguration & planning. In: 2022 IEEE 27th International Conference on Emerging Technologies and Factory Automation (ETFA), pp. 1–8. IEEE (2022)
9. ElMaraghy, H.A.: Changing and evolving products and systems – models and enablers. In: Springer Series in Advanced Manufacturing, pp. 25–45. Springer, London (2009). https://doi.org/10.1007/978-1-84882-067-8_2
10. Ferber, P., Helmert, M., Hoffmann, J.: Neural network heuristics for classical planning: a study of hyperparameter space. In: European Conference on Artificial Intelligence (2020)
11. Ghallab, M., et al.: PDDL - the planning domain definition language. Technical Report CVC TR-98-003/DCS TR-1165 (1998)

12. Goldrick, S., Duran-Villalobos, C.A., Jankauskas, K., Lovett, D., Farid, S.S., Lennox, B.: Modern day monitoring and control challenges outlined on an industrial-scale benchmark fermentation process. Comput. Chem. Eng. **130**, 106471 (2019)
13. Grand, M., Pellier, D., Fiorino, H.: TempAMLSI: temporal action model learning based on STRIPS translation. In: Proceedings of the International Conference on Automated Planning and Scheduling, vol. 32, 597–605 (2022)
14. Hartung, F., et al.: Deep anomaly detection on tennessee eastman process data (2023)
15. Hoffmann, J., Nebel, B.: The FF planning system: fast plan generation through heuristic search. J. Artif. Intell. Res. **14**, 253–302 (2001)
16. Kagermann, H., Helbig, J., Hellinger, A., Wahlster, W.: Recommendations for implementing the strategic initiative INDUSTRIE 4.0: Securing the future of German manufacturing industry; final report of the Industrie 4.0 Working Group. Forschungsunion (2013)
17. Köcher, A., et al.: A research agenda for AI planning in the field of flexible production systems. In: 2022 IEEE 5th International Conference on Industrial Cyber-Physical Systems (ICPS), pp. 1–8 (2022)
18. Klambauer, G., Unterthiner, T., Mayr, A., Hochreiter, S.: Self-normalizing neural networks. In: Advances in Neural Information Processing Systems, vol. 30. Curran Associates, Inc. (2017)
19. Milani, A., Niyogi, R., Biondi, G.: Neural network based approach for learning planning action models. In: Misra, S., et al. (eds.) ICCSA 2019. LNCS, vol. 11624, pp. 526–537. Springer, Cham (2019). https://doi.org/10.1007/978-3-030-24311-1_38
20. Monostori, L.: Cyber-physical production systems: roots, expectations and r&d challenges. Procedia CIRP **17**, 9–13 (2014)
21. Müller, T., Jazdi, N., Schmidt, J.P., Weyrich, M.: Cyber-physical production systems: enhancement with a self-organized reconfiguration management. Procedia CIRP **99**, 549–554 (2021)
22. Multaheb, S., Bauer, F., Bretschneider, P., Niggemann, O.: Learning physically meaningful representations of energy systems with variational autoencoders. In: 2022 IEEE 27th International Conference on Emerging Technologies and Factory Automation (ETFA), pp. 1–6 (2022)
23. Nautrup, H.P., et al.: Operationally meaningful representations of physical systems in neural networks. Mach. Learn.: Sci. Technol. (2022)
24. Niggemann, O., Frey, C.: Data-driven anomaly detection in cyber-physical production systems. At - Automatisierungstechnik **63**(10), 821–832 (2015)
25. van den Oord, A., et al.: WaveNet: a generative model for raw audio. arXiv preprint arXiv:1609.03499 (2016)
26. Toyer, S., Thiébaux, S., Trevizan, F., Xie, L.: ASNets: deep learning for generalised planning. J. Artif. Intell. Res. **68**, 1–68 (2020)
27. Zhang, Y., Lee, K., Lee, H.: Augmenting supervised neural networks with unsupervised objectives for large-scale image classification. In: Proceedings of the 33rd International Conference on International Conference on Machine Learning, vol. 48, pp. 612–621. ICML'16, JMLR.org (2016)

Multi-Mind Dynamics in Intentional Agents

Andreas Brännström[(✉)] and Juan Carlos Nieves

Department of Computing Science, Umeå University, 901 87 Umeå, Sweden
{andreasb,jcnieves}@cs.umu.se

Abstract. This paper introduces an agent framework that integrates the Belief, Desire, Intention (BDI) model with Multi-Context Systems (MCS), particularly for dealing with diverse knowledge sources in belief revision, deliberation and means-end reasoning. By specifying a separate MCS in each BDI-component, the framework manages the interaction between, possibly conflicting, sets of beliefs, desires, intentions and plans generated by specialized sub-systems. A MCS-based BDI-component generates an equilibrium. An approach is introduced for transferring equilibrium between MCSs according to the BDI control loop. This involves the translation of knowledge bases to Answer Set Programming (ASP) to build a shared logic. The proposed framework contributes to the advancement of hybrid intentional agents, where multiple goals and plans must be interwoven in order to deal with a complex multi-modal domain. The potential of the framework is illustrated in a running example, where a driving assistant agent is designed to manage diverse mental states of a human driver, such as emotions, motivations and norms, within each stage of the BDI control loop, producing a plan that is in balance with the diverse contexts.

Keywords: Multi-Context Systems · BDI Agents · Distributed Mind · Contextual Awareness · Concurrency

1 Introduction

The Belief, Desire, Intention (BDI) agent model [31] has been widely recognized as a robust conceptual framework for designing rational agents [18,19,23,30]. The BDI model revolves around an agent's mental attitudes: 'Beliefs', representing the agent's knowledge about the world, 'Desires', representing the objectives to be achieved, and 'Intentions', representing the current course of action being pursued. This enables BDI agents to exhibit a high degree of flexibility and adaptability. There is a range of agent-oriented programming approaches that enable agents to effectively pursue multiple goals simultaneously [14]. Nevertheless, a significant challenge arises when certain concurrent goals or plans clash with one another [24,34]. When an agent attempts to pursue conflicting goals concurrently, it can result in undesirable behavior. Furthermore, as the domain

S. Nowaczyk et al. (Eds.): ECAI 2023 Workshops, CCIS 1948, pp. 346–359, 2024.
https://doi.org/10.1007/978-3-031-50485-3_35

changes, in the time between deliberation and plan execution, a selected intention may no longer be reachable nor wanted [33]. Hence, when a BDI agent is situated in multi-modal dynamic domains, or multi-agent interactions, such as human interactions [21,27], it is, due to an agent's inherent use of contextual information to revise its beliefs, of importance to be contextually aware, considering different aspects of the changing environment [4,16]. This may require operating by considering multiple diverse knowledge sources that are simultaneously active and must be coordinated [26]. However, typically, a BDI agent considers a single knowledge base to inform its deliberation and means-end reasoning processes, making multi-modal coordination a challenging knowledge modeling and engineering task [9].

Addressing the aforementioned challenges involves the fundamental issue of writing statements that hold true simultaneously across multiple contexts of the domain [10], where it is crucial to embrace a rigorous formalization approach, particularly considering the reliability and verifiability of the resulting systems [12]. To tackle these challenges, the field of Multi-Context Systems (MCS) [5,6,10,12,32] has emerged, exploring formal frameworks for interconnecting heterogeneous knowledge sources, so-called contexts, each possibly operating on different logics and semantics, where so-called bridge rules serve as interfaces for managing the flow of information between contexts for reaching an equilibrium, an "agreement" among the contexts.

In this paper, we propose leveraging MCS within the framework of BDI agents to integrate multiple contexts in each BDI component. Our aim is to enhance belief revision, deliberation, and means-end reasoning processes of BDI agents by considering an equilibrium in each step of the process. Previous works which have incorporated MCS in the BDI model [15,18,20,23,25,29,30] have treated the Belief, Desire, and Intention components as individual contexts within an overarching MCS. In this way, they provide a modular framework for designing agents. Nevertheless, given that each component typically is a single context, although modules with multiple sub-contexts has been proposed [29], contextual awareness is not the main focus of the previous works. In contrast, we associate a separate multi-context system to each BDI component. This enables multiple belief contexts, desire contexts, intention contexts and planning contexts. By considering the output of each BDI component as an equilibrium, the agent is provided contextual awareness in belief revision, deliberation, and means-end reasoning. Within the scope of the BDI control loop, the equilibrium of each BDI component serves as input to proceeding BDI components. The end result is a set of intentions and plans that are in balance with all represented contexts of the domain. Let us call agents with such capabilities *multi-mind agents*.

A use-case of interest regards dynamic human interactions and theory of mind, involving tasks where the ability to recognize multiple, potentially heterogeneous, knowledge sources becomes particularly relevant [17,27], such as reasoning about the interaction between emotions [8], motivations [7], and norms [28], each possibly using different forms of representations. By considering a mental domain, such as emotion, as a knowledge base, governed by its own logic and semantics, it becomes essential to explore how other mental domains can be integrated to attain a comprehensive understanding of mental state dynamics. Each separate mental state reasoning process may lead to different beliefs about the domain, different intentions and suitable plans for achieving them. Therefore, an agent must take into account all represented contexts and balance its plans for avoiding unwanted side-effects. Attempting to define a universal logic capable of encompassing all relevant domains is infeasible, both in terms of computational complexity and knowledge engineering [3,13,22].

The rest of this paper is structured as follows. In Sect. 2, the theoretical background in BDI and MCS is covered. In Sect. 3, we introduce the Multi-Mind BDI Agent framework, which includes multi-context belief revision, deliberation, and means-end reasoning. In Sect. 4, a use-case in Theory of Mind reasoning is presented. In Sect. 5, we discuss the approach in comparison with related work. In Sect. 6, the paper is concluded by outlining future research directions.

2 Theoretical Background

In this section, we cover the basic concepts of BDI agents and Multi-context systems on which we base the proposed Multi-Mind BDI agent model.

2.1 Belief, Desire, Intention (BDI) Agent Model

The basic "blind-commitment" BDI (Belief-Desire-Intention) agent architecture [31] follows a control loop (Algorithm 1) guiding its behavior. It initializes beliefs (B) and intentions (I) based on prior knowledge. In each loop iteration, it receives a percept (p) representing the current state. The agent updates beliefs, generates desires (D) based on updated beliefs and initial intentions, deliberates on which goals to pursue, and updates intentions accordingly. Plans (π) are generated based on beliefs and selected intentions. The agent then executes the plans, interacts with the environment, and makes new observations. Let us observe that the agent has a single knowledge base, and single processes for computing desires, intentions and plans.

2.2 Multi-Context Systems (MCS)

The proposed framework follows the theoretical results of Multi-Context Systems (MCS) [10], which we adapt to the purpose of modeling Multi-Mind BDI agents. A MCS is a formal framework for interconnecting heterogeneous knowledge sources, so-called contexts, each possibly operating on different logics and semantics. A *logic* is defined in terms of input and output constraints. For a given knowledge base, particular sets of beliefs are possible for an agent, and a subset of these belief sets are considered acceptable.

Definition 1 (A logic). *[10] A logic $L = (KB_L, BS_L, ACC_L)$ is composed of the following components:*

Algorithm 1: Basic BDI agent control loop

```
   Input: B_0: Initial beliefs
   Input: I_0: Initial intentions
1  B ← B_0;
2  I ← I_0;
3  π ← null;
4  while alive do
5  |  p ← getPercept();
6  |  B ← update(B, p);
7  |  D ← wish(B, I);
8  |  I ← focus(B, D, I);
9  |  π ← plan(B, I);
10 |_ execute(π);
```

1. *KB_L is the set of well-formed knowledge bases of L, where each element of KB_L is a set.*
2. *BS_L is the set of possible belief sets,*
3. *$ACC_L : KB_L \rightarrow 2^{BS_L}$ is a function that assigns to each element of KB_L a set of acceptable sets of beliefs.*

Information flow between different logics is managed by the specification of, so-called, *bridge-rules*. Each context has a set of bridge-rules. The head of a rule corresponds to an element of a knowledge base of a context, while each component of the body corresponds to elements in belief sets of other contexts.

Definition 2 (A bridge rule). *[10] Let $L = \{L_1, \ldots, L_n\}$ be a set of logics and $L_k = (KB_k, BS_k, ACC_k)$, $1 \leq k \leq n$, is a logic. An L_k-bridge rule over L is of the form:*

$$s \leftarrow (r_1 : p_1), \ldots, (r_j : p_j), not(r_{j+1} : p_{j+1}), \ldots, not(r_m : p_m) \tag{1}$$

where $1 \leq r_k \leq n$, and p_k is an element of some belief set of L_{r_k}, and for each $kb \in KB_k : kb \cup \{s\} \in KB_k$. Hence, each conclusion of a bridge rule should also be close in each logic.

A multi-context system connects a set of contexts, each based on a logic, through bridge-rules. This specifies which types of logics that are considered in a particular multi-context system.

Definition 3 (A multi-context system). *[10] A multi-context system $M = (C_1, \ldots, C_n)$ consists of a collection of contexts $C_i = (L_i, kb_i, br_i), 1 \leq i \leq n,$, where $L_i = (KB_i, BS_i, ACC_i)$ is a logic, $kb_i \in KB_i$ is a knowledge base, and br_i is a set of L_i-bridge rules over $\{L_1, \ldots, L_n\}$.*

The semantics of a multi-context system is defined in terms of equilibrium. A so-called belief state defines the simultaneous belief sets of all contexts.

Definition 4 (A belief state). *[10] Let $M = (C_1, \ldots, C_n), 1 \leq i \leq n$, be an MCS, where $C_i = (L_i, kb_i, br_i)$ is a context and $L_i = (KB_i, BS_i, ACC_i)$ is a logic. A belief state is a sequence $S = (S_1, \ldots, S_n)$ such that each S_i is an element of BS_i. We say a bridge rule r of the form $s \leftarrow (r_1 : p_1), \ldots, (r_j : p_j)$, $not(r_{j+1} : p_{j+1}), \ldots, not(r_m : p_m)$, $1 \leq r_k \leq n$, is applicable in a belief state $S = (S_1, \ldots, S_n)$ iff for $1 \leq i \leq j : p_i \in S_{r_i}$ and for $j+1 \leq k \leq m : p_k \notin S_{r_k}$.*

An equilibrium holds when the heads of applicable bridge rules exist in the knowledge base of a context and when the elements of the bodies of applicable bridge rules exist in the acceptable belief sets of other contexts, given a belief state.

Definition 5 (An equilibrium). *[10] A belief state $S = (S_1, \ldots, S_n)$ of a multi-context system $M = (C_1, \ldots, C_n)$, where $C_i = (L_i, kb_i, br_i)$ and $L_i = (KB_i, BS_i, ACC_i)$, is an equilibrium iff, for $1 \leq i \leq n$, the following condition holds:*
$S_i \in ACC_i\ (kb_i \cup \{head(r) \mid r \in br_i \text{ applicable in } S\})$.

3 Multi-Mind BDI Agent

In this section, we introduce the Multi-Mind BDI agent, utilizing multi-context systems for dealing with diverse contexts in each stage of the BDI agent control loop: belief revision, desire recognition, intention selection and planning.

The multi-mind BDI agent architecture incorporates a so-called multi-mind system for each BDI component; This regards a multi-mind belief system (MMB), a multi-mind desire system (MMD), a multi-mind intention system (MMI), and a multi-mind planning system (MMP). To each multi-mind system, there is an associated multi-context system (MCS) tailored to that BDI component. We assume that a context that reasons about, e.g., belief is not necessarily the same context which reasons about desires, intentions or plans. Hence, we assign the contexts to their respective MCS. Specifically, there are four multi-context systems: belief MCS (BC), desire MCS (DC), intention MCS (IC), and planning MCS (PC). The primary aim of these MCSs is to generate an equilibrium between the diverse contexts within its specialization; This regards a belief equilibrium, a desire equilibrium, an intention equilibrium and a plan equilibrium.

In order to deal with the transference of equilibrium between BDI components in accordance with the BDI control loop, we define equilibrium aggregation and equilibrium transference.

Definition 6 (Equilibrium aggregation). *Let the belief state $S = (S_1, \ldots, S_n)$ of a multi-context system $M = (C_1, \ldots, C_n)$, $1 \leq i \leq n$, be an equilibrium, where $C_i = (L_i, kb_i, br_i)$ and $L_i = (KB_i, BS_i, ACC_i)$. An aggregated equilibrium is a set $EQ^S = (S_1 \cup \cdots \cup S_n)$.*

Let us recall that an equilibrium is a belief state, a set of sets. The equilibrium aggregation take the union between the sets to get a single set that we then can transfer to other MCSs.

Definition 7 (Equilibrium transference). *Let the set $EQ^S = (S_1 \cup \cdots \cup S_n)$ be an aggregated equilibrium of the belief state $S = (S_1, \ldots, S_n)$ of a multi-context system $M_1 = (C_1, \ldots, C_n)$, $1 \leq i \leq n$, where $C_i = (L_i, kb_i, br_i)$ and $L_i = (KB_i, BS_i, ACC_i)$. An equilibrium transference to a multi-context system $M_2 = (C_1, \ldots, C_m)$, $1 \leq j \leq m$, where $C_j = (L_j, kb_j, br_j)$ and $L_j = (KB_j, BS_j, ACC_j)$, is the intersection $KB_j \cap EQ^S$.*

The equilibrium transference intersects an aggregated equilibrium with the knowledge bases of another MCS. This enables to integrate the aggregated equilibrium in context inference processes of an other MCS. Equilibrium transference assumes a translation of the aggregated equilibrium set to the logic of the target knowledge base. We further assume a pre-processing step of converting all involved contexts into Answer Set Programming (ASP) [12]. ASP can express all NP-search problems that are solvable using a nondeterministic Turing machine in polynomial time, such that the solutions are encoded in terms of answer sets [11]. ASP being Turing complete makes it interesting for multi-context reasoning due to its possibility of characterizing different logics.

Let us proceed by defining the main components of the multi-mind BDI agent model, where multi-context systems are utilized in each BDI-component.

Definition 8 (Multi-Mind Belief System). *A multi-mind belief system is a tuple $MMB = (BC_n^1, update)$, where BC_n^1 is a multi-context system, such that each BC_i is a belief context. $BC_i = (L_i, kb_i, br_i)$, where $L_i = (KB_i, BS_i, ACC_i)$ is a logic consisting of:*

- *KB_i is the knowledge bases specialized for reasoning about beliefs in BC_i.*
- *BS_i is the set of possible belief sets in BC_i.*
- *$ACC_i : KB_i \rightarrow 2^{BS_i}$ is a function that assigns to each element of KB_i a set of acceptable sets of beliefs. ACC_i is restricted to the (unique) minimal credulous model.*

and $update : \mathcal{B} \times \mathcal{P} \rightarrow \mathcal{B}$ is a function that does the following operations:

- *computes an equilibrium transference $KB_i := KB_i \cap (EQ^B \cup P_n^1)$, $EQ^B \in \mathcal{B}$, $P_n^1 \in \mathcal{P}$, where EQ^B is a prior aggregated belief equilibrium and P_n^1 is a perceived belief state,*
- *computes and returns an aggregated equilibrium $EQ^{B'} = (S_1 \cup \cdots \cup S_n) \in \mathcal{B}$ of the equilibrium $S = (S_1, \ldots, S_n)$ of BC_n^1, such that for $1 \leq i \leq n$, $S_i \in ACC_i$ $(kb_i \cup \{head(r) \mid r \in br_i$ applicable in $S\})$*

where $\mathcal{B}$ are all possible equilibrium aggregations, $\mathcal{P}$ are all possible percepts.

The multi-mind belief system manages beliefs and computes aggregated belief equilibrium. It manages a specialized multi-context system BC_n^1, representing various contexts with associated percepts. The current aggregated belief equilibrium EQ^B serves as the initial state, and the function *update* is used to compute the updated aggregated belief equilibrium $EQ^{B'}$. This updated aggregated belief equilibrium is then passed on to other multi-mind systems through an equilibrium transference.

Definition 9 (Multi-Mind Desire System). *A multi-mind desire system is a tuple $MMD = (DC_m^1, wish)$, where DC_m^1 is a multi-context system, such that each DC_i is a desire context. $DC_i = (L_i, kb_i, br_i)$, where $L_i = (KB_i, DS_i, ACC_i)$ is a logic consisting of:*

- *KB_i is the knowledge specialized for reasoning about desires in DC_i.*
- *DS_i is the set of possible desire sets in DC_i.*
- *$ACC_i : KB_i \rightarrow 2^{BS_i}$ is a function that assigns to each element of KB_i a set of acceptable sets of desires. ACC_i is restricted to the (unique) minimal credulous model.*

and $wish : \mathcal{B} \times \mathcal{I} \rightarrow \mathcal{D}$ is a function that does the following operations:

- *computes an equilibrium transference $KB_i := KB_i \cap (EQ^B \cup EQ^I)$, $EQ^B \in \mathcal{B}$, $EQ^I \in \mathcal{I}$, where EQ^B is a prior aggregated belief equilibrium and EQ^I is a prior aggregated intention equilibrium,*
- *computes and returns an aggregated equilibrium $EQ^D = (S_1 \cup \cdots \cup S_m) \in \mathcal{D}$ of the equilibrium $S = (S_1, \ldots, S_m)$ of DC_m^1, such that for $1 \leq i \leq m$, $S_i \in ACC_i$ $(kb_i \cup \{head(r) \mid r \in br_i$ applicable in $S\})$*

where $\mathcal{B}$ are all possible belief equilibrium aggregations, $\mathcal{I}$ are all possible intention equilibrium aggregations and $\mathcal{D}$ are all possible desire equilibrium aggregations.

The multi-mind desire system manages desires and computes desire equilibrium. It manages a multi-context system DC_m^1, with contexts specialized for generating desires, along with the current belief equilibrium EQ^B and the current intention equilibrium EQ^I. The system incorporates these inputs to generate an aggregated desire equilibrium that is in balance with the desires of all related contexts. This aggregated desire equilibrium is then passed on to the multi-mind intention system.

Definition 10 (Multi-Mind Intention System). *A multi-mind intention system is a tuple $MMI = (IC_k^1, focus)$, where IC_k^1 is a multi-context system, such that each IC_i is an intention context. $IC_i = (L_i, kb_i, br_i)$, where $L_i = (KB_i, IS_i, ACC_i)$ is a logic consisting of:*

- *KB_i is the knowledge specialized for reasoning about intentions in IC_i.*
- *IS_i is the set of possible intention sets in IC_i.*
- *$ACC_i : KB_i \rightarrow 2^{BS_i}$ is a function that assigns to each element of KB_i a set of acceptable sets of intentions. ACC_i is restricted to the (unique) minimal credulous model.*

and $focus : \mathcal{B} \times \mathcal{D} \times \mathcal{I} \rightarrow \mathcal{I}$ is a function that does the following operations:

- *computes an equilibrium transference $KB_i := KB_i \cap (EQ^B \cup EQ^D \cup EQ^I)$, $EQ^B \in \mathcal{B}$, $EQ^D \in \mathcal{D}$, $EQ^I \in \mathcal{I}$, where EQ^B is a prior aggregated belief equilibrium, EQ^D is a prior aggregated desire equilibrium and EQ^I is a prior aggregated intention equilibrium,*

- *computes and returns an aggregated equilibrium* $EQ^I = (S_1 \cup \cdots \cup S_k) \in \mathcal{I}$ *of the equilibrium* $S = (S_1, \ldots, S_k)$ *of* IC_k^1*, such that for* $1 \leq i \leq k$*,* $S_i \in ACC_i$ $(kb_i \cup \{head(r) \mid r \in br_i$ *applicable in* $S\})$

where $\mathcal{B}$ *are all possible belief equilibrium aggregations,* $\mathcal{I}$ *are all possible intention equilibrium aggregations and* $\mathcal{D}$ *are all possible desire equilibrium aggregations.*

The multi-mind intention system is responsible for forming an intention equilibrium. It takes a multi-context system IC_k^1, with contexts specialized on generating intentions, along with the current belief equilibrium EQ^B, the desire equilibrium EQ^D, and the current aggregated intention equilibrium EQ^I. The system incorporates these inputs to generate an updated aggregated intention equilibrium $EQ^{I'}$ that is in balance with the intentions of all related contexts. This aggregated intention equilibrium is then passed on to the multi-mind planning system.

Definition 11 (Multi-Mind Planning System). *A multi-mind planning system is a tuple* $MMP = (PC_g^1, plan)$*, where* PC_g^1 *is a multi-context system, such that each* PC_i *is a planning context. Each planning context* PC_i *is defined as* $PC_i = (L_i, kb_i, br_i)$*, where* $L_i = (KB_i, PS_i, ACC_i)$ *is a logic consisting of:*

- KB_i *is the knowledge specialized for planning in* PC_i*.*
- PS_i *is the set of possible plan sets in* PC_i*.*
- $ACC_i : KB_i \rightarrow 2^{BS_i}$ *is a function that assigns to each element of* KB_i *a set of acceptable sets of plans.* ACC_i *is restricted to the (unique) minimal credulous model.*

and $plan : \mathcal{B} \times \mathcal{I} \rightarrow \Pi$ *is a function that does the following operations:*

- *computes an equilibrium transference* $KB_i := KB_i \cap (EQ^B \cup EQ^I)$*,* $EQ^B \in \mathcal{B}$*,* $EQ^I \in \mathcal{I}$*, where* EQ^B *is a prior aggregated belief equilibrium and* EQ^I *is a prior aggregated intention equilibrium,*
- *computes and returns an aggregated equilibrium* $EQ^\pi = (S_1 \cup \cdots \cup S_g) \in \Pi$ *of the equilibrium* $S = (S_1, \ldots, S_g)$ *of* DC_g^1*, such that for* $1 \leq i \leq g$*,* $S_i \in ACC_i$ $(kb_i \cup \{head(r) \mid r \in br_i$ *applicable in* $S\})$

where $\mathcal{B}$ *are all possible belief equilibrium aggregations,* $\mathcal{I}$ *are all possible intention equilibrium aggregations and* Π *are all possible plan equilibrium aggregations.*

The multi-mind planning system handles the planning process. It takes as input a multi-context system PC_g^1 with contexts specialized for planning, along with the current belief equilibrium EQ^B and the aggregated intention equilibrium EQ^I. Based on this input, the planning system generates an aggregated plan equilibrium. This regards plans which are in balance with the plans of all related contexts toward achieving the intentions specified by the aggregated intention equilibrium.

A Multi-Mind BDI Agent manages the interaction between all multi-mind systems through generation of equilibrium, delivered between BDI components as a dynamic knowledge base utilized in the agent's deliberation and reasoning.

Building on the original BDI agent model, we define a Multi-Mind BDI agent control loop (see Algorithm 2). A distributed knowledge base that incorporates diverse contexts of the domain supports balanced decision-making. The multi-mind belief system initiates by generating a belief equilibrium based on context-specific percepts. Lastly, the multi-mind planning system generates contextually appropriate plans, supporting action-taking that is compatible with all represented contexts.

Algorithm 2: Multi-Mind BDI agent control loop

Input: EQ^{B_0}: Initial beliefs
Input: EQ^{I_0}: Initial intentions
Input: $BC_n^1; DC_m^1; IC_f^1; PC_g^1$: Multi-context systems

1 $EQ^B \leftarrow EQ^{B_0}$;
2 $EQ^I \leftarrow EQ^{I_0}$;
3 $EQ^\pi \leftarrow null$;
4 **while** *alive* **do**
5 $\quad P_n^1 \leftarrow getPercepts()$;
6 $\quad EQ^B \leftarrow MMB.update(EQ^B, P_n^1)$;
7 $\quad EQ^D \leftarrow MMD.wish(EQ^B, EQ^I)$;
8 $\quad EQ^I \leftarrow MMI.focus(EQ^B, EQ^D, EQ^I)$;
9 $\quad EQ^\pi \leftarrow MMP.plan(EQ^B, EQ^I)$;
10 $\quad execute(EQ^\pi)$;

4 Example: A Multi-Mind Driving Assistance Agent

A smart driving assistance system is aiding a driver in decision-making on the road, while maintaining three goal oriented behaviors: 1) maintaining the driver's emotional well-being, 2) motivating eco-driving and 3) adherence to traffic norms. Different perceptions are recognized: driver frustration from heavy traffic (emotional), a strong need to reach the destination quickly (motivational), and adherence to traffic norms (normative). However, determining a balanced driving assistance poses a challenge. If the system prioritizes promoting eco-driving excessively, it may cause increased driver frustration. On the other hand, placing too much emphasis on the driver's emotional state could lead to decisions that prioritize comfort over efficient eco-driving.

A multi-mind BDI agent $MMBDI$ is initialized with four multi-context systems, BC, DC, IC, PC, for managing beliefs, desires, intentions and plans.

- $BC = (E_B, M_B, N_B)$ consisting of three contexts: Emotion (E_B), Motivation (M_B), and Norm (N_B), specialized for belief recognition from observations.

- $DC = (E_D, M_D, N_D)$ consisting of three contexts: Emotion (E_D), Motivation (M_D), and Norm (N_D), specialized for managing desire.
- $IC = (E_I, M_I, N_I)$ consisting of three contexts: Emotion (E_I), Motivation (M_I), and Norm (N_I), specialized for managing intention.
- $PC = (E_P, M_P, N_P)$ consisting of three contexts: Emotion (E_P), Motivation (M_P), and Norm (N_P), specialized for planning.

By considering the knowledge bases and a set of bridge rules for each context in BC, DC, IC, PC, a prior belief equilibrium EQ^B, and a set of percepts P, the Multi-Mind BDI agent generates an aggregated equilibrium (Definition 6) for each BDI component, and conducts an equilibrium transference (Definition 7) in between each step, such that $KB_B \cap (EQ^B \cup P)$, $KB_D \cap (EQ^B \cup EQ^I)$, $KB_I \cap (EQ^B \cup EQ^D \cup EQ^I)$ and $KB_\pi \cap (EQ^B \cup EQ^I)$, where Belief Equilibrium $EQ^B = (S_{E_B} \cup S_{M_B} \cup S_{N_B})$, Desire Equilibrium $EQ^D = (S_{E_D} \cup S_{M_D} \cup S_{N_D})$, Intention Equilibrium $EQ^I = (S_{E_I} \cup S_{M_I} \cup S_{N_I})$, and Plan Equilibrium $EQ^\pi = (S_{E_P} \cup S_{M_P} \cup S_{N_P})$. This chain of equilibrium may contain the following elements:

- $S_{E_B} = \{frustration\}$ is the Emotional belief state.
- $S_{M_B} = \{slow\_driving\}$ is the Motivational belief state.
- $S_{N_B} = \{norm\_compliant\}$ is the Normative belief state.

- $S_{E_D} = \{high\_relax, medium\_relax\}$ is the Emotional desire state.
- $S_{M_D} = \{high\_eco, medium\_eco, low\_eco\}$ is the Motivational desire state.
- $S_{N_D} = \{medium\_norm, low\_norm\}$ is the Normative desire state.

- $S_{E_I} = \{high\_relax\}$ is the Emotional intention state.
- $S_{M_I} = \{medium\_eco\}$ is the Motivational intention state.
- $S_{N_I} = \{low\_norm\}$ is the Normative intention state.

- $S_{E_P} = high\_relax\_plan$ is a set of actions in the Emotional plan.
- $S_{M_P} = medium\_eco\_plan$ is a set of actions in the Motivational plan.
- $S_{N_P} = low\_norm\_plan$ is a set of actions in the Normative plan.

A final plan is constructed by considering the equilibrium aggregation $EQ^\pi = (S_{E_P} \cup S_{M_P} \cup S_{N_P})$, comprised of the set of actions A, such that

$$A \subseteq high\_relax\_plan \cup medium\_eco\_plan \cup low\_norm\_plan.$$

5 Discussion and Related Work

Several previous works have explored the incorporation of Multi-Context Systems (MCS) in the Belief-Desire-Intention (BDI) model [15,18,20,23,25,29,30]. A seminal work [29] proposes an BDI agent specification using multi-context systems, which provide an overarching framework for defining and interrelating the BDI components (Belief, Desire, Intention) as separate contexts. This allows for modular decomposition and encapsulation of the BDI components, supporting efficient specification and execution of complex logics. A proceeding work

[20] extends the multi-context BDI architecture with commitments using multi-context systems. They also model the BDI modalities as individual contexts and introduce a fourth context for commitments, connected to the other mental attitudes via bridge rules. Their work demonstrates the benefits of using multi-context systems for handling normative multiagent systems. In a proceeding study, an extension of the multi-context BDI agent architecture with normative contexts [18] is proposed, allowing agents to acquire norms from their environment and consider norms in their decision-making processes, while maintaining their autonomy. Additionally, a so-called graded BDI agent is proposed [15], building on the previous works in MCS-based BDI agents, extending with the capability to reason about positive and negative, beliefs, desires and intentions, to deal with preferences. The graded BDI model assumes that intentions are determined solely based on the satisfaction of a positive desire and the cost of transforming the world to achieve it. Nevertheless, it overlooks the dynamic and interactive nature of heterogeneous simultaneous contexts. These previous works have treated the components of the BDI model as individual contexts within an overarching MCS. In contrast, our approach introduces a MCS layer on top of each BDI component. A potential with this approach is that it enables equilibrium to be derived at each BDI component to enhance contextual awareness, from belief revision to plan generation.

Limitations of the proposed agent model regard the interactions between MCSs. An equilibrium is assumed to be incorporated in the proceeding MCS as an extended knowledge base. This information flow between MCSs may require sophisticated bridge-rules to manage consistency. The previous works outlined in this section, e.g., [29], dealing with interactions between BDI components using bridge-rules, can be adapted for this purpose.

6 Conclusion and Future Work

The Multi-Mind BDI agent model regards an approach for handling heterogeneous contexts in an agent's beliefs, desires, intentions, and plans. By achieving equilibrium at each stage, the architecture facilitates contextually aware belief revision, deliberation, and means-end reasoning, supporting adaptation to multimodal environments. The decentralized BDI architecture manages conflicts and potential side-effects across diverse knowledge sources at each reasoning stage.

The future horizon lies in the development of hybrid architectures that coordinate the interaction between inductive and deductive contexts in each BDI component. In this direction, future work will explore the possibility of combining the proposed architecture with reinforcement learning methods and deep learning methods. For example, the logic expressed by the method could be encoded as a deep neural network with tuning parameters by the training procedure. Accordingly, different deep neural network approaches could be considered within the proposed architecture [1,2]. Future work will further address consistency between Multi-Context based BDI components. This involves exploring specialized bridge-rules, drawing inspiration from related work in MCS [10] and MCS-BDI [15,29] integrations.

References

1. Amelio, A., et al.: Representation and compression of residual neural networks through a multilayer network based approach. Expert Syst. Appl. **215**, 119391 (2023)
2. Amelio, A., Bonifazi, G., Corradini, E., Ursino, D., Virgili, L.: A multilayer network-based approach to represent, explore and handle convolutional neural networks. Cogn. Comput. **15**(1), 61–89 (2023)
3. Artemov, S., Kuznets, R.: Logical omniscience as infeasibility. Ann. Pure Appl. Logic **165**(1), 6–25 (2014)
4. Baitiche, H., Bouzenada, M., Saidouni, D.E., Berkane, Y., Chama, H.: A context-aware distributed protocol for updating BDI agents abilities. In: Chikhi, S., Amine, A., Chaoui, A., Saidouni, D.E. (eds.) MISC 2018. LNNS, vol. 64, pp. 243–256. Springer, Cham (2019). https://doi.org/10.1007/978-3-030-05481-6_19
5. Besold, T.R., Mandl, S.: Integrating logical and sub-symbolic contexts of reasoning. In: ICAART 2010 – Proceedings of the International Conference on Agents and Artificial Intelligence, Volume 1 - Artificial Intelligence, pp. 494–497 (2010)
6. Besold, T.R., Mandl, S.: Towards an implementation of a multi-context system framework. MRC **2010**, 13 (2010)
7. Brännström, A., Nieves, J.C.: Modelling human mental-states in an action language following the theory of planned behavior. In: ASPOCP 2021: 14th Workshop on Answer Set Programming and Other Computing Paradigms, virtual, September 20–27, 2021, vol. 2970. CEUR-WS (2021)
8. Brännström, A., Nieves, J.C.: Emotional reasoning in an action language for emotion-aware planning. In: Gottlob, G., Inclezan, D., Maratea, M. (eds.) Logic Programming and Nonmonotonic Reasoning. LPNMR 2022. Lecture Notes in Computer Science, vol. 13416, pp. 103–116. Springer, Cham (2022). https://doi.org/10.1007/978-3-031-15707-3_9
9. Braubach, L., Pokahr, A., Lamersdorf, W.: Extending the capability concept for flexible BDI agent modularization. In: Bordini, R.H., Dastani, M.M., Dix, J., El Fallah Seghrouchni, A. (eds.) ProMAS 2005. LNCS (LNAI), vol. 3862, pp. 139–155. Springer, Heidelberg (2006). https://doi.org/10.1007/11678823_9
10. Brewka, G., Eiter, T.: Equilibria in heterogeneous nonmonotonic multi-context systems. In: Proceedings of the Twenty-Second AAAI Conference on Artificial Intelligence, vol. 7, pp. 385–390 (2007)
11. Brewka, G., Eiter, T., Truszczyński, M.: Answer set programming at a glance. Commun. ACM **54**(12), 92–103 (2011)
12. Cabalar, P., Costantini, S., De Gasperis, G., Formisano, A.: Multi-context systems in dynamic environments. Ann. Math. Artif. Intell. **86**, 87–120 (2019)
13. Calvanese, D., De Giacomo, G.: Data integration: a logic-based perspective. AI Mag. **26**(1), 59–59 (2005)
14. Cardoso, R.C., Ferrando, A.: A review of agent-based programming for multi-agent systems. Computers **10**(2), 16 (2021)

15. Casali, A., Godo, L., Sierra, C.: A graded BDI agent model to represent and reason about preferences. Artif. Intell. **175**(7–8), 1468–1478 (2011)
16. Casals, A., Fermé, E., Brandao, A.A.: Domain-specific trust for context-aware BDI agents: preliminary work. In: Proceedings of the 10th International Conference on Agents and Artificial Intelligence (ICAART 2018)-Volume 1, pp. 244–249. Scitepress (2018)
17. Clark, A.: Mindware: An Introduction to the Philosophy of Cognitive Science. Oxford University Press (2000)
18. Criado, N., Argente, E., Botti, V.: A BDI architecture for normative decision making. In: Proceedings of the 9th International Conference on Autonomous Agents and Multiagent Systems: volume 1-Volume 1, pp. 1383–1384 (2010)
19. De Silva, L., Meneguzzi, F.R., Logan, B.: BDI agent architectures: a survey. In: Proceedings of the 29th International Joint Conference on Artificial Intelligence (IJCAI), 2020, Japão. (2020)
20. Gaertner, D., Noriega, P., Sierra, C.: Extending the BDI architecture with commitments. Front. Artif. Intell. Appl. **146**, 247 (2006)
21. Joo, J.: Perception and BDI reasoning based agent model for human behavior simulation in complex system. In: Kurosu, M. (ed.) HCI 2013. LNCS, vol. 8008, pp. 62–71. Springer, Heidelberg (2013). https://doi.org/10.1007/978-3-642-39342-6_8
22. Konar, A.: Cognitive Engineering: A Distributed Approach to Machine Intelligence. Springer Science & Business Media (2007). https://doi.org/10.1007/1-84628-234-9
23. de Mello, R.R.P., Gelaim, T.Â., Silveira, R.A.: Negotiating agents: a model based on BDI architecture and multi-context systems using aspiration adaptation theory as a negotiation strategy. In: Barolli, L., Javaid, N., Ikeda, M., Takizawa, M. (eds.) CISIS 2018. AISC, vol. 772, pp. 351–362. Springer, Cham (2019). https://doi.org/10.1007/978-3-319-93659-8_31
24. Mohajeriparizi, M., Sileno, G., van Engers, T.: Preference-based goal refinement in BDI agents. In: Proceedings of the 21st International Conference on Autonomous Agents and Multiagent Systems, pp. 917–925 (2022)
25. Othmane, A.B., Tettamanzi, A., Villata, S., Le Thanh, N.: A multi-context BDI recommender system: from theory to simulation. In: 2016 IEEE/WIC/ACM International Conference on Web Intelligence (WI), pp. 602–605. IEEE (2016)
26. Ouksel, A.M.: A framework for a scalable agent architecture of cooperating heterogeneous knowledge sources. In: Klusch, M. (eds.) Intelligent Information Agents, pp. 100–124. Springer, Berlin, Heidelberg (1999). https://doi.org/10.1007/978-3-642-60018-0_6
27. Paglieri, F.: Changing minds: the role of beliefs in cognitive dynamics. Synthese **155**, 163–166 (2007)
28. Panagiotidi, S., Nieves, J.C., Vázquez-Salceda, J.: A framework to model norm dynamics in answer set programming. In: MALLOW (2009)
29. Parsons, S., Jennings, N.R., Sabater, J., Sierra, C.: Agent specification using multi-context systems. In: d'Inverno, M., Luck, M., Fisher, M., Preist, C. (eds.) Foundations and Applications of Multi-Agent Systems. LNCS (LNAI), vol. 2403, pp. 205–226. Springer, Heidelberg (2002). https://doi.org/10.1007/3-540-45634-1_13
30. Pinyol, I., Sabater-Mir, J., Dellunde, P.: Cognitive social evaluations for multi-context BDI agents. In: CCIA 2008 (2008)
31. Rao, A.S., Georgeff, M.: BDI agents: from theory to practice. In: Proceedings of the First International Conference on Multiagent Systems, vol. 95, pp. 312–319 (1995)

32. Roelofsen, F., Serafini, L., et al.: Minimal and absent information in contexts. In: IJCAI, vol. 5, pp. 558–563 (2005)
33. Schut, M., Wooldridge, M.: Intention reconsideration in complex environments. In: Proceedings of the Fourth International Conference on Autonomous Agents, pp. 209–216 (2000)
34. Wu, D., Yao, Y., Alechina, N., Logan, B., Thangarajah, J.: Intention progression with maintenance goals. In: Proceedings of the 2023 International Conference on Autonomous Agents and Multiagent Systems, pp. 2400–2402 (2023)

Towards Model-Driven Explainable Artificial Intelligence. An Experiment with Shallow Methods Versus Grammatical Evolution

Dominik Sepioło(✉) and Antoni Ligęza

AGH University of Krakow, Department of Applied Computer Science, al. Mickiewicza 30, 30-059 Krakow, Poland
{sepiolo,ligeza}@agh.edu.pl

Abstract. This paper reports on ongoing and innovative research in the area of *eXplainable Artificial Intelligence* (XAI). An XAI task is considered as finding an explanation of the model generated via Machine Learning by identifying the most influential variables for local decision-making. The proposed approach moves the explanatory process to a new, deeper-level dimension. It is oriented towards Model Discovery, i.e. the internal structure and functions of the components. An experiment on Function Discovery via Grammatical Evolution is reported in brief.

Keywords: explainable artificial intelligence · grammatical evolution · structural regression · model-based explainable artificial intelligence

1 Introduction

Machine Learning (ML) has evolved into a well-established and advanced field of study, offering a wide range of efficient problem-solving techniques and practical applications. Numerous successful projects and implementations in complex domains such as biomedical data analysis, natural language processing or large-scale technological systems are reported, and significant progress w.r.t. variety of ML algorithms and tools is observed. However, it appears that the classical ML paradigm as stated itself, consisting in finding a finite-set decision-making classification or value prediction model, remains a bit too restricted, conservative, where little or no progress is observed concerning *problem formulation.* Practically all the ML data repositories are built according to the same simple scheme of *attributive decision tables*, with no other *knowledge-based components.*

Some of the most challenging and complex AI issues of today, concern real understanding of how intelligent systems work; these include Model-Discovery for Model-Based Reasoning [5], eXplainable Artificial Intelligence (XAI) [1,2], Trustworthy and Responsible Decision-Making, Interpretable and Explainable AI[1] and others. In order to make a step towards building Model-Driven XAI,

[1] https://www.bmc.com/blogs/machine-learning-interpretability-vs-explainability/.

S. Nowaczyk et al. (Eds.): ECAI 2023 Workshops, CCIS 1948, pp. 360–365, 2024.
https://doi.org/10.1007/978-3-031-50485-3_36

incorporation of Knowledge-Based components and more advanced function identification methods (e.g. symbolic regression, grammatical evolution) seems to be necessary and promising.

This short paper[2] is structured as follows: Sect. 2 describes state-of-the-art in XAI and research motivation. Theoretical aspects of Grammatical Evolution are described in Sect. 3. This is followed by a description of an experiment with function identification in Sect. 4. Concluding remarks are presented in Sect. 5.

2 State-of-the-Art in XAI and Motivation

Explainable Artificial Intelligence is focused on providing solutions, decisions and predictions that can be understood by humans. Majority of current ML techniques (e.g. Deep Learning) are based on *black-box* models. In order to assure an appropriate level of transparency, and further justifiability and trustability, man must be aware of the underlying *rules of the game*, i.e. some *Deep Knowledge.*

The current approaches to develop XAI often lean towards using *shallow models.* By sacrificing accuracy, a simple but interpretable model is built upon the one generated with ML technologies. Its work is demonstrated on a subset of the original input data, and there is no way to incorporate auxiliary domain expert knowledge. In [1,2] a vast, representative selection of the proposed shallow approaches and tools is presented.

Local Interpretable Model-Agnostic Explanations (LIME) are the most prominent example of explanations by simplification. LIME algorithm generates an explanation for an individual prediction by creating a simple, interpretable, linear model that approximates the behavior of the opaque model in the neighborhood of the prediction. SHapley Additive exPlanations (SHAP) are another benchmark technique of explainability. SHAP utilizes a game theoretic approach (*Shapley values*) in order to create an explanation that shows feature importance for each prediction. Other methods include visualization techniques and explanations by example. In [7] we provided a comprehensive, critical overview of the current shallow approaches to XAI.

The aforementioned approaches are *shallow*, as they provide explanations that are at a high level of abstraction and do not involve a deep understanding of the model underlying principles and external declarative knowledge. A born-in feature of such shallow methods is the inability to capture the full underlying complexity of the model. It is important that they should be applied only together with other, deep and more transparent, techniques for a more complete understanding of the behavior and structure of the model.

External knowledge components play a crucial role in enriching ML models. One such approach is through the use of Ontologies and Knowledge Graphs, which provide structured and organized knowledge that can enhance the model understanding and reasoning. Another idea consists in using Causal Graphs

[2] A former version of this paper was presented at PP-RAI 2023, a Polish AI conference.

and Functional Components describing the behavior of the system. Context-free grammars are yet another powerful tool to formalize this external knowledge, enabling the creation of well-defined explanation models. By applying these grammars, the structure of the explanation model can be constrained, leading to more interpretable and coherent explanations.

By combining various methods and external knowledge, a more hybrid, more complete and nuanced interpretation of the AI decision-making process can be achieved. This integration of different techniques enables to bridge the gap between interpretability and complexity, leading to a more efficient, reliable and trustworthy AI system.

3 A Note on Grammatical Evolution

Grammatical evolution (GE) is a type of Evolutionary Algorithm (EA) that takes inspiration from the biological evolutionary process to search for solutions to problems [6]. Unlike classical EA, GE combines genetic algorithms with formal language theory. User-defined context-free grammars constrain the structure and syntax of the genome, which allows generating solutions with a well-defined structure. Each solution is then evaluated using a fitness value based on a specified objective function. GE is primarily used to create variable-length linear genome encodings of computer programs. However, it can also be applied to tasks like symbolic regression and identifying functional dependencies. There are numerous implementations of GE algorithms; including PyNeurGen, PonyGE and PonyGE2 for Python, GEVA and ECJ for Java, and GELab for Matlab, gramEvol for R and others[3].

4 An Experiment with Different Explainability Methods

Body Mass Index (BMI) is a simple numeric medical parameter that indicates whether the body weight of a person of a given height is within the healthy range. It can be calculated by dividing the person's weight in kilograms by the square of their height in meters.

A series of experiments, implemented in R language (i.e. gramEvol and caret packages), was performed in order to create models that attempt to discover the BMI function from example data. Beside standard ML methods such as Decision Trees and Random Forest models, Grammatical Evolution was applied. The experiments were conducted with varying amounts of training data. Initially, 10 observations were used to train the models, then this was increased to 50 observations, and finally, the models were trained with 100 observations.

The first applied technique was Decision Tree. For 10 observations the resulting tree had only one node: the root which returned the mean BMI value from input data. The model had 85% accuracy, however, it was overfitted and performed much worse on test data. The increase in training data (50 observations)

[3] https://en.wikipedia.org/wiki/Grammatical_evolution#Implementations.

did not increase accuracy, though the model was more prone to overfitting. Decision tree created with 100 observations performed at around 90% accuracy. Although the advantage of the model was a simple, interpretable structure presented in Fig. 1, the prediction accuracy was disenchanting.

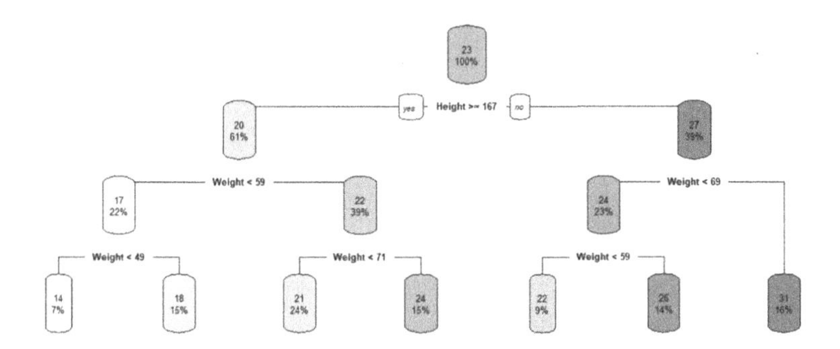

Fig. 1. Resulting decision tree.

Secondly, the Random Forest algorithm was used for BMI calculation. For 10 and 50 observations model accuracy was around 95% but both of the models were overfitted. For 100 training instances, the training accuracy was 97.5% and 93% for test data. As Random Forest is a black-box model, we applied LIME and SHAP methods to generate explanations. For some predictions, explanations proposed by those techniques were significantly different. One example of such discrepancy is presented in Fig. 2. LIME explanation for a given instance shows that the person's height (160–169 cm) increases BMI value, while the person's weight (61.5–74.6 kg) decreases it. The influence of the Height variable on the predicted value is seven times higher than the influence of the Weight variable. In contrast to LIME method, SHAP explanation for the same instance exhibits that both Weight and Height have a negative contribution to the predicted BMI value. Moreover, the Weight variable contributes significantly more to the result than the Height. Potential reasons for this discrepancy include different theoretical assumptions of mentioned explanation techniques but also model instability. Another disadvantage of local explanations technique for BMI prediction is that it assumes that for each prediction BMI coefficient was generated using another formula, while all predictions can be calculated using one simple function.

As there were critical differences in explanations of the model behavior generated by LIME and SHAP techniques for a given prediction, the need for a deeper understanding of the problem structure emerged. For this reason, we decided to implement grammatical evolution approach in order to find causality and functional dependencies in data and create a deep, transparent model.

The definition of the proposed context-free grammar for BMI function identification that expresses external domain knowledge is presented below:

<expr> ::= <op>(<expr>, <expr>) | <func>(<expr>) | <var>

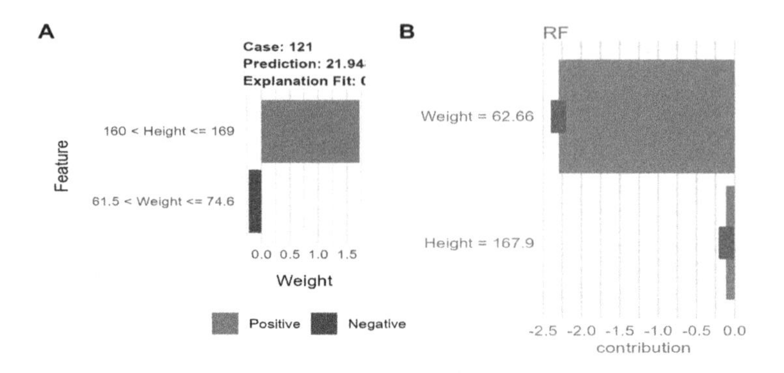

Fig. 2. LIME (A) and SHAP (B) explanation.

```
<func> ::= 'log' | 'sqrt'
<op>   ::= "+" | "-" | "*" | "/" | "^"
<var>  ::= Weight | Height | <n>
<n>    ::= -3 | -2 | -1 | 0 | 1 | 2 | 3
```

We allowed basic functions and arithmetic operations and variables: Weight, Height and $n \in \mathbb{Z}$ from $\langle -3, 3 \rangle$ interval as structure elements of final expression. Only 10 observations were enough in order to correctly identify the formula for the BMI coefficient. The result of grammatical evolution operations is shown below:

```
Best Expression:  Weight * Height^-2
```

The resulting expression (function) is coherent with the BMI formula. The discovered functional model assures 100% accuracy for every instance of input data and outperforms ML solutions. Furthermore, it provides information that enables understanding of the model behavior and structure.

5 Conclusions

The presented experiment shows that using only shallow explainability techniques can lead to inconsistent and misleading explanations for the same prediction. Explanation discrepancies point out the limitations of the shallow, model-agnostic approach. Simple models and explanation techniques that lead to a *deep understanding* of the model behavior and structure should be preferred, as they ensure responsible application of AI solutions. Some early proposal of such approach incorporating Constraint Programming we presented in [3,4].

Grammatical Evolution seems to be a promising technology for extension and further developments in identifying interpretable functional structure. It can be successfully applied to the identification of functional dependencies in data. The reported experiment shows advantages of an accurate model generated with a very limited amount of training data over other shallow methods.

External Knowledge can help to create models that are more robust against uncertainties, missing information or noisy data. Additionally, expert knowledge can support building robust, general solutions, open to new data and scenarios.

Although context-free grammars can be utilized in order to restrict the structure of an explanation model, there is emerging need of penalization of complexity and redundancy of the model. At the moment there are no checks if the proposed genome contains redundant information, so there is no simple way to exclude redundant components. Moreover, it is not straightforward to estimate *a priori* number of building-blocks of a functional model.

Incorporating external knowledge is essential for ensuring ethical and legal compliance. Models must adhere to regulations, privacy standards, and ethical guidelines. By integrating external knowledge that covers these aspects, models can be developed with reliability and responsible decision-making in mind.

References

1. Arrieta, A.B., et al.: Explainable artificial intelligence (XAI): concepts, taxonomies, opportunities and challenges toward responsible AI. Inf. Fusion **58**, 82–115 (2019)
2. Guidotti, R., Monreale, A., Ruggieri, S., Turini, F., Giannotti, F., Pedreschi, D.: A survey of methods for explaining black box models. ACM Comput. Surv. **51**(5), 1–42 (2019). https://doi.org/10.1145/3236009
3. Ligęza, A.: An experiment in causal structure discovery. a constraint programming approach. In: Kryszkiewicz, M., Appice, A., Ślęzak, D., Rybiński, H., Skowron, A., Raś, Z.W. (eds.) Foundations of Intelligent Systems - 23rd International Symposium, ISMIS 2017, Warsaw, Poland, June 26–29, 2017, Proceedings. Lecture Notes in Computer Science, vol. 10352, pp. 261–268. Springer (2017). https://doi.org/10.1007/978-3-319-60438-1_26
4. Ligęza, A., et al.: Explainable artificial intelligence. model discovery with constraint programming. In: Stettinger, M., Leitner, G., Felfernig, A., Raś, Z.W. (eds.) Intelligent Systems in Industrial Applications, 25th International Symposium, ISMIS 2020, Graz, Austria, September 23–25, 2020, Selected Papers from the Industrial Part. Studies in Computational Intelligence, vol. 949, pp. 171–191. Springer (2020). https://doi.org/10.1007/978-3-030-67148-8_13
5. Magnani, Lorenzo, Bertolotti, Tommaso (eds.): Springer Handbook of Model-Based Science. SH, Springer, Cham (2017). https://doi.org/10.1007/978-3-319-30526-4
6. Ryan, C., O'Neill, M., Collins, J.J. (eds.): Handbook of Grammatical Evolution. Springer (2018). https://doi.org/10.1007/978-3-319-78717-6
7. Sepioło, D., Ligęza, A.: Towards explainability of tree-based ensemble models. a critical overview. In: Zamojski, W., Mazurkiewicz, J., Sugier, J., Walkowiak, T., Kacprzyk, J. (eds.) New Advances in Dependability of Networks and Systems, pp. 287–296. Springer, Cham (2022). https://doi.org/10.1007/978-3-031-06746-4_28

AI4AI

AI for AI Education (AI4AI)

Diedrich Wolter[1], Jochen L. Leidner[2,3], Michael Kohlhase[4,5], Ute Schmid[1], and Vania Dimitrova[6]

[1] University of Bamberg, An der Weberei 5, 96047 Bamberg, Germany
Diedrich.Wolter@uni-bamberg.de
[2] Coburg University of Applied Sciences, Friedrich-Streib-Str. 2, 96450 Coburg, Germany
leidner@acm.org
[3] University of Sheffield, Regents Court, 211 Portobello, Sheffield S1 4DP, UK
[4] University Erlangen-Nürnberg, Martensstraße 3, Erlangen 91058, Germany
michael.kohlhase@fau.de
[5] Carnegie Mellon University, 5000 Forbes Avenue, Pittsburgh, PA, USA
[6] University of Leeds, Woodhouse Ln, Leeds, LS2 9JT, UK
V.G.Dimitrova@leeds.ac.uk

Education as an application domain of AI encompasses manifold important use cases and specialised settings, ranging from early education to advanced university programs. Currently, several European countries attribute funding to improving AI education and it thus appears most natural to employ AI techniques for this purpose as well. This workshop brings together researchers involved in these diverse European programs investigating, developing or exploring AI techniques for AI education.

The workshop provided a platform for exchange of ideas and experiences under the general theme of AI for education, specialising on university education in AI, but interpreting AI in a broad sense. We also wish to contribute towards forming a European community on the theme of AI for AI education, and foster basic research as well as the development of intelligent assistance technology (e.g., intelligent tutor systems) in a multi-disciplinary setting in order to improve AI education by making use of AI technology itself: AI4AI.

Out of a total of 16 papers we received, eight contributions were presented in full talks and discussed, along with two additional poster contributions. The eight full contributions featured in this volume tackle different use cases of AI in teaching AI. One group of papers is concerned with the development of intelligent tutor systems for improving programming education that is foundational to most AI curricula. Another group of papers investigates the effect of employing AI techniques in education, especially considering machine learning techniques.

The AI4AI workshop also featured discussions and keynotes by Adish Singla (Max Planck Institute for Software Systems, Germany) and Ken Forbus (Northwestern University, USA). Organization of the workshop was supported by 12 additional reviewers.

The organizers hope that the intense discussions at the workshop will continue and contribute to improving the ability of the AI community to educate the next generation of AI researches.

Enhancing Computer Science Education by Automated Analysis of Students' Code Submissions

Lea Eileen Brauner(✉) and Frank Höppner

Department of Computer Science, Ostfalia University of Applied Sciences, 38302 Wolfenbüttel, Germany
le.brauner@ostfalia.de

Abstract. Lecturers of introductory programming courses are often faced with the challenge of supervising a large number of students. Reviewing a large number of programming exercises is time-consuming, and an automated overview of the available solution approaches would be helpful. In this paper, we focus on source code similarity at the level of students' selected solution approaches. We propose a method to compare Java classes using variable usage paths (VUPs) extracted from modified abstract syntax trees (ASTs). The proposed approach involves matching semantically equivalent functions and attributes between classes by comparing their VUPs. We define a F_1-based similarity measure on how well one student submission matches another. We evaluate our approach using students' submissions from an introductory programming exercise and the results indicate the effectiveness of our method in identifying different solution approaches. The proposed approach outperforms simplified comparisons and the widely used plagiarism detection tool JPlag in accurately grouping submissions by solution approach similarity.

1 Introduction

Lecturers of introductory programming courses often face the challenge of supervising a large number of students. Grading a large number of lab assignments is time-consuming, which is why automated unit tests are frequently used. However, such tests provide only feedback with respect to functionality, not to the efficiency or suitability of the approach. Feedback of this kind can be provided more easily, if code submissions are grouped or clustered according to their (syntactical) similarity, because the same feedback may be used for multiple solutions (see [3] and references therein). However, in this work we are not interested in grading (whereas the authors of [3] are), but feedback that may help students to revise their solution and learn from fellow students. Once an exercise has been solved, a student may benefit from other solutions that follow the same line of thought (but are much more elegant or compact) or alternative solutions that address the problem differently (not just syntactically, but in the underlying idea how the problem has been solved). We thus seek a similarity measure for code

S. Nowaczyk et al. (Eds.): ECAI 2023 Workshops, CCIS 1948, pp. 369–380, 2024.
https://doi.org/10.1007/978-3-031-50485-3_37

(as it is typically written in introductory programming courses) that focusses on structurally different solutions. Note that solutions, which follow different ideas, typically differ syntactically, but syntactical differences do not automatically indicate a difference in the underlying idea.

2 Related Work

The proposed method for program similarity in [1] is based on the use of Graph Neural Networks (GNNs) to analyse Control Flow Graphs (CFGs) of Java functions. The authors state that they wanted to capture both, syntactical similarity as well as semantic similarity. However, this is achieved by estimating the semantics via a syntactic approximation. If the same program constructs are nested in a similar way, this has a positive impact on the semantic similarity. But to our experience this does not necessarily hold for code from novice programmers (cf. next section). Furthermore, single Java functions were used instead of full Java classes to reduce the runtime of the Graph Edit Distance problem, as this significantly reduces the number of nodes in each graph. However, it remains unclear how the approach can generalise to full Java classes with multiple functions.

Some approaches for detecting similar Java classes, like for code clone detection, also use abstract syntax trees (e.g. [6]). In conventional ASTs, a new node is created for each new variable access (even if an already referenced variable is accessed again). Thus, any information about the use of variables and thus about the data flow through the programme is discarded. This is also the problem with plagiarism detection tools like JPlag [5]. Here, all variable identifiers are replaced with generic identifiers, as the naming may not have any influence on plagiarism detection. However, for the detection of solution approaches in student solutions, it is important to obtain information about the data flow.

Many approaches utilize neural networks, which are trained using a large number of open source projects. In [7] individual statements (AST subtrees) are represented as embeddings (e.g. local variable declaration) and a sequence of embeddings is encoded using recurrent networks. However, similar to the clone detection, the sequential representation includes variable declaration statements, but actual dependencies between variables are not captured (that is, which variable is used where). This may not be a problem for well-written code from official repositories, because a tree of statements may suggest a meaningful variable usage itself. It is, however, a problem when source code from novice programmers is used, who struggle not only with the concepts of the language, but also with computational thinking in general. In that case, the wrong variables are used in the wrong places, turning a potentially useful code skeleton into a mess. The fact that conditional statements and loops are composed in a similar manner alone does not mean that the code does something similar.

So for educational purposes (in introductory courses) we consider it as a major problem with other approaches, that they disregard the way in which variables are used. We argue that two submissions follow the same solution approach if they use variables in the same way. This work extends earlier work [2]

```
class Range {

  int getRange(int[] arr) {
    int min = 1000;
    int max = -1000;
    for (int i=0;i<arr.length;++i)
      if (arr[i]<min) min=arr[i]; else
        if (arr[i]>max) max=arr[i];
    return max-min;
  }
}
```

```
class Range {
  int mn = 1000;
  int mx = -1000;

  int getRanges(int[] arr) {
    int min = arr[0], max = arr[0];
    for (int i=1;i<arr.length;++i) {
      if (arr[i]<min) min=arr[i];
      if (arr[i]>max) max=arr[i];
    }
    return max-min;
} }
```

```
class Range {
  int small = 1000;
  int large = -1000;

  void include(int a) {
    if (a<small) small=a; else
      if (a>large) large=a;
  }
  int range(int[] arr) {
    for (int i=0;i<arr.length;++i)
      include(arr[i]);
    return large-small;
} }
```

Fig. 1. Three solutions to the same exercise.

by allowing a full comparison of Java classes (multiple functions and distinction between local variables and attributes) and also addresses the problem of different functional decompositions.

3 Problem Definition

The goal is to detect different approaches to the same problem or exercise. While for an experienced programmer it may look like a task calls for a canonical, straightforward solution, students may find quite different approaches even to standard problems, as they have not yet developed a notion for *standard cases* or struggle with getting the standard approach straight. Figure 1 shows three (potential) solutions to an exercise which requests a function that returns the value range of the passed array (which carries elements of up to three digits only). With respect to the chosen solution approach, all three submissions follow the same idea and are considered similar (in contrast to the examples of Fig. 5, which are syntactically similar to the examples in Fig. 1 but solve a different problem). Keeping the code structure but mixing the variables, however, may easily destroy the functionality completely. A useful notion of similarity has to take into account which variable is used where. But still the similarity is not recognized easily, we are faced with the following challenges: The students have chosen different function names. Some use attributes, others only local variables. There are artefacts that indicate a change in the strategy (the solution in the middle declares some attributes but then decides not to use them). The solution on the right decomposes the problem and uses a second function to solve the task in exactly the same fashion as the solution on the left, but with a more compact code. Syntactically both solutions (left and right) are different, semantically they are identical. Ideally we would like to group code by ideas, but content ourselves with ways to group code by similar variable usage.

4 Proposed Approach

The problem of comparing two classes, say `C` and `D`, is decomposed into two steps, matching functions and then attributes. The use of variables, that is,

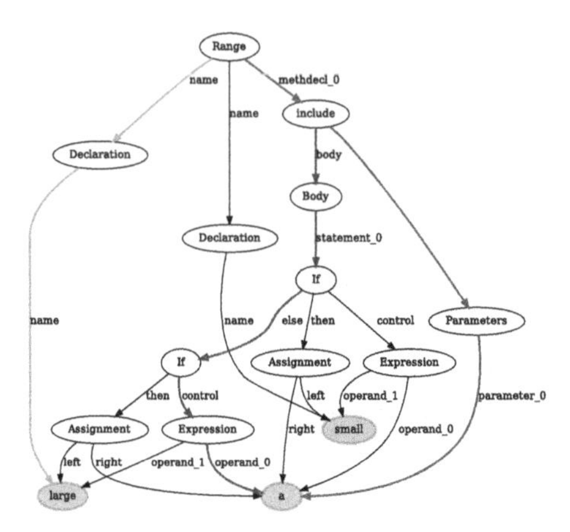

Fig. 2. Modified AST of class **Range** (in Fig. 1(right), only method **include**) where all nodes, that correspond to the same variable (filled red), are unified.

how they are embedded into the control structures, captures the nature of the underlying functionality well and shall form the basis of a similiarity measure. We characterize a variable's usage by inspecting a modified abstract syntax tree (AST), where tree nodes that refer to the same variable are unified into a single node (which turns the AST into a graph). Figure 2 shows an example for the class **Range** (example on the right in Fig. 1, limited to the **include** function). The three variables (argument **a** and attributes **small** and **large**) correspond to nodes shaded red. Whenever a variable is used, there is an incoming edge to these nodes. A variable's usage can thus be described by the set of all paths from the root node (here: Range) to the variable node. (The root node is omitted from the path as it is the same for all paths.) For instance, the blue path **a/parameters/include** tells us that **a** is a parameter of function **include** of class **Range**. The green path a/expression/if/if/body/include informs us, that **a** is used in the control expression of a nested **if**-statement inside the **include** function. The orange path large/Declaration/⊥ misses a function node, because **large** is an attribute that is defined in the scope of the class rather than the scope of a function. We may thus describe a whole class by the set of all *variable usage paths* as follows:

Definition 1 (variable usage path). *Let I be a set of code instruction labels (such as* **if**, **while**, **expression**, *...). For a given Java class C, let V_C be a set of variable identifiers*[1] *and F_C the set of functions declared in C. A* **path** *$p = (v, i_1, \ldots, i_n, f) \in V_C \times I^* \times (F_C \cup \{\bot\}) := \mathcal{P}$ reflects that a variable v is used by instruction i_1, which is itself used by instruction i_2, etc., in function f*

[1] Note that variable names themselves are not valid identifiers, as the same name may be used twice for variables in different functions. From the AST, we extract a unique node identifier for each variable. But in this paper, for simplification and readability, we use the variable names as identifiers.

(or, indicated by $\perp$, directly in the class definition in case of attributes). The **VUP-representation** *(variable usage path) of code C is a set $P_C \subseteq \mathcal{P}$ of all paths occurring in C.*

Classes `C` and `D` may then be compared by comparing the respective VUP representations P_C and P_D:

Definition 2 (VUP similarity). *Given two VUP representations P and Q, we measure their similarity by the F_1-measure:*

$$F_1(P, Q) = 2 \cdot \frac{p \cdot r}{p + r} \quad \textit{where} \quad p = \frac{|P \cap Q|}{|P|}, r = \frac{|P \cap Q|}{|Q|}$$

If, however, function and variable names are disjoint in `C` and `D` (as it is the case in Fig. 1), $F_1(P, Q)$ is undefined, so in this case, we assume $F_1(P, Q) = 0$. We may replace all variable names and all function names by the same identifier, as it is frequently done by other approaches (e.g. plagiarism detection).

Definition 3 (simplified usage path). *Given a class C, let $\sigma : V_C \times I^* \times (F_C \cup \{\perp\}) \to \{\texttt{vn}\} \times I^* \times \{\texttt{fn}, \perp\}$ a transformation, that replaces all variables names by a constant identifier* `vn` *(generic variable name) and all function names f by*

$$f' = \begin{cases} \texttt{fn} \textit{ if } f \neq \perp \\ \perp \textit{ otherwise} \end{cases}$$

where `fn` *is a constant identifier. For a VUP P, we denote $\sigma(P)$ as a simplified VUP representation (SVUP) . By σ_f (σ_v, resp.) we denote the same transformation as σ except that it leaves the variable names (function names, resp.) unaltered.*

The discussed paths would thus read in the simplified representation `vn/Declaration/⊥`, **`vn/parameters/fn`**, and `vn/expression/if/if/body/fn`, resp. Comparing simplified representations $\sigma(P_C)$ usually yields a non-zero value for $F_1(\sigma(P_C), \sigma(P_D))$, but does not distinguish different function and variables at all, and thus gives only a rough similarity estimate.

By visual inspection of the examples in Fig. 1 we *know* that function `getRange` (left) and `range` (right) correspond to each other, but this information is not available to our similarity measure. The simple approach of averaging all possible pairwise similarities, such as comparing `getRange` with `include` and `getRange` with `range` is not a reasonable solution. To accurately assess similarity as realistic as possible, only the corresponding functions (and variables) should be considered (like `getRange` vs `range`). To solve this problem, we need some means to filter for usage paths of certain variables or functions:

Definition 4 (filter π on usage paths). *Let $\pi_{(x,y)} : \mathcal{P} \to \mathcal{P}, P \mapsto \{p \mid p = (v, i_1, \ldots, i_n, f) \in P \wedge (x = v \vee x = *) \wedge (y = f \vee y = *)\}$ be a filtering function that returns a VUP representation of only those paths that refer to variable identifier x (or all variables if $x = *$) and function identifier y (or all functions if $y = *$).*

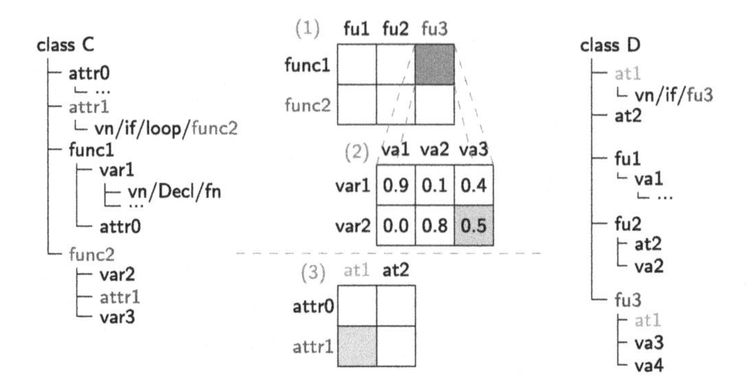

Fig. 3. Schema of class comparison.

The challenge is now to match functions and attributes from different classes dynamically. Figure 3 shows the proposed approach schematically. On the left, class C is decomposed into attributes (here: `attr0` and `attr1`) and functions (here: `func1` and `func2`). Function nodes f have a child node for every variable that is used in the function. The children of some variable v correspond to a simplified VUP representation of all related usage paths of function f, that is, $\sigma(\pi_{(v,f)}(P_C))$. The children of some attribute a correspond to $\sigma_v(\pi_{(a,*)}(P_C))$.

In order to find the best counterparts of functions in `C` among functions in `D`, a cost matrix is created (matrix (1) in Fig. 3). To fill the cost matrix we need to assess the similarity between, say, function `func1` of `C` and `fu3` of `D`, which shall be accomplished by comparing how similar both functions are in terms of their variable usage. To assess this particular value, another cost matrix is constructed (matrix (2) in Fig. 3), which compares all variables of `func1` against all variables of `fu3`. A single cell in this matrix captures the *cost* of assigning a variable from one class to a variable of the other. The cost value is obtained from calculating F_1 of the respective SVUPs ($1 - F_1$ enters the cell, turning similarity F_1 into cost/distance). For the marked cell (`var2` vs `va3`) we obtain its value from

$$1 - F_1 \left(\sigma(\pi_{(\mathtt{var2},\mathtt{func1})}(P_C)) \, , \, \sigma(\pi_{(\mathtt{va3},\mathtt{fu3})}(P_D)) \right)$$

The optimal match of variables is obtained, when the total assignment cost become minimal. This problem is known as an *assignment problem*, which is not trivial. The challenge is to efficiently determine the optimal assignment, as the number of possible combinations grows quickly with the size of the cost matrix. The Munkres algorithm [4] provides a solution by analysing the cost matrix and determining an optimal allocation with minimum total cost in cubic runtime complexity. In cost matrix (2) of Fig. 3 the optimal assignment would be $A_v = \{(\mathtt{var1}, \mathtt{va2}), (\mathtt{var2}, \mathtt{va1})\}$ with a minimal total cost of 0.1.

To reflect the optimal variable assignment for `func1` and `fu3` (as represented by some assignment A), the variable names can be renamed in all paths of P_C and P_D:

Definition 5 (renaming ϱ of usage paths). *Let $A \subset V_C \times V_D$ be the result of an assignment problem for classes C and D, that is, identifiers i_1 and i_2 have been assigned if and only if $(i_1, i_2) \in A$. Let $\varrho_A : \mathcal{P} \to \mathcal{P}$ be a renaming function, which replaces all occurrences of any identifier $(i_1, i_2) \in A$ in all variable usage paths by some new identifier $h(i_1, i_2)$ (e.g. obtained from a hash function h or any other unique, artificially generated name).*

Once the variables are renamed, we can fill in the cost value of the resp. cell in cost matrix (1), which is now obtained from

$$1 - F_1\left(\sigma_f(\varrho_{A_v}(\pi_{(*,\texttt{func1})}(P_C)))\,,\,\sigma_f(\varrho_{A_v}(\pi_{(*,\texttt{fu3})}(P_D)))\right)$$

Having filled out all cells in this way, we obtain the cost-minimal match of functions from another application of the Munkres algorithm [4].

Once all functions have been assigned to one another and all identifiers have been replaced in the usage paths accordingly, the attributes can be assigned in the same fashion by comparing their VUP representations (cost matrix (3) in Fig. 3). With $A_f = \{(\texttt{func1}, \texttt{fu3}), (\texttt{func2}, \texttt{fu2})\}$ being the union of all selected function assignments, the cost of the highlighted cell in cost matrix (3) is obtained from

$$1 - F_1\left(\sigma_v(\varrho_{A_f}(\pi_{(\texttt{attr0},*)}(P_C)))\,,\,\sigma_v(\varrho_{A_f}(\pi_{(\texttt{at1},*)}(P_D)))\right)$$

At this point, all functions and variables (local variables as well as attributes) from class C have been assigned to the respective elements of class D, preserved in the assignments A_f and A_v.[2] The final similarity is then computed as a mixture of function and attribute similarity (we use $\alpha = 0.7$):

$$\alpha \underbrace{F_1(\varrho_{A_f}(P_C), \varrho_{A_f}(P_D))}_{\text{functions}} + (1-\alpha) \underbrace{F_1(\varrho_{A_v}(P_C), \varrho_{A_v}(P_D))}_{\text{attributes}}$$

Functional decomposition. So far, we have not tackled the difference between the code on the left and on the right of Fig. 1, which differs in the functional decomposition. The usage paths will of course differ: `range` (Fig. 1(right)) uses the argument `arr[i]` in the function call `include(arr[i])`, whereas `getRange` (Fig. 1(left)) uses `arr[i]` multiple times in the `if`-statements. To overcome these differences, we modify the way how paths are extracted from the AST in case of function calls. Figure 4 shows the graph for the `range` method, which calls the `include`-method (`call` node with edge to the `include` method). We would extract a path `arr/arrayaccess/call/for/body/range` for the array `arr`, which indicates that it occurs as a parameter in a function call. Whenever a path contains a `call` segment, we modify the path as follows: we replace the single `call` segment with all paths of the respective parameter from the called function, where (1) the argument is removed and (2) the path is cut off at the body of the function. In the case of the `include` function in Fig. 2 we have already discussed

[2] or remain unassigned in case no counterpart exists.

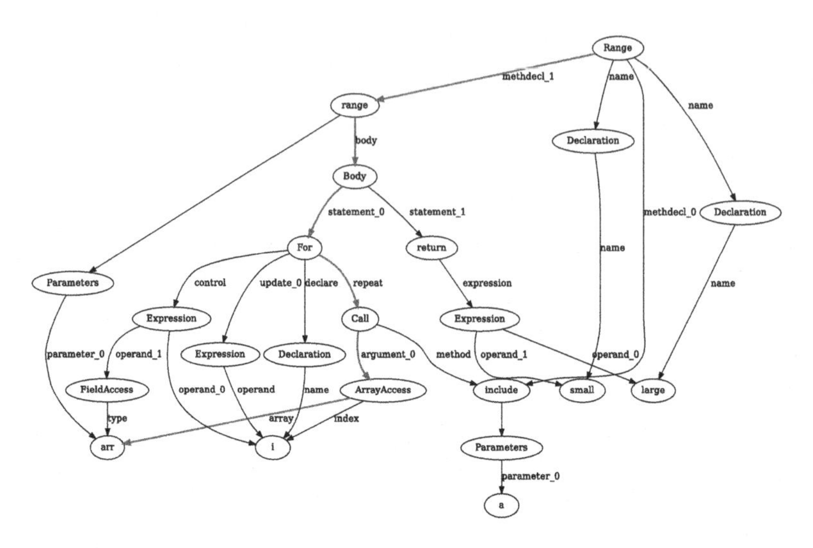

Fig. 4. Modified AST of class `Range` (in Fig. 1(right)), without implementation of `include`.

the path `a/expression/if/if/body/include`. We remove the parameter (`a`) and cut off the path at the body of the function and obtain `expression/if/if`. That is, in the original path of the `include(arr[i])`-call we replace `call` by `expression/if/if` (same for all other paths that include this parameter). This leads us to `arr/arrayaccess/expression/if/if/body/range`, which is the same path we would have obtained if the function `include` was inlined in the `range` function. In this way we generate the same paths that are extracted from Fig. 1(left). Finally, minor transformations are applied to the extracted path sets to purify them, such as filtering out artefacts or nested *bodies* (such that `if(..){{stmt;}}` equals `if(..){stmt;})`.

5 Experimental Evaluation

We first discuss the results for the example classes from Fig. 1. As a distractor we add two more source codes to them, shown in Fig. 5, which are similar in terms of statement nesting, but dissimilar to the others in terms of variable usage. The following sources were compared pairwise: *oddeven* and *oddevenfunc* from Fig. 5, the *left*, *mid*, and *right* code from Fig. 1, an *empty* class and a clone *mid2loop* of *mid* where each of the two conditional statements gets its own for-loop. The result is a 7×7 distance matrix. One cell in this distance matrix then corresponds to the total distance between two classes `C` and `D`. Multidimensional scaling (MDS) was applied to the distance matrix ($R^2 \approx 0.90$), which projects the individual data points in the two-dimensional space, while trying to preserve the pairwise distances. For the final evaluation of the quality of the realised class comparison, hierarchical cluster analysis with the single-linkage method

```
class Range { // oddeven

  int cnt1 = 0;
  int cnt2 = 0;

  int oddeven(int[] a) {
    for (int i=0;i<a.length;++i) {
      if (a[i]%2==0) ++cnt1;
      else ++cnt2;
    }
    return cnt2-cnt1;
  }
}
```

```
class Range { // oddevenfunc
  int cnt1 = 0;
  int cnt2 = 0;

  void f(int a) {
    if (a%2==0) ++cnt1;
    else ++cnt2;
  }

  int oddeven(int[] a) {
    for (int i=0;i<a.length;++i)
      f(a[i]);
    return cnt2-cnt1;
}}
```

Fig. 5. Two sources with similar code structure (conditional statement within loop over array) but different variable usage.

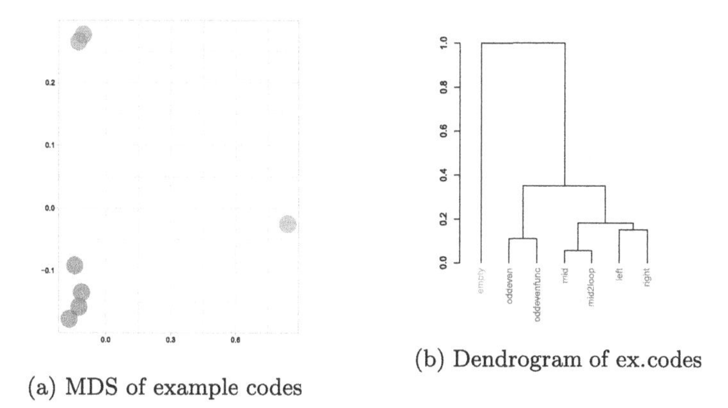

(a) MDS of example codes

(b) Dendrogram of ex.codes

Fig. 6. Evaluation of example codes

was applied to the distance matrices. Figure 6 shows the results. On the left we see the MDS embedding into 2D. The classes that use variables in different ways are optimally separated from each other. This is also reflected in the dendrogram. We can see that the submissions that use variables in a similar way and follow a similar approach are close to each other, as desired (e.g. mid and mid2loop, which barely differ in terms of variable usage).

For a more comprehensive evaluation of the proposed approach, we analysed real students' submissions resulting from different exercises. The evaluation results of one of these exercises are presented below. In the task TimeKeeper (TK), a working time administration had to be implemented. A complete realisation typically contains four methods, a constructor and about four attributes. Two predominant approaches can be found in the submissions, which perform the necessary calculations in a different way (re-calc all values with every change versus calculation of single values upon request). First, the submissions were grouped manually, four clusters were identified. C_{green} contains completely empty classes without implementation, C_{blue} contains an implementation that

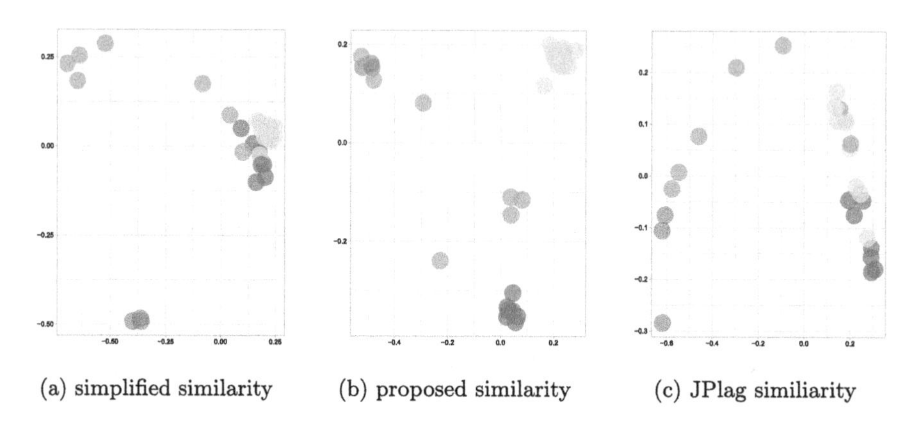

(a) simplified similarity (b) proposed similarity (c) JPlag similiarity

Fig. 7. MDS 2-dimensional projection, C_{green} = empty classes, C_{blue} = partially implemented classes, C_{yellow} and C_{red} = two predominant solution approaches

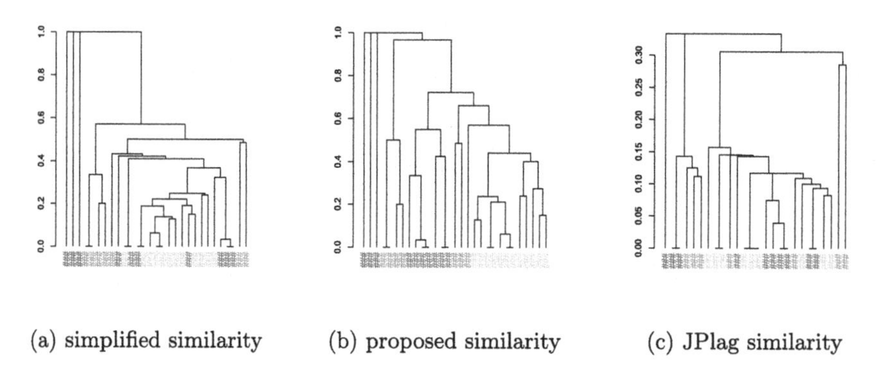

(a) simplified similarity (b) proposed similarity (c) JPlag similarity

Fig. 8. Dendrograms of hierarchical clustering

has been started but for which no specific solution approach is recognisable yet (only some variable and method declarations but only little functionality), and C_{yellow} and C_{red} contain the two predominant solution approaches. We compare the results of the proposed approach with the simplified representation ($F_1(\sigma(P_C), \sigma(P_D))$) and the JPlag [5] tool to derive an additional distance matrix. JPlag is a frequently used and well established tool for source code comparison, most commonly used to detect plagiarisms. Figure 7 shows the results of MDS and Fig. 8 presents the resulting dendrograms. Note that some jitter was applied to the 2D projections to make data points visible that lie very close to each other.

Figure 7a shows the 2D representation of the submissions, which were analysed with the simplified variant. The submissions belonging to C_{green}, representing empty classes, are perfectly separated from the remaining submissions. On the other hand, the submissions in C_{blue}, which represent partially implemented classes, are partially separated from the other groups. Some of these submissions form a distinct cluster in the top-left region. Among these submissions, those that include more code and are gradually evolving towards one of the two solution approaches are more similar to the fully implemented classes. Consequently, they tend to be positioned in close proximity to the fully implemented classes. The fully implemented classes are concentrated in a single cluster. Within this cluster, however, the upper region consists mainly of submissions that follow the yellow approach, while the lower half comprises mostly submissions that follow the red approach. Thus, an approximate separation is already noticeable here using the simplified comparison.

Figure 7c shows the results of the pairwise analysis with the JPlag tool. The empty classes from C_{green} are separated from the other classes, but not as distinctly as in Fig. 7a. This can be explained by the fact that we classified a class as "empty" when no functionality was implemented at all. However, a class declaration or the declaration of the main function may still be present in the file. Thus, the submissions differ in the syntactic comparison with JPlag, but not in their variable usage paths. On the right side of the figure, the fully implemented classes as well as isolated half-finished classes occur in one group. There is a slight tendency to separate the approaches in C_{red} and C_{yellow}, but the approaches are mixed and clusters overlap. Submissions of C_{blue} are widely distributed between the empty and fully implemented classes, two almost reaching C_{yellow}.

Figure 7b analogously shows the results of the proposed similarity presented in the context of this paper. At first glance, four groups and two outliers can be identified. In the upper left there are the empty submissions from C_{green}. Within this group there are two submissions from C_{blue}. This is due to the fact that these two solutions contain only attribute declarations and implement no functionality. Since the declared attributes are never referenced in functions, they are identified as artefacts and removed before class comparison, which results in empty VUP-representations as well. In the middle there is a group of partially implemented submissions (C_{blue}), which have reached a similar stage of completion. Two other partial solutions represent intermediate versions, which are thus located somewhere in between. However, the different approaches have been separated perfectly and form two distinct clusters.

The 2D representation resulting from MDS provides an intuitive way to get an overview of the structure in the data, clusters can be identified with a single glance. However, structures may be present in the data that are not recognisable in 2D space. A coefficient of determination of $R^2 \approx 0.70$ is solid, but not optimal. The dendrograms from a hierarchical cluster analysis are shown in Fig. 8. Again, the proposed approach separates the different approaches (C_{yellow} and C_{red}) best. The dendrograms also show that the proposed comparison is the only one in which the two solutions C_{yellow} and C_{red} can be perfectly separated by a cutplane ($\delta \approx 0.6$). For the other two dendrograms no such separation is feasible.

In summary, the results suggest that the composed comparison is a better discriminating method than the simple one and the JPlag Tool. The sample is small, but it becomes clear that on the test data, with the help of the chosen implementation, manually distinguishable solutions are distinguishable by a machine as well.

6 Conclusion

In conclusion, this paper presents an automated method for improving computer science education by analysing code submitted by students. The proposed approach compares Java classes in a semantic way using variable usage paths (VUPs) extracted from modified abstract syntax trees (ASTs). The method presented in this paper outperforms simplified comparisons and the JPlag tool in accurately grouping submissions by similarity of solution approaches. The evaluation results demonstrate the effectiveness of the approach in identifying different approaches. Through a preliminary evaluation using real student code submissions, it was shown that this method provides valuable insights for students and teachers. Lecturers can get an overview of the prevailing solution approaches in the submissions and specifically discuss individual ones in the lecture. We intend to offer students, who have finished their exercise, a solution from a fellow student that follows a different approach. We then ask the students for pros and cons of both solutions, which encourages students to overthink their own solution as well as comprehending given code (and will also be used to assess the validity of the method on a larger scale). Both applications can have an immediate positive impact on the students' learning success.

Acknowledgements. This work was partly funded by the German Federal Ministry of Education and Research under the grant no. 16DHBKI056 (ki4all).

References

1. Hellendoorn, V.J., Devanbu, P.: Are deep neural networks the best choice for modeling source code? In: Proceedings of the 11th Joint Meeting on Foundation of Software Engineering, pp. 763–773 (2017)
2. Höppner, F.: Grouping source code by solution approaches - improving feedback in programming courses. In: Proceedings of the 14th International Conference on Educational Data Mining (2021)
3. Joyner, D., et al.: From clusters to content: using code clustering for course improvement. In: Proceedings of the 50th ACM Technical Symposium on Computer Science Education, pp. 780–786 (2019)
4. Munkres, M.: Algorithms for the assignment and transportation problems. J. Soc. Ind. Appl. Math. **5**(1), 32–38 (1957)
5. Prechelt, L., Malpohl, G., Phlippsen, M.: JPlag: Finding Plagiarisms Among a Set of Programs. University of Karlsruhe, Tech. rep. (2000)
6. Sager, T., Bernstein, A., Pinzger, M., Kiefer, C.: Detecting similar java classes using tree algorithms. In: Proceedings of the 2006 International Workshop on Mining Software Repositories, pp. 65–71 (2006)
7. Zhang, J., Wang, X., Zhang, H., Sun, H., Wang, K., Liu, X.: A novel neural source code representation based on abstract syntax tree. In: 2019 IEEE/ACM 41st International Conference on Software Engineering, pp. 783–794. IEEE (2019)

Does Starting Deep Learning Homework Earlier Improve Grades?

Edward Raff[1,2,3](✉) and Cynthia Matuszek[2]

[1] Booz Allen Hamilton, McLean, USA
raff.edward@gmail.com
[2] University of Maryland, Baltimore County, Catonsville, USA
[3] Syracuse University, Syracuse, USA

Abstract. Intuitively, students who start a homework assignment earlier and spend more time on it should receive better grades on the assignment. However, existing literature on the impact of time spent on homework is not clear-cut and comes mostly from K-12 education. It is not clear that these prior studies can inform coursework in deep learning due to differences in demographics, as well as the computational time needed for assignments to be completed. We study this problem in a post-hoc study of three semesters of a deep learning course at the University of Maryland, Baltimore County (UMBC), and develop a hierarchical Bayesian model to help make principled conclusions about the impact on student success given an approximate measure of the total time spent on the homework, and how early they submitted the assignment. Our results show that both submitting early and spending more time positively relate with final grade. Surprisingly, the value of an additional day of work is apparently equal across students, even when some require less total time to complete an assignment.

1 Introduction

In developing a course on deep learning for the University of Maryland, Baltimore County (UMBC), we focused on practical coding experience and implementation of deep learning methods for the course content and evaluation. Compared to assignments in some machine learning classes, the course requirement to use a Graphics Processing Unit (GPU) led us to strongly emphasize throughout the semester that students should start their homework early, as they need to have sufficient time to run their code, iterate and try to fix bugs if errors occurred, and ask the instructor for assistance. As the course progressed and assignments were due, students would sometimes ask how early should they start an assignment, and we had no quantifiable justification for our answers. This paper remedies this issue, and studies the overall question: does starting and/or submitting an assignment earlier improve student's grades on that homework?

The literature studying the impact of time spent on homework, at large, is sparse. One set of work studies the impact of "procrastination," measured by comparing the time an assignment is due and the time the assignment was

S. Nowaczyk et al. (Eds.): ECAI 2023 Workshops, CCIS 1948, pp. 381–396, 2024.
https://doi.org/10.1007/978-3-031-50485-3_38

submitted [2,9,10]. This is the easiest form of data to study as it is readily available in modern electronic submission systems. The current studies regularly conclude that those who submit earlier obtain better grades. While we collect the same data, we do not study it directly as it is a proxy for time spent. That is to say, a student who does the assignment the day before and submits the day before has procrastinated, but would not show up in the data as a procrastinator. Similarly a student who starts weeks in advance, and submits at the literal "11'th hour" did not procrastinate, but would be marked a procrastinator when using only submission time. In our study we have the start time of an assignment, and we use that with the time submitted to compute a "total time" spent on the assignment. This is not a contiguous measure of time or effort, but we argue a likely better measure of the quantity we care about: total effort spent on an assignment.

Others have also attempted to look at the total time spent on homework and its relation to performance, and have regularly concluded that too much time spent on homework can result in *reduced* scholastic performance [3,5,12]. All of these works focus on students in high school or earlier, and are focused on overall scholastic outcomes rather than per-assignment results. Similarly, the data is the result of survey information, where our total time is determined via the edit history of the assignment. For this reason we believe our total time measure to be a more reliable, though still not perfect, measure of the goal. In a larger sense, there are numerous differences between our population and those studied before (we study graduate students vs. K-12, homework grade vs. overall performance, and coding and deep learning vs. general Science Technology Engineering and Math subjects). The consistency of the prior studies results' about negative returns for "over-studying" necessitate exploration of the question.

The rest of our paper is organized as follows. First we will give extensive background on our data, the course, and necessary background to interpret and understand the results in Sect. 2. We have $N = 68$ total subjects over three semesters of the course. Next we detail the model we use for understanding the data in Sect. 3, which uses a hierarchical Bayesian approach, as is generally encouraged in studies of this nature [4]. Our results will be presented in Sect. 4, where we conclude that more time spent is better than less, and submitting earlier and spending more time have a statistically significant positive impact on a student's grades. Finally we will review other related works in Sect. 5 and then conclude in Sect. 6.

2 Data Collection and Background

To study the question, our data is collected from a course taught by the author(s) in the Spring 2020, Fall 2020, and Spring 2021 semesters at UMBC. The course content and questions were developed into a book Inside Deep Learning[1] [16]. We note that this immediately introduces a set of biases into our results. Most notably, the semesters involved have occurred at the onset of and through the

[1] Available at https://www.manning.com/books/inside-deep-learning.

COVID-19 pandemic. This has introduced stresses on students and faculty that are beyond the scope of this study. In addition, one set of instructor(s) are involved, and so any instructor modulated response will not be observable.

As part of the course design, students were instructed to write, test, and submit all of their homework within a Google Colaboratory environment. This choice was originally made as a mechanism to satisfy the desiderata:

1. Free or cheap GPU availability to students
2. Avoiding versioning conflicts and software installation issues
3. Having a simple means of running student assignments (also avoiding student vs. teacher package mismatches)
4. Provides an easy way for students to get help/feedback on assignments

An unintended benefit of this course design choice was that Colab kept a *sparse* edit history of the assignments. Different from a normal version control system, Colab will take snapshots that can be differentiated against each other (or the current version) of a document at regular intervals, or as an explicit save request is called. The exact mechanics of this process are not documented, but there does appear to be an age-off process where some subset of snapshots are removed over time, eventually resulting in no edit history.

This edit history, collected close in time to course completion, was initially used as a means of assisting and helping students with feedback on how to perform better in the course. For example, we could see when a student started the homework assignment 40 min before the assignment was due, and thus, was unable to complete the assignment. In such cases the student was coached and advised on time management and the need to reach out to instructors early if something may prevent them from timely completion. Retroactively, this also became the driving force for this study: is there a significant difference in student's grades based on when they begin their assignment?

To answer the question, we went through every student's homework assignments version history, which is available when students submit an editable link to their Colab files (as required by the course submission). It was quickly determined that the first edit in the history was not a reliable method of determining the student's start date, as many students would create the homework file days or weeks before starting the assignment. Small edits to copy questions would also occur. Other faux starts included copying code from the course book that would be used by the homework solution (e.g., assignment says to modify the code), but had not yet started actual modification. For this reason, we subjectively reviewed all edit histories until the first edit that appears to show the student trying to make progress on the assignment, and recorded that as the start date of the assignment. The submission time on the assignment was obtained via email or Blackboard, depending on which method was used to receive homeworks during the given semester.

Combined, this gives us the time of submission and the time between start and submission. A limitation we make explicit is that we cannot reliably measure or quantify the true time spent working on the assignment, because the Colab history is coalesced and undocumented in its triggering frequency/characteristics.

There may be instances where a student in our data "starts early," but does not work on the assignment for an extended period of time. Since we have no way to detect this, we leave the issue to future work.

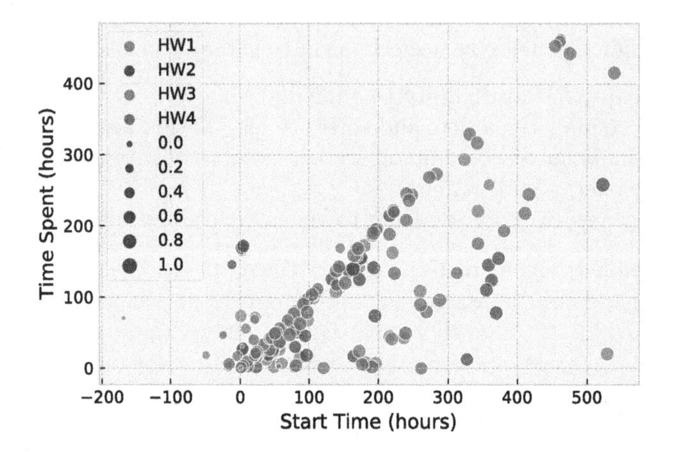

Fig. 1. Visualization of the raw data used in this study. The number of hours in advance of the due date that a student started is on the x-axis, and the number of hours the student appears to have worked on the assignment is the y-axis. Color denotes which homework assignment, and size denotes the grade received on that assignment (1.0 = 100%, 0.0 = 0%). Note most students did well, so many large circles are present. Negative x-axis values occur when students start the assignment after it was due.

A visualization of the resulting data is given in Fig. 1. Note that negative values on the x-axis indicate use of the late submission policy. Most students submit near the deadline, resulting in a strong linear trend. Some students realize they have completed the homework early, and fall to the bottom-right quadrant of the plot.

2.1 Homework Details

Each semester four homeworks were assigned, and their grades were the basis of this study. The design choices of these homeworks impact our modeling of the problem, and the reader's ability to subjectively interpret the applicability of the results to their own curricula and assignments. All four assignments were designed such that someone who knew how to perform all tasks could complete them within 40 min. This reflects the time of an expert practitioner/researcher who has previous done each assignment in the context of a job or research goal, and has over a decade of experience writing code and in machine learning. As such the 40 min is usually not reflective of how long a student will take to complete the assignment, but is done to serve as an upper-bound on the complexity of what is being asked of students to complete. This is not a theory oriented course, and is aimed at students looking to obtain practical knowledge and ultimately write code themselves in the future. The assignments assume that students do not have access to a GPU for days at a time, and so are designed that they can be completed within a day when done correctly. This constraint is born of insufficient funds to purchase GPUs for every student, while also not wanting to burden students with a large capital cost of a GPU when they do not yet know if they will enjoy deep learning.

Each homework assignment consisted of 4 or 5 coding questions with concise summaries in Table 1. Tasks included implementing feature processing, specific neural network architectures, and making specific modifications to an architecture in the book assigned, and comparing the impact of hyper-parameters on total run-time or accuracy of a model.

Table 1. Concise descriptions of the kinds of tasks each homework question(s) required of the students. Each is built from one or more problems from the book written for the course used in this study, Inside Deep Learning. The chapter and question of the full content under the problems column.

HW	Problems	Task
1	C2, Q2	Evaluate a model via AUC
1	C2, Q3-4	Implement checkpointed training
1	C2, Q5	Add more layers to a model
2	C3, Q2	Train a CNN on CIFAR10
2	C4, Q1-3	Train an RNN over text with a custom vocabulary
3	C5, Q6	Perform hyperparameter tuning of a CNN
3	C6, Q2	Train a deeper CNN with BatchNorm
3	C6, Q6	Train an LSTM and compare to an RNN
3	C7, Q1	Train and auto-encoder on MNIST without classes 5 & 9, then evaluate on the missing and included classes
3	C7, Q8	Create an autoregressive loader aware of sentence boundaries
4	C8, Q4	Replace pooling with strided convolutions in a U-Net
4	C9, Q1-2	Implement a convolutional GAN
4	C10, Q1	Combine convolutions and attention for sequential image prediction.

The first and fourth (last) homework were designed to be easier to complete. The first to avoid overwhelming students at the onset, and the second to allow students more time to work on a semester-long final project. There were generally two weeks between each homework assignment and due date, with the next homework being assigned the day the previous was due. The third homework was intentionally designed to be harder, and the instructors suspected students would not give themselves sufficient effort to complete the assignment. For this reason, a 1–2 week extension was baked into the curricula and used every semester. For this reason, student start times can be significantly larger for the third homework.

The course policy included a "no questions asked" late grading policy, that allowed students to submit an assignment up to 72 h late, for −10 points for each day the assignment was late. This meant a total late penalty of -30 h was possible. This penalty was excluded from the data and calculations, as our goal is to make inferences about the value of additional time spent.

Because all courses are different, our results can not be used to infer that every deep learning assignment, class, or set of exercises will follow the results of this paper. Indeed, this will always be the case for any course taught, and no singular study can infer a recommendation appropriate to all universities and classes. Our hope is this study will be informative and help encourage others to study this aspect of education and determine if the results may be applicable and informative to their own instruction.

2.2 Removed Records

Not all student records were kept/used for this study. In total 7 student records are excluded from our analysis due to the following:

- The student did not follow requirements on making the submission editable or starting the homework in Colab, meaning we did not have access to the needed information.
- The student cheated on the homework assignments, making them non-reflective of start time on student grades[2].
- Catastrophic life event such as death of an immediate family member or significant change in medical status.

The final project of the course is excluded from this study. Our experience was that students used multiple Colab instances in clever ways to make further progress on their final projects. This includes running multiple Colabs simultaneously to perform more experiments or using one to run experiments and a second to develop new code. Further, students were allowed to work with external companies/entities on their projects as a means of motivation and to provide more real-world experience (e.g., writing code in support of a favorite charity), and so was not always feasible to perform in a Colab environment. This made data collection on "start" times mostly meaningless, and further exacerbates the importance of true total time spent writing code over the gap between start and submission.

2.3 Institutional Review Board Approval

Our study considers human subjects (our students), and so was required to go through an Institutional Review Board (IRB) for approval. Our study was

[2] Start time potentially impacted propensity to engage in academic misconduct, amongst other stressors with the pandemic. These considerations are critical but beyond our scope and data.

approved by the IRB based on two key factors: 1) Our study's design did not result in any change to student's grades, and was purely observational. 2) Our study did not infringe on any student's rights to privacy.

The later point is particularly important in consideration of limitations in the study's results. As we have stated and will emphasize again, our data does not reflect a granular measure of effort or time spent. We are thus unable to differentiate between a student starting early and spending only a few minutes a day, versus a second student who started later but spent the same amount of time in a single session, to complete the assignment. Getting information at a more granular level would not be passed by our IRB in discussion with them, and we will exemplify two common questions we have received that are not satisfiable by our IRB.

First, one may suggest that the students must engage in the use of some kind of version control system, with positive or negative incentives for frequent use of pushing code changes, such that the total time spent could be inferred from the edit history. This would be a noisy inference, but also would cause the study design to affect student grades or their perception of how they are graded. For this reason our IRB would not approve of a study with this kind of design.

Second, it has been suggested that students should be monitored continuously to track when and for exactly how long they are performing the assignments. Beyond the logistical difficulties of monitoring $\approx$25 students over several months for multiple semesters, this imposes a significant invasion of the student's privacy. Students have an expectation of privacy outside of the classroom, and the monitoring required not only violates that privacy, but is plausibly illegal. This avenue is thus also ill-advised.

For these reasons we find our approach satisfying in allowing us to study the question of interest, at a known and acknowledged level of imprecision. It is logistically feasible, does not alter student grades, and does not infringe on student's privacy rights.

3 Model

To study the impact of student start and "total" time spent on assignments toward the grade received, we will use a linear hierarchical Bayesian model. The overall plate diagram is given in Fig. 2, and the generative story in algorithm 1. Capital Greek letters are used for hyper-priors and lower-case Greek letters for the priors. We use this hierarchical design because of the limited total amount of data, and our assumption is that there is shared information between students in behavior—but some are unique and should be modeled in such a way. Using a hierarchical model allows information sharing to occur across students and homeworks, while simultaneously allowing for variation between them [6]. At a high level, our model incorperates the following design factors with further explenation after.

1. A hierarchical linear model is used to follow best practices to incorporate information sharing (e.g., students working on the same assignment).

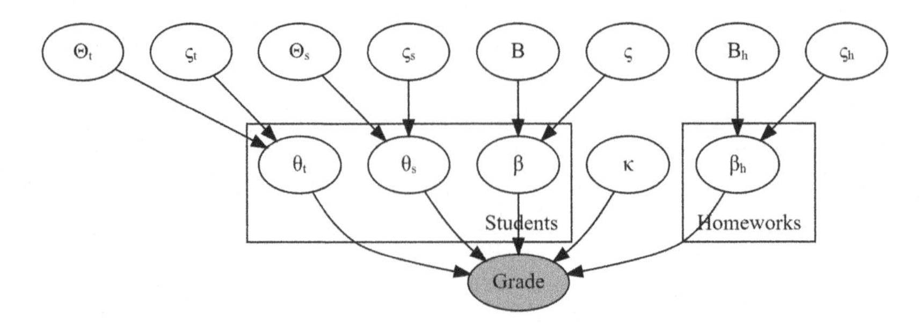

Fig. 2. Plate diagram of the variables used in our model. The box in a plate diagram indicates a repeated measure, as each student receives their own individual bias β (how well does each individual student perform at baseline) and their own coefficients θ_t and θ_s describe their individual benefits from time spent on an assignment and submitting early. Similarly, each homework has a special bias term to quantify if certain homeworks required more time to complete than others. The top level hyper-priors describe the population level averages (Θ_t, Θ_s, B, B_h) and variances (ς_t, ς_s, ς, ς_h) for the variables they point to. The variance for the beta regression κ is inferred on its own as a property of the dataset as a whole.

2. Each student has an independent bias term, which allows the model to account for intrinsic differences in capability to complete the assignment (regardless of the source of those differences, e.g., innate ability or prior exposure).
3. Using the population level hyper-prior to infer population level rates, and the per-student prior to allow for handling of per-student variance.

We will now detail the variables in our model and the logic behind their design. It also allows us to estimate credible intervals, that are a quantified estimate about the uncertainty of each hyper-prior (i.e., population level) and sample prior (i.e., student/homework level) to determine if there is a significant relationship, without being over-encumbered by multiple-test corrections increasing Type II errors in a more frequentist approach [7] . We will use the heavy tailed Cauchy distribution for all hyper-priors as it imposes minimal assumption of the population level values, and a Gaussian distribution for other priors as a reasonable default choice and we do not desire a heavy tail for the coefficients sampled from them.

First, we observe that some students often require less time than others to complete an assignment, and so we feel it would be inappropriate to use a single bias term. For this reason our model allows each of the j students to have their own bias term β^j, determined by its hyper-prior B. Similarly, the homeworks were designed with the intention that the first and last should be easier than the others. So we include additional homework-specific bias terms β_h^i for each of the i different homework assignments.

Using x_t^j and x_s^j to denote the jth's student total time and starting time respectively, we will have corresponding covariance θ_s^j and θ_t^j. Again these are student-specific, so that we may study if individual students benefit differently

Algorithm 1 Generative Story

Input: Student start and total time spent on an assignment x_t and x_s for all students (index by j superscript).

1: $\Theta_t, \Theta_s, B, B_h \sim \text{Cauchy}(0,1)$ # Location hyper-priors
2: $\varsigma_t, \varsigma_s, \varsigma, \varsigma_h, \kappa \sim \text{Cauchy}(0,1)^+$ # Variance hyper-priors, truncated to non-negative values
3: **for** Each Homework i **do**
4: $\beta_h^i \sim \mathcal{N}(B_h, \varsigma_h)$ # Each assignment gets a bias adjustment for difficulty
5: **end for**
6: **for** Each Student j **do**
7: $\beta^j \sim \mathcal{N}(B, \varsigma)$
8: $\theta_t^j \sim \mathcal{N}(\Theta_t, \varsigma_t)$
9: $\theta_s^j \sim \mathcal{N}(\Theta_s, \varsigma_s)$
10: **end for**
11: $\hat{\mu}^{i,j} \leftarrow \sigma\left(\theta_t^j \cdot x_t^j + \theta_s^j \cdot x_s^j + \beta^j + \beta_h^i\right)$
12: measure likelihood against observed grades with eq. (1) using $\mu \leftarrow \hat{\mu}$ and concentration $\kappa \leftarrow \kappa$

from having more time to work on an assignment. The means of the hyper-priors for these two covariates are then Θ_s and Θ_t, and we will look to the hyper-prior posterior after inference to answer the question: *do students at large benefit from more time spent on assignments*. Looking at the student specific θ_s^j and θ_t^j then tells us if students vary in their benefit of more time.

For all hyper-priors (upper-Greek) we sample the mean from a Cauchy distribution, and the variance parameter from the zero truncated Cauchy. This is done to impose little constraint on the location and variance of the hyper-prior. The prior variables (lower-Greek) are samples from Gaussian distributions $\mathcal{N}$(mean, variance) based on the hyper-priors.

The response variable of our model is treated as a Beta regression, and we use the proportional beta formulation as defined by Eq. (1) that allows us to specify a mean μ and non-negative variance κ as it is easier to model[3].

$$\text{Beta\_Prop}(\theta|\mu,\kappa) = \frac{\theta^{\mu\kappa-1}(1-\theta)^{(1-\mu)\kappa-1}}{\mathrm{B}(\mu\kappa,(1-\mu)\kappa)} \tag{1}$$

We use the Beta regression model as it is a popular means of regressing over $(0,1)$ constrained response variables and fits our grade distribution. We prefer to clip the maximum grade of 1.0 (i.e., 100%) to 99.9 and the minimum grade from 0.0 to 0.001, as adding a twice inflated Beta regression would result in a complex to specify model, and complicate analysis due to many 100% grades in our dataset. Functionally a 99% and 100% grade are equal demonstrations of content mastery, but a zero-one inflated model would treat these as meaningfully

[3] In this context B is the beta function, and is not used in this context anywhere else in the manuscript.

different events. To constrain our regression $\hat{\mu}$ of Eq. (1) to the range $(0, 1)$, we use the common sigmoid function as defined by $\sigma(x) = \frac{1}{1+\exp(-x)}$.

This fully specifies our model of student grades and the impact that time, measured by start time and total time spent, impacts students' grades. We use the Numpyro library [13] and the NUTS sampler [8] for our model's inference with 300 burn-in cycles and 600 samples after. This results in a $\hat{r} = 1.00$ for every parameter of the model, indicating full convergence.

4 Results

In this section we present our analysis of the results. We start with the posterior distribution of the hyper-priors shown with a 95% credible interval, which can be found in Fig. 3. First are the global bias term B and the homework specific bias prior B_h. In each case the wide distribution indicates the variability in student behavior. More notably Θ_s and Θ_t show the impact of submitting early and total time spent on an assignment respectively. In both cases the impact is positive and significant as zero is outside the credible interval, with mean values of 0.78 per week early submission and 0.72 per week of additional total time. We remind the reader that this week early corresponds to *starting* the assignment a week early, and not a week of continuous effort.

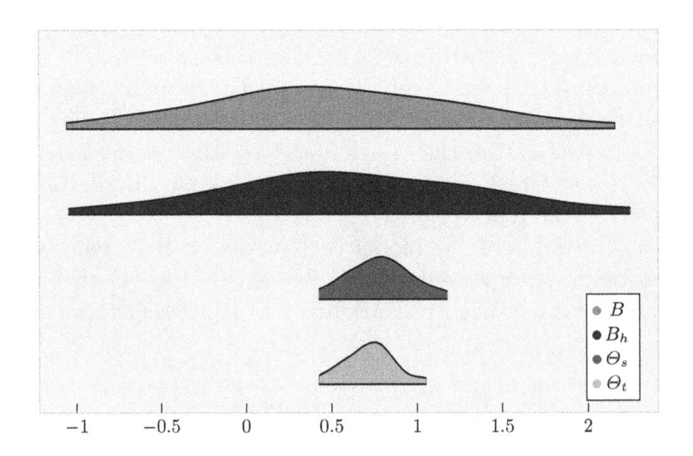

Fig. 3. The 95% credible interval of the hyper-priors B, the global bias term, and B_h, the homework-specific bias prior. Θ_s and Θ_t show the impact of submitting early and total time spent on an assignment; the overall result is a statistically significant positive correlation between these factors and receiving a higher grade.

Crucially, this allows us to examine questions about what the average student can do to improve their grade. One way to look at this is the rate of growth for the function: $\sigma(0.52 + 0.72 \cdot x) - \sigma(0.52)$. This thus returns the impact of starting the assignment earlier, assuming the student will spend all available time to complete it (i.e., submits at the last minute the homework is due). In this form we can infer that starting $x = 2$ weeks early instead of $x = 1$ could yield a 10% improvement in average grade received. This will invariably be affected by individual student performance, and so we must also ask about the distribution of individual students.

Because Θ_s and Θ_t are hyper-priors over the student specific distributions of θ_s and θ_t, we can look at these later distributions to understand the variability of impact. First we consider the total time spent on an assignment θ_t in Fig. 4.

This plot shows the surprisingly consistent benefit that the student receives by spending a week's worth of time on each assignment. This would seem to imply that the benefits are stable and repeatable, and that given we model the problem with a sigmoid σ we suspect corresponds to an implied diminishing return on the benefits of spending more time studying. This would also correspond to the data as shown in Fig. 1, where after starting 200 h (1.2 weeks) before the deadline all students obtain $\geq 85\%$ on their assignments.

We note that the results in submission time are also highly consistent, as shown in Fig. 5. We suspect this is an effect that the submit time x_s can be negative when students submitted late using the 72 h late policy, as shown in Fig. 1. Students *starting* late never received a score better than a 70% before the late penalty was applied. While not an original goal of our study, this does lead us to question the ultimate utility of the late submission policy. If removing the policy would encourage more students to start earlier, because the "backup" of using the late policy does not exist, we may obtain better total outcomes for all students. Simultaneously, our subjective feedback from student reviews and course evaluation is that the late policy is highly appreciated, and could lead to better performance via engagement. Answering this question is beyond the scope of this study, but an important point of future work identified by our data.

While submission and total time have stable distributions across students, students' individual performance biases display more asperity as shown in Fig. 6. In the more extreme cases two students had ≈ -2.5 bias terms, placing them at a deficit of 3 weeks time compared to the mean student. In such a case this would require the student to start each homework assignment immediately in order to obtain the same outcomes. While technically feasible for the course as administered, this requires no other heavy work loads from the student's other courses throughout the semester, and is not realistically possible on all assignments.

This result leads us to question what interventions may be possible to help such students. In our small study, these students are post-hoc identifiable by their performance on the first homework, where most students receive a perfect grade. We lack sufficient examples of such students to statistically confirm that this is reliably the case, but implies the possibility for early intervention may be possible.

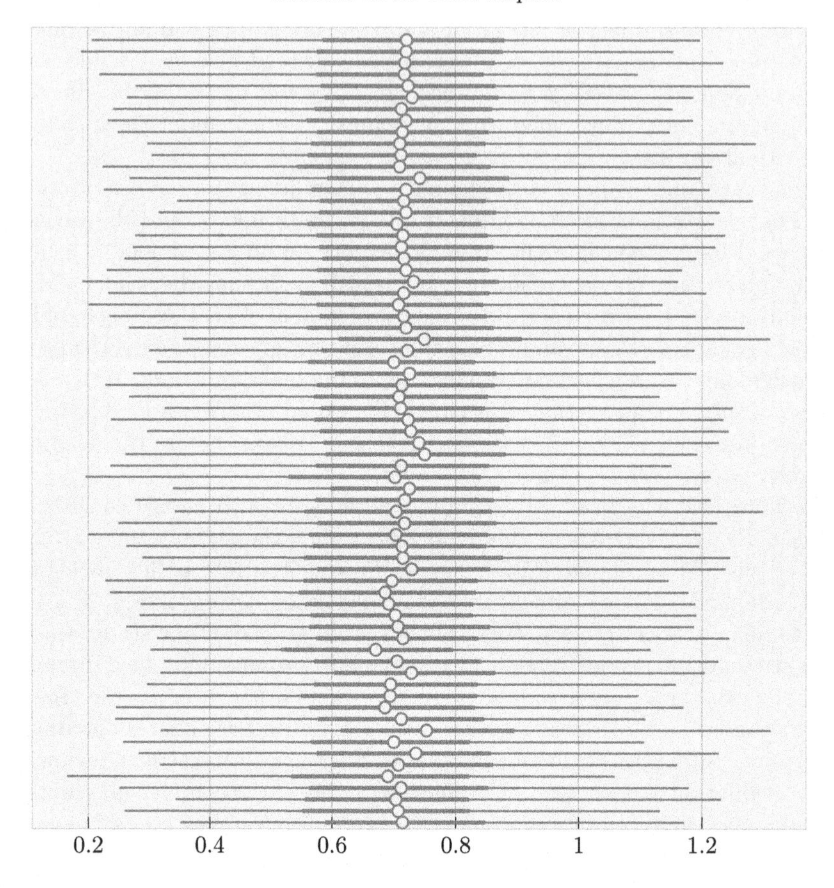

Fig. 4. Forest plot of the 95% credible interval of the student specific distributions θ_t that measure the impact of spending more total time on their final grade. Each line represents a different specific student, the circle showing the median, thick blue lines showing the middle 50% of the interval, and the thin blue lines showing the full 95% credible interval. Results suggest a very consistent cross-population benefit to spending more total time on assignments. (Color figure online)

5 Other Related Work

In our introduction we reviewed two areas of education research that inspire and informed our study. We note that there is little other work regarding the broader question of time to complete or implement deep learning. There has been limited work in studying the amount of time students spend on coding assignments, but most studies are with respect to introductory computer science courses [18]. Empirical reproducibility work has used survival analysis to study the time it takes to replicate machine (and deep) learning papers, finding that most can be done quickly, but a long and heavy tail exists in the effort required [14,15,17].

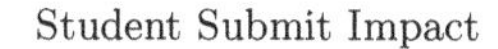

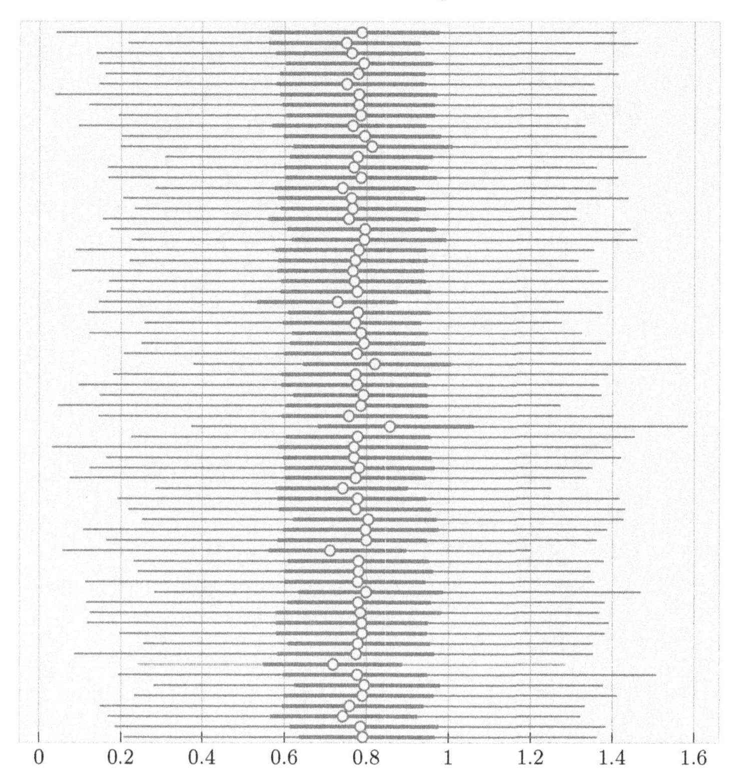

Fig. 5. Forest plot of the 95% credible interval of the student specific distributions θ_s that measure the impact of submitting the homework earlier on individuals' grade. Each line represents a different specific student, with the circle showing the median, thick blue lines showing the middle 50% of the interval, and the thin blue lines showing the full 95% credible interval. Results suggest a consistent correlation between earlier submissions and improved outcomes. (Color figure online)

However, such work is focused on replicated academic peer-reviewed papers, rather than curated assignments in a course. That said, the gap between deep learning graduate course work and implementing academic papers is not too large, and while the annual ML Reproducibility Challenge [19] has demonstrated that students can succeed at such tasks, the additional information of time required has not been recorded. Adding such information to future years could prove valuable to reproducibility work and potentially inform the design of final course projects where attempting to replicate a paper is of a more appropriate scope.

Towards potential interventions, previous work has found that explicitly teaching students how to debug their own code lessens the time they spend on coding assignments [1]. It may be possible to develop similar interventions

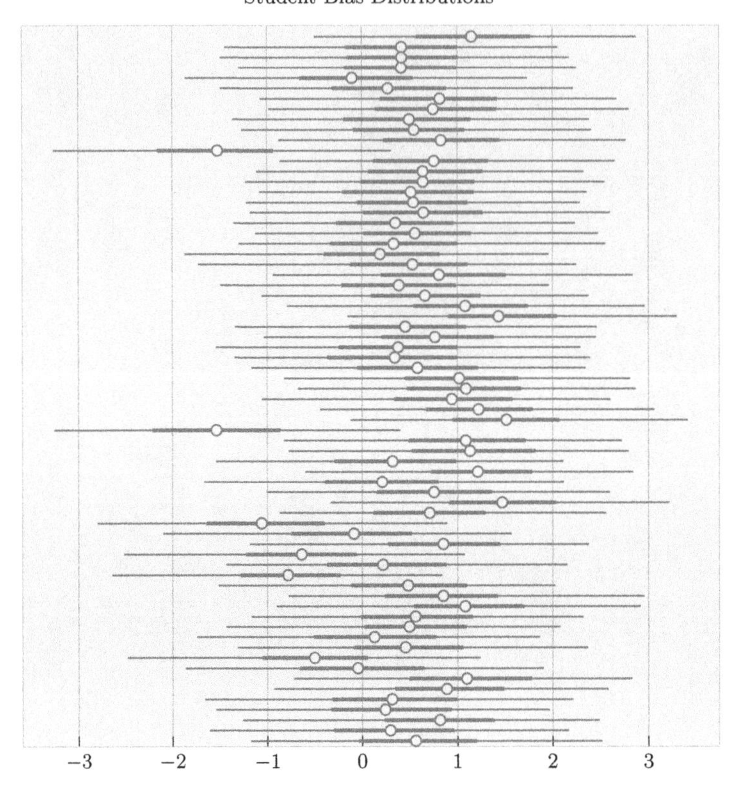

Fig. 6. Forest plot of the 95% credible interval of the student specific distributions β that measure the student specific bias term on individual performance across all assignments. Each line represents a different specific student, the circle showing the median, thick blue lines showing the middle 50% of the interval, and the thin blue lines showing the full 95% credible interval. Students' individual performance bias varies, suggesting that students vary significantly in effort required to complete assignments to a similar level. (Color figure online)

for deep learning, but most work in "debugging" deep learning is still oriented toward researchers[4], and it is not clear to us if the requisite stability in tools and techniques have been distilled to a level for students. We also note that while we are the first (to the best of our knowledge) to estimate time spent on an assignment from version history, we are not the first to use version history in relation to student assessment. In particular, [11] attempted to use version history to try and predict student outcomes on a given assignment, but found little predictive value. While such results could be improved today with better

[4] https://debug-ml-iclr2019.github.io/.

methods for predictive modeling, our more immediate concern would be on how to more precisely quantify actual time spent.

6 Conclusion

We have conducted the first study of the impact of start time (i.e., starting a homework early) and the total time spent on a deep learning assignment on the grade received on the assignment. We find that both factors are statistically significantly correlated with improved scores by a student, which—while intuitive—is not identical to results found in other populations using different methodologies. The current data suggests that students do vary significantly in the base amount of time needed to complete an assignment, but the unit benefit of improvement is remarkably stable across students. This suggests that improved identification and intervention for students who require more time to complete assignments is worth further investigation. Our results suggest the average student may be able to improve their grade by 10% by starting a week earlier than they would otherwise.

Notably, our study is limited to students at a single institution, during three semesters of the COVID-19 pandemic. As such, our results may have selection bias and additional pandemic-related confounding factors. Simultaneously, the current environment suggests that we may unfortunately be operating in a future in which COVID is endemic, and so some of these biases may be relevant to future education concerns. Comparing results across curricula for courses at different institutions, and developing more precise methods of quantifying the actual total time spent, rather than our proxy measure from edit history, are directions for future work to improve upon.

References

1. Chmiel, R., Loui, M.C.: Debugging: from novice to expert. In: Proceedings of the 35th SIGCSE Technical Symposium on Computer Science Education, SIGCSE 2004, pp. 17–21. Association for Computing Machinery, New York, NY, USA (2004)
2. Cormack, S.H., Eagle, L.A., Davies, M.S.: A large-scale test of the relationship between procrastination and performance using learning analytics. Assess. Eval. Higher Educ. **45**(7), 1046–1059 (2020)
3. Fernández-Alonso, R., Suárez-Álvarez, J., Muñiz, J.: Adolescents' homework performance in mathematics and science: Personal factors and teaching practices. J. Educ. Psychol. **107**(4), 1075–1085 (2015)
4. Flunger, B., Trautwein, U., Nagengast, B., Lüdtke, O., Niggli, l., Schnyder, I.: Using multilevel mixture models in educational research: an illustration with homework research. J. Exp. Educ. **89**(1), 209–236 (2021)
5. Galloway, M., Conner, J., Pope, D.: Nonacademic effects of homework in privileged, high-performing high schools. J. Exp. Educ. **81**(4), 490–510 (2013)
6. Gelman, A., Carlin, J.B. Stern, H.S., Dunson, D.B., Vehtari, A., Rubin, D.B.: Bayesian Data Analysis Third edition (with errors fixed as of 13 February 2020), 677, February 2013

7. Gelman, A., Hill, J., Yajima, M.: Why we (usually) don't have to worry about multiple comparisons. J. Res. Educ. Effect. **5**(2), 189–211 (2012)
8. Hoffman, M.D., Gelman, A.: The No-U-Turn sampler: adaptively setting path lengths in Hamiltonian Monte Carlo. J. Mach. Learn. Res. **15**(47), 1593–1623 (2014)
9. Jones, I.S., Blankenship, D.: Year two: effect of procrastination on academic performance of undergraduate online students. Res. Higher Educ. J. **39**, 1–11 (2020)
10. Jones, I.S., Blankenship, D.C.: The effect of procrastination on academic performance of online students at a Hispanic serving institution. J. Bus. Divers. **19**(2), 10–15 (2019)
11. Mierle, K., Laven, K., Roweis, S., Wilson, G.: Mining student CVS repositories for performance indicators. SIGSOFT Softw. Eng. Notes **30**(4), 1–5 (2005)
12. Ozyildirim, G.: Time spent on homework and academic achievement: a meta-analysis study related to results of TIMSS. Psicología Educativa. **28**(1), 13–21 (2021)
13. Phan, D., radhan, N., Jankowiak, M.: Composable Effects for Flexible and Accelerated Probabilistic Programming in NumPyro, arXiv, pp. 1–10 (2019)
14. Raff, E.: A step toward quantifying independently reproducible machine learning research. In: NeurIPS (2019)
15. Raff, E.: Research Reproducibility as a survival analysis. In: The Thirty-Fifth AAAI Conference on Artificial Intelligence (2021)
16. Raff, E.: Inside deep learning: Math, algorithms, models, April 2022
17. Raff, E., Farris, A.L.: A siren song of open source reproducibility, examples from machine learning. In: Proceedings of the 2023 ACM Conference on Reproducibility and Replicability, ACM REP 2023, pp. 115–120. Association for Computing Machinery, New York (2023)
18. Segall, M.: How much time do students spend on programming assignments? A case for self reporting completion times. In: Proceedings of the EDSIG Conference ISSN 2473 3857 (2016)
19. Sinha, K., et al.: ML Reproducibility Challenge 2021. ReScience C. **8**(2), 10 (2022)

Guided Tours in ALeA

Assembling Tailored Educational Dialogues from Semantically Annotated Learning Objects

Jonas Betzendahl(✉), Michael Kohlhase, and Dennis Müller

Friedrich-Alexander University Erlangen-Nürnberg, Erlangen, Germany
jonas.betzendahl@fau.de

Abstract. In times of decreasingly homogeneous educational backgrounds and experiences and increasingly diverse educational target groups and circumstances, the need for educational content that caters to individuals and their specific situations rather than broad groups is rising.

We describe our approach to "guided tours", a framework of educational dialogues that are assembled and tailored on the fly to an individual learner's knowledge and educational experience as part of the intelligent tutoring system ALeA.

1 Introduction

The ALeA system (short for Adaptive Learning Assistant) is an intelligent tutoring system (ITS) that is primarily designed around adapting to the individual learner's knowledge level and preferences. It is an extension of the MMT system [12] which supplies knowledge management functionality based on a domain model expressed as a MMT/OMDoc theory graph [5].

One prominent feature of ALeA are educational dialogues which we call "guided tours". They are designed to allow any user of the system (university students, people studying for a certification, or merely curious souls, henceforth collectively called "learners") to have an interactive, dialogue-like learning experience that starts with *exactly* (ALeA's estimation of) their current understanding of the subject matter and ends with them understanding the concept they originally wanted to learn about.

The key distinction setting guided tours within ALeA apart from other educational dialogues in the context of online learning platforms, is that ALeA possesses a fine-grained (down to the concept level) understanding of any given learner's competencies, and also detailed information about available learning objects. This allows the system to cater to every individual's needs, preferences and current level of understanding.

Detailed information necessary for the above is harvested from *semantically annotated* (university) course materials. The annotations to existing course materials like lecture notes or slide decks introduce structural and topical information about the concepts being talked about in the material, which can then be used to offer a host of educational and didactic services, including guided tours.

S. Nowaczyk et al. (Eds.): ECAI 2023 Workshops, CCIS 1948, pp. 397–408, 2024.
https://doi.org/10.1007/978-3-031-50485-3_39

Modelling Education. We adopt the perspective of Berges et al. [2] that any good educator (human or not) relies on four models for successful instruction of an educatee, independently of concrete context and topic:

1. A **domain model** containing information about concepts in whatever domain of discourse we are interested in, and how they relate to each other.
2. A **learner model** that maintains an estimate of a learner's competencies in regards to the aforementioned concepts. This is achieved by paying attention to the learner and how they interact with the content or educator.
3. A **formulation model** consisting of "formulations" of this knowledge. This includes textual formulations (even in multiple languages) as well as video-files, audio-snippets, podcasts, stone carvings; even interpretive dance performances are thinkable. Anything that even loosely communicates the knowledge in question qualifies as a formulation.
4. A **didactic model** that organises these formulations and their relations to each other, as well as keeping track of their rhetoric classification (is this formulation an introductory video? A quiz question? A hint about a common mistake?) and didactic potential (how should the learner model change when the learner is given this question? When is it appropriate to recommend this musical piece?).

Structure. We use the sTEX format [7,11] for the annotation of the course materials. sTEX is a semantic extension of LATEX, – realised as a LATEX package – that provides macros and environments for embedding functional markup for knowledge items, learning objects, and their relations. sTEX sources can be transformed to semantically annotated HTML, from which MMT/OMDoc representations can be harvested for knowledge management purposes.

The union of all concepts introduced in these annotations and their specified relations to each other forms the ontology that the rest of the system operates on. This means there is no necessity to maintain (and ensure compliance with) a separate ontology. This allows for easy re-use of established concepts, but also (almost) equally easy specification of new concepts or alternative perspectives.

The domain model, as well as the formulation and didactic model, are in practice being managed, organised and served by the MMT system (which we will refer to as the "backend"). There exists an unconnected application managing the learner models (for reasons of separation of concerns and sensitive data) which we will call the LMS (Learner Model Server). Finally, the learners interact directly with a collection of web applications that connect to both the backend and the LMS, which we will call the "frontend".

We are currently working on a domain model for the canonical parts of the undergraduate computer science and AI curricula, and the mathematics they are based upon. The ALEA system is under continuous development and has already been deployed for six courses with over 1000 students total at FAU Erlangen-Nürnberg.

Contribution. The ALEA system itself, its motivation, architecture and individual features, have been thoroughly described in other places in the literature (such as in [8]). Here, we want to focus entirely on the specifics of the tailored educational dialogues under the title "guided tours". We explain the process of guided tours and point out how precise modelling of both learners and domain of discourse improves the experience.

Overview. Section 2 goes further into detail about how individual learners are modelled in ALEA, and how this model can be interacted with and what it informs. In Sect. 3, we will explain the step-by-step flow of a guided tour, what information it draws on during each step, and how it is assembled. Finally, Sect. 4 concludes this paper and discusses ongoing and future work.

2 ALeA Components

2.1 Learner Modelling

The ALEA system keeps a model of a given learner's mastery of concepts in the domain of discourse that they have interacted with before. This is represented as a set of triples $\langle C, D, p\rangle$, where C is a concept, D a cognitive dimension according to Anderson and Krathwohl's revision of Bloom's taxonomy for learning objectives [1,3,4], and $p \in [0,1]$ a probability representing the learner's assumed competency in dimension D; with 0 indicating no previous contact with a concept, and a theoretical maximum of 1 indicating complete and utter mastery.

Specifically, the cognitive dimensions we use are remember, understand, apply, analyze, evaluate and create. Not all cognitive dimensions necessarily apply equally to all concepts (it would be difficult, for example, to assign a meaningful score for create for the Intermediate Value Theorem, even though other dimensions remain useful).

Priming of Learner Models. When learners log into ALEA for the first time, the system knows little about them. In particular, there can be no such thing as a "default" learner model. It might be tempting to install one and assume that every user of the system has a certain educational background (such as arithmetic and trigonometry), but this would paint all learners with the same brush and work antithetically to the goal of providing individualised learning opportunities.

As an alternative, we use an on-boarding dialogue that explains the individual parts of the system to newcomers, but also offers them to *prime* their learner model with their educational history. We give a list of courses and programs the learner might already have completed (such as "Introduction to Databases", but this could also include "Bachelor in Art History at XYZ University" or "German Abitur in Berlin") and ask their grade as a percentage. We then perform a lookup for which concepts of our domain model are being discussed in the course or program in question and set their learner model correspondingly. This allows learners to start with a reasonably accurate and therefore genuinely helpful learner model (e.g. one that reflects a strength in theoretical computer science or a weakness in differential equations, instead of a passing familiarity with both) without having to amass hundreds of interactions first.

Learner Models Fine Tuning. Exactly how a given interaction should affect the learner model is subject to ongoing research. For example, it might seem clear that giving a correct answer to a quiz question involving concepts C_1 and C_2 should increase their values in the learner model. However, it is not obvious by how much. Should they be raised to a set point? Increased by a percentage? If C_1 used to be higher than C_2, should that affect it? Should we also update concepts that one or both depend on, and if so, by how much? What do we do about modelling "forgetting"?

We hope to collect enough data to eventually be able to give evidence-informed opinions on this, by having multiple variations of learner models be informed by the same interaction logs collected over time, and see which predicts the exam grade the best. For now, we rely on an iterative, experimental approach that uses the "quality of semantic services" – e.g. of the generated guided tours as a dependent variable to be optimised.

However useful we might find the data for our own scientific purposes, first and foremost we want learners to be in control of their educational journey (for didactic as well as ethical and legal reasons) and therefore provide them with a way to inspect and change their learner model at any time. They can also initiate a "purge" that erases every bit of information the system stores about them (with the sole exception of the time that such a purge took place), completely resetting their learner model and deleting all interaction logs.

2.2 Learning Objects

In the following, we will use the phrase *learning object* for any formulation that has been semantically annotated with didactic/rhetoric information, all in their respective senses given above. It should be noted, that this differs from how parts of the didactic literature use the term, where it can also mean *"anything that is potentially of use during learning"*.

The information about a learning object L that can be queried in the system will serve as the basis for decisions about the shape and content of the guided tour. It includes:

1. a **string identifier** for L,
2. a **rhetoric classification** for L (definition, example, theorem, problem, ...),
3. the **prerequisites**, $P(L)$, that is to say a collection of pairs (C, D) where C is a concept and D is one of the cognitive dimensions, specifying what parts of the learner model L specifically relies on so that it can be attempted by the learner with reasonable chances of success,
4. the **objectives**, $O(L)$, also a collection of pairs (C, D) as above, but representing the skills displayed by completing the learning object[1],
5. a learner model $M(C, D) \in [0, 1]$ as discussed in Sect. 2.1,
6. a cool-down value $\mathfrak{CD}(L, M)$, that is to say an integer value associated with L per learner.

[1] These may well be different from the prerequisites of L and additionally can be further specified for individual answer classes, as discussed in [9].

3 Guided Tours

We will now explain the step-by-step flow of a guided tour, what information it draws on during each step and how it is assembled. Please also refer to Fig. 1 where you can find a graphical representation of the process.

As a running example, we will show possible dialogue snippets that a learner asking for a guided tour about the Pythagorean Theorem might encounter[2]. We have chosen this example for general familiarity, its simplicity does not restrict the scope of the process. Learner responses in a dialogue like this would be chosen from a list of possible options, not entered as free-form text.

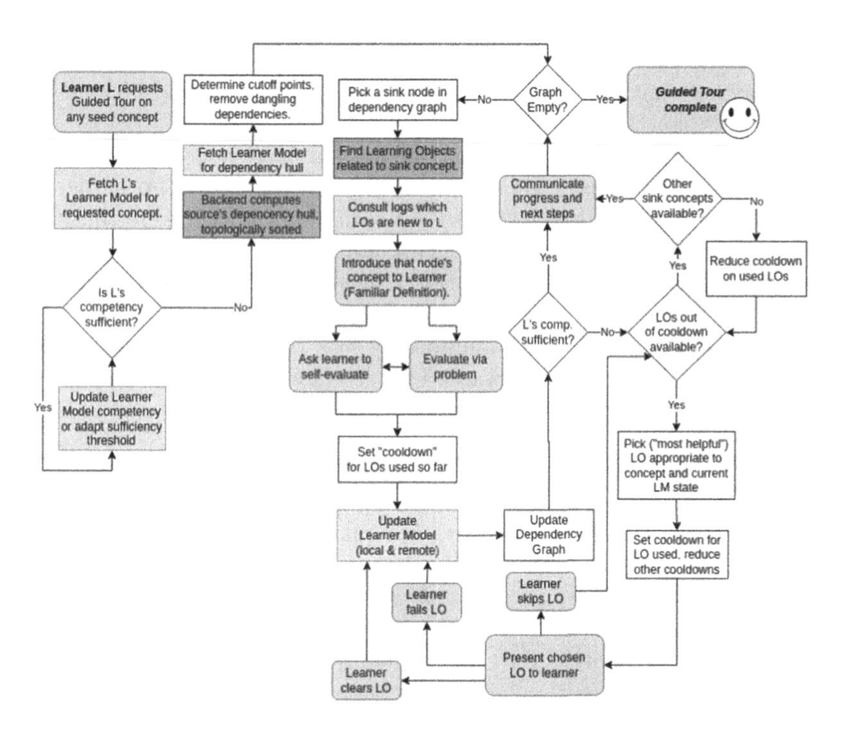

Fig. 1. Overview of the Guided Tours Algorithm. Colour indicates involvement of certain ALEA components. Blue: Frontend, Yellow: Backend, Red: Learner Model Server, Green: Interaction Logs (Color figure online)

3.1 Initial Impetus

Guided tours (GT) can be initiated from any point within the ALEA system – and the respective context serves as an important parameter to GT generation. It could be during a lecture video, from a section in lecture notes, or possibly even from within a forum that students, tutors and professors all frequent.

[2] A more complete version of the prototype dialogue is at https://courses.voll-ki.fau.de/exp/pp_dialogue_tour.

Generally: any place where a learner can interact with a concept, it is possible for them to start a guided tour if they feel like they would benefit from understanding more about it. As soon as the learner opens the guided tour (in our case for the Pythagorean Theorem), they are taken to the dialogue setting.

> Hello!
> You want to learn more about the Pythagorean Theorem?
> Great! Let's get started!

Although it is an important aspect of the process, we will not discuss here what constitutes a "sufficient" level of knowledge for a given concept. The system is parametric in this regard and can adapt to this threshold changing shape or moving for various reasons. A hypothetical learner may, for example, be content with just remembering the definition of a concept as a working baseline during the semester, but insist on also acquiring a good score in other cognitive dimensions before the exam.

However, we do want to highlight one special case: it is of course possible that when a learner starts a GT on a certain subject, that their learner model already fulfils whatever standard we set for sufficient knowledge. In this case, we do not immediately terminate the tour, as might seem to be the obvious step to take, but instead we will either raise/change the standard or downgrade the learner's model for this concept. It is our understanding that the very act of requesting a GT on a concept communicates that the learner is not happy with their current understanding and wants to learn more about it.

3.2 Navigating Dependencies

Once a learner initiates a GT for a certain concept they want to learn about (which we will call the **goal concept**), we query the backend for the complete dependency hull of that goal concept, that is to say the transitive closure of the dependency relation[3]. This graph of concepts will serve as our information what concepts we still need to present to the learner. We also query the LMS for the current learner model for the set of concepts in the dependency hull and associate the values to their respective concepts.

To keep learners engaged in an educational dialogue, it is important that they believe they are not being asked to re-learn things they already understand well. However, in the (usually quite sizeable) dependency hull of the goal concept, there are bound to be concepts a given individual learner is already familiar with (such as "points", "lines" or "triangles"). To make sure not to re-present them to learners unless necessary, the next step involves so-called cut-off points.

For our purposes in guided tours, we use the word *cut-off point* to refer to those concepts in the dependency hull of the goal concept that the learner already has a sufficient understanding of, meaning we don't need to introduce them or any of their dependencies during the course of the GT.

[3] We use "dependency" here to mean that when the definition of a concept C_1 uses concept C_2, then C_1 *depends on* C_2. Note that the dependency relation is a strict partial ordering and thus acyclic.

Note that this does *not* require that the learner's understanding of all dependencies of the cut-off point is sufficient. For example, to explain the Pythagorean Theorem, the learner needs to know about numbers. Those in turn could potentially be defined via (and therefore depend on) some concepts in set theory, but the set-theoretic aspects are of no consequence to the process of learning about the Pythagorean Theorem. So we deliberately make the choice not to require that the learner understands the complete dependency hull of the concept they are interested in. Should it later turn out that they do in fact need a better understanding of a certain concept that was behind a cut-off point and therefore not included in the original GT, they can indicate this at a later point and it will be incorporated in the tour then.

Before moving to the next step in the process, we remove all "dangling dependencies" from our graph, that is concepts that cannot be reached from the goal concept without passing at least one cut-off point.

3.3 Introducing Concepts

We are now ready to introduce the learner to a concept proper. For this, we can pick any of the "sink" nodes (i.e. nodes that other nodes may depend on but do not depend on other nodes themselves) in the dependency graph.

Once we have identified the first concept to talk about, we query the backend for all learning objects that teach something about it, and cross-reference them with the logs to see which of them the learner has interacted with in the past. We are especially interested here in which definition is familiar to the learner, as there can be multiple definitions for the same concept, and we want to start from a place of familiarity.

Next is the presentation and introduction of the concept to the learner. This takes the form of either giving the learner the familiar definition to self-evaluate on or a problem which the learner can answer as a proxy instead. Keep in mind that ALeA is (and therefore guided tours are) designed to work in tandem with traditional learning and studying methods, not to replace them. A student interacting with ALeA in the afternoon could have spent their morning practising a concept by themselves, or maybe weeks have passed without a thought given to this subject, forgetting almost everything. This would both not be reflected (yet) in their learner model, so this part of the interaction tries to catch up to the current state, akin to a human teacher or tutor gauging where exactly to start on a certain topic with their pupil.

My records show that you are already familiar with angles and triangles. The Pythagorean Theorem also concerns *right triangles.*

Do you already feel comfortable with that topic?

I'm not sure...

Okay. Let's find out! Please solve the following problem:

In a right triangle, one of the angles at the longest side is 60°. What would that make the other angle on the longest side?

30°

That is correct!
Let's talk about the Pythagorean Theorem then.

At this point, we're also setting a "cool-down" $\mathfrak{CD}(L, M)$ for the learning objects used in the tour so far (or recently in other contexts, as informed by the interaction logs). This takes the form of an integer associated with both the learner and the learning object. This cool-down will be decreasing over time and is meant to help the system not to show the same learning object multiple times in close succession. This precaution is being taken to avoid frustration. Being presented the same question again that you couldn't answer a minute ago could be perceived as tone-deaf or even mocking by the system or at the very least supremely unhelpful otherwise.

Following the introduction of the concept, the learner has already interacted with one or more learning objects (such as the definition we showed them or the question(s) they self-evaluated with), either successfully or not (more on this below). Both outcomes necessitate an update of the learner model, so we sent the relevant updates to the LMS.

3.4 Working with Concepts

Necessary Updates. After the learner model has been updated based on the newest interaction, we also query the LMS for an updated version of the learner's model for our dependency graph, which we will now have to re-evaluate. Firstly, because we need the updated values to proceed and do not want to re-create the functionality of the LMS within GTs, and secondly because, as discussed in Sect. 2.1, ALEA does not prescribe one true way of updating learner models. Hence, the update we just queued might have affected other parts of the dependency graph. For example, it is possible that cut-off points have moved or that concepts we originally judged to not be sufficiently known now are and therefore don't need to be talked about during the GT any more.

When both learner model and dependency graph have been brought up to date with the newest information, we evaluate if the learner has now reached the "sufficient" level of competency with the concept that is currently in focus. If they have, there does not need to be any further discussion of this concept and we can move on to the next one (see Sect. 3.5).

Choosing Learning Objects. Should the learner's competency not meet our sufficiency standard, we need to select a learning object to improve it.

We originally queried the backend for all learning objects related to the current concept. The results of this query include not only identifiers for the learning objects, but also meta-information about how interacting with it might affect a learner model or which situations or classes of learners it is especially suitable for (see Sect. 2.2). This information can now be used to help identify the appropriate learning object for the current situation.

First, we make sure that there are learning objects available at all that are "out of cool-down". If there are indeed, we can pick the one out of the collection that is the most helpful given the current state of the learner model. There are many approaches to deciding which learning object is the "most helpful", since it strongly correlates with the learning standard we have set. A video detailing how to create your own Diophantine equations is helpful if that is actually what you are currently trying to learn. There might be circumstances though where a learner is happy with just remembering and understanding the definition, and in that situation, a poem that serves as a mnemonic for the definition would be better suited to the task. A "default" way of selecting a fitting learning object does arise, however, from the available information (see Sect. 2.2). Out of the suitable learning objects that involve the current concept and are out of cool-down, select those for which the fulfils the prerequisites $P(L)$. Out of those, filter for the ones with objectives $O(L)$ that best address the lowest scores in cognitive dimensions. If this still returns multiple learning objects, chose randomly.

Of course, theoretically, the judgement about what learning object is most appropriate can become arbitrary complex, all depending on the amount of data and computing resources available. Has the learner ever seen this learning object before? How have other learners with similar competencies reacted to this learning object? Who created this learning object and when and in what context? We hope to give this question of how to pick an appropriate learning object for a given situation the detailed treatment it deserves in the future.

Theorem (Pythagoras).
In a right triangle, the length of the hypotenuse is equal to the sum of the length of the other two sides.
Often, this is expressed with this formula: $a^2 + b^2 = c^2$

Should there *not* be any learning objects available that are out of cool-down, the GT can continue in two ways. If there are other sink concepts to talk about in our dependency graph apart from the current one, we switch. If we have both no learning objects out of cool-down and no other concepts to talk about instead, we accept our fate and decrease all current cool-downs by one level and check again. Maintainers of learning object corpora should make sure that this situation occurs rarely or never.

Interaction with Learning Objects. Once a suitable learning object has been selected, we give it a cool-down value and decrease all other cool-downs by one level. The learning object we picked can now be presented to the learner. At this point, we distinguish three different ways to interact with the learning object:

1. **(Pass)** This is a positive interaction, indicating that one has better understood a concept. This should only increase a learner's modelled competency.
2. **(Fail)** This is a negative interaction, indicating that the learner has not mastered this concept yet. Hence the modelled competency would be reduced.
3. **(Skip)** This is a neutral interaction, merely indicating that the learner didn't fully interact with this learning object (no update to the learner model).

In our running example, one way of such an interaction would be the learner indicating that they do understand the material that was presented to them[4].

There are multiple proofs of this theorem.
Here is one of them:

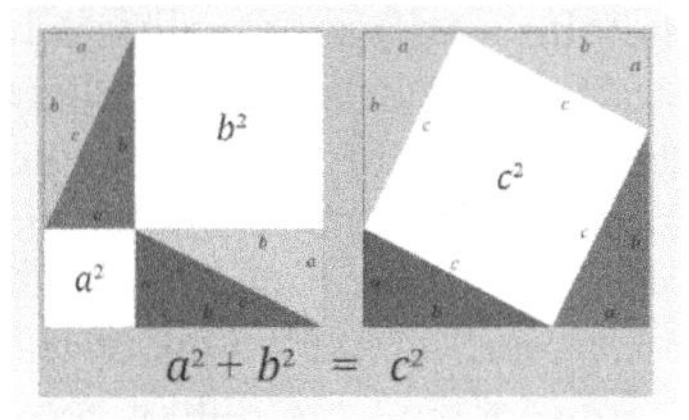

Did that help you understand?

3.5 Da Capo Al Coda

The last step in the cycle is communicating to the learner how the past interactions have shaped their learner model (this can include complimenting them or explaining that it might be better to move to a different topic right now), and moving the conversation to the topic of the next steps, so that the learner remains able to follow the dialogue well.

Having gone through the process of communicating about a concept with the learner once, we now return to our dependency graph of the original goal concept. If it is already empty, we have finished the GT, but in reality this will likely take several rounds of the process above, leaving us with the task of picking a new sink concept from the graph. The selection of a sink concept here could be random, since (to our knowledge) the learner already knows enough about their dependencies. However, we believe that the next concept should be picked by similarity to the last one, preferring concepts that are used or introduced close to each other in the relevant course context. The necessary information already

[4] In the interactive version of the dialogue, this diagram is actually an animation (licensed CC-BY, attribution William B. Faulk), which is easier to understand.

exists in the system and can be queried from the backend, in the hopes of a more coherent narrative in the mind of the learner and avoiding "topic whiplash".

From here on out, the process detailed in Sects. 3.3 and 3.4 repeats, until we have reached an empty dependency graph (the last concept having been the goal concept), at which point the guided tour is complete and we can congratulate the learner for their success. They can then either click away or follow a link to start one of the *other* GTs that are being suggested based off their current learner model...

4 Conclusion and Future Work

In this paper, we introduced and justified the concept of a guided tour, an educational dialogue in the context of the intelligent tutoring system ALeA, that is assembled on the fly and tailor-made specifically for an individual learner.

Precise modelling of the domain of discourse as well as learner's abilities allows us to make informed choices about which topics to discuss and which learning objects to present. This is all to the benefit of the learner, who gets to avoid tedious and unhelpful experiences in online learning, resulting in an educational dialogue that more closely resembles that of a human educator. We hope that this will lead to an increase in successful learning journeys, even in the face of ever more severe budget constraints in public education and ever more heterogeneous educational backgrounds.

Future Work. Continuing work on guided tours, we hope to be able to increase our accuracy in measuring and modelling learner progress. One avenue is introducing another dimension of "certainty" to the learner model, that would allow to differentiate between scores in which we have high or low confidence, say, based on number of interactions involving some concept. This might enable us to skip certain parts of GTs where we gauge the learner's current level, or it might improve the quality of learning object selection.

We also hope to expand the corpus of annotated materials, allowing guided tours (in practice, not just in theory) to not be constrained to only one university course at a time, but be able to draw on connections to other courses and programs that learners have already completed (e.g. "This neural net has a similar structure to the one you know from last semester's course on Computer Vision, with the difference being...").

Acknowledgments. The work reported in this article was conducted as part of the VoLL-KI project (see https://voll-ki.de) funded by the German Research/Education Ministry under grant 16DHBKI089. The work reported here has profited significantly from discussion in the VoLL-KI group.

The design of the ALeA system inherits a lot of the intuitions from the ActiveMath/LeActiveMath system [10], which was based on an early version of OMDoc [6]. The concept of a guided tour discussed in this paper is informed by the realisation – initially suggested by the second author – in ActiveMath, but the representational basis and eventual shape are completely distinct.

References

1. Anderson, L.W., Krathwohl, D.R.: A Taxonomy for Learning, Teaching, and Assessing: A Revision of Bloom's Taxonomy of Educational Objectives. Longman, New York (2009)
2. Berges, M., Betzendahl, J., Chugh, A., Kohlhase, M., Lohr, D., Müller, D.: Learning support systems based on mathematical knowledge managment. In: Intelligent Computer Mathematics (CICM) 2023. LNAI. Springer (2023, in press). https://url.mathhub.info/CICM23ALEA
3. Bloom, B.S., (ed.): Taxonomy of Educational Objectives: The Classification of Educational Goals: Handbook I, Cognitive Domain. Longmans, Green, New York (1956)
4. Fuller, U., et al.: Developing a computer science-specific learning taxonomy. SIGCSE Bull. **39**(4), 152–170 (2007)
5. Kohlhase, M.: Mathematical knowledge management: transcending the one-brain-barrier with theory graphs. EMS Newsl., 22–27 (2014). https://kwarc.info/people/mkohlhase/papers/ems13.pdf
6. Kohlhase, M.: OMDoc – An Open Markup Format for Mathematical Documents [version 1.2]. LNCS (LNAI), vol. 4180. Springer, Heidelberg (2006). https://doi.org/10.1007/11826095. http://omdoc.org/pubs/omdoc1.2.pdf
7. Kohlhase, M., Müller, D.: The sTeX3 Package Collection. https://github.com/slatex/sTeX/blob/main/doc/stex-doc.pdf. Accessed 24 Apr 2022
8. Kruse, T., Berges, M., Betzendahl, J., Kohlhase, M., Lohr, D., Müller, D.: Learning with ALeA: tailored experiences through annotated course material. In: Lecture Notes in Informatics. Gesellschaft für Informatik e.V. (GI) (2023, in press)
9. Lohr, D., Berges, M., Kohlhase, M., Rabe, F.: The potential of answer classes in large-scale written computer-science exams. In: Proceedings of the 10th Symposium on Computer Science in Higher Education HDI 2023, Aachen, Germany (2023, Accepted)
10. Melis, E., et al.: The ActiveMath learning environment. Artif. Intell. Educ. **12**(4), 385–407 (2001)
11. Müller, D., Kohlhase., M.: sTeX3 - a LATEX-based ecosystem for semantic/ active mathematical documents. TUGboat **43**(2), 197–201 (2022). https://kwarc.info/people/dmueller/pubs/tug22.pdf. In: Berry, K. (ed.)
12. UniFormal/MMT - The MMT Language and System. https://github.com/UniFormal/MMT. Accessed 20 July 2023

Performance of Large Language Models in a Computer Science Degree Program

Tim Krüger(✉) and Michael Gref

Niederrhein University of Applied Sciences, Krefeld, Germany
tim.krueger@stud.hn.de, michael.gref@hs-niederrhein.de

Abstract. Large language models such as ChatGPT-3.5 and GPT-4.0 are ubiquitous and dominate the current discourse. Their transformative capabilities have led to a paradigm shift in how we interact with and utilize (text-based) information. Each day, new possibilities to leverage the capabilities of these models emerge. This paper presents findings on the performance of different large language models in a university of applied sciences' undergraduate computer science degree program. Our primary objective is to assess the effectiveness of these models within the curriculum by employing them as educational aids. By prompting the models with lecture material, exercise tasks, and past exams, we aim to evaluate their proficiency across different computer science domains. We showcase the strong performance of current large language models while highlighting limitations and constraints within the context of such a degree program. We found that ChatGPT-3.5 averaged 79.9% of the total score in 10 tested modules, BingAI achieved 68.4%, and LLaMa, in the 65 billion parameter variant, 20%. Despite these convincing results, even GPT-4.0 would not pass the degree program - due to limitations in mathematical calculations.

1 Introduction

In the realm of natural language processing, large language models, hereafter only referenced as LLMs, have now become an integral part of our digital landscape. They have a widespread influence in today's discourse and a ubiquitous presence in various fields and industries [18]. Among these models, ChatGPT-3.5 and GPT-4.0 have emerged as prominent examples, captivating the attention of students, researchers, and developers alike. It is essential to look at these models in the context of higher education because they provide new ways and possibilities to teach, learn and perceive information. Useful for both students and instructors. They could help students, for example, by delivering a more personalized and interactive educational experience and acting as a kind of "learning buddy." For an instructor, the possibilities are also plenty. These models can generate supplementary materials, explanations, or examples [5].

Supported by funds of the *Bundesministerium für Bildung und Forschung*.

S. Nowaczyk et al. (Eds.): ECAI 2023 Workshops, CCIS 1948, pp. 409–424, 2024.
https://doi.org/10.1007/978-3-031-50485-3_40

Alternatively, they could aid in the assessment process by automating the grading procedure for all text-based requirements. A lot of research is currently taking place on this topic. For example, H. Gimpel et al. [5] have written an extensive essay on the opportunities but also the risks that generative AI models bring to higher education by collecting nearly 50 high-quality scholarly sources. They provide guidance for both students and instructors by providing hands-on recommendations for the usage of AI in higher education.

ChatGPT-3.5 and GPT-4.0 are not the only AI models impacting learning and teaching; much more software exists. DeepL Write can improve writing, from fixing grammar and punctuation mistakes to rephrasing entire sentences or sections. The same is true for Grammarly, which offers users an AI text generation functionality for further improvements and suggestions regarding clarity, engagement, and delivery of a text. Even the creation of multimedia content is no problem. Programs like Midjourney and Dall-E allow users the creation of photorealistic images and visualizations with just a few prompts [10]. Furthermore, when Microsoft releases Copilot, their AI support tool, with Office [11], the use of AI will have also arrived in all non-technical disciplines. These tools will then be used passively daily by millions of people, so we must look at the opportunities but also threats that these technologies can bring to higher education and learning/teaching in general.

As part of the research for this paper, we interviewed several professors from our teaching institution. We identified cheating and plagiarism as one of the main concerns. H. Gimpel et al. [5] have also dedicated several pages of their essay to this topic and stressed the importance of rules and guidelines that should be in place for the university environment without denying students access to this new technology. However, as the present work is limited to evaluating the performance of LLMs, this is an aspect to be explored in subsequent work. To accurately assess the benefits of this technology and their usage as educational aids, we set out to evaluate the performance across our undergraduate computer science curriculum. In total, we collected 40 data points, where one data point represents the performance of one LLM or LLM variant in one module of the degree program.

2 Related Work

In this section, we want to explore some of the various research efforts that have examined the performance of LLMs in the field of computer science. The results, some of which differ significantly, inspired us to test the performance of these LLMs in our degree program as well. Table 1 shows a small selection of test and exam results published by OpenAI [14], with the release of their GPT-4.0 model, and one exam (Algorithms and Data Structures) tested by Bordt et al. [2]. The first results are from LeetCode, a popular online platform that provides programming exercises and coding challenges commonly found in technical interviews [7]. The programming exercises and algorithmic problems are divided into three difficulty ranges (easy, medium, and hard) [13].

Table 1. Exam results for GPT-3.5/GPT-4.0 [2, 14]. Values are rounded to the first decimal place.

Test/Exam	GPT-3.5	GPT-4.0
LeetCode (Hard)	0.0%	6.6%
LeetCode (Easy)	29.3%	75.6%
Algorithms & Data Structures	51.3%	60.0%

The platform is aimed at software developers and programmers to enhance their programming skills by solving algorithmic problems [21].

In the *easy* problem section, GPT-3.5 answered 12 out of 41 questions correctly, resulting in a performance of 29.3%. GPT-4.0 answered 31 out of 41 questions correctly, resulting in a performance of 75.6% - an improvement of 47.3% points [14]. The results may depend on the exact category and programming language [13]. Nikolaidis et al. found that in their case, ChatGPT-3.5 solved 45% of 50 randomly selected *easy* LeetCode problems correctly while providing noticeably better results in the programming languages Java and Python.

When tested by OpenAI, GPT-3.5 could not solve a single of the *hard* problems on LeetCode [14]. These results again may depend on the type of problem that had to be solved [13]. Nikolaidis et al. found that ChatGPT-3.5 solved 10 out of 21 *hard* problems correctly, resulting in 47.6% accuracy. ChatGPT-3.5 would then, in fact, even severely outperform GPT-4.0 when tested by OpenAI, which was able to solve 3 out of 45 *hard* problems correctly (6.6% accuracy) [14].

Bordt et al. tested ChatGPT-3.5 and GPT-4.0 on an undergraduate computer science exam in *Algorithms and Data Structures.* The exam was fed to the LLMs in the same way students would receive it. The answers of the models were transferred to paper by the testers and mixed with the solutions of the students [2]. ChatGPT-3.5 scored 20.5 out of 40 possible points (51.25%), allowing it to pass the exam narrowly. GPT-4.0 improved that score by 8.75% points, reaching 60% (24/40 points). With this result, GPT-4.0 outperforms the average student, which scores 23.9 in the mean [2].

Both ChatGPT-3.5 and GPT-4.0 indicate wide-ranging capabilities in the field of computer science. GPT-4.0 also seems to be an improvement over GPT-3.5 in every way. The findings on performance variation are worth noting for our research. The LLMs' answers seem to depend on the corresponding computer science discipline category and the specific programming language asked [13]. It is also relevant to note that the programming errors generated seem to be mainly semantic. The models hardly make syntax errors, but the code, if wrong, can have serious logic errors [13].

3 Methodology

The crux of our methodology is the evaluation of various LLMs by feeding them academic content drawn from a bachelor's degree program in computer science at a university of applied sciences.

Table 2. Overview of our exam data set.

Semester	Written exam	Oral exam
1	0	0
2	2	0
3	2	0
4	2	1
5	2	1
Sum	8	2

We aim to determine each model's overall performance and identify the highest and lowest-scoring modules, grade distributions, and potential affinities for certain topics. Additionally, the study aims to determine whether the models would complete the degree program. Our data set comprised samples of past exams from ten different modules of the degree program, see Table 2. This core data set was complemented with information from questionnaires, practice exercises, and lecture notes to offer a more holistic view of the curriculum. For modules with oral exams, the questions were based on the same data but created in consultation with the supervising professor to simulate realistic exam scenarios. Only examinations for which the professors gave their approval were taken into account for the study.

The criteria for evaluation were adapted for each module. In written exams, we employed the evaluation system and point allocation provided by the supervising professor. In oral exams, we weighted questions according to complexity and difficulty. These questions were finalized in consultation with the supervising professors. Evaluating and assessing the performance involved verifying correctness, compiling and testing program code, and recalculating solutions.

Due to the limitations of certain models in handling multimedia input, we partly excluded those tasks from our assessment. Adjustments were made to the total score and weighting of the exam accordingly. In instances where it was feasible, we transformed such tasks into a suitable textual format with tables and data structures being converted to markdown and diagrams re-imagined into the corresponding UML representation. We tested ChatGPT-3.5, AI-powered Bing (referred to as BingAI) [12], StableLM-Alpha in the 7 billion parameter version, and LLaMa in both the 7 billion and 65 billion parameter versions. Towards the end of our project, we also received access to GPT-4.0 but were restricted in using this model due to time constraints. We viewed these selections as an appropriate mix of open- and closed-access LLMs. StableLM includes various LLMs published by Stability AI. The size of these models ranges from 3 billion to 65 billion parameters. A 175 billion parameter variant is also planned [16]. The models are published in different versions and trained on different datasets. We use the StableLM-Alpha-7B variant, which was trained on a dataset based on *The Pile* [3]. All models are hosted on *The Hugging Face Hub*, and some are accessible through a web interface [17].

LLaMa refers to a collection of different LLMs ranging from 7B to 65B parameters, published by MetaAI [19]. We used LLaMa with the project *llama.cpp*, an open-source C/C++ port of several LLMs [4]. This project supports 8-bit, 5-bit, and 4-bit integer quantization, a technique that significantly reduces the memory requirements of the models. In the case of LLaMa, this allowed us to run the models in RAM instead of GPU memory. We considered this approach a more realistic simulation, as the models otherwise require a significant amount of GPU memory. However, there is the possibility of a degradation in model accuracy. There seems to be a trade-off between model size and quality, depending on the quantization method [22]. In the case of LLaMa-7B, the file size got reduced from 13 GB when using 16-bit floats to 3.5 GB when using 4-bit integer quantization. The perplexity [6] rose from 5.9066 to 6.1565, an increase of only 4.23% [4].

The prompting of the models was a carefully considered aspect of this research project. Prompt engineering has been shown to improve the performance of models in various studies (e.g. [20]). However, to provide a broad overview of the performance across the curriculum, we opted to prompt all models only once and use the first response provided by each model. Before starting the assessment, a generic pre-prompt was given in each case, setting the context that they were interacting in a simulated exam scenario and outlining expectations for responses.

> *I am now going to ask you a few questions from a hypothetical [insert topic or subject] exam of an undergraduate computer science degree program. I want you to answer the questions to the best of your knowledge and capabilities. Please answer briefly and concisely unless I explicitly ask for a more detailed answer! Please answer purely in continuous text or bullet points. If output in chart or table form is desired, I will let you know.*

4 Experimental Results

We tested, between May and July of 2023, ten modules each with ChatGPT-3.5 and BingAI, six modules with GPT-4.0, and fourteen modules in total with StableLM-Alpha-7B, LLaMa-7B, and LLaMa-65B, resulting in forty data points. We have not been able to test every model iteration on every module of the curriculum due to the time constraints of this project. All exam questions were adopted without modification. The following data underpins what we present as a comprehensive insight into the performance of these models across an array of computer science curriculum modules.

Referring to grades in the following, we calculated them according to the *modified Bavarian formula* corresponding to the German grading system [15]. Depending on the university, a conversion may be necessary. If not stated otherwise, 50% of the score are required to pass the exam.

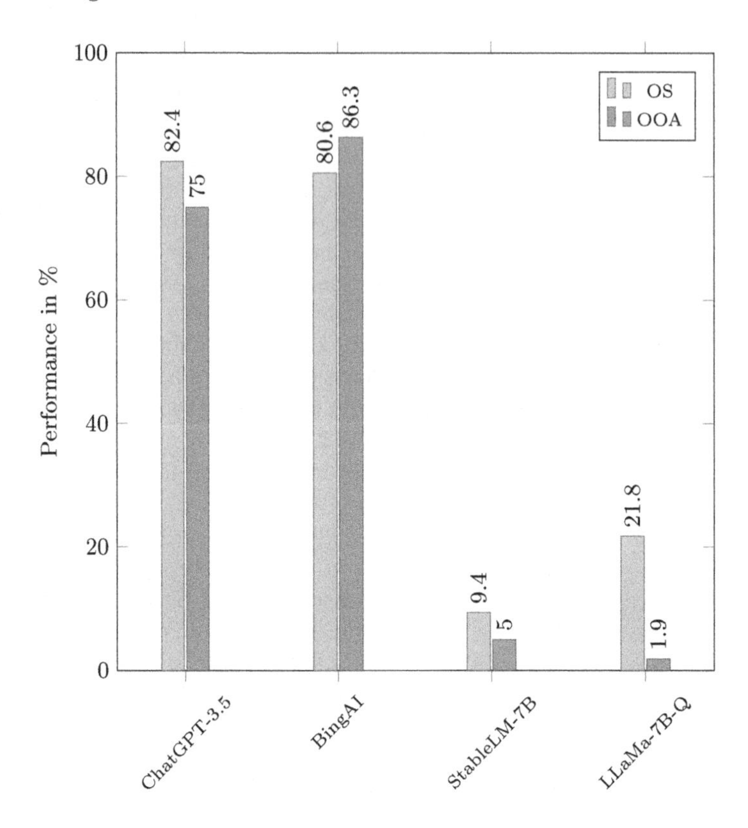

Fig. 1. Exam results for Operating Systems (OS) and Object Oriented Application Development (OOA)

4.1 1st Semester

We have neither received full approval nor the required content for any of the modules of the first semester from the responsible professors. This is left to be explored in subsequent work.

4.2 2nd Semester

We have received approval for two second-semester modules, Operating Systems, and Object-Oriented Application Development. Figure 1 shows the exam results for each LLM in these modules. Operating Systems (OS) is a five credit-point module. In the module, students learn the structure of a modern operating system and algorithms and strategies for managing and allocating resources in it. They also develop programs in a UNIX environment and work out solutions to problems of interprocess communication [8]. Object Oriented Application Development (OOA) is a seven credit-point module. It focuses on teaching the methods and techniques of object-oriented programming.

Requirements are implemented using efficient algorithms and data structures. Programming is done in C++ [8].

ChatGPT-3.5 and BingAI performed quite well in OS, scoring 82.4% and 80.6%, respectively. The 7B parameter models performed significantly worse. LLaMa-7B-Q (quantized) scored 21.8%, and StableLM-7B scored 9.4%. While StableLM-7B could answer almost no questions, LLaMa-7B-Q could still answer questions about shell commands and general operating system terms. Nevertheless, it was too little to pass the exam. ChatGPT-3.5 and BingAI were able to answer many questions. The models did make mistakes when calculating memory usage and applying paging algorithms. This cost them points but kept the good result the same. ChatGPT-3.5 passed this exam with a grade of 2.0 and BingAI with a Grade of 2.1. OOA is the only module in which BingAI performed better than ChatGPT-3.5 in all our testing. The latter LLM scored 75%, whereas BingAI scored 86.3%. This results in grades of 2.5 for ChatGPT-3.5 and 1.8 for BingAI. The score for BingAI is one of the best results for this LLM in all our tests. The biggest problems ChatGPT-3.5 had were with implementing the object-oriented interfaces in C++. The code compiled but either didn't work as it should or implemented something completely different from the task. StableLM-7B performed slightly better than LLaMa-7B-Q in this exam. However, both LLMs had severe problems with the assignments, solving almost no tasks.

4.3 3rd Semester

We have received approval for two modules of the third semester, Web Engineering and Distributed Systems. The results for the modules of the third semester can be seen in Fig. 2. Web Engineering (WEB) is a five credit-point module. It covers the technical fundamentals of modern web-based technologies and architectural, development, and analysis tools for web-based systems. On the front end, students in this module work with HTML, CSS, and JavaScript; on the backend side, with a mixture of Javascript and Python [8]. A student with 33% or more would pass the exam, as determined by the supervising professor. Distributed Systems (DS) is also a five credit-point module. Students of this module learn about distributed system architectures and techniques for synchronization and communication. At the end of this module, they can design, implement and evaluate their own distributed computing structures. The implementation within this module takes place in C/C++ [8]. Our set exam consists of questionnaire material.

WEB was one of the best exam results in all our testing for ChatGPT-3.5, scoring an even 1.0 on the exam with 98.3%. Even the most extensive task, a partial Python implementation of a backend server for the membership management of a business, was solved completely and correctly. BingAI was also able to answer almost every question correctly. Only in the implementation part did BingAI make logical errors and omit required functionalities. This still resulted in 90% or a grade of 1.4. StableLM-7B and LLaMa-7B-Q had surprisingly massive problems in this exam, despite the extensive question part.

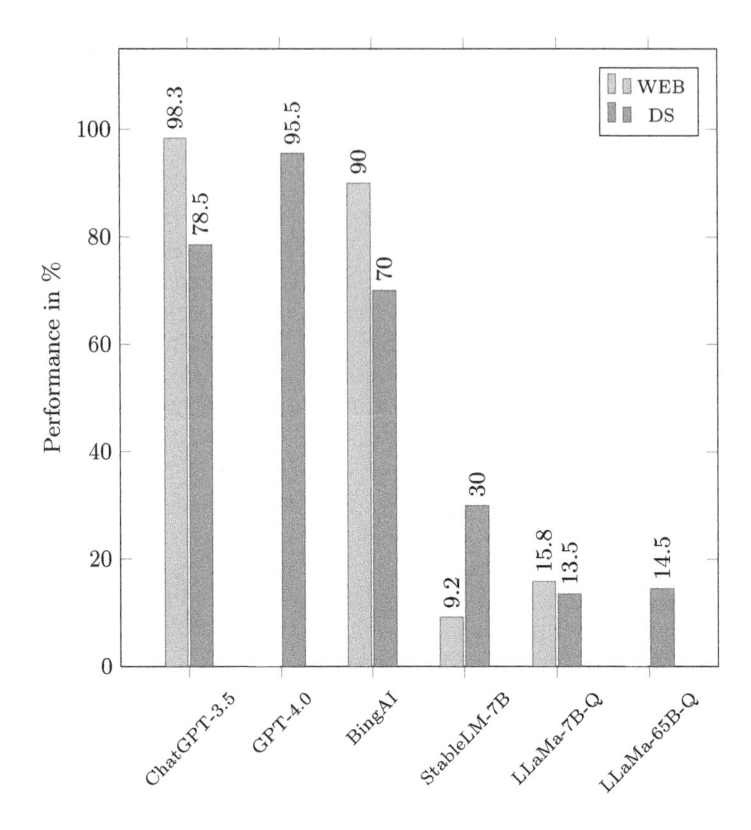

Fig. 2. Exam results for Web-Engineering (WEB) and Distributed Systems (DS)

Almost no question could be answered completely or correctly. Both models also failed the implementation part. LLaMa-7B-Q scored 15.8%, slightly better than StableLM-7B, with 9.2%. In DS, both ChatGPT-3.5 and BingAI performed worse than in WEB. ChatGPT-3.5 got a grade of 2.2 with a result of 78.5%, and BingAI a 2.8 with 70%. The models could answer almost all simple or introductory questions to the topic correctly but had problems with more in-depth questions, e.g., on network data formats or broker implementations. DS was the first module in which we tested GPT-4.0. With a result of 95.5%, it got a grade of 1.2 and topped the grade of ChatGPT-3.5 by a whole level. GPT-4.0 answered almost every question completely and correctly in this exam. StableLM-7B scored 30% in DS, the best result for this LLM in all our tests. Surprisingly, it was able to answer difficult questions on *CORBA*, *SOAP* interfaces, and synchronization mechanisms but failed on simpler, more general questions, like resilience and fault tolerance of distributed systems. Otherwise, it would have had a real chance to pass the exam. In this module, we also tested LLaMa-65B-Q for the first time. With a result of 14.5%, it performed only slightly better than LLaMa-7B-Q with 13.5%. Considering the difference in size, this is a disappointing result.

4.4 4th Semester

We have received approval for three modules of the fourth semester: Data Network Management, Interactive Systems, and Numerical Analysis. The results can be taken from Fig. 3 Data Network Management (DNM) is a six credit-point module. It provides in-depth, application-oriented knowledge of network administration. Students in this module acquire skills in the design, development, and deployment of large-scale computer networks, as well as techniques for securing them [8]. Interactive Systems (IAS) is a five credit-point module. It focuses on software ergonomics and the design and implementation of portable interactive systems. Students of this module learn how to model application-oriented and ergonomic human-machine interfaces [8]. The implementations in this module are web-based in the programming languages JavaScript and Python. As determined by the supervising professor, the module is considered to be passed if 33% of the total points are achieved. Numeric Analysis (NUM) is an elective course in our computer science bachelor's degree program, which gives five credit points. Topics covered include computer arithmetic and rounding errors, systems of linear equations, and linear equilibrium calculus. The module is concluded with an oral examination [8]. This is one of the modules in which we simulated an exam by taking questions from a questionnaire.

DNM is the first module in our tests in which even the larger LLMs have experienced problems. ChatGPT-3.5 barely passed the exam with 51.9% or a grade of 3.8. BingAI had even more difficulties and failed the exam with a score of only 47.1%. The application of firewall rules and routing protocols for custom multi-area networks presented in the exam was particularly problematic for both LLMs. GPT-4.0 performed the best in this exam. It was also unable to completely solve the more difficult tasks but often provided correct partial solutions or made less serious errors than the other two LLMs. GPT-4.0 passed the exam with 65.4% or a grade of 3.0. IAS went very well for ChatGPT-3.5. With 96.7%, it got a grade of 1.1. It answered almost all comprehension and knowledge questions correctly. Even more complex tasks, such as the design of a user interface, were solved completely and correctly. BingAI performed almost 30% points worse in this exam, resulting in one of the biggest gaps between these two LLMs in all our testing. It got a grade of 2.4, or 68.8% of the total score. The grade of 2.4 comes from the fact that the exam is considered passed from 35%, and larger results are offset by the formula linearly. Nevertheless, BingAI had problems with several questions in this exam and either answered incorrectly or omitted information. StableLM-7B and LLaMa-7B-Q had no chance of passing this exam, with a performance of 6.7% and 13.3%, respectively. Nearly every answer had massive errors or large information gaps. The models also lost context in between and started talking about completely different topics. In the simulated oral exam on numerical analysis, mainly comprehension questions were asked, and hardly any calculations had to be done. This led to excellent results for both GPT models. ChatGPT-3.5 got a grade of 1.6, with 90% of the total score, whereas GPT-4.0 increased this to 95% and a grade of 1.3.

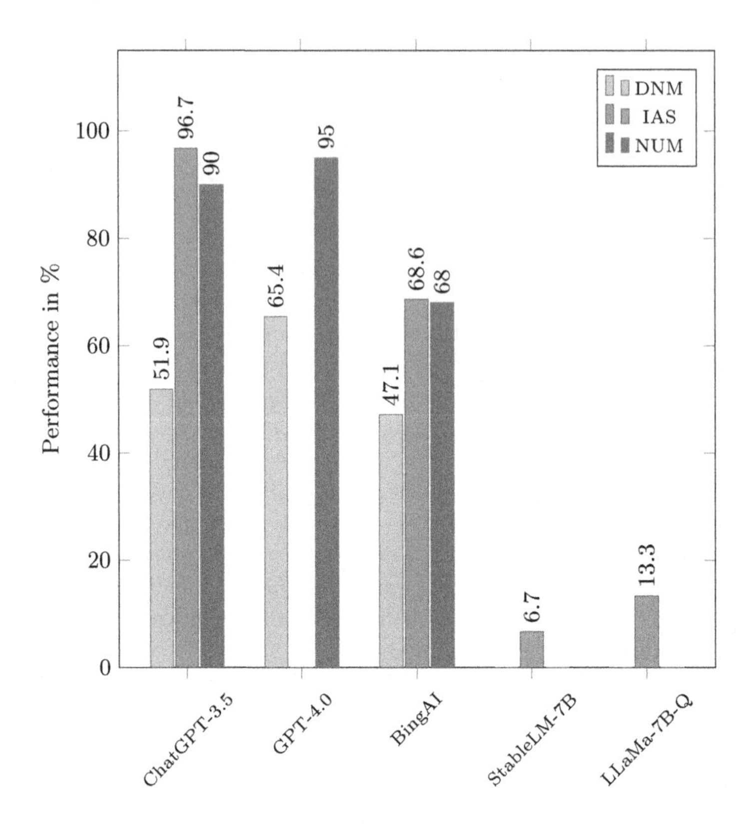

Fig. 3. Exam results for Data Network Management (DNM), Interactive Systems (IAS) and Numerical Analysis (NUM)

Both models could answer almost every question completely and correctly and only made minimal errors. BingAI had great problems in this exam, although it was mainly about knowledge reproduction, and scored well behind the GPT models with 68% of the total score, or a grade of 2.9. BingAI had problems with several questions and made mistakes while reproducing information. For example, when asked about the complexity of the *Gauss Algorithm*, BingAI gave a reference to Wikipedia but then misquoted the article with a complexity of $O(n^2)$.

4.5 5th Semester

We have received approval for three modules of the fifth semester: Data Science, Software Engineering, and Real-Time Systems. The results can be seen in Fig. 4. Data Science (DSC) is an elective course with five credit points. The module provides an introduction to Big Data and Machine Learning. Students of this module will learn to extract, prepare and analyze large data sets [8].

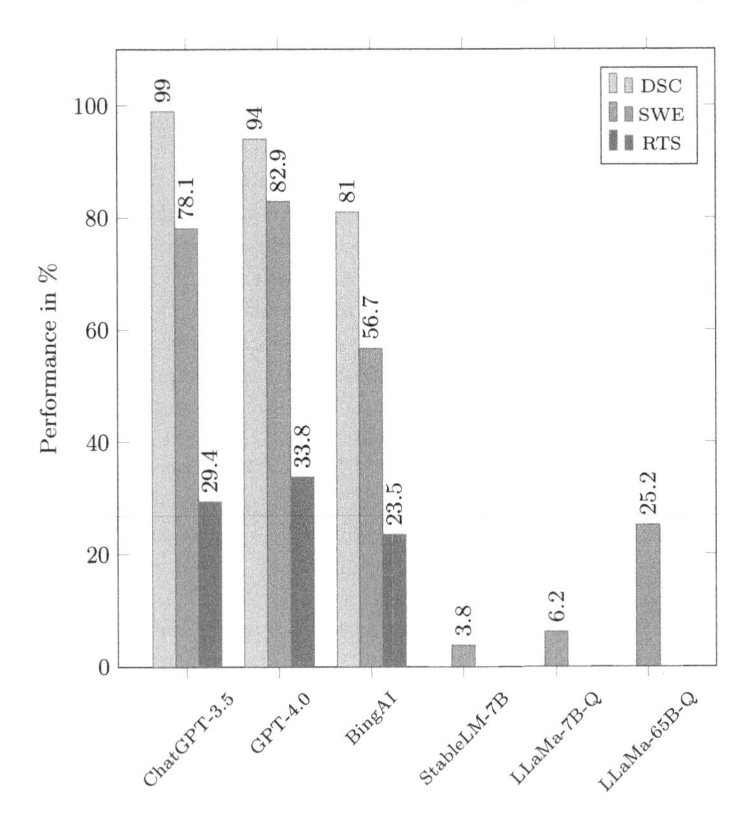

Fig. 4. Exam results for Data Science (DSC), Software Engineering (SWE) and Real-Time Systems (RTS)

The module concludes with an oral exam which we simulated by taking questions from a questionnaire. Software Engineering (SWE) is a five credit-point module. It covers advanced solutions for building, testing, and maintaining large IT systems and techniques for organizing big software projects. A special focus is on effort estimation and (agile) software development processes [8]. As determined by the supervising professor, the module is considered to be passed if 33% of the total points are achieved. Real-Time Systems (RTS) is a five credit-point module. It focuses on the architecture, the concepts, and the functionalities of modern real-time systems. Students learn aspects of concurrent real-time programming and how to deal with time constraints and task management [8]. The module is concluded with a written exam in which a special focus is placed on manual real-time proof for various scheduling methods.

DSC is the best-performing module for ChatGPT-3.5 in all our tests. With 99%, ChatGPT-3.5 scored a 1.0. Every question was answered correctly, from problems in the field of *Big Data* to data preparation, to classification and clustering methods. DSC is also the only module in which ChatGPT-3.5 outperformed GPT-4.0.

The latter model did not score itself badly with 94% and a score of 1.3, but unfortunately gave partially wrong answers to questions about *Eventual Consistency* and *Sharding.* Such results are possible since we only prompt all models once in our tests. BingAI performed again worse than the GPT models. With 81%, it achieved a score of 2.1. It was challenging for BingAI to make its own decisions in tasks, e.g., choosing between an aggregate-oriented or a relational data model. In SWE, the GPT models were again well ahead of BingAI. ChatGPT-3.5 achieved a 1.9 with 78.1%, GPT-4.0 a 1.7 with 82.9%, while BingAI only achieved a 2.9 with 56.7%. The GPT models answered most of the questions completely and correctly but made massive errors in designing test cases for a finite state machine. BingAI could not solve this task either and made errors in explaining design patterns and performing an effort estimation using *Function Point Analysis.* StableLM-7B and LLaMa-7B-Q performed poorly in this module, scoring 3.8% and 6.2%, respectively. LLaMa-65B-Q performed significantly better than the 7 billion parameter version and nearly passed the exam with 25.2%, out of 33% needed. Interestingly, LLaMa-65B-Q was able to partially answer difficult questions on software development principles and the design of component diagrams but failed to explain unit tests. RTS is a demanding exam in which many calculations have to be done. Computational time requirements, core workloads, and a large, manual real-time proof must be calculated. This exam has proven to be extremely difficult for all models tested. ChatGPT-3.5 scored 29.4%, GPT-4.0 scored 33.8%, and BingAI scored 23.5%. Accordingly, all models failed the exam. The models could answer a few simple introductory questions but, early on, miscalculated the computational kernel allocation for a round-robin scheduling procedure. No model was able to solve this task correctly. Likewise, no model was able to calculate the real-time proof correctly. This task is nested, with each intermediate calculation evaluated individually but often a prerequisite for the next calculation. BingAI lost all context in this task after the third partial calculation. The GPT models could continue to calculate but miscalculated fatally early on. Both the calculation path and the result were not correct. When calculating the average execution time for processes of a machine, both ChatGPT-3.5 and GPT-4.0 set up the correct formula, adding all times and dividing by the amount, but only GPT-4.0 also got the correct result; ChatGPT-3.5 miscalculated. All in all, the models were heavily overcharged with this exam.

5 Discussion

An overview of the average performances and results achieved across all tested modules can be seen in Table 3. It is important to note that all data collected is only a snapshot that considers the systems' performance at the time of the assessment. These systems continue to evolve. ChatGPT-3.5 achieved an average of 79.9% of the maximum possible score in the ten modules tested. ChatGPT-3.5 performed particularly well in modules with a high proportion of web development or high-level programming language content, like Python and JavaScript.

Table 3. Summary of the average performance proportionally calculated to all modules taken.

Model	Average score	#Modules	Passed/Failed
GPT-4.0	80.2%	6	5/1
ChatGPT-3.5	79.9%	10	9/1
BingAI	68.4%	10	8/2
LLaMa-65B-Q	20.0%	2	0/2
LLaMa-7B-Q	12.3%	6	0/6
StableLM-7B	10.8%	6	0/6

Even in the field of data science, ChatGPT-3.5 achieved almost full marks. In exams with more complex tasks like Operating Systems or Data Network Management, ChatGPT-3.5 often provided at least an approach to the solution. We noted major difficulties for this LLM with various tasks that required mathematical calculations. The application of scheduling algorithms and the calculation of core utilization and process runtimes posed significant challenges for ChatGPT-3.5. Due to these shortcomings, passing the Real-Time Systems exam is not currently possible. Accordingly, the LLM would not be capable of completely finishing our bachelor's degree program in computer science. However, with an understanding of its strengths and weaknesses, ChatGPT-3.5 shows great potential as an outstanding learning aid for students and lecturers.

GPT-4.0 achieved even better results than ChatGPT-3.5, obtaining an average performance of 80.2%. This score is expected to increase even further if the missing modules are tested with GPT-4.0. A strong focus on specific programming languages or fields of computer science, as observed in ChatGPT-3.5, could not be detected in GPT-4.0. At the same time, GPT-4.0 demonstrated a more consistent overall performance. Like ChatGPT-3.5, GPT-4.0 had difficulties with tasks that required calculations; this also resulted in the failure of the Real-Time Systems exams. For the same reason, GPT-4.0 would not be able to finish the degree program. However, it should be noted that GPT-4.0, despite the identified difficulties, represents an improvement in all areas over ChatGPT-3.5. The use of plugins, for instance, to redirect mathematical computations to a system like WolframAlpha could significantly improve this outcome. This is left to be explored in future studies.

BingAI scored much lower than the GPT models in our tests, with 68.4%. It was the only one of these three models that failed two exams rather than just one, with one of the exams (Data Network Management) being not calculation-intensive. BingAI often encountered problems when the solutions were not directly searchable online. Thus, it made mistakes in extracting information from texts or creating and presenting solutions. Even when the answer to a question could be found via an internet search, BingAI sometimes made inexplicable citation errors. BingAI also provided the shortest responses of all the LLM systems tested, often ignoring aspects of a question. According to the current state, BingAI is inferior to the GPT models.

LLaMa-7B-Q showed poor results, with an average performance of 12.3% in six tested modules. It often had difficulties understanding questions, lost context, or started talking about completely different topics. LLaMa-7B-Q could not solve a single task of an exam. According to our tests, it would not be possible for this LLM to pass any module.

LLaMa-65B-Q showed better results with an average performance of 20.0%, but was also tested only in two modules. It scored one percentage point and 19% points better than its 7 billion parameter counterpart. At this point, more tests are needed to make a final statement about the performance differences between these models. Nevertheless, a trend can be determined: LLaMa-65B-Q performs significantly worse than BingAI, let alone the GPT models. After our tests, whether it would pass a single module is questionable, and it is not suitable for use as a learning aid.

StableLM-7B, tested in six modules, achieved the worst results of all tested LLMs with 10.8%. It was unable to answer any question correctly and completely. Interestingly, StableLM-7B often related questions to a business context or attempted to answer them in such a context. StableLM-7B even understood complex questions from the field of project management but could not establish a reference to computer science or software development. According to our tests, this LLM is also unsuitable as a learning aid.

6 Conclusion

In the presented study, we tested and evaluated the performance of various LLMs across a series of modules in a bachelor's computer science degree program. Our results are in line with existing research (e.g. [1]) by showing strong performances of Generative Pre-training models (GPT) across an undergraduate curriculum while having severe restrictions in key areas. A prevalent worry is the potential for essays to progressively lose significance as evaluation tools within higher education [5]. Our tests show the strength and topic affinities of current LLMs, but also their weaknesses, distinctively in mathematical computations. We conclude from these results that a comprehensive blueprint for our curriculum remains elusive at this point. Despite this, the deployment of these models presents lecturers with challenges, as the detection of plagiarism in AI-generated content is not particularly mature yet [9]. It is imperative to recognize that the GPT models in our tests have completed numerous examinations with scores above 95%. Given that some of our examination rules allow aids, and the pattern of past exams often remains unchanged, the sophisticated capabilities of these models could potentially create near-perfect and legally permissible "cheat" sheets. This, combined with the advancing abilities of current LLMs [5], compels us to reconsider and construct robust examination methods. Oral and written exams without aids remain valid alternative options [5].

The smaller models in our tests exhibit substantial performance deficiencies, with profound disparities encountered in almost all performance-defining areas. Consequently, they currently do not measure up as viable educational aids.

Continued research may examine the performance of existing models in unexplored curriculum modules. Furthermore, additional modules could be examined to provide a broader overview. Future research could also extend to the study of other LLMs, such as Google Bard. Also, broadening the scope to related disciplines, like electrical engineering, would be beneficial to gain a better understanding of domain-specific performance capabilities.

References

1. Binz, M., Schulz, E.: Using cognitive psychology to understand GPT-3. In: Proceedings of the National Academy of Sciences (2023)
2. Bordt, S., von Luxburg, U.: ChatGPT Participates in a Computer Science Exam (2023)
3. Gao, L., et al.: The pile: an 800 GB dataset of diverse text for language modeling. arXiv preprint arXiv:2101.00027 (2020)
4. Gerganov, G.: llama.cpp Github Repository (2023). https://github.com/ggerganov/llama.cpp. Accessed 3 July 2023
5. Gimpel, H., et al.: Unlocking the power of generative AI models and systems such as GPT-4 and ChatGPT for higher education: a guide for students and lecturers. Hohenheim Discussion Papers in Business, Economics and Social Sciences 02–2023, Universität Hohenheim, Fakultät Wirtschafts-und Sozialwissenschaften, Stuttgart (2023). http://hdl.handle.net/10419/270970
6. Gonen, H., Iyer, S., Blevins, T., Smith, N.A., Zettlemoyer, L.: Demystifying prompts in language models via perplexity estimation (2022)
7. Harper, J.: Interview insight: how to get the job. In: A Software Engineer's Guide to Seniority: A Guide to Technical Leadership, pp. 19–28. Springer, Cham (2022). https://doi.org/10.1007/978-1-4842-8783-5_4
8. Niederrhein, H.: Modulhandbuch zum Vollzeit Studiengang Bachelor Informatik nach Prüfungsordnung 2013 (2019). https://www.hs-niederrhein.de/fileadmin/dateien/FB03/Studierende/Bachelor-Studiengaenge/PO2013/modul__bi.pdf. Accessed 26 June 2023
9. Khalil, M., Er, E.: Will ChatGPT get you caught? Rethinking of Plagiarism Detection (2023)
10. Krüger, N.: Künstliche Intelligenz in Training, Weiterbildung und Beratung: 70 direkt anwendbare und erprobte KI-Tools. pitchnext GmbH via Kindle Direct Publishing (2022)
11. Microsoft: Introducing Microsoft 365 Copilot - A whole new way to work (2023). https://www.microsoft.com/en-us/microsoft-365/blog/2023/03/16/introducing-microsoft-365-copilot-a-whole-new-way-to-work/. Accessed 3 July 2023
12. Microsoft: Reinventing search with a new AI-powered Microsoft Bing and Edge, your copilot for the web (2023). https://blogs.microsoft.com/blog/2023/02/07/reinventing-search-with-a-new-ai-powered-microsoft-bing-and-edge-your-copilot-for-the-web. Accessed 4 Sept 2023

13. Nikolaidis, N., Flamos, K., Feitosa, D., Chatzigeorgiou, A., Ampatzoglou, A.: The End of an Era: Can AI Subsume Software Developers? Evaluating Chatgpt and Copilot Capabilities Using Leetcode Problems. Evaluating Chatgpt and Copilot Capabilities Using Leetcode Problems (Preprint) (2023)
14. OpenAI: GPT-4 Technical report (2023). https://arxiv.org/pdf/2303.08774.pdf
15. Sekretariat der ständigen Konferenz der Kultusminister der Länder in der Bundesrepublik Deutschland: Vereinbarung über die festsetzung der gesamtnote bei ausländischen hochschulzugangszeugnissen (2013). https://www.kmk.org/fileadmin/Dateien/pdf/ZAB/Hochschulzugang_Beschluesse_der_KMK/GesNot05.pdf. Accessed 24 June 2023
16. Stability AI: StableLM Github Repository (2023). https://github.com/Stability-AI/StableLM. Accessed 3 July 2023
17. Stability AI: StableLM hugging face (2023). https://huggingface.co/stabilityai. Accessed 3 July 2023
18. Statista: Generative AI - Worldwide (2023). https://www.statista.com/outlook/tmo/artificial-intelligence/generative-ai/worldwide. Accessed 5 July 2023
19. Touvron, H., et al.: LLaMA: open and efficient foundation language models (2023)
20. White, J., et al.: A prompt pattern catalog to enhance prompt engineering with ChatGPT (2023)
21. Wikipedia contributors: Leetcode – Wikipedia, the free encyclopedia (2023). https://en.wikipedia.org/w/index.php?title=Leetcode&oldid=1159537770. Accessed 19 June 2023
22. Yao, Z., Wu, X., Li, C., Youn, S., He, Y.: ZeroQuant-V2: exploring post-training quantization in LLMs from comprehensive study to low rank compensation (2023)

Language-Model Assisted Learning How to Program?

Jochen L. Leidner[1,2(✉)] and Michael Reiche[1]

[1] Coburg University of Applied Sciences, Friedrich Streib-Straße 2, 96450 Coburg, Germany
[2] University of Sheffield, Regents Court, 211 Portobello, Sheffield S1 4DP, UK
leidner@acm.org

Abstract. Foundational language models have forever changed how NLP prototypes may be rapidly constructed, dramatically reducing the "cost of curiosity". This also affects the way we can teach and learn how to program.

In this paper, we explore how well foundational models such as large, pre-trained neural transformers can answer questions pertaining to programming in a "learning to code" context: we present a new dataset comprising questions that students that learn how to program and students of particular programming languages – as offered by typical undergraduate university courses – typically ask. We cover both fundamental concepts in programming and also specific programming language issues. Although our study focuses on English, we believe results would be similar for other human languages due to the multilingual nature of many foundational language models. We explore how well a foundational (generic) pre-trained language model can answer them.

To the best of our knowledge, this is one of the first studies that assesses *how well* generic foundational models and applications like ChatGPT are capable of answering different types of typical programming-related questions. This is a question of primary importance if we consider using such models to assist human students in their struggle to become (good) programmers.

Keywords: Computer-Supported Instruction · AI for Teaching · Improving the Teaching of AI · Pretrained Foundational Models · Education

1 Introduction

1.1 Background and Motivation

Learning how to program is an essential part of studying computer science, because it enables students to implement systems themselves that embody their own (and later, their clients') ideas. It is also an essential and valuable transferable skill: students of other subjects, from architecture to physics, are also often expected to take programming classes, and software developers are above-average earners.

S. Nowaczyk et al. (Eds.): ECAI 2023 Workshops, CCIS 1948, pp. 425–438, 2024.
https://doi.org/10.1007/978-3-031-50485-3_41

Nevertheless, like mastering to play the piano or mastering a foreign language, learning to program entails numerous challenges: to grasp the nature of the problem domain (get the necessary background), to understand a specific problem that a computer program to be written is expected to solve, to decompose the problem, to master the lexis (keywords and operators), syntax (EBNF grammar), semantics (e.g. types), development environment (IDEs or command line, run-time) and libraries of the programming language(s) used, to design the architecture of the program that is the tentative solution, to implement the code by making informed choices between self-coded parts and parts re-used by calling external third-party libraries, commercial or open-source, to handle edge cases and errors, to test the code, to document the code. Therefore, it is hardly surprising that three-year Bachelor programs do not produce experienced programmers, given that programming is only one of the many skills/knowledge areas of the computer science curriculum.

In the past, many efforts have gone into the better or faster teaching of programming by supporting the human learner with computational help, including the use of AI techniques (planning the progress, modeling the learner's grasp of concepts and his/her progress).

Very recently, the introduction of neural transformers and large pre-trained language models (also called "foundational models"), which are trained with general-purpose *un-annotated* human prose language, and sometimes code fragments, has dramatically changes the way natural language applications can be prototyped. Systems like Google's BERT [5], OpenAI's GPT-3, GPT-3.5, GPT-4 and the application ChatGPT [12,13], and many others based on deep neural networks featuring the transformer architecture [18] permit to directly pose a question in English and other languages and get an answer back, also in a human language. Although these models were originally intended to be "just" generative models of *language production*, the fact that they were trained with vast quantities of text, including terabytes of World Wide Web content, means that the language material to train the systems also articulated an enormous amount of *world knowledge*, thus implicitly solving the knowledge bottleneck challenge that prevented progress in AI in the 1980 s.

1.2 Research Question

In this paper, we explore the research question *"How well can a (generic) neural transformer model answer programming questions?"*. It is important to know to what degree pre-trained models can cover answers to such questions, especially as they were not originally designed to provide knowledge (they are language models) and also as they were not *a priori* designed as programming aids (again, they are (human) language models). This research question is distinct from the—more interesting but harder-to-answer—question *"How well can one (learn how to) program when relying (only) on a foundational language model?".*)

To this end, we have manually collected a set of questions from the "learning how to program" domain; while they are not real questions collected from students, they are informed by decades of programming and teaching how to program between the authors, and they are therefore indicative of the nature of questions real students would ask (and have repeatedly asked over the years). Specifically, to what extent can a pre-trained language model such as a neural transformer like ChatGPT provide (1.) code answers or (2.) answers about code that are (i.) correct and that (ii.) do not contain dangerous omissions (e.g. leaving out error handling) or misleading output (foundational models are known to "hallucinate", which means providing untrue output as these models have no notions of truth or falsehood, as they focus on how to say something well).

2 Related Work

Early Computer-Based Initiatives to Support Students. After Carbonell's early and seminal work on intelligent tutoring systems [4], the late 1970 s the 1980 s saw a number of different approaches, including those using traditional AI methods: *BIP-I*, *BIP-II* (basic programming; Barr et al., 1976), *BRIDGE* (programming; Bonar 1985); *Flow Tutor* (FLOW programming language, Genter, 1977), *LISP Tutor* (LISP programming; Anderson and Reiser, 1985); *MALT* (basic machine language programming; Koffman and Blount, 1975); *MENO-Tutor* (basic Pascal programming; Woolf and McDonald, 1984); *PROUST* (Pascal programming; Soloway and Johnson, 1984); *SCENT-3 Advisor* (McCalla et al., 1988); *SPADE* (basic LOGO programming; Goldstein and Miller, 1976); and *TALUS* (basic LISP programming, Murray, 1987).

Robins, Rountree and Rountree review work on teaching and learning programming [11]. Koulouri, Lauria and Macredie [7] evaluate quantitatively alternative approaches to teaching beginners how to program.

Foundational Neural Language Models. OpenAI's GPT-3 [3] and ChatGPT [12] have been early foundational models that have been transformational in natural language processing: they showed how large, pre-trained language models such as neural transformers can dramatically reduce the development time of NLP systems by using large quantities of un-annotated text to train general-purpose "foundational" models. Our experiments use OpenAI's ChatGPT model.

Foundational Models and Programming. Microsoft's *GitHub Copilot* (based on Open AI Inc.'s Codex model[1]) was the first language model aimed at helping coders that was deployed at large-scale (on the Web-based source code revision control service Github.com). [17] describe a human experiment comprising 24 students that use Copilot for three programming tasks and its impact on task completion time and success rate. [1] report on an analysis of how 20 programmers interacted with Copilot. They observed that behavior could be grouped into two modes, acceleration mode, where a programmer uses Copilot to complete the code faster and exploration mode, where a programmer uses Copilot to explore various alternative options for solving a coding problem. [15] report on a Microsoft study that aimed to use a generic neural transformer model to extract

[1] see https://openai.com/blog/openai-codex.

information about locking, exceptions and performance from natural language comments of a large software repository. Bird et al. [2] also describe a case study where a set of subjects got instructed how to use Copilot, and then were given two tasks, namely to create a Tic Tac Toe game and to write code that sends an email programmatically via a Sendmail API. The authors describe how subjects responses to questions indicate an increase in productivity. In 2022, Imai, when studying human-computer "pair" programming found that programming with Copilot helps generate more lines of code (LoC) than human pair-programming in the same period of time, but at a lower quality level [6]. Surameery and Shakor provide a high-level comparison of debugging using Chat GPT versus using traditional debugging tools, and conclude that foundational language models can provide a useful expansion of the debugging toolbox of the future by providing bug prediction and bug explanation capabilities [16]. Sarsa et al. [14] present a very interesting approach: they explore how well foundational LMs can *generate programming exercises*. In a sense, this is the inverse exercise of our RQ1, which explores their ability to *answer* (human-provided) questions.[2] In the context of a next-generation programming education e-book, the same group investigated LMs' power to explain code in an educational context [9]; they let human students rate the usefulness of the automated output.[3] Leinonen et al. also compare code *explanations* created by human students and automatic large language models [8]. They look for differences in accuracy between students and LMs; in contrast, we explore the absolute correctness of human questions against LM answers (as evaluated by a human *expert*).

None of these works uses expert judgment to score a LM's ability to answer coding questions based on an open corpus.

3 Scope

We collected a set of questions based on the author's experience in using (from Scheme over C/C++ to Rust) and teaching (from FORTRAN 90 over Java to Python) various programming languages included general questions of understanding the programming process (c.f. Table 3) as well as questions in or about specific programming languages (c.f. Table 4). To mitigate the problem of personal bias, we checked the programmer help Website `StackExchange.org` for the number of times similar questions have been asked, to ensure that at least for a sizeable subset of questions, we have evidence that they really already occurred (Table 2).

We selected programming concept questions based on the typical topics that create difficulties (recursion, type systems etc.), and we selected programming languages that are important enough (leaving out many others e.g. AWK, FORTH, Erlang) and familiar to the author (leaving out e.g. BCPL, Verilog, Wolfram language, BLISS and Snobol).

---

[2] We thank an anonymous reviewer for making us aware of the work of Sarsa, MacNeil, Leinonen and co-workers.

[3] Questions for code explanations are one of our 4 question types: see type 3 in Table 3.

Table 1. A Sample of Programming Concepts Covered in the Dataset

abstraction	ACID	anonymous function
divide and conquer	domain-specific language	generator function
immutable object	linked list	mailbox
recursion	REST	reusability
singleton class	save data to a file	window

Table 2. A List of Error Types Covered in the Dataset

syntax error	wrong type	lifetime error
scope error	logical error	forgot to initialize
unallocated memory	index out of bounds	null pointer error (

4 Method

We execute the set of questions against the OpenAI Inc. ChatGPT API, one at a time. To implement the processing by the language model, we used a bash script, which sends questions to ChatGPT via the sgpt command[4] and stores the response in an SQL database. Our question dataset was processed on a MacBook Air 10 (2021) with ARM M1 processor in 12:26 min including network round-trip time.

5 Dataset

The resulting questions together with the answers provided by the ChatGPT model and the metadata described in Appendix B is available from our GitHub repository[5] and, at the time of writing, comprises $N = 105$ questions, model responses (as of July 20, 2023, using the May 23 version of the model) and metadata. Tables 4 and 1 provide the number of questions per concept and language in parentheses.

6 Towards an Evaluation

6.1 Quantitative Evaluation

Although we will also provide numbers, our overall evaluation approach is qualitative; due to the small size of our corpus, our numbers are dominated by the small number of examples of each of the many phenomena that should be studied. Nevertheless, as we shall see, a consistent pattern emerged.

[4] see https://github.com/tbckr/sgpt.

[5] see https://github.com/Information-Access-Research-Group-IARG/Prorgramming-Questions-for-ChatGPT.

Table 3. General Question Types Covered in the Dataset

No	Question Type	Example
1	Syntax	*How do I formulate X in language Y*
2	Idiom	*How do I achieve to get X done in language Y*
3	Explain	*What does code X do?*
4	Diagnose	*Why does code X not work?*
		Why does code X not do Y?

Table 4. Programming Languages Covered in the Dataset

Python	C++	Java	C
JavaScript	Julia	Kotlin	Bash/sh
Prolog	Scheme/LISP	Rust	FORTRAN
COBOL	R	Matlab	

We manually graded the answers of the ChatGPT model for all questions, assigning an ordinal rating of 0 for wrong/incorrect responses if *any* syntactic errors, semantic errors, type errors, or logical errors were contained in the response, or if code shown did not implement what was requested. Partially correct answers that were helpful (a rather subjective notion, admittedly) were assigned a rating of 1, and fully correct and relevant answers were assigned a rating of 2. We added the verbatim output and grade to the database.

This way of scoring is admittedly crude, and in future work, more detailed aspect-oriented grading experiments should be carried out. However, out three-point ordinal scoring method worked well enough on the questions we had to swiftly grade the set of questions gathered, and to get a sense of ChatGPT's abilities.

Results. Based on our scoring method, the 105 questions reached 158 points, leading to an arithmetic mean of Avg = 1.7753. Most questions get at least partial credit: only one question was marked 0, because the question about anonymous functions in Kotlin led to an explanation for named functions instead.

This is work in progress; we plan to extend the database with material found to be recurring in student programming classes, and to provide a more extensive evaluation. One could also collect realistic questions from students and validate questions against StackExchange regarding their frequency of occurrence.

6.2 Qualitative Evaluation

How useful are the answers? The are often impeccable. For example:

▶ **Human Question I:**

```
What is divide and conquer? Explain it to me using a chess game as
an example.
```

▶ **Machine Answer I:**

`Divide and conquer is a programming paradigm that involves breaking down a problem into smaller subproblems, solving them independently, and then combining the solutions to solve the original problem. It is often used to solve complex problems more efficiently. In the domain of writing a chess game, an example of using divide and conquer could be implementing the move validation logic. Instead of checking the validity of a move for the entire chessboard, the board can be divided into smaller sections, such as rows or columns. Each section can then be validated independently, reducing the complexity of the problem. For instance, when validating a move for a specific piece, the program can divide the chessboard into rows and check if the move is valid within that row. Similarly, it can divide the board into columns and validate the move within each column. By breaking down the problem into smaller sections, the move validation process becomes more manageable and efficient.`

▶ **Human Question II:**

`What is the difference between String and StringBuffer in Java?`

▶ **Machine Answer II:**

`The main difference between StringBuffer and String in Java is that StringBuffer is mutable, meaning its value can be changed, while String is immutable, meaning its value cannot be changed once it is created. In other words, when you modify a StringBuffer object, it does not create a new object, but instead modifies the existing object. This can be useful when you need to perform a lot of string manipulation operations, as it avoids creating multiple new objects. On the other hand, when you modify a String object, it creates a new object with the modified value, leaving the original object unchanged. This can be less efficient when performing a lot of string manipulation operations, as it involves creating multiple new objects. Another difference is that StringBuffer is synchronized, which means it is thread-safe and can be used in multi-threaded environments without any issues. String, on the other hand, is not synchronized. In summary, if you need to perform a lot of string manipulation operations or if you are working in a multi-threaded environment, StringBuffer is a better choice. If you don't need to modify the string and want to ensure immutability, String is the way to go.`

On the other hand, sometimes functional but incomplete code is returned, as in the following:

▶ **Machine Answer III:**

`You can load a file containing whitespace-separated integers into an array in Python by following these steps:`

```
1. Open the file using the 'open()'function and specify the
file path and mode. For example, to open a file named
''numbers.txt'' in read mode, you can use: (...) file =
open(''numbers.txt'', ''r'') (...)
```

Results. The code in the response is working and well-explained, but a hypothetical "file not found" situation is not handled. However, to be fair, many online Website also lack this level of sophistication.

7 Discussion

7.1 Accomplishments

We reported on an ongoing project to collect questions of the kind that learners of programming concepts and common programming languages may face. Our findings suggest foundational language models are capable of solving programming tasks at the level of a good to very good student, which is remarkable, in particular due to the fact that ChatGPT was not specifically developed as a programming assistant (unlike Copilot).

7.2 Limitations

Our work is still small scale, and our sample suffers from selection bias. We anticipate that a Wizard of Oz experiment with real students could lead to a bigger and better corpus, and well supplement our collection effort. We need to increase the percentage of questions that explain code and that contain bugs in this process. Our work is also limited in that we have not yet conducted any form of inter-coder agreement. Another limitation is that in some countries (e.g. Germany), the student have a right to be taught the correct solutions, so it is not acceptable for e.g. a chatbot to occasionally get the answer wrong ("hallucination"); this could be addressed by warnings to the user. In the box in Table 5, we report on a parallel experiment in which students without programming skills were able to solve a technical assignment assisted by ChatGPT.

However, preliminary experiments by the second author have shown that while task completion probability and task completion time improve when supporting students with a chat-enabled transformer, understanding of programming concepts does not (see Box "A Teaching Experiment" in Table 5).

8 Ethical Reflections

The ability of language models historically came as a surprise: emerging out of the research into large (human) language models that got pre-trained with vast amounts of text, data crawled from the World Wide Web included not just plenty of useful text, but also code repositories, programming discussion forums

Table 5. A Case Study with $N = 2$ Teams of Non-Programmers

In the summer term of 2023, we conducted a controlled experiment "Artificial Intelligence Team Project" at Coburg University of Applied Sciences, with 6 Master's students in business studies. The students were grouped into à 3 students each. The task was to classify an annotated dataset of about 400k German-language feedback messages and numerical ratings of patients' experiences with medical practitioners according to the sentiment polarity expressed (into positive and negative comments) using a simple, two-class logistic regression model. To achieve this, Python code had to be used for data understanding, data preparation and modelling. One question was of how well the students, absent any machine learning experience and hardly any programming experience, could generate functional code fragments and attach them to each other using only a pre-trained language model. It turned out that both groups generated functional Python code, and produced two classifiers with $F1 > 98\%$. OpenAI's ChatGPT (model 3.5 version of May 24, 2023, used with German conversations) as the pre-trained language model used was largely responsible for the success of the project. Indeed, every line of code was generated by ChatGPT, corrected in case of error, and described for the students. This was achieved by adapting prompts, such as instructing ChatGPT to please answer in understandable language or to please correct the previously generated code using an error from Jupyter Notebook or PyCharm. The prompts for generating programme code were formulated without or with hardly any computer science-specific technical terms. A typical prompt for code generation was (translated from German): *"How do i remove stop words in column 3 in a dataframe?"* A typical prompt for code improvement was the following (again, translated from German): *"Instead of the accuracy, it should be output how many were correctly identified with value 0."*

Anecdotal Results: All students reported ChatGPT changed the way they worked, it enabled them to work faster, and to bridge gaps in their knowledge. One group also reported, however, that their understanding of programming did not deepen in this exercise using ChatGPT. ■

etc. One challenge is that the exact set of Web sites included in the training of the proprietary models like OpenAI's ChatGPT remain unpublished.

In any case, this study showed that a model that was *not specifically intended* for this purpose is capable of solving substantial programming sub-tasks. This a case of morally positive unintended use; however, there are also uses that are ethically questionable, such as using a foundational language model for solving exercises when its use is forbidden. It will only be possible to a very limited extent to be able to tell, by humans or machines, whether a foundational model was used in the course of solving a programming exercise. Therefore, if programming exercises are to be graded as part of coursework, either a non-networked environment must be created, or programming has to happen based on pen and paper only (perhaps the latter is less desirable than the former due to its artificial nature, but creating a functional but isolated, secured, non-networked environment is also a challenge, not to mention the pervasiveness of networked mobile devices).

One fundamental danger is that the use of foundational models for programming will become very common (as it no doubt will), and as a result, safety critical code will be in part originate from auto-generated code that contains only insufficient error handling. This scenario is likely due to company's incentives to increase profits and reduce cost rather than maximize quality and minimize software defects.

9 Summary, Conclusion and Future Work

Foundational language models were pre-trained with human language material, and in the process ingested substantial source code in various languages, too; as a consequence, they are *de facto* also models of how to program, despite unreliable ones. We found evidence of programming knowledge could be retrieved on a broad set of tasks and programming languages, which may aid beginners and speed up experts.

In this paper, we looked at one generic (foundational) models' programming abilities, which is a necessary but not sufficient condition for answering the question in this paper's title; we could answer the "ability" question overall affirmatively. Large pre-trained neural transformers like the one underlying the ChatGPT application encode substantial programming and programming language knowledge, which can be accessed using a convenient interface and in many human languages. Whether and how foundational language models can assist humans in the process of learning how to program, the overarching question, further requires us to find out whether they can help learners perform and deepen learner understanding, which should be explored in future work (see also [10] in this volume).

Further work should explore cross-language consistency (many learners are not English native speakers). A comparison of multiple alternative responses of the language model used would also be interesting.[6] Using a detailed prompt may further improve the results; our experience with other transformer experiments has shown that the time to try our various prompts, i.e. prefixing the questions with some prose to set a context, often leads to substantial improvements. One approach could be the collection and clustering of (abstract syntax trees of) problem–answer pairs in terms of code in a way that mixes human-originating answers with machine-generated answers so that students can see that a human solution for their question may already exist, so they do not have to rely on (relatively more error-prone) machine suggestions. Finally, a benchmark evaluation that compares an approach that retrieves human forum answers from StackExchange with automatically synthesized answers from language models would be interesting.

[6] We are grateful to a reviewer for pointing out this idea.

Acknowledgements. We would like to thank our anonymous referees for their valuable feedback, which helped improve the quality of this paper. The research presented in this paper was partially funded by project VoLL-KI (BMBF/German Federal Ministry for Education and Research) under grants 16DHBKI089, 16DHBKI090 and 16DHBKI091, and by an award to the first author under the Hightech Agenda Bavaria; this funding support is gratefully acknowledged. All opinions and errors are solely the authors' and do not necessarily reflect the opinions of any funding agency.

A Some Sample Questions from our Dataset

Show me the C code to start and stop a precise timer for code benchmarking.

In C, how can I generate a random number between 1 and 100?

In C, how can I define a Unicode string?

In C, how can I portably access the elements of the header of a binary file like JPG?

In portable standard ISO C++20, how do you read a *.csv file into RAM without using a library?

In portable standard ISO C++20, how do you read a *.csv file into RAM?

In portable standard ISO C++20, how do you read a *.csv file into RAM using the standard library or an open source library under the MIT, BSD, Apache or LGPL licenses.?

In Python, how can I draw simple graphics using LOGO-like turtle graphics commands?

In Python, how can I professionally render a contingency matrix that shows the performance of a binary classifier?

In Java, how do I iterate over all keys of a hashtable?

In Java, how can I replace all matches of a regular expression?

In C, how can I create a 3-dimensional matrix of float objects that is safe from buffer overflow errors?

In Julia, how can I plot a ROC curve?

In Julia, how can I print a contingency matrix?

In Julia, how can I define a three-dimensional matrix of floats?

In Julia, which library provides an implementation of the Viterbi algorithm for Hidden Markov Models?

Show me the Julia code for generating a random undirected graph.

In Rust, how can I design functions to return errors systematically? In portable standard ISO C++20, how do you read a *.csv file into RAM without using a library?

In portable standard ISO C++20, how do you read a *.csv file into RAM?

In portable standard ISO C++20, how do you read a *.csv file into RAM using the standard library or an open source library under the MIT, BSD, Apache or LGPL licenses.?

In Python, how can I draw simple graphics using LOGO-like turtle graphics commands?

In Python, how can I professionally render a contingency matrix that shows the performance of a binary classifier?

In Java, how can I implement a singleton class?

In C, how can I create a 3-dimensional matrix of float objects that is safe from buffer overflow errors?

In Julia, how can I view the compiled code for a function?

In Rust, how can I design functions to return errors systematically?

In Rust, how do I implement what would be a class in Java or C++?

In Rust, how do I make a struct printable?

Show me a Kotlin class for singly linked lists.

In Rust, how do I implement what would be a class in Java or C++?

In Rust, how do I make a struct printable?

In Rust, which library is best for fast trie lookup in RAM?

In Rust, which library provides efficient B-tree storage on disk?

In Kotlin, how does the minimum code of an Android mobile app look like?

In Kotlin, what is the syntax for anonymous functions?

What does this C++ code do? ...

What does this Python code do? ...

What does the following Python code do? ...

How can I test in Python whether a CUDA GPU is present?

Explain recursion.

Explain the difference between transient and persistent.

In databases, explain the ACID acronym.

Show me an SQL query that computes aggregate statistics about a table.

If I have an SQL table defined by "CREATE TABLE t(...)", how can I insert a new author only if he or she does not already exist?

In FORTRAN 95, how can I multiply two 2×2 matrices of integers A and B?

Can I separate a function's declaration from its implementation in FORTRAN?

Can I separate a function's declaration from its implementation in C++?

Can I separate a function's declaration from its implementation in Java?

Explain tail recursion to me.

Show me all bugs and deficiencies in this C code: void nb__net_init(void) { nb__init_timers(); nb__net_state = malloc(sizeof(nb__net_state)); nb__net_state-_num_conn = 0; }

What is wrong in the following Python code: ... ? Explain all errors or bugs to me.

Show me all errors or bugs in the following C function: ... How does it look like when it is corrected?

Show me a set of C functions for creating a (singly) linked list, inserting data to a linked list, deleting an item from a linked list and freeing a linked list.

B DDL Database Schema

Table 6 shows the Data Definition Language (DDL) specification of the relational database that we use to store and distribute the dataset described in this paper; we use SQlite, which is simple, fast and already pre-installed on many machines. Each question gets a unique ID, the question string is paired with an answer string (the model's response/completion string returned), the name of the programming language is given as a string for reasons of simplicity. The question type refers to the earlier table, and the answer type is incorrect (0), 1 (partially correct) or 2 (correct).

Table 6. DDL Database Schema for the dataset.

```
CREATE TABLE questions(
    id        INTEGER PRIMARY KEY AUTOINCREMENT,
    question  VARCHAR NOT NULL,
    answer    VARCHAR,
    prglang   VARCHAR,
    qtype     INTEGER,
    atype     INTEGER
);
```

References

1. Barke, S., James, M.B., Polikarpova, N.: Grounded Copilot: how programmers interact with code-generating models. Unpublished manuscript. ArXiv.org preprint server, Cornell University, New York, NY, USA (2022). https://arxiv.org/abs/2206.15000
2. Bird, C., et al.: Taking flight with copilot. Commun. ACM **66**(6), 56–62 (2023). https://doi.org/10.1145/3589996
3. Brown, T., et al.: Language models are few-shot learners. In: Larochelle, H., Ranzato, M., Hadsell, R., Balcan, M., Lin, H. (eds.) Advances in Neural Information Processing Systems. vol. 33, pp. 1877–1901. Curran (2020), https://proceedings.neurips.cc/paper_files/paper/2020/file/1457c0d6bfcb4967418bfb8ac142f64a-Paper.pdf
4. Carbonell, J.R.: AI in CAI: an artificial-intelligence approach to computer-assisted instruction. IEEE Trans. Man-Mach. Syst. **11**(4), 190–202 (1970). https://doi.org/10.1109/TMMS.1970.299942
5. Devlin, J., Chang, M.W., Lee, K., Toutanova, K.: BERT: pre-training of deep bidirectional transformers for language understanding. In: Proceedings of the 2019 Conference of the North American Chapter of the Association for Computational Linguistics: Human Language Technologies, Volume 1 (Long and Short Papers), pp. 4171–4186. ACL, Minneapolis, MN, USA (2019). https://doi.org/10.18653/v1/N19-1423
6. Imai, S.: Is GitHub Copilot a substitute for human pair-programming? An empirical study. In: Proceedings of the ACM/IEEE 44th International Conference on Software Engineering: Companion Proceedings, pp. 319–321. ICSE 2022, ACM, New York, NY, USA (2022). https://doi.org/10.1145/3510454.3522684

7. Koulouri, T., Lauria, S., Macredie, R.D.: Teaching introductory programming: a quantitative evaluation of different approaches. ACM Trans. Comput. Educ. **14**(4), 1–28 (2015). https://doi.org/10.1145/2662412
8. Leinonen, J., et al.: Comparing code explanations created by students and large language models (2023). unpublished manuscript, arXiv cs.CY 2304.03938, Cornell University pre-print server
9. MacNeil, S., et al.: Experiences from using code explanations generated by large language models in a web software development E-book. In: Proceedings of the 54th ACM Technical Symposium on Computer Science Education. vol. 1, pp. 931–937. SIGCSE 2023, Association for Computing Machinery, New York, NY, USA (2023). https://doi.org/10.1145/3545945.3569785
10. Reiche, M., Leidner, J.: Bridging the programming skill gap with ChatGPT: A machine learning project with business students. In: Nowacyk et al., S. (ed.) ECAI 2023 Workshops, Kraków, Poland. CCIS, Springer Nature, Cham, Switzerland (2023), Workshop on AI for AI Learning, in this volume
11. Robins, A., Rountree, J., Rountree, N.: Learning and teaching programming: a review and discussion. Comput. Sci. Educ. **13**(2), 137–172 (2003)
12. Roumeliotis, K.I., Tselikas, N.D.: ChatGPT and Open-AI models: a preliminary review. Future Internet **15**(6), 192 (2023). https://doi.org/10.3390/fi15060192,https://www.mdpi.com/1999-5903/15/6/192
13. Sanderson, K.: GPT-4 is here: what scientists think. Nature **615**(7954), 773 (2023)
14. Sarsa, S., Denny, P., Hellas, A., Leinonen, J.: Automatic generation of programming exercises and code explanations using large language models. In: Proceedings of the 2022 ACM Conference on International Computing Education Research - volume 1, pp. 27–43. ICER 2022, Association for Computing Machinery, New York, NY, USA (2022). https://doi.org/10.1145/3501385.3543957
15. Su, Y., Wan, C., Sethi, U., Lu, S., Musuvathi, M., Nath, S.: HotGPT: how to make software documentation more useful with a large language model? In: Proceedings of the 19th Workshop on Hot Topics in Operating Systems, pp. 87–93. HOTOS 2023, Association for Computing Machinery, New York, NY, USA (2023). https://doi.org/10.1145/3593856.3595910
16. Surameery, N.M.S., Shakor, M.Y.: Use ChatGPT to solve programming bugs. Int. J. Inf. Technol. Comput. Eng. **3**(01), 17–22 (2023). https://doi.org/10.55529/ijitc.31.17.22, https://journal.hmjournals.com/index.php/IJITC/article/view/1679
17. Vaithilingam, P., Zhang, T., Glassman, E.: Expectation vs. experience: evaluating the usability of code generation tools powered by large language models. In: Extended Abstracts of the 2022 Conference on Human Factors in Computing Systems, pp. 1–7 (2022), https://dl.acm.org/doi/10.1145/3491101.3519665
18. Vaswani, A., et al.: Attention is all you need. In: Guyon, I., et al. (eds.) Advances in Neural Information Processing Systems 30–31st Annual Conference on Neural Information Processing Systems, Long Beach, CA, 4–9 December 2017, pp. 5999–6010. (NIPS 2017), Curran Associates (2018)

Bridging the Programming Skill Gap with ChatGPT: A Machine Learning Project with Business Students

Michael Reiche[1(✉)] and Jochen L. Leidner[1,2]

[1] Coburg University of Applied Sciences, Friedrich Streib-Strasse 2, 96450 Coburg, Germany
michael.reiche@hs-coburg.de
[2] University of Sheffield, Regents Court, 211 Portobello, Sheffield S1 4DP, UK

Abstract. Foundational language models, i.e. large, pre-trained neural transformer models like Google BERT and OpenAI ChatGPT, GPT-3 or GPT-4 have created considerable general media attention. Microsoft's github.com service has also integrated a foundational model (CodePilot) to make programmers more productive. Some people have gone so far and heralded the end of the programming profession, an unsubstantiated claim.

We investigate the research question to what extent individuals without the necessary technical background can still use such systems to achieve a set task. Our single case study based preliminary evidence suggests that using such systems may lead to a good task completion rate, but without deepening the understanding much on the way.

Keywords: Computer-Supported Instruction · AI for Teaching · Pretrained Foundational Models · Artificial Intelligence in Education · Classroom Case Study

1 Introduction

Increasingly, employees with a business background are also expected to have a high-level understanding of machine learning concepts. Consequently, the textbook *Introduction to Statistical Learning* [2,5] is used to train MBA students at Stanford University. Following this trend, the course "Team Project Artificial Intelligence" was offered as an elective from the area of projects in the winter semester 2022/2023 in the Master's degree program in business studies at the Coburg University of Applied Sciences and Arts.

We borrowed a task from Kaggle.com, namely the task of sentiment analysis of online-feedback about treatment experiences with medics.

Out of 19 participants across all projects of the semester and study program, 6 participants took part in the project. The goal of the project was to impart knowledge for the focus "IT Management", which enables the students to participate in machine learning projects in their later professional life or to be able to comprehend them. In particular, knowledge from the following areas was imparted.

S. Nowaczyk et al. (Eds.): ECAI 2023 Workshops, CCIS 1948, pp. 439–446, 2024.
https://doi.org/10.1007/978-3-031-50485-3_42

- Technical competences:
  - Recognition of machine learning use cases.
  - Implementation of machine learning use cases, especially in the phases of business understanding, data understanding, data preparation, modeling and evaluation.
- Methodical competences:
  - Using ChatGPT for programming.
  - Following a machine learning methodology.
- Social competences:
  - Presenting technical and business results to a group.
  - Discussing in a group.
  - Analyzing, evaluating, and refining one's approach to learning and problem solving.

The project has had another intended impact in addition to building students' competencies. Namely, the generation of data in a controlled experiment to compare two methods with an intervention group and a control group. Therefore, during the planning of the project, dependent (iterations, experimentation, planning, communication) and independent (business case, input data, algorithm, upskilling, domain knowledge, infrastructure) variables as well as behavioral rules were defined to increase the reliability, validity and credibility of the results.

The teaching of the competencies and the performance of the activities required for this purpose were achieved by means of various formats, each of which was selected in such a way that the previously defined dependent and independent variables were subject to as few disturbing influences as possible. An inquiry at the beginning of the project about the theoretical and practical knowledge showed that the participants (as well as the students of the master's program in business administration in general) did not have adequate machine learning or programming knowledge that would have enabled the independent and successful implementation of a machine learning project.

To bridge the gap between the programming skills needed for the project and those brought by the participants, the use of ChatGPT has been suggested for activities with programming content, especially for generating and concatenating Python code fragments and fixing bugs in the program code.

In this paper, we investigate the research question "Can students with no knowledge of computer science and no knowledge of a programming language use ChatGPT to generate all the Python code for a machine learning project?".

2 Related Work

After foundational language models based on the transformer architecture by Google [6] with BERT (Bidirectional Encoder Representations from Transformers) [1] received great attention in the scientific community, more and more so-called large language models (LLM) have emerged [7].

Vaithilingam et al. conducted an experiment with 24 participants, 23 of whom had more than two years of programming experience. They investigated, among other things, whether the LLM Githubs Copilot, which is based on OpenAI's Codex, offers more support to experienced programmers than the code completion tool Intellisense. No significant difference was found. However, participants indicated that Copilot gave them a better start in the programming task. Even in the case of incorrect code, at least a helpful direction was given, which could offer help to novice programmers in particular. 12 of the participants found it difficult to understand or change the code generated by Copilot, which was also due to the fact that the generated code is not commented [5]. Kasneci et al. have critically examined the opportunities and risks of LLM in education. They concluded that LLM offer many opportunities to enhance learners' learning experience, but generated information can also have a negative impact on learners' critical thinking and problem-solving skills. To counteract this, LLM should support learning and not replace human authorities [3].

Controlled experiments in software engineering are a common means of establishing cause-and-effect relationships. A survey of 103 articles found that 87 % of the subjects were students [4].

According to our research, no papers have been published on the use of LLMs or ChatGPT in particular that investigated how well people without a technical background can programme.

3 Method

To answer the research question, various methods were used before, during and after the project.

At the beginning of the project, a survey was conducted to determine the practical experience and theoretical knowledge of each participant. For example, the following closed-ended questions were asked with a free-text option that allowed participants to choose between "yes" and "no" answers, and to be able to explain their answer with an additional answer choice:

- Do you already have practical experience in programming?
- Do you already have theoretical knowledge in Machine Learning Engineering?
- Do you already have practical experience in Machine Learning Engineering?

If one of the questions was answered with "Yes", then the content of the associated free-text option was analyzed and a point value from 0 (no knowledge or experience) to 3 (more than two relevant lectures attended or everyday professional life) was assigned depending on the proficiency.

Two groups (team blue and team red) were formed, which had as equally distributed experience and knowledge as possible in the three questions on programming and machine learning engineering (team blue 3 points and team red 3 points) and in other questions (team blue 25 points and team red 19 points). The two groups differed in that they each had to use one of two machine learning methodologies to carry out the project, which led to different ways of working.

In order to compensate for the lack of technical knowledge and experience, a joint coaching session was held for both groups in the first third of the project before the use of a programming environment. This provided the theoretical foundations of machine learning and a guideline for using ChatGPT to generate the Python code for the project by means of a live demonstration with ChatGPT and Google's development environment Colab.

During the live demonstration, ChatGPT and Google Colab were used in interaction. In ChatGPT, it was shown where prompts are entered, responses generated and regenerated. In Google Colab, it was shown which elements the interface has and in particular how code blocks are inserted and executed. As an example of the interaction between the two web-based interfaces, simple mathematical calculations and a simple data pipeline were generated with ChatGPT and inserted as code blocks in Google Colab. To illustrate the data pipeline, the framework Pandas was imported, a data frame was filled with a data set (CSV), the content of the data frame was sorted and the content of the data frame was visualised. The individual work steps were carried out by the lecturer and by volunteer participants.

The project was implemented in four teamwork sessions per group, three of which included programming. The individual sessions lasted between 83 min and 229 min. However, the average was 181 minutes.

During the project, data such as ChatGPT histories, schedules, project documentation, Python files, presentations and tables with over 250 team activities were generated by the group participants and the lecturer/experiment leader.

The project switched from Google Colab to Jupyter notebooks and JetBrain's PyCharm. The groups were not allowed to use any other tools, information or communication tools than those provided. The project was completed with presentations and final reports by the groups (Fig. 1).

4 Evaluation

The teams interacted with ChatGPT (version 3.5 with German conversations) in different ways. In team blue, one of the three participants was responsible for interacting with ChatGPT and programming in the development environment. In team red, all three participants worked together with ChatGPT most of the time and wrote the programming code for the project. How the prompts were formulated was at the discretion of the participants. Code fragments were asked for with general prompts without project-specific specifications and with specific prompts with detailed specifications that enabled seamless integration into the already existing code.

Although ChatGPT always provided explanations in addition to code, these were rarely read through. There was often a lack of understanding and time to follow the explanations. Instead, the code generated with ChatGPT, including explanatory comments, was copied completely and with hardly any adjustments into a programming environment and executed. In case of errors and unexpected returns, ChatGPT was mostly consulted and in rare cases the lecturer. In some

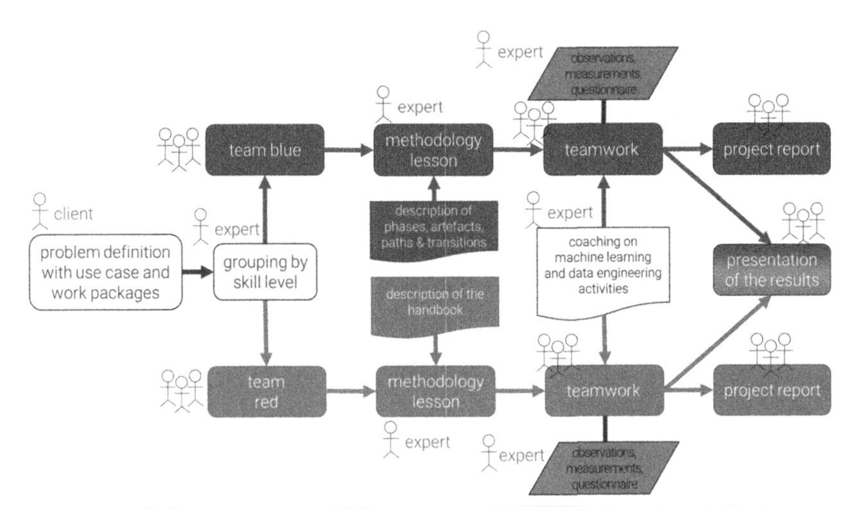

Fig. 1. Controlled Study Design

cases, functions from libraries were mentioned that showed incompatibilities. This is due to the fact that the ChatGPT version used was only trained with data up to 2021.

From a technical point of view, it was clear to the participants what the code fragments should output. Therefore, prompts could be given correctly and the results of the executed code could be interpreted in the development environment.

Interaction behaviour with ChatGPT of the team red: The team generated the programme code for the project with 97 prompts. With specifications such as "In future, please take our data name df into account in the code. Please reissue the code", the group influenced the subsequent response behaviour of ChatGPT so that the generated responses fitted better into the already generated and adopted Python code, which reduced the required understanding about the programming. In one case, the team formulated a prompt without a question. The response was "I'm not sure what exactly you want to customise. If you mean a specific customisation in the DataFrame, please give me more information about it." When the code inserted and executed in the development environment produced unexpected or erroneous results, ChatGPT was interacted with again, for example with the following prompt "what does this mean? Empty DataFrame Columns: [index, rating, comment] Index: []". ChatGPT was also questioned in several stages without inserting code into the development environment in between. Through this, a learning success/progress is recognisable, because the students saw independently that the generated code would not bring the desired result. For example, they were first asked "How do I add a new column?" and then "Add a new column with the title class in df2". Another peculiarity was that when ChatGPT entered the same error code twice (without using regenerate), it gave an off- target answer the first time and a customised and on-target

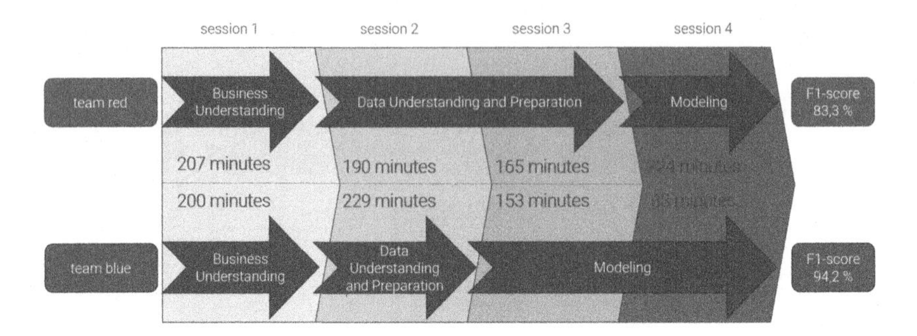

Fig. 2. Teamwork Sessions in Comparison

answer the second time. ChatGPT first replied "Sorry for the misunderstanding. To avoid the SettingWithCopyWarning, you can adjust the code as follows: ..." and then with "Sorry again for the misunderstanding. To avoid the SettingWithCopyWarning, you can correct the code as follows:...". ChatGPT did not always provide the best answers. For example, the bag-of-words method was recommended to convert textual data (online feedback) into numerical features. Nowadays, modern methods exist that would not have lost contextual information or semantic relationships during the conversion, which could have resulted in better classification performance. The participants were not able to understand the generated code in detail and, at least in part, showed little understanding of it. For example, the code for logistic regression was asked twice. The only change in the second prompt was to change the distribution from 90 % training data and 10 % test data to 80 % training data and 20 % test data, which could have been done directly in the development environment by making the smallest changes. Elsewhere, ChatGPT was queried for code to count the frequency of certain words. However, the words searched for were then changed in several iterations directly in the development environment.

Interaction behaviour with ChatGPT of the team blue: The team generated the code for the project using 53 prompts. There was a better understanding of how to adapt the generated code snippets to the previous programming in order to produce executable code. In the group, it took much longer to give ChatGPT specific guidelines that directed the response behaviour so that the generated code needed less customisation and fit better with the given identifiers. Prompts like this "how do I plot an expression in Python that I would otherwise render with print?" show that there was at least a basic understanding of programming. The documentation given in this group on the methodology gave more specific recommendations for action, which is why technical terms such as lemmatisation, stemming or class imbalance reduction were sometimes entered in prompts.

Both groups managed to develop a classifier that can distinguish positive from negative comments by loading a CSV file into a DataFrame, building an understanding of the data, qualitatively enhancing it and implementing a model using the logistic regression algorithm. All without machine learning skills. The created classifiers differ in their F1-scores (team red 83.3 % and team blue 94.2 %) and the time needed for implementation (Fig. 2).

5 Discussion

The current findings should be interpreted with several limitations in mind. Typically, machine learning projects are carried out by people with training in programming or machine learning. In such a more realistic scenario, the use of ChatGPT would have been more effective. The setting, incorporated into a controlled experiment, did not allow the participants to use sources other than ChatGPT, the methodology documents and the lecturers for programming. In other circumstances, the ChatGPT outputs could have been supported with internet research, for example, which might have produced better results.

We would like to stimulate a discussion that sheds light on the relevance and effectiveness of using ChatGPT for programming in a business studies course.

6 Summary, Conclusion and Future Work

We described a case study in which two small teams of business students were given the task of building a sentiment analysis model for German medical practitioner feedback from patients.

In conclusion, our findings support the hypothesis that subjects with little to no relevant training in programming or machine learning can still complete tasks that were traditionally required to require programming skills. However, limitations have been identified that may distinguish the results from those of an experienced machine learning engineering team. In many cases, even simple code fragments were not generated in a functional way in the context of the project, or only after several attempts by ChatGPT. The approaches provided by ChatGPT were helpful for people with programming knowledge even in complex situations, but the students without the necessary know-how could not assess which simple adjustments would be necessary in the code snippet to create executable programme code. According to the authors, at least a basic programming education is necessary to interact effectively and efficiently with ChatGPT for the purpose of creating software.

Feedback indicates that the students' own perception is not that they had a learning experience that deepened their understanding; rather, it was a "gap filling" experience: the foundational language model took the seat that should be filled by a knowledgeable team member.

Elsewhere, we describe how much programming knowledge these models really contain, given that they were conceived to model human language, not programming language(s). In future work, it would be intriguing to explore how Chatbot-based foundational language models could be integrated in tutorial systems that aim at teaching programming principles and programming (language) skills. The need for this is that the demand for programming talent is unmet, not replaced by language models.

Acknowledgements. The authors would like to thank the six participants in the experiment, without whom this article would not have been possible, and the anonymous reviewers for their valuable feedback. Supported by BMBF Grants 16DHBKI089, 16DHBKI090 and 16DHBKI091; we would also like to thank the Free State of Bavaria for funding this research under the Hightech Agenda Bavaria R&D programme.

References

1. Devlin, J., Chang, M.W., Lee, K., Toutanova, K.: BERT: pre-training of deep bidirectional transformers for language understanding. In: Proceedings of the 2019 Conference of the North American Chapter of the Association for Computational Linguistics: Human Language Technologies, Volume 1 (Long and Short Papers), pp. 4171–4186. Association for Computational Linguistics, Minneapolis, Minnesota (2019). https://doi.org/10.18653/v1/N19-1423, https://aclanthology.org/N19-1423
2. James, G., Witten, D., Hastie, T., Tibshirani, R., Taylor, J.: An Introduction to Statistical Learning–with Applications in Python. Springer Texts in Statistics, Springer Nature, Cham, Switzerland (2023). https://doi.org/10.1007/978-3-031-38747-0
3. Kasneci, E., et al.: ChatGPT for good? On opportunities and challenges of large language models for education. Learn. Individ. Differ. **103**, 102274 (2023) https://doi.org/10.1016/j.lindif.2023.102274, https://www.sciencedirect.com/science/article/pii/S1041608023000195
4. Sjoeberg, D., et al.: A survey of controlled experiments in software engineering. IEEE Trans. Software Eng. **31**(9), 733–753 (2005). https://doi.org/10.1109/TSE.2005.97
5. Vaithilingam, P., Zhang, T., Glassman, E.L.: Expectation vs. experience: evaluating the usability of code generation tools powered by large language models. In: Extended Abstracts of the 2022 CHI Conference on Human Factors in Computing Systems. CHI EA 22, Association for Computing Machinery, New York, NY, USA (2022). https://doi.org/10.1145/3491101.3519665, https://doi.org/10.1145/3491101.3519665
6. Vaswani, A., et al.: Attention is all you need (2017). https://arxiv.org/pdf/1706.03762.pdf
7. Zhao, W.X., et al.: A survey of large language models (2023)

Topic Segmentation of Educational Video Lectures Using Audio and Text

Markos Dimitsas[1(✉)] and Jochen L. Leidner[1,2]

[1] Coburg University of Applied Sciences and Arts, Friedrich-Streib-Straße 2, 96450 Coburg, Germany
Markos.Dimitsas@hs-coburg.de

[2] University of Sheffield, Department of Computer Science, Regents Court, 211 Portobello, Sheffield S1 4DP, UK

Abstract. The recent pandemic led to a surge of recorded lecture material available digitally, a resource that can now be used to improve computer-assisted learning. In this paper, we compare two methods for topic segmentation, i.e. the breaking down of a single lecture session into self-contained content units that deal with one or a small set of sub-topics or a set of concepts, respectively. We are interested whether auditory silence or keywords generated by a state-of-the-art keyword extraction tool are superior in segmenting down a session's recording into self- sufficient clips that may be served to student learners of artificial intelligence. To the best of our knowledge, this is the first comparison of silence-based topic segmentation and keyword-based topic segmentation for recorded lecture materials.

Keywords: Topic modeling · Topic segmentation · Detection of thematic shifts · Video analytics · Signal processing · Education applications

1 Introduction

Recent increases in the acceptance of remote work, including remote lecturing, have led to substantial archives with lecture recordings that capture plenty of knowledge. In this paper, we describe an ongoing effort to design and implement methods for effective topic classification and segmentation of video lecture collections, in order to facilitate subsequent search (using a chatbot) and exploration (using a topic browser). While past work has established effective methods for text-based (e.g. [7]; [5]) and audio-based (e.g. c.f. [15]) methods, there is little work that combines modalities and exploits available thematic domain knowledge. Our work forms part of the *VoLL-KI* project ("Learning from Learners"), which aims to develop a toolbox of components that support learners of artificial intelligence and eventually other subjects [3], with a focus on the English and German languages. The remainder of this paper is structured as follows: Sect. 2 briefly summarizes past work in segmentation. Section 3 describes two methods, one using audio and another based on text; Sect. 4 presents our preliminary evaluation and related further plans for discussion. Section 5 discusses our findings before we conclude in Sect. 6.

S. Nowaczyk et al. (Eds.): ECAI 2023 Workshops, CCIS 1948, pp. 447–458, 2024.
https://doi.org/10.1007/978-3-031-50485-3_43

2 Related Work

Topic segmentation (part of topic modeling) is a support task for navigating and understanding large documents or document collections. In traditional document topic segmentation, seminal works by Hearst [7] and Choi [5] laid the foundation for the field. Hearst's TextTiling algorithm is a pioneering method that automatically detects subtopics from expository text. It operates on the observation that a shift in topic is often accompanied by a change in the lexical distribution of a document. The algorithm consists of three steps: First, it tokenizes the text and creates sentence-sized units. Second, it determines a score for each of these units. Finally, in the third step, it detects subtopic boundaries. For the scoring process, three methods have been explored: blocks, vocabulary introductions, and chains. Each of these methods utilizes patterns of lexical co-occurrence and distribution within the text.

On the other hand, Choi's C99 algorithm takes a different approach to topic segmentation. Instead of focusing on lexical shifts, the C99 algorithm uses divisive clustering to detect boundaries in a document. Similar to TextTiling, it also consists of three steps. In the first step, pre-processing and sentence forming occur, along with the measurement of similarity between sentences, resulting in the creation of a similarity matrix. The second step involves ranking the similarity scores between sentences to estimate the order of similarity, thus creating a ranking matrix. The third step involves clustering to determine the location of topic boundaries. Initially, the entire document is considered as one coherent text segment, which is then iteratively divided to maximize the inside density.

More recently, approaches to topic segmentation [1,2,13] have integrated deep learning techniques: they utilize methods such as recurrent neural networks (RNNs), convolutional neural networks (CNNs) and transformers to capture sequential text dependencies and to model complex relationships, consequently enhancing both the accuracy and versatility of topic segmentation.

In the context of topic segmentation on lecture videos, there are multiple approaches to the problem. Most methods for segmenting lecture videos use textual information that is extracted from either audio (e.g., the textual transcript obtained by automatic speech recognition), visual (slide presentation), or a combination of both. Because of this, we can view the text-based part of the task as a problem of textual topic segmentation [6]. In [8] one of the first approaches to lecture video segmentation, they used a linguistic based approach since the existing algorithms for automated video segmentation relied on scene/shot change detection, something that lecture videos are lacking or have very few of. Also topic boundaries are less distinct due to the spontaneous nature of the lecturers speech. For that they propose an algorithm called *PowerSeg* that combines various linguistic segmentation features such as noun phrases, verbs, pronouns and cue phrases.

Shah et al. present TRACE [12], which is designed to perform automatic segmentation of lecture videos using a linguistic-based approach. It leverages Wikipedia articles and the lectures' video transcripts to create feature vectors from blocks of text. These blocks, created using a sliding-window architecture, have a specific length and allow the system to skim through the entire documents. Afterwards, TRACE computes the similarities between the feature vectors of the Wikipedia article blocks and the transcript blocks. Transcript blocks that lead to the maximum similarity score which also exceed a similarity threshold δ are considered as a segment boundary.

In [6] they propose a lecture segmentation algorithm that extracts cue features from the lectures' video transcripts in an attempt to capture the essence of the text. Then these features are turned into vectors for representation purposes. Finally, a sliding window-based method is used to detect the segments in the video. The authors also introduced a new artificially-generated dataset for evaluation, consisting of synthetic lecture transcripts, as detailed in Table 1.

In [10] the authors introduce VISC-L, a comprehensive framework that uses video transcripts for segmenting and characterizing videos, and linking them to their domain. Similar to previous methodologies, it employs knowledge models and a language model to identify primary topics and concepts for each video segment. Unique to VISC-L is its user study evaluation, which assesses the impact of the segmentation and characterization processes on concept learning.

However, relying solely on text for topic segmentation in lecture videos can overlook valuable information present in the audio and visual components of the video. This has led to the development of methods that incorporate audio features, such as silence detection and changes in speaker's tone, into the segmentation process. For instance, Malioutov et al. [9] proposed an unsupervised algorithm for topic segmentation that operates directly on raw acoustic information. Their method predicts topic changes by analyzing the distribution of recurring acoustic patters in the speech signal, demonstrating that audio-based segmentation can perform favorably even without input transcripts.

Moreover, some researchers have explored multimodal approaches, the combination of features extracted from video. These approaches aim to leverage the complementary information present in different modalities and enhance the segmentation process. For example, Soares and Barrere [14] proposed a multimodal approach that leverages both low and high-level audio features for automatic topic segmentation in video lectures. Their method combines frequency and power features from the audio signal, the transcript from automatic speech recognition and annotation features from a knowledge base. Through experiments on a dataset of Portuguese video lectures, they demonstrated that their method can successfully segment video lectures with various characteristics, and the results indicated that combining features from different modalities enhances topic segmentation performance.

Despite the extensive research in topic segmentation, our work introduces a unique perspective that has not been extensively explored in the existing literature. We examine both audio and text modalities individually for segmenting video lectures. While many methods utilize text, audio-visual cues, or their combination, we delve into the distinct strengths of audio and text in isolation. Notably, our use of keyword extraction for this task is a pioneering approach, contrasting the straightforward audio-based method with the intricate text-based one, shedding light on the potential of different speech and text features for segmentation.

3 Methods

3.1 Silence-Based Segmentation

The silence-based segmentation approach exploits natural pauses in speech that during a lecture may signify a transition from one subject to another. This methodology proves especially effective in educational video lectures, where typically a single speaker delivers the content, often accompanied by slide presentations. This format tends to encourage a structured pace and clear distinction between sections and topics. Furthermore, the audio quality in such settings is usually relatively free of noise, simplifying the task of identifying speech pauses. The process encompasses several steps, as outlined in Algorithm 3.1.

The first step involves extracting the audio track from the video lecture (line 2). We then identify pauses (lines 3–6) or silences in the speech by setting a threshold (line 4) and a minimum duration for silence (line 3), then automatically retrieving all the regions where the audio volume falls below this threshold (line 6) as pauses. This is done with the help of the pydub [11] library and its *detect_silence*() function. After identifying the pauses in the audio, we calculate their average length (line 7) and the Standard Deviation (line 8). Pauses that exceed the average length by more than σ standard deviations are considered significant and are marked as potential topic boundaries (line 11), thus creating the segmentations for the lecture video.

Algorithm 1. Audio-based Segmentation

1: **procedure** AudioSegmentation($video$)
2: $audio \leftarrow$ ExtractAudio($video$)
3: $min\_silence \leftarrow 100ms$
4: $silence\_thresh \leftarrow dBFS - 16$
5: $silence\_params \leftarrow \{audio, min\_silence, silence\_thresh\}$
6: $silence\_list \leftarrow$ DetectSilence($silence\_params$)
7: $silence\_mean \leftarrow$ CalculateMean($silence\_list$)
8: $silence\_std \leftarrow$ CalculateStdDev($silence\_list$)
9: $selection\_criteria \leftarrow silence\_mean + \sigma * silence\_std$
10: $selection\_params \leftarrow \{silence\_list, selection\_criteria\}$
11: $silence\_selection \leftarrow$ SelectSilences($selection\_params$)
12: **return** $silence\_selection$
13: **end procedure**

3.2 Keyword Extraction-Based Segmentation

Keyword extraction-based segmentation uses existing models or algorithms for extracting keywords from passages to segment text. For this implementation,

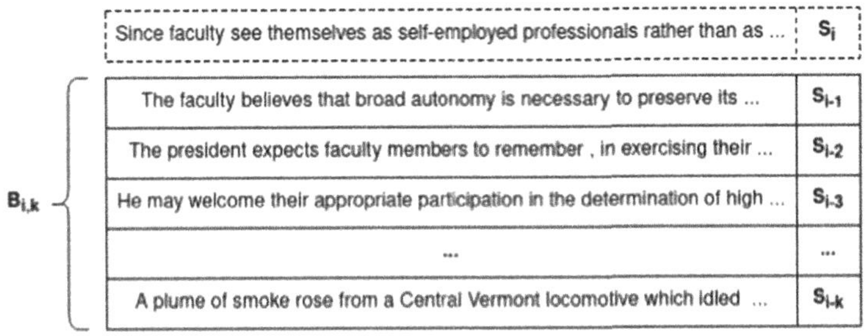

Since faculty see themselves as self-employed professionals rather than as ...	S_i

$B_{i,k}$

The faculty believes that broad autonomy is necessary to preserve its ...	S_{i-1}
The president expects faculty members to remember , in exercising their ...	S_{i-2}
He may welcome their appropriate participation in the determination of high ...	S_{i-3}
...	...
A plume of smoke rose from a Central Vermont locomotive which idled ...	S_{i-k}

Fig. 1. This figure shows the keyword extraction-based approach applied on a document from the Choi dataset [5]

we used the YAKE! method [4], but theoretically this step can be reproduced by any existing keyword extraction methods, or even a vectorization method. The fundamental motivation behind this segmentation approach is put simply, is the hypothesis that a keyword for a given passage can be perceived as a summary describing the topic of that passage. Any change of the underlying topic (*thematic shift*) is expected to result in a change of the associated keyword describing of said passage. This concept can be used to test whether adjacent passages or blocks continue an existing topic or introduce a new, different topic. This is achieved by comparing whether their extracted keywords are equal or not, essentially comparing either individual keywords or sets of keywords.

The way that this idea is implemented is with a "sliding window" buffer architecture. The buffer B has a size limit of k sentences and each sentence i from the document gets compared with the buffer. At the beginning the buffer is empty, and after k iterations it is filled up. In the next iteration $(k+1)$, the first sentence is removed, and the $(k+1)$th sentence is added instead. Afterwards it continues in the same manner, similar to a FIFO queue, until all the sentences of the document will have been compared.

The buffer-sentence comparison is done for every sentence in the document, and it is done in the keyword level. For each iteration of the algorithm, a keyword extraction process is applied to both the buffer B and sentence S_i (line 6 & 7). So, for each iteration, the comparison is done between the keyword set of the buffer and the keyword set of the sentence. The number of keywords extracted from both the buffer and the sentence is kept the same to ensure a fair similarity calculation. For simplicity, we have chosen to extract a number of keywords equal to the buffer size, k. These sets may contain singular words as in keywords, or whole phrases, thus keyphrases. The choice between extracting individual words or phrases can be specified in the keyword extraction process using the *ngram* parameter. Apart from the parameter specifying the number of keywords to be extracted, we use the default values for all other parameters provided by YAKE! [4]. In addition, YAKE! provides a relevance score for each extracted keyword, signifying its importance in the given text. This relevance score is used in the computation of the buffer-sentence similarity score.

Algorithm 2. Keyword Extraction-Based Segmentation

```
 1: Step 1: Calculate Gap Similarity Scores
 2: Set buffer size k
 3: Initialize buffer B and empty list of gap scores GapScores[]
 4: for each sentence S_i in the document D do
 5:     Extract k keywords K[S_i] from S_i
 6:     Extract k keywords K[B] from buffer B
 7:     Calculate sentence score using method A: ScoreA(S_i, B)
 8:     Calculate sentence score using method B: ScoreB(S_i, B)
 9:     Calculate sentence score using method C: ScoreC(S_i, B)
10:     Take the maximum score: ScoreMax(S_i, B) ← max{ScoreA, ScoreB, ScoreC}
11:     Normalize sentence score NormScore(S_i, B) ← 1 − ScoreMax(S_i, B)
12:     Add NormScore(S_i, B) to list of gap scores GapScores[]
13:     Add S_i to buffer B
14:     if length(B) > k then
15:         Remove the first sentence from buffer B
16:     end if
17: end for
18: Step 2: Create Segmentation
19: Set threshold θ
20: Initialize empty list of segmentations Seg[]
21: for each score score in GapScores do
22:     if score ≤ θ then
23:         Append "1" to Seg[]                    ▷ Mark as topic boundary
24:     else
25:         Append "0" to Seg[]                    ▷ Mark as no boundary
26:     end if
27: end for
28: return Seg[]
```

The similarity score for each iteration of the algorithm indicates if a sentence S_i has any similarity with the buffer $B_{i,k}$, i.e. the k previous sentences. If the similarity score is high, it indicates that the sentence is part of the same segment with the sentences of the buffer. If the similarity is low, then the sentence may be the first one of a new segment, indicating a topic shift. Because of the keyword extraction process used, we need to find a way to calculate the similarity between the two keyword sets.

The relevance score of each keyword contributes to calculate the similarity score for each sentence as follows: given the keyword set $K[B_{i,k}]$ of the buffer $B_{i,k}$ and $K[S_i]$ of the sentence S_i. There are three ways to calculate a similarity score (line 9–11), and the best one will be used (line 12).

1. If a keyword from $K[S_i]$ is found in $K[B_{i,k}]$ the relevance score of the keyword from the buffer set gets used for the similarity score. (line 9)
2. If for a keyphrase from $K[S_i]$, a word is found in $K[B_{i,k}]$ as a keyword, the relevance score of the keyword from the buffer set gets used for the similarity score. (line 10)

3. Lastly, for every word that exists in a keyword or keyphrase in $K[S_i]$ is compared with every word that exists in a keyword or keyphrase in $K[B_{i,k}]$. If similarities are found, then the relevance score is divided by the length of the keyphrase $partial\ relevance = kw\ relevance\ score/len(kw)$. (line 11)

After the score calculation, we obtain a list of similarity scores $Sim[S_1, S_N]$ for each of the sentences (line 13). Using a predefined similarity threshold T (line 5), we iterate through this list and begin placing segment breaks $Seg[S_i]$ (lines 14–16). If the similarity score $Sim(S_i)$ for a given sentence is lower than the threshold, this sentence is considered to belong to a new segment, and the algorithm places a segment barrier in front of it. Once all scores have been processed and all segment barriers have been placed, we end up with a segmented document. This is represented by a segmentation list $Seg[D]$ for the document D, containing the indices of the sentences that are preceded by segment barriers.

4 Towards an Evaluation

This chapter outlines the evaluation of the two topic segmentation methods for video lectures developed in this research. In the course of this research, we compiled a list of available datasets relevant to the task of topic segmentation (see Table 1). However, none were suitable for video lectures, thus posing a challenge in assessing our methods' effectiveness.

4.1 Evaluation Datasets

As can be seen from the table, some researchers [5,6] synthesize evaluation data to overcome the lack of available datasets for their segmentation methods. While this is an ingenious approach to address the dataset scarcity issue, it can introduce biases and inaccuracies. Specifically, synthesized data often contain clear topic breaks due to the selection process and the way they are assembled. In contrast, real-world lectures typically feature more subtle topic shifts. Moreover, while synthesized data are usually in text form, which is relatively easy to create, synthesizing data for evaluating a video segmentation method using its audio is not straightforward and can be less accurate, making it less suitable for our purposes.

Given the lack of an existing dataset, we embarked on the evaluation process by manually annotating a video lecture. One of the authors, who also served as the lecturer, segmented the lecture based on slide changes, which served as a reliable indicator of topic transitions, in this case. His intimate understanding of the content guided the segmentation process, ensuring a high degree of accuracy in the annotated data. We acknowledge that evaluating on a single lecture (n=1) may not provide a comprehensive view of the effectiveness of our methods. However, given the constraints, we believe it offers valuable insights and serves as a starting point for further evaluations.

Table 1. Resources for Use in Topic Segmentation Evaluation – A Synopsis

Dataset	Audio	Video	Text	Slides	Source	Lang.	Segmentation Annotation
Hearst [7]	—	—	—	—	1 science article	en	—
Choi [5]	—	—	Orig	—	Brown corpus	en	Synthesized
Wikisection [1]	—	—	Orig	—	Wikipedia	en, de	Collected
ALV [6]	—	—	Auto	—	videolectures.net	en	Synthesized
SB18 [14]	✓	—	Auto	—	Brazilian lecture recordings	pt	Gold data
VoLL-KI [3]	✓	✓	Auto	—	recorded lectures	en, de	*Gold data (planned)*

4.2 Method Hyperparameters

Both methods in this study required hyperparameter tuning. For the silence detection method, the primary hyperparameter is the number of standard deviations σ from the mean silence duration, indicating topic boundaries. The keyword extraction method, however, requires tuning of the buffer size B and the similarity threshold θ. The buffer size influences the granularity of topic segmentation, while the similarity threshold determines sentence segment classification.

4.3 Grid Search

A grid search was employed to explore the hyperparameter space. For the silence detection, standard deviations ranged from 1 to 8. For keyword extraction, buffer sizes between 5 and 15 were tested, and similarity thresholds ranged from 0.05 to 0.95 in increments of 0.05.

4.4 Evaluation Metrics

Performance was assessed using standard metrics: accuracy, precision, recall, and the F1 score. These metrics quantify the effectiveness of each method in segmenting video lectures.

4.5 Evaluation Results

The grid search results and performance evaluations are visualized below. Included are two line graphs for the silence detection method (Fig. 2) and four heatmaps for the keyword extraction method (Figs. 3 and 4).

4.6 Analysis of Results

The results indicate that the optimal parameter for the silence detection method is a standard deviation value of 4, yielding an F1 score of over 40%. This performance significantly surpasses that of the keyword extraction method, which achieves a maximum F1 score of less than 10%. These findings suggest that the silence detection method, with its higher F1 score and inherent simplicity,

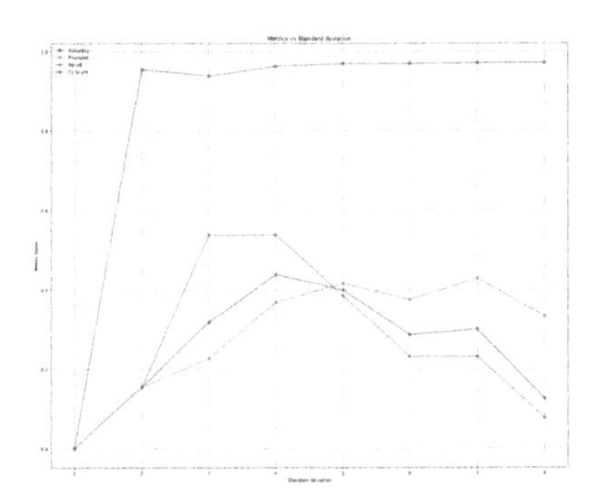

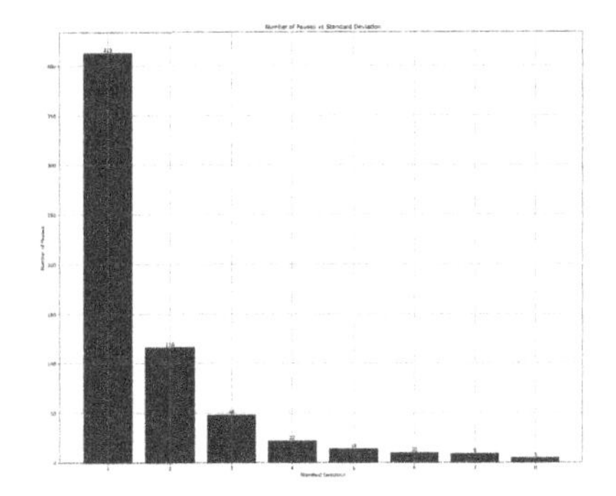

Fig. 2. Left: Performance of the silence-based segmentation method for different standard deviation values. Blue is Accuracy, Orange is Precision, Green is Recall, and Red is F Score. Right: Number of pauses selected as potential topic boundaries for different standard deviation values in the silence-based segmentation method. (Color figure online)

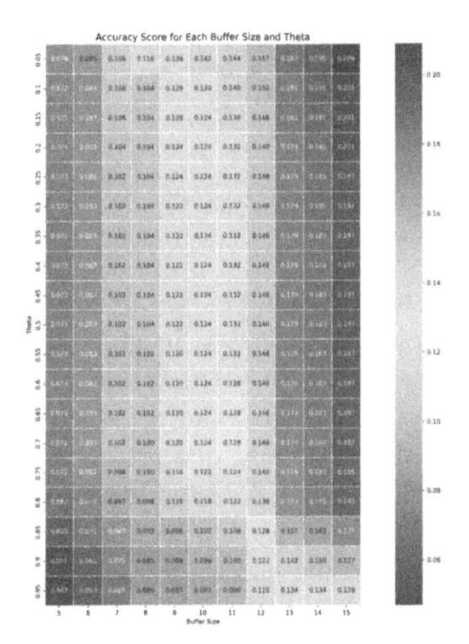

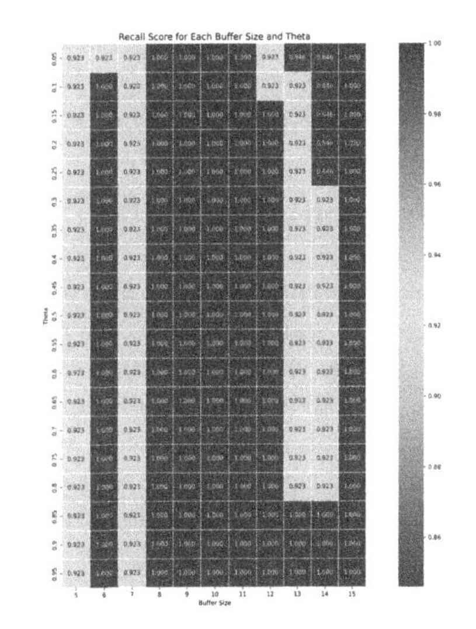

Fig. 3. Heatmaps showing the accuracy (left) and recall (right) of the keyword extraction-based segmentation method for different combinations of buffer size and similarity threshold.

might be more adept at segmenting video lectures into topics. Conversely, the keyword extraction method, despite its current lower performance, should not be dismissed outright. It's worth noting that this study does not demonstrate the ineffectiveness of keyword-based approaches as a whole. Rather, it underscores the need for additional work on this approach. The keyword extraction method, with its complexity and intricacy, could be especially beneficial in scenarios where audio data is unavailable or when the audio quality is poor.

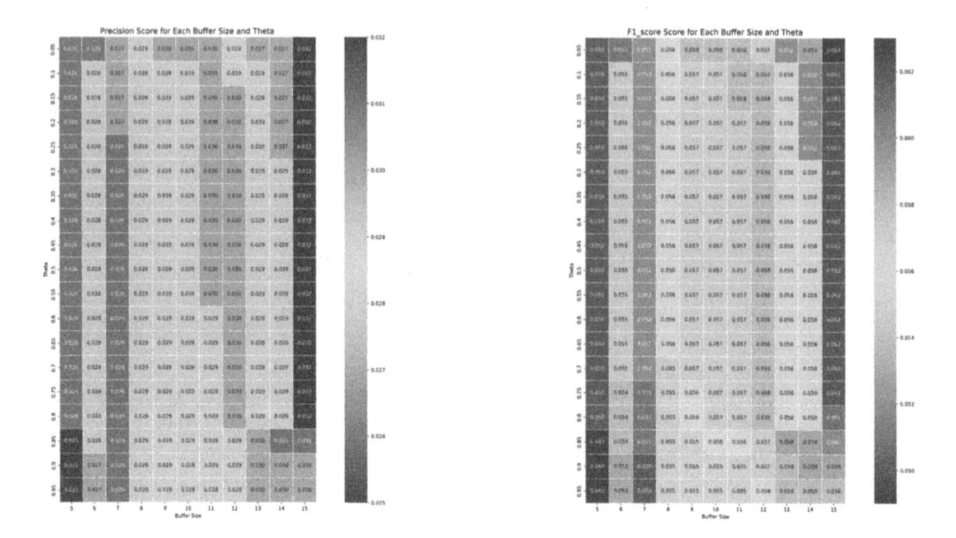

Fig. 4. Heatmaps showing the precision (left) and F1 score (right) of the keyword extraction-based segmentation method for different combinations of buffer size and similarity threshold.

5 Discussion

The results of our study provide valuable insights into the application of silence detection and keyword extraction methods for topic segmentation in video lectures. The silence detection method, despite its simplicity, outperformed the more complex keyword extraction method. This suggests that the presence of significant pauses in speech, which can be easily detected and quantified, is a strong indicator of topic shifts in video lectures. In the context of our study, we found that the silence detection method, which has been used in conjunction with other methods in the literature, showed promise when used independently. This suggests that silence detection can be a useful tool for this task, even without additional methods. On the other hand, our novel application of keyword extraction for this purpose didn't perform as expected. One reason might be the challenge of comparing keyword sets for similarity. While keywords capture main topics, they might not be an effective medium to base the measurement of similarity between two sets, affecting the accuracy of segmentation.

Our study had several limitations. The most significant was the lack of an available dataset for evaluating our methods. We mitigated this by manually annotating a video lecture, but this approach has its own limitations, including potential bias and the difficulty of accurately identifying topic shifts. Furthermore, the use of a single lecture for evaluation limits the generalizability of our findings. Despite these limitations, our study has important implications for the development of automated lecture segmentation tools. Our findings suggest that simple, easily quantifiable features of speech, such as pauses, can be effective indicators of topic shifts. This opens up new possibilities for the design of segmentation algorithms that are both effective and computationally efficient.

6 Summary, Conclusion and Future Work

In this study, we have presented two methods for segmenting video lectures into topics: a silence detection method and a keyword extraction method. Our evaluation results indicate that the silence detection method, with its simpler nature and higher performance, is more effective for this task. However, the keyword extraction method, despite its lower performance, may still have potential applications, particularly in cases where audio data is not available or the audio quality is poor.

Looking ahead, we plan to further enhance our topic segmentation methods. Moving forward, we plan to explore the use of vectorization methods, such as Word2Vec or BERT, as an alternative to the keyword extraction method currently used. Embeddings instead of keywords, could potentially capture more nuanced semantic relationships between words, thereby improving the accuracy of our topic segmentation. In addition, we plan to create a gold data dataset of annotated video lectures. This dataset will serve as a valuable resource for evaluating our methods and for benchmarking future topic segmentation methods. With this dataset, we will be able to retest our methods and potentially combine them into a new, more effective method for topic segmentation.

Acknowledgement. First, we are grateful to all lecture donors. The authors gratefully acknowledge the joint funding from German Federal Ministry of Research (BMBF) and the Free State of Bavaria for the Project grant "VoLL-KI: Von Lernenden Lernen" (Friedrich Alexander University (FAU) Erlangen, Coburg University of Applied Sciences/Otto-Friedrich-University Bamberg, under grants 16DHBKI089, 16DHBKI090 and 16DHBKI091) and to the funding to the second author by the Free State of Bavaria under the Hightech Agenda Bavaria R&D programme. All opinions are the authors' and do not reflect positions of the funding agencies.

References

1. Arnold, S., Schneider, R., Cudré-Mauroux, P., Gers, F.A., Löser, A.: SECTOR: a neural model for coherent topic segmentation and classification. Trans. Assoc. Comput. Linguist. **7**, 169–184 (2019). https://doi.org/10.1162/tacl_a_00261
2. Badjatiya, P., Kurisinkel, L.J., Gupta, M., Varma, V.: Attention-based neural text segmentation. CoRR (abs/1808.09935) (2018). http://arxiv.org/abs/1808.09935
3. Berges, M., et al.: VoLL-KI: Von lernenden lernen. Künstliche Intelligenz (2023, submitted). (currently under review)
4. Campos, R., Mangaravite, V., Pasquali, A., Jorge, A., Nunes, C., Jatowt, A.: YAKE! keyword extraction from single documents using multiple local features. Inf. Sci. **509**, 257–289 (2020). https://doi.org/10.1016/j.ins.2019.09.013
5. Choi, F.Y.Y.: Advances in domain independent linear text segmentation. In: Proceedings of the 1st North American Chapter of the Association for Computational Linguistics Conference, pp. 26–33. NAACL 2000, Association for Computational Linguistics, New York, NY, USA (2000)

6. Galanopoulos, D., Mezaris, V.: Temporal lecture video fragmentation using word embeddings. In: Kompatsiaris, I., Huet, B., Mezaris, V., Gurrin, C., Cheng, W.-H., Vrochidis, S. (eds.) MMM 2019. LNCS, vol. 11296, pp. 254–265. Springer, Cham (2019). https://doi.org/10.1007/978-3-030-05716-9_21
7. Hearst, M.A.: TextTiling: segmenting text into multi-paragraph subtopic passages. Comput. Linguist. **23**(1), 33–64 (1997)
8. Lin, M., Chau, M., Cao, J., Jr., J.F.N.: Automated video segmentation for lecture videos: a linguistics-based approach. Int. J. Technol. Human Interact. (IJTHI) **1**(2), 27–45 (2005). https://ideas.repec.org/a/igg/jthi00/v1y2005i2p27-45.html
9. Malioutov, I., Park, A., Barzilay, R., Glass, J.R.: Making sense of sound: Unsupervised topic segmentation over acoustic input. In: Carroll, J., van den Bosch, A., Zaenen, A. (eds.) ACL 2007, Proceedings of the 45th Annual Meeting of the Association for Computational Linguistics, 23–30 June 2007, Prague, Czech Republic. The Association for Computational Linguistics (2007). https://aclanthology.org/P07-1064/
10. Mohammed, A., Dimitrova, V.: Video segmentation and characterisation to support learning. In: Hilliger, I., Muñoz-Merino, P.J., De Laet, T., Ortega-Arranz, A., Farrell, T. (eds.) Educating for a New Future: Making Sense of Technology-Enhanced Learning Adoption. EC-TEL 2022. LNCS, vol. 13450, pp. 229–242. Springer, Cham (2022). https://doi.org/10.1007/978-3-031-16290-9_17
11. Robert, J., Webbie, M., et al.: Pydub (2018). http://pydub.com/
12. Shah, R.R., Yu, Y., Shaikh, A.D., Zimmermann, R.: TRACE: linguistic-based approach for automatic lecture video segmentation leveraging Wikipedia texts. In: 2015 IEEE International Symposium on Multimedia, ISM 2015, Miami, FL, USA, December 14–16, 2015, pp. 217–220. IEEE Computer Society (2015). https://doi.org/10.1109/ISM.2015.18
13. Sheikh, I., Fohr, D., Illina, I.: Topic segmentation in ASR transcripts using bidirectional RNNs for change detection. In: IEEE Automatic Speech Recognition and Understanding Workshop. ASRU 2017, Okinawa, Japan (2017). https://hal.science/hal-01599682
14. Soares, E.R., Barrére, E.: Automatic topic segmentation for video lectures using low and high-level audio features. In: Proceedings of the 24th Brazilian Symposium on Multimedia and the Web. pp. 189–196. WebMedia 2018, Association for Computing Machinery, New York, NY, USA (2018). https://doi.org/10.1145/3243082.3243096, https://doi.org/10.1145/3243082.3243096
15. Theodorou, T., Mporas, I., Fakotakis, N.: An overview of automatic audio segmentation. Int. J. Inf. Technol. Comput. Sci. **11**, 1–9 (2014). https://doi.org/10.5815/ijitcs.2014.11.01

Model-Based-Diagnosis for Assistance in Programming Exercises

Moritz Bayerkuhnlein(✉) and Diedrich Wolter

University of Bamberg, An der Weberei 5, 96047 Bamberg, Germany
{moritz.bayerkuhnlein,diedrich.wolter}@uni-bamberg.de

Abstract. Implementing AI methods can be an effective way to understand their inner workings, in particular when learners have to locate bugs. However, programming tasks are time consuming and can be extremely challenging for students. In order to provide assistance, code evaluation platforms have been developed that give immediate feedback in the form of discrepancies between expected and actual output for test cases. While such tests clearly indicate wether or not an implementation is faulty, they do not assist learners in locating the fault in their implementation. We propose to diagnose solution attempts, explaining potential faults with respect to abstract behavior. By framing programming tasks as functional models, we can diagnose the underlying concepts of a task and provide feedback. In this paper we focus on abstract data types as a basis for AI algorithms. The diagnosis method described in this paper produces an explanation of a fault in the form of a description based on a reconstruction of hidden program states. Applying the method to student submissions in a programming class shows that the proposed method can effectively identify and locate faults.

Keywords: Model-Based Diagnosis · Fault Localization · Intelligent Tutor System

1 Introduction

The classic AI textbook "Paradigms of AI Programming" by Peter Norvig [16] prominently quotes Alan Perlis stating that learners can only be certain to fully understand an algorithm if they are able to implement – hence also debug – it. We consider programming exercises to be a crucial part in education, helping students to understand and demystify the inner workings of an AI method. Programming tasks operate on multiple levels of abstraction, from the concrete syntax of the programming language to the abstract concepts of the task, all involving a number of *mental models* [13,18].

For algorithms that operate on these abstract representations, debugging can be difficult for learners since a faulty behavior cannot easily be traced back to a

This work has been carried out in context of the VoLL-KI project (grant 16DHKBI091), funded by Bundesministeriums für Bildung und Forschung (BMBF).

S. Nowaczyk et al. (Eds.): ECAI 2023 Workshops, CCIS 1948, pp. 459–470, 2024.
https://doi.org/10.1007/978-3-031-50485-3_44

location in the source code. Multiple program components interact in a complex way and faulty intermediate results may only occur under certain conditions and remain hidden in internal program states. While experienced programmers are able to craft decisive test cases that test special cases, students need to learn about such cases first.

Immediate feedback and automated assistance enables novices to learn from a programming task as they face, without overly indulging in handholding the student. This requires automated means to provide feedback for submitted solution attempts, for example using evaluation platforms that run automated tests [10]. Such platforms present an assistance systems to students while developing a solution attempt. Although feedback given in the form of discrepancies between expected and actual output has already been found helpful [11], such approach only assesses correctness of a submitted solution at whole and does not differentiate the abstract representations underlying the task. In other words, existing tools only state whether or not an implementation is faulty. They do not explain *why*, nor do they provide hints to the learner *where* the bug is. We are motivated – also by feedback from our students that suffered interpreting test feedback from existing tools – to develop means for automated feedback that is capable of explaining program faults more intuitively.

We propose to relate faults identified in programming tasks to explicit functional models by means of diagnosis and explicit reconstruction of the faulty system's internal state, providing feedback on level that is close to how underlying concepts are taught. Our approach builds on the common infrastructure of automated test cases, but extends it with model-based diagnosis. This means we do not inspect the actual source code but treat it as a black box, allowing the method to be applied independent of the programming language used. To achieve our aim we propose a model of functional circuits that is related to classical diagnosis domains like electrical circuits. In this paper we consider implementation of Abstract Data Types (ADTs) (e.g., stack, tree, etc.) which underly AI methods (e.g., for managing the fringe in search methods). ADTs are challenging to debug for novices since ADTs are based on information hiding, concealing the internal state.

Figure 1 gives an example of the feedback generated by the method described in this paper for a faulty implementation. In the corresponding programming exercise, a binary search tree had to be implemented. In Sect. 2 we describe how model-based diagnosis can be applied and relate the approach to other techniques for fault localization. Based on a logic model, we apply diagnosis to programs (Sect. 3) and with the help of computational logic tools we then determine a model (Sect. 4) of the faulty behavior that reconstructs hidden states of the program to explain the fault (Sect. 5). As can be seen in Fig. 1, our system produces hypotheses of possible faults, aiming to direct students to bugs in the code. Both, textual and graphical presentations can be provided. In Sect. 5.1 we give first results regarding the effectiveness of the proposed method we obtained for student submissions in an introduction course.

```
1      public void addRec(int key, Node current){
2          if(root.getKey() < current.getKey()){
3              if(current.getLeft() != null){
4                  addRec(key,current.getLeft());
5              }else{
6                  current.setLeft(new Node(key));
7              }
8          }else if(current.getRight() != null){ //...
```

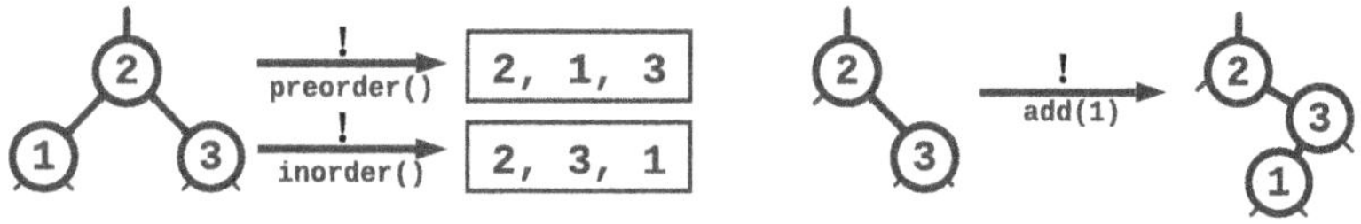

preorder() ! 2, 1, 3

inorder() ! 2, 3, 1

add(1) !

[Hypothesis 1] **add**-method(s) are faulty, we suspect for example:

example: calling add(1) on tree(nil,2,tree(nil,3,nil)) may have produced tree(nil,2,tree(tree(nil,1,nil),3,nil))

[Hypothesis 2] **inorder and preorder**-method(s) are faulty, we suspect for example:

example: calling inorder() on tree(tree(nil,1,nil),2,tree(nil,3,nil)) may have produced [2,1,3]
example: calling preorder() on tree(tree(nil,1,nil),2,tree(nil,3,nil)) may have produced [2,3,1]

Fig. 1. Excerpt from faulty student code of a binary search tree which always compares the current node's key with the root key, no the provided key (line 2). The resulting diagnosis as text with additional illustration is shown below.

2 Model-Based Diagnosis and Debugging

In this section we discuss approaches to fault localization and show how the problem of localizing faults within a system can be posed as a diagnosis problem, using reasoning from the first principles [9,17], that is, model-based diagnosis (MBD). Following Reiter [17], diagnosis employs a *structural* and a *behavioral* model of a system.

Definition 1 (Diagnosis System). *A diagnosis system consists of* (SD, COMP)*, where* COMP *is a set of components that reside within the system, and the description of the system* SD *defines the behavior of the components in their interaction based on their structure.*

A functionally correct system consists of components that exhibit the behavior of SD. If the system is observed to behave abnormally, i.e. it produces unexpected output, then diagnosis traces back this abnormality to one or more potentially abnormal components $\{\text{AB}(c_1), ..., \text{AB}(c_n)\}$. We define all observable inputs and outputs on terminals of a system as a finite set OBS.

In the consistency-based approach to model-based diagnosis, a component c is admitted to show arbitrary behavior regardless of the specification in SD only if it is declared by $\text{AB}(c)$ to act abnormally [17]. Diagnosis is thus the task of determining minimal sets of components such that their conjectured abnormality explains all observations.

Definition 2 (Diagnosis). *For a system* (SD, COMP) *and* OBS *formalized as logical sentences, a diagnosis is a set* $\Delta \subseteq$ COMP *iff* SD $\cup$ OBS $\cup \{\text{AB}(c)|c \in \Delta\} \cup \{\neg\text{AB}(c)|c \in (\text{COMP} \setminus \Delta)\}$ *is consistent. A diagnosis* Δ *is minimal if there is no alternative diagnosis* $\Delta' \subset \Delta$.

2.1 Model-Based Software Debugging

Applying MBD to debugging has been done in the form of Model-Based Software Debugging (MBSD) initially in Logic Programming [7], but has since been adapted to functional [20] and object-oriented paradigms [23]. MBSD derives a system model directly from the source code and the programming language semantics. Statements and expressions constitute set COMP, and, in contrast to MBD, SD does not provide the specification; rather, it mirrors the faulty implementation. Similarly, the role of OBS is flipped, as they now represent the expected output according to a test oracle [21]. MBSD is aimed at an application for experienced programmers [21]. It is generally assumed that the experienced programmer knows what they are doing, bugs are expected to be infrequent and are most likely repairable by slight modifications [21]. In the context of a learning support system, de Barros et al. [3] use structural abstraction and a hierarchical model-based approach to reason about specified code patterns as abstract components, with the goal of establishing a better dialog when communicating errors to students in terms of their problem solving strategies. A challenge when referring to source code (aside from adaption efforts to specific programming languages) lies in the fact that diverse implementations can produce the same behavior using dramatically different techniques.

2.2 Fault Localization

Lately, even machine learning methods have been applied to fault localization and automated repair of code [2]. By contrast, classical models are based on formal specification and testing against a formal specification, hence ensuring correctness of the output. While well-designed complex tests can be very effective to verify correctness of a program, they provide no direct pointers to bugs in the code. Moreover, it requires much care to design a minimal set of test cases that is able to detect all reasonable faults. It is therefore attractive to run many tests in an exhaustive manner. As a downside of exhaustive testing, test output may be overwhelming. A further challenge faced in testing is that a single fault can cause multiple tests to fail. Several methods have been proposed to compile test failures into a ranked set of fault candidates, a prominent example being the family of spectrum-based fault analysis [19] which has also been applied to the challenging task of multiple fault localization [1]. The idea of spectrum-based based methods is to compute a metric that derives the likelihood of a component being faulty from the number of faulty tests the component was used (along other components) in relation to participation in passed tests. While computing such metrics can be done efficiently, they only provide an estimate and rely on an appropriate balancing of the test cases. In contrast to such heuristic methods,

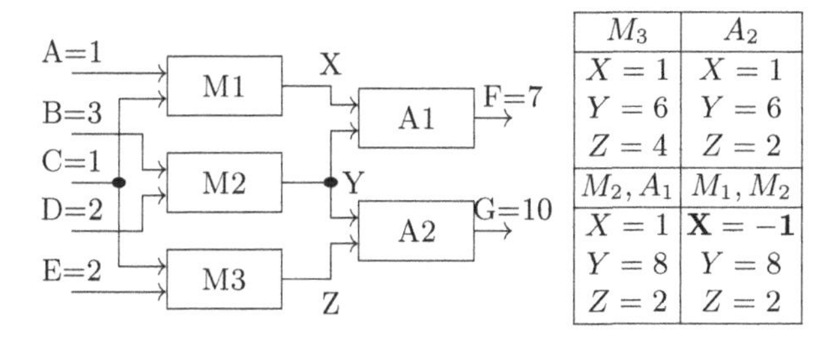

M_3	A_2
$X = 1$	$X = 1$
$Y = 6$	$Y = 6$
$Z = 4$	$Z = 2$
M_2, A_1	M_1, M_2
$X = 1$	$\mathbf{X = -1}$
$Y = 8$	$Y = 8$
$Z = 2$	$Z = 2$

Fig. 2. Functional circuit on a range of [0,15] (4-bit), diagnosed component sets and their context as corresponding variable values.

model-based diagnosis has the advantage of giving correct results and is able to provide justification in form of a logic model.

3 Modelfinding for Diagnosis

The presence of a fault introduces unknown behavior into a system, which manifests itself as symptoms. Diagnosing involves identifying and isolating a cause from the observed symptoms. This form of reasoning is known as abductive reasoning. *Abductive diagnosis*, as defined by Console in [8], uses strong fault models that explicitly model faulty system behavior. By restricting the outcome to a set of possible causes that act as justifications, stronger fault models reduce the number of candidate diagnoses. However, additional modelling effort is required.

Instead, and unlike abductive diagnosis, our approach reconstructs the system state from the observations made. Related approaches to model-based diagnosis from the field of constraint programming have been termed *constructive abduction* [14]. To illustrate the benefit of constructive abduction over consistency-based diagnosis, consider a classic example of a circuit consisting of multiplier components {M1, M2, M3} and adder components {A1, A2}, as shown in Fig. 2, where the components perform operations on 4-bit integer values from 0 to 15. Ports A to E are the inputs and ports F, G are the observable system outputs. The system thus computes $F = (A{\cdot}C)+(B{\cdot}D)$ and $G = (B{\cdot}D)+(C{\cdot}E)$. The inputs shown in Fig. 2 indicate a discrepancy, since $G = 10$ differs from the expected value $(3 \cdot 2) + (1 \cdot 2) = 8$.

The diagnoses generated by the consistency-based approach in accordance with Definition 2 are $\Delta = \{\{\text{M3}\}, \{\text{A2}\}, \{\text{M2}, \text{A1}\}, \{\text{M1}, \text{M2}\}\}$, i.e. four possible minimal sets of abnormal components. If we consider the diagnostic system as a system of equations, and the abnormal components output X, Y as *free variables*, we obtain the equations $X + Y = 7$ and $Y + 2 = 10$. We thus have $X + 8 = 7$, which has no solution over the domain of non-negative 4-bit integers, but all other solutions actually provide a justification based on the value assumed to be the output of an abnormal component. In conclusion, diagnosis {M1, M2} is not a feasible explanation for the observed error. As a side product, we also obtain values that support a diagnosis, essentially determining a satisfying model or context C such that

$$C \models \mathrm{SD} \cup \mathrm{OBS} \cup \{ab(c) \mid c \in \Delta\} \tag{1}$$

The method can be formulated as a Constraint Satisfaction Problem (CSP), where an assignment of variables is sought from a finite domain, in our case the context C. A practical method can easily be obtained by first-order model finding, using answer set programming (ASP) or SMT solvers.[1]

To find the minimal diagnosis, we use an incremental approach, directly specifying the number of abnormal operations or components we want to diagnose, and incrementally increasing the value; the consistency check by the solver can only consider models that satisfy the exact number of abnormal operations [22].

Once a constellation of abnormal operations is found, the framework excludes it from further diagnosis, so that no super sets are generated. For the scope of this paper we focus on the modelling aspects as the main contribution.

4 Model-Based Diagnosis of Programming Exercises

Different implementations can achieve the same behavior using a variety of underlying mechanisms, yet the behavior follows a common specification. In our work we assume that a specification of the ADT to be implemented is given as an algebraic specification.

Definition 3 (Algebraic Specification). *An algebraic specification (AS) is a tuple* (Σ, E) *where signature* Σ *has a finite set of sorts* S *(i.e. type names) and operations of structure* $op : s_1 \times ... \times s_n \rightarrow s \mid s_i \in S$*. Semantics of* op *is defined by equations, as a set of axioms* E*.*

A natural level of abstraction for components in the sense of a diagnostic system is then the level of individual methods defined by the ADT and in use in a sequence of operation calls. During diagnosis, we model each operation call as a single component in order to differentiate between different conditions in which a component is in use. For example, a stack implementation is composed of components that implement initialisation, PUSH, POP, etc. Two successive PUSH operations are modelled as two different components PUSH_1, PUSH_2. Component behavior is defined as input and output pairs or functions that pass values, but not all values are observable. For example, the result of a PUSH operation modifies the stack and usually does not return a directly observable value. Consequently, values appearing at the terminals of intermediate components must be reconstructed during diagnostic reasoning. We say that if the output produced by a component c differs from what is specified in a given AS, it behaves abnormally, written $ab(c)$. For observable outputs, abnormality can

[1] For experiments, specifications are formalised in the interactive theorem prover Isabelle/HOL [15] using its integrated model finding capabilities [5] to perform the constructive abduction.

be inferred from observations. For unobservable components, abnormality can only be inferred by reasoning about their behavior within a network of components as a whole. Abnormality of a component is treated as a justification for any output produced by the component, both in conflict with and in accordance with the specification. Since components of the same functional type, e.g. PUSH_i, $i = 1, 2, \ldots$, are based on a single implementation, we introduce a rule that propagates an inferred abnormality to all components of that type: $ab(c) \wedge type(c, op_i) \wedge type(c', op_i) \rightarrow ab(c')$.

The goal of diagnosis is to identify (i) a set of individually faulty components, or (ii) a faulty mechanic that may be spread across multiple components and cannot be attributed to a single component. To this end, we use compound statements of the form $a, b \in \text{COMP}$: $a \wedge b$ to express that either there are problems in both the mechanics implementing a and b, or there is a common mechanic that is broken by both, including side effects of one that affect the other. Analogously, $a \vee b$ denotes an alternative diagnosis that either a or b is abnormal, and occurs whenever some uncertainty remains from the observations made.

4.1 Algebraic Specification as Diagnosis System

Given an AS (Σ, E), we construct test cases by arbitrarily composing the methods of the ADT, i.e. the set of non-primitive functions occurring in op and determining the expected results according to E, for an example see Fig. 3. Each test case is then applied to the code and fully executed to be diagnosed, collecting the observable outputs. Each test case is fully executed, thus the actual output can deviate on multiple occasions from the expected output which aids identifying aftereffects of faults. The method calls occurring in the tests then constitute the

```
definition create:: "nat ⇒ S"  ("create'(_')") where "create N ≡ (empty,N)"
definition push :: "S ⇒ E ⇒ S" ("push'(_,_')") where "push(P,E) ≡ (E on fst P,snd P)"
axiomatization
  size :: "S ⇒ nat"    ("size'(_')") and
  pop :: "S ⇒ S × E"   ("pop'(_')") and
  isEmpty :: "S ⇒ bool" ("isEmpty'(_')") and
  isFull :: "S ⇒ bool"  ("isFull'(_')") and
  capacity :: "S ⇒ nat" ("capacity'(_')")
where
 AA: "capacity(S)<size(S) ⟶ err(S)"  and AB: "err (pop(create(N)))" and
 A1: "fst pop(push(s,e)) = s"          and A2: "snd pop(push(s,e)) = e" and
 A3: "isEmpty(push(s,e)) = False"  and A4: "isEmpty(create(N)) = True" and
 A5: "size(create(N)) = 0"             and A6: "size(push(s,e)) = size(s)+1 " and
 A7: "capacity(create(N)) = N"       and A8: "capacity(push(s,e)) = capacity(s)" and
 A9: "isFull(S) = (size(S)=capacity(S))"
```

Fig. 3. Specification of capacity bounded abstract datatype stack formalized in Isabelle/HOL using definitions on pairs and inductive datatypes for constructors and axiomatization to specify the remaining behavior

set of components $\textsc{comp}_{AS}$ of the diagnosis system $(\textsc{comp}_{AS}, \textsc{sd}_{AS})$. Behavior representation $\textsc{sd}_{AS}$ and observations $\textsc{obs}_{AS}$ is given by test cases.
A Diagnosis Δ of $\textsc{sd}_{AS}$ is then: $\textsc{sd}_{AS} \cup \textsc{obs} \cup \{\textsc{ab}(c)|c \in \Delta\} \cup \{\neg\textsc{ab}(c)|c \in \textsc{comp}_{AS} \setminus \Delta\}$

As opposed to primitive datatypes such as boolean and integer, ADTs perform information hiding. There is usually not even a method to test for equality. So we can only check the tests on the basis of *observable sorts.* This has implications for the representation of values propagated through the components of a diagnostic system, since instead checking instances of non-observable sorts (i.e. ADTs) it is only possible to check whether they are *observational equal.* That is, instances cannot be distinguished by "experiments", as in any sequence of operations that results in an observable sort [4].

As a means of transferring information between the components of $\textsc{comp}_{AS}$, we choose to represent values of unobservable sorts as first-order ground terms using the constructors of the ADT (e.g. `node(Key,LeftChild, rightChild)` for a binary tree). Through constructive abduction we effectively reconstruct values for the purpose of justification whenever a feasible diagnosis is found. Using this representation, we anchor any justification we make to the structure and state of the data type. However, this assumes that the observations made can be deterministically reconstructed while relying only on this simplified representation. Whenever the value represented here is the product of a faulty component, we will refer to it as a *corrupt* value or state.

Example 1. Let component $\textsc{pop}_i$ represent the operation $\textsc{pop} : stack \longrightarrow stack \times char$. Provided with input term $t_1 = \textsc{push}(\textsc{create}(3), \texttt{a})$, i.e. a stack of size 3 containing only literal 'a', the output of $\textsc{pop}_i$, namely $\textsc{pop}(\textsc{push}(\textsc{create}(3), \texttt{a}))$, can be rewritten as $\textsc{create}(3)$ using the axiom $\textsc{pop}(\textsc{push}(s, e)) = (s, e)$. Assuming $\textsc{pop}_i$ to act normally, one can only infer from the element e returned that the state of the data structure before calling $\textsc{pop}_i$ is consistent with t_1, not that it must be identical to t_1.

5 Inferring Hidden Values from Testcases

Identifying faulty components within a system requires tracing symptoms through the propagation of the components. A key part of this propagation and reconstruction of the state of the system is determined by how we structure and relate the observations, forming a *structural model.* The model of a physical device is defined by the actual physical connections between each component. This is not necessarily the case for a more abstract system. *Connections* between calls to the datatype are the datatype values or states and any other value passed between calls. We consider *components* as the operation calls, where the implementing operation is the type of that component. Values, including the representation of ADT states, are passed from one operation call to the next, usually terminating in an observing operation that returns a primitive value.

If we want to effectively describe and reason about a failure, information hiding must be overcome by reconstructing states. A call to a component flagged as abnormal means that no guarantees can be made about the output of that operation. This induces the possibly of corrupted states through the observed context, i.e. the sequence of calls following the values output by the observers, resulting in a context with (at least) a behaviorally equivalent representation [12]. As shown in Fig. 4 (right), we structure the connection model in a branching fashion in order to relate the information. Where a path through the diagram represents a test, tests share the same history and therefore the same state. Whenever a test sequence branches from another, the values present on both branches must be identical. Following the notation introduced in [6], we formalize these branches using shared variables, so that any constraint imposed on one variable affects all its branches.

Example 2. Expression 2 represents two test sequences that overlap until op_3, where one test, represented by the shared variable **b**, observes and terminates with f, while the other test continues to manipulate the state to c, d and e.

$$\exists\, a\, b\, c\, d\, e\, f. \mathrm{create}_1(3, a) \wedge \mathrm{push}_2(a, 1, \mathbf{b}) \wedge \mathrm{push}_3(\mathbf{b}, 2, c) \wedge \mathrm{pop}_3(\mathbf{b}, f, 1) \wedge \mathrm{pop}_4(c, d, 2) \wedge \mathrm{pop}_5(d, e, 2) \quad (2)$$

Therefore, when generating tests for an implementation, we require a certain amount of overlap in the test cases so that operations operate on the same state according to the structural model. In the case of abstract data type implementations and other API-like specifications, tests can be generated using for example a breadth-first search.

5.1 Constructing Diagnosis

From the consistency-based definition 2, a regular diagnosis result identifies the bug by providing a set of components $\{c \mid c \in \mathrm{COMP} \wedge ab(c)\}$ that need to be repaired. In our case, this set includes a set of operations from the specification that must deviate from the specification. An operation may implement multiple cases, or have behavior that depends on a particular range of values, in which case it is helpful to contextualize the diagnosis. As mentioned in Sect. 3 using the reconstructed values, a diagnosis can also be justified when faced with a discrepancy based on the inferred input and output values.

Fig. 4 (left) illustrates Example 2 as a component connection model. On an operation-call level, i.e. distinguishing between the individual calls during diagnosis, we obtain the (4) minimal diagnoses: The minimal diagnoses are searched for incrementally following [22] by allowing only a fixed number of abnormal components.
(i) $ab(pop_5)$, justified by $d = push(create(3), 1)$ but returning 2. (ii) $ab(pop_4)$, justified by $c = push(push(create(3), 1), 2)$ producing $d = push(\_, 2)$[2]. (iii) $ab(push_3)$, justified by $b = push(create(3), 1)$ but returning $c =$

[2] Wildcard (_) denotes assignment where no context constrains the value.

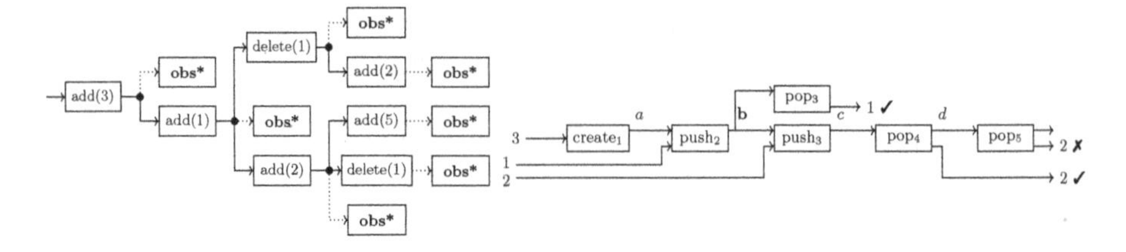

Fig. 4. Visual Representation of test cases as circuits. Binary Search Tree test cases represented as a branching functional circuit (left). Sequence of stack operations annotated with observations (right).

$push(push(\_, 2), 2)$. (iv) $ab(push_2)$, justified by $a = create(3)$ but producing $b = push(\_, 2)$ and $ab(pop_3)$ justified by $b = push(\_, 2)$ but returning 1.

Qualitatively, these justifications can now be scrutinized to assess their plausibility. For example, just by aggregating and looking at the diagnosis operation by operation, as described in Sect. 4, we can check whether reconstructed values still induce deterministic functions from their inputs and outputs.

In the following, we demonstrate the quality of diagnosis that the approach can provide. For demonstration, we modeled a programming task to implement an ADT stack and implemented the approach. We asked students in a first-year introductory course on algorithms and data structures at our university to implement the stack based on an array in Java at the beginning of the semester as part of their homework. The submitted code was stored and evaluated using the INGInious platform [10]. 74 students submitted multiple attempts to solve their homework. In total, 267 submissions were recorded, of which 49 had solution errors in their stack implementation, detected by manually written test cases and the INGInious platform. We demonstrate the use of the approach by localiszing the incorrect behavior of the implementations.

Table 1 shows the types of erroneous implementations that we identified by manually scanning all submissions. The table also shows the corresponding diagnosis found by the proposed method, based on testing against a stack using an exhaustive test suite. Note that the correctness of a diagnosis here depends on the coverage of the test suite. The diagnosis found for the faulty implementations is correct, i.e. the diagnosis covers the actual faults in the implementation, although there are false positives among the conjunctions. However, these can be checked using the reconstructed values. For example, if there are several possible values for a variable, the justification is not deterministic and therefore not plausible.

We can use a reduced test set to get good, potentially equivalent diagnoses. As shown in the results obtained for a binary tree datatype implementation of Table 1. Where the implementations have only been tested on the circuit shown in Fig. 4 (left). However, this does affect the ability to effectively reconstruct values as the presence of the constraint decreases. The ground-truths are found by the diagnosis and here listed first.

Table 1. Observed errors in the student submission for an array-based stack data type and binary search tree. For all error classes, the diagnosis covered the actual errors in the code. (*)-Asterisk marks conjunctions that suggested an implausible justification based on non-determinism.

ID	Description	Diagnosis Δ		
$\mathbf{ar}_1$:	Array not initialized	*create*	$\vee$	*push*
$\mathbf{ar}_2$:	Array indexing starts at 1	*push*	$\vee$	$(create \wedge full)$
$\mathbf{ie}_1$:	empty is inverted	*empty*	$\vee$	$(create \wedge push \wedge pop)^*$
$\mathbf{if}_1$:	full is inverted	*full*	$\vee$	$(create \wedge push \wedge pop)^*$
$\mathbf{ieif}_1$:	both empty and full are inverted	$(empty \wedge full)$	$\vee$	$(create \wedge push \wedge pop)^*$
$\mathbf{po}_1$:	pop on empty returns constant	*pop*	$\vee$	$(create \wedge push \wedge empty)^*$
$\mathbf{po}_2$:	pop always returns constant	*pop*		
$\mathbf{po}_3$:	pop only observes	*pop*	$\vee$	$(push \wedge full)^*$
$\mathbf{pu}_1$:	push on full no exception	*push*	$\vee$	$(pop \wedge empty \wedge full)^*$
$\mathbf{pu}_2$:	push on full overwrites top element	*push*	$\vee$	$(pop \wedge empty \wedge full)^*$
$\mathbf{lst}_1$	tree is list structured	*add*	$\vee$	$(find \wedge inorder)$
$\mathbf{dl}_1$	delete has no effect	*delete*		
$\mathbf{dl}_2$	delete removes subtree	*delete*	$\vee$	$(add \wedge find \wedge inorder)$
$\mathbf{ip}_1$	in- implements postorder	*inorder*	$\vee$	$(add \wedge find)$
$\mathbf{co}_1$	exception if not contained	*find*		

6 Conclusion and Future Work

As an effort to provide more informative automated feedback for student programming tasks, we design a computational logic model in an adaption of model-based diagnosis. The model presented here is able to isolate faults and reason explicitly about the internal state of the faulty system by means of constructive abduction. The approach bridges automated testing to abstract reasoning, allowing intuitive explanations of a fault.

In future work we want to investigate diagnosis of complex AI algorithms. This poses challenges with respect to efficiency of the diagnosis and with respect to handling components that influence the control flow of a program. Last but not least, we plan to conduct a user study to learn about most suitable levels of abstractions when communicating a fault to the student.

References

1. Abreu, R., Zoeteweij, P., Gemund, A.J.V.: Spectrum-based multiple fault localization. In: Proceedings of IEEE/ACM International Conference on Automated Software Engineering, pp. 88–99. IEEE (2009)
2. Allamanis, M., Jackson-Flux, H., Brockschmidt, M.: Self-supervised bug detection and repair. In: Proceedings of 35th Conference on Neural Information Processing Systems (NeurIPS 2021) (2021)
3. de Barros, L.N., Pinheiro, W.R., Delgado, K.V.: Learning to program using hierarchical model-based debugging. Appl. Intell. **43**(3), 544–563 (2015)
4. Bidoit, M., Hennicker, R., Wirsing, M.: Behavioural and abstractor specifications. Sci. Comput. Program. **25**(2–3), 149–186 (1995)

5. Blanchette, J.C., Nipkow, T.: Nitpick: a counterexample generator for higher-order logic based on a relational model finder. In: Kaufmann, M., Paulson, L.C. (eds.) ITP 2010. LNCS, vol. 6172, pp. 131–146. Springer, Heidelberg (2010). https://doi.org/10.1007/978-3-642-14052-5_11
6. Camilleri, A., Gordon, M., Melham, T.: Hardware verification using higher-order logic. University of Cambridge, Computer Laboratory, Technical report (1986)
7. Console, L., Friedrich, G., Dupré, D.T.: Model-based diagnosis meets error diagnosis in logic programs. In: Fritzson, P.A. (ed.) AADEBUG 1993. LNCS, vol. 749, pp. 85–87. Springer, Heidelberg (1993). https://doi.org/10.1007/BFb0019402
8. Console, L., Torasso, P.: A spectrum of logical definitions of model-based diagnosis 1. Comput. Intell. **7**(3), 133–141 (1991)
9. Davis, R.: Diagnostic reasoning based on structure and behavior. Artif. Intell. **24**(1–3), 347–410 (1984)
10. Derval, G., Gego, A., Reinbold, P., Frantzen, B., Van Roy, P.: Automatic grading of programming exercises in a MOOC using the INGinious platform. In: European Stakeholder Summit on Experiences and Best Practices in and Around MOOCs (EMOOCS 2015), pp. 86–91 (2015)
11. Hao, Q., et al.: Towards understanding the effective design of automated formative feedback for programming assignments. Comput. Sci. Educ. **32**(1), 105–127 (2022)
12. Hennicker, R.: Context induction: a proof principle for behavioural abstractions and algebraic implementations. Formal Aspects Comput. **3**, 326–345 (1991)
13. Johnson-Laird, P.N.: Mental Models. MIT Press, Cambridge (1989)
14. Ligeza, A., et al.: Constraint programming for constructive abduction. A case study in diagnostic model-based reasoning. In: Kościelny, J.M., Syfert, M., Sztyber, A. (eds.) DPS 2017. AISC, vol. 635, pp. 94–105. Springer, Cham (2018). https://doi.org/10.1007/978-3-319-64474-5_8
15. Nipkow, T., Wenzel, M., Paulson, L.C.: Isabelle/HOL. A Proof Assistant for Higher-Order Logic. LNCS, vol. 2283. Springer, Heidelberg (2002). https://doi.org/10.1007/3-540-45949-9
16. Norvig, P.: Paradigms of AI Programming: Case Studies in Common Lisp. Morgan Kaufmann (1992)
17. Reiter, R.: A theory of diagnosis from first principles. Artif. Intell. **32**(1), 57–95 (1987)
18. Robins, A., Rountree, J., Rountree, N.: Learning and teaching programming: a review and discussion. Comput. Sci. Educ. **13**(2), 137–172 (2003)
19. de Souza, H.A., Chaim, M.L., Kon, F.: Spectrum-based software fault localization: A survey of techniques, advances, and challenges. Technical report. arXiv:1607.04347 (2016)
20. Stumptner, M., Wotawa, F.: Debugging functional programs. In: IJCAI, vol. 99, pp. 1074–1079. Citeseer (1999)
21. Wieland, D.: Model-based Debugging of Java Programs using Dependencies. Ph.D. thesis, Technische Universität Wien (2001)
22. Wotawa, F., Kaufmann, D.: Model-based reasoning using answer set programming. Appl. Intell. **52**, 1–19 (2022)
23. Wotawa, F., Stumptner, M., Mayer, W.: Model-based debugging or how to diagnose programs automatically. In: Hendtlass, T., Ali, M. (eds.) IEA/AIE 2002. LNCS (LNAI), vol. 2358, pp. 746–757. Springer, Heidelberg (2002). https://doi.org/10.1007/3-540-48035-8_72

Author Index

S. Nowaczyk et al. (Eds.): ECAI 2023 Workshops, CCIS 1948, pp. 471–473, 2024.
https://doi.org/10.1007/978-3-031-50485-3